For students:

GradeMax is a powerful tool for students, too.

- For planning: Individual reports guide students on where to apply their study time.

- For improvement: Topic specific review modules provide immediate opportunities to work on areas of weakness.

- For success: Each instance of a test is unique. Students can easily see their improvement by re-taking chapter tests without getting the same questions.

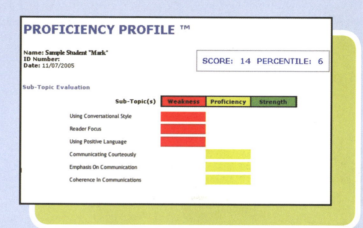

Put GradeMax to work in your class.

Making GradeMax part of your course gives you tremendous control through the robust administrative tracking and reporting features. You have the option to receive powerful graphic reporting at both the class and student level to help adjust teaching emphasis.

Even if you do not plan to require GradeMax, recommending it to your students allows them to take advantage of the testing, reporting, and remediation to improve their grades.

The power of knowledge gap assessment, reporting, and remediation for students and instructors.

GradeMax supports the way you teach, however you teach.

GET READY FOR GRADEMAX!

McGraw-Hill/Irwin is pleased to provide you access to GradeMax, a revolutionary adaptive testing tool created specifically for the Business Communication course. This dynamic online-based system is designed to maximize interactive learning between instructors and students.

FOR INSTRUCTORS, GRADEMAX ALLOWS YOU TO:

- Administer unique, text-specific tests to each student to assess his or her understanding of each concept in a chapter.

- Receive powerful graphic reporting at both the class and student level to help adjust teaching emphasis.

- Assign lessons to reinforce weaker comprehension areas.

FOR STUDENTS, GRADEMAX ALLOWS YOU TO:

- Test your knowledge of business communication concepts.

- Access resource materials to sharpen your business communication know-how.

GRACIAARTUNOCRUZ
SAMART12

Your personal password is:

MH3943GM1306

TO GAIN ACCESS TO GRADEMAX:

- Go to the GradeMax Registration Page at http://grademax.assetlearning.com/card.aspx

- Enter in your personal password listed above.

- Follow the registration instructions.

- During the registration process, you'll be asked to set up your account under your instructor's class. If there is no class present, let your instructor know you'd like to take advantage of GradeMax's many benefits in your class. (You can also access GradeMax through the Online Learning Center that accompanies this text—the URL is listed on the back cover or inside cover of the text).

Free access is provided for purchasers of a new book.
*Your registration code can be used only once to establish access. It is not transferable.

ISBN-13: 978-0-07-328600-6
ISBN-10: 0-07-328600-1

Business Communication

MAKING CONNECTIONS IN A DIGITAL WORLD

ELEVENTH EDITION

Raymond V. Lesikar, Ph.D.
EMERITUS, LOUISIANA STATE UNIVERSITY

Marie E. Flatley, Ph.D.
SAN DIEGO STATE UNIVERSITY

Kathryn Rentz, Ph.D.
UNIVERSITY OF CINCINNATI

Boston   Burr Ridge, IL   Dubuque, IA   New York   San Francisco   St. Louis
Bangkok   Bogotá   Caracas   Kuala Lumpur   Lisbon   London   Madrid   Mexico City
Milan   Montreal   New Delhi   Santiago   Seoul   Singapore   Sydney   Taipei   Toronto

McGraw-Hill
Irwin

BUSINESS COMMUNICATION: MAKING CONNECTIONS IN A DIGITAL WORLD
Published by McGraw-Hill/Irwin, a business unit of The McGraw-Hill Companies, Inc., 1221
Avenue of the Americas, New York, NY, 10020. Copyright © 2008 by The McGraw-Hill Companies, Inc.

Some ancillaries, including electronic and print components, may not be available to customers outside the
United States.

This book is printed on acid-free paper.

5 6 7 8 9 0 CCI/CCI 0 9 8

ISBN: 978-0-07-305036-2
MHID: 0-07-305036-9

Editorial director: *John E. Biernat*
Publisher: *Andy Winston*
Sponsoring editor: *Barrett Koger*
Developmental editor: *Anna M. Chan*
Editorial assistant: *Kelly I. Pekelder*
Marketing manager: *Trent Whatcott*
Senior media producer: *Damian Moshak*
Project manager: *Gina F. DiMartino*
Production supervisor: *Gina Hangos*
Designer: *Cara David*
Photo research coordinator: *Lori Kramer*
Photo researcher: *PoYee Oster*
Media project manager: *Joyce J. Chappetto*
Cover design: *Krysten Brown*
Interior design: *Cara David*
Typeface: *10.5/12 Times Roman*
Compositor: *Interactive Composition Corporation*
Printer: *Courier Kendallville*

Library of Congress Cataloging-in-Publication Data

Lesikar, Raymond Vincent.
   Business communication : making connections in a digital world / Raymond V. Lesikar,
Marie E. Flatley, Kathryn Rentz.—11th ed.
      p. cm.
   Rev. ed. of: Basic business communication. 10th ed. c2005.
   Includes index.
   ISBN: 978-0-07-305036-2 (alk. paper)
   MHID: 0-07-305036-9 (alk. paper)
   1. Commercial correspondence. 2. English language–Business English. 3. Business
communication. I. Flatley, Marie Elizabeth. II. Rentz, Kathryn. III. Lesikar, Raymond
Vincent. Basic business communication. IV. Title.
HF5721.L37 2008
651.7'4–dc22   2006024235

www.mhhe.com

To our families, our friends, and all the dedicated teachers and researchers in the Association for Business Communication.

—Raymond V. Lesikar
Marie E. Flatley
Kathryn Rentz

Dr. Raymond V. Lesikar has served on the faculties of the University of North Texas, Louisiana State University at Baton Rouge, The University of Texas at Austin, and Texas Christian University. He served also as a visiting professor at the University of International Business and Economics, Beijing, China. His contributions to the literature include six books and numerous articles.

Dr. Lesikar has been active in consulting, serving over 80 companies and organizations. Included in this group are Kaiser Aluminum, Goodyear, Exxon, Sears, Ethyl, U.S. Department of Agriculture, Veterans Administration, Crown Zellerbach, Gulf States Utilities, Dow Chemical, Ford Motor Company, Gulf-South Executive Development Program, and the Air War College. He is a Fellow, Distinguished Member, and former president of the Association for Business Communication. In addition, he has served ABC in many capacities over the years. He also holds membership in the Federation of Administrative Disciplines and is a former president of the Southwest Social Science Association. His distinguished teaching career was highlighted by his service as major professor for 23 recipients of the doctoral degree.

Dr. Marie E. Flatley is a Professor of Information and Decision Systems at San Diego State University, where she teaches various courses in business communication. Additionally, she has served as a Fellow at the university's Center for Teaching and Learning and as a Qualcomm Fellow in the pICT (people, Information, Communication, and Technology) program. She received her B.B.A., M.A., and Ph.D. from the University of Iowa.

Dr. Flatley is active in numerous professional organizations, including the Association for Business Communication, the California Business Education Association, Delta Pi Epsilon, and the National Business Education Association. She has served as president of the Association for Business Communication and is a distinguished member of the Association. The California Business Education Association recently named her Business Educator of the year for the senior college/university level. Additionally, she has served as an editorial board member for the *Delta Pi Epsilon Journal,* associate editor for the *Journal of Business Communication* and editor for the *NABTE Review.* Currently she is a reviewer and member of the editorial review board for the *Journal of Education for Business.*

Her current research interests involve using technology to assist with the communication process. Her research spans the investigation of the effective use of blogs to making good channel choices to using video email and various wireless technologies.

Dr. Kathryn Rentz is an Associate Professor in the English Department at the University of Cincinnati. She taught her first business writing class as a doctoral student at the University of Illinois in the early 1980s and has been teaching workplace writing ever since. She helped establish the University of Cincinnati's professional writing program and has served as its coordinator. She has also won the English Department's teaching award, directed the department's graduate program, and helped direct the composition program.

Dr. Rentz's affiliation with the Association for Business Communication goes back to her beginnings as a business writing teacher. She has performed many roles for the association, including serving on the board of directors, organizing a conference, and chairing the publications board. She served two terms as an Associate Editor of the *Journal of Business Communication* and was Interim Editor from 2000–2001, for which she won the Francis W. Weeks Award of Merit.

Dr. Rentz has published articles and commentary on pedagogy, genre theory, narrative, and ethics in such journals as *Business Communication Quarterly,* the *Journal of Business Communication, Technical Communication Quarterly,* and the *Journal of Business and Technical Communication.* She has participated in many professional meetings and seminars over the years and is always learning from her colleagues and her students.

Our overall objective in this revision was to produce the most technologically current and pedagogically effective book in the field. We modestly believe we have succeeded. Because in a sense business communication is technology in today's digital business world, to thoroughly emphasize technology wherever it applies was a logical first goal in our efforts. In working to produce the most pedagogically effective book possible, we continued to pursue the goals that enabled preceding editions to enjoy wide acceptance. These goals were to produce the most authoritative, thorough, learnable, and teachable book possible. Our specific efforts in pursuing all these goals are summarized as follows.

TECHNOLOGICALLY CURRENT

Because the computer and the Internet have affected business communication in so many ways, we worked this subject into the book wherever applicable. Where technology is integral to the way business communicates today, we integrated it into the text discussion. In those cases where technology helps students perform special tasks, we presented it in boxes. Additionally, both the textbook cases and the Web cases use technology in ways typical of today's businesspeople. We believe these efforts will enable students to leverage the power of the computer to save time and improve work quality.

AUTHORITATIVE

The authors are an interdisciplinary team with diverse training and experience who have worked to bring you the subject matter authoritatively from a thorough review of the field. In addition to being well-respected teachers, scholars, and leaders themselves, they have integrated their ideas with information from other researchers and practitioners in the mainstream of business communication, providing the enhanced value of multiple perspectives.

Throughout the text are realistic examples of current business problems and practices. You will find that business information is integrated into examples, message models, reports, text boxes, and end-of-chapter questions, problems, and cases. The extensive range of cases covers both internal and external communication as well as a wide variety of business environments. Furthermore, the cases cover a broad spectrum of challenges that students are likely to find in the workplace—from routine, everyday cases to complex scenarios requiring research and extensive analysis.

THOROUGH

We worked diligently to cover the subject thoroughly. The content of the earlier editions was based on the results of two extensive surveys of business communication teachers. In this edition we supplemented the results of those surveys with suggestions from the highly competent professionals who reviewed the book. And we implemented the research findings and suggestions we heard from colleagues at professional meetings. The result is a book whose content has been developed and approved by experts in the field. It includes sound advice on writing and speaking for business in both internal and external communication situations, using graphics or visuals, and leveraging technological tools to improve the process and the product. Additionally, it incorporates material that meets the needs of both beginning and advanced students. As well as we can determine, this edition covers every topic that today's business communication leaders say it should have.

LEARNABLE

As in earlier editions, we worked hard to make the book serve the student in every practical way. Our goal was to make the learning experience easy and interesting. The book's structured problem-solving approach guides students through the analytical process for various kinds of business messages, blending concrete advice with a focus on critical thinking, judgment, and creativity. To support this we include the following features, all of which have proved to be highly successful in preceding editions:

Readable writing. The writing is in plain, everyday English—the kind the book instructs the students to use.

Learning objectives. Placed at the beginning of all chapters, clearly worded objectives emphasize the learning goals and are tied in to the chapter summaries.

Introductory situations. A realistic description of a business scenario introduces the student to each topic, providing context for discussion and examples.

Outlines of messages. To simplify and clarify the instructions for writing the basic message types, outlines of message plans follow the discussions.

Margin notes. Summaries of content appear in the margins to help students emphasize main points and to review text highlights.

Full document illustrations. Well-written models with detailed margin comments are provided for all kinds of documents—text messages, emails, letters, memos, proposals, and short and long reports.

Specialized report topics. A list of research topics by major business discipline is available for teachers who prefer to assign reports in the students' areas of specialization.

Communication matters. Boxes containing anecdotal and authoritative communication messages add interest and make points throughout the book.

Abundant real business illustrations. Both good and bad examples with explanatory criticisms show the student how to apply the text instructions.

Cartoons. Carefully selected cartoons emphasize key points and add interest.

Photographs. Full-color photographs throughout the text emphasize key points and add interest to content. Teaching captions enhance the textual material.

Computer and web-based Internet applications. Computer and web-based applications have been integrated throughout the book wherever appropriate—into topics such as readability analysis, graphics, research methods, and formatting.

Computer use suggestions. For students who want to know more about how useful computers can be in business communication, pertinent suggestions appear in boxes and on the text website.

Chapter summaries by learning objectives. Ending summaries in fast reading outline form and by learning objectives enable students to recall text highlights.

Critical thinking problems. Fresh, contemporary, in-depth business cases are included for all message and report types—more than in any competing text.

Critical thinking exercises. Challenging exercises test the student's understanding of text content.

Critical thinking questions. End-of-chapter questions emphasize text concepts and provide material for classroom discussion.

New cases. As in past editions, the realistic and thorough case problems are new and updated.

Student Resource portion of the Online Learning Center <www.mhhe.com/lesikar11e>. Additional resources are provided on a comprehensive, up-to-date website. Included are online quizzes, PowerPoint slides, web cases, video cases, an extensive collection of annotated links to relevant websites organized by topic, and more.

TEACHABLE

Perhaps more valuable than anything we can do to help the teacher teach is to help the student learn. The features designed to provide such help are listed above. But there are additional things we can do to help the teacher teach. We worked very hard to develop these teaching tools; and we think we were successful. We sincerely believe the following list of features created for this edition is the most useful and effective ever assembled for a business communication textbook.

Instructor's Resource Manual. The following support material is available for easy use with each lecture:

Sample syllabi and grading systems (rubrics).

Summary teaching notes.

Teaching suggestions with notes for each kind of message.

Illustrated discussion guides for the slides/transparencies.

Answers to end-of-chapter critical thinking questions.

Answers to end-of-chapter critical thinking exercises.

Sample solutions to selected cases.

Case problems from the previous edition (online).

Grading checklists and software. (Part of the Online Learning Center). Lists of likely errors keyed to marking symbols are available for messages and reports. Similarly, symbols for marking grammatical and punctuation errors are available. They help the teacher in the grading process and provide the students with explanations of their errors. Similarly, a software tool coordinated with the text grading symbols is available. It's particularly helpful with students' documents received digitally.

PowerPoint slides. Complete full-chapter slide shows are available for the entire text. These colorful slides provide summaries of key points, additional examples, and examples to critique.

Transparency package. Available on request.

Video DVD to accompany Business Communication. These video cases are presented by real business people, focusing on the importance of communication in the workplace. Each segment presents a real business problem for student interpretation and classroom discussions. In addition to being motivational and informative, these videocases give the students practice to develop their listening skills. (Contact your McGraw-Hill/Irwin representative for more information.)

Test bank. This comprehensive collection of objective questions covers all chapters.

Computerized testing software. This advanced test generator enables the teacher to build and restructure tests to meet specific preferences.

Instructor resources portion of the Online Learning Center. <www.mhhe.com/lesikar11e> An up-to-date website fully supports the text. It includes a database of cases, new web cases that entail using web resources to write solutions, an author-selected collection of annotated links to relevant websites organized by topic, enhanced links for technology chapter, and other active learning material.

Blackboard/WebCT plug-ins for testing and review.

eBook in online and downloadable formats. A customizable version of the text is available as an ebook. One version can be subscribed to and viewed on the Web for anytime/anyplace access. Another version is downloadable for use with a new Zinio reader, an especially desirable option for students with tablets (or laptops) using Clear Type. For more information go to <http://www.zinio.com>.

Tools and Techniques Blog. This blog, accessible on the instructor's website, will include up-to-date material for lectures and assignments as well as a place to communicate with the authors.

ORGANIZATION OF THE BOOK

Because the reviewers and adopters generally approve of the organization of the book, we made no major organization changes. Thus the plan of presentation that has characterized this book through ten successful editions remains as follows:

Part I begins with an introductory summary of the role of communication in the organization, including a description of the business communication process.

Part II is a review of the basic techniques of writing and an introduction to messages and the writing process. Here the emphasis is on clear writing, the effect of words, and applications to messages, especially to email.

Part III covers the patterns of business messages—the most common direct and indirect ones.

Part IV concentrates on report writing. Although the emphasis is on the shorter reports and proposals, the long, analytical reports also receive complete coverage.

Part V reviews the other forms of business communication. Included here are communication activities such as participating in meetings, telephoning, dictating, and listening as well as giving presentations.

Part VI consists of special topic chapters for flexible use as customized for particular classes. The part includes chapters on cross-cultural communication, correctness, technology-assisted communication, and business-research methods.

Because teachers use these topics in different ways and in different sequences, they are placed in this final part so that they can be used in the sequence and way that best fit each teacher's needs.

RETAINED FEATURES

Many of our reviewers have commented on the value of particular items that we have kept and in some cases polished. Some are well tested and widely used while others, such as blogs, were in their infancy in the last edition. Here are just a few you will find here again.

- Ethical issues are integrated throughout with particular focus on ethical treatment of the reader and on ethical persuasion.

- Students are walked through the writing process and given effective strategies for planning, drafting, and revising.

- Traits of all major forms of business writing are discussed, from letters, memos, and reports to email, text messaging, and instant messaging.

- A building-block approach to writing skills is taken, providing advice on word choice, sentences, and paragraphs before discussions of major message types.

- Foundational advice is provided on report writing topics from data gathering and analysis to level of formality, structure, and format.

- Research is thoroughly covered, including gathering primary and secondary information and the use of databases and the Internet.

- Cross-cultural communication is discussed, with emphasis on using English with non-native English speakers.

- A full chapter on correctness is offered, using contemporary examples along with clear explanations.

ADDITIONS TO CONTENT

As with previous editions, we thoroughly updated this edition. We expanded coverage wherever we and our reviewers thought it would improve content. Our most significant additions or expansions are the following:

- Information about technology has been updated and integrated throughout with new emphasis on web-based applications and Office 12.
- The communication model has been adapted to business communication with special emphasis on business-related contexts and the communicators' relationship.
- Coverage of general persuasion concepts, including reader benefits and persuasive appeals (logical, emotional, and character based), has been expanded.
- Sections on internal messages have been added to Chapters 6 and 7 with new information on operational messages and negative announcements.
- The section on proposals has been extended, covering different purposes, types, and strategies.
- A new section on delivering virtual presentations has been included, along with expanded coverage on the use of photos as graphics or visuals.
- Updated material on job search, research, and documentation has been provided.

Finally, the website has updated online quizzes and new web-based and video cases. The web-based cases include ones for iPods (and mp3 devices).

ACKNOWLEDGMENTS

Any comprehensive work such as this must owe credit to a multitude of people. Certainly, we should acknowledge the contributions of the pioneers in the business communication field, especially those whose teachings have become a part of our thinking. We are especially indebted to those business communication scholars who served as reviewers for this and past editions. They truly deserve much of the credit for improvements in this book. It is with a sincere expression of gratitude that we recognize them:

James J. Balakier, *University of South Dakota*

Lecia Barker, *University of Colorado*

Melissa Barth, *Appalachian State University*

Rathin Basu, *Ferrum College*

Linda Bell, *Reading Area Community College*

Sandra K. Christianson, *National American University*

Sara Cushing, *Piedmont Technical College*

Mary Beth Debs, *University of Cincinnati*

Norma J. Dexter, *Florida State University—Panama City*

Gloria Diemer, *Suffolk County Community College*

Carolyn Embree, *The University of Akron*

Donna Everett, *Morehead State University*

Lu Ann Farrell, *Clinton Community College*

Dale Fike, *Redlands Community College*

Alicen Fiosi, *Lamar University*

Sheryl Fitzpatrick, *Waldorf College*

Fernando Ganivet, *Florida International University*

Glenn Good, *Front Range Community College*

Katherine Gotthardt, *National American University*

Diana Green, *Weber State University*

Frances K. Griffin, *Oklahoma State University*

Lisa E. Gueldenzoph, *North Carolina AT&T University*

Susan A. Heller, *Reading Area Community College*

Deborah Holder, *Piedmont Technical College*

Robert Insley, *University of North Texas*

Jane Johansen, *University of Southern Indiana*

Susan King, *Union County College*

Melinda Knight, *University of Rochester*

Marianna Larsen, *Utah State University*

John La Lone, *Tarleton State University—Central Texas*

Robert J. McMahon, *National American University*

Elizabeth Metzger, *University of South Florida*

Richard R. Meza, *Columbia College of Missouri*

Dr. R. Wayne Preslar, *Methodist College*

Zane Quible, *Oklahoma State University*

Pamela L. Ramey, *Kent State University*

Lillie A. Robinson, *North Carolina AT&T University*

Janet Sebesy, *Cuyahoga Community College*

Stacey Short, *Northern Illinois University*

Julie Simon, *Clarkson College*

Eric Soares, *California State University, East Bay*

Sandy Thomas, *Kansas City Kansas Community College*

David Ward, *University of Wisconsin—Madison*

Gary T. Ward, *Reedley College*

Karen Schelter Williams, *San Diego Mesa College*

Laura Williams, *Lipscomb University*

In addition, over the life of this book many of our professional colleagues have made a variety of inputs. Most of these were made orally at professional meetings. Our memories will not permit us to acknowledge these colleagues individually. Nevertheless, we are grateful to all of them.

Finally, on our respective home fronts, we acknowledge the support of our loved ones. Kathy acknowledges the support of Dave, Caroline, and Michael Rentz; her sister, Rebecca Horn; and friends in the English Department at the University of Cincinnati. Marie acknowledges her immediate family, friends, and San Diego State University colleagues. Ray acknowledges all his family members, both present and departed, who have provided love and inspiration over the years. Without the support of all these dear people this book would not exist.

Raymond V. Lesikar
Marie E. Flatley
Kathryn Rentz

A Quick Look

BUSINESS COMMUNICATION by Raymond Lesikar, Marie Flatley, and Kathryn Rentz attends to the dynamic, fast-paced, and ever-changing means by which business communication occurs by being the most technologically current and pedagogically effective book in the field. The 11th edition continues to set the standard by incorporating a multitude of real business examples and a thorough treatment of technology-driven business communication.

NEW PART OPENERS

Each section in the book begins with part openers featuring quotes from distinguished business leaders from recognized companies such as Dell Computer and ABC Television. These illustrate for students the importance of business communication skills in the real world.

Part Three

Basic Patterns of Business Messages

5   The Writing Process and an Introduction to Business Messages
6   Directness in Good-News and Neutral Messages
7   Indirectness in Bad-News Messages
8   Indirectness in Persuasive Messages
9   Strategies in the Job-Search Process

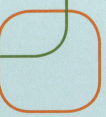

In 1992, Michael Dell was the youngest CEO ever to be listed in the Fortune 500 ranks. His continued success comes from thinking about how Dell products and services can bring value to customers.

"Whenever we're having our discussions with product teams or teams that are focused on unique kinds of customers, we talk about market trends and operating trends—'What are you seeing?' 'What are customers asking for?' 'What are customers buying?' And when I'm out in the field talking to customers, I spend a fair amount of time understanding what our customers are doing, why they're doing it, and where they're going."

Michael Dell, Chairman and CEO, Dell Computer

part six

Cross-Cultural Communication, Correctness, Technology, Research

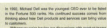

16   Techniques of Cross-Cultural Communication
17   Correctness of Communication
18   Technology-Enabled Communication
19   Business Research Methods

Named one of the "25 Most Influential Global Executives" (*Time* magazine/CNN) and one of *Fortune* magazine's "50 most powerful women in business," Andrea Jung is widely recognized for connecting Avon's international operations into a global "Company for Women." By setting up and listening to an advisory council from every level of the company, Jung has revitalized the 140-country sales force and increased sales around the globe. Being able to adapt to cultural and market differences is essential to communicating with customers.

"Avon does business in more than 100 countries, and engaging in an active dialogue with women is critical in helping us meet the beauty and lifestyle aspirations of our 5 million Avon Sales Representatives and 300 million customers from diverse cultures. We are a major global corporation but our roots are in local communities, and the person-to-person relationships we build through our direct sales model are a source of competitive advantage."

Andrea Jung, Chairman and CEO, Avon Products, Inc.

GOOD AND BAD EXAMPLES

Numerous good and bad examples of various business documents—from messages to memos to reports—are featured throughout the text. These writing samples allow students to learn by example. For easy reference, good examples are highlighted with a checkmark and bad examples are denoted by a crossout sign.

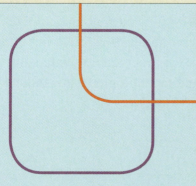

Contrasting Examples of Claim Messages

The following two email messages show contrasting ways of handling Tri-Cities Hardware's problem with the Old London lamppost lights. The first is slow and harsh. The second is courteous, yet to the point and firm.

> ● The following contrasting messages show bad and good handling of a claim.

A Slow and Harsh Message. The first message starts slowly with a long explanation of the situation. Some of the details in the beginning sentence are helpful, but they do not deserve the emphasis this position gives them. The problem is not described until the second paragraph. The wording here is clear but much too strong. The words are angry and insulting, and they talk down to the reader. Such words are more likely to produce resistance than acceptance. The negative writing continues into the close, leaving a bad final impression.

Subject: Our Order No. 7135

Mr. Goetz

As your records will show, on March 7 we ordered 30 Old London lamppost lights (our Order No. 7135). The units were received by us on March 14 (your Invoice No. 715C).

At the time of delivery, our shipping and receiving supervisor noticed that some of the cartons had broken glass inside. Upon further inspection, he found that the glass on 17 of the lamps was broken. Further inspection showed that your packers had been negligent as there was insufficient packing material in each carton.

It is hard for me to understand a shipping system that permits such errors to take place. We had advertised these lights for our annual spring promotion, which begins next Saturday. We want the lights by then or our money back.

Megan Adami

> This message is slow and harsh.

A Firm Yet Courteous Message. The second message follows the plan suggested in preceding paragraphs. A subject line quickly identifies the situation. The message begins with a clear statement of the problem. Next, in a tone that shows firmness without anger, it tells what went wrong. Then it requests a specific remedy and asks what to do with the damaged goods. The ending uses subtle persuasion by implying confidence in the reader. The words used here leave no doubt about the writer's interest in a continued relationship.

Subject: Broken glass in 17 Old London lamppost lights received

Mr. Goetz

Seventeen of the 30 lamppost lights we received today arrived with glass coverings broken.

At the time of delivery, our shipping and receiving manager noticed broken glass in some of the cartons. Upon further inspection, he found that 17 were in this condition. It was apparent to him that insufficient packing material was the cause of the problem.

Because we had advertised these lights for our annual spring promotion, which begins Saturday, please get replacements to us by that date. If delivery is not possible, we request a refund for the broken units. In either event, please instruct me on what to do with the damaged lamps.

I am aware, of course, that situations like this will occur in spite of all precautions. And I am confident that you will replace the units with your usual courtesy.

Megan Adami

> This better message follows text recommendations.

CHAPTER 6 Directness in Good-News and Neutral Messages   117

In addition, the two Case Illustrations show good handling of inquiries. The handwritten comments in the margins of these examples should be especially useful.

As you read the first example below, note that it is marked by a "" icon in the side panel. We use this icon throughout the book wherever we show bad examples. Take care not to confuse the bad with the good examples, which are marked by a "✓" icon.

The Old-Style Indirect Message. The less effective message begins slowly and gives obvious information. Even if one thinks that this information needs to be communicated, it does not deserve the emphasis of the opening sentence. The writer gets to the point of the message in the second paragraph. But there are no questions here—just hints for information. The items of information the writer wants do not stand out but are listed in rapid succession in one sentence. The close is selfish and stiff.

> This letter's indirect and vague beginning makes it slow.

Dear Mr. Piper:

We have seen your advertisement for 3,200 square feet of office space in the *Daily Journal*. As we are interested, we would like additional information.

Specifically, we would like to know the interior layout, annual cost, availability of transportation, length of lease agreement, escalation provisions, and any other information you think pertinent.

If the information you give us is favorable, we will inspect the property. Please send your reply.

Sincerely

The Direct and Effective Message. The second example begins directly by asking for information. The explanation is brief but complete. The questions, with explanation worked in where needed, are made to stand out; thus, they help to make answering easy. The message closes with a courteous and appropriate request for quick action.

> This direct and orderly letter is better.

Dear Mr. Piper:

Will you please answer the following questions about the 3,200-square-foot office suite advertised in the June 28 issue of the *Daily Journal*? It appears that this space may be suitable for the new regional headquarters we are opening in your city in August.

- Is the layout of these offices suitable for a work force of two administrators, a receptionist, and seven office employees? (If possible, please send us a diagram of the space.)
- What is the annual rental charge?
- Are housekeeping, maintenance, and utilities included?
- What is the nature of the walls and flooring?
- Does the location provide easy access to mass transportation and the airport?
- What are your requirements for length of lease agreement?
- What escalation provisions are included in the lease agreement?

If your answers meet our needs, we would like to arrange a tour of the offices as soon as possible.

Sincerely,

116   PART 3 Basic Patterns of Business Messages

THEMATIC BOXES

Each chapter features thematic boxes to highlight and reinforce important topics.

INTRODUCTORY SITUATION

Each box presents a realistic business scenario and provides students with a context for the topics discussed in the text.

TECHNOLOGY IN BRIEF

These boxes reflect how current technologies affect business communication, covering topics such as text messaging, email etiquette, and software tools and technologies that students will encounter in the workplace.

COMMUNICATION MATTERS

Communication Matters boxes contain anecdotal and authoritative commentary to emphasize communication concepts from each chapter.

MARGIN NOTES

Extensive, running margin notes highlight important key concepts for student review and study.

REAL BUSINESS CASE ILLUSTRATIONS

Numerous examples feature real business companies with explanatory criticisms to show students how to apply the concepts discussed in the text.

A Wealth

GRADEMAX FOR BUSINESS COMMUNICATION

GradeMax is a new testing and remediation program that helps instructors assess student skill levels and provides students with customized assistance.

This adaptive testing engine tests students on the core concepts in each chapter or unit of *Business Communication: Making Connections in a Digital World*. As students answer each question, GradeMax alters the difficulty level of successive questions based on the student's response. The result is a unique, detailed view of each student's mastery of each chapter's core concepts. Following the tests, GradeMax provides proficiency reports of each student's comprehension. This allows instructors to adjust their teaching accordingly and also guide students on where to apply their study time. GradeMax offers topic-specific review modules for students to work on areas of weakness.

INSTRUCTOR'S RESOURCE CD-ROM

Included on the IRCD is the Instructor's Manual, the Test Bank, and an annotated PowerPoint presentation, including new slides with voiceovers. To ensure that the supplements affectively tie into the book's concepts, each item on the Instructor's CD is developed and created by the authors.

# of Supplements

ONLINE LEARNING CENTER

Numerous resources are available for both instructors and students online at **www.mhhe.com/lesikar11e**. Downloadable supplements for the Instructor include an Instructor's Manual, Test Bank, and PowerPoint slides. Students can access self-grading quizzes, review material, or work through interactive exercises.

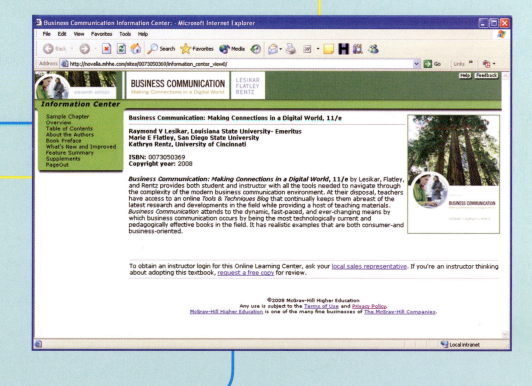

BRIEF CONTENTS

CONTENTS

PART THREE

Basic Patterns of Business Messages

Contents **xxi**

PART FIVE

Other Forms of Business Communication

PART SIX

Cross-Cultural Communication, Correctness, Technology, Research

APPENDIXES

1 Communication in the
Workplace

Norm Fjeldheim credits much of the success in his career to learning and developing his business writing and reporting skills. As a leader in a leading company in the digital wireless communications industry, he relies heavily on these well-honed skills. In overseeing all aspects of Qualcomm's information technology, he interacts with people in a wide variety of positions including QUALCOMM senior executives and board members, senior executives of customers and suppliers, and occasionally even the Department of Justice and the FBI on security issues. He also keeps his direct reports and customers informed and on track. By far the most important tools he uses daily for the majority of his work are Eudora, PowerPoint, and Word.

When asked about the most important class to take, he definitively answers " Business Communication." He says, "Even if you have great technical skills, your career will get stalled without good communication skills. In fact, the better your communication skills, the further you will go. While technology changes over time, being able to communicate well will always be valuable."

Norm Fjeldheim, Senior Vice President and CIO
Qualcomm

chapter one

Communication in the Workplace

LEARNING OBJECTIVES

Upon completing this chapter, you will understand the role and nature of communication in business. To achieve this goal, you should be able to

1 Explain the importance of communication to you and to business.

2 Describe the three main forms of communication in the business organization.

3 Describe the formal and informal communication networks in the business organization.

4 Describe factors that affect the types and amount of communicating that a business does.

5 Describe the various contexts for each act of business communication.

6 Describe the communication process.

7 Explain why business communication is a form of problem solving.

8 Explain three basic truths about communication.

9 Understand the importance of adaptation to successful communication.

10 Describe the goal and plan of this book.

THE ROLE OF COMMUNICATION IN BUSINESS

Your work in business will involve communication—a lot of it—because communication is a major and essential part of the work of business.

● Communication is important to business.

The Importance of Communication Skills to You

Because communication is so important in business, businesses want and need people with good communication skills. Evidence of the importance of communication in business is found in numerous surveys of executives, recruiters, and academicians. Without exception, these surveys have found that communication (especially written communication) ranks at or near the top of the business skills needed for success.

● Business needs good communicators,

Typical of these surveys is one by Robert Half International of the 1,000 largest employers in the United States. According to 96 percent of the executives surveyed, today's employees must have good communication skills to advance professionally.[1] A study of skills and competencies needed by accountants strongly supports the value of writing, speaking, and listening.[2] Similar results were found in an unpublished survey made by the Jones Graduate School of Management, Rice University, in 2000. The deans of the 90 programs surveyed reported that they see communication as one of the greatest teaching priorities of an MBA program. Most recently, NFI Research, a private organization that regularly surveys over 2,000 executives and senior managers, found that 94 percent of the members "rank 'communicating well' as the most important skill for them to succeed today and tomorrow."[3] These words to job seekers in *The Wall Street Journal* lend additional support to the importance of communication: "To stand out from the competition, you must demonstrate the unwritten requirements that are now most in demand: leadership and communication skills . . . ."[4]

Unfortunately, business's need for employees with good communication skills is all too often not fulfilled. Most employees, even the college trained, do not communicate well. In fact, surveys show that, in the opinion of their employees, even managers and executives who think they communicate well actually fall short.[5] Effective communicators are, therefore, in high demand. Not surprisingly, there is a high correlation between communication skills and income. Even among college graduates, those with higher scores in literacy (use of printed and written information) earn 47 percent more than lower scoring graduates earn.[6] A study by Office Team concluded that such skills as writing and speaking well, displaying proper etiquette, and listening attentively will probably determine career success. This study also reported that technology magnifies the exposure of one's communications skills, forcing workers to communicate more effectively and articulately because these skills will be showcased more. Email often results in a sender's language skills being placed in front of different people simultaneously, while audio and video will reveal the caliber of one's verbal and diplomacy strengths as well.[7]

● but most people do not communicate well.

The communication shortcomings of employees and the importance of communication in business explain why you should work to improve your communication skills. Whatever position you have in business, your performance will be judged largely by your ability to communicate. If you perform (and communicate) well, you are likely to

● By improving your communication ability, you improve your chances for success.

---

[1] Ann Fisher, "The High Cost of Living and Not Writing Well," *Fortune* 7 December 1998: 244.

[2] *Keying In: Newsletter of the National Business Education Association* 10.3 (2000): 4.

[3] Chuck Martin, *Tough Management: The 7 Winning Ways to Make Tough Decisions Easier, Deliver the Numbers, and Grow the Business in Good Times and Bad* (New York: McGraw-Hill, 2005) 1.

[4] David Perry, "Do You Have the Skills Most in Demand Today?" *Career Journal, The Wall Street Journal*, 20 May 2002, Dow Jones and Company, Inc 6 June 2003 <http:www.careerjournal.com/columnist/perspective/20020520-fmp.html>.

[5] "Study Offers Insights on Effective Communication from the Perspective of Employees," *Towers Perrin Monitor* 7 January 2005, Towers Pernn HR Services 8 January 2006 <http://www.towersperrin.com/hrservices/webcache/towers/TP_Monitor/jsp/showdoc_fromtowers.jsp?webc=../../TP_Monitor/2005/01/articles/m,on_article_-1-5c.htm>.

[6] Paul T. Decker et al., *Education and the Economy: An Indicators Report* (Washington, DC: Government Printing Office, 1997) 131.

[7] "The Challenge Facing Workers in the Future," *HR Focus* August 1999: 6 ff.

Some Quotes on Communication by Business Professionals

Communication is the most used skill in almost every job. How you communicate your accomplishments to others is a reflection of the quality of your work. Sure, you must know how to do your tasks to accomplish great results, but that is only a portion of professional success. Good communication skills are required to report your results to others, persuade colleagues to take action, and (most importantly at review time) sell your successes to management.

Don Zatyko, Senior Program Manager
IT Asset Management, Intuit

Communication is essential to building trust and teamwork among employees. To become a successful leader, you must have a great team. Just look at Michelangelo. He didn't paint the Sistine Chapel by himself, but with the help of his team. It is considered one of the best works in history. It's all about the team.

Mark Federighi, Fine Wine Sales Director
E & J Gallo Winery

Your message will get lost if it's not clear, concise and high impact! Get to the point quickly, let the recipient know exactly what you want, and use attention-grabbing techniques whenever possible.

Amy Betterton, IT Manager
San Diego Hospice and Palliative Care

Whenever I see a business document that has uncorrected typos and other grammatical mistakes, I wonder whether the author is (a) not very bright or (b) sloppy.

Glenda K. Moehlenpah, CPA, CFP®
Financial Bridges

Good communication skills are vital for your success on the job. They make the difference in how well your writing and spelling are perceived by others (if you can't explain it, maybe you don't know it), in your confidence in speaking to customers or giving presentations (which helps your company bring in revenue), and in your ability to be productive and efficient when working in a team (takes advantage of collective knowledge and shared resources).

Doris J. Towne, Manager, Technical Communications
Computer Associates, Int'l

Good communication is necessary in order to continually apply research findings and improve business operations.

Rosemary Lenaghan, Transportation Policy Analyst, Research
and Analysis Section
Illinois Commerce Commission

be rewarded with advancement. And the higher you advance, the more you will need your communication ability. The evidence is clear: Improving your communication skills improves your chances for success in business.

Why Business Depends upon Communication

• Communication is vital to every part of business.

Every business, even a one-person business, is actually an economic and social system. To produce and sell goods and services, any business must coordinate the activities of many groups of people: employees, suppliers, customers, legal advisors, community representatives, government agencies that might be involved, and others. This feat is achieved largely through communication.

Consider, for example, the communications of a pharmaceutical manufacturer. Throughout the company employees send and receive information about all aspects of the company's business, from sales to business strategy to manufacturing. They process information with computers, write messages, fill out forms, give and receive orders, talk

Peter Drucker, on the Importance of Communication in Business

Peter Drucker, recipient of the Presidential Medal of Freedom and one of the most respected management consultants, educators, speakers, and writers of our time, made these observations about communication:

> Colleges teach the one thing that is perhaps most valuable for the future employee to know. But very few students bother to learn it. This one basic skill is the ability to organize and express ideas in writing and speaking.
>
> As soon as you move one step from the bottom, your effectiveness depends on your ability to reach others through the spoken or the written word. And the further away your job is from manual work, the larger the organization of which you are an employee, the more important it will be that you know how to convey your thoughts in writing or speaking. In the very large organization . . . this ability to express oneself is perhaps the most important of all the skills a person can possess.

over the telephone, and meet face to face. Salespeople receive instructions and information from the home office and send back orders and regular reports of their contact with customers. Executives use written and oral messages to conduct business with customers and other companies, manage company operations, and perform strategic planning. Production supervisors receive work orders, issue instructions, receive status reports, and submit production summaries. Shop floor supervisors deliver production orders to the employees on the production line, communicate and enforce guidelines for safety and efficiency, troubleshoot problems that arise, and bring any concerns or suggestions back to management. Marketing professionals gather market information, propose new directions for company production and sales efforts, coordinate with the research and development staff, and receive direction from the company's executives. Research specialists receive or propose problems to investigate, make detailed records of their research, monitor lab operations for compliance with government regulations, and communicate their findings to management. Numerous communication-related activities occur in every other niche of the company as well: finance and accounting, human resources, legal, information systems, and others. Everywhere workers receive and send information as they conduct their work, and they may be doing so across or between continents as well as between buildings or offices.

Oral communication is a major part of this information flow. So, too, are various types of forms and records, as well as the storage and retrieval facilities provided by computers. Yet another major part consists of various forms of written communication—instant messaging, text messaging, email, letters, and reports.

- Information is managed and exchanged through many oral, written, and electronic forms.

All of this communicating goes on in business because communication is essential to the organized effort involved in business. Simply put, communication enables human beings to work together.

Main Categories of Business Communication

The importance of communication to business becomes even more apparent when we consider the communication activities of an organization from an overall point of view. These activities fall into three broad categories: internal operational, external operational, and personal.

- There are three categories of communication in business:

Internal-Operational Communication. All the communication that occurs in conducting work within a business is internal operational. This is the communication among the business's workers that is done to create, implement, and track the success of the business's operating plan. By *operating plan* we mean the procedure that the business has developed to do whatever it was formed to do—for example, to manufacture products, provide a service, or sell goods.

- (1) Internal operational—the communicating done in conducting work within a business,

"The shipment will be delayed. We were supposed to order
the trucks to get loaded at 9:00 AM, but we accidentally
ordered the truckers to get loaded at 9:00 AM."

- such as giving orders, assembling reports, and writing email.

Internal-operational communication takes many forms. It includes the ongoing discussions that senior management undertakes to determine the goals and processes of the business. It includes the orders and instructions that supervisors give workers, as well as oral exchanges among workers about work matters. It includes reports that workers prepare concerning sales, production, inventories, finance, maintenance, and so on. It includes the email messages that workers write in carrying out their assignments and contributing their ideas to the business.

Much of this internal-operational communication is performed on computer networks. Workers send electronic mail and post information on company intranets or portals for others throughout the business, whether located down the hall, across the street, or around the world. As you will learn in Chapter 18, the computer assists the business writer and speaker in many other aspects of communication as well.

- (2) External operational—work-related communication with people outside the business,

External-Operational Communication.
The work-related communicating that a business does with people and groups outside the business is external-operational communication. This is the business's communication with its publics—suppliers, service companies, customers, government agencies, the general public, and others.

Companies often use portals or intranets to communicate with employees such as this one at John Deere.

External-operational communication includes all of the business's efforts at direct selling: salespeople's "spiels," descriptive brochures, telephone callbacks, follow-up service calls, and the like. It also includes the advertising the business does to retain and generate new customers. Radio and television messages, newspaper and magazine advertising, website advertising, product placement, and point-of-purchase display material obviously play a role in the business's plan to achieve its work objective. Also in this category is all that a business does to improve its public relations, whether through planned publicity or formal and informal contacts between company representatives and the outside world. In fact, every act of communication with an external audience can be regarded as a public-relations message, conveying a certain image of the company. For this reason, all such acts should be undertaken with careful attention to both content and tone.

The importance of external-operational communication to a business hardly requires supporting comment. Because the success of a business depends on its ability to satisfy customers' needs, it must communicate effectively with those customers. But businesses also depend on each other in the production and distribution of goods and services. Coordinating with contractors, consultants, and suppliers also requires skillful communication. In addition, every business must communicate to some extent with government agencies, such as the Internal Revenue Service, the Securities and Exchange Commission, or the Environmental Protection Agency. Like internal communication, external communication is vital to business success.

Personal Communication. Not all the communication that occurs in business is operational. In fact, much of it is without apparent purpose as far as the operating plan of the business is concerned. This type of communication is personal. Do not make the mistake of underestimating its importance. Personal communication helps make and sustain the relationships upon which business depends.

Personal communication is the exchange of information and feelings in which we human beings engage whenever we come together. We are social animals. We have a need to communicate, and we will communicate even when we have little or nothing to say. You may have noticed that even total strangers are likely to communicate when they are placed together, as on an airplane flight, in a waiting room, or at a ball game. Such personal communication also occurs in the workplace, and it is a part of the communication activity of any business. Although not an obvious part of the business's plan of operation, personal communication can have a significant effect on the success of that plan. This effect is a result of the influence that personal communication can have on the attitudes of the employees and those with whom they communicate.

The employees' attitudes toward the business, each other, and their assignments directly affect their productivity. And the nature of conversation in a work situation affects attitudes. In a work situation where heated words and flaming tempers are often present, the employees are not likely to give their best efforts to their jobs. Likewise, a rollicking, jovial work situation can undermine business goals. Wise managers cultivate the optimum balance between employees' focus on job-related tasks and their freedom to bring their personal selves to work. They also know that chat around the water cooler or in the break room encourages a team attitude and can often be the medium in which actual business issues get discussed.

Even communication that is largely internal operational will often include personal elements that relieve the tedium of daily routine and enable employees to build personal relationships. Similarly, communication with external parties will naturally include personal remarks at some point. Sometimes you may find yourself writing a wholly personal message to a client, as when he or she has won a major award or experienced a loss of some kind. Other times, you may compose an external-operational message that also includes a brief personal note, perhaps thanking a client for a pleasant lunch or referring to a personal matter that came up in the course of a business meeting. Personal communication on the job is inevitable. When wisely undertaken, it makes business more successful, pleasant, and fulfilling.

- such as personal selling, telephoning, advertising, and writing messages.

- Every external message conveys an image of the company.

- Both internal and external communications are vital to business success.

- (3) Personal communication— non-business-related exchanges of information and feelings among people.

- Personal communication affects employee attitudes.

- And attitudes affect employee performance.

- The kinds of personal communication allowed and encouraged in the company affect employee attitudes.

- Personal communication elements can enhance internal and external business communication.

Communication Networks of the Organization

Looking over all of a business's communication (internal, external, and personal), we see an extremely complex system of information flow and human interaction. We see dozens, hundreds, or even thousands of individuals engaging in untold numbers of communication events throughout each workday.

There are, in fact, two complex networks of information in virtually any organization—one formal and one informal. Both are critically important to the success of the business.

The Formal Network. In simplified form, information flow in a modern business is much like the network of arteries and veins in the body. Just as the body has blood vessels, the business has major, well-established channels for information exchange. These are the formal channels—the main lines of operational communication. Through these channels flows the bulk of the communication that the business needs to operate. Specifically, the flow includes the upward, lateral, and downward movement of information in the form of reports, memos, email, and such within the organization; the downward movement of orders, instructions, advisories, and announcements; the broad dissemination of company information through the organization's newsletter, bulletin boards, email, intranet, or portal; and the channeling of company information outward to its various publics in forms of external-operational communication.

These officially sanctioned lines of communication cause certain forms of communication, or *genres*, to exist within the organization. For example, it may be customary in one company for project leaders to require a weekly report from team members. Or the executives in another company may hold monthly staff meetings. Whatever the established form (genre) it will bring with it certain expectations about what can and cannot be said, who may and may not say it, and how the messages should be structured and worded. This means that the favored forms (genres) will advance certain practices in the organization and discourage others. It is, therefore, important that the main channels in the formal communication network be carefully thought out and changed as the needs of the business change.

The Informal Network. Operating alongside the formal network is the informal network (see Figure 1–1). It comprises the thousands upon thousands of personal communications that may or may not support the formal communication network of a business. Such communications follow no set pattern; they form an ever-changing and infinitely complex structure linking the members of the organization.

The complexity of this informal network, especially in larger organizations, cannot be overemphasized. Typically, it is really not a single network but a complex relationship of smaller networks consisting of certain groups of people. The relationship is made even more complex by the fact that these people may belong to more than one group and that

- Information flow in a business can be said to form two complex networks, one formal and one informal.

- The formal network consists of the official, more stable lines of communication.

- Each company has its preferred communication forms, or *genres*, for conducting its business.

- The informal network, consisting largely of personal communications, is highly complex and ever changing.

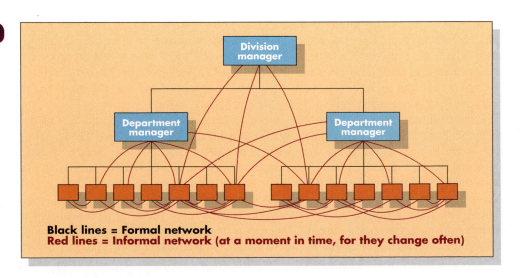

Figure 1–1

Formal and Informal Communication Networks in a Division of a Small Business

Black lines = Formal network
Red lines = Informal network (at a moment in time, for they change often)

group memberships and the links between and among groups are continually changing. The department you belong to, the other employees whom you see in the course of your work day, and even random personal connections, such as having the same home town or having kids the same age, can cause links in this network to form.

Known as the *grapevine* in management literature, this communication network is more valuable to the company's operations than a first impression might indicate. Certainly, it carries much gossip and rumor, for this is the nature of human conversation. And it is as fickle and inaccurate as the human beings who are a part of it. Even so, the grapevine usually carries far more information than the formal communication system, and on many matters it is more effective in determining the course of an organization. Skillful managers recognize the presence of the grapevine, and they know that the powerful people in this network are often not those at the top of the formal organizational hierarchy. They find out who the talk leaders are and give them the information that will do the most good for the organization. They also make management decisions that will cultivate positive talk.

Variation in Communication Activity by Business

- How much and what kinds of communicating a business does depends on the nature of the business, its operating plan, its environment, its geographic dispersion, and the people involved.

Just how much and what kind of communicating a business does depends on several factors. The nature of the business is one. For example, insurance companies have a great need to communicate with their customers, especially through letters and mailing pieces, whereas housecleaning service companies have little such need. The business's operating plan affects the amount of internal communication. Relatively simple businesses, such as repair services, require far less communication than complex businesses, such as automobile manufacturers. The business's relation to its environment also influences its communication practices. Businesses in a comparatively stable environment, such as textile manufacturing or commercial food processing, will tend to depend on established types of formal communication in a set organizational hierarchy, whereas those in a volatile environment, such as software development or telecommunications, will tend to improvise more in terms of their communications and company structure. Yet another factor is the geographic dispersion of the operations of a business. Obviously, internal communication in a business with multiple locations differs from that of a one-location business. Also, the people who make up a business affect its volume of communication. Every human being is unique. Each has unique communication needs and abilities. Thus, varying combinations of people will produce varying needs for communication.

- Each business has its own particular *culture*, which profoundly affects, and is affected by, its communication.

Each business can also be said to possess a certain organizational *culture,* which has a strong effect upon, and is strongly affected by, the company's communication. The concept of organizational or corporate culture was popularized in the early 1980s, and it continues to be a central focus of management consultants and theorists.[8] You can think of a given company's culture as its customary, often unexpressed, ways of perceiving and doing things. It is the medium of preferred values and practices in which the company's members do their work. Recall places you've worked or businesses you've patronized. In some, the employees' demeanor suggests a coherent, healthy culture in which people seem to know what to do and be happy doing it. At the other extreme are companies where employees exhibit little affiliation with the business and may even be sabotaging it through poor customer service or lack of knowledge about their jobs. The content and quality of the company's communication has a great deal to do with employees' attitudes and behavior.

- The officially publicized and the real company culture may not be the same.

Take care to note that the official culture and the actual culture in a company are not necessarily the same thing. Officially, the company management may announce and try to promote a certain culture through formal communication such as mission statements and mottoes. But the actual culture of a company is a dynamic, living realm of meaning constructed daily through infinite behaviors and communications at all levels of the company. Having your antennae out for the assumptions that actually drive people's conduct in your or your client's workplace will help you become a more effective communicator.

THE BUSINESS COMMUNICATION PROCESS

- The following discussion describes business communication as an interpersonal, goal-directed process.

Although we may view the communication of a business as a network of information flow, we must keep in mind that a business organization consists of people and that communication with those inside and outside the organization occurs among people. It is also helpful to bear in mind that, by and large, each act of business communication is designed to achieve particular goals. The following discussion highlights the main steps in tackling business communication problems.

---

[8] See Edgar H. Schein, *Organizational Culture and Leadership,* 3rd ed. (San Francisco: Jossey-Bass, 2004), which reviews the literature and offers a current perspective.

Figure 1–2

The Business Communication Process

Communicator 1 ...

1. senses a communication need
2. defines the problem
3. searches for possible solutions
4. selects a course of action (message type, contents, style, format, channel)
5. composes the message
6. delivers the message

The Larger Context
Business-Economic, Sociocultural, Historical

Communicator 1's World
Organizational
Professional
Personal

The Communicators' Relationship

initial message

1–6

Communicator 2's World
Organizational
Professional
Personal

7-10

responding message

Communicator 2 ...

7. receives the message
8. interprets the message
9. decides on a response
10. may send a responding message

A Model of Business Communication

Figure 1–2 shows the basic elements of a business communication event. Even though people can, and often do, communicate inadvertently, this communication model focuses on what happens when someone *deliberately* undertakes to communicate with someone else to achieve particular business-related goals.

You'll notice that the two communicators in the figure are labeled simply "Communicator 1" and "Communicator 2," instead of "Sender" and "Receiver" or "Communicator" and "Audience." Certainly any communication event begins with someone deciding that communication is needed and initiating that communication, with an intended "receiver" (a popular term in speech communication) or "audience" (the preferred term in composition) on the other end. But in many situations, especially those involving real-time conversation, the two parties work together to reach a mutual understanding. Even in situations where a communicator is attempting to deliver a complete, carefully prepared message—as in a letter, report, or oral presentation—the intended recipients have in a sense already participated in the construction of the message via the imaginative efforts of the writer or presenter, who has kept them in mind when composing and designing the message. The labels in this model are thus intended to convey the cooperative effort behind every successful communication event.

- Both parties in a communication event influence the outcome of that event.

The Contexts for Communication. Certain features of the communication situation are already in place as the communicators in our model begin to communicate.

The *larger context* includes the general business-economic climate; the language, values, and customs in the surrounding culture; and the historical moment in which the communication is taking place. Think about how these contexts might influence communication. For example, if the country's economy or a particular industry is flourishing, a communicator's message and the recipient's response may well be different than they would be in an economic slump. The sociocultural context also affects how they communicate. Whether they are communicating in the context of U.S. urban culture, for instance, or the culture of a particular region or another country, or whether they are communicating across cultures, their communication choices will be affected. The particular historical context of their communication can also be a factor. Consider how the terrorist attacks of 9/11 brought to the fore language about religion, war, and patriotism. Such shifts in language and values can trickle down into daily acts of communication. The skillful communicator is sensitive to these larger contexts, which always exert an influence and, to some extent, are always changing.

- Business communication always takes place within certain contexts, including

- (1) such larger contexts as the general business-economic climate, the surrounding culture, and the historical timing of the communication;

(2) the relationship of the communicators; and

(3) the particular contexts—organizational, professional, and personal—of each communicator.

The *relationship of the communicators* also forms an important context for communication. Certainly, communication is about moving information from point A to point B, but it also about interaction between human beings. Your first correspondence with someone begins a relationship between the two of you, whether as individuals, people in certain roles, or both. All future messages between you will need to take this relationship into account.

The communicators' *particular contexts* exert perhaps the strongest influence on the act of communication. These interrelated contexts can be

- *Organizational contexts.* As we've discussed, the type and culture of the organization you represent will shape your communication choices in many ways, and the organizational contexts of your audiences will, in turn, shape their responses. In fact, in every act of business communication, at least one of the parties involved is likely to be representing an organization. What you communicate and how you do so will be strongly shaped by the organization for whom you speak. In turn, the organization to which your audience belongs—its priorities, its current circumstances, even how fast or slow its pace of work—can strongly influence the way your message is received.

- *Professional contexts.* You know from school and experience that different professionals—whether physicians, social workers, managers, accountants, or those involved in other fields—possess different kinds of expertise, speak differently, and tend to focus on different things. What gets communicated and how can be heavily influenced by the communicators' professional roles. Be aware that internal audiences as well as external ones can occupy different professional roles and, therefore, favor different kinds of content and language. Employees in management and engineering, for example, have been demonstrated to have quite different priorities, with the former focusing on financial benefit and the latter on technological achievement.[9] Part of successful communication is being alert to your audiences' different professional contexts.

- *Personal contexts.* Who you are as a person comes from many sources: the genes you inherited, your family and upbringing, your life experiences, your schooling, the many people with whom you've come in contact, the culture in which you were reared. Who you are as a person also, to some extent, depends on your current circumstances. Successes and failures, current relationships, financial ups and downs, the state of your health, your physical environment—all can affect a particular communicative act. Since much business communication is between individuals occupying organizational roles, personal matters are usually not disclosed. But it is well to keep in mind the effect that these can have on the communicators.

The process of initiating a communication act can be said to have six basic stages:

(1) sensing a need for communication,

(2) defining the situation,

The Process of Communication. No one can know exactly what occurs inside the minds of communicators when they undertake to create a message, but researchers generally agree that the process includes the following activities, generally in this order:

1. Sensing a communication need. A problem has come to your attention, or you have an idea about how to achieve a certain goal. Perhaps someone has written an email of complaint and you must answer it, or perhaps you've noticed that the company could benefit from automating a certain procedure. Whatever the case, you find that an action is in order, and you believe that some form of communication will help you achieve the desired state.

2. Defining the situation. To create a successful message or plan a communication event, you need to have a well-informed sense of the situation. For example, if you

---

[9] See research by Dorothy A. Winsor, most recently *Writing Power: Communication in an Engineering Center* (Albany: SUNY Press, 2003).

Channel Choice Affects Message Success

"Its [sic] official, you no longer work for JNI Traffic Control and u [sic] have forfided (sic) any arrangements made." Can you imagine getting such a text message? The Sydney employer was sued over this inappropriate choice of a communication channel for firing an employee; in settling the matter the commissioner went further in stating that email, text messages, and even answering machines were inappropriate for official business communication. Or what about being notified by text message of an overdue bill? While some might think of that as a service, others regard it as much too invasive and inappropriate.

Historically, the importance of channel choice has been disputed, with some arguing that it is simply a means for transmitting words and others arguing that the chosen channel is, in itself, a message. However, today most people realize that the appropriate choice of communication channel contributes significantly, along with the words, to the success of the message. While early research in media richness provided guidelines for understanding when to use very lean (printed material) to very rich (face-to-face) channels, more recent studies as well as new technologies and laws have added new dimensions to this theory. Not only are there no clear-cut rules or guidelines, but the smallest change in context may lead to different choices.

In selecting a channel, a communicator needs to weigh several factors. Some of these include the message content, the communicators' levels of competency with the channel, the recipient's access to the channel, and the recipient's environment. Appropriate choice of a communication channel helps people communicate clearly, improving both their productivity and personal relationships.

have received a letter of complaint from a customer, what exactly is the problem here? Does the customer have a legitimate point? What further information might you need to acquire in order to understand the situation? In what ways is this problem like or unlike others you have solved? How might you or your organization's goals be hindered or helped depending on your communication choices?

3. Considering possible communication strategies. As your definition of the situation takes shape, you will start considering different options for solving it. What kind of communication event will you initiate, and what will you want to achieve with it? What image of yourself, your company, and your communication partners might you project in your message? To generate a good solution, you will need to think about and research your potential audiences and their contexts, your own goals and contexts, your relationship with each audience, and any relevant larger contexts.

    ● (3) considering possible communication strategies,

4. Selecting a course of action. Considering the situation as you've defined it and looking at your communication options, you will consider the potential costs and benefits of each option and select the optimum one. Your decision will include preliminary choices about the message type, contents, structure, verbal style, and visual format, and about the channel you will use to deliver the message.

    ● (4) selecting a course of action,

5. Composing the message. Here is where you either craft your message, carefully working out its contents, structure, verbal style, and visual format, or plan your strategy for discussing your solution with your audience. If you have decided to present or initiate your message orally, you will make careful notes or perhaps even write out your whole message or presentation and design any visuals you may need. If you have decided to write your message, you will use your favorite strategies for composing effectively. See the section on "The Process of Writing" in Chapter 5 for the strategies that writing researchers recommend.

    ● (5) composing the message, and

6. Sending the message. When your message is prepared or carefully planned, you are ready to deliver it to your intended recipients in the channel you have chosen. You choose a good time to deliver it, realizing, for example, that Monday morning may not be the best time to make an important phone call to a busy

    ● (6) sending the message.

executive. You also consider sending auxiliary messages, such as a "heads-up" phone call or email, that could increase your main message's chances of success. You want to do all you can to ensure that your message doesn't get lost amidst all the other stimuli competing for your intended audience's attention.

While these activities tend to form a linear pattern, the communicator often needs to revisit earlier steps while moving through the different activities. In other words, solving a communication problem can be a recursive process. This is particularly true for situations that invite many different solutions or heavily involve the audience in the communication process. A communicator may begin a communication event with a certain conception of the situation and then discover, upon further analysis or the discovery of new or additional facts, that this conception needs to be revised in order to take into account all the involved parties and their goals.

If all goes as planned, here is what will happen on the recipient's end:

7. Receiving the message. Your chosen channel has delivered your message to each intended recipient, who has perceived and decides to read or listen to your message.

8. Interpreting the message. Just as you had to interpret the situation that prompted your communication, your recipient now has to interpret the message you sent. This activity will involve not only extracting information from the message but also guessing your communication purpose, forming judgments about you and those you represent, and picking up on cues about the relationship you want to promote between the communicators. If you have anticipated the particular contexts and interests successfully, your recipient will form the impressions that you intended. The recipient may prompt the initiating communicator for help with this interpretive act, especially if the communication is a live conversation.

9. Deciding on a response. Any time you send a message, you hope for a certain response from your audiences, whether it be increased goodwill, increased knowledge, a specific responding action, or a combination of these. If your message has been carefully adapted to the recipient, it has a good chance of achieving the desired response.

10. Replying to the message. The recipient's response to your message will often take the form, at least in part, of replying to your message. When this is the case, the receiver is acting as communicator, following the process that you followed to generate your message.

Figure 1–3 lists the main questions to consider when developing a communication strategy. Taking this analytical approach will help you think consciously about each stage of the process and give you the best chance of achieving the desired results with your messages.

Business Communication as Problem Solving

As you look ahead to all the business communication tasks you may face, it can help to think about business communication as a problem-solving activity. Researchers in many fields—management, medicine, writing, psychology, and others—have studied problem solving. In general, they define *problem* as simply "a gap between where you are now and where you want to be."[10] Within this framework, a problem isn't always something negative; it can also be an opportunity to improve a situation or do things in a better way. As a goal-focused enterprise, business is all about solving problems, and so, therefore, is business communication.

- While the message-creation process tends to be linear, it can also be recursive, involving a return to earlier steps.

- The recipient of the message will then go through these basic stages:

- (7) receiving the message,

- (8) interpreting the message,

- (9) deciding on a response, and

- (10) replying to the message.

- Taking an analytical approach to each communication situation will give you the best chance for success.

- Business communication can be thought of as a problem-solving activity.

- A problem, as defined here, is not only a negative situation that needs to be remedied; it can also be an opportunity to gain something positive.

---

[10] For discussions of problem solving, see John R. Hayes, *The Complete Problem Solver*, 2nd ed. (Hillsdale, NJ: Lawrence Erlbaum, 1989); Janet E. Davidson and Robert J. Sternberg, eds., *The Psychology of Problem Solving* (Cambridge, UK: Cambridge University Press, 2003); Rosemary J. Stevenson, *Language, Thought, and Representation* (Chichester, UK: John Wiley, 1993); and Arthur B. VanGundy, *Techniques of Structured Problem Solving* (New York: Van Nostrand Reinhold, 1988).

Carefully thinking through the elements of each situation will give you the best odds of communicating successfully.

What is the situation?

• What has happened to make you think you need to communicate?

• What background and prior knowledge can you apply to this situation? How is this situation like or unlike others you have encountered?

• What do you need to find out in order to understand every facet of this situation? Where can you get this information?

What are some possible communication strategies?

• To whom might you communicate? Who might be your primary and secondary audiences? What are their different organizational, professional, and personal contexts? What would each care about or want to know? What, if any, is your prior relationship with them?

• What purpose might you want to achieve with each recipient? What are your organizational, professional, and personal contexts?

• What are some communication strategies that might help you achieve your goals?

• How might the larger business/economic, sociocultural, and historical contexts affect the success of different strategies?

Which is the best course of action?

• Which strategies are impractical, incomplete, or potentially dangerous? Why?

• Which of the remaining strategies looks like the optimum one? Why?

• What will be the best message type, contents, structure, style, and format for your message?

• What channel will you use to deliver it?

What is the best way to design the chosen message?

• Given your goals for each recipient, what information should your message include?

• What logical structure (ordering and grouping of information) should you use?

• What kind of style should you use? How formal or informal should you be? What kinds of associations should your language have? What image of yourself and your audience should you try to convey? What kind of relationship with each recipient should your message promote?

• How can you use text formatting, graphics, and/or supporting media to make your message easier to comprehend?

• What are your recipients' expectations for the channel you've chosen?

What is the best way to deliver the message?

• Are there any timing considerations related to delivering your message?

• Should you combine the main message with any other messages?

• How can you best ensure that each intended recipient receives and reads or hears your message?

The problem-solving literature divides problems into two main types: well defined and ill defined. The former can be solved by following a formula, such as when you are computing how much money is left in your department's budget. But most real-world problems, including business communication problems, cannot be solved this way. They do not come to us in neat packages with the path to the best solution clearly implied. Instead, they require research, analysis, creativity, and judgment. One reason why this is the case in business communication is that, as in any communication situation, people are involved—and people are both complex and unique. But the business context itself is often complex, presenting you with multiple options for handling any given situation. For example, if a customer has complained, what will you do about it? Nothing? Apologize? Imply that the customer was at fault? Give a conciliatory discount? Refuse to adjust the bill? Even a "simple" problem like this one requires thinking through the likely short- and long-term effects of several possible solutions.

• There are well-defined and ill-defined problems. Most business communication situations can be categorized as ill-defined problems, requiring analysis, creativity, and judgment.

Words of Wisdom

Students should practice managerial skills in the same way they practice writing and other communication skills. Just as reading a book about driving will not result in a skilled driver, students who only hear about ethical issues, leadership, and critical thinking will not be accomplished practitioners of these skills.

Paula E. Brown, Northern Illinois University
Jean Mausehund, University of Wisconsin, Whitewater

Paula E. Brown and Jean Mausehund, "Integrating Managerial Ethics into the Business Communication Curriculum," *Business Communication Quarterly* 60. 1 (1997): 89.

* *Heuristics* (problem-solving aids such as prior examples, analytical processes, or established communication plans) can help you solve business communication problems more efficiently, but they must be adapted to each unique situation.

Solving ill-defined problems involves combining existing resources with innovation and good judgment. Although this book presents basic plans for several common types of business communication messages, you will not be able to solve particular communication problems by just filling in the blanks of these plans. The plans can be thought of as *heuristics*—"rules of thumb" that keep you from reinventing the wheel with each new problem. But the plans do not tell you all you need to do to solve each unique communication problem. You must decide how to adapt each plan to the given situation.

What this means is that successful business communication is both more challenging and more exciting than you may have thought. You will need to draw on your own powers of interpretation and decision making to succeed with your human communication partners.

Some Basic Truths about Communication

* The communication process reveals some basic truths.

Business communication shares with other kinds of communication three foundational truths, each having to do with the challenge of getting others to share our points of view. Skillful communicators have a healthy respect for these truths and are motivated by them to plan and construct messages carefully.

* Because we all inhabit different perceptual and verbal worlds, the meaning extracted from a message can differ from the intended meaning.

Meaning Is in the Mind, and No Two Minds Are Alike. No experience comes to us unmediated by our own "filters"—our preconceptions, frames of reference, abilities, and circumstances. In the process of understanding and solving a communication problem, you use the mental resources you have to construct a vision of the situation and a sense of purpose. These, in turn, direct your communication choices. When your recipients receive your message, they have to use their unique mental resources to guess what you intended and evaluate it within their particular contexts. It is actually quite an accomplishment for your communication successfully to cross the divide between yourself and others.

* Meanings are unstable and imperfectly represented by symbols.

The Symbols for Communicating Are Imperfect, and So Are Our Best Communication Efforts. We often take for granted that the language we use has dependable, stable meanings. But there is no intrinsic relationship between any symbols, including words, and what they are being used to represent. As the semanticist Alfred Korzybski wrote, "The map is not the territory." Instead, the connection between words and reality depends on social convention. If enough people agree that a word will have a certain meaning, then it will—until new social influences cause the meaning to change. But even at their most stable, words are crude substitutes for the real thing.

The word *house* can refer to structures ranging from shanties to palatial mansions. The word *family* can stand for many different kinds of human connections. Cultural differences can cause drastic variations in terminology and the assumed meanings of words. Even more problematic is that two people can use the same word but mean entirely different things. For example, what does the word *liberal* mean? Or *fairness*? How about *teamwork* or *boss*? The meanings with which people fill these verbal slots can vary enormously in connotation and even denotation. When communicators are—unbeknownst to themselves—using the same term but with very different meanings, they are experiencing a form of miscommunication known as "bypassing." Being alert to the slippery nature of the linkage between words and things can help you avoid such communication problems.

- Bypassing occurs when communicators are unaware that they are using the same word in different ways.

Managing the tenuous connection between symbols and what they represent is not your only challenge, however. Virtually every significant communication task that you will face will involve assessing a unique configuration of factors that requires at least a somewhat unique solution. This means that there is no one right answer to a communication problem. Different people will handle different cases somewhat differently, depending on who they are, how they interpret the situation, and who they imagine their recipients to be. Does this mean that all communication solutions are equally valid? Not at all. While there is no perfect solution, there can be many bad ones that have been developed without enough analysis and effort. Focused thinking, research, and planning will not guarantee success in the shifting, complex world of human communication, but they will make your chances of success as high as possible.

- While there is no one perfect solution to any given communication problem, some solutions are definitely better than others.

Communication Is about Information *and* Relationships. A common mistake that inexperienced business communicators make is to assume that the point of communicating is solely to transfer information. Getting important information from one place to another is critical to the success of any business or organization, and much of this book is about getting your message across as clearly as possible. But as we have said, the creation and maintenance of positive human relations is also essential to successful business communication. Every act of communication carries with it an implied view of the communicators' relationship. When planning and crafting your messages, be careful not to neglect this important dimension, which can make or break your communication efforts. See Chapter 4, in particular, for ways to build goodwill between yourself and your audience.

- Conveying information is not the only important goal of business communication. Cultivating positive relationships is also critical to successful communication.

Because communication always involves human relations, it also involves ethics. Each message is an effort to engage other persons, shape their attitudes, and influence their behavior. In the realm of business, it is also an occasion to help, hinder, or otherwise affect your organization and those whose welfare depends upon it. Words and other symbols have the power to achieve positive or negative effects. You have an obligation to avoid deception, to enable people to make informed decisions, and to consider all the likely effects of your messages on others.

- Every act of communication involves ethics.

The Importance of Adaptation

As you can see, conveying your meaning to another person in such a way that you receive the desired response can be a challenge. The unstable nature of language and the uniqueness of each person threaten to make successful communication impossible. Your key strategy for overcoming these difficulties is *adaptation*.

By *adaptation* we mean fitting every facet of your communication solution to your intended recipients. From figuring out what you want to say to deciding on each word, putting your audience at the heart of your communication efforts is your best strategy for success. As you will see, adaptation is the foundation for our review of communication principles in the pages ahead. The ability to analyze your intended communication partners and direct your message to them is perhaps *the* central communication skill, and it is one that will serve you well personally and professionally.

- Your best ally when facing the challenge of communicating with others is adaptation (adapting your message to your intended recipients).

THE GOAL AND PLAN OF THIS BOOK

The preceding discussion shows that communication is important to business, that it is performed in various and complex ways, and that it involves numerous stages of analysis and decision making. Helping you develop the communication skills you'll need in order to achieve your business purposes is the goal of this book.

The Plan: Situations, Solutions, Summaries

To achieve this goal, the book introduces each major topic through a business communication situation that realistically places you in the business world. Each situation describes a possible communication problem. Then the following material instructs you on how to solve this kind of problem. For your study convenience, summaries of the text material appear in the margins. A general summary by learning objectives appears at the end of each chapter.

An Overarching Rule: Ethical Communication

As we have said, the human-relations dimension of communication makes it an activity that involves ethics. But business communication in particular brings ethical considerations into play. The fundamental purpose of a business is to stay in business and, most would say, to maintain or increase stakeholder wealth. When a business is in trouble or the owners are greedy, it can be tempting to try to serve this purpose by using communication in unethical ways—for example, lying about or omitting critical information, promoting unfair employment practices, or generating unhealthy needs on the part of consumers. In the pages ahead you will learn how words can be selected and organized to achieve desired goals. These goals can range from good to bad extremes. Without exception, our emphasis will be on achieving effects consistent with honorable goals.

SUMMARY BY LEARNING OBJECTIVES

1 Explain the importance of communication to you and to business.

1. Business needs and rewards people who can communicate, for communication is vital to business operations.
   - But good communicators are scarce.
   - So, if you can improve your communication skills, you increase your value to business and advance your own career as well.

2 Describe the three main forms of communication in the business organization.

2. Communicating in business falls into three categories:
   - *Internal-operational* communication is the communicating a business does to implement its operating plan (its procedure for doing what it was formed to do).
   - *External-operational* communication is the communicating a business does with outsiders (customers, other businesses, the public, government agencies, and such).
   - *Personal* communication is informal exchanges of information not formally related to operations but nevertheless important to an organization's success.

3 Describe the formal and informal communication networks in the business organization.

3. The flow of communication in a business organization forms a complex and ever-changing network. Information continually flows from person to person—upward, downward, and laterally.
   - The communicating that follows the formal structure of the business comprises the *formal* network. Primarily, operational information flows through this network, which is sustained by particular forms of communication (*genres*).
   - The flow of personal communication forms the *informal* network, or *grapevine*.

4. The kind and amount of communicating a business does depend upon such factors as
   - The nature of the business.
   - Its operating plan.
   - Its environment.
   - The geographic dispersion of its members.
   - Its people.
   - Its organizational *culture* (an organization's customary, often unexpressed, ways of perceiving and doing things).

4 Describe factors that affect the types and amount of communicating that a business does.

5. Business communication takes place in these contexts:
   - The larger business-economic, sociocultural, and historical contexts.
   - The relationship of the communicators.
   - The communicators' own worlds: organizational, professional, and personal.

5 Describe the various contexts for each act of business communication.

6. The process of communication involves these activities, which tend to be linear in nature but are often *recursive* (revisiting earlier steps):

   The initiator
   - Senses a communication need.
   - Defines the situation.
   - Considers possible communication strategies.
   - Selects a course of action (message type, contents, style, format, channel).
   - Composes the message.
   - Sends the message.

   The intended recipient
   - Receives the message.
   - Interprets the message.
   - Decides on a response.
   - May send a responding message.

6 Describe the communication process.

7. Business communication can be thought of as a problem-solving activity.
   - Finding communication solutions requires analysis, creativity, and judgment.
   - *Heuristics* (problem-solving devices such as common communication plans) can help make your communication problem-solving more efficient.
   - The common communication plans must still be adapted to each situation.

7 Explain why business communication is a form of problem solving.

8. The communication process reveals these truths:
   - Meaning is in the mind, and no two minds are alike.
   - The symbols for communicating are imperfect, and so are our best communication efforts.
   - Communication is about information and relationships.

8 Explain three basic truths about communication.

9. Your best strategy for overcoming communication challenges is adaptation (fitting every facet of your communication solution to your intended recipients).

9 Understand the importance of adaptation to successful communication.

10. The plan of this book is to introduce you to the primary types of business communication strategies through realistic situations.
    - You are placed in a situation that involves a particular communication problem.
    - You are shown how to solve it by using problem analysis, common communication strategies, and adaptation.
    - And always the emphasis is on ethics.

10 Describe the goal and plan of this book.

1 "If there's no definitive solution, then all ways of handling a business communication problem are equally good." Using the discussion of business communication problem solving in this chapter, explain why this statement is false.

2 Think of a recent transaction you had with a business person or a staff person at your school. Describe the contexts of your communication, from the larger context (business-economic, sociocultural, and historical) down to the personal (to the extent you know them). How did these help determine the outcome of your communication?

3 Is the ability to communicate more important to the successful performance of a supervisor than to the successful performance of a company president? Defend your answer.

4 Make a list of types of companies requiring extensive communication. Then make a list of types of companies requiring little communication. What explains the difference in these two groups?

5 List the types of external-operational and internal-operational communication that occur in an organization with which you are familiar (school, fraternity, church, or such).

6 Identify the types of technology used primarily in internal- and external-operational communication to transmit messages. Explain what you think might account for the differences.

7 "Never mix business with personal matters—it just leads to damaged relationships, poor business decisions, or both." In what ways might this be a fair statement? In what ways is it unwise advice?

8 Describe the network of communication in an organization with which you are familiar (preferably a simple one). Discuss and explain.

9 In *Images of Organization* (2nd ed., Thousand Oaks, CA: Sage, 1997), management scholar Gareth Morgan has analyzed companies using a variety of metaphors. For example, he has looked at those elements of a company that make it appear to run like a machine (with rigidly organized, specific job roles), an organism (with elements that make it dependent upon and responsive to its environment), a brain (with self-managing teams and employees who can do a variety of jobs as needed), and a political system (with employees vying for power and influence). Think of an organization you know well and decide upon its dominant cultural metaphor. Is it one of Morgan's? Or is it a family? A team? A community? A prison? A mixture of several kinds? Once you settle on your metaphor, be prepared to explain how this organization's culture affects, and is affected by, its communication practices.

10 As this chapter said, companies develop specific forms of communication, or genres, that enable them to get their work done. In a place where you have worked or another organization you have been a member of, what were the main forms of communication with the employees or members? To what extent were these uniquely adapted to the needs of the organization?

11 Using this chapter's discussion of communication, explain how people reading or hearing the same message can disagree on its meaning.

12 Give an example of a word or phrase used in business, in the news, or in our general culture and explain why it can be construed in several ways depending on the interpreter's point of view.

1 Find two websites of companies in the same industry—for example, two manufacturers of household products or two wireless service providers. Using the evidence presented on their websites, compare their company cultures. Look at their stated mission (if any), their history (if provided), the gender and qualifications of their personnel (if given), their employee benefits, their information for job applicants, their information for investors, the company image projected by the visual elements on the site—anything that suggests who they are or want you to think they are. Write up your comparison in a well-organized, well-supported message to your instructor.

2 Megan Cabot is one of 12 workers in Department X. She has strong leadership qualities, and all her co-workers look up to her. She dominates conversations with them and expresses strong viewpoints on most matters. Although she is a good worker, her dominating personality has caused problems for you, the new manager of Department X. Today you directed your subordinates to change a certain work procedure. The change is one that has proven superior wherever it has been tried. Soon after giving the directive, you noticed the workers talking in a group, with Megan the obvious leader. In a few minutes she appeared in your office. "We've thought it over," she said. "Your production

change won't work." Explain what is happening. How will you handle the situation?

3   After noticing that some workers were starting work late and finishing early, a department head wrote this message to subordinates: It is apparent that many of you are not giving the company a full day's work. Thus, the following procedures are implemented immediately:

a. After you clock in, you will proceed to your workstations and will be ready to begin work promptly at the start of the work period.

b. You will not take a coffee break or consume coffee on the job at the beginning of the work period. You will wait until your designated break times.

c. You will not participate in social gatherings at any time during the workday except during designated break periods.

d. You will terminate work activities no earlier than 10 minutes prior to the end of the work period. You will use the 10 minutes to put up equipment, clean equipment, and police the work area.

e. You will not queue up at the exit prior to the end of the work period.

The message was not well received by the workers. In fact, it led to considerable anger, misunderstanding, and confusion. Using the discussion of communication planning in this chapter, explain where the department head's problem-solving process went awry. What did he or she fail to take into account?

4   Find an article in the business press or general news about a recent incident involving a company—for example, a merger or acquisition, a scandal or crisis, or the launching of a new product. What kind of communication challenges might this event pose for the company, both internally and externally? What kinds of messages would probably need to be written, and to whom?

5   Times are hard for RoboSolutions, a small local company that creates assembly-line robotics. Lately, the clients have been few and far between. But today the sales staff got encouraging news: James Pritchett, president of a nearby tool and die company, has inquired about the possibility of your company's designing a series of computer-run robots for key processes in the plant. There's a hitch, though: it's Sarah McCann's turn to try to snare his business (and the commission)—and Pritchett is known to prefer dealing with men. Do you, as president, send Sarah anyway, or do you send in one of your male salespeople to get Pritchett's business, giving Sarah a shot at the next potential client? How would you solve this communication—and ethics—problem?

With a net worth of around $42 billion, Warren Buffett is ranked by *Forbes Magazine* as the second-richest person in the world, after Microsoft co-founder and chairman Bill Gates. Buffett made his first stock purchase at the age of 11, but sold before the stock skyrocketed. This early lesson taught him to study hard and carefully analyze potential investments. The result was the development of one of the world's largest holding companies, Berkshire Hathaway, Inc.

Although best known for his ability to pick stocks, Buffett was honored in 2006 by the National Commission on Writing for America's Families, Schools, and Colleges for writing Berkshire Hathaway's annual report. Buffett writes, "One way or another, you have to project your ideas to other people. Writing isn't necessarily easy . . . But you get better and better at it, and I encourage everybody to do that."

Warren E. Buffett, CEO of Berkshire Hathaway, Inc.

chapter two

Adaptation and the Selection of Words

Upon completing this chapter, you will be able to adapt your language to specific readers and to select the most effective words for use in business communication. To reach this goal, you should be able to

1 Explain the role of adaptation in selecting words that communicate.

2 Simplify writing by selecting familiar and short words.

3 Use technical words and acronyms appropriately.

4 Write concretely and use active verbs.

5 Write with clarity and precision by selecting the right words and by using idioms correctly.

6 Use words that do not discriminate.

Choosing Words That Communicate

As a means of introducing yourself to business communication, place yourself in a hypothetical situation. You are the entrepreneurial manager of a struggling small business. You work very hard to make certain that all aspects of your business function effectively and efficiently. At the moment your attention is focused generally on the communicating done by your subordinates. Specifically, you are concerned about the communicating of Max Elliott, your assistant manager.

You have before you an email report from Max. Following your instructions, he investigated your company's use of available space. He has summarized his findings in this report. At first glance you are impressed with Max's work. But after reading further, you are not sure just what his investigation has uncovered. Here is a typical paragraph:

In the interest of ensuring maximum utilization of the subterranean components of the building currently not apportioned to operations departments, it is recommended that an evaluation of requisites for storage space be initiated. Subject review should be initiated at the earliest practicable opportunity and should be conducted by administrative personnel not affiliated with operative departments.

Max's problem is altogether too commonplace in business. His words, though properly used, do not communicate quickly and easily. This and the following chapter show you what you can do about writing like this.

THE IMPORTANCE OF ADAPTATION

Clear writing begins with adapting your message to your specific readers. As Chapter 1 explains, readers occupy particular organizational, professional, and personal contexts. They do not all have the same kind or level of vocabulary, knowledge, or values. And you do not have the same relationship with all of them.

- For writing to be clear, it must be adapted to your readers.

To choose words that communicate clearly and with the appropriate tone, you should learn everything possible about those with whom you wish to communicate and take into account any prior correspondence with them. Then you should word your message so that it is easy for them to understand it and respond favorably. Tailoring your message to your readers is not only strategically necessary, it is also a sign of consideration for their time and energy. Everyone benefits when messages are clear and appropriate to the correspondents' situation.

- Use all your knowledge of your readers to adapt your messages to them.

Technique of Adapting

In many business situations, adapting to your reader means writing on a level lower than the one you would normally use. For example, you will sometimes need to communicate with people whose educational level is below your own. Or you may need to communicate with people of your educational level who simply do not know much about the subject of your message.

- Often you will need to write at levels lower than your own.

To illustrate, assume that you need to write a message to a group of less-educated workers. You know that their vocabularies are limited. If you are to reach them, you will have to use simple words. If you do not, you will not communicate. On the other hand, if you had to write the same message to a group of highly educated people, you would have a wider choice of words. These people have larger vocabularies than the first group. In either case, however, you would select words that the intended readers understand.

- In writing to less-educated workers, for example, you may need to simplify. You may write differently for highly educated people.

Adaptation Illustrated

The following paragraphs from two company annual reports illustrate the basic principle of adaptation. The writer of the first report apparently viewed the readers as people who were not well informed in finance.

Last year your company's total sales were $117,400,000, which was slightly higher than the $109,800,000 total for the year before. After deducting for all expenses, we

A Classic Case of Adaptation

There is a story told around Washington about a not-too-bright inventor who wrote the Bureau of Standards that he had made a great discovery: Hydrochloric acid is good for cleaning clogged drains.

He got this response: "The efficacy of hydrochloric acid is indisputable, but the corrosive residue is incompatible with metallic permanence."

Believing that these big words indicated agreement, this not-so-bright inventor wrote back telling how pleased he was that the bureau liked his discovery.

The bureaucrat tried again: "We cannot assume responsibility for the production of toxic residue with hydrochloric acid and suggest alternative procedure."

The inventor was even more gratified. He again expressed his appreciation to the bureau for agreeing with him.

This time the bureaucrat got the message. He replied in words any inventor would be certain to understand: "Don't use hydrochloric acid. It'll eat hell out of pipes."

---

had $4,593,000 left over for profits, compared with $2,830,000 for 2003. Because of these increased profits, we were able to increase your annual dividend payments per share from the 50 cents paid over the last 10 years.

The writer of the second report saw the readers as being well informed in finance. Perhaps this writer believed the typical reader would come from the ranks of stockbrokers, financial managers, financial analysts, and bankers. So this writer adapted the annual report to these readers with language like this:

> The corporation's investments and advances in three unconsolidated subsidiaries (all in the development stage) and in 50 percent–owned companies was $42,200,000 on December 31, 2003, and the excess of the investments in certain companies over net asset value at dates of acquisition was $1,760,000. The corporation's equity in the net assets as of December 31, 2006, was $41,800,000 and in the results of operations for the years ended December 31, 2003 and 2004, was $1,350,000 and $887,500, respectively. Dividend income was $750,000 and $388,000 for the years 2003 and 2004, respectively.

Which writer was right? Perhaps both. Perhaps neither. The answer depends on what the stockholders of each company were really like. Both examples illustrate the technique of adaptation. They use different words for different audiences, which is what you should try to do.

Adapting to Multiple Readers

- Writing to multiple readers can be a challenge.

Adapting your message to one reader requires considerable care, but what if, as often happens, you need to address your message to several different readers? What if your readers vary widely in education, knowledge of the subject, and so on? How can you write your message in such a way that you communicate to everyone? The solution is to write in such a way that everyone can find and follow the parts of your message that are intended for and of value to them.

For example, assume that you are the assistant director of marketing for a telecommunications company and you need to report some complex marketing data to your boss in marketing, to the sales manager, and to the president of the company. How might you design your report so that all three, with their differing levels of familiarity with market research techniques, could understand it?

For the sales manager and the president, the nonexperts, you will need to define any specialized vocabulary you use. You will also spell out the implications of your findings for their domains of interest. For example, the sales manager in our example will need

In talking to a child, we naturally adapt the language to the child. Similarly, in business communication we need to adapt the language to the reader.

you to say what your findings mean for the sales staff, while the president will want to understand how your findings could enhance the financial health of the company.

Accommodating the nonexperts need not alienate or bore the expert readers. They often can benefit from seeing the bigger picture themselves, and they usually are not bothered when definitions and explanations are provided. Often it is helpful to to provide clearly worded headings in your message so that readers looking for different things can find those parts, read them carefully, and then skim or skip the rest.

- Accommodating nonexperts usually does not impair your communication with experts.

Adaptation: Your Best Strategy for Effective Wording

As with every other element of your messages, your choice of words needs to be guided by your audience and purpose. For example, knowing that your writing should be "clear and concise" is not enough; What this means will depend a great deal on the situation. As we have suggested above, what is clear for one person may not be clear at all for another. People occupy different language domains, and anything outside their domains will not be clear unless it is explained in their language. As for conciseness, you must be careful not to sacrifice effectiveness for brevity. If you cut your communications too short for your readers—for example, by omitting important details in a persuasive message or critical information in a report—you have written an incomplete, not a concise, message.

- Write in the reader's language, and don't sacrifice effectiveness for brevity.

SUGGESTIONS FOR SELECTING WORDS

The advice in the following paragraphs will stand you in good stead in most business communication situations. But, as we have said, you must use them with good judgment. The words that communicate best will be those that appeal to your particular readers and enable them easily to understand what you are trying to say.

Several of these suggestions support simplicity in writing. This approach is justified for three good reasons. The first is that many of us tend to write at too difficult a level. Instead of being ourselves, we change character when we write. Rather than being friendly, normal people, we become cold and stiff. We work to use big words and complex structures. Winston Churchill referred to this tendency when he made his classic remark: "Little men use big words; big men use little words." We would do well to follow the example of this well-regarded communicator.

The second reason for simplicity is that the writer usually knows the subject of the message better than the reader. Thus, the two are not equally equipped to communicate

- Use the following suggestions for selecting words with good judgment.

- These suggestions stress simplicity for three reasons: (1) many people tend to write at a difficult level;

- (2) the writer usually knows the subject better than the reader; and

on the matter. If the writer does not work at reducing the message to the reader's level, communication will be difficult.

The third reason for simplicity is that convincing research supports it. According to the readability research of such experts as Gunning, Dale, Chall, and Flesch, writing slightly below the reader's level of understanding communicates best.

- (3) the results of research support simplicity.

Use Familiar Words

The foremost suggestion for word selection is to use familiar words. These are the everyday words—the words with sharp and clear meanings in the mind. Because words that are familiar to some people may be unfamiliar to others, you will need to select familiar words with care. You have no choice but to rely on your judgment.

- Familiar words communicate. Use them. Use your judgment in determining what words are familiar.

Specifically, using familiar words means using the language that most of us use in everyday conversation. We should avoid the stiff, more difficult words that do not communicate so precisely or quickly. For example, instead of using the more unfamiliar word *endeavor,* use *try.* Instead of using *terminate,* use *end.* Prefer *use* to *utilize, do* to *perform, begin* to *initiate, find out* to *ascertain, stop* to *discontinue,* and *show* to *demonstrate.*

The suggestion to use familiar words does not rule out some use of more difficult words. You should use them whenever their meanings fit your purpose best and your readers understand them clearly. The mistake that many of us make is to overwork the more difficult words. We use them so much that they interfere with our communication. A good suggestion is to use the simplest words that carry the meaning without offending the readers' intelligence. Perhaps the best suggestion is to write the words you would use in face-to-face communication with your readers.

- Difficult words are not all bad. Use them when they fit your needs and are understood.

The following contrasting examples illustrate the communication advantages of familiar words over less familiar ones.[1] As you read the examples, consider the effect on communication of an entire message or report written in the styles illustrated.

Unfamiliar Words	Familiar Words
This machine has a tendency to develop excessive and unpleasant audio symptoms when operating at elevated temperatures.	This machine tends to get noisy when it runs hot.
Ms. Smith's idiosyncrasies supply adequate justification for terminating her employment status.	Ms. Smith's peculiar ways justify firing her.
This antiquated mechanism is ineffectual for an accelerated assembly-line operation.	This old robot will not work on a fast assembly line.
The most operative assembly-line configuration is a unidirectional flow.	The most efficient assembly-line design is a one-way flow.
The conclusion ascertained from a perusal of pertinent data is that a lucrative market exists for the product.	The data studied show that the product is in good demand.
Company operations for the preceding accounting period terminated with a substantial deficit.	The company lost much money last year.

An example supporting the use of familiar words came from Cape Kennedy while scientists were conducting research in preparation for long spaceflights. In one experiment, a monkey was placed in a simulated spaceship with enough food to last many days. With an unlimited supply of food available, the monkey simply ate too much and died. A scientist used these words to record the incident: "One monkey succumbed unexpectedly apparently as a result of an untoward response to a change in feeding regimen." Most readers of the report missed the message. Why didn't the scientist report in everyday language, "One monkey died because it ate too much"?

---

[1] For some of these examples, we are indebted to students and friends who gave them to us over the years.

An old but classic example involved President Franklin D. Roosevelt in World War II. Across his desk came a memorandum advising federal workers to do the following in the event of an air raid:

Such preparations shall be made as will completely obscure all federal buildings and nonfederal buildings occupied by the federal government during an air raid for any period of time from visibility by reason of internal or external illumination. Such obscuration may be obtained either by blackout construction or by termination of the illumination.

Irked by the heavy wording, FDR sent this memorandum to the author:

Tell them that in buildings where they have to keep the work going to put something over the windows; and, in buildings where they can let the work stop for a while, turn out the lights.

In this and the preceding examples, the familiar words are clearly better. Readers understand them.

Use Slang and Popular Clichés with Caution

At any given time in any society some slang words and clichés are in vogue. As this book goes to press, "yada, yada, yada," "master of your domain" (*Seinfeld*), "voted off the island" (*Survivor*), and "Is that your final answer?" (*Who Wants to Be a Millionaire*) are widely used. Such expressions may convey a desired effect in a communication. But they are likely to be meaningful only for the moment. They may be out of vogue tomorrow along with "Where's the beef?" "$64,000 question," "to beat sixty," and the countless others from past generations. Thus, you should use such expressions sparingly and always only in informal communication with people who know and appreciate them.

- Use popular slang and clichés only when meaningful and appropriate.

Choose Short Words

According to studies of readability, short words generally communicate better than long words. Of course, part of the explanation is that short words tend to be familiar words. But there is another explanation: A heavy use of long words—even long words that are understood—leaves an impression of difficulty that hinders communication.

- Generally, short words communicate better.

The suggestion that short words be chosen does not mean that all short words are easy and all long words are hard. Many exceptions exist. Few people know such one-syllable words as *gybe, verd,* and *id*. Even children know such long words as *hippopotamus, automobile,* and *bicycle*. On the whole, however, word length and word difficulty are related. Thus, you should concentrate on short words and use long words with caution. Use a long word only when you think your readers know it.

- Some exceptions exist.

This point is illustrated by many of the examples presented to support the use of familiar words. But the following illustrations give it additional support. In some of them, the long-word versions are likely to be understood by more highly-educated readers. Even so, the heavy proportion of hard words clouds the message. Without question, the short-word versions communicate better. Note that the long words and their short replacements are in italics.

Long Words	Short Words
The decision was *predicated* on the *assumption* that an abundance of *monetary* funds was *forthcoming*.	The decision was *based* on the *belief* that there *would be more money*.
They *acceded* to the *proposition* to *terminate* business.	They *agreed to quit* business.
During the *preceding* year the company *operated* at a *financial deficit*.	*Last year* the company *lost money*.
Prior to *accelerating productive operation*, the supervisor inspected the machinery.	Before *speeding up* production, the supervisor inspected the machinery.

Long Words	Short Words
Definitive action was *effected subsequent* to the reporting date.	*Final* action was *taken after* the reporting date.
The *unanimity* of current forecasts is not *incontrovertible evidence* of an *impending* business acceleration.	*Agreement* of the forecasts is not *proof* that business *will get better*.
This *antiquated merchandising* strategy is *ineffectual* in *contemporary* business *operations*.	This *old sales* strategy *will not work* in *today's* business.

Mark Twain understood the value of using short words when he made this often-quoted statement: "I never use a word like *metropolis* when I can get the same price for *city*." One bureaucrat who did not understand the principle created a position to improve communication and gave it the title of Coordinator for the Obliteration of Proliferation of Obfuscation!

Use Technical Words and Acronyms with Caution

- All fields have technical words.

Every field of business—accounting, information systems, finance—has its technical language. This language can be so complex that in some cases specialized dictionaries are compiled. Such dictionaries exist for computers, law, finance, and other business specialties. There are even dictionaries for subareas such as databases, ecommerce, and real estate.

- These words are useful when you communicate with people in your field. But they do not communicate with outsiders. Use them with caution.

As you work in your chosen field, you will learn its technical words and acronyms. In time you will use these terms freely in communicating with people in your field. This is as it should be, for such terms are useful. Frequently, one such word will communicate a concept that would otherwise take dozens of words to describe. Moreover, specialized language can signal to other specialists that you are qualified to communicate on their level.

A problem comes about, however, when you use technical terms with people outside your field. Because these words are everyday words to you, you tend to forget that not everyone knows them. The result is miscommunication. You can avoid such miscommunication by using technical words with extreme caution. Use them only when your readers know them.

- Some examples are *covered employment, cerebral vascular accident, annuity, bobtail.* These words are well known to people in special fields, but not to most outsiders.

Examples of misuse of technical writing are easy to find. To a worker in the Social Security Administration, the words *covered employment* commonly mean employment covered by social security. To some outsiders, however, they could mean working under a roof. When a physician uses the words *cerebral vascular accident* with other physicians, they understand. Most people would get little meaning from these words, but they could understand a *minor stroke. Annuity* has a clear meaning to someone in insurance. A *contract that guarantees an income for a specified period* would have more meaning to uninformed outsiders. Computer specialists know C# and Java to be popular programming languages, but these words may have different meanings for others. To a trucker *bobtail* means a tractor cab without trailer. Nontruckers might get other meanings from that word—or perhaps no meaning at all.

- Use initials cautiously. Spell out and define as needed.

Initials (including acronyms) should be used with caution, too. While some initials, such as IBM, are widely recognized, others, such as XML (extensible markup language), are not. Not only might your readers not know certain initials, they might confuse them with others. For example, if you saw SARS, you might think of the virus, severe acute respiratory syndrome, and someone else might think of segmentation and reassembly sublayer. And a South African might think of South African Revenue Service. If you have any question as to whether your reader is familiar with the initials, the best practice is to spell out the words the first time you use them and follow them with the initials. Also, if you are writing a long document with several pages between where you defined initials originally and where you use them again, it is courteous to your reader to spell them out again.

Technical Language?

When an ordinary person wants to give someone an orange, he or she merely says, "Have an orange." But when a lawyer does it, the words are something like this: "Know all persons by these present that I hereby give, grant, bargain, sell, release, convey, transfer, and quitclaim all my right, title, interest, benefit, and use whatever in, of, and concerning this chattel, otherwise known as an orange, or *Citrus orantium*, together with all the appurtenances thereto of skin, pulp, pip, rind, seeds, and juice, to have and to hold the said orange together with its skin, pulp, pip, rind, seeds, and juice for his own use and behoof, to himself and his heirs, in fee simple forever, free from all liens, encumbrances, easements, limitations, restraints, or conditions whatsoever, any and all prior deeds, transfers, or other documents whatsoever, now or anywhere made, to the contrary notwithstanding, with full power to bite, cut, suck, or otherwise eat the said orange or to give away the same, with or without its skin, pulp, pip, rind, seeds, or juice."

Probably the most troublesome technical language is that of the legal profession. Legal terms too often have worked their way into business communication. The result has been to add unnecessary words as well as words not understood by many business readers. Such words also produce a dull and formal effect.

• Legal language has worked its way into business writing.

Among the legal words that may add little real meaning are *thereto, therein, whereas, herewith,* and *herein.* For example, "the land adjacent thereto" can be written "the adjacent land" without loss in meaning. In addition, legal wordings such as *cease and desist* and *bequeath and devise* contain needless repetition.

• Words like *thereto, herewith,* and *ipso facto* are examples.

Some legal words can be replaced with plain words. *Despite* can replace *notwithstanding. Ipso facto, sub judice,* and other such Latin phrases can be replaced by plain language with the same meaning.

• Replace legal language with plain words.

Your technical language may not be any of the ones illustrated here, but you will have one. You will need to be careful not to use it when you write to people who do not understand it.

Use Concrete Language

Good business communication is marked by words that tend to form sharp and clear meanings in the mind. These are the concrete words. You should prefer them in your writing.

• Use concrete words.

Concrete is the opposite of abstract. Abstract words are vague. In contrast, concrete words stand for things the reader can see, feel, taste, or smell. Concrete words hold interest, for they refer to the reader's experience.

• Concrete words are specific words.

Among the concrete words are those that stand for things that exist in the real world. Included are such nouns as *chair, desk, computer, road, automobile,* and *flowers.* Also included are words that stand for creatures and things: *Meg Whitman, Tiger Woods, Mickey Mouse, Barney,* the *Empire State Building,* and *Rodeo Drive.*

• They stand for things that exist in the real world: *deck, chair, road.*

Abstract nouns, on the other hand, cover broad meanings—concepts, ideas, and the like. Their meanings are general, as in these examples: *administration, negotiation, wealth, inconsistency, loyalty, compatibility, conservation, discrimination, incompetence,* and *communication.* Note how difficult it is to visualize what these words stand for.

• Abstract nouns have general meanings: *administration, negotiation.*

Concreteness also means being specific. Exact or specific wordings are concrete; vague and general wordings are abstract. For example, take the case of a researcher who must report the odor of a newly developed cleaning agent. The researcher could use such general words as "It has an offensive, nauseating odor." Now note how much more concrete language communicates: "It has the odor of decaying fish." The second example is concrete because it recalls an exact odor from memory. Notice the difference in communication effect in these contrasting pairs of wordings:

• Concreteness also means exactness: *a 53 percent loss, the odor of decaying fish.*

Grammar and Style Checkers Help Writers with Word Selection

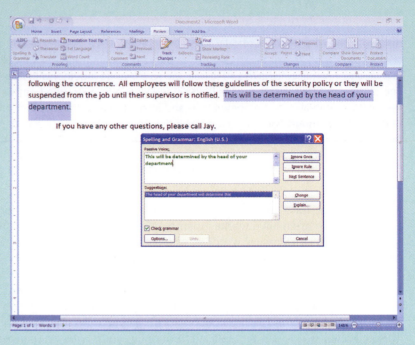

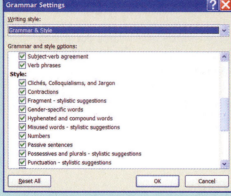

Today, word processors will help writers with grammar and style as well as with spelling. By default Word checks spelling and grammar automatically, using red and green underlines to distinguish between them. But as you see in the grammar settings screen shots here, writers can specify whether or not they want help and even which rules are applied to their documents. And they can choose to correct as they go along or to correct on demand. Although grammar and style checkers are not as accurate as spelling checkers, they will identify words, phrases, and sentences that could be improved. In fact, they often suggest a way to fix problems along with an explanation of correct usage.

In the example shown here, the checker found the use of passive voice and suggested a change to active voice. However, the writer decides whether to accept the suggestion, revise, or ignore the suggestion. The writer needs to determine whether this passive voice was used intentionally for one of the reasons discussed in this chapter or whether it was used by accident and should be changed.

Abstract	Concrete
A significant loss	A 53 percent loss
Good attendance record	100 percent attendance record
The leading company	First among 3,212 competitors
The majority	62 percent
In the near future	By noon Thursday
A labor-saving robot	A robot that does the work of seven workers
Light in weight	Featherlight
Substantial amount	$3,517,000

Now let us see the difference concreteness makes in the clarity of longer passages. Here is an example of abstract wording:

It is imperative that the firm practice extreme conservatism in operating expenditures during the coming biennium. The firm's past operating performance has been ineffectual for the reason that a preponderance of administrative assignments have been delegated to personnel who were ill-equipped to perform in these capacities. Recently instituted administrative changes stressing experience in operating economies have rectified this condition.

Written for concreteness, this message might read as follows:

We must reduce operating expenses at least $2 million during 2008–09. Our $1,350,000 deficit for 2004–05 was caused by the inexperience of our two chief administrators, Mr. Sartan and Mr. Ross. We have replaced them with Ms. Pharr and Mr. Kunz, who have had 13 and 17 years, respectively, of successful experience in operations management.

Another illustration of concreteness is the story of the foreign nation that competed strenuously with the United States in an international automobile show. In one category, only automobiles from these two countries were entered. One would surely win first place, the other second. The U.S. automobile won. The government-controlled press of the losing country gave this report to its people: "In worldwide competition, our excellent entry was judged to be second. The entry from the United States was rated next to last." The words sound concrete—*second, next to last.* But they omitted one fact needed for ethical concreteness—that only two automobiles were entered.

Use Active Verbs

Of all parts of speech, verbs do the most to make your writing interesting and lively, for a good reason: they contain the action of the sentence.

But not all verbs add vigor to your writing. Overuse of the verb "to be" and passive voice can sap the energy from your sentences. To see the difference between writing that relies heavily on forms of "to be" and writing that uses active verbs, compare the following two passages (the forms of "to be" and their replacements are italicized):

There *are* over 300 customers served by our help desk each day. The help desk personnel's main tasks *are* to answer questions, solve problems, and educate the callers about the software. Without their expert work, our customer satisfaction ratings *would be* much lower than they *are*.

Our help desk personnel *serve* over 300 customers each day. They *answer* questions, *solve* problems, and *educate* the users about the software. Without their expert work, our customer satisfaction ratings *would drop* significantly.

As these examples show, using active verbs adds impact to your writing, and it usually saves words as well.

In addition to minimizing your use of "to be" verbs, you can make your verbs more active by using what grammarians refer to as *active voice*. As you may recall, a sentence with a verb that can take a direct object (the recipient of the action) can be written either in a direct (active) pattern or an indirect (passive) pattern. For example, the sentence "the auditor inspected the books" is in active voice. In passive voice, the sentence would read: "The books were inspected by the auditor." For further support of the advantages of active over passive voice, compare the following sentences:

- Strong verbs make your writing lively and interesting

- Prefer active verbs to forms of "to be."

- Prefer the active voice to the passive voice.

Passive	Active
The results were reported in our July 9 letter.	We reported the results in our July 9 letter.
This policy has been supported by our union.	Our union supported this policy.
The new process is believed to be superior by the investigators.	The investigators believe that the new process is superior.
The policy was enforced by the committee.	The committee enforced the policy.
The office will be inspected by Mr. Hall.	Mr. Hall will inspect the office.
A gain of 30.1 percent was reported for hardware sales.	Hardware sales gained 30.1 percent.

Passive	Active
It is desired by the director that this problem be brought before the board.	The director desires that the secretary bring this problem before the board.
A complete reorganization of the administration was effected by the president.	The president completely reorganized the administration.

- Passive voice has a place. It is not incorrect.

The suggestion that active voice be preferred does not mean passive voice is incorrect or you should never use it. Passive voice is correct, and it has a place. The problem is that many writers tend to overuse it, especially in report writing. Writing is more interesting and communicates better when it uses active voice.

- Passive is better when the doer of the action is not important.

Your decision on whether to use active or passive voice is not simply a matter of choice. Sometimes passive voice is preferable. For example, when identifying the doer of the action is unimportant to the message, passive voice properly de-emphasizes the doer.

> Advertising is often criticized for its effect on price.

> Petroleum is refined in Texas.

- Passive helps avoid accusing the reader.

Passive voice may enable you to avoid accusing your reader of an action:

> The damage was caused by exposing the material to sunlight.

> The color desired was not specified in your order.

- Passive is better when the performer is not known.

Passive voice also may be preferable when the performer is unknown, as in these examples:

> During the past year, the equipment has been sabotaged seven times.

> Anonymous complaints have been received.

- It is also better when the writer prefers not to name the performer.

Yet another situation in which passive voice may be preferable is one in which the writer does not want to name the performer:

> The interviews were conducted on weekdays between noon and 6 pm.

> Two complaints have been made about you.

In other instances, passive voice is preferable for reasons of style.

Avoid Overuse of Camouflaged Verbs

- Avoid camouflaged verbs—verbs embedded in nouns.

An awkward construction that should be avoided is the camouflaged verb. When a verb is camouflaged, the verb describing the action in a sentence takes the form of a noun. Then action words have to be added. For example, suppose you want to write a sentence in which *eliminate* is the action to be expressed. If you change *eliminate* into its noun form, *elimination,* you must add action words—perhaps *was effected*—to have a sentence. Your sentence might then be: "Elimination of the surplus was effected by the staff." The sentence is indirect and passive. You could have avoided the camouflaged construction with a sentence using the verb *eliminate:* "The staff eliminated the surplus."

- For example, if *cancel* becomes *cancellation,* you must add "to effect a" to have action.

Here are two more examples. If we take the good action word *cancel* and make it into a noun, *cancellation,* we would have to say something like "to effect a cancellation" to communicate the action. If we change *consider* to *consideration,* we would have to say "give consideration to." So it would be with the following examples:

Action Verb	Noun Form	Wording of Camouflaged Verb
acquire	acquisition	make an acquisition
appear	appearance	make an appearance
apply	application	make an application
appraise	appraisal	make an appraisal
assist	assistance	give assistance to
cancel	cancellation	make a cancellation
commit	commitment	make a commitment
discuss	discussion	have a discussion

The plain language movement crosses many continents. The European Union (EU) has written a booklet entitled, "How to Write Clearly, Fight the Fog." It is designed for all writers of English at the European Commission. The first section is about the readers of Commission documents—EU insiders, outside specialists, and the general public. The public is to be considered the most important audience.

Paula J. Pomerenke, Illinois State University

Paula J. Pomerenke, "Challenges for ABC Members in 2,000," *Journal of Business Communication* 38 (2001): 6.

Action Verb	Noun Form	Wording of Camouflaged Verb
investigate	investigation	make an investigation
judge	judgment	make a judgment
liquidate	liquidation	effect a liquidation
reconcile	reconciliation	make a reconciliation
record	recording	make a recording

Note the differences in overall effect in these contrasting sentences:

Camouflaged Verb	Clear Verb Form
An *arrangement was made* to meet for breakfast.	We *arranged* to meet for breakfast.
Amortization of the account *was effected* by the staff.	The staff *amortized* the account.
Control of the water *was not possible*.	They *could not control* the water.
The new policy *involved the standardization of* the procedures.	The new policy *standardized* the procedures.
Application of the mixture *was accomplished*.	They *applied* the mixture.
We must *bring about a reconciliation of our* differences.	We must *reconcile* our differences.
The *establishment* of a wellness center *has been accomplished* by the company.	The company *has established* a wellness center.

From these illustrations you can see that our suggestion on camouflaged verbs overlaps our two preceding suggestions. First, camouflaged verbs are abstract nouns. We suggested that you prefer concrete words over abstract words. Second, camouflaged verbs frequently require passive voice. We suggested that you prefer active voice.

- Avoid camouflaged verbs by (1) writing concretely and (2) preferring active voice.

You can comply with these related suggestions by following two helpful writing hints. The first is to make the subjects of most sentences either persons or things. For example, rather than write "consideration was given to . . . ," you should write "we considered . . . ." The second is to write most sentences in normal order (subject, verb, object), with the doer of the action as the subject. Involved, strained, passive structures often result from attempts at other orders.

- To comply with these suggestions, (1) make subjects persons or things and (2) write sentences in normal order.

Select Words for Precise Meanings

Obviously, writing requires considerable knowledge of the language being used. But beyond basic familiarity with vocabulary, good writers possess a sensitivity to words' shades of meaning. Words, like people, have personalities. Some are forceful and some timid; some are positive and some negative; some are formal and some informal. Any

- Writing well requires sensitivity to words' meanings.

given word can occupy a place on many different scales of tone and meaning. Your task, as a writer attempting to achieve deliberate effects, is to choose the words that will achieve those effects with your intended readers.

Consider the differences among *tycoon, industry giant, eminently successful entrepreneur,* and *prominent business executive.* All four terms indicate a person who has acquired wealth and power in business, but you would use these terms in different circumstances. For example, *tycoon* calls to mind the robber barons of the late 19th and early 20th centuries, with their diamond tie pins and ruthless air, whereas *prominent business executive* suggests a less flashy, less greedy person who has achieved success within the constraints of a corporation. Similarly, *fired, dismissed, canned, separated, terminated,* and *discharged* refer to the same action but have different shades of meaning. So it is with each of the following groups of words:

die, decease, pass on, croak, kick the bucket, check out, expire, go to one's reward

money, funds, cash, dough, bread, finances

boy, youth, young man, lad, shaver, stripling

fight, brawl, fracas, battle royal, donnybrook

thin, slender, skinny, slight, wispy, lean, willowy, rangy, spindly, lanky, wiry

ill, sick, poorly, weak, delicate, cachectic, unwell, peaked, indisposed, out of sorts

- You should learn the shades of difference in the meanings of similar words.

- You should learn the specific meanings of other words.

Though the words in each list share the same denotation (barebones meaning), they vary widely in their connotations (their social and emotional associations). Being attentive to how different words are used will make you a more skillful and effective writer.

Knowledge of language also enables you to use words that carry the meanings you want to communicate. For example, *fewer* and *less* mean the same to some people. But careful users select *fewer* to mean "smaller numbers of items" and *less* to mean "reduced value, degree, or quantity." The verbs *affect* and *effect* are often used as synonyms. But those who know language select *affect* when they mean "to influence" and *effect* when they mean "to bring to pass." They use *feel* to express physical contact, perception, or such—not as a substitute for *believe* or *think.* Similarly, careful writers use *continual* to mean "repeated but broken succession" and *continuous* to mean "unbroken succession." They write *farther* to express geographic distance and *further* to indicate "more, in addition." They know that *learn* means "to acquire knowledge" and *teach* means "to impart knowledge."

- Use correct idiom. *Idiom* is the way ideas are expressed in a language.

In your effort to be a precise writer, you should use correct idiom. By *idiom* we mean the way things are said in a language. Much of our idiom has little rhyme or reason, but if we want to be understood, we should follow it. For example, what is the logic in the word *up* in the sentence "Look up her name in the directory"? There really is none. This is just the wording we have developed to cover this meaning. "Independent of" is good idiomatic usage; "independent from" is not. What is the justification? Similarly, you "agree to" a proposal, but you "agree with" a person. You are "careful about" an affair, but you are "careful with" your money. Here are some additional illustrations:

- There is little reason to some idioms, but violations offend the reader.

Faulty Idiom	Correct Idiom
authority about	authority on
comply to	comply with
different than	different from
enamored with	enamored of
equally as bad	equally bad
in accordance to	in accordance with
in search for	in search of
listen at	listen to
possessed with ability	possessed of ability
seldom or ever	seldom if ever
superior than	superior to

SUGGESTIONS FOR NONDISCRIMINATORY WRITING

Although discriminatory words are not directly related to writing clarity, our review of word selection would not be complete without some mention of them. By discriminatory words we mean words that do not treat all people equally and with respect. More specifically, they are words that refer negatively to groups of people, such as by sex, race, nationality, sexual orientation, age, or disability. Such words run contrary to acceptable views of fair play and human decency. They do not promote good business ethics, and thus have no place in business communication.

Many discriminatory words are a part of the vocabularies we have acquired from our environments. We often use them innocently, not realizing how they affect others. We can eliminate discriminatory words from our vocabularies by examining them carefully and placing ourselves in the shoes of those to whom they refer. The following review of the major forms of discriminatory words should help you achieve this goal.

- Avoid words that discriminate against sex, race, nationality, age, sexual orientation, or disability.

- We often use discriminatory words without bad intent.

Use Gender-Neutral Words

All too prevalent in today's business communication are words that discriminate by gender ("sexist" words). Although this form of discrimination can be directed against men, most instances involve discrimination against women because many of our words suggest male superiority. This condition is easily explained. Our language developed in a society in which it was customary for women to work in the home and for men to be the breadwinners and decision makers. As a result, our language reflects this male dominance. For reasons of fair play and to be in step with today's society in which gender equality is the goal, you would do well to use gender-neutral words. Suggestions for doing this follow.

Masculine Pronouns for Both Sexes. Perhaps the most troublesome sexist words are the masculine pronouns (*he, his, him*) when they are used to refer to both sexes, as in this example: "The typical State University student eats *his* lunch at the student center." Assuming that State is coeducational, the use of *his* suggests male supremacy. Historically, of course, the word *his* has been classified as generic—that is, it can refer to both sexes. But many modern-day businesspeople do not agree and are offended by the use of the masculine pronoun in this way.

- Avoid using the masculine pronouns (he, him, his) for both sexes.

Pepper ... and Salt

Believe me, if there w as any sexism in this office, my girl Friday here would know about it."

SOURCE: From *The Wall Street Journal*—Permission, Cartoon Features Syndicate.

- You can do this (1) by rewording the sentence;

You can avoid the use of masculine pronouns in such cases in three ways. First, you can reword the sentence to eliminate the offending word. Thus, the illustration above could be reworded as follows: "The typical State University student eats lunch at the student center." Here are other examples:

Sexist	Gender-Neutral
If a customer pays promptly, *he* is placed on our preferred list.	A customer who pays promptly is placed on our preferred list.
When an unauthorized employee enters the security area, *he* is subject to dismissal.	An employee who enters the security area is subject to dismissal.
A supervisor is not responsible for such losses if *he* is not negligent.	A supervisor who is not negligent is not responsible for such losses.
When a customer needs service, it is *his* right to ask for it.	A customer who needs service has the right to ask for it.

- (2) by making the reference plural,

A second way to avoid sexist use of the masculine pronoun is to make the reference plural. Fortunately, the English language has plural pronouns (*their, them, they*) that refer to both sexes. Making the references plural in the examples given above, we have these nonsexist revisions:

- as illustrated here;

If customers pay promptly, *they* are placed on our preferred list.

When unauthorized employees enter the security area, *they* are subject to dismissal.

Supervisors are not responsible for such losses if *they* are not negligent.

When customers need service, *they* have the right to ask for it.

In business today, men and women, the young and the old, and people of all races work side by side in roles of mutual respect. It would be unfair to use words that discriminate against any of them.

Meaning and the Appearance of a Word

A real-life illustration of how words don't always mean what they may appear to mean is the case of the ombudsman to the mayor of Washington, DC. The ombudsman, who is white, used these words in commenting on his budget: "I will have to be 'niggardly' with these funds . . ."

The word "niggardly" means "miserly." It is derived from a Scandinavian word and has no racial origin or meaning. Even so, the mayor's office was deluged with protest calls from the black community. So intense were the objections that the ombudsman resigned, and his resignation was accepted.

The appropriateness of the resignation was intensely argued. Those favoring the resignation generally argued that the ombudsman should have been more sensitive in his choice of words—that he should have known that the word's sound would offend. Those opposing generally argued that the man should not be criticized because of the ignorance of others. After considerable argument was heard, the mayor appointed the man to another position.

What is to be learned from this incident? Does the sound of a word affect its meaning?

A third way to avoid sexist use of *he*, *his*, or *him* is to substitute any of a number of neutral expressions. The most common are *he or she*, *he/she*, *s/he*, *you*, *one*, and *person*. Using neutral expressions in the problem sentences, we have these revisions:

- or (3) by substituting neutral expressions,

> If a customer pays promptly, he or she is placed on our preferred list.

> When an unauthorized employee enters the security area, he/she is subject to dismissal.

- as in these examples.

> A supervisor is not responsible for such losses if *s/he* is not negligent.

> When *one* needs service, *one* has the right to ask for it.

You should use such expressions with caution, however. They tend to be somewhat awkward, particularly if they are used often. For this reason, many skilled writers do not use some of them. If you use them, you should pay attention to their effect on the flow of your words. Certainly, you should avoid sentences like this one: "To make an employee feel he/she is doing well by complimenting her/him insincerely confuses her/him later when he/she sees his/her co-workers promoted ahead of him/her."

- Neutral expressions can be awkward; so use them with caution.

Words Derived from Masculine Words. As we have noted, our culture was male dominated when our language developed. Because of this, many of our words are masculine even though they do not refer exclusively to men. Take *chairman*, for example. This word can refer to both sexes, yet it does not sound that way. More appropriate and less offensive substitutes are *chair*, *presiding officer*, *moderator*, and *chairperson*. Similarly, *salesman* suggests a man, but many women work in sales. *Salesperson*, *salesclerk*, or *sales representative* would be better. Other sexist words and gender-neutral substitutes are as follows:

- Avoid words suggesting male dominance,

Sexist	Gender-Neutral
man-made	manufactured, of human origin
manpower	personnel, workers
congressman	representative, member of Congress
businessman	business executive, businessperson
mailman	letter carrier, mail carrier
policeman	police officer
fireman	fire fighter
repairman	repair technician
cameraman	camera operator

- such as these examples.

Many words with *man*, *his*, and the like in them have nonsexist origins. Among such words are *manufacture*, *management*, *history*, and *manipulate*. Also, some clearly sexist words are hard to avoid. *Freshperson*, for example, would not serve as a substitute for *freshman*. And *personhole* is an illogical substitute for *manhole*.

- Do not use words that lower one's status.

Words that Lower Status by Gender. Thoughtless writers and speakers use expressions belittling the status of women. You should avoid such expressions. To illustrate, male executives sometimes refer to their female secretaries as *my girl*, as in this sentence: "I'll have my girl take care of this matter." Of course, *secretary* or *assistant* would be a better choice. Then there are the many female forms for words that refer to work roles. In this group are *lady lawyer, authoress, sculptress,* and *poetess.* You should refer to women in these work roles by the same words that you would use for men: *lawyer, author, sculptor, poet.* Using words such as *male nurse* or *male teacher* can be demeaning as well.

Examples of sexist words could go on and on. But not all of them would be as clear as those given above for the issue is somewhat complex and confusing. In deciding which words to avoid and which to use, you will have to rely on your best judgment. Remember that your goal should be to use words that are fair and that do not offend.

Avoid Words That Stereotype by Race, Nationality, or Sexual Orientation

- Words depicting minorities in a stereotyped way are unfair and untrue.

Words that stereotype all members of a group by race, nationality, or sexual orientation are especially unfair, and frequently they reinforce stereotypical beliefs about this group. Members of any minority vary widely in all characteristics. Thus, it is unfair to suggest that Jews are miserly, that Italians are Mafia members, that Hispanics are lazy, that African Americans can do only menial jobs, that gays are perfectionists, and so on. Unfair references to minorities are sometimes subtle and not intended, as in this example: "We conducted the first marketing tests in the low-income areas of the city. Using a sample of 200 African-American families, we . . . " These words unfairly suggest that only African Americans live in low-income areas.

- Words that present members of minorities as exceptions to stereotypes are also unfair.

Also unfair are words suggesting that a minority member has struggled to achieve something that is taken for granted in the majority group. Usually well intended, words of this kind can carry subtle discriminatory messages. For example, a reference to a "neatly dressed Hispanic man" may suggest that he is an exception to the rule—that most Hispanics are not neatly dressed, but here is one who is. So can references to "a generous Jew," "an energetic Puerto Rican," "a hardworking African American," and "a Chinese manager."

- Eliminate such references to minorities by treating all people equally and by being sensitive to the effects of your words.

Eliminating unfair references to minority groups from your communication requires two basic steps. First, you must consciously treat all people equally, without regard to their minority status. You should refer to minority membership only in those rare cases in which it is a vital part of the message to be communicated. Second, you must be sensitive to the effects of your words. Specifically, you should ask yourself how those words would affect you if you were a member of the minorities to which they are addressed. You should evaluate your word choices from the viewpoints of others.

Avoid Words That Stereotype by Age

- Words that label people as old or young can arouse negative reactions.

Your sensitivity in not discriminating by sex also should be extended to include discriminating by age—against both the old and the young. While those over 55 might be retired from their first jobs, many lead lives that are far from the sedentary roles in which they are sometimes depicted. They also are not necessarily feeble, forgetful, or forsaken. While some do not mind being called *senior citizens*, others do. Be sensitive with terms such as *mature, elderly,* and *golden ager,* also. Some even abhor *oldster* as much as the young detest *youngster.* The young are often called *teenagers* or *adolescents* although *young person, young man,* and *young woman* are much fairer. Some slang terms show lack of sensitivity, too—words such as *brat*, *retard*, and *dummy*. Even harsher are *juvenile delinquent*, *truant*, and *runaway*, for these labels often are put on the young based on one behavior over a short time period. Presenting both the old and the young objectively is only fair.

As we have suggested, use labels only when relevant, and use positive terms when possible. In describing the old, be sensitive to terms such as *spry*, which on the surface might be well intended but also can imply a negative connotation. Present both groups fairly and objectively when you write about them.

Avoid Words That Typecast Those with Disabilities

People with disabilities are likely to be sensitive to discriminatory words. Television shows those with disabilities competing in the Special Olympics, often exceeding the performance of an average person, and common sense tells us not to stereotype these people. However, sometimes we do anyway. Just as with age, we need to avoid derogatory labels and apologetic or patronizing behavior. For example, instead of describing one as *deaf and dumb*, use *deaf*. Avoid slang terms such as *fits*, *spells*, *attacks*; use *seizures*, *epilepsy*, or other objective terms. Terms such as *crippled* and *retarded* should be avoided because they degrade in most cases. Work to develop a nonbiased attitude, and show it through carefully chosen words.

- Disabled people are sensitive to words that describe their disabilities.

In Conclusion about Words

The preceding review of suggestions for selecting words is not complete. You will find more—much more—in the pages ahead. But you now have in mind the basics of word selection. The remaining suggestions are refinements of these basics.

As you move along, you should view these basics as work tools. Unfortunately, the tendency is to view them as rules to memorize and give back to the instructor on an examination. Although a good examination grade is a commendable goal, the long-run value of these tools is their use in your writing. So do yourself a favor. Resolve to keep these basics in mind every time you write. Consciously use them. The results will make you glad you did.

- More about words appears in the following pages.

- The preceding suggestions are realistic ways to improve your writing. Use them.

SUMMARY BY LEARNING OBJECTIVES

1. To communicate clearly, you must adapt to your reader.
   - Adapting means using words the reader understands.
   - It also involves following the suggestions below.
2. Select words that your reader understands.
   - These are the familiar words (words like *old* instead of *antiquated*).
   - They are also the short words (*agreed to quit* rather than *acceded to the proposition to terminate*).
3. Use technical words and acronyms with caution.
   - For example, use a *minor stroke* rather than a *cerebral vascular accident*.
   - Spell out and define acronyms as needed.
   - However, technical words are appropriate among technical people.
4. Prefer the concrete words and active verbs.
   - Concrete words are the specific ones. For example, *57 percent majority* is more concrete than *majority*.
   - Action verbs are more vigorous and interesting than forms of "to be."
   - In active voice, the subject acts; in passive voice, it receives the action. For example, use *we reported the results* rather than *the results were reported by us*.

1 Explain the role of adaptation in selecting words that communicate.

2 Simplify writing by selecting familiar and short words.

3 Use technical words and acronyms appropriately.

4 Write concretely and use active verbs.

- Active voice is stronger, more vigorous, and more interesting. But passive voice is correct and has a place in writing.
- Avoid overuse of camouflaged verbs—making a noun of the logical verb and then having to add a verb (*appear* rather than *make an appearance*).

5. Write more clearly and precisely by following these suggestions:

- Develop a feeling for the personalities of words.
- Select words for their precise meanings (involves studying words to detect shades of difference in meaning—for example, differences in *fight, brawl, fracas, donnybrook, battle royal*).
- Also, learn the specific ways that words are used in our culture (called *idiom*).

6. Avoid discriminatory words.

- Do not use words that discriminate against women. (For example, using *he, him,* or *his* to refer to both sexes and words such as *fireman, postman, lady lawyer,* and *authoress.*)
- Do not use words that suggest stereotyped roles of race, nationality, or sexual orientation (African Americans and menial jobs, Italians and the Mafia, gays and perfectionists), for such words are unfair and untrue.
- Do not use words that discriminate against age or disability.

1 A fellow student says, "So I'm not a good writer. But I have other places to put my study time. I'm a management major. I'll have secretaries to handle my writing for me." Give this student your best advice, including the reasoning behind it.

2 Evaluate this comment: "I'm not going to simplify my writing for my readers. That would be talking down to them. Plus, if they can't understand clear English, that's their problem."

3 Explain how you would apply the basic principle of adaptation to your choice of words for each of the following writing assignments:

   a. An editorial in a company newsletter.
   b. A message to Joan Branch, a supervisor of an information systems department, concerning a change in determining project priorities.
   c. A report to the chief engineer on a technical topic in the engineer's field.
   d. A message to employees explaining a change in pension benefits.
   e. A letter to company stockholders explaining a change in company reporting dates.

4 "Some short words are hard, and some long words are easy. Thus, the suggestion to prefer short words doesn't make sense." Discuss.

5 "As technical language typically consists of acronyms and long, hard words, it contributes to miscommunication. Thus, it should be avoided in all business communication." Discuss.

6 Using examples other than those in the book, identify some technical terms that would communicate effectively to others in the field but would need to be clarified for those outside the field.

7 Define and give examples of active and passive voice. Explain when each should be used.

8 In his book *Style: Ten Lessons in Clarity and Grace* (8th ed., Boston: Longman, 2005), Joseph M. Williams advises writers to avoid monotonous-sounding writing — that is, writing that has a droning, "blah-blah" effect when read aloud. What advice in this chapter might help you avoid a monotonous style?

9 Discuss this statement: "When I use *he, him,* or *his* as a generic, I am not discriminating against women. For many years these words have been accepted as generic. They refer to both sexes, and that's the meaning I have in mind when I use them."

10 List synonyms (words with similar meanings) for each of the following words. Then explain the differences in shades of meaning as you see them.

   a. fat
   b. skinny
   c. old
   d. tell
   e. happiness
   f. customer
   g. boss
   h. misfortune
   i. inquire
   j. stop
   k. lie
   l. mistake

11 Discuss this statement: "Mr. Williams scolded Susan in a grandfatherly manner."

CRITICAL THINKING EXERCISES

Using Familiar Words

Instructions, Sentences 1–20: Assume that your readers are at about the 10th-grade level in education. Revise these sentences for easy communication to this audience.

1 We must terminate all deficit financing.

2 We must endeavor to correct this problem by expediting delivery.

3 A proportionate tax consumes a determinate apportionment of one's monetary flow.

4 Business has an inordinate influence on governmental operations.

5 It is imperative that consumers be unrestrained in determining their preferences.

6 Mr. Sanchez terminated Kevin's employment as a consequence of his ineffectual performance.

7 Our expectations are that there will be increments in commodity value.

8 Can we ascertain the types of customers that have a predisposition to utilize our instant-credit offer?

9 The preponderance of the businesspeople we consulted envision signs of improvement from the current siege of economic stagnation.

10 If liquidation becomes mandatory, we shall dispose of these assets first.

11 Recent stock acquisitions have accentuated the company's current financial crisis.

12 Mr. Coward will serve as intermediary in the pending labor–management parley.

13 Ms. Smith's idiosyncrasies supply adequate justification for terminating her employment.

14 Requisites for employment by this company have been enhanced.

15 The unanimity of current forecasts is not incontrovertible evidence of an impending business acceleration.

16 People's propensity to consume is insatiable.

17 The company must desist from its deficit financing immediately.

18 This antiquated merchandising strategy is ineffectual in contemporary business operations.

19 Percentage return on common stockholders' equity averaged 23.1 for the year.

20 The company's retained earnings last year exceeded $2,500,000.

Instructions: Exercise 21 concerns adaptation and technical language. As you must find your own sentences for it, this exercise differs from the others.

21 From a scholarly business journal, select a paragraph (at least 150 words long) that would be difficult for a student less advanced in the subject than you. Rewrite the paragraph so that this student can understand it easily.

Instructions, Sentences 22–53: Revise these sentences to make them conform to the writing suggestions discussed in the book. They are grouped by the suggestion they illustrate.

Selecting Concrete Words

22 We have found that young men are best for this work.

23 She makes good grades.

24 John lost a fortune in Las Vegas.

25 If we don't receive the goods soon, we will cancel.

26 Profits last year were exorbitant.

27 Some years ago she made good money.

28 His grade on the aptitude test was not high.

29 Here is a product with very little markup.

30 The cost of the online subscription was reasonable.

31 We will need some new equipment soon.

Limiting Use of Passive Voice

32 Our action is based on the assumption that the competition will be taken by surprise.

33 It is believed by the typical union member that his or her welfare is not considered to be important by management.

34 We are serviced by the Bratton Company.

35 Our safety is the responsibility of management.

36 You were directed by your supervisor to complete this assignment by noon.

37 It is believed by the writer that this company policy is wrong.

38 The union was represented by Cecil Chambers.

39 These reports are prepared by the salespeople every Friday.

40 Success of this project is the responsibility of the research department.

41 Our decision is based on the belief that the national economy will be improved.

Avoiding Camouflaged Verbs

42 It was my duty to make a determination of the damages.

43 Harold made a recommendation that we fire Mr. Schultz.

44 We will make her give an accounting of her activities.

45 We will ask him to bring about a change in his work routine.

46 This new equipment will result in a saving in maintenance.

47 Will you please make an adjustment for this defect?

48 Implementation of the plan was effected by the crew.

49 Acceptance of all orders must be made by the chief.

50 A committee performs the function of determining the award.

51 Adaptation to the new conditions was performed easily by all new personnel.

52 Verification of the amount is made daily by the auditor.

53 The president tried to effect a reconciliation of the two groups.

Selecting Precise Words

Instructions, Sentences 54–65: Following is an exercise in word precision. Explain the differences in meaning for the word choices shown. Point out any words that are wrongly used.

54 Performance during the fourth quarter was (average) (mediocre).

55 This merchandise is (old) (antique) (secondhand) (preowned) (used).

56 The machine ran (continually) (continuously).

57 The mechanic is a (woman) (lady) (female person).

58 His action (implies) (infers) that he accepts the criticism.

59 Her performance on the job was (good) (topnotch) (excellent) (superior).

60 On July 1 the company will (become bankrupt) (close its door) (go under) (fail).

61 The staff members (think) (understand) (know) the results were satisfactory.

62 Before buying any material, we (compare) (contrast) it with competing products.

63 I cannot (resist) (oppose) her appointment.

64 Did you (verify) (confirm) these figures?

65 This is an (effective) (effectual) (efficient) plan.

Using Proper Idiom

Instructions, Sentences 66–75: These sentences use faulty and correct idioms. Make any changes you think are necessary.

66 The purchasing officer has gone in search for a substitute product.

67 Our office has become independent from the Dallas office.

68 This strike was different than the one in 2000.

69 This letter is equally as bad.

70 She is an authority about mutual funds.

71 When the sale is over with, we will restock.

72 Our truck collided against the wall.

73 We have been in search for a qualified supervisor since August.

74 Murphy was equal to the task.

75 Apparently, the clock fell off the shelf.

Avoiding Discriminatory Language

Instructions, Sentences 76–85: Change these sentences to avoid discriminatory language.

76 Any worker who ignores this rule will have his salary reduced.

77 The typical postman rarely makes mistakes in delivering his mail.

78 A good executive plans his daily activities.

79 The committee consisted of a businessman, a banker, and a lady lawyer.

80 A good secretary screens all telephone calls for her boss and arranges his schedule.

81 An efficient salesman organizes his calls and manages his time.

82 Our company was represented by two sales representatives, one Hispanic engineer, and one senior citizen.

83 Three people applied for the job, including two well-groomed black women.

84 Handicap parking spaces are strictly for use by the crippled.

85 He is one of the best gay designers in the city.

chapter three

Construction of Clear Sentences and Paragraphs

LEARNING OBJECTIVES

Upon completing this chapter, you will be able to construct clear sentences and paragraphs by emphasizing adaptation, short sentences, and effective paragraph design. To reach this goal, you should be able to

1 Explain the role of adaptation in writing clear sentences.

2 Write short, clear sentences by limiting sentence content and economizing on words.

3 Design sentences that give the right emphasis to content.

4 Employ unity and clarity in writing effective sentences.

5 Compose paragraphs that are short and unified, use topic sentences effectively, and communicate coherently.

Writing Sentences and Paragraphs That Communicate

Introduce yourself to this chapter by continuing in the role of small business manager and immediate superior to Max Elliott (preceding chapter). Max's writing problem would be of concern in any business, but it is especially important in small businesses such as yours. Your company is struggling to survive with its competition. It must be more efficient in every aspect of its operations if it is to survive. Communication is one of these aspects. This is why you are concerned about what you see in Max's writing.

As you continue your review of Max's writing, you detect more than problems with word choice. Something else is wrong. His sentences just do not convey sharp, clear meanings. Although grammatically correct, they appear to be needlessly complex and heavy. His long and involved paragraphs also cause you concern.

What you have seen in Max's writing are problems concerning two other determinants of readability: the sentence and the paragraph. As you will learn in the pages ahead, these two writing units play major roles in communicating. This chapter will show you (and Max) how to construct sentences and paragraphs that produce readable writing.

THE IMPORTANCE OF ADAPTATION

As you have seen, choosing the right words is basic to clear communication. Equally basic is the task of arranging those words into clear sentences and the sentences into clear paragraphs. Like choosing words, constructing clear sentences and paragraphs involves adaptation to the minds of the intended readers.

- Sentences should be adapted to readers.

Fitting your writing to your readers requires the reader analysis we discussed in Chapter 1. You should study your readers to find out what they are like—what they know, how they think, and what their contexts are. Then write in a way that will communicate with them.

In general, this procedure involves using the simpler sentence structures to reach people with lower communication abilities and people not knowledgeable about the subject. It involves using the more complex sentence structures only when communicating with more verbal, knowledgeable people. As we will see, even with knowledgeable people, simplicity is sometimes needed for the best communication effect.

- Use the simpler sentence structures for those less able to understand; use the more complex structures when appropriate.

You should aim a little below the level of your reader. Readability research tells us that writing communicates best when it does not tax the reader's comprehension skills. Thus, some simplification is desirable for all readers. Keep this point in mind as you read through the rest of this chapter.

Writing effectively also requires managing the emphasis in your sentences, making each sentence express a main idea, and ordering the sentence elements according to accepted rules of grammar and logic. The next section will help you see how to achieve these goals.

This chapter then offers advice about how to turn your well-constructed sentences into well-constructed paragraphs—paragraphs that are united, efficient, forward moving, and coherent. Delivering your contents in easy-to-digest chunks is one of your most powerful strategies for engaging and informing your busy readers.

CARE IN SENTENCE DESIGN

When you sit down to write a given message, you have many bits of information at hand. How will you turn them into a clear, coherent message?

Your first task will probably be grouping and ordering the information—that is, planning the message's overall pattern of organization or structure. But sooner or later, writing a successful message comes down to figuring out how to stitch your contents together in a series of sentences. How much information will you put into each sentence? And in what order will that information be?

- Writing effective sentences involves grouping and ordering the information.

- Your familiarity with different sentence elements—whether or not you know their grammatical labels—will help you design sentences that manage the information.

Deciding how to use sentences to group your information is a fundamental challenge for writers. Fortunately, you have a powerful resource at your disposal: your own storehouse of knowledge about the many kinds of clauses, phrases, and types of modifiers that can be used. You may not know the names of all these elements, but you can still use them to good effect. The building blocks for sentences are already part of your competency as an English speaker, whether or not you are conscious of them.

For example, how might we turn the following bits of information about a retiring employee into the opening of an article for a company newsletter?

Bill Jones is a drill press operator. He has been employed by Allied Manufacturing. He has been employed by the company for 15 years. He is retiring. He is retiring on June 15.

Surely we would not report each bit of information separately in this way. It would be too hard for the reader to put the facts together, and the writing would sound childish. Instead, we would combine some of the facts, and we would draw upon our storehouse of possible sentence elements to do it. We might write

Bill Jones, a drill press operator who has been with Allied Manufacturing for 15 years, will be retiring on June 15.

Or we might write

Bill Jones will be retiring on June 15. He has been a drill press operator with Allied Manufacturing for 15 years.

Both ways indicate that "Bill Jones will be retiring" is an important idea, because it occupies a main clause, the central statement in any sentence. The first version adds the other facts as modifying phrases, whereas the second version gives certain additional facts a bit more significance by putting them in their own sentence. Which way is better? It depends on the effect you want to achieve and on how much information you think your readers can digest at once.

- Cultivating an awareness of the different sentence types and elements will help make you a better writer.

Of course, you won't start out with all your bits of information as neatly separated as they were in this example. But you will still have to decide how much and what kind of information to put into each sentence, and in what form and order. The more consciously you control the information in your sentences, the more consciously you control your meaning and your reader's response to it. Paying attention to examples of clear, smooth writing and learning more about the different sentence elements will help you with this goal.

So will the advice in the following sections. But remember: adaptation is critical. Your ultimate guide to communicating well is your awareness of your particular readers' skills and likely responses.

Using Short Sentences

- Your readers are busy. Writing efficient sentences can save them time and effort.

Business audiences tend to prefer simple, efficient sentences over long, complex ones. Having too much to do in too little time is a chronic problem in business. A recent study found that 95 percent of executives and managers make a to-do list for each day, but 99 percent of them do not complete the tasks on those lists.[1] No one, whether executive or first-level employee, wants to read writing that wastes time.

- Short sentences communicate better because of mind limitations.

Favoring short sentences can save your readers time. It can also prevent miscommunication. Readability research tells us that the more words and the more relationships there are in a sentence, the greater is the possibility for misunderstanding. This finding suggests that the mind can hold only so much information at one time. Thus, to give it too much information in your sentences is to risk falling short of your communication purpose.

- Short means about 16–18 words for middle-level readers.

What constitutes a short, readable sentence is related to the reader's ability. Readability studies suggest that writing intended to communicate with the middle-level

---

[1] Chuck Martin, *Tough Management: The 7 Winning Ways to Make Tough Decisions Easier, Deliver the Numbers, and Grow the Business in Good Times and Bad* (New York: McGraw-Hill, 2005) xiv.

Readability Statistics Help Writers Evaluate Document Length and Difficulty

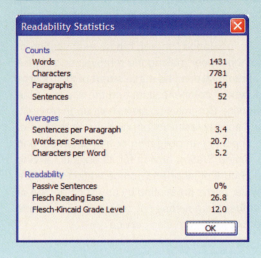

Readability Statistics

Counts
Words	1431
Characters	7781
Paragraphs	164
Sentences	52

Averages
Sentences per Paragraph	3.4
Words per Sentence	20.7
Characters per Word	5.2

Readability
Passive Sentences	0%
Flesch Reading Ease	26.8
Flesch-Kincaid Grade Level	12.0

OK

Grammar and style checkers give writers the option of reporting readability statistics. These statistics report the number of words, characters, paragraphs, and sentences in a document along with averages of characters per word, words per sentence, and sentences per paragraph.

The report you see here was generated for a scholarly manuscript. It reports an average of 20.7 words per sentence, a bit high for a business document but probably at an acceptable level for a scholarly document's readers. The Flesch-Kincaid score confirms that the reading grade level is 12.0, too high for business documents but likely appropriate for a scholarly audience. However, the Flesch Reading Ease score should give the writer cause to review the document for accessibility, even for its targeted audience. The 26.8 score is well below the 60–70 range Microsoft recommends.

adult reader should average about 16 to 18 words per sentence. For more advanced readers, the average may be higher. For less advanced readers, it should be lower.

Our emphasis on short sentences does not mean that you should use all short sentences. In fact, you should avoid overusing them. The overuse of short sentences results in a choppy effect and suggests primer simplicity. You should use moderately long sentences occasionally. They are sometimes useful in subordinating information and in increasing interest by adding variety. And sometimes the information needed to convey a thought requires a long sentence. Even so, you should take care not to make the long sentences excessively long. Always you should make certain that they are clear.

- But avoid excessive use of short sentences.

The following sentence from an employee handbook illustrates the effect of long sentences on communication:

> When an employee has changed from one job to another job, the new corresponding coverages will be effective as of the date the change occurs, unless, however, if due to a physical disability or infirmity as a result of advanced age, an employee is changed from one job to another job and such change results in the employee's new job rate coming within a lower hourly job-rate bracket in the table, in which case the employee may, at the discretion of the company, continue the amount of group term life insurance and the amount of accidental death and dismemberment insurance that the employee had prior to such change.

The chances are that you did not get a clear message from this sentence when you first read it. The explanation is not in the words used; you probably know them all. Neither is it in the ideas presented; they are relatively simple. The obvious explanation is the length of the sentence. So many words and relationships are in the sentence that they cause confusion. The result is vague communication at best—complete miscommunication at worst. Now look at the message written in all short sentences. The meanings may be clear, but the choppy effect is distracting and irritating. Imagine reading a long document written in this style.

A Marathon Sentence (308 Words) from U.S. Government Regulations

That no person in the classified civil service of the United States shall be removed therefrom except for such cause as will promote the efficiency of said service and for reasons given in writing, and the person whose removal is sought shall have notice of the same and of any charges preferred against him, and be furnished with a copy thereof, and also be allowed a reasonable time for personally answering the same in writing; and affidavits in support thereof; but no examination of witnesses nor any trial or hearing shall be required except in the discretion of the officer making the removal; and copies of charges, notice of hearing, answer, reasons for removal, and of the order of removal shall be made a part of the records of the proper department or office, as shall also the reasons for reduction in rank or compensation; and the copies of the same shall be furnished to the person affected upon request, and the Civil Service Commission also shall, upon request, be furnished copies of the same: *Provided, however,* that membership in any society, association, club, or other form of organization of postal employees not affiliated with any outside organization imposing an obligation or duty upon them to engage in any strike, or proposing to assist them in any strike, against the United States, having for its objects, among other things, improvements in the condition of labor of its members, including hours of labor and compensation therefore and leave of absence, by any person or groups of persons in said postal service, or the presenting by any such person or groups of persons of any grievance or grievances to the Congress or any Member thereof shall not constitute or be cause for reduction in rank or compensation or removal of such person or groups of persons from said service.

An employee may change jobs. The change may result in a lower pay bracket. The new coverage is effective when this happens. The job change must be because of physical disability. It can also be because of infirmity. Old age may be another cause. The company has some discretion in the matter. It can permit continuing the accidental death insurance. It can permit continuing the dismemberment insurance.

The following paragraph takes a course between these two extremes. Clearly, it is an improvement. Generally, it emphasizes short sentences, but it combines content items where appropriate.

The new insurance coverage becomes effective when because of disability, infirmity, or age an employee's job change results in lower pay. But at its discretion, the company may permit the old insurance coverage to continue.

- Short sentences are achieved in two ways.

You can shorten and simplify sentences in two basic ways: (1) by limiting sentence content and (2) by using words economically. The following pages contain specific suggestions for doing this.

Limiting Sentence Content

- Limiting content is one way to make short sentences.

Limiting sentence content is largely a matter of mentally selecting thought units and making separate sentences of most of them. Sometimes, of course, you should combine thoughts into one sentence, but only when you have good reason. You have good reason, for example, when thoughts are closely related or when you want to deemphasize content. The advantage of limiting sentence content is evident from the following contrasting examples:

Long and Hard to Understand

This letter is being distributed with enrollment confirmation sheets, which are to serve as a final check on the correctness of the registration of students and are to be used later when obtaining semester grades from the regline system, which are to be available two weeks after the term officially ends.

Short and Clear

This letter is being distributed with enrollment confirmation sheets. These sheets will serve now as a final check on student registration. Later, the codes on them will be used to access course grades through the regline system; the grades will be available two weeks after the term officially ends.

Long and Hard to Understand	**Short and Clear**
Some authorities in human resources object to expanding normal salary ranges to include a trainee rate because they fear that through oversight or prejudice probationers may be kept at the minimum rate longer than is warranted and because they fear that it would encourage the spread from the minimum to maximum rate range.	Some authorities in human resources object to expanding the normal salary range to include a trainee rate for two reasons. First, they fear that through oversight or prejudice probationers may be kept at the minimum rate longer than is warranted. Second, they fear that expansion would increase the spread between the minimum and the maximum rate range.
Regardless of their seniority or union affiliation, all employees who hope to be promoted are expected to continue their education either by enrolling in the special courses to be offered by the company, which are scheduled to be given after working hours beginning next Wednesday, or by taking approved online courses selected from a list, which may be seen on the company portal.	Regardless of their seniority or union affiliation, all employees who hope to be promoted are expected to continue their education in either of two ways. (1) They may enroll in special courses to be given by the company. (2) They may take approved online courses selected from the list on the company portal.

Without question, the long sentences in the examples are hard to understand, and the shorter versions are easy to understand. In each case, the difference is primarily in sentence length. Clearly, the shorter sentences communicate better. They give more emphasis to content and to organization of the subject matter.

Economizing on Words

A second basic technique of shortening sentences is to use words economically. Anything you write can be expressed in many ways, some shorter than others. In general, the shorter wordings save the reader time and are clearer and more interesting.

- Another way to shorten sentences is through word economy.

Economizing on words generally means seeking shorter ways of saying things. Once you try to economize, you will probably find that your present writing is wasteful and that you use uneconomical wordings.

- Seek shorter ways of saying things.

To help you recognize these uneconomical wordings, a brief review of the most common of them follows. This review does not cover all the possibilities for wasteful writing, but it does cover many troublesome problems.

- Following are some suggestions.

Cluttering Phrases. An often used uneconomical wording is the cluttering phrase. This is a phrase that can be replaced by shorter wording without loss of meaning. The little savings achieved in this way add up.

- Avoid cluttering phrases. Substitute shorter expressions.

Here is an example of a cluttering phrase:

In the event that payment is not made by January, operations will cease.

The phrase *in the event that* is uneconomical. The little word *if* can substitute for it without loss of meaning:

If payment is not made by January, operations will cease.

Similarly, the phrase that begins the following sentence adds unnecessary length:

In spite of the fact that they received help, they failed to exceed the quota.

Although makes an economical substitute:

Although they received help, they failed to exceed their quota.

You probably use many cluttering phrases. The following partial list (with suggested substitutions) should help you cut down on them:

Source: Reprinted with Special Permission of King Features Syndicate.

Cluttering Phrase	Shorter Substitution
Along the lines of	Like
At the present time	Now
For the purpose of	For
For the reason that	Because, since
In accordance with	By
In the amount of	For
In the meantime	Meanwhile
In the near future	Soon
In the neighborhood of	About
In very few cases	Seldom
In view of the fact that	Since, because
On the basis of	By
On the occasion of	On
With regard to, with reference to	About
With a view to	To

● Eliminate surplus words.

Surplus Words. To write economically, eliminate words that add nothing to sentence meaning. As with cluttering phrases, we often use meaningless extra words as a matter of habit. Eliminating these surplus words sometimes requires recasting a sentence, but sometimes they can just be left out.

The following is an example of surplus wording from a business report:

It will be noted that the records for the past years show a steady increase in special appropriations.

The beginning words add nothing to the meaning of the sentence. Notice how dropping them makes the sentence stronger—and without loss of meaning:

The records for the past years show a steady increase in special appropriations.

Here is a second example:

His performance was good enough *to enable him* to qualify for the promotion.

The words *to enable* add nothing and can be dropped:

His performance was good enough to qualify him for the promotion.

The following sentences further illustrate the use of surplus words. In each case, the surplus words can be eliminated without changing the meaning.

With the advent of computers, the way business messages are composed has changed, but the mental process involved remains unchanged. One still must select words and build sentences that form precise meanings in the minds of readers.

Contains Surplus Words	Eliminates Surplus Words
He ordered desks *that are of the executive type.*	He ordered executive-type desks.
There are four rules *that* should be observed.	Four rules should be observed.
In addition to these defects, numerous other defects mar the operating procedure.	Numerous other defects mar the operating procedure.
The machines *that were* damaged by the fire were repaired.	The machines damaged by the fire were repaired.
By *the* examining *of* production records, they found the error.	By examining production records, they found the error.
In the period between April and June, we detected the problem.	Between April and June we detected the problem.
I am prepared to report *to the effect* that sales increased.	I am prepared to report that sales increased.

Roundabout Constructions. As we have noted, you can write anything in many ways. Some of the ways are direct. Some cover the same ground in a roundabout way. Usually the direct ways are shorter and communicate better.

- Avoid roundabout ways of saying things.

This sentence illustrates roundabout construction:

The department budget *can be observed to be decreasing* each *new* year.

Do the words *can be observed to be decreasing* get to the point? Is the idea of *observing* essential? Is *new* needed? A more direct and better sentence is this one:

The department budget decreases each year.

Here is another roundabout sentence:

The union *is involved in the task of reviewing* the seniority provision of the contract.

Now if the union is *involved in the task of reviewing,* it is really *reviewing.* The sentence should be written in these direct words:

The Starbucks Study

Supporting all we present in this text is the Starbucks Study conducted by Fugere, Hardaway, and Warshawsky. These researchers selected two actual writing samples. One was written in what they called typical corporate speak—big words and long sentences. The other was written in the straight, clear way stressed in this text. The identities of the companies were hidden. The researchers asked a sample of customers at an Atlanta Starbucks coffee shop to select from a list of 30 common psychological traits (15 good and 15 bad) the ones they would associate with each writing sample. The Starbucks customers did not like the corporate-speak sample, selecting mostly words such as *obnoxious, rude, stubborn,* and *unreliable.* They liked the straight and clear writing sample, selecting words such as *likeable, energetic, friendly, inspiring,* and *enthusiastic.*

Brian Fugere, Cheksea Hardaway, and Jon Warshawsky, *Why Business People Speak Like Idiots* (New York: The Free Press, 2005) 17.

The union *is reviewing* the seniority provision of the contract.

The following sentence pairs further illustrate the advantages of short, direct wording over roundabout wording:

Roundabout	Direct
The president *is of the opinion that* the tax was paid.	The president *believes* the tax was paid.
It is essential that the income be used to retire the debt.	The income *must* be used to retire the debt.
Reference is made to your May 10 report *in which you concluded* that the warranty is worthless.	Your May 10 report *concluded* that the warranty is worthless.
The supervisors *should take appropriate action to determine* whether the absentee reports are being verified.	The supervisors *should determine* whether the absentee reports are being verified.
The price increase *will afford* the company *an opportunity* to retire the debt.	The price *will enable* the company to retire the debt.
During the time she was employed by this company, Ms. Carr was absent once.	*While* employed by this company, Ms. Carr was absent once.
He criticized everyone he *came in contact with.*	He criticized everyone he *met.*

● Repeat words only for effect and emphasis.

Unnecessary Repetition of Words or Ideas. Repeating words obviously adds to sentence length. Such repetition sometimes serves a purpose, as when it is used for emphasis or special effect. But all too often it is without purpose, as this sentence illustrates:

We have not received your payment covering invoices covering June and July purchases.

It would be better to write the sentence like this:

We have not received your payment covering invoices for June and July purchases.

Another example is this one:

He stated that he believes that we are responsible.

The following sentence eliminates one of the *thats:*

He stated that he believes we are responsible.

Repetitions of ideas through the use of different words that mean the same thing (*free gift, true fact, past history*) also add to sentence length. Known as redundancies, such repetitions are illogical and can rarely be defended. Note the redundancy in this sentence:

● Avoid repetitions of ideas (redundancies).

The provision of Section 5 provides for a union shop.

The duplication, of course, is in the meaning of *provides.* By definition, a *provision* provides. So the repetition serves no purpose. The following sentence is better:

Section 5 provides for a union shop.

You often hear this expression:

In my opinion, I think the plan is sound.

Do not *in my opinion* and *I think* express the same thought? Could you possibly think in an opinion other than your own? The following sentence makes better sense:

I think the plan is sound.

Here are other examples of redundancies and ways to eliminate them:

Needless Repetition	Repetition Eliminated
Please *endorse your name on the back* of this check.	Please *endorse* this check.
We must *assemble together* at 10:30 AM *in the morning.*	We must *assemble* at 10:30 AM.
Our new model *is longer in length* than the old one.	Our new model *is longer* than the old one.
If you are not satisfied, *return it back* to us.	If you are not satisfied, *return* it to us.
Tod Wilson is the *present incumbent.*	Tod Wilson is the *incumbent.*
One should know the *basic fundamentals* of clear writing.	One should know the *fundamentals* of clear writing.
The *consensus of opinion* is that the tax is unfair.	The *consensus* is that the tax is unfair.
By acting now, we can finish *sooner than if we wait until a later date.*	By acting now, we can finish *sooner.*
At the present time, we *are* conducting two clinics.	We *are* conducting two clinics.
As a matter of interest, I am interested in learning your procedure.	I am *interested* in learning your procedure.
We should *plan in advance for the future.*	We should *plan.*

Determining Emphasis in Sentence Design

The sentences you write should give the right emphasis to content. Any written business communication contains a number of items of information, not all of which are equally important. Some are very important, such as a conclusion in a report or the objective in a message. Others are relatively unimportant. Your task as a writer is to form your sentences to communicate the importance of each item.

● You should give every item its due emphasis.

Sentence length affects emphasis. Short, simple sentences carry more emphasis than long, involved ones. They stand out and call attention to their contents. Thus, they give the reader a single message without the interference of related or supporting information.

● Short sentences emphasize contents.

Longer sentences give less emphasis to their contents. When a sentence contains two or more ideas, the ideas share emphasis. How they share it depends on how the

● Long sentences deemphasize contents.

sentence is constructed. If two ideas are presented equally (in independent clauses, for example), they get about equal emphasis. But if they are not presented equally (for example, in an independent and a dependent clause), one gets more emphasis than the other.

To illustrate the varying emphasis you can give information, consider this example. You have two items of information to write. One is that the company lost money last year. The other is that its sales volume reached a record high. You could present the information in at least three ways. First, you could give both items equal emphasis by placing them in separate short sentences:

> The company lost money last year. The loss occurred in spite of record sales.

Second, you could present the two items in the same sentence with emphasis on the lost money.

> Although the company enjoyed record sales last year, it lost money.

Third, you could present the two items in one sentence with emphasis on the sales increase:

> The company enjoyed record sales last year, although it lost money.

● Determining emphasis is a matter of good judgment.

Which way would you choose? The answer depends on how much emphasis each item deserves. You should think the matter through and follow your best judgment. But the point is clear: Your choice makes a difference.

The following paragraphs illustrate the importance of thinking logically to determine emphasis. In the first, each item of information gets the emphasis of a short sentence and none stands out. However, the items are not equally important and do not deserve equal emphasis. Notice, also, the choppy effect that the succession of short sentences produces.

> The main building was inspected on October 1. Mr. George Wills inspected the building. Mr. Wills is a vice president of the company. He found that the building has 6,500 square feet of floor space. He also found that it has 2,400 square feet of storage space. The new store must have a minimum of 6,000 square feet of floor space. It must have 2,000 square feet of storage space. Thus, the main building exceeds the space requirements for the new store. Therefore, Mr. Wills concluded that the main building is adequate for the company's needs.

In the next paragraph, some of the items are subordinated, but not logically. The really important information does not receive the emphasis it deserves. Logically, these two points should stand out: (1) the building is large enough and (2) storage space exceeds minimum requirements. But they do not stand out in this version:

> Mr. George Wills, who inspected the main building on October 1, is a vice president of the company. His inspection, which supports the conclusion that the building is large enough for the proposed store, uncovered these facts. The building has 6,500 square feet of floor space and 2,400 square feet of storage space, which is more than the minimum requirement of 6,000 and 2,000 square feet, respectively, of floor and storage space.

The third paragraph shows good emphasis of the important points. The short beginning sentence emphasizes the conclusion. The supporting facts that the building exceeds the minimum floor and storage space requirements receive main-clause emphasis. The less important facts, such as the reference to George Wills, are treated subordinately. Also, the most important facts are placed at the points of emphasis—the beginning and ending.

> The main building is large enough for the new store. This conclusion, reached by Vice President George Wills following his October 1 inspection of the building, is based on these facts. The building's 6,500 square feet of floor space exceed the minimum requirement by 500 square feet. The 2,400 square feet of storage space exceed the minimum requirement by 400 square feet.

The preceding illustrations show how sentence construction can determine emphasis. You can make items stand out, you can treat them equally, or you can deemphasize them. The choices are yours. But what you do must be the result of good, sound thinking and not simply a matter of chance.

Giving the Sentences Unity

Good sentences have unity. For a sentence to have unity, all of its parts must combine to form one clear thought. In other words, all the things put in a sentence should have a good reason for being together.

- All parts of a sentence should concern one thought.

Violations of unity in sentence construction fall into three categories: (1) unrelated ideas, (2) excessive detail, and (3) illogical constructions.

- There are three causes of unity error.

Unrelated Ideas. Placing unrelated ideas in a sentence is the most obvious violation of unity. Putting two or more ideas in a sentence is not grammatically wrong, but the ideas must have a reason for being together. They must combine to complete the single goal of the sentence.

- First, placing unrelated ideas in a sentence violates unity.

You can give unity to sentences that contain unrelated ideas in three basic ways: (1) You can put the ideas in separate sentences. (2) You can make one of the ideas subordinate to the other. (3) You can add words that show how the ideas are related. The first two of these techniques are illustrated by the revisions of the following sentence:

- You can avoid this error by (1) putting unrelated ideas in separate sentences, (2) subordinating an idea, or (3) adding words that show relationship.

Mr. Jordan is our sales manager, and he has a degree in law.

Perhaps the two ideas are related, but the words do not tell how. A better arrangement is to put each in a separate sentence:

Mr. Jordan is our sales manager. He has a law degree.

Or the two ideas could be kept in one sentence by subordinating one to the other. In this way, the main clause provides the unity of the sentence.

Mr. Jordan, our sales manager, has a law degree.

Adding words to show the relationship of ideas is illustrated in the revision of the following example:

Our production increased in January, and our equipment is wearing out.

The sentence has two ideas that seem unrelated. One way of improving it is to make a separate sentence of each idea. A closer look reveals, however, that the two ideas really are related. The words just do not show how. Thus, the sentence could be revised to show how:

Even though our equipment is wearing out, our production increased in January.

The following contrasting pairs of sentences further illustrate the technique:

Unrelated	Improved
Our territory is the southern half of the state, and our salespeople cannot cover it thoroughly.	Our territory is the southern half of the state. Our salespeople cannot cover it thoroughly.
Using the cost-of-living calculator is simple, but no tool will work well unless it is explained clearly.	Using the cost-of-living calculator is simple, but, like any tool, it will not work well unless it is explained clearly.
We concentrate on energy-saving products, and 70 percent of our business comes from them.	As a result of our concentration on energy-saving products, 70 percent of our business comes from them.

• Excessive detail is another cause of lack of unity. If the detail is important, put it in a separate sentence. This means using short sentences.

Excessive Detail. Putting too much detail into one sentence tends to hide the central thought. If the detail is important, you should put it in a separate sentence.

This suggestion strengthens another given earlier in the chapter—the suggestion that you use short sentences. Obviously, short sentences cannot have much detail. Long sentences—full of detail—definitely lead to lack of unity, as illustrated in these contrasting examples:

Excessive Detail	Improved
Our New York offices, considered plush in the 1990s, but now badly in need of renovation, as is the case with most offices that have not been maintained, have been abandoned.	Considered plush in the 1990s, our New York offices have not been maintained properly. As they badly need repair, we have abandoned them.
We have attempted to trace the Plytec insulation you ordered from us October 1, and about which you inquired in your October 10 message, but we have not yet been able to locate it, although we are sending you a rush shipment immediately.	We are sending you a rush shipment of Plytec insulation immediately. Following your October 10 inquiry, we attempted to trace your October 1 order. We were unable to locate it.
In 2006, when I, a small-town girl from a middle-class family, began my studies at Bradley University, which is widely recognized for its business administration program, I set my goal for a career with a large public company.	A small-town girl from a middle-class family, I entered Bradley University in 2006. I selected Bradley because of its widely recognized business administration program. From the beginning, my goal was a career with a large public company.

• Illogical constructions can rob a sentence of unity.

Illogical Constructions. Illogical constructions destroy sentence unity. These constructions result primarily from illogical thinking. Illogical thinking is too complex for meaningful study here, but a few typical examples should acquaint you with the possibilities. Then, by thinking logically, you should be able to reduce illogical constructions in your writing.

The first example contains two main thoughts in two correct clauses. But one clause is in active voice (*we cut*), and the other is in passive voice (*quality was reduced*).

> First we cut prices, and then quality was reduced.

We achieve unity by making both clauses active, as in this example:

> First we cut prices, and then we reduced quality.

The mixed constructions of the following sentence do not make a clear and logical thought. The technical explanation is that the beginning clause belongs with a complex sentence, while the last part is the predicate of a simple sentence.

> Because our salespeople are inexperienced caused us to miss our quota.

Revised for good logic, the sentence might read:

> The inexperience of our salespeople caused us to miss our quota.

These sentences further illustrate the point:

• Active and passive voice in the same sentence can violate unity.

• So can mixed constructions.

Illogical Construction	Improved
Job rotation is when you train people by moving them from job to job.	Job rotation is a training method in which people are moved from job to job.
Knowing that she objected to the price was the reason we permitted her to return the goods.	Because we knew she objected to the price, we permitted her to return the goods.
I never knew an executive who was interested in helping workers who had got into problems that caused them to worry.	I never knew an executive who was interested in helping worried workers with their problems.
My education was completed in 2006, and then I began work as a manager for Home Depot.	I completed my education in 2006 and then began work as a manager for Home Depot.

Arranging Sentence Elements for Clarity

As you know, various rules of grammar govern the structure of sentences. You know, for example, that modifying words must follow a definite sequence—that altering the sequence changes meaning. "A venetian blind" means one thing. "A blind Venetian" means quite another. Long-established rules of usage determine the meaning.

Many such rules exist. Established by centuries of use, these rules are not merely arbitrary requirements. Rather, they are based on custom and on logical relationships between words. In general, they are based on the need for clear communication.

Take the rule concerning dangling modifiers. Dangling modifiers confuse meaning by modifying the wrong words. On the surface, this sentence appears correct: "Believing that the price would drop, our purchasing agents were instructed not to buy." But the sentence is correct only if the purchasing agents did the believing—which is not the case. The modifying phrase dangles, and the intended meaning was probably this: "Believing that the price would drop, we instructed our purchasing agents not to buy."

Other rules of grammar also help to make writing clear. Unparallel constructions leave wrong impressions. Pronouns that do not clearly refer to a definite preceding word are vague and confusing. Subject–verb disagreements confuse the reader. The list goes on and on. The rules of grammar are useful in writing clear sentences. You should know them and follow them. You will want to study Chapter 17 for a review of these rules and complete the diagnostic exercise at the chapter end for feedback on your understanding of them.

• Clear writing requires that you follow the established rules of grammar.

• These rules are based on custom and logical relationships.

• For example, dangling modifiers confuse meaning.

• So do unparallel constructions, pronouns without antecedents, and subject–verb disagreements.

CARE IN PARAGRAPH DESIGN

- Paragraphing shows and emphasizes organization.

- It involves logical thinking.

Paragraphing is also important to clear communication. Paragraphs show the reader where topics begin and end, thus helping organize information in the reader's mind. Paragraphs also help make ideas stand out.

How one should design paragraphs is hard to explain, for the procedure is largely mental. Designing paragraphs requires the ability to organize and relate information. It involves the use of logic and imagination. But we can say little that would help you in these activities. The best we can do is give the following points on paragraph structure.

Giving the Paragraphs Unity

- The contents of a paragraph should concern one topic or idea (unity).

- But unity can vary in breadth. Paragraph unity concerns a narrow topic.

Like sentences, paragraphs should have unity. When applied to paragraph structure, unity means that a paragraph builds around a single topic or idea. Thus, everything you include in a paragraph should develop this topic or idea. When you have finished the paragraph, you should be able to say, "Everything in this paragraph belongs together because every part concerns every other part."

Unity is not always easy to determine. As all of a message or a report may concern a single topic, one could say that the whole message or report has unity. One could say the same about a major division of a report or a long paper. Obviously, paragraph unity concerns smaller units than these. Generally, it concerns the next largest unit of thought above a sentence.

A violation of unity is illustrated in the following paragraph from an application letter. As the goal of the paragraph is to summarize the applicant's coursework, all the sentences should pertain to coursework. By shifting to personal qualities, the third sentence violates paragraph unity. Taking this sentence out would correct the fault.

> At the university I studied all the basic accounting courses as well as specialized courses in taxation, international accounting, and computer security. I also took specialized coursework in the behavioral areas, with emphasis on human relations. Realizing the value of human relations in business, I also actively participated in organizations, such as Sigma Nu (social fraternity), Alpha Kappa Psi (professional fraternity), Intramural Soccer, and A cappella. I selected my elective coursework to round out my general business education. Among my electives were courses in investments, advanced business report writing, financial policy, and management information systems. A glance at my résumé will show you the additional courses that round out my training.

Keeping Paragraphs Short

- Generally, paragraphs should be short.

- Short paragraphs show organization better than long ones.

- Most readers prefer to read short paragraphs.

- About eight lines is a good average length.

As a general rule, you should keep your paragraphs short. This suggestion overlaps the suggestion about unity, for if your paragraphs have unity, they will usually be short.

As noted earlier, paragraphs help the reader follow the writer's organization plan. Writing marked by short paragraphs identifies more of the details of that plan. In addition, such writing is inviting to the eye. People simply prefer to read writing with frequent paragraph breaks.

This last point is easily proved by illustration. Assume you have a choice of reading either of two business reports on the same subject. One report has long paragraphs. Its pages appear solid with type. The second report has short paragraphs and thus provides frequent rest stops. You can see the rest stops at first glance. Now, which would you choose? No doubt, you would prefer the report with short paragraphs. It is more inviting, and it appears less difficult. Perhaps the difference is largely psychological, but it is a very real difference.

How long a paragraph should be depends on its contents—on what must be included to achieve unity. Readability research has suggested an average length of eight lines for longer papers such as reports. Shorter paragraphs are appropriate for messages.

Words of Wisdom

I notice that you use plain, simple language, short words and brief sentences. That is the way to write English—it is the modern way and the best way.

—Mark Twain

In all pointed sentences, some degree of accuracy must be sacrificed for conciseness.

—Samuel Johnson

Everything must be made as simple as possible, but not simpler.

—Albert Einstein

Keep in mind that these suggestions concern only an average. Some good paragraphs may be quite long—well over the average. Some paragraphs can be very short—as short as one line. One-line paragraphs are an especially appropriate means of emphasizing major points in business messages. A one-line paragraph may be all that is needed for a goodwill closing comment.

- But length can and should vary with need.

A good rule to follow is to question the unity of all long paragraphs—say, those longer than 10 lines. If after looking over such a paragraph you conclude that it has unity, leave it as it is. But you will sometimes find more than one topic. When you do, make each topic into a separate paragraph.

- A good practice is to question paragraphs over 10 lines.

Making Good Use of Topic Sentences

One good way of organizing paragraphs is to use topic sentences. The topic sentence expresses the main idea of a paragraph, and the remaining sentences build around and support it. In a sense, the topic sentence serves as a headline for the paragraph, and all the other sentences supply the story. Not every paragraph must have a topic sentence. Some paragraphs, for example, introduce ideas, relate succeeding items, or present an assortment of facts that lead to no conclusion. The central thought of such paragraphs is difficult to put into a single sentence. Even so, you should use topic sentences whenever you can. You should use them especially in writing reports that discuss a number of topics and subtopics. Using topic sentences forces you to find the central idea of each paragraph and helps you check paragraph unity.

- Topic sentences can help make good paragraphs. But not every paragraph must have a topic sentence.

How a topic sentence should fit into a paragraph depends primarily on the subject matter and the writer's plan. Some subject matter develops best if details are presented first and then followed by a conclusion or a summary statement (the topic sentence). Other subject matter develops best if it is introduced by the conclusion or the summary statement. Yet other arrangements are possible. You must make the decision, and you should base it on your best judgment. Your judgment should be helped, however, by a knowledge of the paragraph arrangements most commonly used.

- Placement of the topic sentence depends on the writer's plan.

Topic Sentence First. The most common paragraph arrangement begins with the topic sentence and continues with the supporting material. As this arrangement fits most units of business information, you should find it useful. In fact, the arrangement is so appropriate for business information that one company's writing manual suggests that it be used for virtually all paragraphs.

- The topic sentence can come first.

To illustrate the writing of a paragraph in which the topic sentence comes first, take a paragraph reporting on economists' replies to a survey question asking their view of business activity for the coming year. The facts to be presented are these: 13 percent of the economists expected an increase; 28 percent expected little or no change; 59 percent expected a downturn; 87 percent of those who expected a downturn thought it would come in the first quarter. The obvious conclusion—and the subject for the topic sentence—is that the majority expected a decline in the first quarter. Following this reasoning, we would develop a paragraph like this:

A majority of the economists consulted think that business activity will drop during the first quarter of next year. Of the 185 economists interviewed, 13 percent looked for continued increases in business activity, and 28 percent anticipated little or no change from the present high level. The remaining 59 percent looked for a recession. Of this group, nearly all (87 percent) believed that the downturn would occur during the first quarter of the year.

- It can come last.

Topic Sentence at End. The second most common paragraph arrangement places the topic sentence at the end, usually as a conclusion. Paragraphs of this kind usually present the supporting details first, and from these details they lead readers to the conclusion. Such paragraphs often begin with what may appear to be a topic sentence. But the final sentence covers their real point, as in this illustration:

The significant role of inventories in the economic picture should not be overlooked. At present, inventories represent 3.8 months' supply. Their dollar value is the highest in history. If considered in relation to increased sales, however, they are not excessive. In fact, they are well within the range generally believed to be safe. *Thus, inventories are not likely to cause a downward swing in the economy.*

- Or it can come in the middle.

Topic Sentence within the Paragraph. A third arrangement places the topic sentence somewhere within the paragraph. This arrangement is rarely used, for good reason. It does not emphasize the topic sentence, although the topic sentence usually deserves emphasis. Still, you can sometimes justify using this arrangement for special effect, as in this example:

Numerous materials have been used in manufacturing this part. And many have shown quite satisfactory results. *Material 329, however, is superior to them all.* When built with material 329, the part is almost twice as strong as when built with the next best material. It is also three ounces lighter. Most important, it is cheaper than any of the other products.

Leaving Out Unnecessary Detail

- In writing paragraphs, leave out unnecessary information.

You should include in your paragraphs only the information needed. The chances are that you have more information than the reader needs. Thus, a part of your communication task is to select what you need and discard what you do not need.

- But deciding what to include is a matter of judgment.

What you need, of course, is a matter of judgment. You can judge best by putting yourself in your reader's place. Ask yourself questions such as these: How will the information be used? What information will be used? What will not be used? Then make your decisions. If you follow this procedure, you will probably leave out much that you originally intended to use.

The following paragraph from a message to maintenance workers presents excessive information.

In reviewing the personnel records in our company database, I found that several items in your file were incomplete. The section titled "work history" has blanks for three items of information. The first is for dates employed. The second is for company name. And the third is for type of work performed. On your record only company name was entered, leaving two items blank. Years employed or your duties were not indicated. This information is important. It is reviewed by your supervisors every time you are considered for promotion or for a pay increase. Therefore, it must be completed. I request that you sign on the company portal and update your personnel record at your earliest convenience.

The message says much more than the reader needs to know. The goal is to have the reader update the personnel record, and everything else is of questionable value. This revised message is better:

> Please sign on the company portal at your earliest convenience to update your personnel record.

Making Paragraphs Coherent

Like well-made sentences, well-made paragraphs move the reader logically and smoothly from point to point. They clearly indicate how the different bits of information are related to each other, in terms of logic and the writer's apparent purpose. This quality of enabling readers to proceed easily through your message, without side trips and backward shifts, is called *coherence*.

- Paragraphs should be coherent. The relationships of parts should be clear.

The best thing you can do to give your message coherence is to arrange its information in a logical order—an order appropriate for the strategy of the case. So important are such decisions to message writing that we devote whole chapters to different patterns of organization. But logical organization is not enough. Various techniques are needed to tie the information together. These techniques are known as transitional devices. Here we will discuss three major ones: repetition of key words, use of pronouns, and the use of transitional words. The next chapter will say more about achieving coherence on the document level.

- Presenting information in a logical order helps coherence.

Repetition of Key Words. By repeating key words from one sentence to the next, you can make smooth connections of successive ideas. The following successive sentences illustrate this transitional device (key words in italics). The sentences come from a message refusing a request to present a lecture series for an advertising clinic.

- Repetition of key words connects thoughts.

> Because your advertising clinic is so well planned, I am confident that it can provide a really *valuable* service to practioners in the community. To be truly *valuable,* I think you will agree, the program must be given the time a thorough preparation requires. As my time for the coming week is heavily committed, you will need to find someone who is in a better position to do justice to your program.

Use of Pronouns. Because pronouns refer to words previously used, they make good transitions between ideas. So use them from time to time in forming idea connections. Especially use the demonstrative pronouns (*this, that, these, those*) for these words clearly relate ideas. The following sentences (with the demonstrative pronouns in italics) illustrate this technique.

- Pronouns connect with the words to which they relate.

> Ever since the introduction of our Model V nine years ago, consumers have suggested only one possible improvement—voice controls. During all *this* time, making *this* improvement has been the objective of Atkins research personnel. Now we proudly report that *these* efforts have been successful.

Transitional Words. When you talk in everyday conversation, you can connect many of your thoughts with transitional words. But when you write, more than likely you do not use them enough. So be alert for places where providing such words will help move your readers through your paragraphs.

- Use transitional words in your paragraphs.

Among the commonly used transitional words are *in addition, besides, in spite of, in contrast, however, likewise, thus, therefore, for example,* and *also.* A more extensive list appears in Chapter 10, where we review transition in report writing. That these words bridge thoughts is easy to see, for each gives a clue to the nature of the connection between what has been said and what will be said next. *In addition,* for example, tells the reader that what is to be discussed next builds on what has been discussed. *However* clearly shows a contrast in ideas. *Likewise* tells that what has been said resembles what will be said.

- Transitional words tell the thought connection between following ideas.

Notice how the transitional expressions (in italics) in the following paragraph signal the relations among the parts and move the reader steadily forward through the ideas:

Three reasons justify moving from the Crowton site. *First,* the building rock in the Crowton area is questionable. The failure of recent geologic explorations in the area appears to confirm suspicions that the Crowton deposits are nearly exhausted. *Second,* the distances from the Crowton site to major markets make transportation costs unusually high. Obviously, any savings in transportation costs will add to company profits. *Third,* the obsolescence of much of the equipment at the Crowton plant makes this an ideal time for relocation. The old equipment at the Crowton plant could be scrapped.

The transition words *first, second,* and *third* bring out the paragraph's pattern of organization and make it easy for the reader to follow along.

- Do not use transitional words arbitrarily.

But a note of caution: do not use transitional words just for the sake of using them. Be sure that they fit your intended meaning and will truly help the reader's comprehension.

SUMMARY BY LEARNING OBJECTIVES

1 Explain the role of adaptation in writing clear sentences.

1. Writing that communicates uses words that the reader understands and sentence structures that organize the message clearly in the reader's mind. It is writing that is *adapted* to the reader.

2 Write short, clear sentences by limiting sentence content and economizing on words.

2. In general, you should use short sentences, especially when adapting to readers with low reading ability. Do this in two ways:
   - Limit sentence content by breaking up those that are too long.
   - Use words economically by following these specific suggestions:
     — Avoid cluttering phrases (*if* rather than *in the event that*).
     — Eliminate surplus words—words that contribute nothing (*It will be noted that*).
     — Avoid roundabout ways of saying things (*decreases* rather than *can be observed to be decreasing*).
     — Avoid unnecessary repetition (*In my opinion, I think*).

3 Design sentences that give the right emphasis to content.

3. Give every item you communicate the emphasis it deserves by following these suggestions:
   - Use short sentences to emphasize points.
   - Combine points in longer sentences to de-emphasize them.
   - But how you combine points (by equal treatment, by subordination) determines the emphasis given.

4 Employ unity and clarity in writing effective sentences.

4. Achieve unity and clarity in your sentences.
   - Make certain all the information in a sentence belongs together—that it forms a unit. These suggestions help:
     — Eliminate excessive detail.
     — Combine only related thoughts.
     — Avoid illogical constructions.
   - Ensure clarity by following the conventional rules of writing (standards of punctuation, grammar, and such).

5 Compose paragraphs that are short and unified, use topic sentences effectively, and communicate coherently.

5. Design your paragraphs for clear communication by following these standards:
   - Give the paragraphs unity.
   - Keep the paragraphs short.
   - Use topic sentences effectively, usually at the beginning but sometimes within and at the end of the paragraph.
   - Leave out unessential details.
   - Use transitional devices for coherence.

1 How are sentence length and sentence design related to adaptation?

2 Discuss this comment: "Long, involved sentences tend to be difficult to understand. Therefore, the shorter the sentence, the better."

3 Discuss ways to give ideas more or less emphasis in your sentences.

4 How can unity apply equally well to a sentence, to a paragraph, and to longer units of writing?

5 What are the principal causes of lack of unity in sentences?

6 Discuss this comment: "Words carry the message. They would carry the same meanings with or without paragraphing. Therefore, paragraphing has no effect on communication."

7 Defend the use of short paragraphs in report writing.

8 "Topic sentences merely repeat what the other sentences in the paragraph say. As they serve only to add length, they should be eliminated." Discuss.

CRITICAL THINKING EXERCISES

Instructions, Sentences 1–8: Break up these sentences into shorter, more readable sentences.

1 Records were set by both the New York Stock Exchange Composite Index, which closed at 8,001.40 up 27.08 points, topping its previous high of 7,986.50, set Wednesday, and Standard & Poor's 500 Index, which finished at 1,264.03, up 6.90, moving up significantly, also set a five-day high.

2 Dealers attributed the rate decline to several factors, including expectations that the U.S. Treasury will choose to pay off rather than refinance some $4 billion of government obligations that fall due next month, an action that would absorb even further the available supplies of short-term government securities, leaving more funds chasing skimpier stocks of the securities.

3 If you report your income on a fiscal-year basis ending in 2007, you may not take credit for any tax withheld on your calendar-year 2007 earnings, inasmuch as your taxable year began in 2006, although you may include, as a part of your withholding tax credits against your fiscal 2008 tax liability, the amount of tax withheld during 2007.

4 The Consumer Education Committee is assigned the duties of keeping informed of the qualities of all consumer goods and services, especially of their strengths and shortcomings, of gathering all pertinent information on dealers' sales practices, with emphasis on practices involving honest and reasonable fairness, and of publicizing any of the information collected that may be helpful in educating the consumer.

5 The upswing in business activity that began in 2007 is expected to continue and possibly accelerate in 2008, and gross domestic product should rise by $664 billion, representing an 8 percent increase over 2007, which is significantly higher than the modest 5 percent increase of 2006.

6 As you will not get this part of Medicare automatically, even if you are covered by Social Security, you must sign up for it and pay $88.50 per month, which the government will match, if you want your physician's bills to be covered.

7 Students with approved excused absences from any of the hour examinations have the option of taking a special makeup examination to be given during dead week or of using their average grade on their examinations in the course as their grade for the work missed.

8 Although we have not definitely determined the causes for the decline in sales volume for the month, we know that during this period construction on the street adjacent to the store severely limited traffic flow and that because of resignations in the advertising department promotion efforts dropped well below normal.

9 Assume that you are the assistant manager of a hotel and are describing your hotel's meeting room to a prospective customer who is thinking of holding a seminar there. Turn the following pieces of information into coherent writing, making paragraph breaks where you think appropriate. Be ready to explain why you grouped the information and managed the emphasis the way you did. You may need to add some words or information to make the facts flow smoothly.

We have a meeting room.

It will be available on the date you requested.

It can seat 100 people.

The seating can be arranged to your specifications.

It is quiet.

It is on the ground floor.

It is not near the guest rooms.

The lounge has live music on occasion.

The lounge is at the opposite end of the hotel from the meeting room.

The meeting room has a lectern.

It has a projector.

It has a screen.

It has a laptop hookup.

We can rent additional equipment.

We can rent it at no charge to you.

The charge for the room is $300.

This is the charge for one day.

Instructions, Sentences 10–39: Revise the following sentences for more economical wording.

10 In view of the fact that we financed the experiment, we were entitled to some profit.

11 We will deliver the goods in the near future.

12 Mr. Watts outlined his development plans on the occasion of his acceptance of the presidency.

13 I will talk to him with regard to the new policy.

14 The candidates who had the most money won.

15 There are many obligations that we must meet.

16 We purchased coats that are lined with rabbit fur.

17 Mary is of the conviction that service has improved.

18 Sales can be detected to have improved over last year.

19 It is essential that we take the actions that are necessary to correct the problem.

20 The chairperson is engaged in the activities of preparing the program.

21 Martin is engaged in the process of revising the application.

22 You should study all new innovations in your field.

23 In all probability, we are likely to suffer a loss this quarter.

24 The requirements for the job require a minimum of three years of experience.

25 In spite of the fact that the bill remains unpaid, they placed another order.

26 We expect to deliver the goods in the event that we receive the money.

27 In accordance with their plans, company officials sold the machinery.

28 This policy exists for the purpose of preventing dishonesty.

29 The salespeople who were most successful received the best rewards.

30 The reader will note that this area ranks in the top 5 percent in per capita income.

31 Our new coats are made of a fabric that is of the wrinkle-resistant variety.

32 Our office is charged with the task of counting supplies not used in production.

33 Their salespeople are of the conviction that service is obsolete.

34 Losses caused by the strike exceeded the amount of $640,000.

35 This condition can be assumed to be critical.

36 Our goal is to effect a change concerning the overtime pay rate.

37 Mr. Wilson replaced the old antiquated machinery with new machinery.

38 We must keep this information from transpiring to others.

39 The consensus of opinion of this group is that Wellington was wrong.

Instructions, Paragraphs 40–44: Rewrite the following paragraphs in two ways to show different placement of the topic sentence and variations in emphasis of contents. Point out the differences in meaning in each of your paragraphs.

40 Jennifer has a good knowledge of office procedures. She works hard. She has performed her job well. She is pleasant most of the time, but she has a bad temper, which has led to many personal problems with the work group. Although I cannot recommend her for promotion, I approve a 5 percent raise for her.

41 Last year our sales increased 7 percent in California and 9 percent in Arizona. Nevada had the highest increase, with 14 percent. Although all states in the western region enjoyed increases, Oregon recorded only a 2 percent gain. Sales in Washington increased 3 percent.

42 I majored in marketing at Darden University and received a B.S. degree in 2007. Among the marketing courses I took were marketing strategy, promotion, marketing research, marketing management, and consumer behavior. These and other courses prepared me specifically for a career in retailing. Included, also, was a one-semester internship in retailing with Macy's Department Stores.

43 Our records show that Penn motors cost more than Oslo motors. The Penns have less breakdown time. They cost more to repair. I recommend that we buy Penn motors the next time we replace worn-out motors. The longer working life offsets Penn's cost disadvantage. So does its better record for breakdown.

44 Recently China ordered a large quantity of wheat from the United States. Likewise, Germany ordered a large quantity. Other countries continued to order heavily, resulting in a dramatic improvement in the outlook for wheat farming. Increased demand by Eastern European countries also contributed to the improved outlook.

chapter four

Writing for Effect

LEARNING OBJECTIVES

Upon completing this chapter, you will be able to write business communications that emphasize key points and have a positive effect on human relations. To reach this goal, you should be able to

1 Explain the need for effect in writing business messages.

2 Use a conversational style that eliminates the old language of business and "rubber stamps."

3 Use the you-viewpoint to build goodwill.

4 Employ positive language to achieve goodwill and other desired effects.

5 Explain the techniques of achieving courtesy.

6 Use the four major techniques for emphasis in writing.

7 Write documents that flow smoothly through the use of a logical order helped by the four major transitional devices.

Affecting Human Relations through Writing

To prepare yourself for this chapter, once again play the role of a small business manager and Max Elliott's superior. As you review Max's writing, you see more evidence of how his communication shortcomings affect your company's effectiveness as it strives to compete. This new evidence appears in the messages Max writes—primarily letters and email. These messages go to the people inside and outside the company. They affect the human relationships that go far to determine the success of the operation. Poorly written, insensitive messages can produce serious negative reactions. Typical of Max's messages is the following letter:

Dear Mr. Morley:

Your December 3d complaint was received and contents noted. After reviewing the facts, I regret to report that I must refuse your claim. If you will read the warranty brochure, you will see that the shelving you bought is designed for light loads—a maximum of 800 pounds. You should have bought the heavy-duty product.

　　I regret the damage this mistake caused you and trust that you will see our position. Hoping to be of service to you in the future, I remain,

Sincerely yours,

In this message you detect more than just the readability problem you saw in Max's reports. The words are not polite. Instead of showing concern for the reader, they are blunt, tactless, and unfriendly. Overall, they leave a bad impression in the reader's mind—the impression of a writer, and a business, unconcerned about the needs for good human relations. This chapter will show you how to avoid such impressions.

THE IMPORTANCE OF EFFECT

- Written communication within a business primarily requires clarity.

Clarity is a primary concern in most of the writing you will do in business—especially your writing within the organization. Much of this writing concerns matters that do not involve the readers personally. Thus you can communicate the information in a matter-of-fact way. Your primary concern will be to communicate, and you will want to do so quickly and accurately. This is the way your fellow workers want and expect you to write. Even so, you will want to maintain the courtesy and friendliness that is so vital to good working relationships.

- Good business writing, especially to external audiences, requires both clarity and the goodwill effect.

When you write messages that tend to be more personal, however, you will be concerned about more than just communicating information. This will especially be the case when you communicate with people outside the organization and a major concern is to gain or maintain favorable relationships. Email messages or letters written for a company to its customers are examples of such communications. The information in these messages will be important, of course. In fact, probably it will be the most important part. But you also will need to achieve certain effects—effects that will contribute to a favorable image of the company.

One effect you should strive for in virtually any message is the goodwill effect. Building goodwill through written messages is good business practice. Wise business leaders know that the success of their business is affected by what people think about the business. They know that what people think about a business is influenced by their human contact with that business: the services they receive, how they are treated, the manners displayed, and such. The written word is a major form of human contact.

- Most people enjoy building goodwill.

The goodwill effect in messages is not desirable for business reasons alone. It is, quite simply, the effect most of us want in our relations with people. The things we do and say to create goodwill are the things we enjoy doing and saying. They are friendly,

. . . you-attitude requires writers first to view a real-world situation from the reader's perspective and then to show in the text of the document a sensitivity to the reader's perspective. . . . While simply using "you" and "yours" rater than "I" or "mine" will sometimes help to express a you-attitude, it would be both simple-minded and incorrect to equate you-attitude with the dominance of "you" in the text.

Lilita Rodman, University of British Columbia

Lilita Rodman, "You-Attitude: A Linguistic Perspective," *Business Communication Quarterly* 64.4 (2001): 11–12.

courteous things that make relations between people enjoyable. Most of us would want to do and say them even if they were not profitable. Clearly, they display the good manners of business practice. They display good business etiquette.

As you read the following chapters, you will see that other effects help ensure the success of written messages. For example, in writing to persuade a reader to accept an unfavorable decision, you can use the techniques of persuasion. In applying for a job, you can use writing techniques that emphasize your qualifications. And in telling bad news, you can use techniques that play down the negative parts. These are but a few ways to manage the effects of your writing.

- For their success, letters and some email messages often require achieving other effects.

Getting positive effects with your messages is largely a matter of skillful writing and of understanding how people respond to words. It involves keeping certain attitudes in mind and using certain writing techniques. The following review of these attitudes and techniques should help you get the effects you need.

- Getting the desired effects is a matter of writing skill and of understanding people.

CONVERSATIONAL STYLE

One technique that helps build the goodwill effect is to write in conversational language. By conversational language we mean language that resembles conversation. It is warm and natural. Such language leaves an impression that people like. It is also the language we use most and understand best. Because it is easily understood, it is courteous to use it.

- Writing in conversational language has a favorable effect.

Resisting the Tendency to Be Formal

Writing conversationally is not as easy as you might think, because most of us tend to write formally. When faced with a writing task, we change character. Instead of writing in friendly, conversational language, we write in stiff and stilted words. We seek the big word, the difficult word. The result is a cold and unnatural style—one that doesn't produce the goodwill effect you want your messages to have. The following examples illustrate this problem and how to correct it.

- Writing in conversational language is not easy, for we tend to be stiff and formal.

Stiff and Dull

Reference is made to your May 7 email, in which you describe the approved procedure for initiating a claim.

Enclosed herewith is the brochure about which you make inquiry.

In reply to your July 11 letter, please be informed that your adherence to instructions outlined therein will greatly facilitate attainment of our objective.

Conversational

Please refer to your May 7 email in which you tell how to file a claim.

Enclosed is the brochure you asked about.

By following the procedures you listed in your July 11 letter, you will help us reach our goal.

Grammar and Style Checkers Help Identify Clichés, Colloquialisms, and Jargon

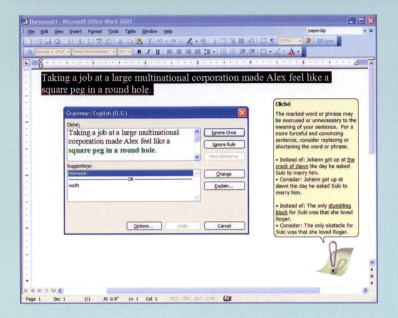

While not perfect, grammar and style checkers can help writers identify some clichés, colloquialisms, and jargon that creep into their writing. The checker here illustrates that it found a cliché and offers two suggestions for correcting it. By clicking on the explain button, the office assistant will tell the writer what it determines is the case here. Although this software can help, writers still need to be able to identify the trite and overused expressions the software misses. Also, writers need to be able to recast the sentences for clarity and sincerity.

Stiff and Dull

This is in reply to your letter of December 1, expressing concern that you do not have a high school diploma and asking if a GED would suffice as prerequisite for the TAA Training Program.

I shall be most pleased to avail myself of your kind suggestion when and if prices decline.

Conversational

The GED you mention in your December 1 letter qualifies you for the TAA Training Program.

I'll gladly follow your suggestion if the price falls.

Cutting Out "Rubber Stamps"

- Rubber stamps are expressions used by habit every time a certain type of situation occurs.

- They give the effect of routine treatment. It is better to use words written for the present case.

Rubber stamps (also called *clichés*) are expressions used by habit every time a certain type of situation occurs. They are used without thought and do not fit the present situation exclusively. As the term indicates, they are used much as you would use a rubber stamp.

Because they are used routinely, rubber stamps communicate the effect of routine treatment, which is not likely to impress readers favorably. Such treatment tells readers that the writer has no special concern for them—that the present case is being handled in the same way as others. In contrast, words specially selected for this case are likely to impress. They show the writer's concern for and interest in the readers. Clearly, specially selected wording is the better choice for producing a goodwill effect. Some examples of rubber stamps you have no doubt heard before are listed below. These phrases, while once quite appropriate, have become stale with overuse.

a blessing in disguise	last but not least
as good as gold	learning the ropes
back against the wall	leave no stone unturned
call the shots	to add insult to injury

Some of the rubber stamps used today are relics from the old language of business—a way of writing that was in vogue over a century ago. In the early days of business writing, a heavily formal, stilted, and unnatural style developed. Messages typically began with expressions such as "your letter of the 7th inst. received . . ." and "your esteemed favor at hand . . ." They ended with dangling closes such as "trusting to be favored by your response . . ." and "thanking you in advance, I remain . . ." Messages were filled with expressions such as "deem it advisable," "beg to advise," "this is to inform," and "wherein you state." Fortunately, these awkward and unnatural expressions have faded from use. Even so, a few of the old expressions remain with us, some with modern-day changes in wording. One example is the "thank you for your letter" form of opening sentence. Its intent may be sincere, but its roots in the old language of business and its overuse make it a rubber stamp. Another is the "if I can be of any further assistance, do not hesitate to call on me" type of close. Other examples of rubber stamps in this category are the following:

- Expressions from the old language of business are rubber stamps. Some new ones exist.

I am happy to be able to answer your message.

I have received your message.

This will acknowledge receipt of . . .

According to our records . . .

This is to inform you that . . .

In accordance with your instructions . . .

You do not need to know all the rubber stamps to stop using them. You do not even need to be able to recognize them. You only need to write in the language of good conversation, for these worn-out expressions are not a part of most conversational vocabularies.

- You can avoid rubber stamps by writing in your conversational vocabulary.

Proof through Contrasting Examples

The advantages of conversational writing over writing marked by old business language and rubber stamps are best proved by example. As you read the following contrasting sentences, note the overall effects of the words. The goodwill advantages of conversational writing are obvious.

Dull and Stiff	**Friendly and Conversational**
This is to advise that we deem it a great pleasure to approve subject of your request as per letter of the 12th inst.	Yes, you certainly may use the equipment you asked about in your letter of August 12.
Pursuant to this matter, I wish to state that the aforementioned provisions are unmistakably clear.	These contract provisions are clear on this point.
This will acknowledge receipt of your May 10th order for four dozen Docker slacks. Please be advised that they will be shipped in accordance with your instructions by UPS on May 16.	Four dozen Docker slacks should reach your store by the 18th. As you instructed, they were shipped today by UPS.
The undersigned wishes to advise that the aforementioned contract is at hand.	I have the contract.
Please be advised that you should sign the form before the 1st.	You should sign the form before the 1st.

Dull and Stiff	Friendly and Conversational
Hoping this meets with your approval . . .	I hope you approve.
Submitted herewith is your notification of our compliance with subject standards.	Attached is notification of our compliance with the standards.
Assuring you of our continued cooperation, we remain . . .	We will continue to cooperate.
Thanking you in advance . . .	I'll sincerely appreciate . . .
Herewith enclosed please find . . .	Enclosed is . . .
I deem it advisable . . .	I suggest . . .
I herewith hand you . . .	Here is . . .
Kindly advise at an early date.	Please let me know soon.

YOU-VIEWPOINT

- The you-viewpoint produces goodwill and influences people favorably.

- The you-viewpoint emphasizes the reader's interests. It is an attitude of mind involving more than the use of *you* and *yours*.

Writing from the you-viewpoint (also called *you-attitude*) is another technique for building goodwill in written messages. As you will see in following chapters, it focuses interest on the reader. Thus, it is a technique for persuasion and for influencing people favorably. It is fundamental in the practice of business communication.

In a broad sense, you-viewpoint writing emphasizes the reader's interests and concerns. It emphasizes *you* and *your* and de-emphasizes *we* and *our*. But it is more than a matter of just using second-person pronouns. *You* and *your* can appear prominently in sentences that emphasize the we-viewpoint, as in this example: "If you do not pay by the 15th, you must pay a penalty." Likewise, *we* and *mine* can appear in sentences that emphasize the you-viewpoint, as in this example: "We will do whatever we can to protect your investment." The point is that the you-viewpoint is an attitude of mind. It is the attitude that places the reader in the center of things. Sometimes it just involves being friendly and treating people the way they like to be treated. Sometimes it involves skillfully handling people with carefully chosen words to make a desired impression. It involves all these things and more.

The You-Viewpoint Illustrated

Although the you-viewpoint involves much more than word selection, examples of word selection help explain the technique. First, take the case of a person writing to present good news. This person could write from a self-centered point of view, beginning with such words as "I am happy to report . . ." Or he or she could begin with the you-viewpoint words "You will be happy to know . . ." The messages are much the same, but the effects are different.

Or consider the case of a writer who must inform the reader that a request for credit has been approved. A we-viewpoint beginning could take this form: "We are pleased to have your new account." Some readers might view these words favorably. But some would sense a self-centered writer concerned primarily with making money. A you-viewpoint beginning would go something like this: "Your new charge account is now open for your convenience."

Advertising copywriters know the value of the you-viewpoint perhaps better than any other group. So no advertising copywriter would write anything like this: "We make Kodak digital cameras for three levels: beginner, intermediate, and professional." An advertising copywriter would probably bring the reader into the center of things and write about the product in reader-satisfaction language: "So that you can choose the one camera that is just right for you, Kodak makes cameras for you in three models: basic, standard, and full-featured."

The you-viewpoint can even be used in bad-news messages. For example, take the case of an executive who must say no to a professor's request for help on a research

project. The bad news is made especially bad when it is presented in we-viewpoint words: "We cannot comply with your request to use our staff on your project, for it would cost us more than we can afford." A skilled writer using the you-viewpoint would look at the situation from this reader's point of view, find an explanation likely to satisfy this reader, and present the explanation in you-viewpoint language. The you-viewpoint response might take this form: "As a business professor well acquainted with the need for economizing in all phases of support, you will understand why we must limit our staff to work in our office."

The following contrasting examples demonstrate the different effects that changes in viewpoint produce. With a bit of imagination, you should be able to supply information on the situations they cover.

- Even a bad-news situation can benefit from you-viewpoint wording.

We-Viewpoint	You-Viewpoint
We are happy to have your order for Hewlett-Packard products, which we are sending today by UPS.	Your selection of Hewlett-Packard products should reach you by Saturday as they were shipped by UPS today.
We sell the Chicago cutlery set for the low price of $24 each and suggest a retail price of $36.50.	You can reap a $12.50 profit on each Chicago Cutlery set you sell at $36.50, for your cost is only $24.00.
Our policy prohibits us from permitting outside groups to use our equipment except on a cash-rental basis.	Our policy of cutting operating costs by renting our equipment helps us make efficient use of your tax dollars.
We have been quite tolerant of your past-due account and must now demand payment.	If you are to continue to enjoy the benefits of credit buying, you must clear your account now.
We have received your report of May 1.	Thank you for your report of May 1.
So that we may complete our file records on you, we ask that you submit to us your January report.	So that your file records may be completed, please send us your January report.
We have shipped the two dozen Cross desk sets you ordered.	Your two dozen Cross desk sets should reach you with this letter.
We require that you sign the sales slip before we will charge to your account.	For your protection, you are charged only after you have signed the sales slip.

A Point of Controversy

- Some say that the you-viewpoint is insincere and manipulative. It can be insincere, but it need not be. Using the you-viewpoint is being courteous. Research supports its use.

The you-viewpoint has been a matter of some controversy. Its critics point out two major shortcomings: (1) it is insincere and (2) it is manipulative. In either event, they argue, the technique is dishonest. It is better, they say, to just "tell it as it is."

These arguments have some merit. Without question, the you-viewpoint can be used to the point of being insincere; and it can be obvious flattery. Thus it can be used to pursue unethical goals. But those who favor the technique argue that insincerity, flattery, and unethical manipulation need not—in fact, should not—be the result of you-viewpoint effort. The objective is to treat people courteously—the way they like to be treated. People like to be singled out for attention. They are naturally more interested in themselves than in the writer. Overuse of the technique, the defenders argue, does not justify not using it. Their argument is supported by research comparing readers' responses to a case written to determine the effect of the you-attitude. The study evaluated the readers' perception of the writer's tone, commitment to comply to the message, and satisfaction. It found support for using the you-viewpoint.[1]

- The you-viewpoint can manipulate. But condemn the goal, not the technique.

On the matter of manipulative use of the you-viewpoint, we must again concede a point. It is a technique of persuasion, and persuasion may have bad as well as good goals. Supporters of the you-viewpoint argue that it is bad goals and not the techniques used to reach them that should be condemned. Persuasion techniques used to reach good goals are good.

- A middle-ground approach is best. Use the you-viewpoint when it is the right thing to do.

The correct approach appears to lie somewhere between the extremes. You do not have to use the you-viewpoint exclusively or eliminate it. You can take a middle ground. You can use the you-viewpoint when it is friendly and sincere and when your goals are ethical. In such cases, using the you-viewpoint is "telling it as it is"—or at least as it should be. With this position in mind, we apply the technique in the following chapters.

ACCENT ON POSITIVE LANGUAGE

Whether your written message achieves its goal often will depend on the words you use. As you know, one can say anything in many ways, and each way conveys a different meaning. Much of the difference lies in the meanings of words.

- Of the many ways of saying anything, each has a unique meaning.

Effects of Words

- Positive words are usually best for message goals, especially when persuasion and goodwill are needed.

Positive words are usually best for achieving your message goals. This is not to say that negative words have no place in business writing. Such words are strong and give emphasis, and you will sometimes want to use them. But your need will usually be for positive words, for such words are more likely to produce the effects you seek. When your goal is to change someone's position, for example, positive words are most likely to do the job. They tend to put the reader in the right frame of mind, and they emphasize the pleasant aspects of the goal. They also create the goodwill atmosphere we seek in most messages.

- Negative words stir up resistance and hurt goodwill.

Negative words tend to produce the opposite effects. They may stir up your reader's resistance to your goals, and they are likely to be highly destructive of goodwill. Thus, to reach your writing goals, you will need to study carefully the negativeness and positiveness of your words. You will need to select the words that are most appropriate in each case.

- So beware of strongly negative words (*mistake, problem*), words that deny (*no, do not*), and ugly words (*itch, guts*).

In doing so you should generally be wary of strongly negative words. These words convey unhappy and unpleasant thoughts, and such thoughts usually detract from your goal. They include such words as *mistake, problem, error, damage, loss,* and *failure.* There are also words that deny—words such as *no, do not, refuse,* and *stop.* And there

---

[1] Annette N. Shelby and Lamar Reinsch, Jr., "Positive Emphasis and You-Attitude: An Empirical Study," *Journal of Business Communication* 32 (1995): 319.

6/3

"They called it a pack of lies —
I called it a sales presentation."

are words whose sounds or meanings have unpleasant effects. Examples would differ from person to person, but many would probably agree on these: *itch, guts, scratch, grime, sloppy, sticky, bloody,* and *nauseous.* Or how about *gummy, slimy, bilious,* and *soggy?* Run these negative words through your mind and think about the meanings they produce. You should find it easy to see that they tend to work against most of the goals you may have in your messages.

Examples of Word Choice

To illustrate your positive-to-negative word choices in handling written messages, take the case of a company executive who had to deny a local civic group's request to use the company's meeting facilities. To soften the refusal, the executive could let the group use a conference room, which might be somewhat small for its purpose. The executive came up with this totally negative response:

> We *regret* to inform you that we *cannot* permit you to use our auditorium for your meeting, as the Sun City Investment Club asked for it first. We can, however, let you use our conference room, but it seats *only* 60.

The negative words are italicized. First, the positively intended message "We *regret* to inform you" is an unmistakable sign of coming bad news. "*Cannot* permit" contains an unnecessarily harsh meaning. And notice how the good-news part of the message is handicapped by the limiting word *only.*

Had the executive searched for more positive ways of covering the same situation, he or she might have written:

> Although the SunCity Investment Club has reserved the auditorium for Saturday, we can instead offer you our conference room, which seats 60.

Not a single negative word appears in this version. Both approaches achieve the primary objective of denying a request, but their effects on the reader differ sharply. There is no question as to which approach does the better job of building and holding goodwill.

For a second illustration, take the case of a writer granting the claim of a woman for cosmetics damaged in transit. Granting the claim, of course, is the most positive ending that such a situation can have. Even though this customer has had a somewhat unhappy experience, she is receiving what she wants. The negative language of an unskilled writer, however, can so vividly recall the unhappy aspects of the problem that the happy solution is moved to the background. As this negative version of the message illustrates, the effect is to damage the reader's goodwill:

> We received your claim in which you contend that we were responsible for *damage* to three cases of Estée Lauder lotion. We assure you that we sincerely *regret* the *problems* this has caused you. Even though we feel in all sincerity that your receiving clerks may have been *negligent,* we will assume the *blame* and replace the *damaged* merchandise.

Obviously, this version grants the claim grudgingly, and the company would profit from such an approach only if there were extenuating circumstances. The phrase "in which you contend" clearly implies some doubt about the legitimacy of the claim. Even the sincerely intended expression of regret only recalls to the reader's mind the event that caused all the trouble. And the negatives *blame* and *damage* only strengthen the recollection. Certainly, this approach is not conducive to goodwill.

In the following version of the same message, the writer refers only to positive aspects of the situation—what can be done to settle the problem. The job is done without using a negative word and without mentioning the situation being corrected or suspicions concerning the honesty of the claim. The goodwill effect of this approach is likely to maintain business relations with the reader:

> Three cases of Estée Lauder lotion are on their way to you by FedEx and should be on your sales floor by Saturday.

For additional illustrations, compare the differing results obtained from these contrasting negative-positive versions of messages (italics mark the negative words):

Negative	Positive
You *failed* to give us the fabric specifications of the chair you ordered.	So that you may have the one chair you want, will you please check your choice of fabric on the enclosed card?
Smoking is *not* permitted anywhere except in the lobby.	Smoking is permitted in the lobby only.
We *cannot* deliver until Friday.	We can deliver the goods on Friday.
Chock-O-Nuts do not have that *gummy, runny* coating that makes some candies *stick* together when they get hot.	The rich chocolate coating of Chock-O-Nuts stays crispy good throughout the summer months.
You were *wrong* in your conclusion, for paragraph 3 of our agreement clearly states	Please read paragraph 3 of our agreement, which explains . . .
We *regret* that we *overlooked* your coverage on this equipment and apologize for the *trouble* and *concern* it must have caused you.	You were quite right in believing that you have coverage on the equipment. We appreciate your calling the matter to our attention.
We *regret* to inform you that we must deny your request for credit.	For the time being, we can serve you on a cash basis only.
You should have known that the camera lens *cannot* be cleaned with tissue, for it is clearly explained in the instructions.	The instructions explain why the camera lens should be cleaned only with a non-scratch cloth.
Your May 7 *complaint* about our remote control is *not* supported by the evidence.	Review of the situation described in your May 7 email explains what happened when you used the remote control.

COURTESY

A major contributor to goodwill in business documents is courtesy. By courtesy we mean treating people with respect and friendly human concern. It produces friendly relations between people. The result is a better human climate for solving business problems and doing business.

A French General's Justification of Politeness

Once, at a diplomatic function, the great World War I leader Marshal Foch was maneuvered into a position in which he had to defend French politeness.

"There is nothing in it but wind," Foch's critic sneered.

"There is nothing in a tire but wind," the marshal responded politely, "but it makes riding in a car very smooth and pleasant."

As with every other facet of your communications, how to be courteous ultimately depends on the given situation. Including "please," "thank you," "we're sorry," and other standard expressions of politeness do not necessarily make a message courteous. Rather than focusing on stock phrases, consider what will make your reader feel most comfortable, understood, and appreciated. A message with no overtly polite expressions whatsoever can still demonstrate great courtesy by being easy to read, focusing on the writer's interests, and conveying the writer's feelings of goodwill.

- Courtesy involves the preceding goodwill techniques.

Still, courtesy generally is enhanced by using certain techniques. We have already discussed three of them: writing in conversational language, employing the you-viewpoint, and choosing positive words.

Focusing Your Message on Your Reader

One of the other techniques is to write directly to your specific reader. Messages that appear routine have a cold, impersonal effect. On the other hand, messages that appear to be written for one reader tend to make the reader feel important and appreciated.

- It also involves writing directly for the one reader.

To design your message for the specific reader, you should write for the one situation. What you say throughout the document should make it clear that the reader is getting individual treatment. For example, a message granting a professor permission to quote company material in the professor's book could end with "We wish you the best of success on the book." This specially adapted comment is better than one that fits any similar case: "If we can be of further assistance, please let us know." Using the reader's name in the message text is another good way to show that the reader is being given special treatment. We can gain the reader's favor by occasionally making such references as "You are correct, Ms. Brock" or "As you know, Helen."

- This means writing for the one situation.

Refraining from Preaching

You can help give your documents a courteous effect by not preaching—that is, by avoiding the tone of a lecture or a sermon. Except in the rare cases in which the reader looks up to the writer, a preaching tone hurts goodwill. We human beings like to be treated as equals. We do not want to be bossed or talked down to. Thus, writing that suggests unequal writer–reader relations is likely to make the reader unhappy.

- The effect of courtesy is helped by not preaching (lecturing).

Preaching is usually not intended. It often occurs when the writer is trying to convince the reader of something, as in this example:

- Usually preaching is not intended. It often results from efforts to persuade.

You must take advantage of savings like this if you are to be successful. The pennies you save pile up. In time you will have dollars.

It is insulting to tell the reader something quite elementary as if it were not known. Such obvious information should be omitted.

- Elementary, flat, and obvious statements often sound preachy.

Likewise, flat statements of the obvious fall into the preachy category. Statements like "Rapid inventory turnover means greater profits" are obvious to the experienced retailer and would probably produce negative reactions. So would most statements including such phrases as "you need," "you want," "you should," and "you must," for they tend to talk down to the reader.

Another form of preachiness takes this obvious question-and-answer pattern: "Would you like to make a deal that would make you a 38 percent profit? Of course you would!" What intelligent and self-respecting businessperson would not be offended by this approach?

Doing More Than Is Expected

- Doing more than necessary builds goodwill.

One sure way to gain goodwill is to do a little bit more than you have to do for your reader. We are all aware of how helpful little extra acts are in other areas of our personal relationships. Too many of us, however, do not use them in our messages. Perhaps in the mistaken belief that we are being concise, we include only the barest essentials in our messages. The result is brusque, hurried treatment, which is inconsistent with our efforts to build goodwill.

The writer of a message refusing a request for use of company equipment, for example, needs only to say no to accomplish the primary goal. This answer, of course, is blunt and totally without courtesy. A goodwill-conscious writer would explain and justify the refusal, perhaps suggesting alternative steps that the reader might take. A wholesaler's brief extra sentence to wish a retailer good luck on a coming promotion is worth the effort. So are an insurance agent's few words of congratulations in a message to a policyholder who has earned some distinction.

Likewise, a writer uses good judgment in an acknowledgment message that includes helpful suggestions about using the goods ordered. And in messages to customers a writer for a sales organization can justifiably include a few words about new merchandise received, new services provided, price reductions, and so on.

- As the extras add length, they appear not to be concise. But conciseness means word economy—not leaving out essentials.

To those who say that these suggestions are inconsistent with the need for conciseness, we must answer that the information we speak of is needed to build goodwill. Conciseness concerns the number of words needed to say what you must say. It never involves leaving out information vital to any of your objectives. On the other hand, nothing we have said should be interpreted to mean that any kind or amount of extra information is justified. You must take care to use only the extra information you need to reach your goal.

Avoiding Anger

Expressing anger in messages—letting off steam—may sometimes help you emotionally. But anger helps achieve the goal of a message only when that goal is to anger the reader. The effect of angry words is to make the reader angry. With both writer and reader angry, the two are not likely to get together on whatever the message is about.

To illustrate the effect of anger, take the case of an insurance company employee who must write a message telling a policyholder that the policyholder has made a mistake in interpreting the policy and is not covered on the matter in question. The writer, feeling that any fool should be able to read the policy, might respond in these angry words:

● Rarely is anger justified in messages. It destroys goodwill.

> If you had read Section IV of your policy, you would know that you are not covered on accidents that occur on water.

One might argue that these words "tell it as it is"—that what they say is true. Even so, they show anger and lack tact. Their obvious effect is to make the reader angry. A more tactful writer would refer courteously to the point of misunderstanding:

> As a review of Section IV of your policy indicates, you are covered on accidents that occur on the grounds of your residence only.

Most of the comments made in anger do not provide needed information but merely serve to let the writer blow off steam. Such comments take many forms: sarcasm, insults, exclamations. You can see from the following examples that you should not use them in your writing:

> No doubt, you expect us to hold your hand.
>
> I cannot understand your negligence.
>
> This is the third time you have permitted your account to be delinquent.
>
> We will not tolerate this condition.
>
> Your careless attitude has caused us a loss in sales.
>
> We have had it!
>
> We have no intention of permitting this condition to continue.

Being Sincere

Courteous treatment is sincere treatment. If your messages are to be effective, people must believe you. You must convince them that you mean what you say and that your efforts to be courteous and friendly are well intended. That is, your messages must have the quality of sincerity.

The best way of getting sincerity into your writing is to believe in the techniques you use. If you honestly want to be courteous, if you honestly believe that you-viewpoint treatment leads to harmonious relations, and if you honestly think that tactful treatment spares your reader's sensitive feelings, you are likely to apply these techniques sincerely. Your sincerity will show in your writing.

● Efforts to be courteous must be sincere.

● Sincerity results from believing in the techniques of courtesy.

Overdoing the Goodwill Techniques. Being sincere will help you avoid two problems. The first is the overdoing of your goodwill techniques. Perhaps through insincerity or as a result of overzealous effort, the goodwill techniques are frequently overdone. For example, you can easily refer too often to your reader by name in your efforts to write to the one person. Also, as shown in the following example, you-viewpoint effort can go beyond the bounds of reason.

● The goodwill effort can be overdone. Too much you-viewpoint sounds insincere.

> So that you may be able to buy Kantrell equipment at an extremely low price and sell it at a tremendous profit, we now offer you the complete line at a 50 percent price reduction.

The following example, included in a form letter from the company president to a new charge customer, has a touch of unbelievability:

> I was delighted today to see your name listed among Macy's new charge customers.

Or how about this one, taken from an adjustment message of a large department store?

> We are extremely pleased to be able to help you and want you to know that your satisfaction means more than anything to us.

- Exaggerated statements are obviously insincere.

Exaggerating. The second danger that you should avoid is exaggerating the positive. It is easy to see through most exaggerated statements; thus, they can give a mark of insincerity to your message. Exaggerations are overstatements of facts. Although some puffery is conventional in sales writing, even here bounds of propriety exist. The following examples clearly overstep these bounds:

> Already thousands of new customers are beating paths to the doors of Martin dealers.

> Never has there been, nor will there be, a fan as smooth running and whispering quiet as the North Wind.

> Everywhere coffee drinkers meet, they are talking about the amazing whiteness Rembrandt gives their teeth.

- Superlatives (*greatest*, *finest*, *strongest*) often suggest exaggeration.

Many exaggerated statements involve the use of superlatives. All of us use them, but only rarely do they fit the reality about which we communicate. Words like *greatest*, *most amazing*, *finest*, *healthiest*, and *strongest* are seldom appropriate. Other strong words may have similar effects—for example, *extraordinary*, *stupendous*, *delicious*, *more than happy*, *sensational*, *terrific*, *revolutionary*, *colossal*, and *perfection*. Such words cause us to question; we rarely believe them.

THE ROLE OF EMPHASIS

- Emphasis also determines effect. Every item communicated should get the proper emphasis.

Getting desired effects in writing often involves giving proper emphasis to the items in the message. Every message contains a number of facts, ideas, and so on that must be presented. Some of these items are more important than others. For example, the main goal of a message is very important. Supporting explanations and incidental facts are less important. A part of your job as a writer is to determine the importance of each item and to give each item the emphasis it deserves.

- There are four basic emphasis techniques.

To give each item in your message proper emphasis, you must use certain techniques. By far the most useful are these four: position, space, structure, and mechanical devices. The following paragraphs explain each.

Emphasis by Position

- Position determines emphasis. Beginnings and endings carry emphasis.

The beginnings and endings of a writing unit carry more emphasis than the center parts. This rule of emphasis applies whether the unit is the message, a paragraph of the message, or a sentence within the paragraph (see Figure 4–1.). We do not know why this is so. Some authorities think that the reader's fresh mental energy explains beginning emphasis. Some say that the last parts stand out because they are the most recent in the reader's mind. Whatever the explanation, research has suggested that this emphasis technique works.

Figure 4–1

Emphasis by Position

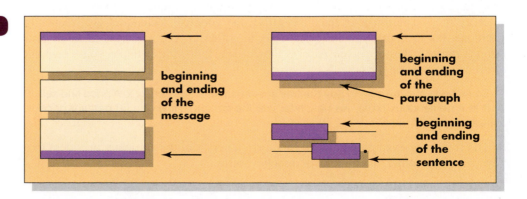

In the message as a whole, the beginning and the closing are the major emphasis positions. Thus, you must be especially mindful of what you put in these places. The beginnings and endings of the internal paragraphs are secondary emphasis positions. Your design of each paragraph should take this into account. To a lesser extent, the first and last words of each sentence carry more emphasis than the middle ones. Even in your sentence design, you can help determine the emphasis that your reader will give the points in your message. In summary, your organizational plan should place the points you want to stand out in these beginning and ending positions. You should bury the points you do not want to emphasize between these positions.

- The first and last sentences of a message, the first and last sentences of a paragraph, and the first and last words of a sentence all carry more emphasis than the middle parts.

Space and Emphasis

The more you say about something, the more emphasis you give it; and the less you say about something, the less emphasis you give it. If your message devotes a full paragraph to one point and a scant sentence to another, the first point receives more emphasis. To give the desired effect in your message, you will need to say just enough about each item of information you present.

- The more space a topic is given, the more emphasis the topic receives.

Sentence Structure and Emphasis

As we noted in Chapter 3, short, simple sentences call attention to their content and long, involved ones do not. In applying this emphasis technique to your writing, carefully consider the possible sentence arrangements of your information. Place the more important information in short, simple sentences so that it will not have to compete with other information for the reader's attention. Combine the less important information, taking care that the relationships are logical. In your combination sentences, place the more important material in independent clauses and the less important information in subordinate structures.

- Sentence structure determines emphasis. Short, simple sentences emphasize content; long, involved ones do not.

Mechanical Means of Emphasis

Perhaps the most obvious emphasis techniques are those that use mechanical devices. By *mechanical devices* we mean any of the things that we can do physically to give the printed word emphasis. The most common of these devices are the underscore, quotation marks, italics, boldface type, and solid capitals. Lines, arrows, and diagrams also can call attention to certain parts. So can color, special type, and drawings.

- Mechanical devices (underscore, color, diagrams, and the like) also give emphasis to content.

COHERENCE

As we noted in the previous chapter, your documents are composed of independent bits of information. But if these bits are to communicate your message, they will need to be put together in such a way that the relationships among them are clear. Making the relationships among facts clear is the task of giving coherence to your message.

Arranging your information in a logical order, as we have said, is fundamental to coherence. If related things are put too far apart from each other or the order of your information violates a logical pattern that the reader expects, no other strategies can save the coherence of your document. And when your document is incoherent, your reader is in for a frustrating experience. We include coherence in this chapter on writing for effect because it is central to having a positive effect on your reader.

If your points are in a logical, reader-oriented order, you can use four main transitional devices to enhance your document's coherence: repeating key words, using pronouns to refer back to earlier facts, using transitional expressions (such as *in contrast*, *for example*, or *first*, *second*, and *third*), and using tie-in sentences (sentences that pick up on and continue what the preceding sentence said). Chapter 3 discussed how to use these devices on the paragraph level. They are also useful on the document level, in between paragraphs—to tie thoughts together, keep the focus on the message sharp, and move your reader smoothly from point to point.

- Messages should be coherent. The relationships among the parts should be clear.

- Presenting information in a logical order is central to coherence.

- You can use transitional devices to enhance the coherence of your documents.

SUMMARY BY LEARNING OBJECTIVES

1 Explain the need for effect in writing business messages.

1. Although clarity is a major concern in all business writing, you also will be concerned with effect.
   - Specifically, you will need to communicate the effect of goodwill, for it is profitable in business to do so.
   - Sometimes you will need to communicate effects that help you persuade, sell, or the like.
   - To achieve these effects, you will need to heed the following advice.

2 Use a conversational style that eliminates the old language of business and "rubber stamps."

2. Write messages in a conversational style (language that sounds like people talking).
   - Such a style requires that you resist the tendency to be formal.
   - It requires that you avoid words from the old language of business (*thanking you in advance, please be advised*).
   - It requires that you avoid the so-called rubber stamps—words used routinely and without thought (*this is to inform, in accordance with*).

3 Use the you-viewpoint to build goodwill.

3. In your messages, you will need to emphasize the you-viewpoint (*your refund is enclosed . . .* rather than *I am happy to report . . .*).
   - But be careful not to be or appear to be insincere.
   - And do not use the you-viewpoint to manipulate the reader.

4 Employ positive language to achieve goodwill and other desired effects.

4. You should understand the negative and positive meanings of words.
   - Negative words have unpleasant meanings (*We cannot deliver until Friday*).
   - Positive words have pleasant meanings (*We can deliver Friday*).
   - Select those negative and positive words that achieve the best effect for your goal.

5 Explain the techniques of achieving courtesy.

5. You should strive for courtesy in your messages by doing the following:
   - Practice the goodwill techniques discussed above.
   - Focus on your reader (write for the one person).
   - Avoid preaching or talking down.
   - Avoid displays of anger.
   - Be sincere (avoiding exaggeration and overdoing the goodwill techniques).

6 Use the four major techniques for emphasis in writing.

6. Use the four major techniques for emphasis in writing.
   - Determine the items of information the message will contain.
   - Give each item the emphasis it deserves.
   - Show emphasis in these ways:
     - By position (beginnings and endings receive prime emphasis).
     - By space (the greater the space devoted to a topic, the greater is the emphasis).
     - By sentence structure (short sentences emphasize more than longer ones).
     - By mechanical means (color, underscore, boldface, and such).

7 Write documents that flow smoothly through the use of a logical order helped by the four major transitional devices.

7. You should write messages that flow smoothly.
   - Present the information in logical order—so that one thought sets up the next.
   - Help show the relationships of thoughts by using these transitional devices:
     - Tie-in sentences.
     - Word repetitions.
     - Pronouns.
     - Transitional words.

1 Discuss this comment: "Getting the goodwill effect requires extra effort. It takes extra time, and time costs money."

2 "Our normal conversation is filled with error. Typically, it is crude and awkward. So why make our writing sound conversational?" Discuss.

3 "If a company really wants to impress the readers of its messages, the messages should be formal and should be written in dignified language that displays knowledge." Discuss.

4 After reading a message filled with expressions from the old language of business, a young administrative trainee made this remark: "I'm keeping this one for reference. It sounds so businesslike!" Evaluate this comment.

5 "If you can find words, sentences, or phrases that cover a general situation, why not use them every time that general situation comes about? Using such rubber stamps would save time, and in business time is money." Discuss.

6 Discuss this comment: "The you-viewpoint is insincere and deceitful."

7 Evaluate this comment: "It's hard to argue against courtesy. But businesspeople don't have time to spend extra effort on it. Anyway, they want their documents to go straight to the point—without wasting words and without sugar coating."

8 "I use the words that communicate the message best. I don't care whether they are negative or positive." Discuss.

9 "I like writers who shoot straight. When they are happy, you know it. When they are angry, they let you know." Discuss.

10 A writer wants to include a certain negative point in a message and to give it little emphasis. Discuss each of the four basic emphasis techniques as they relate to what can be done.

11 Using illustrations other than those in the text, discuss and illustrate the four major transitional devices.

12 Imagine that a customer has written to complain about the lack of attention that she received when visiting a paint store. The manager's responding letter explains why the sales staff were so busy, offers to make a special appointment with the customer to discuss her decorating needs, and then ends with the following paragraph: "We do apologize again for any inconvenience that this situation caused you. We thank you for your understanding. Please do not hesitate to contact us again if we ever fall short of the superior service that you have come to expect from us." If the manager asked for your feedback on this letter, what would you say? It's full of polite expressions. Is it a good concluding paragraph? Discuss.

Instructions, Rewrite Sentences 1–16 in conversational style.

1 I hereby acknowledge receipt of your July 7 favor.

2 Anticipating your reply by return mail, I remain . . .

3 Attached please find receipt requested in your May 1st inquiry.

4 We take pleasure in advising that subject contract is hereby canceled.

5 You are hereby advised to endorse subject proposal and return same to the undersigned.

6 I shall appreciate the pleasure of your reply.

7 Referring to yours of May 7, I wish to state that this office has no record of a sale.

8 This is to advise that henceforth all invoices will be submitted in duplicate.

9 Agreeable to yours of the 24th, we have consulted our actuarial department to ascertain the status of subject policy.

10 Kindly be advised that permission is hereby granted to delay remittance until the 12th.

11 In conclusion would state that, up to this writing, said account has not been profitable.

12 Replying to your letter of the 3rd would state that we deem it a great pleasure to accept your kind offer to serve on the committee.

13 I beg to advise that, with regard to above invoice, this office finds that partial payment of $312 was submitted on delivery date.

14 In replying to your esteemed favor of the 7th, I submit under separate cover the report you requested.

15 In reply to your letter of May 10, please be informed that this office heretofore has generously supported funding activities of your organization.

16 Kindly advise the undersigned as to your availability for participation in the program.

Instructions, Sentences 17–32: Write you-viewpoint sentences to cover each of the situations described.

17 Company policy requires that you must submit the warranty agreement within two weeks of sale.

18 We will be pleased to deliver your order by the 12th.

19 We have worked for 37 years to build the best lawn mowers for our customers.

20 Today we are shipping the goods you ordered February 3.

21 (From an application letter) I have seven years of successful experience selling office supplies.

22 (From an email to employees) We take pleasure in announcing that, effective today, the Company will give a 20 percent discount on all purchases made by employees.

23 Kraff files are made in three widths—one for every standard size of record.

24 We are happy to report approval of your application for membership.

25 Items desired should be checked on the enclosed order form.

26 Our long experience in the book business has enabled us to provide the best customer service possible.

27 So that we can sell at discount prices, we cannot permit returns of merchandise.

28 We invite you to buy from the enclosed catalog.

29 Tony's Red Beans have an exciting spicy taste.

30 We give a 2 percent discount when payment is made within 10 days.

31 I am pleased to inform you that I can grant your request for payment of travel expenses.

32 We can permit you to attend classes on company time only when the course is related to your work assignment.

Instructions, Sentences 33–48: Underscore all negative words in these sentences. Then rewrite the sentences for positive effect. Use your imagination to supply situation information when necessary.

33 Your misunderstanding of our January 7 email caused you to make this mistake.

34 We hope this delay has not inconvenienced you. If you will be patient, we will get the order to you as soon as our supply is replenished.

35 We regret that we must call your attention to our policy of prohibiting refunds for merchandise bought at discount.

36 Your negligence in this matter caused the damage to the equipment.

37 You cannot visit the plant except on Saturdays.

38 We are disappointed to learn from your July 7 email that you are having trouble with our Model 7 motor.

39 Tuff-Boy work clothing is not made from cloth that shrinks or fades.

40 Our Stone-skin material won't do the job unless it is reinforced.

41 Even though you were late in paying the bill, we did not disallow the discount.

42 We were sorry to learn of the disappointing service you have had from our sales force, but we feel we have corrected all mistakes with recent personnel changes.

43 We have received your complaint of the 7th in which you claim that our product was defective, and have thoroughly investigated the matter.

44 I regret the necessity of calling your attention to our letter of May 1.

45 We have received your undated letter, which you sent to the wrong office.

46 Old New Orleans pralines are not the gummy kind that stick to your teeth.

47 I regret to have to say that I will be unable to speak at your conference, as I have a prior commitment.

48 Do not walk on the grass.

Instructions, Numbers 49 and 50: The answers to these questions should come from message examples to be found in following chapters.

49 Find examples of each of the four major emphasis techniques discussed in this chapter.

50 Find examples of each of the four transitional devices discussed in this chapter and Chapter 3.

In 1992, Michael Dell was the youngest CEO ever to be listed in the Fortune 500 ranks. His continued success comes from thinking about how Dell products and services can bring value to customers.

"Whenever we're having our discussions with product teams or teams that are focused on unique kinds of customers, we talk about market trends and operating trends—'What are you seeing?' 'What are customers asking for?' 'What are customers buying?' And when I'm out in the field talking to customers, I spend a fair amount of time understanding what our customers are doing, why they're doing it, and where they're going."

Michael Dell, Chairman and CEO, Dell Computer

chapter five

The Writing Process and an Introduction to Business Messages

LEARNING OBJECTIVES

Upon completing this chapter, you will understand the role of messages in business and the process of writing them. To reach this goal, you should be able to

1   Describe the writing process and effective writing strategies.

2   Explain the importance of readable formatting.

3   Describe the development and current usage of the business letter.

4   Describe the purpose and form of memorandums.

5   Understand the phenomenal growth and nature of email.

6   Follow email conventions and organize and write clear email messages.

7   Understand the nature and business uses of text messaging.

8   Understand how instant messaging works.

The Nature of Business Messages

Introduce yourself to this chapter by shifting to the role of Max Elliott (your subordinate in the preceding chapters). As Max, you are grateful to your boss for deftly instructing you in readable and sensitive writing. You have been convinced of the importance of good communication to the success of a struggling small business. You are especially grateful because most of the work you do involves communicating with fellow employees, customers, and suppliers. Every day you process dozens of internal email messages. Occasionally you write and receive memorandums. Then there are the more formal communications you exchange with people outside the company—both email and hard copy. This chapter introduces you to these messages and the process of writing them.

The preceding chapters (Part II) have focused on selecting words and arranging them into sentences and paragraphs that create a desired effect. Now we turn to the application of this knowledge to the writing of business documents. We begin with a review of the writing process, covering the three main stages in the process and providing helpful tips for each.

• We now turn to the writing of shorter business documents.

As part of this discussion, we include a brief section on making wise formatting decisions. The advice on these topics will help you make all your messages, whatever the type, more successful acts of communication.

• We begin with a discussion of the writing process.

We then discuss the major types of business documents, with specific suggestions for writing them. In the current part (Part III) we cover first the shorter forms of messages—letters, memorandums, email, text messaging, and instant messaging. Chapters 6, 7, and 8 divide short messages into a different set of categories based upon purpose and typical structure: good-news or neutral messages, bad-news messages, and persuasive messages. In the next part (Part IV) we cover documents called reports.

• We then cover the major forms of short business messages.

THE PROCESS OF WRITING

Writing researchers have been studying the composing process since the 1970s. They have found, not surprisingly, that each person's way of developing a piece of writing for a given situation is unique. On the other hand, they have also come to some general conclusions about the nature of the process and about strategies that can help it along. Familiarizing yourself with these findings will help make you a more deliberate, effective writer.

• Taking charge of your writing process will make you a more effective writer.

As Figure 5–1 shows, there are essentially three stages in preparing any piece of writing: planning, drafting, and revising. These stages can be defined, roughly, as figuring

• The writing process consists of three main stages: planning, drafting, and revising.

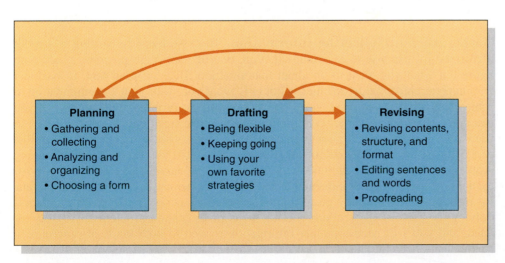

Figure 5–1

A Model of the Writing Process

- These stages are *recursive,* not strictly linear.

out what you want to say, saying it, and then saying it better. Each of these stages can be broken down into various specific activities, which the next section will describe. But as the arrows in the figure suggest, it is important not to think of the three stages as strictly chronological or separate. In practice, there are interrelations among the stages—that is, like the steps for solving business communication problems described in Chapter 1, they are *recursive.* For example, a writer in the planning stage may start writing pieces of the draft. Or, he or she may find, when drafting, that more gathering of information is necessary. Or, he or she may decide that it's necessary to revise a piece of the document carefully before continuing on with the drafting. An undue emphasis on keeping the stages separate and chronological will hinder the success of your messages. Allow yourself to blend these stages as necessary.

- Student writers should spend roughly a third of their writing time in each stage.

A good rule of thumb for student writers is to spend roughly a third of their writing time in each of the three stages. A common mistake that such writers make is to spend too much time on drafting and too little on the other two stages, planning and revising. Preparing to write and improving what you have written are as critical to success as the drafting stage, and careful attention to all three stages can actually make your writing process more efficient. Once you have become an experienced business writer, you will be able to write many routine messages without as much planning and revising. Even so, some planning and revising will still be essential to getting the best results with your messages.

Planning the Message

- The problem-solving guide in Chapter 1 is a good guide for the planning stage of writing.

The guide for solving business problems presented in Figure 1–3 of Chapter 1 is also a good guide for the planning stage of writing. As the questions indicate, you will need to develop a definition of the problem that you are trying to address. To find a solution, you will need an informed sense of your audiences and their individual contexts—organizational, professional, and personal. You will also need to think about your own organizational, professional, and personal contexts and their possible impact on your communication goal. And you will need to think about the larger contexts in which your act of communication will be taking place, including the context of your relationship with your reader. All these deliberations will help you figure out what you want your message to achieve.

Once you have chosen your message's purpose, you'll need to figure out the best way to achieve it. You'll consider the different kinds of content you could include and choose what will best serve your purpose. You will develop a rough idea of how to organize and format that content, decide on the kind of channel you will use, and settle on a general sense of the style you will use. Most people, before drafting, have at least some sense of how they want to handle these elements.

- Planning consists of three general activities:

For simplicity's sake, we might group all these planning activities into three categories: gathering and collecting information; analyzing and organizing the information; and choosing the form, channel, and format it will take.

- gathering and collecting information,

Gathering and Collecting Information. Because business writing is largely performed in response to a certain situation, one of your main planning goals is to figure out what you want to do about that situation. Bear in mind that, in business communication, "what to do" means not only what you want your communication to achieve but also any action related to the larger business problem. For example, if you manage a hotel where the air conditioning has stopped functioning, you will need to decide what, if anything, to communicate to your guests about this problem. But this decision is related to other decisions. How and when will you get the air conditioning problem solved? In the meantime, will you simply apologize? Make arrangements for each guest to have a free continental breakfast or complementary beverages? Rent fans for meeting rooms and any guest rooms occupied by people with health problems? Solving the general problem and solving the communication problem are closely related, and you will need to gather information related to both kinds of problems to tackle business communication tasks.

Gathering information means doing some research. In many cases this research can be informal—finding past correspondence; consulting with other employees or with outside advisors; getting sales records, warranties, and product descriptions; and so forth. In other cases you will do such formal research as conducting surveys or reviewing the literature on a certain subject. Chapters 10 and 19 discuss various methods and sources at your disposal for this kind of research. In general, you will collect any information that can help you decide what to do and what to say in your message.

But collecting information by using your memory, imagination, and creativity is also important. Visualizing your readers and bearing their interests in mind is an excellent planning technique. Making a list of pertinent facts is helpful. Brainstorming, or generating possible solutions without censoring them, will allow you to come up with creative solutions. Drawing a diagram of your ideas can also enable you to collect your thoughts. Let yourself use any strategy that shows promise of contributing to a solution.

Analyzing and Organizing Information.

Once you have a goodly number of ideas, you will start to assess them. If your data are numerical, you will do the calculations that will enable you to see patterns and meaning in the numbers. You will put other kinds of data together as well to see what course of action they might indicate, weighing what the parties involved stand to gain or lose from each possible solution.

- analyzing and organizing information,

As you ponder what to do and say with your message, you will, of course, keep your readers in mind. What kind of information will most matter to them? In the scenario described above, will the hotel guests most likely want information about what caused the air conditioning problem or about when it will be fixed and what they can do to stay comfortable in the meantime? As always, your intended readers are your best guide to what information to include.

They are also your guide for organizing the information. Whatever order will draw the most positive reaction from your readers is the best order to use. If you have information that your readers will want, put it first. This plan, called using the *direct order,* is discussed in the next chapter. On the other hand, if you think your information could run the risk of evoking a negative response, you will use an *indirect order,* using your message's opening to prepare the reader to receive the news as positively as possible. As you will see in Chapter 7, such a message usually requires a more skillful use of organization and word choice than one written in direct order. Regardless of the situation, all readers appreciate a logical pattern for the information. Chapter 10 will discuss different logical plans that you might use to put your thoughts in order and present them in an easy-to-follow way.

Choosing a Form, Channel, and Format.

Writers in school typically produce writing of two types: essays or research papers. But on the job you have a wide range of established forms of communication (genres) to choose from. Which one you think you will use has a huge impact on your planning. For instance, if you want to advertise your company's services, how will you do it? Write potential customers a letter? Email them? Include a brochure? Create a website? Use some combination of these? Each form has its own formatting and stylistic conventions, and even conventions about content. Business writers do not launch into writing a document without some sense of what kind of document it will be. The medium itself helps them know what to say and how to say it. On the job, choosing the type of document to be written is an important part of planning.

- and choosing the form, channel, and format for the message.

Specific decisions about a document's format, or visual design, can be made at any point in the writing process, but usually the planning stage involves preliminary decisions along these lines. Will you be dividing up the contents with headings? How about with a bulleted or numbered list? How long or short will the paragraphs be? Will there be any visual elements, such as a logo or picture or diagram? Anticipating the format can help you plan an inviting and readable message.

Formatting devices have such a large impact on readers' reactions that we will discuss them separately in the next section. But decisions about formatting are an integral part of the business writer's writing process, even in the planning stage.

Drafting

Writing experts' main advice about drafting boils down to these words: "Be flexible." Writers often hamstring themselves by thinking that they have to write a finished document all at once, with the parts in their correct order and with perfect results. Writing is such a cognitively difficult task that it is better to concentrate only on certain things at a time. The following suggestions can help you draft your messages as painlessly and effectively as possible.

- Avoiding perfectionism helps you include all important information and makes you more willing to revise.

Avoid Perfectionism When Drafting. Trying to make your first draft a perfect draft causes two problems. First, spending too much energy perfecting the early parts can make you forget important pieces and purposes of the later parts. Second, premature perfectionism can make drafting frustrating and slow, thus keeping you from wanting to revise your message when you're done. You will be much more inclined to go back over your message and improve it if you have not put blood, sweat, and tears into drafting.

- Keep going, making each statement just good enough to let you move on.

Keep Going. When turning your planning into a draft, don't let minor problems with wording or grammar distract you from your main goal—to generate your first version of the document. Have an understanding with yourself that you will draft relatively quickly, to get the ideas down on paper or onto the screen, and then go back and carefully revise. Expressing your points in a somewhat coherent, complete, and orderly fashion is hard enough. Allow yourself to save close reexamination and evaluation of what you've written for the revision stage.

- Use any other strategies that help you to keep making progress.

Use Any Other Strategies That Will Keep You Working Productively. The idea with drafting is to keep moving forward at a reasonably steady pace with as little agonizing as possible. Do anything you can think of that will make your drafting relatively free and easy. For example, write at your most productive time of day, write in chunks, start with a favorite part, talk aloud or write to yourself to clarify your thoughts, take breaks, let the project sit for a while, create a setting conducive to writing—even promise yourself a little reward for getting a certain amount accomplished. Your goal is to get the first orderly expression of your planned contents written out just well enough so that you can go back and work with it.

Revising

- Revision requires going back over your message carefully—several times.

Getting your draft ready for your reader requires going back over it carefully—again and again. Did you say what you mean? Could someone misunderstand or take offense at what you wrote? Is your organization best for the situation? Is each word the right one for your goals? Are there better, more concise ways of structuring your sentences? Can you move the reader more smoothly from point to point? Does each element of format enhance readability and highlight the structure of the contents? When revising, you turn into your own critic. You challenge what you have written and look for possibly better alternatives.

- Professional writers recommend editing in levels.

There are so many facets to any given message that it can help to use what professional writers call "levels of edit." There are three main levels of edit, commonly referred to as *revision, editing,* and *proofreading*.

- The three main levels are revision of contents, organization, and format;

With revision, you look at top-level concerns: whether or not you included all necessary information, if the pattern of organization is logical and as effective as possible, if the overall meaning of the message comes through, if the formatting is appropriate and helpful.

- editing of sentences and words; and

You then move to the editing level, focusing on your style. You examine your sentences to see if they pace the information in such a way that the reader can easily follow it, if they emphasize the right things, and if they combine pieces of information coherently. You also look at your word choices to see if they best serve your purpose.

- proofreading your document for typos, spelling errors, and other mechanical or grammatical problems.

Finally, you proofread, looking at particular mechanical and grammatical elements—spelling, typography, punctuation, and any particular grammar problems that tend to give you trouble. Editing functions in your word-processing program can help you with this task. Careful attention to each level will result in a polished, effective message.

One last word about revision: Get feedback from others. As you may well know, it is difficult to find weaknesses or errors in your own work. Seek out assistance from willing colleagues, and if they give you criticism, receive it with an open mind. Better to hear it from them, not from your intended readers, when costly mistakes may have already been made.

- Get others' opinions on your message.

THE IMPORTANCE OF READABLE FORMATTING

Have you ever opened up a letter or a reading for a class, seen long, unbroken blocks of text, and dreaded jumping into the piece? Business readers are even more likely to have this kind of reaction. They are far too bombarded with messages to have patience with this kind of document. If you want your readers actually to read what you wrote and get your ideas and information, you must pay attention to an important element of any message: its physical format.

- Do not put off your readers with a daunting physical format.

Decades ago, you might well have been able to rely on a secretary or typist to format your documents for you. But widespread use of the personal computer, with its full-featured publishing capabilities, has placed the responsibility for readable formatting much more on the writer. Except for projects that will involve a graphic designer, it will largely be up to you to make the key formatting decisions for your messages. What kind and size of type will you use? What kind of headings? Will you use any means of typographical emphasis? How about numbered or bulleted lists? Should the document include such visual elements as logos, textboxes, pictures, or diagrams? Smart decisions on such matters will not only increase your readers' motivation to read but also enable them quickly to comprehend the main points and structure of the message.

- The writer is responsible for making the important formatting decisions.

For example, below is the starting text of a memo (sent by email) from a university registrar to the faculty, with the subject line "'X' and 'WX' Grades Effective for Autumn '05 Grading." How inviting do you find the format of the following message, and how easy is it to extract the information about the two new grades?

At its October 20, 2005, meeting, the Faculty Senate, having received a favorable recommendation from the Academic Affairs Committee, voted to approve the creation and Autumn Quarter implementation of two new grades: "X" and "WX." Instructors will record an "X" on the final grade roster for students who never attended any classes and did not submit any assigned work. The "X" will appear on the transcript and will carry zero (0.00) quality points, thus computed into the GPA like the grades of "F" and "UW." Instructors will record a "WX" for those students who officially withdrew from the class (as denoted on the grade roster by either EW or W) but who never attended any classes and did not submit any assigned work. The "WX" may be entered to overwrite a "W" appearing on the grade roster. An assignment of "WX" has no impact on the student's GPA. A "W" will appear on the student's online grade report and on the transcript. The "WX" recognizes the student's official withdrawal from the class and only records the fact of nonparticipation. The need to record nonparticipation is defined in "Rationale" below. With the introduction of the "X" and "WX" grades to denote nonparticipation, by definition all other grades can only be awarded to students who had participated in the class in some way. Instructors will record a "UW" (unofficial withdrawal) only for students who cease to attend a class following some participation. Previously, instructors utilized the "UW" both for those students who had never attended classes and for those who had attended and participated initially but had ceased to attend at some point during the term. In cases of official withdrawal, instructors have three options available at the time of grading: "W," "WX," and "F." If the student has officially withdrawn from the class, a "W" (withdrawal) or "EW" (electronic withdrawal) will appear on the grade roster. If the student participated in the class and the withdrawal was in accordance with the instructor's withdrawal policy as communicated by the syllabus, the instructor may retain the student's "W" grade by making no alteration to the grade roster. . . .

Now look at the first part of the actual message that was sent out. What formatting decisions on the part of the writer made this document much more readable?

At its October 20, 2005, meeting, the Faculty Senate, having received a favorable recommendation from the Academic Affairs Committee, voted to approve the creation and Autumn Quarter implementation of two new grades: "X" and "WX."

Definition of "X" and "WX" Grades, Effective Autumn Quarter 2005

- "X" (nonattendance):

Instructors will record an "X" on the final grade roster for students who never attended any classes and did not submit any assigned work.

The "X" will appear on the transcript and will carry zero (0.00) quality points, thus computed into the GPA like the grades of "F" and "UW."

- "WX" (official withdrawal, nonattending):

Instructors will record a "WX" for those students who officially withdrew from the class (as denoted on the grade roster by either EW or W) but who never attended any classes and did not submit any assigned work.

The "WX" may be entered to overwrite a "W" appearing on the grade roster. An assignment of "WX" has no impact on the student's GPA. A "W" will appear on the student's online grade report and on the transcript. The "WX" recognizes the student's official withdrawal from the class and only records the fact of nonparticipation. The need to record nonparticipation is defined in "Rationale" below.

Participation and Nonparticipation Grades

With the introduction of the "X" and "WX" grades to denote nonparticipation, by definition all other grades can only be awarded to students who had participated in the class in some way.

Instructors will record a "UW" (unofficial withdrawal) only for students who cease to attend a class following some participation. Previously, instructors utilized the "UW" both for those students who had never attended classes and for those who had attended and participated initially but had ceased to attend at some point during the term.

Official Withdrawals

In cases of official withdrawal, instructors have three options available at the time of grading: "W," "WX," and "F."

1. *If the student has officially withdrawn from the class,* a "W" (withdrawal) or "EW" (electronic withdrawal) will appear on the grade roster. If the student participated in the class and the withdrawal was in accordance with the instructor's withdrawal policy as communicated by the syllabus, the instructor may retain the student's "W" grade by making no alteration to the grade roster. . . .

Reprinted with permission from Dr. Douglas Burgess, Registrar, University of Cincinnati.

- An attractive, readable format is critical to any message's success.

The remaining sections of this chapter describe specific purposes and traits of different message types. Appendix B provides in-depth advice about their physical design. No matter what you're writing, taking time to make careful formatting decisions during your writing process will significantly enhance your chances of achieving your communication goals.

LETTERS

- Letters are the oldest form. The early civilizations used them.

Letters are the traditional form of business messages. They are the oldest form. In fact, they have existed since the early days of civilization. The use of letters has been documented in virtually all the great early civilizations. The ancient Chinese wrote letters. So did the early Egyptians, Romans, and Greeks. Although many of these early letters pertained to military and personal matters, some clearly concerned business.

From these early days letters have continued to be used in business. Although the history of their development would be interesting, we need only be concerned with the end product—with the business letter as it has evolved to date. Specifically, we need to consider three aspects: its general purpose, its format, and its composition.

- We should know about the letter purpose, format, and composition.

The general purpose of a letter is to represent the writer and his or her topic rather formally to the recipient. For this reason, letters are used primarily for corresponding with people outside your organization. When you write to internal readers, they are often familiar to you—and even if they are not, you all share the connection of being in the same company. Your messages to such audiences tend to use less formal media. But when you write to customers, to suppliers, to citizens and community leaders, and to other external audiences, you will often want to put your company's best foot forward by choosing the letter format, complete with an attractive company letterhead and the elements of courtesy built into this traditional format. And your readers will expect this gesture of respect. Once you have established friendly relations with them, you may well conduct your business through emails and phone calls. But especially when corresponding with an external party whom you do not know well, a letter is usually the most appropriate form to use.

- Letters are primarily for external audiences.

The format of the business letter probably already is known to you. Although some variations in format are generally acceptable, typically these information items are included: date, inside address, salutation (Dear Ms. Smith), body, and complimentary close (Sincerely yours). Other items sometimes needed are attention line, subject line, return address (when letterhead paper is not used), and enclosure information. Placement of these items as well as guidelines for processing the text of the letter are presented in Appendix B.

- Letter format is described in Appendix B.

Current techniques of composing business letters have been developed by various business scholars and leaders over time, but especially in the past century. In the early days (a century ago) emphasis was on word choice, especially on use of a stiff and stilted manner of expressing courtesy. We referred to this manner of expression in Chapter 4 as "the old language of business."

- In the early days, techniques emphasized a stilted manner of expressing courtesy.

In more recent times emphasis shifted to structure and strategy of content and humanness of wording. As the preceding chapters explain, unduly formal, impersonal writing has now fallen out of favor, and the communication strategy for any business message, including the letter, needs as careful attention as the wording. Despite its heightened formality, the letter should always be regarded as an exchange between real people as well as a strategic means for accomplishing business goals.

- Current emphasis is on strategy and humanness, which are covered in detail in this book.

MEMORANDUMS

Defining Memorandums

Memorandums (memos) are a form of letter written inside the business. In rare cases, they may be used in communicating outside the business. They are written messages exchanged by employees in the conduct of their work. They may be distinguished from other messages primarily by their form. Originally, they were used only in hard copy, but with the advent of computers they are now often processed electronically as faxes. In fact, their function of communicating within the business has been largely taken over by email. Even so, they still are a part of most company communication. They are especially useful in communicating with employees who do not use computers in their work.

- Memos are internal letters. Email is taking over their function.

As we shall see in Chapter 11, some memorandums communicate factual, problem-related information and are classified as reports. Those not classified as reports are the memorandums that concern us now. Even so, much of the following discussion applies to both types.

- Some memos may be classified as reports.

Businesses with multiple locations send many of their documents by fax, email, or text messages.

Figure 5–2

Illustration of Good Form for the Memorandum Using the MS Word Professional Template

Lenaghan Financial

Memo

To: Matthew Lenaghan, President

From: Payton Kubicek, Public Relations

CC: Katheleen Lenaghan, Chair

Date: June 1, 2007

Re: May meeting of Plant Safety Committee

As we agreed on March 30 meeting of the Environmental Impact Committee, we will meet again on May 12. I am requesting agenda items and meeting suggestions from each (etc.) . . .

Determining Memorandum Form

As we have noted, memorandums are distinguished from other messages primarily by their form. Some companies have stationery printed especially for memorandums, while many used standard or customized templates in word processors. Sometimes the word *memorandum* appears at the top in large, heavy type. But some companies prefer other titles, such as *Interoffice Memorandum* or *Interoffice Communication*. Below this main heading come the specific headings common to all memorandums: *Date, To, From, Subject* (though not necessarily in this order). This simple arrangement is displayed in Figure 5–2. Because memorandums are often short, some companies use $5 \times 8^1/2$-inch stationery for them as well as the conventional $8^1/2 \times 11$-inch size. Hard-copy memorandums are usually initialed by the writer rather than signed.

Large organizations, especially those with a number of locations and departments, often include additional information on their memorandum stationery. *Department, Plant, Location, Territory, Store Number,* and *Copies to* are examples (see Figure 5–3). Since in some companies memorandums are often addressed to more than one reader, the heading *To* may be followed by enough space to list a number of names.

- Most large companies use standard memo templates or printed memorandum stationery with *Date, To, From, and Subject* headings.

- Some larger companies have additional headings (*Department, Plant, Territory, Store Number,* and such).

Viewing Memorandum Formality

Because memorandums usually are messages sent and received by people who work with and know one another, they tend to use casual or informal language. Even so, their degree of formality ranges from one extreme to the other. At one end are the casual

- Memorandums vary widely in formality.

PENNY-WISE STORES, INC.

MEMORANDUM

To: _____   Date: _____
                            From: _____
Store: _____   Store: _____
At: _____   At: _____
Territory: _____   Territory: _____
Copies to: _____

Subject: Form for in-house letters (memos)

This is an illustration of our memorandum stationery. It should be used for written communications within the organization.

Notice that the memorandum uses no form of salutation. Neither does it have any form of complimentary close. The writer does not need to sign the message. He or she needs only to initial after the typed name in the heading.

Notice also that the message is single-spaced with double spacing between paragraphs.

Figure 5–3

Memorandum Stationery with Special Headings Adapted to the Needs of an Organization with Multiple Locations

notes that workers exchange. At the other are the formal messages written by lower-ranking workers to their top administrators. The typical memorandum falls somewhere between these extremes.

Writing Memorandums

- Because the situations involved are similar, the techniques for writing memos and email are similar.

The techniques for writing memorandums (memos) are much like those for writing the other business messages (letters and email). Short, simple memos are often written in casual or informal language, much like short, simple email messages. Longer, more formal memorandums are appropriately organized in the patterns appropriate for longer, more formal messages discussed in Chapters 6–8. Like most of the other business messages, most memorandums are appropriately written in a direct pattern, usually beginning with the most important point and working down. And memorandums conveying sensitive or negative information appropriately are written in an indirect order. Direct and indirect patterns are discussed in detail in following chapters.

EMAIL

- Recent growth of email has been phenomenal.

The rapid growth of email has been the most exciting business communication development in recent years. In just a short time, email has emerged as a mainstream form of business communication. Its volume surpasses that of the U.S. Postal Service. According to one authority, "there are more emails sent every day than telephone calls." It has become widely used in both small and large organizations. The explosive growth of email continues. And it is likely to continue for some time to come.

Evaluating Email's Pros and Cons

- It has grown because it

The reasons for this rapid growth are the advantages email has over other communication forms, especially over its principal competitor, the telephone. Among the reasons, the following are most significant:

- eliminates "telephone tag,"

- Email eliminates "telephone tag"—the problem of trying to contact busy people who are not always available for telephone calls. Messages sent to them can be stored in their electronic mailboxes until they are ready to read them.

- saves time,

- Conversely, email saves the time of these busy people. They are spared the interruptions of telephone calls.

- facilitates fast decisions,

- Email can speed up the process of making business decisions because it permits rapid exchanges from all involved in the decisions.

- is cheap,

- Email is cheap. It permits unlimited use at no more than the cost of an Internet connection.

- and provides a written record.

- It provides a written record.

Internal email forms a significant part of the communication used to coordinate the work in small and large businesses alike.

Figure 5–4

Typical Electronic Mail Clients

Email also has its disadvantages. The following stand out:

- Email is not confidential. "It's just about as private as a postcard you drop in the mail box."[1]

- Email doesn't communicate the sender's emotions well. Voice intonations, facial expressions, body movements, and such are not a part of the message. They are in telephone, video, and face-to-face communication.

- Email may be ignored or delayed. The volume of email often makes it difficult for some respondents to read and act on all of their messages.

Including the Prefatory Elements

The mechanical parts of the email message are generally standardized and are a part of the template of the software you use in constructing the message. But the second part of your effort, writing the message, is far from standardized. Although the following review covers both, the writing receives the greater emphasis. It is here that you are likely to need the most help.

Although the various email systems differ somewhat, the elements are standardized (see Figure 5–4). They include the following parts:

- **To:** Here the sender places the email address of the recipients. It must be perfect, for any error will result in failure to reach the recipient.

- It has disadvantages, too.

- It is not confidential,

- doesn't show emotions, and

- may be ignored or delayed.

- These standard parts precede the message.

---

[1] Monique I. Cuvelier, "Take Control of Your Inbox," *Guide to Email & More* 8, no. 7 (2000): 104.

- **Cc:** If someone other than the primary recipient is to receive a *courtesy copy,* his or her address goes here.
- **Bcc:** This line stands for *blind courtesy copy.* The recipient's message will not show this information; that is, he or she will not know who else is receiving a copy of the message.
- **Subject:** This line describes the message as precisely as the situation permits. The reader should get from it a clear idea of what the message is about.
- **Attachments:** In this area you can enter a file that you desire to send along with the message. As will be emphasized later, you should make certain that what you attach is really needed.
- **The message:** The information you are sending goes here. How to write it is the subject of much of the following discussion.

Beginning the Message

- Begin with the recipient's name or a greeting. Identify yourself if necessary.

Typically, email messages begin with the recipient's name. If writer and reader are acquainted, first name only is the rule. If you would normally address the reader as Ms., Dr., Mr., and such, address him or her this way in an initial email. But you can change the salutation in subsequent messages if the person indicates that informality is desired. A friendly generic greeting such as "Greetings" is appropriate for a group of people with whom you communicate. Use of the recipient's full name also is acceptable. The salutations commonly used in letters (Dear Mr., Dear Ms.) are rarely used in email. When writing to someone or a group you do not know, it is appropriate to identify yourself early in the message. This identification may include your purpose and your company. Your title and position also may be helpful.

Organizing the Contents

- Organize short messages by presenting information in descending order of importance.

Even though email messages often are written under time pressure, you would do well to organize them carefully. For most short, informative messages, a "top-down" order is appropriate. This plan, used in newspaper writing, involves presenting the most important material first. The remaining information follows in descending order of importance. Such an arrangement permits a busy reader to get the essential facts first, and the reader accessing email on a smartphone or other small screen to get the essential facts more easily. Many writers routinely follow this practice.

- Longer messages usually follow more complex patterns.

Longer, more complex, and formal email messages frequently follow more involved and strategic organization patterns. The most common of these are reviewed in Chapters 6, 7, 8, and 9. As you will see, these patterns vary depending on how the reader will likely perceive the writer's objective. In general, those messages that are likely to be received positively or neutrally are written in a direct pattern. That is, they get to the goal right away and then present their contents systematically and quickly. Those messages that are likely to be received negatively are appropriately written in an indirect pattern. Their negative content is preceded by conditioning and explanatory words that prepare the reader to receive the bad news.

- Some resemble business reports.

Some long email messages may resemble business reports. With these messages, you well may follow the organization and writing instructions for business reports (Chapters 10–12). You should use your knowledge of report presentation in writing them. In fact, business reports can be communicated by email just as business letters can. Some memorandums are communicated by email. The variety of email messages covers the entire spectrum of written business communication.

Writing the Email Message: Formality Considerations

- Email messages range from highly informal to formal.

A review of email writing is complicated by the fact that email messages are extremely diverse. They run the range from highly informal to formal. The informal messages often resemble face-to-face oral communication; some even sound like chitchat that occurs between acquaintances and friends. Email messages are often written in a fast-paced environment with little time for deliberation.

Because of this diversity, discussing the formality of email writing is difficult. One approach is to view the language used from three general classifications: casual, informal, and formal.[2]

Casual. By casual language we mean the language we use in talking with close friends in everyday situations. It includes slang and colloquialisms. It uses contractions and personal pronouns freely. Its sentences are short—sometimes incomplete. It uses mechanical emphasis devices and initialisms (to be discussed later). Although in actual practice it may be subject to grammatical incorrectness, as we stress elsewhere this practice is not helpful to the communication and should be avoided. Casual language is best limited to your communications with close friends. Following is an example of casual language:

> Hi Cindy:
>
> High-five me! Just back from confab with pinheads. They're high on our marketing plan. But as you crystal balled it, they want a special for the jumbos. ASAP, they said. Let's meet, my cell, 10 A.M., Wed.?
>
> TTFN
>
> Brandon

Most of your personal email (messages to friends) are likely to be casually written. This is the way friends talk, and their email should be no different. Probably some of the email you will write in business also will fall in this category. Much of it will be with your fellow employees and friends in business. But here some words of caution should be expressed. You would be wise to use casual language only when you know your readers well—when you know they expect and prefer casual communication. Never should you use slang, initialisms, emphasis devices, or such that are not certain to communicate clearly and quickly.

Informal. Informal language retains some of the qualities of casual writing. It makes some use of personal pronouns and contractions. Its sentences are relatively short. It occasionally may use colloquialisms, but more selectively than in casual writing. It has the effect of conversation, but it is proper conversation—not chitchat. Its sentences are short, but they are well structured and organized. They have varied patterns that produce an interesting literary style. In general, it is the writing that you will find in most of the illustrations in Chapters 6–9. It is the language that appears in the text of this book. You should use it in most of your business email messages, especially when writing to people you know only on a business basis. An example of an email message in informal language is the following:

> Cindy:
>
> The management team has heartily approved our marketing plan. They were most complimentary. But as you predicted, they want a special plan for the large accounts. As they want it as soon as possible, let's get together to work on it. Can we meet Wednesday, 10 A.M., my office?
>
> Brandon

Formal. A formal style of writing maintains a greater distance between writer and reader than informal style. It avoids personal references and contractions. Its sentences are well structured and organized. Although there is a tendency to create longer sentences in formal writing, this tendency should be resisted. Formal style is well illustrated in the examples of formal reports in Chapters 11 and 12. It is appropriate to use in email messages resembling formal reports, in messages to people of higher status, and to people not known to the writer.

- The language may be casual, informal, or formal.

- Casual language uses slang, colloquialisms, contractions, short sentences.

- Use casual language when writing to friends.

- Informal language resembles proper conversation.

- Formal language keeps a distance between writer and reader.

---

[2] Heidi Schultz. *The Elements of Electronic Communication* (Boston: Allyn and Bacon, 2000) 43–47.

Writing the Email Message: General Considerations

Instructions for writing email messages are much the same as those given in Chapters 2, 3, and 4 for other types of messages. For the purpose of email writing, we may group the more important of these instructions under three heads: conciseness, clarity, and etiquette. A fourth, correctness (covered in Chapter 17), is equally vital. Each of these important qualities for email writing is briefly reviewed in the following paragraphs.

- Follow the writing instructions in preceding chapters.

Conciseness. As we have mentioned, email often is written by busy people for busy people. In the best interests of all concerned, email messages should be as short as complete coverage of the subject matter will permit. This means culling out the extra information and using only that which is essential. It means also that the information remaining should be worded concisely. In the words of one email authority, "Keep it short. If your email message is more than two paragraphs, maybe you should use the telephone."[3]

- Cut nonessentials and write concisely.

Frequently in email communication, a need exists to refer to previous email messages. The easiest way, of course, is to tell your mailer to include the entire message. Unless the entire message is needed, however, this practice adds length. It is better either to paraphrase the essentials from the original or to quote the selected parts that cover the essentials. All quoted material should be distinguished from your own words by the sign > at the beginning and the sign < at the end of the quoted part. Another technique is to place three of these signs (>>>) at the beginning of all parts you write and three of these signs (<<<) at the beginning of all parts you are quoting from previous messages.

- Minimize references to previous communications.

Clarity. Especially important in email writing is clarity of wording. As suggested in Chapters 2 and 3, you should know and practice the techniques of readable writing. You should select words that quickly create clear meanings. Typically, these are the short, familiar ones. You should strive for concreteness, vigor, and precision. Your sentences should be short, and so should your paragraphs. In fact, all of the advice given in Chapters 2 and 3 is applicable to the writing of clear email messages.

- Use the techniques of clear writing.

Etiquette. It goes without saying that courtesy should be practiced in all business relations. We all want to receive courteous and fair treatment. In fact, this is the way we human beings prefer to act. Even so, the current literature has much to say about anger among email participants. "Flaming," as the practice of sending abusive or offensive language is called, has no place in business. Good email etiquette should prevail. As you will recall, Chapter 4 emphasized using courteous language. The skillful use of positive language and you-viewpoint also can be effective in email. So can the use of conversational language. Nondiscriminatory language also helps, as can emphasis on sincerity. In fact, virtually all the instructions given on goodwill building apply here. Also in the interest of good email etiquette, you will want to let your reader know when no response is required to your message.

- Be courteous, as suggested in preceding chapters.

Correctness. One would think that the need for correctness in email writing would be universally accepted. Unfortunately, such is not the case. Because of the fast pace of email communication, some practitioners argue that "getting the message out there" is the important goal—that style need not be a matter of concern. In the view of one in this group, "You should not add stylistic and grammatical refinements to your email messages because they'll slow you down."[4]

- Write correctly. Some critics disagree.

---

[3] Kim Komando, "8 Email Mistakes That Make You Look Bad," 2006, Microsoft, 09 May 2006 <http://www.microsoft.com/smallbusiness/resources/technology/communications/8_email_mistakes_that_make_you_look_bad.mspx>.

[4] Guy Kawasaki, as quoted in David Angell and Brent Heslop, *Elements of Email Style* (Reading, MA: Addison-Wesley, 1994) 3.

Using Good Email Etiquette Helps Writers Convey Intended Message

Using proper email etiquette is as easy as applying a bit of empathy to your messages: send only what you would want to receive. The following additional etiquette guides will help you consider a variety of issues when using email.

- Is your message really needed by the recipient(s)?
- Is your message for routine rather than sensitive messages?
- Are you sure your message is not spam (an annoying message sent repeatedly) or a chain letter?
- Have you carefully checked that your message is going where you want it to go?
- Has your wording avoided defamatory or libelous language?
- Have you complied with copyright laws and attributed sources accurately?

- Have you avoided humor and sarcasm your reader may not understand as intended?
- Have you proofread your message carefully?
- Is this a message you would not mind having distributed widely?
- Does your signature avoid offensive quotes or illustrations, especially those that are religious, political, or sexual?
- Is your recipient willing or able to accept attached files?
- Are attached files a size that your recipient's system can handle?
- Are the files you are attaching virus free?

We cannot accept this view. *How* one communicates is very much a part of the message. As expressed by one authority, "People still judge you on how well you communicate. . . . Commercial email represents your company and your brand. There's no room for excuses."[5] Bad spelling, illogical punctuation, awkward wording, and such stand out like sore thumbs. Such errors reflect on the writer. And they can reflect on the credibility of the message. If one knows correctness, it is easy enough to get it right the first time. What is the logic of doing something wrong when you know better? Clearly, an error-filled message strongly suggests the writer's ignorance.

- Correctness is a part of the message.

To avoid any such suggestion of ignorance, you should follow the grammatical and punctuation instructions presented in Chapter 17. And you should follow the basic instructions for using words, constructing sentences, and designing paragraphs presented in the writing chapters. Before pressing the Send button, proofread your message carefully.

Closing the Email Message

Most email messages end with just the writer's name—the first name alone if the recipient knows the writer well. But in some messages, especially the more formal ones, a closing statement may be appropriate. "Thanks" and "Regards" are popular. In casual messages, acronyms such as THX (thanks) and TTFN (ta-ta for now) are often used. The conventional complimentary closes used in traditional letters (sincerely, cordially) are not widely used, but they are appropriate in messages that involve formal business relationships. In messages to other businesses, it is important that you include your company and position.

- End with your name and perhaps a closing statement.

---

[5] Jim Sterne and Anthony Priore, *Email Marketing: Using Email to Reach Your Target Audience and Build Customer Relationships* (New York: John Wiley & Sons, 2000) 141.

Although e-mail is an essential communication medium in business today, many businesspeople and business students take it casually and fail to realize its full potential. It's easy to assume that since e-mail can be produced quickly and easily, readers can comprehend e-mail messages quickly and easily too. Yet overly speedy e-mail writing can result in much slower e-mail reading and even miscommunication.

Mary Munter, Dartmouth College
Priscilla S. Rogers, University of Michigan
Jone Rymer, Wayne State University

Mary Munter, Priscilla S. Rogers, Jone Rymer, "Business E-mail: Guidelines for Users," *Business Communication Quarterly* 66.1 (2003): 26.

Today most email software has a signature feature that will automatically attach a signature file to a message. Most programs even allow the writer to set up an alternative signature, giving users the flexibility to choose between a standard, one alternate, and none attached at all. Writers sometimes set up a formal full signature in one file and an informal signature in another. The important point to remember is to close with a signature that gives the reader the information he or she needs to know.

Using Emphasis Devices in Email

- Email has limited use of emphasis devices. These substitutes have been developed.

When you write email messages, you may find that certain elements of style are missing either on your system or on your readers' systems. While most of the current versions of Windows and Macintosh email programs support mechanical devices such as underscoring, font variations, italics, bold, color, and even graphics, some older or mainframe-based systems do not. Email writers have attempted to overcome the limitations of these older systems by developing alternative means of showing emphasis. To show underscoring, they use the sign _ at the beginning of the words needing underscoring. They use asterisks (*) before and after words to show boldface. Solid capital letters are another means of emphasis, although some critics believe this practice is greatly overused. In the words of one critic "Don't use solid capital letters. People will think you're shouting."[6] A sign they use to emphasize items in a list is the bullet. Since there is no standardized bullet character that will display on all computers, many writers of email use substitute characters. One is the asterisk (*) followed by a tab space. Another is the dash (—) followed by a tab space. Probably these devices are used best in the email messages written in casual language.

Using Initialisms Cautiously

- Initialisms have been developed to save time. But use them cautiously.

Probably as a result of the early informal development of email, a somewhat standardized system of initialisms has developed. Their purpose has been to cut message length and to save the writer's time. In spite of these apparent advantages, you would be wise to use them cautiously. They have meaning only if readers know them. Even so, you should be acquainted with the more widely used ones, such as those below.[7] You are likely to find others created by your email correspondents.

ASAP	as soon as possible
BTW	by the way
FAQ	frequently asked question

---

[6] Mark Kakkurik, "E-mail FAQs," *Guide to E-mail & More* 8, no. 7 (2000): 14.

[7] Linda Lamb and Jerry Peek, *Using Email Effectively* (Sebastopol, CA: O'Reilly and Associates, Inc., 1995), 107.

FWIW	for what it's worth
FYI	for your information
IMHO	in my humble opinion
LOL	laughing out loud
TIA	thanks in advance
TTFN	ta-ta for now

As noted previously, initialisms are appropriate primarily in casual messages.

It is important to keep in mind that these practices and some of the other pointers given in this review apply only to current usage. Computers and their use are changing almost daily. The techniques of email writing also are likely to change over time.

Avoiding Inappropriate Use of Email

In spite of its popularity and ease of use, email is not always a good medium for your communications. As summarized by two authorities, "it should not be used when:

- The message is long, complicated, or requires negotiation.
- Questions or information need clarification and discussion.
- The information is confidential or sensitive, requires security, or could be misinterpreted.
- The message is emotionally charged and really requires tone of voice or conversational feedback to soften the words or negotiate meaning.
- The message is sent to *avoid* direct contact with a person, especially if the message is unpleasant and uncomfortable or seems too difficult to say face-to-face.
- The message contains sensitive issues, relays feelings, or attempts to resolve conflict. Email can make conflict worse."[8]

- Don't use email when

- the message involves these aspects.

TEXT MESSAGING

Probably you are already well acquainted with text messaging. Although a recent technological innovation, it is widely used, especially by young people. With about 170 million active mobile phones in the United States in 2006, it is estimated that about 7.2 billion text messages are sent a month.[9] As you read this text, the number is likely growing as the use of text messaging is increasing rapidly.

- Text messaging is widely used today.

Text messaging, also called short message service (SMS), allows one to use a mobile phone to send, receive, and view short messages using the phone's keypad and screen. Typically, its messages are limited to 160 characters. Some carriers allow longer messages but may break them into multiple messages when forwarding them to receivers. The input screens count the characters as you enter them, helping you keep your message concise. Some even allow you to customize for shortcuts, and most use predictive technology to complete the spelling of words quickly. In addition to being able to send messages between mobile phones, users can use their email programs on desktop, laptop, or hand-held hardware to send text messages.

- It enables one to send and receive short messages by wireless phones and personal computers.

Although text messaging currently is used primarily for personal communications, it is beginning to find a place in business communication. Marketers have begun to test its potential. McDonald's and Budweiser have used it in their advertising campaigns. It is especially useful in businesses with a mobile work force, permitting communication between home office and sales representatives, maintenance support staff, field service engineers, and such. It is a good way to keep in touch with staff while at a meeting, on the road, or otherwise indisposed.

- It is beginning to find a place in business.

---

[8] Vera Terminello and Marcia G. Reed, *Email: Communicate Effectively* (Upper Saddle River, NJ: Pearson Education, 2003) 13.

[9] Kevin Manley, "Surge in Text Messaging Makes Cell Operators :-)," *USA Today,* http://www.usatoday.com/money/2005-07-27-text-messaging_x.htm.

Figure 5–5

An Illustration of a Web-Based Text Messaging Application

- The writing involved stresses brevity and uses abbreviations.

The writing of text messages is quite different from that of other messages. As the message generally is limited to 160 characters, the emphasis is on brevity. You include only the bare essentials. The need for brevity has led to the use of many abbreviations. Some examples: b4 (before), u (you), gr8 (great), BTW (by the way), ASAP (as soon as possible), CU (see you), NP (no problem) FB (fine by me), HRY (how are you), TC (take care), TYT (take your time). So many of these abbreviations have developed that one might say that a new language has developed. In fact, a dictionary of over 300 of these abbreviations has been compiled at *Webopedia,* an online computer technology encyclopedia (http://www.Webopedia.com/quick_reft/textmessageabbreviations.asp). In addition to abbreviations, typed symbols are used to convey emotions. Generally called smileys, here are some of them: :) (standard smiley), :-! (foot in mouth), :*) (drunk smiley), :-((sad or frown), :-0 (yell), and (((H))) (hugs). Other smileys may be found in the *Webopedia* dictionary previously cited. Because text messaging is less formal than other types of messages, these shortcuts are often used and accepted. However, they still force the reader to stop and interpret the meaning. You should avoid using them whenever there is a likelihood they will not communicate quickly and clearly.

- Text messages should convey ideas completely with minimal need for response.

In composing text messages, the writer's objective should be to convey all critical information the receiver needs and to keep needed responses as short as possible. For example, if you learn that an important visiting customer is a vegetarian and you have reservations for lunch at Ruth's Chris Steakhouse, you might need to let your boss know—before the lunch meeting. However, the boss is leading an important meeting where a phone call would be disruptive and inappropriate. So you decide to send a text message. An immediate thought might be to send something like this: *Marina Smith is a vegetarian. Where should we take her for lunch today? Zeke* Although it does convey the major fact and is only 77 characters counting spaces, it forces the recipient to enter a long response—the name of another place. It might also result in more message exchanges about availability and time. A better version might be this: *Marina Smith is a vegetarian. Shall we go to 1-Fish House, 2-Souplantation, 3-Mandarian House? All are available at noon. Zeke* This version conveys the major fact in 130 characters and allows the recipient to respond simply with a 1, 2, or 3. However, before sending this message, the writer took the initiative to identify appropriate alternatives, perhaps

Pepper ... and Salt

"Miss Pearson, send me a text message."

SOURCE: From *The Wall Street Journal*—Permission, Cartoon Features Syndicate.

with the help of others, through firsthand knowledge of the boss's preferences, or some basic research. As you will read later in the chapter, gathering needed information is a prerequisite to writing clear, complete messages.

While text messaging is relatively new for business use, you will find it a valuable tool if your messages are clear, complete, and concise with a pleasant and professional tone.

INSTANT MESSAGING

Another type of electronic message that continues to grow in popularity is instant messaging. Commonly referred to as IM-ing, instant messaging, or online chatting, is much like a telephone conversation.

- Another popular kind of electronic message is instant messaging.

As with a phone call, the parties communicate in real time (immediately). It differs primarily in that it uses text-based (typed) rather than voice-based communication, although recent developments have made voice-based instant messaging possible. With some exceptions, in instant messaging both parties are logged into their instant message server at the same time. They communicate in much the same way as in email. Instant messaging allows you to develop a list of people with whom you wish to communicate (often called a "buddy list"). You can engage in instant messaging with any of these people as long as they are online when you are. When you send a message, a small window opens where you and the other person can type. Both of you can see these messages immediately. You continue exchanging these message bits until you have achieved your objective.[10]

- Instant messaging is like a telephone conversation, but it uses type rather than voice.

You should write instant messages much as you would talk in conversation with the other person. If the person is a personal friend, your language should reflect this friendship. If the person is the president of your company, a business associate, or a fellow worker, this relationship should guide you. The message bits presented in instant messaging are determined largely by the flow of information. Responses often are impromptu. Even so, in business situations you should consciously direct the flow toward your objective.

- Write instant messages as you would talk to the other person.

---

[10] Jeff Tyson, "How Instant Messaging Works," 1998–2006, HowStuffWorks, Inc., 09 May 2006 <http://computer.howstuffworks.com/instant-messaging.htm>.

Figure 5–6

Enterprise Instant
Messaging Often
Looks and Works Like
Typical Free IM, But
It Gives Businesses
Added Security and
Recordkeeping Benefits

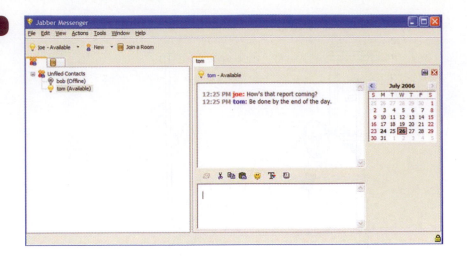

- Your instant messages
  may be monitored

In writing instant messages you should keep in mind that your instant messages may not be just between you and the other person. Companies often use enterprise instant messaging software to monitor and log employee instant messaging. This communication management software is designed to audit and control instant message use. Specifically, it detects excessive use, inappropriate or unethical behavior, disclosure of proprietary information, use of sexually explicit language, and attachments with viruses. It also has features that protect the company from legal liabilities.

SUMMARY BY LEARNING OBJECTIVES

1 Describe the writing process of writing and successful writing strategies.

1. The writing process consists of three main stages:
   - Planning includes the following activities:
     — Gathering and collecting information.
     — Analyzing and organizing the information.
     — Choosing a form, channel, and format.
   - Drafting needs to be flexible.
     — Avoid perfectionism when drafting.
     — Keep going—don't stop for excessive tinkering.
     — Pursue any strategy that will help you make progress on the draft.
   - Revising involves three main levels of edit:
     — Revising for content, organization, and format.
     — Editing sentences and words.
     — Proofreading to catch mechanical and grammatical errors.
   - The three stages are *recursive*—you can revisit earlier stages at any time.

2 Explain the importance of readable formatting.

2. Making good formatting decisions is critical to your messages' success.
   - Good formatting makes your messages inviting.
   - Good formatting makes your information easier to find and follow.

3 Describe the development and current usage of the business letter.

3. These are the highlights of the development of business letters:
   - The early civilizations (Chinese, Greek, Roman, Egyptian) used them.
   - They are now used largely in more formal situations, especially with external audiences.
   - Letter formats are standardized (see Appendix B).
   - Early business letters used a stilted language.
   - Strategic organization and humanized language mark recent developments.

4. The memorandum is a form of letter written inside the business.

   • Hard-copy memorandums usually are processed on special stationery (*Memorandum* at the top; *Date, To, From,* and *Subject* follow).

   • Large organizations often include more information (*Department, Plant, Location, Copies to, Store Number,* etc.)

4 Describe the purpose and form of memorandums.

5. Today, email is a mainstream form of business communication.

   • It has grown because it
     — Eliminates "telephone tag."
     — Saves time.
     — Speeds up decision making.
     — Is cheap.
     — Provides a written record.

   • But it has disadvantages:
     — It is not confidential.
     — It doesn't show emotions.
     — It may be ignored or delayed.

   • Email should be avoided when
     — The message is long, complicated, or needs negotiating.
     — Content needs discussion.
     — Content needs softening in tone, voice, or words.
     — The message is used to avoid unpleasant and uncomfortable personal contact.
     — The message contains sensitive issues.

5 Understand the phenomenal growth and nature of email.

6. The way to write good email messages is as follows:

   • Use standardized prefatory parts.

   • Begin with recipient's name or a greeting.

   • Organize logically.
     — For short messages, present the information in descending order of importance.
     — For long messages, use the organization that best presents the information.

   • Make the message short.

   • Write correctly.

   • Close with your name or a closing statement.

   • Use asterisks, dashes, solid caps, and such, as needed, to show emphasis.

   • Sometimes initialisms are useful, but use them cautiously.

6 Follow conventional procedures and organize and write clear email messages.

7. Text messaging is an important new type of business message.

   • It is widely used today.

   • It enables one to send and receive short messages by wireless phones and personal computers.

   • It is finding a place in business communication.

   • The writing stresses brevity and uses shortcuts—but never at the expense of clarity.

7 Understand the nature and business uses of text messaging.

8. Another popular type of electronic message is instant messaging (IM-ing).

   • Instant messaging is like a telephone conversation, but it uses type rather than voice.

   • Write your instant messages as though you were talking to the other person.

   • Be aware that your instant messaging may be monitored in an organizational environment.

8 Understand how instant messaging works.

1 Identify and explain the steps in the writing process.

2 Think about a writing project that you recently completed. Using the terminology in this chapter, describe the process that you used. How might using different strategies have made the project more pleasant and productive? What helpful strategies did you use, if any, that were not mentioned in this chapter?

3 Think about a letter you received or wrote recently, and explain why it was appropriate to use a letter in this situation.

4 Will hard-copy letters diminish in importance as email continues to grow? Become obsolete? Vanish?

5 a. Discuss the reasons for email's phenomenal growth.

   b. Is this growth likely to continue?

6 Some authorities say that concerns about correctness inhibit a person's email communication. Does this stand have merit? Discuss.

7 Some authorities say that shortcuts in text messaging will lead to users' inability to spell properly in more formal contexts. Discuss.

8 Memorandums and email messages differ more than letters in their physical makeup. Explain and discuss.

9 Explain the logic of using negative words in email and memorandums to fellow employees that you would not use in letters carrying similar messages.

10 Discuss and justify the wide range of formality used in memorandums and email messages.

11 What factors might determine whether or not instant messaging would be an appropriate medium to use in a given situation?

1 Interview a working professional about his or her writing process. In addition to asking about general strategies for different kinds of writing, ask how he or she tackled a particularly difficult writing situation. Write up the results of your findings in a brief memo report to your instructor.

2 Find a sample of business writing and evaluate its use of formatting elements. If they are effective, say why; if not, explain what you would do differently.

3 Using various formatting devices, turn the following contents into a readable, attractive flyer or email announcing a health club's new rates for employees of a nearby hospital. (You may want to consult Appendix B's advice on formatting.)

New Special Rates for Metropolitan Hospital Staff! The Health Club is now offering special rates for all Metropolitan Hospital employees. The Club is a full-service exercise club located at 42 Adams Street, just across from the hospital. Our facilities may be a good option for Metropolitan employees to explore. We offer the following membership types for Metropolitan employees or retirees: Single Standard, 1 year prepaid ($200/year); Single Standard, by the month ($15/month plus a one-time $50 enrollment fee); Single Deluxe, 1 year prepaid ($300/year). Single Deluxe includes your personal locker and a towel service. Metropolitan employees' spouses or domestic partners are eligible for a 20 percent discount on the Club's normal rates. You can take a tour, join the Club, or ask any questions by calling 555-5555. We have a large free-weight room; new Cybex (Nautilus-style) machines; ellipticals, treadmills, bikes, steppers, and rowers; an Olympic-size swimming pool; aerobics, Pilates, and yoga classes; racquetball and handball courts; a large gym/basketball court; a whirlpool; a steam room and saunas; shower and locker room facilities; and free parking. A small fee for some classes may apply. Our hours are Monday through Friday, 5 AM to 10 PM; Saturday, 7 AM to 8 PM, and Sunday 7 AM to 6 PM— Our website address is www.healthclubin.org.

4 Instructions: Write a text message in less than 160 characters for each of the cases below. Be sure your message is both clear and complete.

   a. You own three coffee shops around your area. Although you have a loyal base of regular customers, you realize that there is both room to grow this base and a real need to compete with the growing presence of Starbucks and other competitors. Your coffee is good and reasonably priced, but your emphasis on seasonal fruit has long been your specialty. You serve fruit fresh in muffins and as toppings for pancakes, French toast, and waffles. In fact, since the local television station included your shop in a healthy eating segment, your low-fat muffins are selling out every day even though you have been increasing production. When some of your loyal customers started grumbling about not always being able to get them, you knew you wanted to serve them better.

Because most of them have mobile phones, text messaging seemed like an obvious solution. You decided to offer an opt-in polling service that would ask their preference for a particular low-fat muffin or fresh fruit. Your customers could select the days of the week they would be interested in getting the poll. Although they would not be placing an order, they would be helping you plan. You'd also be spending well-targeted promotion dollars while creating good-will with your loyal customers. Now you need to write this poll question.

b. You are on your way to the airport for a trip to a week-long conference when you remember a file you were supposed to send to a customer. So many last-minute details came up that you really don't remember if you sent it. Unfortunately, you cannot access your work computer from outside the company firewall, but you have a colleague, Chris VanLerBerghe, who would be able to check your email outbox to confirm whether or not you sent it. Chris could also send the file, if necessary. However, you cannot reach her by phone now because she is in an important planning meeting, so you decide to send a text message with the exact names and data she will need. Be sure your message is both clear and complete.

c. As you are in the morning sales meeting, your mobile phone vibrates, indicating you have an incoming call. You recognize the source—Yesaya Chan, the high school student you are mentoring/tutoring in math. When you are finally able to listen to the call, you learn that Yesaya needs your help tonight because his teacher moved a test up a couple of days. He wants to know if you can meet him at the local library at 5 PM, noting that it will be open late tonight. You will say yes, but the earliest you can be there on such short notice is 6 PM. Suggest that he still go to the library at 5 PM and work as many of the review problems on his own as he can. You will help him with the others when you get there. Because he is probably in class now, you will send your response as a text message so it won't interrupt his class.

chapter six

Directness in Good-News and Neutral Messages

LEARNING OBJECTIVES

Upon completing this chapter, you will be able to write direct-order messages effectively. To reach this goal, you should be able to

1 Properly assess the reader's reaction to your message.

2 Describe the general plan for direct-order messages.

3 Write clear, well-structured routine requests for information.

4 Write direct, orderly, and friendly answers to inquiries.

5 Compose adjustment grants that regain any lost confidence.

6 Write order acknowledgments that cover problems and build goodwill.

7 Write claims that objectively and courteously explain the facts.

8 Write clear and effective operational communications.

Most business messages use a direct organizational pattern. That is, the message leads with its most important point and then moves to additional or supporting information. If you will recall what Chapter 1 observed about the nature of business, you will understand why. Communication is central to organized human activity. Especially in business, people need to know what to do, why, and how. They undertake any job understanding that they have a certain function to perform, and they need information to be able to perform it well. When external audiences interact with companies, they also expect and need certain kinds of information, presented as expeditiously as possible. It is fair to say that direct messages are the lifeblood of virtually any business activity.

• Direct order is used in most business messages.

There are, of course, unlimited kinds of direct messages. Each business is unique in some ways, and each, therefore, will have developed its own direct-message types—its preferred purposes, patterns, styles, and formats for these messages. Still, one can identify a certain basic plan for the direct message. Moreover, certain situations calling for a direct approach have occurred so often that we can identify several common types of these messages.

This chapter will first describe a general plan for writing all messages of this type. Then we will adapt this general plan to some of the more common business situations that generally can be organized by it. We will show why each of these situations requires special treatment and how to handle each. Although our coverage is not complete, we believe that by noting these special requirements, you will be able to adapt to any related situation not covered.

• A general direct plan is presented and then adapted to specific situations.

PRELIMINARY ASSESSMENT

As discussed in Chapter 1, any message other than those for the most mechanical, routine circumstances will require careful thinking about the situation, your readers, and your goals. When determining your message's basic plan, a good beginning is to assess your reader's probable reaction to what you have to say. If the reaction is likely to be negative, a strategic organization plan is in order. These plans are discussed in following chapters. But if the reaction is likely to be positive, or even neutral, your best approach is likely to be a direct one—that is, one that gets to the objective right away without delaying explanation or conditioning words. The general plan for this direct approach is the following.

• Begin by assessing the reader's probable reaction. A positive or neutral reaction calls for directness; a negative reaction, indirectness.

THE GENERAL DIRECT PLAN

Beginning with the Objective

Begin with your objective. If you are seeking information, start by asking for it. If you are giving information, start giving it. Whatever is your objective, lead with it.

• Start with the objective.

In some cases, you might need to open with a brief orienting phrase, clause, or even sentence. Especially if your reader is not expecting to hear from you or is not familiar with you or your company, you may need to preface your main point with a few words of background. But get to the point as soon as possible. For example, the sentence "We have received your May 7th inquiry" does nothing but state the obvious. Keep any prefatory remarks brief and get to the real message without delay. Then stop the first paragraph. Let the rest of the message fill in the details.

• You may need to lead with brief orienting information.

Covering the Remaining Part of the Objective

Whatever else must be covered to complete the objective makes up the bulk of the remainder of the message. If you cover all of your objective in the beginning (as in an inquiry in which a single question is asked), nothing else is needed. But if additional questions, answers, or such are needed, you cover them. And you cover them systematically—perhaps listing them or arranging them by paragraphs. If these parts have their own explanations or commentary, you include them. In short, you cover everything else that needs to be covered.

• Complete the objective systematically—perhaps by listing or paragraphing.

Ending with Adapted Goodwill

- End with a goodwill comment
- specifically adapted.

Because it is the natural thing for friendly people to do, you end this message with some appropriate friendly comment. This is how you would end a face-to-face communication with the reader. There is no reason to do otherwise in writing.

These final goodwill words will receive the best reader reaction if they are selected to fit the one case. Such general closes as "A prompt reply will be appreciated" and "Thank you in advance for your response" are positive, for they express a friendly thank-you. And there is nothing wrong with a thank-you sincerely expressed here or elsewhere. The problem is in the routine, rubber-stamp nature of many of these expressions. A more positive reaction results from an individually tailored expression that fits the one case—for example: "If you will answer these questions about Ms. Hill right away, she and I will be most grateful."

Now let us see how you can adapt this general plan to fit the more common direct message situations.

ROUTINE INQUIRIES

INTRODUCTORY SITUATION

Routine Inquiries

Introduce yourself to routine inquiries by assuming you are the assistant to the vice president for administration of Pinnacle Manufacturing Company. Pinnacle is the manufacturer and distributor of an assortment of high-quality products. Your duties involve helping your boss cover a wide assortment of activities. Many of these activities involve writing messages.

At the moment, your boss is working with a group of Pinnacle executives to select offices for a new regional headquarters. They have chosen the city. Now they must find the best possible offices in this city. As chair of this committee, your boss has accepted responsibility for finding office locations from which to choose. Of course, your boss has delegated much of the work to you.

Already you have found three possible office suites in the chosen city. Now you must get the pertinent information about each so that the executives can make their selection. The first of these you found in the classified advertisements of the local newspaper. It is a 3,200-square-foot office suite, but the ad tells little more. So now you must write the advertiser a routine inquiry seeking the information the management team needs.

Choosing from Two Types of Beginnings

- Routine inquiries appropriately begin asking either of two types of questions:

- (1) a specific question that sets up the information wanted or

The routine inquiry appropriately begins with the objective, just as described in the general plan. Since your objective is to ask for information, this means beginning by asking a question. But here a variation unique to the routine-inquiry message is appropriate. This opening question can be either of two types.

First, it can be one of the specific questions to be asked (assuming more than one question needs to be asked). Preferably it should be a question that sets up the other questions. For example, if your objective is to get answers to specific questions about test results of a company's product, you might begin with these words:

Will you please send me test results showing how Duro-Press withstands high temperatures and exposure to sunlight?

In the body of the message you would include the more specific questions concerning temperatures and exposure to sunlight.

- (2) a general request for information.

Second, the opening question could be a general request for information. The specific questions come later. This beginning sentence illustrates a general request:

Will you please answer the following questions about Duro-Press fabric?

Answering inquiries that do not include adequate explanation can be frustrating.

The "will you" here and in the preceding example may appear to be unnecessary. The basic message would not change if the words were eliminated. In the minds of some experienced writers, however, including them softens the request and is worth the additional length.

Informing and Explaining Adequately

To help your reader answer your questions, you may need to include explanation or information. If you do not explain enough or if you misjudge the reader's knowledge, you make the reader's task difficult. For example, answers to questions about a computer often depend on the specific needs or characteristics of the company that will use it. The best-informed computer expert cannot answer such questions without knowing the facts of the company concerned.

- Somewhere in the message, explain enough to enable the reader to answer.

Where and how you include the necessary explanatory information depend on the nature of your message. Usually, a good place for general explanatory material that fits the entire message is before or after the direct request in the opening paragraph. This information helps reduce any startling effect that a direct opening question might have. It often fits logically into this place, serving as a qualifying or justifying sentence for the message. In messages that ask more than one question, you will sometimes need to include explanatory material with the questions. If this is the case, the explanation fits best with the questions to which it pertains. Such messages may alternate questions and explanations.

- Place the explanation anywhere it fits logically.

Structuring the Questions

If your inquiry involves just one question, you can achieve your primary objective with the first sentence. After any necessary explanation and a few words of friendly closing comment, your message is done. If you must ask a number of questions, however, you will need to consider their organization.

- If the inquiry involves just one question, begin with it.

Whatever you do, you will need to make your questions stand out. You can do this in a number of ways. First, you can make each question a separate sentence with a bullet, a symbol (for example, ●, ○, ■) used to call attention to a particular item. Combining two or more questions in a sentence de-emphasizes each and invites the reader to overlook some.

- If it involves more than one, make each stand out. Do this by (1) placing each question in a separate sentence,

Second, you can give each question a separate paragraph, whenever this practice is logical. It is logical when your explanation and other comments about each question justify a paragraph.

- (2) structuring the questions in separate paragraphs,

- (3) ordering or ranking the questions, and

Third, you can order or rank your questions with numbers. By using words (*first, second, third,* etc.), numerals (1, 2, 3, etc.), or letters (*a, b, c,* etc.), you make the questions stand out. Also, you provide the reader with a convenient check and reference guide to answering.

- (4) using the question form of sentence.

Fourth, you can structure your questions in question form. True questions stand out. Sentences that merely hint at a need for information do not attract much attention. The "It would be nice if you would tell me . . ." and "I would like to know . . ." types are really not questions. They do not ask—they merely suggest. The questions that stand out are those written in question form: "Will you please tell me . . . ?" "How much would one be able to save . . . ?" "How many contract problems have you had . . . ?"

- But take caution in asking questions that produce yes or no answers.

You may want to avoid questions that can be answered with a simple *yes* or *no.* An obvious exception, of course, would be when you really want a simple *yes* or *no* answer. For example, the question "Is the chair available in blue?" may not be what you really want to know. A better wording probably is "In what colors is the chair available?" Often you'll find that you can combine a yes/no question and its explanation to get a better, more concise question. To illustrate, the wording "Does the program run with Windows? We use Windows Vista." could be improved with "What operating system does the program run on?" or "Does the program run with Windows Vista?"

Ending with Goodwill

- End with a friendly comment that fits the one case.

The goodwill ending described in the general plan is appropriate here, just as it is in most business messages. And we must emphasize again that the closing words do the most toward creating goodwill when they fit the one case.

Reviewing the Order

In summary, the plan recommended for the routine inquiry message is as follows:

- Begin directly with the objective—either a specific question that sets up the entire message or a general request for information.
- Include necessary explanation—wherever it fits.
- If a number of questions are involved, ask them.

Picture Bullets Allow Writers to List Equal Items with a Bit of Flair

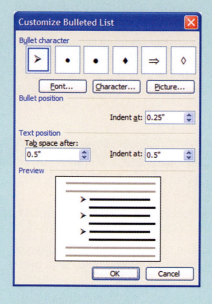
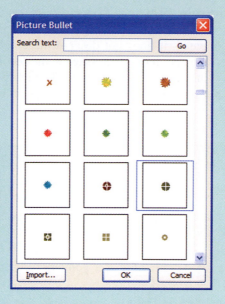
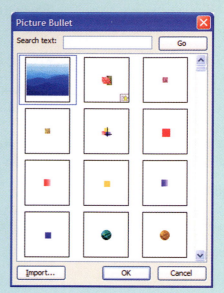

Word processing software allows writers to list items easily with bullets or numbers. Writers generally use numbers to show ordering or ranking and bullets to list unranked or equal items. One way to add interest to lists is to use picture bullets, an easy task today. Rather than selecting one of the six standard bullets, writers can easily customize them with pictures. Microsoft Word includes a nice selection of picture bullets in various colors and styles, some that you see above. However, writers can also select other images to import for use as a bullet. By simply pointing and clicking on the image to import, a writer instantly creates a bullet and resizes it automatically for bullet use.

In a message to its members meeting in Washington, DC, the executive director of the Association for Business Communication might use one picture bullet to list items members should bring with them for tours of national monuments. The writer might suggest that members bring these items:

 Binoculars for taking in spectacular views.

 All-weather jacket with a hood for protection from sudden showers.

 Cameras with wide lenses for panoramic photos.

The same message might use a different picture bullet for a list of items for a side trip to the Smithsonian. Clearly, these bullets could add interest through color and convey differentiation of the lists as well. Through careful use, picture bullets can help writers present lists that get attention.

- Make the questions stand out (using bullets, numbering, paragraphing, question form).
- End with goodwill words adapted to the individual case.

Contrasting Examples

Illustrating bad and good techniques are the following two routine inquiry messages about office space for a new Pinnacle regional headquarters (recall the introductory situation). The first example follows the indirect pattern that was popular in days gone by. The second is direct. Here they are presented as letters, as indicated by the "Dear" in the salutation and the "Sincerely" closing. In following parts of this book, similar illustrations are presented in email format. As you know, email format uses the conventional subject beginning, name-only salutation, and no complimentary close. The format we use is of little consequence. Our emphasis is on the message, which could be letter, fax, or email. We make this distinction in format only as a matter of clarification.

- Following are bad and good examples. They could be email, fax, or letter.

In addition, the two Case Illustrations show good handling of inquiries. The handwritten comments in the margins of these examples should be especially useful.

As you read the first example below, note that it is marked by a "⊘" icon in the side panel. We use this icon throughout the book wherever we show bad examples. Take care not to confuse the bad with the good examples, which are marked by a "✔" icon.

The Old-Style Indirect Message. The less effective message begins slowly and gives obvious information. Even if one thinks that this information needs to be communicated, it does not deserve the emphasis of the opening sentence. The writer gets to the point of the message in the second paragraph. But there are no questions here—just hints for information. The items of information the writer wants do not stand out but are listed in rapid succession in one sentence. The close is selfish and stiff.

This letter's indirect and vague beginning makes it slow.

Dear Mr. Piper:

We have seen your advertisement for 3,200 square feet of office space in the *Daily Journal.* As we are interested, we would like additional information.

Specifically, we would like to know the interior layout, annual cost, availability of transportation, length of lease agreement, escalation provisions, and any other information you think pertinent.

If the information you give us is favorable, we will inspect the property. Please send your reply.

Sincerely

The Direct and Effective Message. The second example begins directly by asking for information. The explanation is brief but complete. The questions, with explanation worked in where needed, are made to stand out; thus, they help to make answering easy. The message closes with a courteous and appropriate request for quick action.

This direct and orderly letter is better.

Dear Mr. Piper:

Will you please answer the following questions about the 3,200-square-foot office suite advertised in the June 28 issue of the *Daily Journal?* It appears that this space may be suitable for the new regional headquarters we are opening in your city in August.

- Is the layout of these offices suitable for a work force of two administrators, a receptionist, and seven office employees? (If possible, please send us a diagram of the space.)
- What is the annual rental charge?
- Are housekeeping, maintenance, and utilities included?
- What is the nature of the walls and flooring?
- Does the location provide easy access to mass transportation and the airport?
- What are your requirements for length of lease agreement?
- What escalation provisions are included in the lease agreement?

If your answers meet our needs, we would like to arrange a tour of the offices as soon as possible.

Sincerely,

Routine Inquiries (Getting Information about a Training Program) This email message is from a company training director to the director of a management-training program. The company training director has received literature on the program but needs additional information. The message seeks this information.

Direct— a general request sets up the specific question

Numbered questions stand out— helps reader in responding

Reference to website tells what writer knows—helps reader in responding

Explanations worked into questions where needed

Favorable forward look makes goodwill close

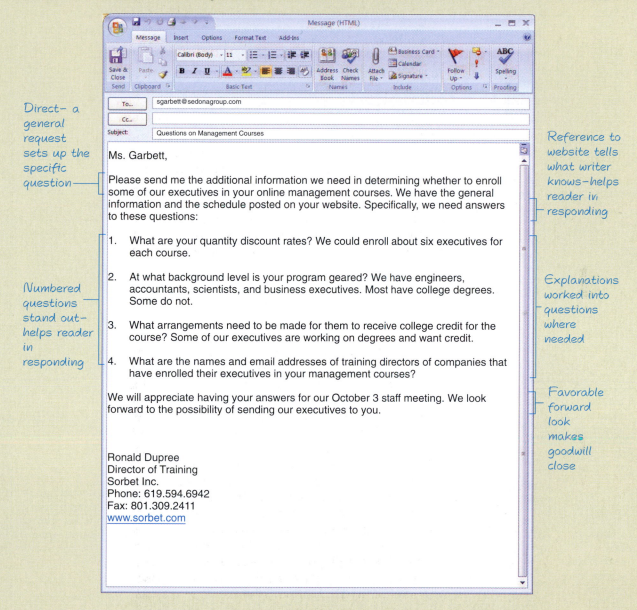

To... sgarbett@sedonagroup.com

Cc...

Subject: Questions on Management Courses

Ms. Garbett,

Please send me the additional information we need in determining whether to enroll some of our executives in your online management courses. We have the general information and the schedule posted on your website. Specifically, we need answers to these questions:

1. What are your quantity discount rates? We could enroll about six executives for each course.

2. At what background level is your program geared? We have engineers, accountants, scientists, and business executives. Most have college degrees. Some do not.

3. What arrangements need to be made for them to receive college credit for the course? Some of our executives are working on degrees and want credit.

4. What are the names and email addresses of training directors of companies that have enrolled their executives in your management courses?

We will appreciate having your answers for our October 3 staff meeting. We look forward to the possibility of sending our executives to you.

Ronald Dupree
Director of Training
Sorbet Inc.
Phone: 619.594.6942
Fax: 801.309.2411
www.sorbet.com

117

Routine Inquiries (An Inquiry about Hotel Accommodations) This fax message to a hotel inquires about meeting accommodations for a professional association. In selecting a hotel, the company's managers need answers to specific questions. The message covers these questions.

Visit us: www.womensmedia.com

TO: Ms. Connie Briggs, Manager
COMPANY: Drake Hotel
FAX: 312.787.1431
DATE: July 17, 2007

FROM: Patti Wolff, Chair of the Site Selection Committee
COMPANY: WomensMedia.com
PHONE: 619.401.9600
FAX: 619.401.9444
EMAIL: pwolff@womensmedia.com

TOTAL PAGES *(including cover):* 1

Direct—a courteous general request that sets up the specific question

COMMENTS: Will you please help WomensMedia.com decide whether we can meet at the Drake hotel?

Explanation of situation provides background information

We have selected Chicago for our 2009 meeting, which will be held August 16, 17, and 18. In addition to the Drake, the conference committee is considering the Marriott and the Hilton. In order to decide, we need the information requested in the following questions.

Can you accommodate a group of about 600 employees on these dates? They will need about 400 rooms.

What are your room rates? We need assurance of having available a minimum of 450 rooms, and we could guarantee 400. Would you be willing to set aside this size block of rooms?

Specific questions— with explanations where needed

What are your charges for conference rooms? We will need eight for each of the three days, and each should have a minimum capacity of 60. On the 18th, for the half-hour business meeting, we will need a large ballroom with a capacity of at least 500.

Questions stand out— in separate paragraphs

Also, will you please send me your menu selections and prices for group dinners? On the 17th we plan our presidential dinner. About 500 can be expected for this event.

Individually tailored goodwill close

As meeting plans must be announced by September, may we have your response right away? We look forward to the possibility of being with you in 2009.

Some Words of Advice on Letter Writing from the Old Masters

A letter is a deliberate and written conversation.

Gracian

Remember this: write only as you would speak; then your letter will be good.

Goethe

There is one golden rule to bear in mind always: that we should try to put ourselves in the position of our correspondent, to imagine his feelings as he writes his letters, and to gauge his reaction as he receives ours. If we put ourselves in the other man's shoes we shall speedily detect how unconvincing our letters can seem, or how much we may be taking for granted.

Sir Ernest Gowers

Do not answer a letter in the midst of great anger.

Chinese proverb

Seeking an epistle hath chieflie this definition hereof, in that it is termed the familiar and mutual task of one friend to another: it seemeth the character thereof should according thereunto be simple, plain and of the lowest and neatest stile utterly devoid of any shadow of lie and lofty speeches.

Angel Day, *The English Secretorie,* 1586
(early book on letter writing)

And to describe the true definition of an Epistle or letter, it is nothing but an Oration written, containing the mynd of the Orator, or wryter, thereby to give to him or them absent, the same that should be declared if they were present.

William Fulwood, *The Enemie of Idlenesse,* 1568
(earliest known book on letter writing in English)

Answering inquiries about people requires the most careful thought, for the lives and rights of human begins are affected.

CHAPTER 6   Directness in Good-News and Neutral Messages

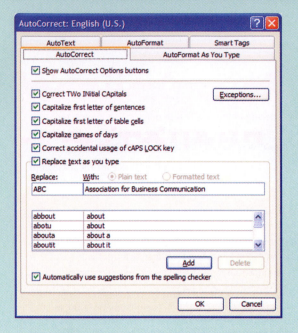

Shortcuts help writers save time and improve quality. One of the easiest to use is the AutoCorrect tool in Word (shown here) or the similar QuickCorrect tool in Word-Perfect. This tool will automatically replace a word entered with another word set up to replace that particular word. The default setting is generally set up to correct common misspellings and typos. However, it also can be used to expand acronyms or phrases used repeatedly.

If you worked frequently with the Association for Business Communication, you might set up the AutoCorrect tool to replace the acronym ABC with the full name, as you see at the left. Not only will this shortcut enable you to save time, but it also will improve the quality by inserting a correctly spelled and typed replacement every time.

GENERAL FAVORABLE RESPONSES

INTRODUCTORY SITUATION

General Favorable Responses

Continue in your role as assistant to the vice president for operations of Pinnacle Manufacturing Company and answer some of the messages sent to you.

Most of the incoming messages you answer favorably. That is, you tell the reader what he or she wants to know. In today's inbox, for example, you have a typical problem of this type. It is a message from a prospective customer for Pinnacle's Chem-Treat paint. In response to an advertisement, this prospective customer asks a number of specific questions about Chem-Treat. Foremost, she wants to know whether the paint is really mildewproof. Do you have evidence of results? Do you guarantee results? Is the paint safe? How much does a gallon cost? Will one coat do the job?

You can answer all but one of the questions positively. Of course, you will report this one negative point (that two coats are needed to do most jobs), but you will take care to give it only the emphasis it deserves. The response will be primarily a good-news message. Because the reader is a good prospect, you will work for the best goodwill effect.

When you answer inquiries favorably, your primary goal is to tell your readers what they want to know. Because their reactions to your goal will be favorable, directness is in order.

Beginning with the Answer

- Begin by answering. If there is one question, answer it; if there are more than one, answer the most important.

As you can deduce from the preceding examples, directness here means giving the readers what they want at the beginning. Thus you begin by answering. When a response involves answering a single question, you begin by answering that question.

"First the good news — if I cure you, I'll become world famous."

SOURCE: From *The Wall Street Journal*—Permission Cartoon Features Syndicate.

When it involves answering two or more questions, one good plan is to begin by answering one of them—preferably the most important. In the Chem-Treat case, this opening would get the response off to a fast start:

Yes, you can use Chem-Treat to prevent mildew.

An alternative possibility is to begin by stating that you are giving the reader what he or she wants—that you are complying with the request. Actually, this approach is really not direct, for it delays giving the information requested. But it is a favorable beginning that does respond to the inquiry, and it does not run the risk of sounding abrupt, which is a criticism of direct beginnings. These examples illustrate this type of beginning:

- Or begin by saying that you are complying with the request.

The following information should tell you what you need to know about Chem-Treat.

Here are the answers to your questions about Chem-Treat.

Identifying the Message Being Answered

Because this message is a response to another message, you should identify the message you are answering. Such identification helps the reader recall or find the message being answered. If you are writing an email response, the original message is appended to your message. Hard-copy messages may use a subject line (Subject: Your April 2nd inquiry about Chem-Treat), as illustrated in Appendix B. Or you can refer to the message incidentally in the text ("as requested in your April 2 inquiry"). Preferably you should make this identification early in your message.

Logically Arranging the Answers

If you are answering just one question, you have little to do after handling that question in the opening. You answer it as completely as the situation requires, and you present whatever explanation or other information is needed. Then you are ready to close the message.

- If one answer is involved, give it directly and completely.

If, on the other hand, you are answering two or more questions, the body of your message becomes a series of answers. As in all clear writing, you should work for a logical order, perhaps answering the questions in the order your reader used in asking them. You may even number your answers, especially if your reader numbered the questions. Or you may decide to arrange your answers by paragraphs so that each stands out clearly.

- If more than one answer is involved, arrange the answers so that each stands out.

Skillfully Handling the Negatives

When your response concerns some bad news along with the good news, you may need to handle the bad news with care. Bad news stands out. Unless you are careful,

- Emphasize favorable responses; subordinate unfavorable responses.

How Routine Responses Were Written in the Late 1800s

The following model letter for answering routine inquiries appears on page 75 of O. R. Palmer's *Type-Writing and Business Correspondence*. Published in 1896, the book was a leader in its field.

Dear Sirs:

Your favor of Dec. 18th, enclosing blue prints for tank, received. In reply thereto we beg to submit the following:

[*Here was a listing of materials for the tank.*]

Trusting that our price may be satisfactory to you, and that we shall be favored with your order, we beg to remain,

Very truly yours,

---

it is likely to receive more emphasis than it deserves. Sometimes you will need to subordinate the bad news and emphasize the good news.

• Place favorable responses at beginnings and ends. Give them more space. Use words skillfully to emphasize them.

In giving proper emphasis to the good- and bad-news parts, you should use the techniques discussed in Chapter 4, especially position. That is, you should place the good news in positions of high emphasis—at paragraph beginnings and endings and at the beginning and ending of the message as a whole. You should place the bad news in secondary positions. In addition, you should use space emphasis to your advantage. This means giving less space to bad-news parts and more space to good-news parts. You also should select words and build sentences that communicate the effect you want. Generally, this means using positive words and avoiding negative words. Your overall goal should be to present the information in your response so that your readers feel good about you and your company.

Considering Extras

• The little extra things you do for the reader will build goodwill.

To create goodwill, as well as future business, you should consider including extras with your answers. These are the things you say and do that are not actually required. Examples are a comment or question showing an interest in the reader's problem, some additional information that may prove valuable, and a suggestion for use of the information supplied. In fact, extras can be anything that does more than skim the surface with hurried, routine answers. Such extras frequently make the difference between success and failure in the goodwill effort.

Illustrations of how extras can be used to strengthen the goodwill effects of a message are as broad as the imagination. A business executive answering a college professor's request for information on company operations could supplement the requested information with suggestions of other sources. A technical writer could amplify highly technical answers with simpler explanations. In the Chem-Treat problem, additional information (say, how much surface area a gallon covers) would be helpful. Such extras encourage readers to take the extra step in building a business relationship with you.

Closing Cordially

As in the other direct messages, your ending should be cordial, friendly words that fit the one case. For example, you might close the Chem-Treat message with these words:

If I can help you further in deciding whether Chem-Treat will meet your needs, please email me again.

Reviewing the Plan

When we review the preceding special considerations, we produce the following plan for the general favorable response message:

- Begin with the answer, or state that you are complying with the request.
- Identify the message being answered either incidentally or in a subject line.
- Continue to give what is wanted in orderly arrangement.
- If negative information is involved, give it reduced emphasis.
- Consider including extras.
- End with a friendly comment adapted to your reader.

Contrasting Illustrations

Contrasting email messages in answer to the Chem-Treat inquiry illustrate the techniques of answering routine inquiries. The first message violates many of the standards set in this and earlier chapters. The second meets the requirements of a good business message. It takes into account the reader's needs and the writer's business goals.

• Following are bad and good examples of response messages.

An Indirect and Hurried Response. The not-so-good message begins indirectly with an obvious statement referring to receipt of the inquiry. Though well intended, the second sentence continues to delay the answers. The second paragraph begins to give the information sought, but it emphasizes the most negative answer by position and by wording. This answer is followed by hurried and routine answers to the other questions asked. Only the barest information is presented. There is no goodwill close.

Subject: Your inquiry of April 3

Ms. Motley

I have received your April 3 message, in which you inquire about our Chem-Treat paint. I want you to know that we appreciate your interest and will welcome your business.

In response to your question about how many coats are needed to cover new surfaces, I regret to report that two are usually required. The paint is mildewproof. We do guarantee it. It has been well tested in our laboratories. It is safe to use as directed.

George Moxley

This email is indirect and ineffective.

Routine Response Message (Favorable Response to a Professor's Request) This email message responds to a professor's request for production records that will be used in a research project. The writer is giving the information wanted but must restrict its use.

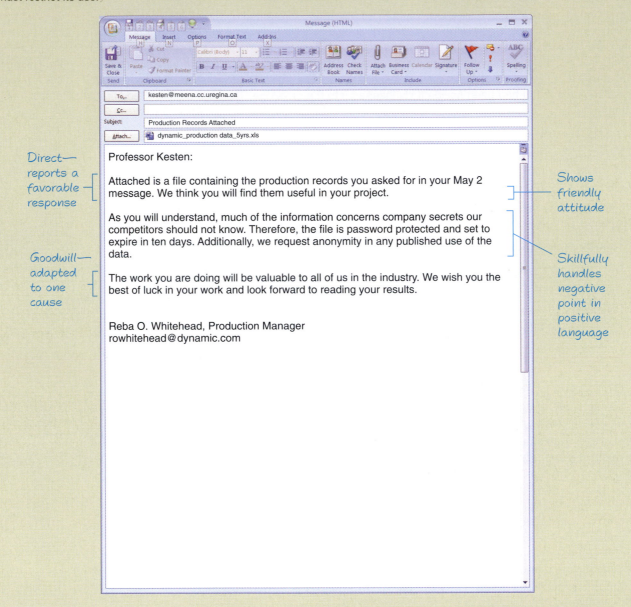

Direct—reports a favorable response

Goodwill—adapted to one cause

Shows friendly attitude

Skillfully handles negative point in positive language

To... kesten@meena.cc.uregina.ca

Cc...

Subject: Production Records Attached

Attach... dynamic_production data_5yrs.xls

Professor Kesten:

Attached is a file containing the production records you asked for in your May 2 message. We think you will find them useful in your project.

As you will understand, much of the information concerns company secrets our competitors should not know. Therefore, the file is password protected and set to expire in ten days. Additionally, we request anonymity in any published use of the data.

The work you are doing will be valuable to all of us in the industry. We wish you the best of luck in your work and look forward to reading your results.

Reba O. Whitehead, Production Manager
rowhitehead@dynamic.com

Routine Response Message (A Request for Detailed Information) Answering an inquiry about a company's experience with executive suites, this letter numbers the answers as the questions were numbered in the inquiry. The opening appropriately sets up the numbered answers with a statement that indicates a favorable response.

Merck & Co., Inc.
One Merck Drive
P.O. Box 100, WS1A-46
Whitehouse Station NJ 08889

 **MERCK**

August 7, 2007

Ms. Ida Casey, Sales Manager
Liberty Insurance Company
1165 Second Ave.
Des Moines, IA 50318-9631

Dear Ms. Casey:

Direct—tells that writer is complying

Following is the information about our use of temporary executive suites you requested in your August 3 fax. For your convenience, I have numbered my responses to correspond with the sequence you used.

Sets up listing

Orderly listing of answers

1. Our executives have mixed feelings about the effectiveness of the center. At the beginning, majority opinion was negative; but it appears now that most of the antagonism has faded.

2. The center definitely has saved us money. Rental costs in the suburbs are much less than downtown costs; annual savings are estimated at nearly 30 percent.

3. The transition did create a morale problem among those remaining downtown even after we assured them that their workloads would not increase.

4. We began using executive suites at the request of several sales representatives who had read about other companies using them. We pilot-tested the program in one territory for a year using volunteers before we implemented it companywide.

5. We are quite willing to share with you the list of facilities we plan to use again. Additionally I am enclosing a copy of our corporate policy, which describes details of use.

Complete yet concise answers

Friendly—adapted to the one case

If after reviewing this information you have any other questions, please write me again. And if you want to contact our sales representatives for firsthand information, please do so. I wish you the best of luck in implementing these suites in your operations.

This extra builds good-will

Sincerely,

David M. Earp

David M. Earp
Office Manager

Enclosure

Effectiveness in Direct Response. The better message begins directly, with the most favorable answer. Then it presents the other answers, giving each the emphasis and positive language it deserves. It subordinates the one negative answer, by position, volume of treatment, and structure. More pleasant information follows the negative answer. The close is goodwill talk, with some subtle selling strategy thrown in. "We know that you'll enjoy the long-lasting beauty of this mildewproof paint" points positively to purchase and successful use of the product.

This direct email does a better job.

Subject: Your April 3 inquiry about Chem-Treat

Ms. Motley

Yes, Chem-Treat paint will prevent mildew or we will give you back your money. We know it works because we have tested it under all common conditions. In every case, it proved successful.

When you carefully follow the directions on each can, Chem-Treat paint is guaranteed safe. As the directions state, you should use Chem-Treat only in a well-ventilated room—never in a closed, unvented area.

One gallon of Chem-Treat is usually enough for one-coat coverage of 500 square feet of previously painted surface. For the best results on new surfaces, you will want to apply two coats. For such surfaces, you should figure about 200 square feet per gallon for a long-lasting coating.

We sincerely appreciate your interest in Chem-Treat, Ms. Motley. This mildewproof paint will bring you five years or more of beautiful protection.

George Moxley

ADJUSTMENT GRANTS

INTRODUCTORY SITUATION

Adjustment Grants

Continuing in your role with Pinnacle, this time you find on your computer an email message from an unhappy customer. It seems that Ms. Bernice Watson, owner of Tri-Cities Hardware, is upset because some of the 30 Old London lampposts she ordered from Pinnacle arrived in damaged condition. "The glass is broken in 17 of the units," she writes, "obviously because of poor packing." She had ordered the lights for a special sale. In fact, she notes, she had even featured them in her advertising. The sale begins next Friday. She wants a fast adjustment—either the lamps by sale time or her money back.

Of course, you will grant Ms. Watson's request. You will send her an email message saying that the goods are on the way. And because you want to keep this good customer, you will try to regain any lost confidence with an honest explanation of the problem. This message is classified as an adjustment grant.

- Good news in adjustment grants justifies directness.

When you can grant an adjustment, the situation is a happy one for your customer. You are correcting an error. You are doing what you were asked to do. As in other positive situations, a message written in the direct order is appropriate.

Considering Special Needs

- Follow the good-news pattern, but consider two special needs.

The adjustment-grant message has much in common with the message types previously discussed. You begin directly with the good-news answer. You refer to the message

126   PART 3   Basic Patterns of Business Messages

In most face-to-face business relations, people communicate with courteous directness. You should write most business messages this way.

you are answering. And you close on a friendly note. But because the situation stems from an unhappy experience, you have two special needs. One is the need to overcome the negative impressions that the experience leading to the adjustment has formed in the reader's mind. The other is the need to regain any confidence in your company, its products, or its service that the reader may have lost from the experience.

Need to Overcome Negative Impressions. To understand the first need, just place yourself in the reader's shoes. As the reader sees it, something bad has happened—goods have been damaged, equipment has failed, or sales have been lost. The experience has not been pleasant. Granting the claim will take care of much of the problem, but some negative thoughts may remain. You need to work to overcome any such thoughts.

- Negative impressions remain; so overcome them.

You can attempt to do this using words that produce positive effects. For example, in the opening you can do more than just give the affirmative answer. You can add goodwill, as in this example:

- Overcome them through positive writing.

> The enclosed check for $89.77 is our way of proving to you that we value your satisfaction highly.

Throughout the message you should avoid words that recall unnecessarily the bad situation you are correcting. You especially want to avoid the negative words that could be used to describe what went wrong—words such as *mistake, trouble, damage, broken,* and *loss.* Even general words such as *problem, difficulty,* and *misunderstanding* can create unpleasant connotations.

Also negative are the apologies often included in these messages. Even though well intended, the somewhat conventional "we sincerely regret the inconvenience caused you . . ." type of comment is of questionable value. It emphasizes the negative happenings for which the apology is made. If you sincerely believe that you owe an apology, or that one is expected, you can apologize and risk the negative effect. But do it early and move on, and don't repeat it at the end. In most instances, however, your efforts to correct the problem will show adequate concern for your reader's interests.

- Even apologies may be negative.

Need to Regain Lost Confidence. Except in cases in which the cause of the difficulty is routine or incidental, you also will need to regain the reader's lost confidence. Just what you must do and how you must do it depend on the facts of the situation. You will need to survey the situation to see what they are. If something can be done to correct a bad procedure or a product defect, you should do it. Then you should tell your reader what has been done as convincingly and positively as you can.

- Regain lost confidence through convincing explanation.

If what went wrong was a rare, unavoidable event, you should explain this. Sometimes you will need to explain how a product should be used or cared for. Sometimes you will need to resell the product. Of course, whatever you do must be ethical—supported by truth and integrity.

Reviewing the Plan

Applying these two special needs to the general plan previously reviewed, we come up with this specific plan for the message granting an adjustment:

- Begin directly—with the good news.
- Incidentally identify the correspondence that you are answering.
- Avoid negatives that recall the problem.
- Regain lost confidence through explanation or corrective action.
- End with a friendly, positive comment.

Contrasting Adjustments

- Following are examples of bad and good adjustment messages.

The techniques previously discussed are illustrated by the following adjustment messages. The first, with its indirect order and grudging tone, is ineffective. The directness and positiveness of the second clearly make it the better message.

A Slow and Negative Treatment. The ineffective message begins with an obvious comment about receiving the claim. It recalls vividly what went wrong and then painfully explains what happened. As a result, the good news is delayed for an additional paragraph. Finally, after two delaying paragraphs, the message gets to the good news. Though well intended, the close leaves the reader with a reminder of the trouble.

This email is indirect and negative.

Subject: Your broken Old London lights

Ms. Watson,

We have received your May 1 claim reporting that our shipment of Old London lamppost lights reached you with 17 broken units. We regret the inconvenience caused you and can understand your unhappiness.

Following our standard practice, we investigated the situation thoroughly. Apparently the fault is the result of an inexperienced temporary employee's negligence. We have taken corrective measures to assure that future shipments will be packed more carefully.

I am pleased to report that we are sending replacements today. They should reach you before your sale begins. Our driver will pick up the broken units when he makes delivery.

Again, we regret all the trouble caused you.

Stephanie King

The Direct and Positive Technique. The better message uses the subject line to identify the transaction. The opening words tell the reader what she most wants to hear in a positive way that adds to the goodwill tone of the message. With reader-viewpoint explanation, the message then reviews what happened. Without a single negative word, it makes clear what caused the problem and what has been done to prevent its recurrence. After handling the essential matter of picking up the broken lamps, the message closes with positive resale talk far removed from the problem.

Subject: Your May 1 report on invoice 1248

Ms. Watson,

Seventeen carefully packed Old London lamppost lamps should reach your sales floor in time for your Saturday promotion. Our driver left our warehouse today with instructions to special deliver them to you on Friday.

Because your satisfaction with our service and products is our top priority, we have thoroughly checked our shipping procedures. It appears that the shipment to you was packed by a temporary employee who was filling in for a hospitalized veteran packer. We now have our veteran packer back at work, and have taken measures to ensure better performance by our temporary staff.

As you know, the Old London lamppost lights have become one of the hottest products in the lighting field. Their authentic Elizabethan design has made them a smashing success. We are confident they will play their part in the success of your sale.

Stephanie King

This message is direct and positive.

ORDER ACKNOWLEDGMENTS

INTRODUCTORY SITUATION

Order Acknowledgments

The next work you take from your in-box is an order for paints and painting supplies. It is from Mr. Tony Lee of the Central City Paint Company, a new customer whom Pinnacle has been trying to attract for months. You usually acknowledge orders with routine messages, but this case is different. You feel the need to welcome this new customer and to cultivate him for future sales.

After checking your current inventory and making certain that the goods will be on the way to Lee today, you are ready to write him a special acknowledgment.

Acknowledgments are sent to let people who order goods know the status of their orders. Most acknowledgments are routine. They simply tell when the goods are being shipped. Many companies use form or computer-generated messages for such situations. Some use printed, standard notes with check-off or write-in blanks. But individually written acknowledgments are sometimes justified, especially with new accounts or large orders.

Skillfully composed acknowledgments can do more than acknowledge orders, though this task remains their primary goal. These messages also can build goodwill through their warm, personal, human tone. They can make the reader feel good about doing business with a company that cares and want to continue doing business with that company. To maintain this goodwill for repeat customers, you will want to revise your form acknowledgments regularly.

- Businesses usually acknowledge orders with forms, but they sometimes use written messages.

- Acknowledgments can serve to build goodwill.

Adjustment Grant Messages (Explaining a Human Error) This email message grants the action requested in the claim of a customer who received a leather computer case that was monogrammed incorrectly. The writer has no excuse, for human error was to blame. His explanation is positive and convincing.

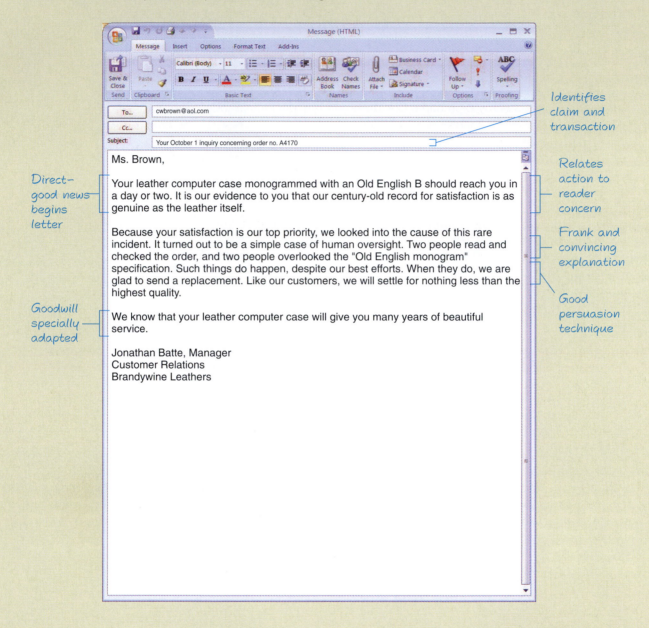

Annotations (left):
- Direct—good news begins letter
- Goodwill specially adapted

Annotations (right):
- Identifies claim and transaction
- Relates action to reader concern
- Frank and convincing explanation
- Good persuasion technique

Email content:

To... cwbrown@aol.com

Subject: Your October 1 inquiry concerning order no. A4170

Ms. Brown,

Your leather computer case monogrammed with an Old English B should reach you in a day or two. It is our evidence to you that our century-old record for satisfaction is as genuine as the leather itself.

Because your satisfaction is our top priority, we looked into the cause of this rare incident. It turned out to be a simple case of human oversight. Two people read and checked the order, and two people overlooked the "Old English monogram" specification. Such things do happen, despite our best efforts. When they do, we are glad to send a replacement. Like our customers, we will settle for nothing less than the highest quality.

We know that your leather computer case will give you many years of beautiful service.

Jonathan Batte, Manager
Customer Relations
Brandywine Leathers

Tables Help Writers Organize Data for Easy Reading

Setting up tables within a document is an easy task. The tables feature allows writers to create tables as well as import spreadsheet and database files. In both instances, you can arrange information in columns and rows, inserting detail in the cells. Headings can be formatted and formulas can be entered in the cells. The table you see here could be one the writer created for use in a favorable response to an inquiry about possible locations for a meeting in Chicago.

Organizing information with tables makes it easier for both the writer and the reader. A careful writer will include column and row labels as needed, helping the reader extract information both quickly and accurately.

Hotel Name	Address	Convention Room Rate for Standard Rooms	Rating
Marriott Chicago Downtown	540 North Michigan Avenue, Chicago, IL 60611-3869	$187	☆☆☆
Drake Hotel	140 East Walton Street, Chicago, IL 60611-1545	$229	☆☆☆☆
Palmer House Hilton	17 East Monroe Street, Chicago, IL 60603-5605	$162	☆☆☆☆

Using Directness and Goodwill Building

Like the other preceding messages, the acknowledgment message appropriately begins with its good news—that the goods are being shipped. And it ends on a good-will note. Except when some of the goods ordered must be delayed, the remainder of the message is devoted to goodwill building. This goodwill building can begin in the opening by emphasizing receipt of the goods rather than merely sending the goods:

> The Protect-O paints and supplies you ordered April 4 should reach you by Wednesday. They are leaving our Walden warehouse today by Arrow Freight.

It also can include a warm expression of thanks for the order, especially when a first order is involved. Anything else you can say that will be helpful to the reader is appropriate in this regard—information about new products, services, or such. Specially adapted forward look to continued business relations is an appropriate goodwill gesture in the close.

• Directness and goodwill mark the message.

Being Tactful with Shipment Delays

Sometimes the task of acknowledging is complicated by your inability to send the goods requested right away. You could be out of them; or perhaps the reader did not give you all the information you need to send the goods. In either case, a delay is involved. In some cases, delays are routine and expected and do not pose a serious problem. In others, they can lead to major disappointments. When this is the case, you will need to use tact.

Using tact involves minimizing the negative effect of the message. In the case of a vague order, for example, you should handle the information you need without appearing to accuse the reader of giving insufficient information. To illustrate, you gain nothing by writing "You failed to specify the color of phones you want." But you gain goodwill by writing "So that we can send you precisely the phones you want, please check your choice of colors on the space below." This sentence handles the matter positively and makes the action easy to take. It also shows a courteous attitude.

• When goods must be delayed, handle this news tactfully.

• In vague orders, request the needed information positively.

Similarly, you can handle back-order information tactfully by emphasizing the positive part of the message. For example, instead of writing "We can't ship the ink jet cartridges until the 9th," you can write "We will rush the ink jet cartridges to you as soon as our stock is replenished by a shipment due May 9." If the back-order period is longer than the customer expects or longer than the 30 days allowed by law, you may choose to give your customer an alternative. You could offer a substitute product or service. Giving the customer a choice builds goodwill. A more complete discussion of how to handle such negative news is provided in Chapter 7.

Summarizing the Structure of Order Acknowledgments

Applying these special considerations to the general plan for direct messages, we arrive at this specific plan for order acknowledgments:

- Give status of order, acknowledging incidentally.
- Include some goodwill—sales talk, reselling, or such efforts.
- Include a thank-you.
- Report frankly or handle tactfully problems with vague or back orders.
- Close with adapted, friendly comment.

Contrasting Acknowledgments

The following two messages show bad and good technique in acknowledging Mr. Lee's order. As you would expect, the good version follows the plan described in the preceding paragraphs.

Slow Route to a Favorable Message. The bad example begins indirectly, emphasizing receipt of the order. Although intended to produce goodwill, the second sentence further delays what the reader wants most to hear. Moreover, the letter is written from the writer's point of view (note the we-emphasis).

This one delays the important news.

Dear Mr. Lee:

Your April 4 order for $1,743.30 worth of Protect-O paints and supplies has been received. We are pleased to have this nice order and hope that it marks the beginning of a long relationship.

As you instructed, we will bill you for this amount. We are shipping the goods today by Blue Darter Motor Freight.

We look forward to your future orders.

Sincerely,

Fast-Moving Presentation of the Good News. The better message begins directly, telling Mr. Lee that he is getting what he wants. The remainder of the message is a customer welcome and subtle selling. Notice the good use of reader emphasis and positive language. The message closes with a note of appreciation and a friendly, forward look.

Dear Mr. Lee:

Your selection of Protect-O paints and supplies was shipped today by Blue Darter Freight and should reach you by Wednesday. As you requested, we are sending you an invoice for $1,743.30, including sales tax.

Because this is your first order from us, I welcome you to the Protect-O circle of dealers. Our representative, Ms. Cindy Wooley, will call from time to time to offer whatever assistance she can. She is a highly competent technical adviser on paint and painting.

Here in the home plant we also will do what we can to help you profit from Protect-O products. We'll do our best to give you the most efficient service. And we'll continue to develop the best possible paints—like our new Chem-Treat line. As you will see from the enclosed brochure, Chem-Treat is a real breakthrough in mildew protection.

We genuinely appreciate your order, Mr. Lee. We are determined to serve you well in the years ahead.

Sincerely,

This message is better.

CLAIMS

INTRODUCTORY SITUATION

Claims

Introduce yourself to claim messages by playing the role of Ms. Bernice Watson, one of Pinnacle's customers and the owner of Tri-Cities Hardware. For the past few days you have been preparing for your annual spring promotion. You have ordered widely, and you have advertised the items to be featured. All has gone well until today when Pinnacle's shipment of Old London lamppost lights arrived. You ordered 30, and the glass coverings on 17 of them are broken. Obviously, the lamps were poorly packed.

Now you must make a fast claim for adjustment. You will send Pinnacle an email message requesting replacement by the sale date or your money back. This message is classified as a claim.

When something goes wrong between a business and its customers, usually someone begins an effort to correct the situation. Typically, the offended party calls the matter to the attention of those responsible. This claim can be made in person, by telephone, or by written message (email or letter). Our concern here is how to make it in a written message. You would probably choose this more formal medium if you wanted a record of the interchange or if you were not on informal terms with the recipient.

• Claims are written to collect for damages.

Using Directness for Bad News

Claim situations may appear to be bad-news situations. As you may know, usually bad-news situations are handled in indirect order. But claims are exceptions—for two good reasons. First, most businesspeople want to know when something is wrong with their products or services so they can correct the matter. Thus, there is no reason for delay. Second, as we have noted, directness lends strength, and strength in a claim enhances the likelihood of a satisfactory response.

• Use directness for this bad news because (1) the reader wants to know and (2) it adds strength.

Choosing the Right Tone

Your goal in a claim message is to convince your recipient that you deserve some kind of compensation or remedy for a situation that has occurred. But even if you

• Your tone should suggest the reasonableness of reader and writer.

are completely in the right, you will not advance your cause with accusatory, one-sided language. When writing this kind of message, project an image of yourself as a reasonable person. Just as importantly, project an image of the reader as a reasonable person. Give him or her a chance to show that, if presented with the facts, he or she will do the right thing. Do not give in to the temptation to blame or whine. Keep your tone as objective as you can while also making sure that the reader understands the problems caused by the situation. Focus as much as possible on facts, not feelings.

Identifying the Problem in a Direct Beginning

• Identify the problem in the direct beginning.

Because of their uniqueness, claim situations involve more special concerns than other direct-order messages. First is the need to identify the transactions involved. This you can do early in the message as a part of the direct beginning that tells what went wrong. One way is to put the identification in the subject head in an email message or in the subject line of a letter, as in this example:

> Subject: Damaged condition of fire extinguishers on arrival, your invoice C13144

If you use a subject line, choose your words with care. Such negatively charged words as *complaint* or *disappointment* can put your readers on the defensive before you've even had a chance to make your case.

Stating the Problem Directly

• State the problem clearly in the opening.

The beginning words appropriately state the problem. They should be courteous yet firm. And they should cover the problem completely, giving enough information to permit the reader to judge the matter. If there were consequences of what happened, you may benefit your case by naming them. This beginning sentence illustrates the point:

> The Model H freezer (Serial No. 713129) that we bought from you September 17 suddenly quit working, ruining $517 of frozen foods in the process.

Giving Choice in Correcting the Error

• Handle the claim by either stating what you want or letting the reader decide.

The facts you present should prove your claim. So your next step is to follow logically with the handling of the claim. How you handle the claim, however, is a matter for you to decide. You have two choices: You can state what you want (money back, replacement), or you can leave the decision to the reader. Because most businesspeople want to do the right thing, often the latter choice is the better one.

Overcoming Negativeness with a Fair-Minded Close

• Your closing words should show your cordial attitude.

Your final friendly words should leave no doubt that you are trying to maintain a positive relationship. For added strength, when strength is needed to support a claim, you could express appreciation for what you seek. This suggestion does not support use of the timeworn "Thanking you in advance." Instead, say something like "I would be grateful if you could get the new merchandise to me in time for my Friday sale." Whatever final words you choose, they should clearly show that yours is a firm yet cordial and fair request.

Outlining the Claim Message

Summarizing the foregoing points, we arrive at this outline for the claim message:

- Begin directly. Tell what is wrong.
- Identify the situation (invoice number, product information, etc.) in the text or in a subject line.
- Present enough of the facts to permit a decision.
- Seek corrective action.
- End positively—friendly but firm.

Order Acknowledgment This routine acknowledgment illustrates good practice in Internet selling. It gives the customer all that is needed to track the status of the order.

To: marie.flatley@sdsu.edu
From: ship-confirm@amazon.com
Subject: Your Amazon.com order has shipped (#002-0212016-9528012)
Date: Sun, 11 May 2007 07:59:16 +0000 (GMT)

Greetings from Amazon.com.

Direct, tells that the goods are on the way.

We thought you'd like to know that we shipped your gift today, and that this completes your order.

Thanks for shopping at Amazon.com, and we hope to see you again soon.

You can track the status of this order, and all your orders, online by visiting Your Account at http://www.amazon.com/your-account/

There you can:
* Track order and shipment status
* Review estimated delivery dates
* Cancel unshipped items
* Return items
* And do much more

Presents additional ordering information with you-viewpoint.

The following items were included in this shipment:

Qty Item   Price Shipped Subtotal
----
1   Google Hacks $17.47 1 $17.47
1   First Look Microsoft Office 20 $13.99 1 $13.99
1   Graphically Speaking: A Visual $23.09 1 $23.09

Item Subtotal: $54.55
Shipping & Handling: $5.97

Giftwrap: no charge
Super Saver Discount: −$5.97

Total: $54.55

Reminds reader of the details of the order and shipping instructions.

This shipment was sent to:

Marie E. Flatley
12912 Via Grimaldi
Del Mar CA 92014

via USPS (5-9 business days).

For your reference, the number you can use to track your package is 91020493900094076192782. You can refer to our Web site's Help page or:

http://www.amazon.com/wheresmystuff

to retrieve current tracking information. Please note that tracking information may not be available immediately.

Gives helpful information about how to track the order.

If you've explored the links on the Your Account page but still need to get in touch with us about your order, you can find an e-mail form in our Help department at http://www.amazon.com/help/

Please note: This e-mail was sent from a notification-only address that cannot accept incoming e-mail. Please do not reply to this message.

Invites inquiries about the order.

Thank you for shopping with us

Ends with an expression of gratefulness

Amazon.com
Earth's Biggest Selection
http://www.amazon.com/

Order Acknowledgment Letters (Acknowledgment with a Problem) This letter concerns an order that cannot be handled exactly as the customer would like. Some items are being sent, but one must be placed on back order and one cannot be shipped because the customer did not give the information needed. The letter skillfully handles the negative points.

LOWE'S
Companies, Inc.

One of the "100 Best Companies to Work for in America"

October 7, 2007

Mr. Fred K. Fletcher, President
Fletcher Machine Works
4772 Worth Road
Detroit, MI 48201

Dear Mr. Fletcher:

Direct—tells about goods being sent

By noon tomorrow, your three new Baskin motors and one Dawson 110 compressor should reach your Meadowbrook shops. As you requested, we marked them for your West Side loading dock and sent them by Warren Motor Express. *Positive emphasis on delivery*

Negative information presented with you-viewpoint emphasis

So that we can be certain of sending you the one handcart for your special uses, will you please review the enclosed description of the two models available? As you will see, the Model M is our heavy-duty design; but its extra weight is not justified for all jobs. When you have made your choice, please mark it on the enclosed card and mail the card to us. We'll send your choice right away. *Helpful explanation—aids reader in making choice*

Tactful—emphasis on receipt of goods

Your three dozen 317 T-clamps should reach you by the 13th. As you may know, these very popular clamps have been in short supply for some time now, but we have been promised a limited order by the 11th. We are marking three dozen for rush shipment to you.

We are always pleased to do business with Fletcher Machine Works and will continue to serve you with quality industrial equipment. *Friendly forward look*

Sincerely,

Shannon E. Kurrus

Shannon E. Kurrus
Sales Manager

SEK:bim
Enclosure

Contrasting Examples of Claim Messages

The following two email messages show contrasting ways of handling Tri-Cities Hardware's problem with the Old London lamppost lights. The first is slow and harsh. The second is courteous, yet to the point and firm.

• The following contrasting messages show bad and good handling of a claim.

A Slow and Harsh Message. The first message starts slowly with a long explanation of the situation. Some of the details in the beginning sentence are helpful, but they do not deserve the emphasis that this position gives them. The problem is not described until the second paragraph. The wording here is clear but much too strong. The words are angry and insulting, and they talk down to the reader. Such words are more likely to produce resistance than acceptance. The negative writing continues into the close, leaving a bad final impression.

This message is slow and harsh.

Subject: Our Order No. 7135

Mr. Goetz

As your records will show, on March 7 we ordered 30 Old London lamppost lights (our Order No. 7135). The units were received by us on March 14 (your Invoice No. 715C).

At the time of delivery, our shipping and receiving supervisor noticed that some of the cartons had broken glass inside. Upon further inspection, he found that the glass on 17 of the lamps was broken. Further inspection showed that your packers had been negligent as there was insufficient packing material in each carton.

It is hard for me to understand a shipping system that permits such errors to take place. We had advertised these lights for our annual spring promotion, which begins next Saturday. We want the lights by then or our money back.

Megan Adami

A Firm Yet Courteous Message. The second message follows the plan suggested in preceding paragraphs. A subject line quickly identifies the situation. The message begins with a clear statement of the problem. Next, in a tone that shows firmness without anger, it tells what went wrong. Then it requests a specific remedy and asks what to do with the damaged goods. The ending uses subtle persuasion by implying confidence in the reader. The words used here leave no doubt about the writer's interest in a continued relationship.

This better message follows text recommendations.

Subject: Broken glass in 17 Old London lamppost lights received

Mr. Goetz

Seventeen of the 30 lamppost lights we received today arrived with glass coverings broken.

At the time of delivery, our shipping and receiving manager noticed broken glass in some of the cartons. Upon further inspection, he found that 17 were in this condition. It was apparent to him that insufficient packing material was the cause of the problem.

Because we had advertised these lights for our annual spring promotion, which begins Saturday, please get replacements to us by that date. If delivery is not possible, we request a refund for the broken units. In either event, please instruct me on what to do with the damaged lamps.

I am aware, of course, that situations like this will occur in spite of all precautions. And I am confident that you will replace the units with your usual courtesy.

Megan Adami

Claim Letters (Polite Firmness in a Claim about Defective Carpeting) In this letter a hotel manager presents a claim about defective carpeting. She makes the claim directly and forcefully—yet politely. She explains the problem clearly and emphasizes the effect of the damage.

September 17, 2007

Mr. Luther R. Ferguson, President
Rich Carpet, Inc.
13171 Industrial Boulevard
Seattle, WA 98107

Dear Mr. Ferguson:

Direct statement of problem

Subject: Color fading of your Kota-Tuff carpeting, your invoice 3147 dated January 3, 2007.

Clearly states problem and identifies transaction

Emphasis on effect

The Kota-Tuff carpeting you installed for us last January has faded badly and is an eyesore in our hotel pool area.

As you can see in the enclosed photograph, the original forest green color now is spotted with rings of varying shades of white and green. The spotting is especially heavy in areas adjacent to the pool. Probably water has caused the damage. But your written warranty says that the color will "withstand the effects of sun and water."

Explains nature and extent of defect

Establishes case firmly

Suggests solution

Because the product clearly has not lived up to the warranty, we ask that you replace the Kota-Tuff with a more suitable carpeting. If you are unable to find a satisfactory carpeting, we request a refund of the full purchase price, including installation.

Justifies claim

I will appreciate your usual promptness in correcting this problem.

Sincerely,

Luella E. Dabbs
Luella E. Dabbs
Manager

tos
Enclosure (photograph)

2-201 East 15th Street
North Vancouver, BC V7M 1S2
604-678-9080
FAX: 604-678-9076

Truthful (?) Reporting in Recommendation Letters

Some choice double entendres (two-meaning sentences) to be used in letters of recommendation when you don't want to lie or to hurt the person involved:

To describe a lazy person: "In my opinion, you will be very fortunate to get this person to work for you."

To describe an inept person: "I most enthusiastically recommend this candidate with no qualifications whatsoever."

To describe an ex-employee who had problems getting along with fellow workers: "I am pleased to say that this candidate is a former colleague of mine."

To describe a job applicant who is not worth further consideration: "I would urge you to waste no time in making this candidate an offer of employment."

To describe a person with lackluster credentials: "All in all, I cannot say enough good things about this candidate or recommend him too highly."

Robert Thornton

INQUIRIES AND RESPONSES ABOUT JOB APPLICANTS

Once widely written, messages seeking and reporting information about prospective employees are rarely written today. For one reason, many companies refuse to provide such information because of legal concerns. Another reason is the advantage the telephone has for such purposes. Often information will be given orally that would not be put in writing. Even so, some of these messages are written. They are appropriately written according to the direct order outlines presented previously for the direct request and direct response. But some special considerations for each message type are involved.

Because this exchange of information concerns the lives of people, in your inquiries you should take special care to protect the rights of these people. You should make the request only if the subject has authorized it. You should ask only questions related to the job involved. You should avoid personal questions (race, religion, gender, disabilities, pregnancy, and such). You should make it clear that the information given will be held in confidence. And you should structure the inquiry around the requirements of the job involved.

Your responses to these inquiries should clearly rely on facts. If you give an opinion, clearly label it as opinion; but even opinions should be based on facts. In reporting you should strive to give every bit of information the emphasis it is due, knowing that negative information tends to stand out. You should respect the personal considerations reviewed in the preceding paragraph. And above all, you should take care to present an accurate report—one that is fair to the applicant, to the prospective employer, and to you.

- These two message forms are rarely written today. Legal reasons and the telephone explain why.

- Personnel inquiries should protect the subject's rights.

- Responses should be based on facts, each given its proper weight.

OPERATIONAL COMMUNICATIONS

As Chapter 1 explained, operational communications are those messages that stay within a business. They are messages to and from employees that get the work of the organization done. The memorandums discussed in Chapter 5 are one form of operational communication. Internal email messages are another. And so are the various documents posted on bulletin boards, mailed to employees, uploaded on intranets, or distributed as handouts.

The formality of operational messages ranges widely. At one extreme are the informal, casual memorandum and email exchanges between employees concerning

- Operational communications are messages to and from employees.

- They range from highly informal to formal.

work matters. At the other are formal documents communicating company policies, directives, procedures, and such. Then, of course, there are the various stages of formality in between.

The documents at the bottom of the formality range typically resemble conversation. Usually they are quick responses to work needs. Rarely is there time or need for careful construction and wording. The goal is simply to exchange the information needed in the conduct of the company's work. Because of the informal nature of these messages, we give no instruction on their construction except to emphasize that clarity of expression and courtesy should prevail.

Frankness describes the tone of these highly casual messages as well as many of the messages at more formal levels. The participants exchange information, views, and such forthrightly. They know that the audience will interpret their words impersonally. They write with the understanding that all participants are working for a common goal—usually what is best for the company. They know that people working together in business situations want and expect straightforward communication.

Messages in the midlevel formality range tend to resemble the messages discussed earlier in this chapter. Usually they require more care in construction. And usually they follow a direct pattern. The most common arrangement begins with the most important point and works down. Thus, a typical beginning sentence is a topic (theme) statement. In messages in memorandum form, the opening repeats the subject-line information and includes the additional information needed to identify the situation. The remainder of the message consists of a logical, orderly arrangement of the information covered. When the message consists of items in sequence, the items can be numbered and presented in this sequence.

Suggestions for writing the somewhat formal internal messages are much the same as those for writing the messages covered previously. Clarity, correctness, and courtesy should guide your efforts. The following example of a hard-copy memorandum illustrates these qualities. It is moderately formal, distinctly above casual writing. Yet it is conversational. It is clearly written and organized in direct order, beginning with the objective and then systematically and clearly covering the vital bits of information. It is straightforward yet courteous.

DATE: April 1, 2007

TO: Remigo Ruiz

FROM: Becky Pharr

SUBJECT: Request for cost information concerning meeting at Timber Creek Lodge

As we discussed in my office today, please get the necessary cost information for conducting our annual sales meeting at the Timber Creek Lodge, Timber Creek Village, Colorado. Our meeting will begin on the morning of Monday, June 5; we should arrange to arrive on the 4th. We will leave after a brief morning session on June 9.

Specifially, we'll need the following information:

- Travel costs for all 43 participants, including air travel to Denver and ground travel between the airport and the lodge. I have listed the names and home stations of the 43 participants on the attached sheet.
- Room and board costs for the five-day period, including cost with and without dinner at the lodge. As you know, we are considering the possibility of allowing participants to purchase dinners at nearby restaurants.
- Costs for recreational facilities at the lodge.
- Costs for meeting rooms and meeting equipment (projectors, lecterns, and such). We will need a room large enough to accommodate our 43 participants.

I'd like to have the information by April 15. If you need additional information, please contact me at ×3715 or Pharr@yahoo.com.

The most formal of the operational messages deserve our special attention. These are the messages presenting policies, directives, and procedures. Usually written

---

- The highly informal messages are like conversation—frank and casual.

- Frankness is expected in most internal exchanges.

- Most follow a direct pattern.

- The writing should follow the techniques previously covered.

- The memorandum begins directly–with the objective. The necessary explanation follows.

- Then the specific information needed is listed in logical order.

- The memorandum ends with courteous words.
- The most formal operational messages are policies, directives, and procedures.

by executives for their subordinates, these administrative messages are often compiled in manuals, perhaps kept in loose-leaf form and updated as new material is developed.

Some of these more formal documents are designed to keep employees informed about the company. Convincing research strongly supports the value of these messages about the company.[1] It shows that employees want to know more about their roles in the company's successes, their company's customers, their compensation plans, their company's products, and more. And they want to get this information from their bosses. As the study also shows that the employees prefer these messages in hard copy, memorandums appear to be appropriate for these messages.

- Others present company information employees want to know.

As we have implied, these higher-level messages are more formally written than most of the internal communications. Their official status explains why. Usually they follow a direct order, although the nature of their contents can require variations. The goal should be to arrange the information in the most logical order for quick understanding. Since the information frequently involves a sequence of information bits, numbering these bits can be desirable. And since these documents must be clearly understood and followed, the writing must be clear to all, including those with low verbal skills. The following example illustrates these desirable qualities:

- These official documents are more formally written.

DATE: June 10, 2007

TO: All Employees

FROM: Terry Boedeker, President

SUBJECT: Energy conservation

To help us keep costs low, the following conservation measures are effective immediately:

- The beginning is direct and immediately identifies the situation.

- Thermostats will be set to maintain temperatures of 78 degrees Fahrenheit throughout the air-conditioning season.
- Air conditioners will be shut off in all buildings at 4 PM Monday through Friday.
- Air conditioners will be started as late as possible each morning so as to have the buildings at the appropriate temperature within 30 minutes after the start of the workday.
- Lighting levels will be reduced to approximately 50 to 60 foot-candles in all work areas. Corridor lighting will be reduced to 5 to 10 foot-candles.
- Outside lighting levels will be reduced as much as possible without compromising safety and security.

- Clear writing and listing result in good readability.

In addition, will each of you help in conservation areas under your control? Specifically, I ask that you do the following:

- Separate listing of other measures gives order and enchances understanding.

Turn off lights not required in performing work.

Keep windows closed when the cooling system is operating.

Turn off all computer monitors and printers at the end of the day.

I am confident that these measures will reduce our energy use significantly. Your efforts to follow them will be greatly appreciated.

- Closing personal remarks add to effectiveness.

Even though this message is straightforward, note the writer's courtesy and his use of *us* and *our*. When writing direct messages, skillful managers make use of such strategies for maintaining good relations with employees. Remembering this goal becomes especially important in situations where managers have news to convey or requests to make that employees may not be ready to accept. In fact, in these situations an indirect order will be more appropriate, as Chapters 7 and 8 will discuss. For most operational communication, however, the direct order will be both expected and appreciated.

- Sometimes indirectness may be better, as discussed in following chapters.

---

[1] "Study Offers Insights on Effective Communication from the Perspective of Employees," *Towers Perrin Monitor,* January 2005, Towers Perrin, 06 May 2006 <http://www.towersperrin.com/hrservices/webcache/towers/TP_Monitor/jsp/showdoc_fromtowers.jsp?webc=../../TP_Monitor/2005/01/articles/mon_article_0105c.htm>.

OTHER DIRECT MESSAGE SITUATIONS

- Other direct message situations occur.

- You should be able to handle them by applying the techniques covered in this chapter.

In the preceding pages, we have covered the most common direct message situations. Others occur, of course. You should be able to handle them with the techniques that have been explained and illustrated.

In handling such situations, remember that whenever possible, you should get to the goal of the message right away. You should cover any other information needed in good logical order. You should carefully choose words that convey just the right meaning. More specifically, you should consider the value of using the you-viewpoint, and you should weigh carefully the differences in meaning conveyed by the positiveness or negativeness of your words. As in all cordial human contacts, you should end your message with appropriate and friendly goodwill words.

SUMMARY BY LEARNING OBJECTIVES

1 Properly assess the reader's reaction to your message.

1. Properly assess the reader's reaction to your message.
   - If the reaction is negative, indirect order is your likely choice.
   - If it is positive or neutral, you probably will want directness.

2 Describe the general plan for direct-order messages.

2. Describe the general plan for direct-order messages.
   - Begin with the objective.
   - Cover any necessary explanation.
   - Systematically present any remaining parts of the objective.
   - End with adapted goodwill.

3 Write clear, well-structured routine requests for information.

3. The routine inquiry is a basic direct-order message.
   - Begin it with a request—either (1) a request for specific information wanted or (2) a general request for information.
   - Somewhere in the message explain enough to enable the reader to answer.
   - If the inquiry involves more than one question, make each stand out—perhaps as separate sentences or separate paragraphs.
   - Consider numbering the questions.
   - And word them as questions.
   - End with an appropriate friendly comment.

4 Write direct, orderly, and friendly answers to inquiries.

4. When responding to inquiries favorably, you should begin directly.
   - If the response contains only one answer, begin with it.
   - If it contains more than one answer, begin with a major one or a general statement indicating you are answering.
   - Identify the message being answered early, perhaps in a subject line.
   - Arrange your answers (if more than one) logically.
   - And make them stand out.
   - If both good- and bad-news answers are involved, give each answer the emphasis it deserves, perhaps by subordinating the negative.
   - For extra goodwill effect, consider doing more than was asked.
   - End with appropriate cordiality.

5 Compose adjustment grants that regain any lost confidence.

5. As messages granting adjustments are positive responses, write them in the direct order.
   - But they differ from other direct-order messages in that they involve a negative situation.
     — Something has gone wrong.
     — You are correcting that wrong.
     — But you also should overcome the negative image in the reader's mind.
   - You do this by first telling the good news—what you are doing to correct the wrong.

- In the opening and throughout, emphasize the positive.
- Avoid the negative—words like *trouble, damage,* and *broken.*
- Try to regain the reader's lost confidence, maybe with explanation or with assurance of corrective measures taken.
- End with a goodwill comment, avoiding words that recall what went wrong.

6. Write order acknowledgments in the form of a favorable response.
   - Handle most by form messages or notes.
   - But in special cases use individual messages.
   - Begin such messages directly, telling the status of the goods ordered.
   - In the remainder of the message, build goodwill, perhaps including some selling or reselling.
   - Include an expression of appreciation somewhere in the message.
   - End with an appropriate, friendly comment.

6 Write order acknowledgments that cover problems and build goodwill.

7. Claims are a special case. Even though they carry bad news, they are best written in the direct order. The reason: the reader usually wants to correct the problem and requires only that the facts be presented; also, directness strengthens the claim. Follow this general plan:
   - Somewhere early in the message (in a subject line or incidentally in the first sentence) identify the transaction.
   - Then state what went wrong, perhaps with some interpretation of the effects.
   - Follow with a clear review of the facts, without showing anger.
   - You may want to suggest a remedy.
   - End with cordial words.

7 Write claims that objectively and courteously explain the facts.

8. Operational (internal) communications must also be clear and effective. The following instructions explain how to write operational communications:
   - Organize most of them in direct order.
   - Write the casual ones like good conversation.
   - But make them clear and courteous.
   - Give administrative communications (policies, directives, procedures) the importance due them.
   - Organize them logically; strive for clarity.

8 Write clear and effective operational communications.

CRITICAL THINKING QUESTIONS

1 When is the direct order appropriate in inquiries? When would you use the indirect order? Give examples.

2 "Explanations in inquiries merely add length and should be eliminated." Discuss.

3 Discuss why just reporting truthfully may not be enough in handling negative information in messages answering inquiries.

4 Defend a policy of doing more than asked in answering routine inquiries. Can the policy be carried too far?

5 What can acknowledgment messages do to build goodwill?

6 Discuss situations where each of the following forms of an order acknowledgment would be preferred: form letter, merged letter, and a special letter.

7 Discuss how problems (vague orders, back orders) should be handled in messages acknowledging orders.

8 Why is it usually advisable to do more than just grant the claim in an adjustment-grant message?

9 Usually bad-news messages are appropriately written in the indirect order. Why should claims be exceptions?

10 Justify the use of negative words in claims. Can they be overused? Discuss.

11 Discuss the use of directness in operational communications. Why is it desirable? Can it be overdone? When might indirectness be appropriate?

1 Point out the shortcomings in this email response to an inquiry about a short course in business communication taught by a professor for the company's employees. The inquiry included five questions: (1) How did the professor perform? (2) What was the course format (length, meeting structure)? (3) What was the employee evaluation of the instruction? (4) Was the course adapted to the company and its technical employees? (5) Was homework assigned?

Subject: Course evaluation

Mr. Braden:

Your January 17 inquiry addressed to the Training Director has been referred to me for attention since we have no one with that title. I do have some training responsibilities and was the one who organized the in-house course in clear writing. You asked five questions about our course.

Concerning your question about the instructor, Professor Alonzo Britt, I can report that he did an acceptable job in the classroom. Some of the students, including this writer, felt that the emphasis was too much on grammar and punctuation, however. He did assign homework, but it was not excessive.

We had class two hours a day from 3:00 to 5:00 PM every Thursday for eight weeks. Usually the professor lectured the first hour. He is a good lecturer but sometimes talks over the heads of the students. This was the main complaint in the evaluations the students made at the end of the course, but they had many good comments to make also. Some did not like the content, which they said was not adapted to the needs of a technical worker. Overall, the professor got a rating of B– on a scale of A to F.

We think the course was good for our technical people, but it could have been better adapted to our needs and our people. I also think it was too long—about 10 hours (five meetings) would have been enough. Also, we think the professor spent too much time lecturing and not enough on application work in class.

Please be informed that the information about Professor Britt must be held in confidence.

Casey Webster

2 Point out the shortcomings in this message granting a claim for a fax machine received in damaged condition. Inspection of the package revealed that the damage did not occur in transit.

Dear Ms. Orsag:

Your May 3 letter in which you claim that the Rigo FAX391 was received in damaged condition has been carefully considered. We inspect all our machines carefully before packing them, and we pack them carefully in strong boxes with Styrofoam supports that hold them snugly. Thus we cannot understand how the damage could have occurred.

Even so, we stand behind our product and will replace any that are damaged. However, we must ask that first you send us the defective one so we can inspect it. After your claim of damage has been verified, we will send you a new one.

We regret any inconvenience this situation may have caused you and assure you that problems like this rarely occur in our shipping department.

Scott Hilderbran

3 List your criticisms of this email message inquiring about a convenience store advertised for sale:

Subject: Store details needed

Mr. Meeks:

This is in response to your advertisement in the May 17 *Daily Bulletin* in which you describe a convenience store in Clark City that you want to sell. I am very much interested since I would like to relocate in that area. Before I drive down to see the property, I need some preliminary information. Most important is the question of financing. I am wondering whether you would be willing to finance up to $50,000 of the total if I could come up with the rest, and how much interest you would charge and for how long. I also would like to have the figures for your operations for the past two or three years, including gross sales, expenses, and profits. I also need to know the condition of the building, including such information as when built, improvements made, repairs needed, and so on.

Hoping that you can get these answers to me soon so we can do business.

4 Criticize the following email claim.

Subject: Your shipment of candy

Mr. Stanton:

For many years now I have bought your candies and have been pleased with them. However, last June 4 I ordered 48 boxes of your Swiss Decadence chocolates, and it appears you tried to push off some old stock on me. I have sold some of the boxes, and already three customers have returned the candy to me. The candy is rancid—obviously old. Probably the whole lot was bad and I now have a bunch of dissatisfied customers.

I have taken the remaining boxes off the shelves and will send them back to you—after I get my money back.

5 Criticize the following operational message from a hotel manager:

Housekeeping staff,

It has come to my attention that the cleanliness of our rooms is substandard. We will therefore hold mandatory training sessions over the next three weeks. See your shift supervisor to plan your work schedule so that you can attend.

Management

Routine Inquiries

1 Move the calendar 10 years ahead and make the unlikely assumption that you are not satisfied with the progress you have made professionally. So you are thinking about launching a new career.

Why not go in business for yourself, you reason. Specifically, your thoughts turn to obtaining a franchise for a Pet Haven outlet in your city. A friend told you about a person she knew who got one two or three years ago and is enjoying great success with it. You are interested. You love animals and would enjoy working with them. You have found what you think is an ideal location for it—heavy traffic and no competition in the area. You are not sure about financing. You could raise about $40,000 from savings and the cash value of your life insurance. And you think you have good credit at your bank. Would that be sufficient?

You know very little about how this franchise operates. How much help do they give the owner? (You would need a lot.) And what controls does the company maintain? In fact, you'll need to know the answers to all the questions involved in making an intelligent decision. So you will write the company for it. You have their email as well as their mailing address.

---

2 At today's meeting of your civic club, you heard one of your friends mention an online management-training course being offered by the Extension Division of Benton University. As the training director for Goetz-Morris Industries, you have been sending four of your middle managers each year to the on-campus management development program at Wimberly University. This expensive ($14,500) three-week program has been hard on your budget. No doubt, an online program would be less expensive and would permit you to train more people. You will look into the matter.

As your friend explained the program to you, it consists of 20 online lessons. The students study assigned reading material, view specially adapted audio lectures, and submit answers to questions. The questions are graded by senior Wimberly faculty. A final examination ends the course.

You like the plan, especially the fact that it costs under $3,000 (your friend thinks). But you need much more information, so you'll make an inquiry to get it. Of course, you'll ask for the printed brochure that your friend said they have. Then there is the matter of possible course credit. (You know that some of your executives are working nights on degree programs.) And does it matter that your executives have different academic backgrounds—liberal arts, engineering, business? Also, you'll need to verify the cost information you heard, discounts for quantity enrollments, and reports on the students' work. If the company pays, can it be informed of the grades earned, or is this privileged information? Other questions may come to mind before you complete your inquiry.

Send your inquiry to the Director of Extension. You have the Division of Extension email address.

---

3 Today you received the good news that you have been appointed director of Chinese operations for Acton-Walters, Inc., manufacturers of a line of farm machinery. You are excited, of course, but you are also frightened. You don't know the language! Although at the beginning you will have a full-time interpreter, you know that eventually you will need to know Chinese.

In discussing your fears with a co-worker recently returned from assignment in China, you learn of a retired Chinese professor of English in Beijing who conducts a two-week intensive training course. As your co-worker explained it, "Wang Tingbi is a master teacher. He works with you 10 hours every day—every minute of every hour. You start talking Chinese early in the course, and you end the course carrying on a decent conversation."

You are interested. As you have five weeks before you begin the new assignment, you could arrive two weeks early and have the training behind you before beginning work. But first you'll need the answers to some questions. Most important, you need to know whether the professor can schedule the training in the time you have available before your assignment begins. There is the question regarding cost. You know about how much your co-worker paid, but that was three years ago. And what about housing? Your furnished quarters won't be available until shortly before your duties begin. There might be other questions, so think through the problem carefully.

Your co-worker gave you professor Wang's email address. Now write him.

---

4 As assistant to the president of Atlas Micro Systems, Inc., you have been given the assignment of getting information on a possible property to buy for corporate retreats. This morning your boss showed you an advertisement he saw in *The Wall Street Journal*. "This could be just what we're looking for," he tells you. "Check it out. You know our requirements and limitations." Here is the advertisement he showed you:

Boca Raton, FL., 15,500 square feet, lodge on 7 acres, suitable for corporate retreat, 575 feet ocean front, 3 guest cottages, Helipad, 9 garages, Olympic pool, 2 tennis courts, theater room, 20 minutes from commercial airport, $8.2 million. doranrealty@aol.com.

Now you will write the advertiser for the information you need. As you understand the company's requirements, the price must be under $10 million, so the price is right. The place must house a maximum of 20 executives, each in a private bedroom. There must be a meeting room large enough to accommodate all 20. Much of what you need could be given in pictures—or a brochure, if they have one. Age of the property is also important, and so are taxes. Probably you will think of other information that will be needed in making the decision. If the information given meets the company's requirements, your boss will want to inspect the place. Now write the message.

5 As the director of human resources for Mid-Continental Utilities, you have been authorized to hire up to 10 interns for the coming summer. They may come from the liberal arts or any of these business fields: accounting, economics, finance, information systems, management, and marketing. And they will come from your old university.

You decide that the simplest way is to write to the director of employment (or whatever the title is at your school). You don't know her (or him) personally, but you have entered into intermittent correspondence with this person in the past few years. You will write the employment director explaining that Mid-Continental is seeking serious, competent juniors who might consider careers with the company after graduation. The intern appointment would be for 10 weeks in the coming summer. Interns would work directly under a member of senior management. Of course, there would be no obligation involved for either party. But if a mutual fit becomes apparent, a permanent job could be expected after graduation. Pay for the 10 weeks is $5,000.

You will ask that those interested write you directly describing their personal history, degree progress, and career goals. Now write the message to the director.

6 For this assignment you are the purchasing agent for Atlas Micro Systems, Inc. The company management has decided to reward its loyal customers with gifts this Christmas. The gift can be anything appropriate under $75—fruits, cheeses, candy, meats, and such. You have been requested to search for such a gift and to recommend one to management.

You will begin your search by looking through *Business Week, The Wall Street Journal,* trade association publications, and the like for advertisements of possible products. Then you will select one and write (letter or email) for the information that will be needed in making a decision—prices, shipping procedures, quantity discounts, timing requirements, and more. So that your instructor may better evaluate your inquiry, attach a copy of the advertisement to your message.

7 Today you received a sales letter and brochure from Dr. Jim Atterbury, a professional in the field of creativity training, inviting your company to purchase his consulting services. To sell you on the idea, this material cites experts who claim that creativity is critical to business survival, it tells you that Dr. Atterbury has helped "dozens" of businesses in your geographic area improve their bottom line through creativity, and it provides enthusiastic testimonials from some of Dr. Atterbury's clients. It so happens that, as president of Natural Designs, a landscaping company serving primarily residential customers, you've been toying with the idea of bringing in some kind of creativity expert. Your "sales-and-marketing department"—consisting of yourself and another manager—regularly scans the industry for new products and practices, but you don't think this is enough. Your three crew bosses, their crews, your four support staff, your finance/accounting person, and even you could benefit from being more open to creative ideas. Times are hard for nonessential services like yours, and you need as sharp a competitive edge as you can get.

You check Dr. Atterbury's website to learn more about his business, but there isn't much more there than was in the mailing you received. So you decide to email Dr. Atterbury to investigate the possibility of his conducting some form of creativity training for Natural Design's employees. You want everyone in your company to become more alert to better ways of doing things. On the other hand, you've heard and read things about this kind of training, and some of it seems just plain silly. You don't want to waste your money, and you don't want your employees to regard a creativity workshop as a waste of time. Dr. Atterbury would need to be able to help your employees draw direct connections between his ideas and better business practices.

Write to Dr. Atterbury to find out whether or not you want to purchase training from him. Tell him about your company, including any details that might help him see how to help you. Find out more about what kinds of training he offers and what his fees are (the amount of time and money that you could spend would be limited). You also want a better sense of who he is. What are his credentials? Is he practical as well as interesting? It would be great if you could talk to some of his prior clients to see if they found his training worthwhile. Try to get enough information to be able to make a reasonably confident decision on this important issue. (You might look at some creativity-training websites or articles to help you decide what to say and ask.)

8 Assume that you are Vice President of Operations for Tourist Publications. Your company's main product is a promotional magazine, *Be Our Guest,* that hotels and motels distribute free of charge to their customers. Each issue of the magazine contains a few articles of general interest on traveling, but it consists mostly of specific information tailored to local businesses. You finance the magazine by selling ad and story space to these local businesses.

There has been friction of late in the company, caused by the fact that this family-owned business was recently sold. The new president and owner brought you in to run day-to-day operations, and personnel problems are causing you real headaches. Some employees who were close friends of the previous owners still remain in the company, and you'd like them to stay on if possible. They have valuable experience and knowledge. On the other hand, you and the new owner have brought in some talented new writers, ad salespersons, and trade-publication people who have ideas about better ways to do things. You can sense that there is tension between the old and new guard and have even seen a shouting match or two.

In looking for a solution to your problem, you did an Internet search combining the name of your city and the phrase "conflict management." One local firm that came up, Personnel Solutions, looks promising. They seem to have considerable experience with small businesses, and their trainers' credentials look solid. But you'd like to learn more about their ability to help you.

Specifically, you'd like to know whether the training would be a general, one-size-fits-all kind of course or if it could be tailored to meet your specific needs. For example, you know that some conflict-resolution training focuses on helping managers resolve conflict, but you'd like your employees as well as the managers to learn how to defuse confrontation, and you

want them to be persuaded that it's in their best interest to do so. That is, you would want all 16 people in your company to participate in the training and feel that their time had been well spent. What kind of strategies does Personnel Solutions teach, exactly, and can everyone benefit?

You also want to be sure that, if you arrange such training for your people, it doesn't convey too negative an impression. The act of bringing in a "conflict management" expert could be taken as a public announcement that the company has serious personnel problems. Can the people at Personnel Solutions help you figure out how to arrange the training without its being interpreted as a really negative commentary on the company?

Also, of course, you wonder about what kinds of training are offered and what the fee for each kind is. And you wonder if the training might be set up for sometime near the end of the month—so that your company can start getting the benefits as soon as possible.

Write the email message, using the address on Personnel Solutions' website, that will get you the information you need. (You might look at some conflict-management websites to get a fuller idea of what to say and ask.)

---

9 You are the personnel director for Professional Billing Services. Today you read an article in one of your human-resources magazines about flextime—the practice of letting the employees determine, within limits, their own work schedules. The article pointed out many benefits of the practice: savings in overhead costs (because employees on different schedules can share office space and expensive equipment), the ability to attract and retain employees who need to balance job and home responsibilities, and overall improved morale. You think this practice might be attractive to some of your people.

While considering the idea, you recall that at last year's meeting of the International Society for Office Administration you heard a presentation on the subject. It was made by Frank Schott, the vice president of administration for an insurance company. You meant to pursue the idea then but apparently forgot about it. You recall that Frank reported on a three-month experiment with flextime at his company. But you don't remember the particulars. You know Frank relatively well. He might be glad to hear from you and to fill you in on the details.

Specifically, you would like to know how flextime worked at his company. What were the ground rules for employees' choosing their own schedules? Did the employees like the change? What were the cost savings for his company? You also wonder if it was difficult for employees to coordinate their activities when they couldn't count on seeing each other during "regular" office hours. How were meetings managed when people were on different schedules? Did the managers feel that it was difficult to coordinate everyone's activities? And what, if anything, happened to the spirit of camaraderie among the employees when they didn't see each other as much during the day? Does Frank's company still feel positively about the change? As you think about what you want to know, you realize that, if you do decide to propose this idea to your bosses, you'll want to be sure you have the facts they will consider important.

Write Frank a message asking for the information that will help you think through this possible change for your company. As you prepare the message (and check Internet resources on flextime), other questions may come to mind. And you won't forget the personal touch that will reinforce your good relationship with Frank.

---

10 As the business manager for Dr. Michelle Matthews, you are responsible for making all arrangements for this nutrition expert's workshops. Today you find that a scheduled workshop in Richmond, Virginia, cannot be held at the city's main convention hotel on the 23rd of next month. It turns out that there is a scheduling conflict. With their apologies, the hotel staff recommended that you try the York Hotel, just off I-81, in a part of town away from the downtown area.

You find the York's website on the Internet and see that it is indeed in a convenient location. The room rates also look relatively reasonable. But there isn't much detail about the hotel's facilities—no floor plan or meeting room information, for example. Here are the things you'd like to know:

- Is the hotel attractive and well maintained, and is it in a decent neighborhood? You know you can't ask these things point blank, but it would be good to be reassured that this hotel, away from the main tourist traffic, will give a good impression to Dr. Matthews's attendees.
- Does the hotel have a meeting room suitable for Dr. Matthews's lecture? You expect about 75 attendees. Dr. Matthews will want to be able to show a slide presentation. She'll also want to be able to divide the attendees up into groups for part of the workshop, and she'll need flip charts and markers for the groups to be able to record and share their work. The workshop will last from 9:00 AM to 5:00 PM with a lunch break.

- Where should the attendees eat lunch? Are there places to get lunch near the hotel, or might the guests be better off eating at the hotel?
- Usually a certain percentage of the attendees stay the night, while another percentage come by car. You saw the room rates on the website. What's the hotel's policy on group rates?

How many attendees would need to reserve rooms, and by when, in order to get a group rate? As for those who'll drive to the workshop, will there be ample parking for them?

As you think through the situation, you may find a need for additional information. Send the message by fax to the manager at a number given on the website, 521-365-2000.

11 Assume that, as a student in your college or university's professional practice course—a course that gets students thinking about, and prepared for, applying for jobs—you are required to "shadow" a professional in your anticipated career for a day. Assume that you'll be writing a brief report on the experience for your professor. Also assume that you have already called a company and gotten an appropriate person's name, title, and email address.

Write this person an email message asking if you may shadow him or her for a day. But before you do, think carefully about what the person will want or need to know, and about what you want to get out of the experience. Use your best you-attitude in this direct inquiry.

12 You recently read about a new movie technology from MovieBeam. With their box ($199 at BestBuy and Sears) attached to your television, you can rent up to 10 movies a week. You learned on moviebeam.com that movies are beamed via an antenna to the box and are available for 24 hours. The rental fees start at $1.99 for standard viewing and go up to $4.99 for high definition viewing. You are billed only for what you view—no subscription or late fees, no driving to the video store only to discover your favorite picks are taken, and no hard-to-use interface.

On the surface this looks perfect for you. Once you buy the box, you pay only for what you use, so costs are in your control. One big question is the near-term available selection of movies. It seems to you that the payback period for the cost of the box is short even at only one movie a week, assuming

there are good choices. So you need to ask about the selection along with lag times from release dates for the kind of films you like to watch.

You also read on the website that the box plugs into a phone jack, which is supposedly used for billing to determine what you've downloaded. Right now your primary phone is a cell phone. You wonder if there is any kind of adapter to use or any other alternative to the phone jack connection. And you wonder if you can take the box with you when you travel to a second home or on the road for business. Or perhaps you can tap into it via your computer when away from home.

Write an inquiry that includes these questions along with any others you need answers for before buying the box. Send your email to Alex Kubicek, Director of Sales at sales@moviebeam.com.

13 You are Terry Lenaghan, the owner of a relatively new web business that specializes in providing nonmusic content for the iPod. Your business is beginning to take off as owners of iPods look to expand their use of them and as business travelers buy them, too. In fact, one of your company's new products includes kiosks at airports where iPod users can download your content easily. However, during your first presentation to a focus group, one finding revealed that iPod users were willing to download content but reluctant to pay through the kiosk.

One member of the focus group, Megan Adami, mentioned that if there had been a familiar privacy seal displayed on it, such as the BBBonline seal or any of the other major seals, she would have been more likely to trust it. You have seen these seals displayed on other sites, but you've never

pursued getting one for your web business. You thought they looked expensive and were primarily for larger businesses, but perhaps for the kiosk business it would be a necessary cost of doing business.

So you decide to look into it further by asking the president of your website design company, Alison Gomez, more about it. Since her company designs for a variety of clients, she may know more about them. She might even be able to recommend which privacy seal would be most appropriate for your targeted audience of business travelers. Write her an inquiry asking questions that cover not only a recommendation for which privacy seal to use but also questions about pricing, return on investment, and any other topics you need information on before deciding whether or not to secure one. You can write Alison at alison@webdesigns.com.

14 As Don Zatyko, a network specialist for a small but growing local business, a major part of your job is both giving access to information to employees and keeping information assets secure from hackers. You have set up the wireless network in your office to be relatively secure from outsiders tapping in, but serious hackers could find a way. You even read a story recently of a company losing information through someone attaching a travel network (the size of a deck of cards) to

an employee's workstation, as easy as plugging in a phone. So when you read in *BusinessWeek* of BAE Systems' new development, a wallpaper that blocks Wi-Fi signals from escaping through walls while letting through mobile phone and radio signals, you thought it was worth looking into further.

BAE's website did not give you much information. The *BusinessWeek* story you read reported that the wallpaper was made of thin sheets of copper and plastic and cost as little as

$300 to screen one floor of an office building. That seems very inexpensive for the protection it provides, so you wonder if there are other costs involved. What size office does $300 cover? Is any special technique or technically skilled labor needed to install it? What kind of maintenance is required? What is the length of the warranty period? Is it aesthetically pleasing or will you need to hide it with other wall-paper, paint, or paneling? What references can they provide of other businesses in your area that have installed it?

Feel free to add other questions to your inquiry that you need answered in order to decide whether this technology is worth the time and effort to get. Direct your inquiry to the Vice President of Sales at BAE, Amy Betterton, at agbetterton@bae.co.uk.

15 At Cell2Recycle.com you learned about an organization whose goal is keeping rechargeable batteries and cell phones out of our nation's solid waste stream and preserving natural resources.

It does this by collecting and recycling them. Recovered materials can be used to make new products—the cadmium is used to make new batteries, while the nickel and iron are used to make stainless steel products. Cell phones are refurbished and resold when possible. And a portion of the proceeds from the resale of the cell phones will benefit select charities.

And the program is simple—the company provides pre-paid, preaddressed collection boxes. When they are full, you send them to the recycling company.

As Kevin Stamper, Director of Corporate Relations for a small document delivery service, you think collecting phones from both your fellow employees and your clients might be a valuable community service project. And it's something that a small business can do without much cost. But before you propose the idea to company president and owner Kate Troy, asking her to allow the company to participate in this effort, you need a few questions answered.

Which charities are helped by this effort? Can your employees select from a list of needy charities or organizations or even designate specific ones, such as your local schools, police, and fire department? Although you realize that this is a nonprofit, public service organization, you still wonder what percentage of the profits go to these charities. What happens to the components that aren't recycled? You've heard stories of waste materials being dumped in other countries, which seems inappropriate to you. If your company decides to hold a phone drive, will someone at Call2Recycle be designated a contact person for your company should anything else come up that needs their direction or expertise? You'll need answers to these questions before you submit the idea to your boss, so a prompt reply would be greatly appreciated.

16 As Rebecca Makely, the new Marketing Director at New Feet, you are just beginning to initiate some new programs that you think will help the business and its employees. While the company already sponsors and promotes several walks and runs, one idea you have is to complement those activities with another aspect of a healthy lifestyle—eating well.

To do this, you'd like the company to participate in a program to raise awareness and money for Meatout.org, but you'll need to inquire if some of your ideas are possible. First, you'd like to organize a Meat Out Day, where all food choices in the company cafeteria are plant-based foods. Second, you would like to have at least one plant-based entrée available every Monday in the cafeteria. And finally, you'd like to raise money for the organization by raffling off the annual use of a reserved parking place. You are willing to do most of the work for the raffle yourself, but you need to know if a primo space is available and how to go about arranging for it.

Send an email to the CEO, Steven Copp, asking if these things can be done in time to coincide with National Meat Out Day (March 20th this year).

Favorable Responses

17 As franchise manager for Pet Haven (see Problem 1 for background details), answer the message about your franchise. At the moment you will cover only the basic matters. The specific facts will come later after negotiations have proceeded further.

You are always pleased to get inquiries about your franchise operations, for Pet Haven is trying hard to expand its operations into all areas of the country. But franchises are awarded only after careful investigation. Locations must be checked and approved by the company. This is a safety feature, you think, and explains why not one outlet has failed in the company's history.

Total investment in a franchise ranges from $75,000 to $200,000, depending on the size of the store and local cost variations. A minimum of $30,000 in cash is required. The company can assist in finding financing, but usually the owner handles it locally. All basic merchandise is purchased through the company, but exceptions are made for some local and specialty products. Actually, this policy assures quality products and permits significant economies.

The company provides a six-week training program for all new owners (included in the franchise fee), and it has expert consultants who visit each outlet on a regular basis. These consultants help with just about any problem the owner may have. For the best interest of all, the company does maintain some control over operations, although each outlet is basically an independent operation. The controls exercised largely pertain to building appearance, services provided, product quality, and such. The company firmly believes that these controls are for the owner's protection and explain the remarkable success record of the franchises.

With this information in mind, write an email message answering the questions that were asked (or should have been asked) in the inquiry.

18 You, the director of the Extension Division of Benton University, must answer the inquiry of the Goetz-Morris training director (see Problem 2 for background details). First, you will send the descriptive brochure that describes your online management development program. As the reader will see, the course presents the highlights of the basic business disciplines (accounting, economics, finance, information systems, management, marketing) from the manager's perspective. Senior Benton faculty members conduct each area. They assign readings, present lectures, assign and grade homework, and test each student at the end of the course.

Grades in the course are privileged information, but before beginning the course the student can agree to permit the employer to receive the final grades. As to course credit, three semester hours of elective credit is given for work in Benton business programs. Whether the credit can be transferred and applied to programs at other institutions is a matter for that institution to determine. Cost for the course is $3,250 per student. As the program is not designed to make a profit, no quantity discounts can be given.

Now write the message that will answer the director's questions and get the company's education business.

19 Today play the role of Wang Tingbi, retired professor from the University of International Business and Economics, Beijing, China, and respond to the inquiry of the Acton-Walters executive (see Problem 3 for background details). Yes, you'd like to teach the executive Chinese, and the dates he or she needs are open. The question about where to live is an easy one. You would be very willing to include room and board in your $1,000 (U.S.) for the two weeks of instruction. You have an extra bedroom since your mother-in-law died, and your wife is an excellent cook. Both of you like Americans and would enjoy the experience.

You can point out further that your wife assists in the instruction. And with the executive living in the house, the instruction would continue beyond the 10-hour day. Furthermore, if the executive will give the arrival time, you will meet him or her at the airport and escort him or her to your residence. The excess baggage and personal things the executive is bringing can be kept in a storage bin at your apartment complex. And when the instruction is over, you can arrange for moving these items to the executive's permanent residence. You will write the message using the direct order you learned while in the States as an exchange professor at the University of North Texas. As a professor of English, you are naturally quite proficient in the language.

20 At the Doran Realty office in Boca Raton, this morning's email includes an inquiry from the assistant to the president of Atlas Micro Systems (see Problem 4 for background details). The company's management is interested in the huge waterfront property you listed last week as a possible corporate retreat. Yes, you can answer the questions positively.

You don't have a brochure on the place, but you do have nine photographs and two short videos that show most of the highlights. You are attaching them to your email response. The buildings can easily accommodate 20 executives. Including the three cottages, each with two bedrooms, there are 28 total bedrooms with private baths. The large living area with connecting dining hall has accommodated more than 30 people. The theater room also will seat 30 people comfortably. The property was built in the 1960s but has been maintained to perfection. Current annual property taxes are $115,740.

Of course, you would be pleased to show the property at any time the Atlas Micro Systems people choose. Now write the message that will maintain the reader's interest and lead to a big sale.

21 Select an advertisement (Internet, magazine, newspaper) or brochure describing a product a business executive might want to get more information on before buying. The product can be one for resale or one to be consumed or used by the business. Next, make a list of questions the executive needs answered before buying (minimum of four). Your questions should be ones not covered in the advertisement or brochure.

Then assuming that an executive included these questions in an inquiry to the company selling this product, write the company's response. For class purposes submit to your instructor your list of questions and the advertisement or brochure you used. Make certain that your message does not parrot the language in the advertisement or brochure. That is, use your own words.

22 Assume the role of Dr. Jim Atterbury, professional creativity consultant (see Problem 7 for background details). Today you received an email inquiry in response to the promotional letter and brochure you recently mailed to a number of local businesses. The inquiry is from Jasmine Parker, president of the residential landscaping company Natural Designs. She has a company of approximately 20 employees (three landscaping crews, three managers, office staff, and a finance/accounting person). She is looking for a competitive edge for her business, and she wonders if your creativity training is the answer.

She asks you to describe your training, and your own credentials, in more detail. She didn't come right out and say it, but you can tell that she worries about such training being too "out there" and not related enough to bottom-line results. She also wonders to what extent the training can be tailored to the particular client. You need to convince her that your services will be a good match for her needs and that you will do a good job.

You can tailor the training to the client to some extent. Usually what you do is conduct a long interview, either by phone or in person, with the management of the potential customer to find out what made them contact you in the first place—that is, what kinds of problems the company is having or what goals it wants to meet. You can then work this information into your standard approach for such training (to find out what that might be, do some research on creativity training on the web and/or on your school's business-literature databases).

You can offer several different levels of training. The minimal version would be to have the employees meet—preferably off-site—for an afternoon of instruction, which would include several fun but effective exercises. A more extensive version would be a day-long retreat, enabling different participant groups to do creative problem solving based on actual company situations and then share their results with the rest of the employees at the end of the day. With the day-long training, clients wind up with more applicable results than they do with the half-day training, which really can cover only the basics. Or, some of your clients actually retain you on a regular basis to come and do a "creativity" brown-bag lunch once a month. This can be a great follow-up to the workshop, keeping the creativity dialog going. You charge $500 for the half-day workshop, $1,000 for the day-long workshop, and $100 for each brown-bag lunch (clients have to buy a minimum of six of these). You can give Ms. Parker a list of places where you've held your workshops in the past—places that (for a price) offer refreshments and a nice locale for this kind of team building. You might even describe one or two of these.

Ms. Parker also wondered if she could contact some of your past clients, so you will include names and contact information for three of these. But to help overcome her skepticism, you will also relate some impressive claims from the creativity literature (such as the article "Cashing in on Creativity," from the September/October 2000 issue of *Psychology Today* magazine). And of course, you need to supply more information about your credentials, as Ms. Parker asked. You have a Ph.D. from Temple University, in English literature. You got interested in creativity while taking and teaching creative writing. Your spouse is actually Business Editor for the local paper, and that has been a big part of your business education. But over the nine years that you have been doing creativity training, you have learned much more about what creativity can do for almost any kind of business. You've been teaching at a local community college while growing your consulting business, so you don't have that many clients—but you've consulted for some impressive local companies, and they have given you excellent evaluations. In fact, you have kept in touch with many of these companies, and they've given you a lot of attractive quotes to put in your promotional material. You're a member of the American Creativity Association and are a Certified Creavity Coach (awarded for successful completion of the ACA's training program).

Tell Ms. Parker what she needs to know, what you recommend she do, and what the next step would be. (You might want to look at some creativity-training websites or articles to get a fuller sense of what to include in your message.)

---

23 Your boss at Personnel Solutions, a human-resources consulting firm, just forwarded an email to you that the company's webmaster sent to him. The email is from Glenn Estes, Vice President of Operations at Tourist Publications (for background, see the related Problem 8). Mr. Estes reports a classic management problem: The company was recently sold to new ownership, and now there is friction between the old and new employees. Mr. Estes pulled up your company's website on a search for conflict management training, and he wants more information to help him decide if the kind of training you offer along these lines can help solve his problem.

Your task, as one of two conflict resolution specialists at Personnel Solutions, is to answer Mr. Estes's questions—in such a way, you hope, that you attract his business. You jot down the following notes:

- You have three years of experience as a conflict management trainer, 12 years of personnel management experience, and certification from the American Association of Conflict Management Consultants.
- You've worked with a lot of small companies, maybe some he's heard of. You also have particular experience with just the kind of situation that Mr. Estes describes—the selling of a company and the resulting personnel problems. (You can research or discuss in class what kinds of personnel problems a buy-out often creates.)
- You've found that it's usually best to train the top-level management and the employees in separate sessions. When

the powerful people are present, employees tend to clam up and just watch what the executives do.

- For the employees, you can offer an afternoon workshop ($499), a full day ($999), or an ongoing series (price to be negotiated). All materials for up to 20 people would be included in the fee. If the company doesn't have a meeting room appropriate for the workshop, you can recommend some suitable, relatively inexpensive sites. For upper management, you can deliver a presentation on-site that summarizes the techniques (no charge if supplementing an employee workshop; $300 if by itself).
- In your training, you focus on specific techniques, but you don't tailor the contents much to the individual client. You've found that, at least for short-term consulting, it's best not to get too far into employees' actual problems. When you do that, things get worse before they get better, and a short engagement doesn't provide enough time for extensive counseling of those involved.
- Your techniques have been proven to reduce friction and increase harmony in organizations (see sample websites and/or articles to gather information on such techniques).
- Yes, you can help Mr. Estes frame the training in such a way that it doesn't emphasize "conflict." Usually you recommend that the training be described as "team building," but you'd need to consult more with Mr. Estes to determine the best strategy for announcing the workshop in his case.
- Write the email telling Mr. Estes what he needs—and what you want him—to know. In your forward-looking ending, anticipate the next steps in the process.

24 As Vice President of Administration at the home office of United Insurance Companies, you just received an inquiry from Sandra Thompson, Personnel Director of Professional Billing Services. You know Sandra fairly well and are happy to hear from her. She recalls that you gave a presentation on flextime at the last meeting of the International Society for Office Administration. Now she is considering proposing that her company adopt some form of flextime, and she wants more details about how it has been working at your company (see the related Problem 9 for the questions she asked).

You started a pilot flextime program in one department six months ago. It worked so well in its first three months that it was approved for other departments' adoption and has now become a widespread company practice. There are two options for flextime at United Insurance Companies: working five days a week but on an earlier or later schedule than the usual 8:00–5:00 workday or working a compressed schedule of four 10-hour days per week with an extra day off. Someone must be in each department during regular business hours every day, everyone must be on the job during certain core hours, and employees have to get their weekly work done. Also, when something is declared a priority project, everyone involved must be able to come in during regular business hours until the project is completed. But outside these requirements, it's up to each department and its personnel to determine how they want to implement flextime. Some personnel—certain managerial and support staff—are excluded from the flextime options, but pretty much all other employees can choose flextime if it's worked out with the department supervisors.

In order for flextime to work, there has to be clear communication between the supervisors and their staff about everyone's work schedule. Coordinating and communicating the schedules does create some extra work for the supervisors. Getting everyone together for meetings hasn't really been a problem. The core hours make it relatively easy to schedule meetings when everyone involved can be there, and instant messaging makes it possible to conduct discussions online when people can't be physically present. Your flextime program used to involve obligatory two-hour meetings once a week for participating departments, but employees complained about this requirement, and your supervisors report that eliminating it has not appreciably reduced their ability to coordinate their people's efforts. You do think that having flextime makes it doubly important for a company to maintain certain regular social functions for all employees.

Each supervisor at United Insurance Companies keeps an ongoing assessment of how flextime is working, specifically in the areas of absenteeism, coverage of the work, employee turnover, and number of internal and external complaints. On all these counts, the experiment seems to be succeeding (you can give Sandra some data to prove the point). This initiative is too young for the company to have realized cost savings in the form of shared office space and computer equipment; maybe these benefits will occur. But all supervisors involved agree that employees' morale is higher and that their work is better (you don't have actual statistics on this, but you can cite a persuasive example or two). You and other executives have concluded that this experiment in accommodating employees' needs is paying off. You know that some companies haven't had such good experiences, so Sandra will probably want to check around to see if flextime will have a good chance of working at her company.

You hope that your information will help Sandra, and her supervisors, make a wise decision about flextime.

---

25 Assume the position of Assistant Manager for the York Hotel in Richmond, Virginia, and answer the inquiry you have received from Dr. Michelle Matthews's business manager (see related Problem 10 for background).

Yes, the York does have a meeting room that would appear to be perfect for Dr. Matthews's nutrition workshop. It can accommodate 100 people, and the seating can be arranged in any way that Dr. Matthews would like. The room is off the main lobby—easy to find but away from the lounge, restaurant, and guest rooms. It is the only meeting room. You can promise that it will be equipped with all the lecture and workshop equipment that Dr. Matthews will need. She will have only to mention what she needs and you will make certain it is there even if you have to rent it. The room rents for $800 a day. You might schedule another event in this room for the evening, so Dr. Matthews will need to be sure to be out of the room no later than 5:30 PM.

You can offer any of Dr. Matthews's group who will be spending the night a 10 percent discount on the regular room rates. There is also a free continental breakfast for hotel guests. If you know how many people to expect, you can block out a section of rooms for the event, but you can hold the rooms only up until 72 hours before the day of the event. After that, you'll need to release them for other guests.

There's plenty of free parking in the large hotel parking lot (an advantage of not being downtown), but only those guests staying the night will be allowed to park in front of the hotel; any of Dr. Matthews's guests who are attending just for the day will need to park in the back lot.

Yours is a nice, relatively new hotel, having been built just six years ago. The lobby is an atrium with a skylight, plants, and comfortable chairs. The hotel is located at the entrance to an attractively landscaped business park, and most of its customers are business clientele (with an occasional wedding or retirement party thrown in). Your 100-room hotel has a small but classy restaurant with a menu that, as Dr. Matthews may be interested to know, contains a wide assortment of healthy selections. In fact, if she likes, she can reserve a portion of the restaurant for her attendees' lunch, and she can also, for a fee, have your restaurant supply refreshments during the day for her workshop. You're including more information on these options with your message. You suppose it's only fair to mention that there are also two other restaurants within walking distance of the hotel.

Since the business manager communicated by fax, you'll respond the same way. Include any additional appropriate details that you think Dr. Matthews and her attendees might be interested in.

26 As Kate Troy, president and owner of a small business that delivers documents and small parcels, you are delighted to respond to an email from Kevin Stamper, Director of Corporate Communications, requesting that the company participate in a cell phone recycling program (see Problem 15 for background). He told you in his email about a company, Call2Recycle, that collects and refurbishes phones. In addition to helping the environment, the company will donate a portion of the proceeds to a charity that it can select.

Not only do you think it's a good idea, but it is especially timely during this week, National Cell Phone Recyle Week,

October 11–17. You may want to suggest that if Kevin heads up the program for your company, he can help identify which charity to choose. He might also want to release a PR blurb on the company's efforts to encourage other small businesses to do the same thing. In fact, you're willing to volunteer your company's services in collecting phones and delivering them to the local drop centers. Your small business should gain more visibility and goodwill while helping the community. Let Kevin know how much you appreciate his idea.

---

27 As Steven Copp, president and CEO of a mid-size retail company, New Feet Solutions, you need to respond to a request from an employee, Rebecca Makely. Rebecca's been working for you as director of marketing for about a year. She has quickly learned the ropes of your company and is beginning to show some initiative in proposing a variety of new projects and products. Her latest is a request for the company to participate in activities supporting a national Meat Out Day observation (see Problem 16 for background). This year's observation is on Friday, March 20th, but her request is to begin an annual observation of this day held near the first day of spring each year.

Before agreeing to this seemingly healthy idea, you decide to learn more about the program. When checking out the website at <http://www.meatout.org>, you notice that one of their major sources of fundraising is sponsoring nationwide walks, an activity very compatible with your business's mission. And while it's an organization devoted to vegetarianism, its activities raise funds primarily to educate people and promote the benefits of a plant-based diet. You know there are other highly respected organizations also promoting the benefits of a plant-based diet such as the American Cancer Society, the

National Cancer Institute, and the American Heart Association. Although the Meatout organization does have some connection to the more radical PETA group, its purpose is in line with your company's mission—to help people gain good health.

While your company is already involved in sponsoring numerous walks across the country, Rebecca is interested in targeting this health program internally at your own employees. She wants the company to promote its own employees' health through diet to complement the exercise activities that the company already has in place. She has requested that on March 20th the employee cafeteria offer only plant-based items, and she asks that at least one of the entrees be solely plant-based on every Monday for the next six months. Furthermore, Rebecca would like to raise both awareness and money for the group through a raffle of the use of a reserved parking space for a year. She has offered to conduct the raffle on her own time; she just needs your approval.

You decide to send her an email message responding favorably to her request, giving her the formal permission she needs to begin making arrangements. You suggest that she contact Margaret Kiley, the office manager, to identify the new privileged parking space.

---

28 You were delighted today to receive a suggestion from Kate Grey, one of your top-notch customer service reps, that looks like it will not only save you money and lots of work but also improve the quality of your customer communication.

As a small business that specializes in selling quality commercial printers, you regularly exhibit at trade shows to expose your products to special audiences. You've pretty well mastered coordinating the set-up process at these shows for the printers, but the print material you distribute there varies from show to show and with the timing of special promotions. So you often end up carting these newly printed documents in extra luggage and boxes with you on flights to various cities. And you've often had to pay extra baggage or overweight charges, since the handouts can be heavy.

For the meeting in Miami next month, Kate suggested she try using Kinko's virtual printing program. Unlike Kinko's

older program where documents had to be uploaded to their servers, the new program prints on their printers from your site. Paper and binding can be specified from a large selection, and users pay online. So you can pick up the documents at the local Kinko's (in Miami it's across the street from the meeting site) without having to worry about packing and transporting them. Also, the documents will have up-to-the-minute accuracy, and more can be printed as needed rather than your having to overestimate the need to be on the safe side as you have done in the past.

Kate's idea is so logical, you wish you had thought of it before. So, as Linda Hittle, co-owner of PrintSafe, you'll give her the approval she needs for this trial. And you'll tell her how much you appreciate her efforts to improve the communication with your customers, including her recent efforts to improve your company's website also.

---

29 Jane Marion, one of the most loyal and cost-conscious employees in your school's administration, recently suggested that the university use a technology she saw on a recent *CSI: NY* episode—DataDots. These dots help with asset identification and theft deterrence.

DataDots are microscopic and encoded with unique identification linked to the owner. About the size of a grain of sand, they are applied with a special adhesive that can be visible or hidden, and they are read with an ultraviolet light that police and campus security departments use. She wants you both to suggest the campus bookstore stock them and to recommend their use to new students in your letter welcoming them to the College of Business. Not only are the dots inexpensive at $19.95 a package, but students can also apply them easily to cell phones, iPods, PDAs, laptops, bicycles, televisions, cameras, and much more. And they've been proven effective. She told you that more information about them could be found at <http://www.datadotsusa.com>.

As Edwardo Paul, Dean of the College of Business, you will respond favorably. You know that parents pay a lot of money for the items students pack up and take to school with them, so knowing there's a technology that will help protect them against loss as well as assist in getting lost or stolen items returned will be greatly appreciated. Write Jane a letter agreeing to her suggestions and telling her how you plan to implement them. Of course, you will thank her for making the suggestion.

Adjustment Grants

30 Play the role of the marketing manager for European Holidays, Inc. (see Problem 45 for background information). The professor does indeed have a valid claim, and you will correct the problem. But you want to go further than just correcting the error. You want to protect the good reputation your company has built over the years. What happened just isn't representative of your operation.

Apparently the new tour guide assigned to the professor's group confused this group with one scheduled for his next assignment—a tour for American industrialists who preferred to arrange their own dinners. When the tour guide called the home office to determine whether dinners were included, the clerk answering the call must have pulled the wrong contract. So the professor's tour guide got the wrong information. It was an honest mistake, but the fault lies entirely with European Holidays.

Now you will email the professor. You will clearly state that a check for payment of the full amount is on the way. And you will explain what happened apologetically, taking full blame for the mistake.

31 As the marketing manager for BioTech Inc. (see Problem 46 for background information), you are embarrassed as you read the claim message from the Cherokee Springs Country Club manager. Nothing like this has happened before, so you are eager to find out what happened.

In assessing the facts of the case, you talk with your warehouse supervisor. He was the one who supervised the loading of the seed trucks before they went out to the Cherokee Springs job. The supervisor remembers that one of your suppliers stacked some seed sacks incorrectly several months back, mixing some SB13 with SB18. However, your warehouse supervisor thought he'd caught the mistake. But such a mix-up would certainly account for the problems at Cherokee Springs.

If SB18, a hybrid seed for colder climates, were mixed with SB13, a hybrid for warmer climates, the effect could be exactly what the Cherokee Springs manager described—different and irregular growth patterns of the fairways, tee boxes, and greens on the golf course. You conclude that you are at fault and that the claim is valid.

Of course, you will refund the money—all $94,600 of it. And you will explain what happened and take full responsibility for the mishap. In addition, you will offer to meet with the club's board of directors to explain what happened. Because you want to keep the business of this affluent club, you will offer to do the job over next spring at a 20 percent discount.

32 For this assignment you are the sales manager for the Sleepwell Mattress Company. You have just received an email message from the West Side Furniture Company. Mr. William Braddock, owner-manager, claims that he received 50 damaged mattresses (see Problem 44 for background information). The claim is valid, and you've already instructed your shipping clerk to deliver 50 replacement mattresses immediately. They will arrive tomorrow. Your driver will pick up the damaged goods.

It is important to you to maintain the goodwill of this aggressive and prosperous furniture business, so you'll try to present an honest explanation of the facts behind the error. And you'll try to assure the man that such a slip-up is not likely to recur. After investigating the situation, you come up with a weak but possibly understandable explanation.

In short, things around the warehouse haven't been normal since the damaging fire last month. You had to put on a number of extras to do salvage work and assist in moving the warehouse stores to a temporary location. Obviously, in the confusion of moving, some of the damaged mattresses that were to be shipped to numerous used-furniture buyers were erroneously stored with the undamaged ones. So when West Side's order was filled, the mattresses taken from the stacks that were believed to consist of first-class goods turned out to be damaged. One of your regular employees, you believe, would have detected the error.

By next week the old hands will be in complete charge again. And, to prevent similar errors, all mattresses on future shipments will be personally inspected by the shipping clerk. Unless there is another fire, West Side Furniture's future orders will receive the careful treatment that Mr. Braddock has a right to expect.

33 As Director of Hospitality at the Mandarin Hotel, you have to answer a letter of complaint by a new customer, Roberto Calderon, President of Calderon Construction.

Mr. Calderon held a company event at your hotel a few weeks ago, and he was not pleased (see Problem 47).

He has two complaints. One is that the room in which you placed his event was next to a meeting room in which a boisterous party, complete with live band, was going on. Mr. Calderon complains that his guests could hardly converse and that they had great difficulty hearing his speech to the group. The other, bigger problem is that he was disappointed with the food. He expected coconut shrimp and sushi to be served along with the other hors d'oeuvres, but, instead, his party got spring rolls and chicken fingers, which apparently did not please. Now he wants an adjustment to his bill. In all honesty, you have to agree that he has a point on both counts.

You did know that a live band would be in the meeting room next to his, but you'd hoped that, because there was a solid wall rather than a partition between the two rooms, his party would be able to tolerate the noise level. You'd also supplied the room with a microphone to ensure that any speakers could be heard. You could have given his party a quieter room if the company had made its reservation earlier, but they gave you only six weeks' lead time, and, considering that the target date was in December, at the height of your busiest season for parties, you thought you'd done well just getting them in. True, at the time the company made its request, you'd had two rooms available and had assigned them the one further from the party with the live band, but when an important repeat customer had requested a room shortly afterwards, you'd bumped Calderon's party into the louder room to give the better room to your favored customer. In your own defense, you knew that the repeat customer's event,

an awards banquet, would be a quiet affair, whereas you had no way of knowing how loud the Calderon party might be or how much they might be bothered by music from an adjoining room. Now that you know what kind of event Calderon's party is, you will be sure to give the party a quiet room—if they come back, and if they make their reservation far enough in advance.

As for the food complaint, the problem was that, at the last minute, your supplier of fresh seafood had failed to come through with the shrimp and sushi, and your catering staff hadn't had time to prepare anything more imaginative than the spring rolls and chicken fingers. Such occurrences are rare, but they do happen, and that is why you put the disclaimer on your party menu about not being able to guarantee the exact fare on the menu. Still, you can understand Mr. Calderon's disappointment, and you'd have to agree that the spring rolls and chicken fingers, while of higher quality than he gives them credit for, were less impressive and appetizing than the fresh seafood would have been. It's too bad, because usually your guests rave about your food, and you'd have liked for Mr. Calderon to have gotten a good first impression.

In an effort to repair his confidence in your services and turn him into a repeat customer, write Mr. Calderon a letter that grants him the reasonable (you decide what it is) discount that he is requesting. Add any details that will help your case—and leave out the ones that won't.

---

34 You've just received a package in the mail from one Sarah Ronstadt, of Xenia, Ohio. In it is the leather jacket that she purchased from the upscale women's clothing store where you work, Elaine's, in Laguna Beach, California. With the jacket is a request that you refund her money both for the jacket and for the cost of shipping it back to you (she had also purchased delivery confirmation for the package).

You remember this nice customer. She was visiting the area in order to attend a professional conference being held there. In exploring the mall where your store is located, she had expressed delight in finding that all your leather goods were on sale. And high-quality goods they are, too—all made by Angaro's of Italy. Ms. Ronstadt had gotten a $700 jacket for $379. And it had looked great on her. All in all, you remember feeling pleased by the experience.

But now Ms. Ronstadt reports that the jacket turned out to be defective. When she got it home and into the daylight, she

noticed that one panel of the jacket was a somewhat different color than the other panels. You take it over to a window to look, and you see what she means. While some variations in the leather, a natural material, are to be expected, the one panel does jump out as being different from the rest of the coat. The thing is, many signs above the sale racks had proclaimed "All sales final." If there were any evidence that Ms. Ronstadt had mistreated the merchandise, you would certainly stand by this advertised policy. But clearly, the coat was flawed from the start, and neither she nor you had been able to see this fact in the store lighting. Also, you know that you can ship the coat back to Angaro's for your own refund, so in refunding Ms. Ronstadt's money, you won't actually take much of a loss.

Write Ms. Ronstadt to grant her request. In the process, let her know more about other Elaine's stores across the country. Who knows? With your gracious handling of this situation, you just might create more business for your company down the road.

---

35 Mary Adami is right. The $500 deductible should not have been applied twice in settling the insurance claim she made recently on her totaled car (see details in Problem 50). You'll write her immediately letting her know that is the case. While you are not sure how that happened, you think it might be that gap insurance coverage is relatively new and you have not had much experience with claims on it yet.

You also realize you need to work hard to retain her goodwill and her future business. You may want to let her know

you are glad she was not hurt when she ran into the fire truck, and you can compliment her on being smart enough to have elected to pay the extra $20 for the gap insurance. It saves her from having to go into debt for a car she no longer has. Remind her that you will be paying off the finance company this week. In addition, you might consider telling her that you really appreciate her family's long-time business with you and look forward to her future business.

36 As Chris VanLerBerghe, Senior Customer Care Representative for Office Depot, you were not too surprised to get a message today reporting that one of your customers, Carol Acord, had had trouble with the chair from a desk set you sold last summer (see details in Problem 52). Due to two other injuries suffered from the chair breaking, the Consumer Product Safety Commission has recalled that desk set. While Carol was disappointed that the chair did not hold up, she reported that an acquaintance had fallen off it but was not injured. You are certainly glad no one was hurt, and you will gladly offer to replace the chair.

You appreciated Carol's thoroughness in including the model number along with a copy of her receipt. It makes it much easier for you to meet her request in a timely manner. In granting her request, you will need to get the chair back even in its broken condition to reduce any future liability with it. You will offer Carol a gift card for the full value of the set, $80, but she needs to return the chair to get it.

To help maintain her goodwill and to encourage her to purchase from Office Depot in the future, you may want to remind her that at Office Depot all purchases can be exchanged or refunded within 30 days with the original receipt. You may even want to do some promotion that might interest her.

Order Acknowledgments (with Problems)

37 At your desk in the sales office of Pauling-Ward Paper Company, you have just received by email a first order from Jonathan Marcus of Marcus Printers. For some time you have been trying to acquire this account. But now that you have landed it, you have a problem. The order doesn't give you the information you need. It doesn't specify the finish desired on seven reams of Bosco Wood Grain cover stock. It is a two-ply cardboard imitating wood-grain finishes, and comes in mulberry, gum, walnut, cypress, and pine. You'll just have to ask his preference before you can send the product.

Now you will have to email Mr. Marcus in the most constructive way you can. You'd be happy to send samples for him to look at, but this would take time. And, of course, you'll give him a new-customer welcome.

38 Six months ago your rather conservative and elegant importing and jobbing house (you name it) got its first shipment of Wellington china (a long-established, middle-priced line) from England, and hurried to put out a promotion to department stores, jewelry houses, and gift shops. It worked. Some profitable new accounts were generated, and you welcomed each with a friendly and dignified personal message.

Today you received another such order, this one in email form from Beverly's Gift Shop in Arlington, VA. Beverly Walzel, the manager, wants a rush shipment of Wellington sets totaling $2,340. You are pleased to have this new customer, but unfortunately you cannot deliver. Your stock has been exhausted for almost a month. You have contacted the Wellington people and have been assured that a shipment is now on a ship in the Atlantic and on the way to you. It should be in your warehouse in 10 days. It will be sufficient to take care of all orders, including Beverly's. You can rush her order to her as soon as you have the china.

Now you must write a cordial email message to Beverly welcoming her as a new customer and reporting the problems so constructively that she will be very willing to wait.

39 Your university store (you name it) ordered 1,500 sun visors, assorted colors, at $2.47 each (total of $3,705) from your hat manufacturing firm, Chapeaux, Inc. Also, it ordered 1,250 baseball caps in your school's colors and with a caricature of the school's mascot in front at $3.34 each (total of $4,175). The store paid the full amount with the order. A note with the order said that the caps are needed before August 23, the day freshman orientation begins. It is now late July.

You are sending the sun visors right away. But because of other rush orders you have promised, you can't have the baseball caps ready for three weeks. The summer months are your busiest times, and it is all you can do to meet the orders already on your production schedule. You know that what you can promise will be "cutting it close," but it is the best you can do. Anyway, caps that don't sell during the orientation period will be marketable throughout the year.

Write the acknowledgment message (email or letter) that will keep the goodwill of this long-time customer.

40 As vice president and part-owner of your parents' restaurant, Zorah's, you've just received a new order via the email address on your website. Apparently the nearby university is having its World Village celebration next week, and the person in charge of the opening-ceremonies buffet, Neil Dormer, would like to feature your Middle Eastern cuisine in addition to that of other regions. He indicated that he would like to purchase enough tabouli, hummus and pita bread, rice flavored with almonds and pine nuts, slow-roasted chicken (your specialty), and baklava for 120 people. He is not sure what that comes to, though, because your website says that, for large orders, these items are offered by the half or full tray, and he isn't certain how many people a half or full tray will serve. He hopes that, since it is for a worthy cause, you might also give him a bit of a price break on the order. He and his staff would need to come pick up the order at 11:00 AM. next Saturday for the noon event.

Email Mr. Dormer to tell him that you are happy to have his order. For his information, a half tray serves about 20 and a whole tray about 40, so he would need three full trays of each item he ordered. One problem is that you can't have the chicken ready that early in the day because you have to use your rotisserie all morning to cook chicken for your dine-in customers. That's why the chicken is available only for dinner parties. But your grape leaves stuffed with lamb are extremely popular. They're a classic Middle-Eastern dish—and they're not as messy to eat as the chicken, either! Add up the full trays

of tabouli ($60), hummus and pita bread ($50), and flavored rice ($60), plus the grape leaves ($.75 apiece—you'd recommend two per person), to come up with a price for Mr. Dorner. You will give him a little extra on all the trays and also include a full order of olives (priced at $20) at no charge. You'll also waive the $100 deposit that you usually require for large orders. Make Mr. Dormer feel that he is making a good choice in selecting your cuisine for the event—and be sure that all the details are clear.

41 You run a small specialty store, We R Flags, that makes and sells custom flags and banners. Today you received an order from the community council of Fernside, a neighborhood in your city, for banners to hang from the lampposts along the two main entrances to the neighborhood. Their representative, Kay Gillespie, had spoken with you earlier during an office visit about the design and price of the banners, and she has now emailed you to confirm that the council would like to go ahead with them.

They'll need 20 banners altogether—10 for each of the two entrances to the neighborhood. Of the three possible designs that she and you discussed, the council would like the one featuring the fern leaves in the background and the words "Welcome to Fernside" in the "Seabird SF" font appliquéd to the banner. As you and she agreed, the price will be $47 per banner, or $940 not including tax. She asks that the banners be

ready in four weeks, in time for the neighborhood picnic and clean-up day.

But there's the rub—you can't have the banners ready by then. A critical cog in your production, Jeff Smith, is out on sick leave and will not return for at least another week. Jeff is the one who gets the design from your artist, superimposes it on the fabric, and cuts out the pieces for the sewing people to appliqué to the banner. He is the only one who knows how to run the cutting machine. He has already been out one week, and business has backed up. You simply cannot move this job ahead of all the others that customers are waiting for.

Reply to Ms. Gillespie confirming the details of her order but also telling her about this hitch. You look on the Fernside Community Council website and see that the neighborhood has another special event coming up later. Perhaps it will be acceptable for you to have the banners ready by then.

42 You work in the distribution center at 3M, where you have received an unusual order for your privacy filters from an important customer BuyOnlineNow.com, an office supply superstore. The order was for an extraordinarily large number of privacy filters in 12.1", 14.1", and 17.0" sizes and none in the comparable widescreen sizes. In fact, your inventory management software flagged this order as one to check.

While your own statistics reveal that the sales of laptops is up considerably, which likely accounts for the large size of the order, the newest stats you have show that sales of the widescreen models have outsold the square screen models since 2004.

Therefore, before filling the order with all square filters, you'll write the buyer, Sandra Hernandez, at sandra@BuyOnlineNow.com to confirm her intentions. You might want to share some of your current statistics for the sales of widescreen laptops with her as well as the model numbers for the widescreen filters for these sizes—PF12.1W, PF14.1W, and PF17.0W—so she can place a new order online if she prefers.

Make it clear that you are only delaying filling the order to ensure that she gets exactly the sizes she needs. Retaining the order is your primary goal, but keeping this important customer's goodwill is critical as well.

43 Boy, have your sales of the TheStick, a massage tool, been hot lately. Your CEO, Jay Suverkrup, has been doing an excellent job of promoting the benefits of it for both health and athletic uses. He's appeared on the Today Show, talking about its benefits for those with fibromyalgia. And he's been quoted in major newspapers across the country talking about its use by a wide variety of athletes in both amateur and professional sports. On top of all this, TheStick was shown in an HBO special on the NFL.

Until today, most of the orders placed on your website, <http://www.thestick.com>, have been for the Original Body Stick. This 24" model for the average person addresses the

most muscle groups. And you've been able to fill all the orders placed so far.

However, today's order from the athletic director at [your school] for 200 of the travel sticks took you by surprise. Apparently, an alum, who saw Jay on television and who is a confirmed user after being introduced to it through a friend on the USA Cycling Team, donated the funds to your school to provide one for every varsity athlete who wants one.

As Sally Short, sales manager for TheStick, you'll confirm receiving the order but will need to send it in two batches—the 150 that you have on hand will be sent immediately with the remaining 50 in about two weeks.

Claims

44 While on spring break you visited your uncle William's furniture store (West Side Furniture) just in time to witness the

receipt of a shipment of badly damaged Sleepwell mattresses. Uncle William had ordered 50 of them at $145 each (total

$7,250) and had featured them in his annual spring sale scheduled to begin in three days. As the sale had been heavily promoted in local newspaper and television advertising, Uncle William was understandably upset. You followed him into his office and watched him prepare a claim message to the company. After a few minutes, Uncle William threw up his hands in disgust. "I'm too upset to do it right," he said. "You told me about that business communication course you're taking. You write it for me."

As you look over what Uncle William has composed, you agree that he does indeed need your help. Here is what you read:

Sleepwell Sales Manager:

Are you people trying to put something over on me? Today the 50 mattresses I ordered arrived in terrible condition, some smoke damaged and some water damaged. They aren't fit for sale. They weren't damaged in shipment. The paper covering was perfect. There must have been a fire at your place and you are trying to push the damaged ones off on an old customer. I'd ask for my money back, but I have already spent a bundle on advertising them in my big spring sale that begins in three days. If you don't get me good ones in time, I'll sue.

Uncle William was right. He does need your help. Now write the message as you were instructed in your course.

45 Play the role of a professor of industrial management at your school. You have just returned from a 15-day tour of a German industry with 21 of your industrial management students. You worked up the tour through European Holidays, Ltd., a London-based tour company. The agreement with European Holidays called for a package price of $3,600 per person, including all travel, housing, and food.

The tour was excellent in most respects. The accommodations, tour guide, itinerary, and travel were as proposed by the tour company. But there was one serious shortcoming. Dinners were not paid for by European Holidays. The tour guide, who was excellent in every respect, said he had no authorization to have European Holidays cover the meals. So you and the students paid for dinners personally. After returning home, you reviewed the written agreement with the tour company. As you remembered, it clearly stated that dinners would be included in the price. You conclude that out-of-pocket expenses for dinners were about $16 a day—a total of $240 per person. Including your dinners, the total comes to $5,280.

You will insist that European Holidays return this part of the total cost. It can pay individually (to each of the 21 students) or it can send the total amount to you to distribute to the students. Now you will write the claim (email or letter) that will get the results you want.

46 Your job as grounds superintendent at the prestigious Cherokee Springs Country Club involves keeping the golf course in tip-top shape for its 655 affluent members. Early last spring you contracted with BioTech, Inc., professionals in sodding, building, and maintaining sports-related grass areas. They reseeded all your fairways, tee boxes, and greens with the newest hybrid grasses designed to withstand the intense summer heat in your area.

Today is July 30. You have noticed over the past three weeks that the fairways show brown spots in several places. Also, there are thatched spines in several areas in irregular patterns on the greens. When you first noticed these problems, you reported them to BioTech. They told you that regular fertilizing and watering would bring the grass to its proper growth and consistency. Despite your maintenance crew's attempts to revive the turf, the problem seems to be getting worse instead of better.

One of the club members, a chemical agronomist, told you that there appear to be two different kinds of grasses. The fading ones are not the same pattern as the other. Could it be that different types of grass were planted? So you took samples and had them analyzed by your county agricultural extension agent. The results confirmed your original suspicions. Different hybrids exist in the samples. The fading grass was developed for a much colder climate.

Now you must write BioTech about your unsatisfactory experiences with their service and products. First, you want an explanation of what happened. You will have to report to your board of directors about what happened and why. So you want the details. It will be at least a year before you can have the turf in good playing shape. The club paid $94,600 for the job, and you think it is entitled to a refund. BioTech simply botched this job. Whether they will be contracted to redo the job will depend on the reasons for their mistakes.

47 You're the co-owner and president of a midsized construction company specializing in residential projects. You recently held your big end-of-the-year appreciation party for your employees at the Mandarin Hotel. Now you stare at the bill for the event. It's for $1,280.70, which includes the room rental and food and drinks for 80 people. As you reflect on the quality of the party, you realize that you're going to have to write a letter asking for an adjustment.

Yes, the hotel gave you a private party room as your administrative assistant had requested when he made the reservation six weeks ago, but the room was very loud, thanks to a boisterous party that was going on in the next room (complete with live band). Your guests could hardly hear each other talk, and you had to shout, even with a microphone, to share your words of appreciation with the group.

But the bigger problem was the food. You had expected such elegant fare as coconut shrimp, sushi, and miniature quiches, along with the standard offerings of cheese cubes, veggies, and fruit. You did get the quiches, but the other warm hors d'oeuvres consisted of miniature spring rolls and chicken fingers that looked and tasted as if they'd come straight out of a box in the freezer. Yes, when your assistant had arranged the event, it had been pointed out (and the menu had said) that the listed food options were samples and not necessarily exactly what your party would get. But you don't feel that the hors d'oeuvres you were served came close to what the hotel's hospitality staff or its printed material had led you and your assistant to expect.

You were disappointed and embarrassed by these problems. The annual dinner is supposed to be a reflection of how much the company values its employees, and it looked bad that you hadn't managed to arrange things better for them. You'd heard good things about the hotel and its catering service, and you did find the room to be attractive and the service staff to be professional and courteous. But given your experience, you don't feel that you should pay the full amount of the bill. Decide what you do want to pay and write the letter to the center telling them that this is the amount you feel is fair, in light of the problems you experienced. You may or may not hold another company function there, depending on their answer.

---

48 You are a CPA who runs your own one-person tax-consulting business out of your home, a set-up that enables you to be the primary caregiver for your kids. Your clients are private citizens who need help getting their annual income taxes filed. Essentially, you tell them what forms and documentation they need, they get all these together, and then you come over with your laptop to prepare their taxes with them. The process usually takes only an hour or two, but at $100 an hour, you make a decent income. Plus, once you serve a client, he or she tends to stay on with you year after year, so you have built up a nice amount of repeat business. It has all worked out quite well.

But there's the occasional disaster, like the one that occurred last week. Your laptop suddenly went on the blink. You could bring up nothing on the screen but programming code that you didn't understand. You called IT Solutions to come troubleshoot the problem, and the service person, Ray, discovered that your hard drive had gone bad. Yes, you'd kept backup files on an alternative drive, but it turned out that you had to go through the main hard drive to get to the other one, so when the main drive stopped working, the backup drive was inaccessible.

After several hours' work, however, Ray managed to recover your customer information (names, addresses and contact information, and dates serviced) and your business information (income, expenses, and so forth). What a relief! He also put new internal and external hard drives in place. He was not sure of the pricing for the new hardware, so he said that he would send you a final bill once he got all the information he needed.

Two days later you receive an itemized bill for $510. The service part of the bill came to $200—which you would be happy to pay if you hadn't discovered after Ray's visit that, in fact, some of the customer records and financial records have become garbled or lost. You are missing key pieces of information on which your business depends. The equipment part of the bill shows that IT Solutions charged a considerably higher price for the internal and external hard drives than you could have gotten on the Internet or at a local computer center. In light of these facts, you do not feel that it is fair to pay the full amount of the bill—certainly not until your records are fully recovered.

To get a quick response, email IT Solutions telling them of the problems and requesting a fair solution.

---

49 As a staff person for a real estate office, you have been directed by your boss to return and get a refund on a set of photographs that were developed by a mail-order photo-developing company, Olympia PhotoService. Your boss had received several ads in the mail from this company. Their prices certainly did undercut those of any local photo shop, and they had guaranteed to deliver high-quality pictures or else redevelop them for free. Yes, you'd had to wait a good while for the pictures to come in the mail, but your boss had figured that the low price would make the wait worthwhile. Plus, there wasn't a hurry on these particular pictures. You use printed-out digital photographs for your usual flyers and web listings, but the pictures in question were taken with a film camera and were intended for a gallery of properties to display proudly on a table in the office.

The thing is, you have already sent these pictures back once to be redeveloped, and the replacements have turned out

to be no better than the first set. To make sure the problem wasn't with the original film, you took the negatives to a local photo-developing shop and, at some expense, had had them developed. The pictures had turned out fine. Neither you nor your boss has any confidence left that Olympia will do a good job, and these photographs are too important to make a less-than-perfect job acceptable. You will return the second set of faulty pictures and ask for a reimbursement to cover both the developing fee and the mailing costs. Too bad the company can't reimburse you for your lost time as well. But you know you'll have to control your temper. You'll be asking Olympia to go beyond their stated customer-satisfaction policy, and your chances for success will be low if you adopt an offensive tone. Write the message that will get you the result that your boss wants and end your business with this company on at least a civil note.

---

50 Yesterday one of your good friends, Mary Adami, told you about a serious car accident she had had on the way to school. While neither she nor the other driver was seriously injured personally, her brand new car was totaled. And she seemed a bit rattled when she told you about her insurance dilemma.

While she had bought her insurance through an independent agent her family had known for years, the policy was a new one that the agent hadn't sold before. But the agent thought it was particularly good for her because for about $20 per year extra it included gap coverage. This covers the difference between the value and what is owed on the car. Because she was buying a new car that was almost completely financed, she thought it was probably a good idea to have this coverage. And right now she's very glad she spent the extra $20 on the gap coverage because the Toyota Corolla she bought for $19,000 with $1,000 down and an $18,000 loan was valued at only $16,000 by the insurance company now—just eight months later. The company, however, is telling her that her $500 deductible applies to both her regular coverage and to the gap coverage. So instead of having to come up with the $500 deductible to clear the loan, she has to come up with $1,000.

That did not seem quite right to you either, so you asked to see the policy. As you read it, the gap protection was part of the basic policy rather than an added-on policy. The policy clearly states that it will cover the difference between what is owed on the vehicle and its value. There is no mention of the deduction applying here again. And you recall from the business law class you took last semester that deductibles can be applied only once per incident. It seems very clear to you that the company should subtract only the $500 deductible once. So you decide to write a claim message for Mary to James Andrews, the director of customer relations, at Mary's insurer [you supply a name and address here] to help her get the second $500 deduction dropped from their computation. You feel good about helping a friend and glad you can put your business law and communication knowledge to work.

---

51 Today's mail brought a postcard on the status of a $90 rebate from Daewoo for a flat panel monitor you bought at Fry's. Basically, it said that your rebate was denied because it was postmarked past the eligibility period. You are certain that you mailed it well before the March 4 closing date because you made a point to set the monitor up and mail in the required UPC code and receipt before classes started. In fact, you had the computer tech in the dorm set it up for you, and you are certain you can get a copy of the tech's work log to prove the date it was set up. However, you can't prove the date it was received or entered at the company. In fact, when you called Daewoo to get more information, you learned that their records show receiving it on March 6. But in your business law class you learned that businesses that rely on the post office to do business must use the date postmarked as the date received.

Since the $90 could pay for a book for one of your classes next semester, it is clearly worth your time to write for the rebate you deserve. Write Fry's a claim message for the rebate. Be sure to make it clear that you expect the rebate promptly.

---

52 Just before school started in August, you purchased what looked like the perfect desk and chair set at Office Depot. Not only were you delighted at its $80 price, but you also thought its size was perfect for the small apartment you would be sharing with a friend. And you liked the idea that the chair didn't look like a typical office chair; it was similar to a deck chair on wheels. It had a tubular frame with a leather-look black seat and back. So you thought you could use it for additional seating when people stopped by.

Until last night it seemed to serve the purpose well as both a desk and table chair. However, you were both embarrassed and frightened last night when it broke and your computer tutor, Tom McLaughlin, fell to the floor. He wasn't hurt, but he could have been. He's a slim guy, and the two of you were just working quietly on a laptop together. There wasn't anything at all that caused it, and the chair hasn't had rough or extensive use either.

While it's not the end of world, you decide to write Office Depot about it. You think they should know about it in case the product is faulty, but you'd also like to have a new chair. Luckily you saved both the receipt and the box with the desk set's model number (NF913232) on it. From their website you learned that you can contact their customer service representative at custcare@4sure.com.

---

53 As the sales manager for Computer Depot, a wholesale outlet for computer components, you conceived a plan to keep your company's name on your customers' minds throughout the year. The plan was to give subscriptions to *Golf World* or *Racquet* at Christmas to your established customers. The magazine given would depend on the customer's interest in either golf or tennis or a racquet sport. By special agreement with the publisher, the mailer wrapping on each issue would carry the name of the gift donor. So you reasoned that with each monthly issue, the customer would receive a reminder of Computer Depot. You ordered complimentary subscriptions for the 243 people whom your sales representatives recommended. The cost was $15.50 per subscription for either magazine. (Both are published by the Forsythe Company.)

Christmas was a month ago. Now you are getting reports from your sales representatives that the customers haven't received their first copies—nor have they even been notified that they have been given subscriptions. Something is wrong here. You are embarrassed. Your salespeople have told their customers of your intentions, and they are waiting for their magazines.

Now you must write the Forsythe circulation manager a claim message that will ask for an explanation of what went wrong. You think the publisher should write to each customer involved explaining what happened and relieving Computer Depot of any responsibility. And, of course, they should start sending the magazines. The damage to your goodwill should be apparent. Write this email message in a calm, rational, yet forceful way.

Operational Messages

54 Move into the role of secretary to the board of directors of Central National Bank. At last week's meeting of the board, the discussion centered on the inappropriate attire and grooming of too many of the bank's employees. The general thought was that the bank's image is suffering and that something should be done about it.

The meeting concluded with President Wilma Hughes directing you to prepare a first draft of dress and grooming regulations for your sex. (Another person will do the same for the opposite sex.) These proposed regulations will be discussed at next month's board meeting.

President Hughes's words give you a general idea of what is wanted: "Be careful not to make us appear to be prudes, but give us something that will protect the bank image. We all know that things aren't as they once were. We have to loosen up a bit. But we still have to draw the line somewhere. Use your very best judgment. What we want are employees whose appearances enhance the bank's image in today's world. And don't be upset if the board rejects parts of what you propose."

So now you must begin planning the content. When you have finished, you will write the regulations in the bank's usual memorandum form. Prepare it for the signature of President Hughes. Make sure that your regulations are in orderly form and are easy for all to understand. And work hard to make them acceptable to the employees.

---

55 You, the president of Goliath Manufacturing Company, have just concluded a long conversation with Ellie Lopez, your training director. For the past few months, Ellie has been working on an educational program for company employees. Her plan is to encourage employees to take advantage of the extensive night offerings made available by the local university, and perhaps even more important, to assist them financially.

As Ellie explained her plan, any employee could take one course a semester as long as it was in an approved degree program. The company would pay all tuition and required fees plus an allowance of up to $150 for books and supplies. Satisfactory completion of the course (meaning a grade of C or better) would be a requirement for registering for another course. This requirement could be waived on appeal.

Employees who progress in a degree plan to the point that they can complete all degree requirements in one academic year would be permitted to take a leave with pay plus tuition, fees, books, and supplies. But they would have to agree to stay with the company for two years after this leave. Actually, this payment would be in the form of a loan that would be forgiven after the completion of two years of work with the company.

You like the plan very much, especially after Ellie supported it with strong reasoning. The resulting enlightened work force would improve management quality. And certainly the plan would be a boost to morale. So you enthusiastically accepted the proposal.

Now you must write a memorandum to all employees explaining the program and encouraging them to participate. For class purposes, you may add any reasonable provisions that Ellie may have overlooked.

---

56 You're the president and primary owner of a small software-development firm. Your part-time marketing person, Roger Evans, has been acting as the company webmaster, but he has simply had too many other duties to be able to do this job well. As a result, you recently purchased several site licenses for a computer program that, when installed on various employees' computers, will enable them to make changes directly to the company website. Every page of the site is based on the same template, so the various new "webmasters" will not be able to alter the essential look of the pages—which is good, since you don't want your website to be a hodgepodge of different designs. But by using the new program, the people who know the different functional areas of the company best will be able to maintain the content portion of the website that pertains to their operations, rather than their having to route everything (slowly) through the busy Roger. Roger will still be responsible for general oversight and maintenance of the site, but the new procedure will relieve him of a great deal of busy work, freeing him up for more important things.

Write an email announcement to the relevant employees in sales, product development, training, and, of course, to Roger, informing them that, as some of them may know, you have purchased the licenses for this program; that they will need to attend a training and testing session for the new program on the first Saturday of next month, from 9:00 to noon; and that, from now on, they'll be responsible for keeping their part of the website updated. The employees don't usually work on Saturdays, but you can't spare them for a three-hour chunk of time during the week. You also need to hold the training on a Saturday because your information technology person will need to bring people's computers into one meeting room so that the trainees can learn and share notes together, and if she were to do this setting up during regular work hours, people would be without their computers and, therefore, unable to work.

Your company has a positive, team-like culture, so the employees are not likely, overall, to view this news negatively. You know they've been frustrated with having to pressure Roger, politely, to get things updated on the website, so they may well be relieved that they can now just take matters into their own hands. On the other hand, nobody really wants to come in to work on a Saturday morning, and nobody really wants extra responsibilities, either. So anything you can say to get a positive reception for your message would be a good idea. You also want to anticipate any questions that these employees may have and give them enough information so that the plan seems well thought out and reasonable.

57 As chief operations officer at FunDreams, a company that makes toys and children's furniture, you find yourself in a position that you always dread but that is, unfortunately, a fact of life for the makers of children's products: having to issue a safety recall for one of your products. Child safety laws are very strict, so whenever you get a clear hint that one of your products could be hazardous, you initiate a voluntary safety recall campaign. Much as you hate to take such steps, they can keep people from getting hurt—and it would be folly to wait for someone to file a lawsuit against your company, generate terrible publicity, and perhaps ultimately have a judge force you to pay damages as well as recall the faulty product. For your conscience as well as your company's image, you announce a safety recall whenever it seems warranted, and in this case, it does.

Four retailers who sell your bunk beds have contacted your company now to say that they have received complaints about the top bed of your newest model collapsing onto the bottom bed. Fortunately, no one, as far as you know, was hurt. While one isolated incident could be attributed to misuse of the bed (the instructions for assembling the bed clearly state that the top bunk will not support more than 200 pounds), four different cases, reported so soon after the release of your new model, do not bode well. You have discussed the complaints with your top materials engineer, and it appears that the engineering department misjudged the sturdiness of the

metal tubing used for the frame of the bed. You've also gotten the advice of your company's legal adviser. Costly as it is, you must initiate a recall campaign.

Part of the campaign will be to write your employees to tell them what's going on. Tell them why the bed is being recalled and how this will occur. Specifically, your company will be sending letters to any customer who sent in the warranty card that came with the product; you'll send recall notices to your retailers and to pediatricians' offices for them to post; you'll run a recall notice in the most popular parenting magazines; and you'll post the announcement on your company website. All announcements will include the information that customers should stop using the beds immediately and return these to the retailer to get free brackets to put on the supports for the top bed. You'll be sending all your retailers a supply of the brackets. If it's not feasible for customers to return the product to the original retailer, they can contact your customer service department directly and have the brackets sent to them.

Several departments of the company will be involved in this effort, and you'll be talking further with the supervisors of those departments.

Use this unfortunate situation as an opportunity to build pride in the company's integrity and to show that FunDreams has the kind of management that keeps its employees informed on important company matters.

---

58 While your company has been doing well, you've noticed a sense of detachment of employees from each other that concerns you. In the past, their ability to work well as a team seemed to help them be successful on a variety of projects. But the detachment seemed to start when employees were allowed to bring iPods to work and listen to their own music. Initially, this seemed motivational, and employees seemed to enjoy it as far as you could tell by the proliferation of people with earphones. However, you're not sure they are talking with each other as much as they used to do.

When some employees who did not own iPods asked to be able to listen to music of their choice over headphones but streaming from the Internet, you thought it was only fair and

permitted it. However, that extended to online news videos first, then to *Desperate Housewives,* and sometimes now even to movies. And some are even IM-ing now. Clearly none of these activities are promoting the collaborative environment you once had. So you've made a decision to limit the amount of time employees can use these technologies to the first and last hour of the working day and the lunch hour unless such use is directly related to the work at hand.

To communicate this new policy, write a message that explains it along with the benefits it is likely to bring both the company and employees. This message will be sent to all employees by email as well as posted on the company portal.

---

59 An article in *BusinessWeek* reported on the benefits of meditation in relieving stress, naming companies and CEOs that practice it regularly. While once thought to be a religious or spiritual practice, meditation is being investigated by scientists at the National Institute of Health, the University of Wisconsin, and the Mind/Body Institute at Harvard. New technologies are showing what happens to the brain during and after meditation.

The results reveal that during meditation the left prefrontal cortex of the brain is much more active in meditators than in the brains of nonmeditators. This change in neural physiology enables meditators to respond to events with less emotion and to think options through more clearly. Even the Mayo Clinic is recommending that meditation be used along with other medications to treat a variety of conditions, including stress.

Dr. Herbert Benson, at Harvard, recommends that businesses set aside a quiet room for people to carry out a meditative behavior of their choice. So you've decided try it, including providing lessons in basic meditation as well as yoga, tai chi, Qi gong and even walking meditation.

Write a memo that will go to all employees, telling them that you will set up basic lessons for learning a variety of meditative practices and provide a quiet room on site for them to use on a regular basis. Encourage them to choose a form of meditation that fits them and their lifestyle and to schedule a time into their days to practice regularly at a time that works best for them. Show that you are offering this benefit as an opportunity for maintaining good health.

chapter seven

Indirectness in Bad-News Messages

Upon completing this chapter, you will be able to write indirect responses to convey bad news. To reach this goal, you should be able to

1 Determine which situations require using the indirect order for the most effective response.

2 Write indirect-order messages following the general plan.

3 Use tact and courtesy in refusals of requests.

4 Write adjustment refusals that minimize and overcome bad impressions.

5 Compose tactful, yet clear, credit refusals that foster goodwill.

6 Write negative announcements that maintain goodwill.

SITUATIONS REQUIRING INDIRECTNESS

- Usually bad-news messages should be in the indirect order.

As explained in Chapter 6, when a message is primarily bad news, you usually should write in the indirect order. The indirect order is especially effective when you must say no or convey other disappointing news. The main reason for this approach is that negative messages are received more positively when an explanation precedes them. An explanation may even convince the reader that the writer's position is correct. In addition, an explanation cushions the shock of bad news. Not cushioning the shock makes the message unnecessarily harsh, and harshness destroys goodwill.

- There is exceptions, as when the bad news is routine or when the reader prefers frankness.

You may want to use directness in some bad-news situations. If, for example, you think that your negative answer will be accepted routinely, you might choose directness. For example, in many buyer–seller relationships in business, both parties expect backorders and order errors to occur now and then. Thus messages reporting this negative information are considered routine and are written in direct order. You also might choose directness if you know your reader well and feel that he or she will appreciate frankness. And you might choose directness anytime you are not concerned about goodwill. But such instances are not the rule. Usually you would be wise to use indirectness in refusals.

- Following is a general plan for bad-news messages and four applications.

As in the preceding chapter, we first describe a general plan. Then we adapt this plan to specific business situations—four in this case. First is the refusal of a request. We cover it in detail. Next we cover the refusal of a request for adjustment and refusals of credit. Since these last two situations are similar to the first one, we cover them briefly. The focus here is on special considerations involving each type. Finally, we cover negative announcements, which are a form of bad-news messages with unique characteristics.

THE GENERAL INDIRECT PLAN

Using a Strategic Buffer

- Use a buffer in indirect bad-news messages.
- Begin with a buffer that identifies the subject.
- Use a neutral or positive buffer without raising readers' hopes.

Indirect messages presenting bad news often begin with a strategic buffer. By buffer we mean an opening that identifies the subject of the message but does not indicate overtly that negative news is coming. That is, it raises the topic of the message but does not indicate what the rest of the message will say about it.

A buffer can be neutral or positive. A neutral buffer might simply acknowledge your receipt of the reader's earlier message and indicate your awareness of what it said. A positive buffer might thank the reader for bringing a situation to your attention or for being a valued customer or employee. You do need to use care when opening on a positive note. You do not in any way want to raise the reader's hopes that you are about to deliver the news that he or she may be hoping for. That would only make your task of maintaining good relations more difficult.

- Sometimes the direct approach is best, especially if ethical issues are involved.

Some may argue that not starting with the good news is, for savvy readers, a clear tip-off that bad news is coming. If this is the case, then why not just start with the bad news? True, for some readers in some situations, a direct approach may be the best. For example, if you are writing to tell customers that there is a defective part in a car they have purchased and that they should return the car to the dealership immediately for repairs, it would be almost unethical not to feature this important information in the opening paragraph. Most readers in most situations, however, appreciate a more gradual introduction to the message's main negative point. It gives them a chance to prepare for the news—and even if they suspect that it will be negative, the use of a buffer indicates consideration for their feelings.

Setting Up the Negative News

- Follow the buffer with an explanatory strategy before presenting the negative news.

For each case, you will have thought through the facts involved and decided that, to some extent, you will have to say no or present some other kind of negative news. You then have to figure out how you will present your reasons in such a way that your reader will accept the news as positively as possible. Your strategy might be to explain the fairness of a certain action. It might be to present facts that clearly make the decision necessary. Or you might cite the expert opinion of authorities whom both you and your reader respect. It might even be possible to show that your reasons for the negative decision actually will benefit the reader in the long run. Whatever explanatory strategy you have chosen, these reasons should follow your buffer and precede the negative news itself. In other words, the paragraph after the buffer should start explaining the situation in such a way that, by the time the negative news comes, the reader should be prepared to receive it in the most favorable light possible. Examples of how to accomplish this follow.

Presenting the Bad News Positively

Next, you present the bad news. If you have developed your reasoning convincingly, this bad news should appear as a logical outcome. And you should present it as positively as the situation will permit. In doing so, you must make certain that the negative message is clear—that your positive approach has not given the wrong impression.

• Refuse as positively as the situation permits.

One useful technique is to present your reasoning in first and third person, avoiding second person. To illustrate, in a message refusing a request for money back and return of product, one could write these negative words: "Since you have broken the seal, state law prohibits us from returning the product to stock." Or one could write these more positive words emphasizing first and third person: "State law prohibits us from returning to stock all such products with broken seals."

• Avoiding second person can reduce the negative impact.

It is sometimes possible to take the sting out of negative news by linking it to a reader benefit. For example, if you preface a company policy with "in the interest of fairness" or "for the safety of our guests," you are indicating that all of your patrons, including the reader, get an important benefit from your policy.

• Linking negative news to a reader benefit can also lessen the sting.

Your efforts to present this part of the message positively should stress the positive word emphasis described in Chapter 4. In using positive words, however, you must make certain your words truthfully and accurately convey your message. Your goal is to present the facts in a positive way. In no way should your ethics be in question.

• Be certain that you are honest and clear.

Offering an Alternative Solution

For almost any negative-news situation that you can think of, there is something you can do to help the reader with his or her problem.

• Help solve the reader's problem.

If someone seeks to hold an event on your company grounds and you must say no, you may be able to suggest other sites. If someone wants information that you cannot give, you might know of another way that he or she could get similar information. If you cannot volunteer your time and services, perhaps you know someone who might, or perhaps you could invite the reader to make the request again at a later, better time. If you have to announce a cutback on an employee benefit, you might be able to suggest ways that employees can supplement this benefit on their own. Taking the time to help the reader in this way is a sincere show of concern for the reader's situation. For this reason, it is one of your most powerful strategies for maintaining goodwill.

• Showing concern maintains goodwill.

Ending on a Positive Note

Since even a skillfully handled bad-news presentation can be disappointing to the reader, you should end the message on a forward-looking note. Your goal here is to shift the reader's thoughts to happier things—perhaps what you would say if you were in face-to-face conversation with the person. Preferably your comments should fit the one case, and they should not recall the negative message to the reader's mind. They should make clear that you value your relationship with the reader and still regard it as a positive one.

• End with specially adapted goodwill.

Following are adaptations of this general plan to four of the more common negative business message situations. From these applications you should be able to see how to adapt this general plan to almost any other negative message situation.

REFUSED REQUESTS

INTRODUCTORY SITUATION

Refused Requests

As in Chapter 6, assume again the role of assistant to the Pinnacle vice president. Today your boss assigned you the task of responding to a request from the local chapter of the National Association of Peace Officers. This worthy organization has asked Pinnacle to contribute to a scholarship fund for certain needy children.

The request is persuasive. It points out that the scholarship fund is terribly short. As a result, the association is not able to take care of all the needy children. Many of them are the children of officers who were killed in the line of duty. You have been moved by the persuasion, and you would like to comply, but you cannot.

You cannot contribute now because Pinnacle policy does not permit it. Even though you do not like the effects of the policy in this case, you think the policy is good. Each year Pinnacle earmarks a fixed amount—all it can afford—for contributions. Then it doles out this amount to the causes that a committee of its executives considers the most worthy. Unfortunately, all the money earmarked for this year has already been given away. You will have to say no to the request, at least for now. You can offer to consider the association's cause next year.

Your response must report the bad news, though it can hold out hope for the future. Because you like the association and because you want it to like Pinnacle, you will try to handle the situation delicately. The task will require your best strategy and your best writing skills.

● Refusing a request involves both saying no and maintaining goodwill.

The refusal of a request is definitely bad news. Your reader has asked for something, and you must say no. Your primary goal, of course, is to present this bad news. You could do this easily with a direct refusal. But as a courteous and caring businessperson, you have the secondary goal of maintaining goodwill. To achieve this second goal, you must convince your reader that the refusal is fair and reasonable.

Developing the Strategy

● Think through the situation, looking for a good explanation.

Finding a fair and reasonable explanation involves carefully thinking through the facts of the situation. First, consider why you are refusing. Then, assuming that your reasons are just, you should try to find the best way of explaining them to your reader. In doing this, you might well place yourself in your reader's shoes. Try to imagine how the explanation will be received. What comes out of this thinking is the strategy you should use in your message.

One often-used explanation is that company policy forbids compliance. This explanation may be valid, but only if this company policy is defensible. Justification of the policy may well be a part of the explanation. Often you must refuse simply because the facts of the case justify a refusal—that is, you are right and the reader is wrong. In such cases, your best course is to review the facts, taking care not to accuse or insult and to appeal to the reader's sense of fair play. There are other explanations, of course. You select the one that best fits your situation.

Setting Up the Explanation in the Opening

● Begin with words that set up the explanation.

Having determined the explanation, you begin the message with words that set up discussing it. For example, take the case described at the beginning of this discussion—refusing an association's request for a donation. The following opening meets this case's requirements well:

> Your organization is doing a commendable job of educating its needy children. It deserves the help of those who are in a position to give it.

This beginning, on-subject comment clearly marks the message as a response to the inquiry. It implies neither a yes nor a no answer. The statement, "It deserves the help of those who are in a position to give it," sets up the explanation, which will point out that the company is not in a position to give. Also, it puts the reader in an agreeable or open frame of mind—ready to accept the explanation that follows.

Presenting the Explanation Convincingly

As with the general plan, you next present your reasoning. To do this you use your best persuasion techniques: positive wording, proper emphasis, convincing logic, and supporting detail. In general, you use all your presentation skills in your effort to convince your reader.

- Then present your explanation.

Handling the Refusal Positively

Your handling of the refusal follows logically from your reasoning. If you have built the groundwork of explanation and fact convincingly, the refusal comes as a logical conclusion and as no surprise. If you have done your job well, your reader may even support the refusal. Even so, because the refusal is the most negative part of your message, you should not give it too much emphasis. You should state it quickly, clearly, and positively. You should keep it away from positions of emphasis, such as paragraph endings.

- The refusal should flow logically from the reasoning. Do not emphasize it.

To state the refusal quickly, you should use as few words as possible. Laboring the refusal for three or four sentences when a single clause would do gives it too much emphasis.

- State the refusal quickly,

Still, you should make certain that the reader has no doubt about your answer. In the effort to be positive, writers sometimes become evasive and unclear. Take, for example, a writer who attempts to show that the facts of the case justify the company policy on which a refusal is based. Such words as "these facts clearly support our policy of . . ." would not communicate a clear refusal to some people. Another example is that of a writer who follows justifying an explanation with a compromise offer. In this case, such words as "it would be better if . . ." would make for a vague refusal.

- clearly,

Telling people news they don't want to hear requires your most careful communication effort.

● and positively.

To state the refusal positively, you should study carefully the effects of your words. Such harsh words as *I refuse, will not,* and *cannot* stand out. So do such timeworn apologies as "I deeply regret to inform you . . ." and "I am sorry to say . . ." You can usually phrase your refusal in terms of a positive statement of policy. For example, instead of writing "your insurance does not cover damage to buildings not connected to the house," write "your insurance covers damage to the house only." Or instead of writing "We must refuse," a wholesaler could deny a discount by writing "We can grant discounts only when . . ." In some cases, your job may be to educate the reader. Not only will this be your explanation for the refusal, but it also will build goodwill.

Using a Compromise When Practical

● If a compromise is
practical, use it to imply
what you cannot do.

If the situation justifies a compromise, you can use it in making the refusal positive. More specifically, by saying what you can do (the compromise), you can clearly imply what you cannot do. For example, if you write "The best we can do is to (the compromise) . . . ," you clearly imply that you cannot do what the reader requested. Such statements contain no negative words and usually are as positive as the situation will permit.

Closing with Goodwill

● End with a pleasant
off-subject comment.

Even a skillfully handled refusal is the most negative part of your message. Because the news is disappointing, it is likely to put your reader in an unhappy frame of mind. That frame of mind works against your goodwill goal. To leave your reader with a feeling of goodwill, you must shift his or her thoughts to more pleasant matters.

● Adapt the close to the
one case.

The best closing subject matter depends on the facts of the case, but it should be positive talk that fits the one situation. For example, if your refusal involves a counterproposal, you could say more about the counterproposal. Or you could make some friendly remark about the subject of the request as long as it does not remind the reader of the bad news. In fact, your closing subject matter could be almost any friendly remark that would be appropriate if you were handling the case face to face. The major requirement is that your ending words have a goodwill effect.

● Avoid ending with the
old, negative apologies.

Ruled out are the timeworn, negative apologies. "Again, may I say that I regret that we must refuse" is typical of these. Also ruled out are the equally timeworn appeals for understanding, such as "I sincerely hope that you understand why we must make this decision." Such words emphasize the bad news.

Fitting the General Plan to Refused Requests

Adapting the preceding analysis to the general plan, we arrive at the following outline for the refused request:

- Begin with words that indicate a response to the request, are neutral as to the answer, and set up the strategy.
- Present your justification or explanation, using positive language and you-viewpoint.
- Refuse clearly and positively, including a counterproposal or compromise when appropriate.
- End with an adapted goodwill comment.

Contrasting Refusals

The advantage of the indirect order in refusal messages is evident from the following contrasting examples. Both refuse clearly. But only the one that uses the indirect order is likely to gain reader goodwill.

Harshness in the Direct Refusal. The first example states the bad news right away. This blunt treatment puts the reader in an unreceptive frame of mind. The result is that the reader is less likely to accept the explanation that follows. The explanation is clear, but note the unnecessary use of negative words (*exhausted, regret, cannot consider*). Note also how the closing words leave the reader with a strong reminder of the bad news.

Subject: Your request for donation

Subject: Your request for donation

Ms. Cangelosi:

We regret to inform you that we cannot grant your request for a donation to the association's scholarship fund.

So many requests for contributions are made of us that we have found it necessary to budget a definite amount each year for this purpose. Our budgeted funds for this year have been exhausted, so we simply cannot consider additional requests. However, we will be able to consider your request next year.

We deeply regret our inability to help you now and trust that you understand our position.

Mark Stephens

This bad email is harsh because of its directness.

Tact and Courtesy in an Indirect Refusal. The second example skillfully handles the negative message. Its opening words are on subject and neutral. They set up the explanation that follows. The clear and logical explanation ties in with the opening. Using no negative words, the explanation leads smoothly to the refusal. Note that the refusal also is handled without negative words and yet is clear. The friendly close fits the one case.

Subject: Your scholarship fund request

Ms. Cangelosi:

Your efforts to build the scholarship fund for the association's needy children are most commendable. We wish you good success in your efforts to further this worthy cause.

We at Pinnacle are always willing to assist worthy causes whenever we can. That is why every January we budget for the year the maximum amount we believe we are able to contribute to such causes. Then we distribute that amount among the various deserving groups as far as it will go. Since our budgeted contributions for this year have already been made, we are placing your organization on our list for consideration next year.

We wish you the best of luck in your efforts to help educate the deserving children of the association's members.

Mark Stephens

This email using the indirect approach is better.

ADJUSTMENT REFUSALS

INTRODUCTORY SITUATION

Adjustment Refusals

Sometimes your job at Pinnacle involves handling an unhappy person. Today you have to do that, for the morning email has brought a strong claim for adjustment on an order for Pinnacle's Do-Craft fabrics. The claim writer, Ms. Arlene Sanderson, explains that a Do-Craft fabric her upholstering company used on some outdoor furniture has faded badly in less than 10 months. She even includes photographs of the fabric to prove her point. She contends that the product is defective, and she wants her money back—all $2,517 of it.

Inspection of the photographs reveals that the fabric has been subjected to strong sunlight for long periods. Do-Craft fabrics are for inside use only. Both the Pinnacle brochures on the product and the catalog description stress this point. In fact, you have difficulty understanding how Ms. Sanderson missed it when she ordered from the catalog. Anyway, as you see it, Pinnacle is not responsible and does not intend to refund the money. At the same time, it wants to keep Ms. Sanderson as a repeat customer. Now you must write the message that will do just that. The following discussion tells you how.

Refused Request Message (Refusing a Request for Examples). Tact and strategy mark this refusal in which an office manager turns down a textbook author's request. The author has asked for model email messages that can be used as examples in a communication guidebook. The office manager reasons that complying with this request would take more time than he is willing or able to give.

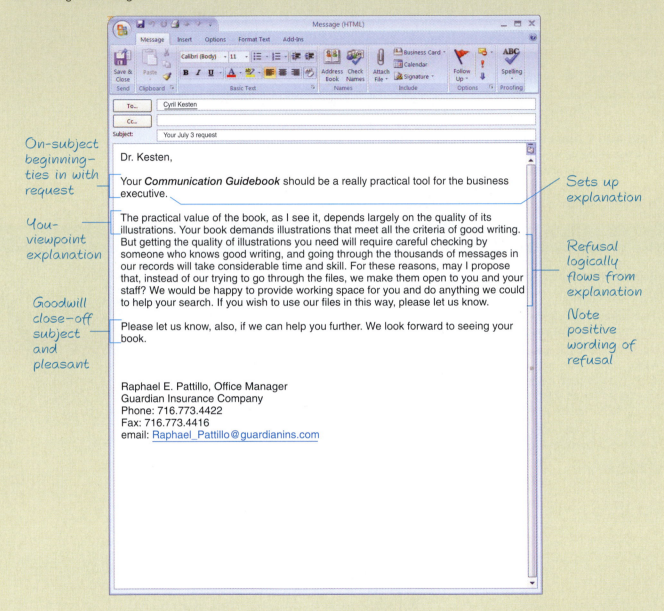

On-subject beginning—ties in with request

You-viewpoint explanation

Goodwill close—off subject and pleasant

Sets up explanation

Refusal logically flows from explanation

Note positive wording of refusal

Email content:

To... Cyril Kesten

Subject: Your July 3 request

Dr. Kesten,

Your *Communication Guidebook* should be a really practical tool for the business executive.

The practical value of the book, as I see it, depends largely on the quality of its illustrations. Your book demands illustrations that meet all the criteria of good writing. But getting the quality of illustrations you need will require careful checking by someone who knows good writing, and going through the thousands of messages in our records will take considerable time and skill. For these reasons, may I propose that, instead of our trying to go through the files, we make them open to you and your staff? We would be happy to provide working space for you and do anything we could to help your search. If you wish to use our files in this way, please let us know.

Please let us know, also, if we can help you further. We look forward to seeing your book.

Raphael E. Pattillo, Office Manager
Guardian Insurance Company
Phone: 716.773.4422
Fax: 716.773.4416
email: Raphael_Pattillo@guardianins.com

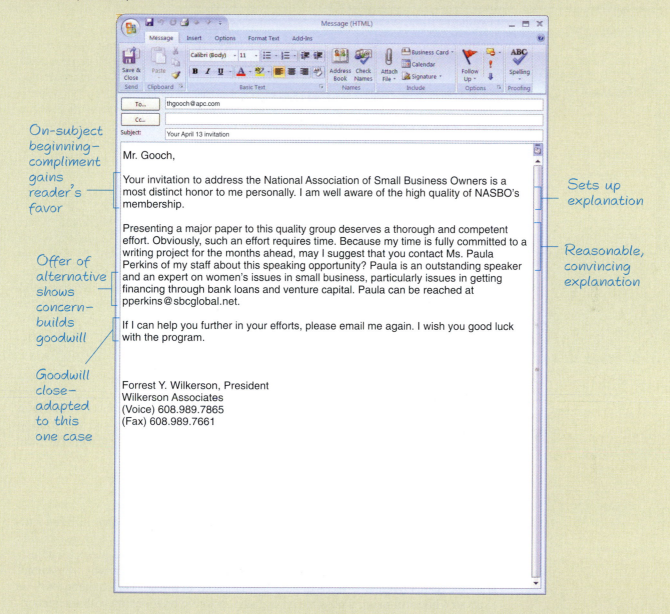

Refused Request Message (Turning Down a Speaking Invitation). This example shows good strategy in turning down a request to speak at a convention.

On-subject beginning—compliment gains reader's favor

Offer of alternative shows concern—builds goodwill

Goodwill close—adapted to this one case

Sets up explanation

Reasonable, convincing explanation

To... thgooch@apc.com

Cc...

Subject: Your April 13 invitation

Mr. Gooch,

Your invitation to address the National Association of Small Business Owners is a most distinct honor to me personally. I am well aware of the high quality of NASBO's membership.

Presenting a major paper to this quality group deserves a thorough and competent effort. Obviously, such an effort requires time. Because my time is fully committed to a writing project for the months ahead, may I suggest that you contact Ms. Paula Perkins of my staff about this speaking opportunity? Paula is an outstanding speaker and an expert on women's issues in small business, particularly issues in getting financing through bank loans and venture capital. Paula can be reached at pperkins@sbcglobal.net.

If I can help you further in your efforts, please email me again. I wish you good luck with the program.

Forrest Y. Wilkerson, President
Wilkerson Associates
(Voice) 608.989.7865
(Fax) 608.989.7661

Email Merge Tool Allows Writers to Customize Frequent Messages

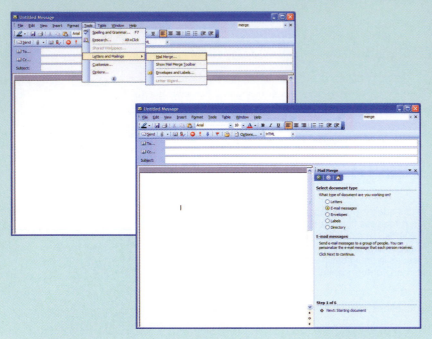

If you use Word as your editor in Outlook, you can use the merge tool to create form documents for those responses you send often. A writer simply creates the message first or uses an existing template or document. Saving it with a descriptive file name is important so that you can identify it easily the next time you need to send the same information. You can insert fields for information you know will be variable and modify other items as needed.

As you see here, once you select Mail Merge from the Tools/Letters and Mailings menus, you will be prompted through a series of steps to create documents that can be customized efficiently. By spending time creating well-written messages to start with, you can let the tool take care of repeated use of them.

Adjustment refusals are a special type of refused request. Your reader has made a claim asking for a remedy. Usually you grant claims. Most are legitimate, and you want to correct any error for which you are responsible. But such is not the case here. The facts do not justify correction. You must say no.

Determining the Strategy

The primary difference between this and other refusal messages is that in these situations, as we are defining them, your company will probably have clear, reasonable guidelines for what should and should not be regarded as legitimate requests for adjustment. You will, therefore, not have to spend much time figuring out why you cannot grant the reader's request. You will have good reasons to refuse. The challenge will be to do so while still making possible an ongoing, positive relationship with the reader.

Setting Up Your Reasoning

• Begin with words that set up your reasoning.

With your strategy in mind, you begin with words that set it up. Since this message is a response to one the reader has sent, you also acknowledge this message. You can do this by a date reference early in the message. Or you can do it with words that clearly show you are writing about the specific situation.

• A point of common agreement is one good possibility.

One good way of setting up your strategy is to begin on a point of common agreement and then to explain how the case at hand is an exception. To illustrate, a case involving a claim for adjustment for failure of an air conditioner to perform properly might begin thus:

> You are correct in believing that an 18,000 BTU Whirlpool window unit should cool the ordinary three-room apartment.

The explanation that follows this sentence will show that the apartment in question is not an ordinary apartment.

Another strategy is to build the case that the claim for adjustment goes beyond what can reasonably be expected. A beginning such as this one sets it up:

> Assisting families to enjoy beautifully decorated homes at budget prices is one of our most satisfying goals. We do all we reasonably can to reach it.

The explanation that follows this sentence will show that the requested adjustment goes beyond what can be reasonably expected.

● Another is to show that the claim goes beyond what is reasonable.

Making Your Case

In presenting your reasons for refusal, explain your company's relevant policy or practice. Without accusing the reader, call attention to facts that bear on the case—for example, that the item in question has been submerged in water, that the printed material warned against certain uses, or that the warranty has expired. Putting together the policy and the facts should lead logically to the conclusion that the adjustment cannot be granted.

● Explain your refusal by associating the facts of the case with a policy or practice.

Refusing Positively and Closing Courteously

As in other refusal messages, your refusal derives from your explanation. It is the logical result. You word it clearly, and you make it as positive as the circumstances permit. For example, this one is clear, and it contains no negative words:

> For these reasons, we can pay only when our employees pack the goods.

If a compromise is in order, you might present it in positive language like this:

> In view of these facts, the best we can do is repair the equipment at cost.

As in all bad-news messages, you should end this one with some appropriate, positive comment. You could reinforce the message that you care about the reader's business or the quality of your products. In cases where it would not seem selfish, you could write about new products or services, industry news, or such. Neither negative apologies nor words that recall the problem are appropriate here.

● Refuse positively and end with goodwill.

Adapting the General Plan

When we apply these special considerations to the general plan, we come up with the following specific plan for adjustment refusals:

- Begin with words that are on subject, are neutral as to the decision, and set up your strategy.
- Present the strategy that explains or justifies, being factual and positive.
- Refuse clearly and positively, perhaps including a counterproposal.
- End with off-subject, positive, forward-looking, friendly words.

Contrasting Adjustment Refusal Messages

Bad and good treatment of Pinnacle's refusal to give money back for the faded fabric are illustrated by the following two messages. The bad one, which is blunt and insulting, destroys goodwill. The good one, which uses the techniques described in the preceding paragraphs, stands a fair chance of keeping goodwill.

Bluntness in a Direct Refusal. The bad email begins bluntly with a direct statement of the refusal. The language is negative (*regret, must reject, claim, refuse, damage,* *inconvenience*). The explanation is equally blunt. In addition, it is insulting ("It is difficult to understand how you failed . . ."). It uses little tact, little you-viewpoint. Even the close is negative, for it recalls the bad news.

The bad email shows little concern for the reader's feelings.

Subject: Your May 3 claim for damages

Ms. Sanderson,

I regret to report that we must reject your request for money back on the faded Do-Craft fabric.

We must refuse because Do-Craft fabrics are not made for outside use. It is difficult for me to understand how you failed to notice this limitation. It was clearly stated in the catalog from which you ordered. It was even stamped on the back of every yard of fabric. Since we have been more than reasonable in trying to inform you, we cannot possibly be responsible.

We trust that you will understand our position. We regret very much the damage and inconvenience our product has caused you.

Marilyn Cox, Customer Relations

Tact and Indirect Order in a Courteous Refusal. The good message begins with friendly talk on a point of agreement that also sets up the explanation. Without accusations, anger, or negative words, it reviews the facts of the case, which free the company of blame. The refusal is clear, even though it is made by implication rather than by direct words. It is skillfully handled. It uses no negatives, and it does not receive undue emphasis. The close shifts to helpful suggestions that fit the one case—suggestions that may actually result in a future sale. Friendliness and resale are evident throughout the message, but especially in the close.

This better email is indirect, tactful, and helpful.

Subject: Your May 3 message about Do-Craft fabric

Ms. Sanderson,

Certainly, you have a right to expect the best possible service from Do-Craft fabrics. Every Do-Craft product is the result of years of experimentation. And we manufacture each yard under the most careful controls. We are determined that our products will do for you what we say they will do.

Because we do want our fabrics to please, we carefully inspected the photos of Do-Craft Fabric 103 you sent us. It is apparent that each sample has been subjected to long periods in extreme sunlight. Since we have known from the beginning that Do-Craft fabrics cannot withstand exposure to sunlight, we have clearly noted this in all our advertising, in the catalog from which you ordered, and in a stamped reminder on the back of every yard of the fabric. Under the circumstances, all we can do concerning your request is suggest that you change to one of our outdoor fabrics. As you can see from our catalog, all of the fabrics in the 200 series are recommended for outdoor use.

You may also be interested in the new Duck Back cotton fabrics listed in our 500 series. These plastic-coated cotton fabrics are most economical, and they resist sun and rain remarkably well. If we can help you further in your selection, please contact us at service@pinnacle.com.

Marilyn Cox, Consumer Relations

Adjustment Refusal Letter (Refusing a Refund for a Woman's Dress). An out-of-town customer bought an expensive dress from the writer and mailed it back three weeks later, asking for a refund. The customer explained that the dress was not a good fit and that she really did not like it anymore. But perspiration stains on the dress proved that she had worn it. This letter skillfully presents the refusal.

MARIE'S
Fashions

103 BREAKER RD. HOUSTON, TX 77015 713-454-6778 Fax: 713-454-6771

February 19, 2007

Ms. Maud E. Krumpleman
117 Kyle Avenue E
College Station, TX 77840-2415

Dear Ms. Krumpleman:

On-subject opening—neutral point from claim letter

We understand your concern about the exclusive St. John's dress you returned February 15. As always, we are willing to do as much as we reasonably can to make things right.

Sets up explanation

Review of facts supports writer's position

What we can do in each instance is determined by the facts of the case. With returned clothing, we generally give refunds. Of course, to meet our obligations to our customers for quality merchandise, all returned clothing must be unquestionably new. As you know, our customers expect only the best from us, and we insist that they get it. Thus, because the perspiration stains on your dress would prevent its resale, we must consider the sale final. We are returning the dress to you. With it you will find a special alteration voucher that assures you of getting the best possible fit free of charge.

Good restraint—no accusations, no anger

Note positive language in refusal

Emphasis on what store can do helps restore goodwill

Friendly goodwill close

So, whenever it is convenient, please come by and let us alter this beautiful St. John's creation to your requirements. We look forward to serving you.

Sincerely,

Marie O. Mitchell

Marie O. Mitchell
President

dm

CREDIT REFUSALS

INTRODUCTORY SITUATION

Credit Refusals

Although Chester Carter, your boss at Pinnacle, is in charge of the credit department, you do not normally get involved in credit work. But exceptions occur. Today, for example, the credit manager consulted with Chester about a request for credit from Bell Builders Supply Company, one of Pinnacle's longtime cash customers. The financial information Bell submitted with the request does not justify credit. Bell has more debt than it can afford, and still more debt would only make matters worse.

Because a refusal appears to be best for all concerned, Pinnacle will turn down Bell's request. The decision is fair, but it will not be good news to Bell. In fact, it might even end this firm's cash business with Pinnacle. Handling the situation is obviously a delicate task.

The importance of the case prompts Chester to ask you to write the refusal for his signature. A refusal from a top executive, Chester thinks, just might be effective. Now you are faced with the task of writing the message that will refuse the request yet keep the reader as a cash customer.

• Because credit is personal, use tact in refusing it.

Messages that refuse credit are more negative than most refusals. The very nature of credit makes them so. Credit is tied to personal characteristics, such as industriousness, stability, and trustworthiness. So, unless skillfully handled, a credit refusal can be viewed as a personal insult. For the most positive results, such a refusal requires the indirect order and a strategy that demonstrates careful courtesy.

• Some think tact is not necessary.

Some will argue that you need not be concerned about the reader's reactions in this situation. Since you are turning down the reader's business, why spend time trying to be tactful? Why not just say no quickly and let it go at that? If you will study the situation, the answer will become obvious.

• But treating people tactfully pleases us personally.

In the first place, being kind to people is personally pleasing to all of us. At least, it should be. The rewards in business are not all measured in dollars and cents. Other rewards exist, such as the good feelings that come from treating people with courtesy and respect.

• It also gains future customers for your business.

In the second place, being kind to people is profitable in the long run. People who are refused credit still have needs. They are likely to satisfy those needs somewhere. They may have to buy for cash. If you are friendly to them, they just might buy from you. In addition, the fact that people are bad credit risks now does not mean that they will never be good credit risks. Many people who are good credit accounts today were bad risks at some time in the past. By not offending bad risks now, you may keep them as friends of your company until they become good risks.

Selecting the Strategy

• Begin by working out the refusal strategy. You can imply the reason with bad character risks.

As in the other bad-news situations, your first step is to work out your strategy—in this case, your reason for refusing credit. If you are refusing because the applicant is a bad character risk (one who pays slowly or not at all), you have a very difficult assignment. You cannot just say bluntly that you are refusing because of bad character. Anyone would bristle at this approach. In such cases, you might choose a roundabout approach. For example, you might imply the reason. Since the applicant knows his or her credit reputation, a mere hint should indicate that you also know it.

• But some authorities favor offering an explanation.

Some credit authorities in the United States prefer a more direct approach for bad character risks, citing the Equal Credit Opportunity Act of 1975 as support. This act states that applicants refused credit are entitled to written explanation of the reasons for the refusal. One way of implementing this approach is to follow the refusal with an invitation to come in (or telephone) to discuss the reasons. This discussion could be followed by a written explanation, if the applicant wants it. Opponents of this approach argue that the applicants already know the facts—that very few of them would pursue the matter further.

A Not-So-Successful Refusal

Trusty old Mr. Whiffle bought an umbrella from a mail-order company. When the umbrella did not function to his requirements, Mr. Whiffle wrote the company a letter asking for his money back.

The mail-order company answered with a well-written letter of refusal.

Again Mr. Whiffle wrote, and again the company replied with a nicely written refusal.

Mr. Whiffle wrote a third time. The mail-order company refused a third time.

So angry was Mr. Whiffle that he boarded a bus, traveled to the home office of the mail-order company, and paid a visit to the company's adjustment correspondent. After a quick explanation of his purpose, Mr. Whiffle broke the umbrella over the adjustment correspondent's head. The correspondent then gave Mr. Whiffle his money.

"Now why didn't you do this before?" Mr. Whiffle asked. "You had all the evidence."

Replied the correspondent, "But you never explained it so clearly before."

If you are refusing because your applicant's financial condition is weak, your task is easier. Weak finances are not necessarily a reflection on character, for instead of being related to personal qualities, they can be related to such factors as illness, unemployment, and bad luck. Thus, with applicants whose finances are weak, you can talk about the subject more directly. You also can talk more hopefully about granting credit in the future. In actual practice, credit-refusal cases do not fit neatly into these two groups. But you should be able to adapt the suggestions that follow to the facts of each case.

● Frank discussion is effective with weak financial risks.

Auto crashes such as this are bitter disappointments to those involved. Messages about the matter should not unnecessarily recall this scene.

Adapting the General Plan

The credit-refusal message clearly follows the general plan for bad-news messages. The opening sets up your strategy, and it is neutral as to the decision. It might well refer to the order or credit application involved, as in this example:

> Your January 22 order for Rock-Ware roofing shows good planning for the rush months ahead. As you will agree, it is good planning that marks the path of business success.

The strategy this opening sets up is to explain that well-managed businesses hold down indebtedness—something the reader needs to do.

A popular and appropriate strategy is to begin with a simple expression of gratitude for the credit application and then lead into a courteous explanation and refusal. Although it is usually effective, the timeworn "Thank you for your application" variety is better replaced with different wording, such as this:

- A thank-you for the request is an appropriate and popular strategy.

> We are sincerely grateful for your credit application and will do all that we reasonably can to help you get your business started.

The following explanation will show that the facts of this case make granting credit something beyond what the writer can reasonably do.

- Explanations to bad character risks can be vague.

The explanation set up by the opening can be an additional point of difference. If you are refusing because of the reader's bad credit character, you need to say little. Bad character risks know their records. You need only to imply that you also know. For example, this sentence handles such an explanation well, and it also gives the answer.

> Our review of your credit record requires that we serve you only on a cash basis at this time.

- Explanations to weak financial risks with good character can be more open.

Your explanation to applicants with good character but weak finances can be more open financial discussions of the facts of the case. Even so, you should select your words carefully to avoid any unintended negative effect. In some cases, you might want to show concern for the reader's credit problem.

- Refuse clearly and positively.

Whatever explanation you use, your words should lead to a clear but positive refusal. For a good character risk with bad finances, this one does the job well:

> Thus, in the best interest of both of us, we must postpone extending credit until your current assets-to-liabilities ratio reaches 2 to 1.

"Shorty, your job is to 'minimize' the bad news.
Stretch, your job is to 'stretch the truth'
for good news."

SOURCE: 2004 Tribune Media Services, Inc.

As in the other bad-news messages, you should end the credit refusal with words of goodwill. Preferably, avoid anything routine, and make the words fit the one case. A suggestion for cash buying or comments about merchandise or service can be effective. So can a forward look to whatever future relations appear appropriate. This closing meets these requirements:

● Close with positive, friendly words that fit the one case.

> As one of Print Safe's cash customers, you will continue to receive the same courtesy, quality merchandise, and low prices we give to all our customers. We look forward to serving you soon.

Fitting the General Plan to the Credit Refusal

Adapting the preceding comments to the general plan, the following structure for credit-refusal messages emerges:

- Begin with words that set up the strategy (explanation), are neutral as to the decision, and tie in with the application.
- Present the explanation.
- Refuse tactfully—to a bad character risk, by implication; to a person with weak finances or in a weak economic environment, positively and with a look to the future.
- End with adapted goodwill words.

Contrasting Credit Refusal Illustrations

The following two contrasting messages refusing Bell's credit application clearly show the advantages of tactful indirect treatment. The bad message does little other than refuse. The good one says no clearly, yet it works to build goodwill and cultivate cash sales.

● The following messages contrast credit refusal techniques.

Harshness as a Result of Tactless Treatment. The weaker email does begin indirectly, but the opening subject matter does little to soften the bad news. This obvious subject matter hardly deserves the emphasis that the opening gives it. Next comes the refusal—without any preceding explanation. It uses negative words (*regret, do not meet, weak, deny*). Explanation follows, but it is scant. The appeal for a cash sale is weak. The closing words leave a negative impression in the reader's mind.

Subject: Credit request

Mr. Bell,

We have received your May 3 order and accompanying request for credit.

After carefully reviewing the financial information you submitted, we regret to report that you do not meet our requirements for credit. It is our considered judgment that firms with your weak assets-to-liabilities ratio would be better off buying with cash. Thus, we encourage you to do so.

We would, of course, be pleased to serve you on a cash basis. In closing, let me assure you that we sincerely regret that we must deny you credit at this time.

Terrence Patrick

This email is tactless.

Courtesy and Tact in a Clear Refusal. The better email generally follows the plan outlined in preceding pages. Its on-subject, neutral opening sets up the explanation. The explanation is thorough and tactful. Throughout, the impression of genuine concern for the reader is clear. Perhaps the explanation of the values of cash buying would be out

Credit Refusal Message (A Form Refusal for Bad Character Risks). As the merge information in the address area indicates, this is a department store's form letter refusing credit to bad character risks. Such stores ordinarily use form letters because they must handle credit on a mass basis. Because form letters must fit a variety of people and cases, they tend to be general.

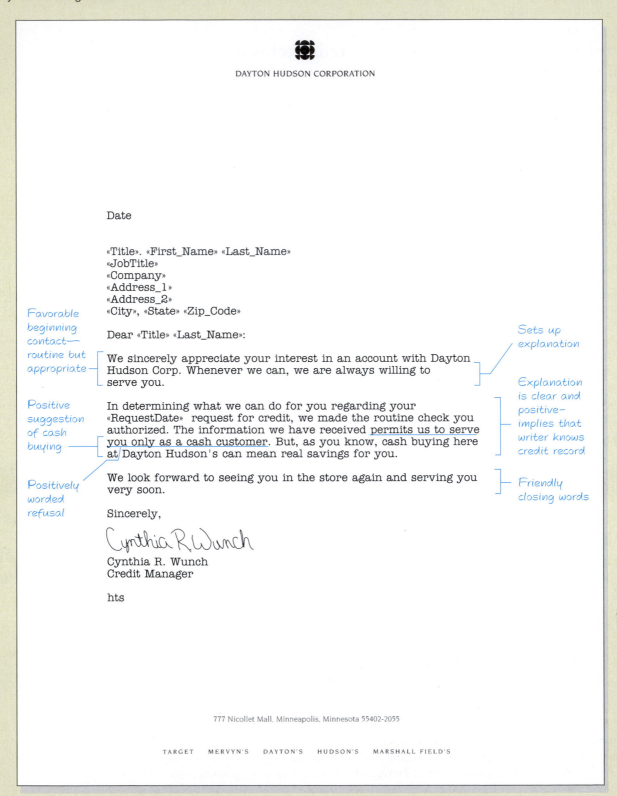

DAYTON HUDSON CORPORATION

Date

«Title». «First_Name» «Last_Name»
«JobTitle»
«Company»
«Address_1»
«Address_2»
«City», «State» «Zip_Code»

Favorable beginning contact— routine but appropriate

Dear «Title» «Last_Name»:

We sincerely appreciate your interest in an account with Dayton Hudson Corp. Whenever we can, we are always willing to serve you.

Sets up explanation

Positive suggestion of cash buying

In determining what we can do for you regarding your «RequestDate» request for credit, we made the routine check you authorized. The information we have received permits us to serve you only as a cash customer. But, as you know, cash buying here at Dayton Hudson's can mean real savings for you.

Explanation is clear and positive— implies that writer knows credit record

Positively worded refusal

We look forward to seeing you in the store again and serving you very soon.

Friendly closing words

Sincerely,

Cynthia R. Wunch
Cynthia R. Wunch
Credit Manager

hts

777 Nicollet Mall, Minneapolis, Minnesota 55402-2055

TARGET   MERVYN'S   DAYTON'S   HUDSON'S   MARSHALL FIELD'S

Words of Wisdom

Some scholars argue that authors delivering a negative message should use an indirect organization, which consists of delaying the main point. Such an approach is believed to secure reader understanding before risking the loss of the reader's attention by delivering bad news. . . . The current results (of the authors' research) appear to support the use of an indirect organization scheme in a negative situation.

Annette Shelby, Georgetown University
N. Lamar Reinsch, Jr., Georgetown University

Annette N. Shelby and N. Lamar Reinsch, Jr., "Positive Emphasis and You-Attitude: An Empirical Study," *Journal of Business Communication* 32 (1995): 322.

of place in some cases. In this case, however, the past relationship between reader and writer justifies it. The message ends with pleasant words that look to the future.

Subject: Credit request

Mr. Bell,

Your May 3 order for Pinnacle paints and supplies suggests that your company is continuing to make good progress.

To assure yourself of continued progress, we feel certain that you will want to follow the soundest business practices possible. As you may know, most financial experts say that maintaining a reasonable indebtedness is a must for sound growth. About a 2-to-1 ratio of current assets to liabilities is a good minimum, they say. In the belief that this minimum ratio is best for all concerned, we extend credit only when it is met. As soon as you reach this ratio, we would like to review your application again. Meanwhile, we will strive to meet your needs on a cash basis.

We appreciate your interest in Pinnacle paints and look forward to serving you.

Terrence Patrick

This good email refuses tactfully.

NEGATIVE ANNOUNCEMENTS

INTRODUCTORY SITUATION

Negative Announcements

In your role as assistant to Pinnacle's vice president for administration, you have been given the difficult assignment of writing a bad-news message for your boss. She has just returned from a meeting of the company's top executives in which the decision was made to deduct 25 percent of the employees' medical insurance premiums from their paychecks. Until now, Pinnacle has paid it all. But the rising cost of health coverage is forcing the company to cut back on these benefits, especially since Pinnacle's profits have declined for the past several quarters. Something has to give if Pinnacle is to remain competitive while also avoiding lay-offs. The administrators decided on a number of cost-cutting measures including this reduction in Pinnacle's payment for medical insurance. The message you will write to Pinnacle employees is a negative announcement.

- Sometimes negative announcements are necessary.

Occasionally, businesses must announce bad news to their customers or employees. For example, a company might need to announce that prices are going up, that a service or product line is being discontinued, or that a branch of the business is closing. Or a company might need to tell its employees that the company is in some kind of trouble, that people will need to be laid off, or, as in the example above, that employee benefits must be reduced. Such announcements generally follow the instructions previously given in this chapter.

Determining the Strategy

- First decide whether to use direct or indirect organization.

- Indirect order usually is better.

When faced with the problem of making a negative announcement, your first step should be to determine your overall strategy. Will you use direct or indirect organization?

In most cases the indirect (buffer) arrangement will be better. This route is especially recommended when it is reasonable to expect that the readers would be surprised, particularly disappointed, or even angered by a direct presentation. When planning an indirect announcement, you will need to think about what kind of buffer opening to use, what kind of explanation to give, how to word the news itself, and how to leave your readers feeling that you have taken their interests into account.

Setting Up the Bad News

- Select a strategy that prepares the reader to accept the bad news.

As with the preceding negative message types, you should plan your indirect (buffer) beginning carefully. You should think through the situation and select a strategy that will set up or begin the explanation that justifies the announcement. Perhaps you will begin by presenting justifying information. Or maybe you will start with complimentary or cordial talk focusing on the good relationship that you and your readers have developed. Whatever you choose should be what will be most likely to prepare your reader to accept the coming bad news.

Positively Presenting the Bad News

- The bad news should follow logically from your opening.

- Word it positively, and include all necessary details.

In most cases, the opening paragraph will enable you to continue with background reasons or explanations in the next paragraph, before you present the negative news. Such explaining will help you put the negative news in the middle of the paragraph rather than at the beginning, where it would be emphasized.

As in other negative situations, you should use positive words and avoid unnecessary negative comments when presenting the news itself. Since this is an announcement, however, you must make certain that you cover all the factual details involved. People may not be expecting this news. They will, therefore, want to know the why's and what's of the situation. And if you want them to believe that you have done all you can to prevent the negative situation, you will need to provide evidence that this is true. If there are actions the readers must take, these should be covered clearly as well. All questions that may come to the readers' minds should be anticipated and covered.

Focusing on Next Steps or Remaining Benefits

- Help people solve their problem and focus on any positive aspects.

In many cases negative news will mean that things have changed. Customers may no longer be able to get a product that they have relied upon, or employees may have to find a way to pay for something that they have been getting free. For this reason, a skillful handling of a negative announcement will often need to include an effort to help people solve the problem that your news just created for them. In situations where you have no further help to offer—for example, when announcing certain price increases—you can still help people feel better about your news by calling attention to the benefits that they will continue to enjoy. You can focus on the good things that have not changed and perhaps even look ahead to something positive or exciting on the horizon.

Negative Announcement (A Message Reporting a Price Increase). Here a TV cable company informs a customer of a rate increase. The cordial opening makes friendly contact that leads to an explanation of the action. Then the news is presented clearly yet positively. The goodwill close continues the cordiality established earlier in the message.

Heartland Cable TV, Inc.
37411 Jester Road, Kansas City, MO 64106

Ms. Ellen Butler
396 Scott Street
Kansas City, MO 64109
Ph: 815.555.1212
Fax: 815.555.1213
www.heartlandcabletv.com

March 14, 2007

Dear Ms. Butler:

Cordial opening contact —

Your cable company has been working extra hard to provide you with the highest-quality TV entertainment. We think we have succeeded. The quantity of programming as well as its quality has continued to improve over the past year.

Explanation sets up bad news

Bad news presented in terms of reader interests

We have also been working hard to keep the cost of these services as low as possible and continue to maintain high standards. Last year we were able to do this and pass along savings of up to 20 percent on two of our premium services. As you may have heard in the news, our costs continue to increase. Thus, in order to continue to maintain our goals of high quality at the lowest possible cost, we are announcing a price adjustment effective April 1. The monthly cost of your basic package of 59 stations will increase $1.50 (from $37.99 to $39.49) The cost of all premium services (HBO, Cinemax, Encore, Starz, and Showtime) will remain the same.

Positive information ends paragraph —

Friendly forward look follows bad news

In our continuing efforts to improve your total entertainment value, we are planning a number of exciting new projects. We will announce them before the year's end.

Cordial words end the message —

We appreciate your business and assure you that we will continue to bring you the very best in service and entertainment.

Sincerely,

Carlos H. Rodriguez

Carlos H. Rodriguez
President

183

Closing on a Positive or Encouraging Note

- Close with goodwill.

The ending words should cement your effort to cover the matter positively. They can be whatever is appropriate for this one situation—a positive look forward, a sincere expression of gratitude, an affirmation of your positive relationship with your readers.

Reviewing the Plan

Applying the preceding instructions to the general plan, we arrive at this specific plan for negative announcements written in indirect order:

- Start with a buffer that begins or sets up justification for the bad news.
- Present the justification material.
- Give the bad news positively but clearly.
- Help solve the problem that the news may have created for the reader.
- End with appropriate goodwill talk.

Contrasting Negative Announcements

- Following are good and bad examples.

Good and bad techniques in negative announcements are shown in the following two messages. The bad one is direct, which in some circumstances may be acceptable but clearly is not in this case. The good one follows the pattern just discussed.

Directness Here Alarms the Readers. This bad example clearly upsets the readers with its abrupt announcement in the beginning. The readers aren't prepared to receive the negative message. Probably they don't understand the reasons behind the negative news. The explanation comes later, but the readers are not likely to be in a receptive mood when they see it. The message ends with a repetition of the bad news.

Directness here sends a negative message.

To our employees:

Pinnacle management sincerely regrets that effective February 1 you must begin contributing 25 percent of the cost of your medical insurance. As you know, in the past the company has paid the full amount.

This decision is primarily the result of the rising costs of health insurance, but Pinnacle's profits also have declined the last several quarters. Given this tight financial picture, we needed to find ways to reduce expenses.

We trust that you will understand why we must ask you to help us get out of this predicament.

Sincerely,

Convincing Explanation Begins a Courteous Message. The better example follows the recommended indirect pattern. Its opening words begin the task of convincing the readers of the appropriateness of the action to be taken. After more convincing explanation, the announcement flows logically. Perhaps it will not be received positively by all recipients, but it is a reasonable deduction from the facts presented. After the announcement comes an offer of assistance to help readers deal with their new situation. The last paragraph reminds readers of remaining benefits and reassures them that management understands their interests. It ends on an appreciative, goodwill note.

To All Employees:

Probably you have heard or read in the news that companies all across the United States, no matter how large or small, are struggling to keep up with the rising cost of healthcare. Just last week, an article in *The Wall Street Journal* reported that health care costs represent "a business crisis that Congress can no longer afford to ignore." Legislators, healthcare providers, and businesspeople everywhere are struggling to find a solution to the skyrocketing cost of health insurance.

We are feeling this situation here in our own company. The premiums that we pay to cover our health benefits have increased by 34 percent over the last two years, and they now represent a huge percentage of our expenditures. Meanwhile, as you know, our sales have been lower than usual for the past several quarters. At least in the short run, it is imperative that we find a way to cut overall costs. Your management has considered many options and rejected such measures as cutting salaries and reducing personnel. Of the solutions that will be implemented, the only change that affects you directly concerns your medical insurance. On March 1 we will begin deducting 25 percent of the cost of the premium. The other savings measures will be at the corporate level.

Jim Taylor in the Personnel Office will soon be announcing an informational meeting about your insurance options. Switching to spousal coverage, choosing a less expensive plan with lighter deductibles, or setting up a flexible spending account may be right for you. You can also see Jim after the meeting to arrange a personal consultation. He is well versed in the many solutions available and can give you expert advice for your situation.

Our healthcare benefits are some of the best in our city and in our industry, and those who continue with the current plan will not see any change in their medical coverage or their co-pays. Your management regards a strong benefits program as critical to the company's success, and we will do all we can to maintain these benefits while keeping your company financially viable. We appreciate your cooperation and understanding.

Sincerely,

This indirect example follows the bad-news pattern.

Using Directness in Some Cases

In some cases it is likely that the reader will react favorably to a direct presentation of the bad news. If, for example, the negative news is expected (as when the news media have already revealed it), its impact may be viewed as negligible. There is also a good case for directness when the company's announcement will contain a remedy or announce new

• Directness is appropriate when the news is expected or will have little negative impact,

---

Dear Ms. Cato:

As a long-time customer, you will be interested in knowing that we are discontinuing our Preferred Customer program so that we may offer several new promotions.

Effective January 1 we will take your accumulated points and convert them to a savings coupon worth as much as or more than your points total. Your new points total is on the coupon enclosed with this letter. You may apply this coupon in these ways:

• When shopping in our stores, present your coupon at the register.
• When shopping from our catalogs, give the coupon number to the telephone service agent, enclose your coupon with your mail order, or enter it with your web order.

In all these cases we will deduct your coupon value from your purchase total. If you have any questions, please call us at 1-800-343-4111.

We thank you very much for your loyalty. You'll soon hear about exciting new opportunities to shop and save with us.

Sincerely,

• as in this example.

benefits that are designed to offset the effects of the bad news. As in all announcements with some negative element, this part must be handled in good positive language. Also, the message should end on a goodwill note. The preceding example of a mail-order/department store's announcement discontinuing a customer program illustrates this situation.

OTHER INDIRECT MESSAGES

- Adapt the techniques of this chapter.

The types of indirect messages covered in the preceding pages are the most common ones. There are others. Some of these (persuasive messages, and job applications) are rather special types. They are covered in the following chapters. You should be able to handle all the other indirect types that you encounter by adapting the techniques explained and illustrated in this chapter.

SUMMARY BY LEARNING OBJECTIVES

1 Determine which situations require using the indirect order for the most effective response.

1. When the main point of your message is bad news, use the indirect order.
   - But exceptions exist, as when you believe that the news will be received routinely.
   - Make exceptions also when you think the reader will appreciate directness.

2 Write indirect-order messages following the general plan.

2. In general, bad-news messages follow this general plan.
   - Begin with a buffer that sets up the strategy.
   - Develop the strategy.
   - Present the bad news as a logical result of the strategy.
   - Try to offer an alternative solution.
   - End on a positive note.

3 Use tact and courtesy in refusals of requests.

3. The refusal of a request is one bad-news situation that you will probably choose to treat indirectly.
   - In such situations, strive to achieve two main goals:
     — to refuse and
     — to maintain goodwill.
   - Begin by thinking through the problem, looking for a logical explanation (or reasoning).
   - Write an opening that sets up this explanation.
   - Then present your explanation (reasoning), taking care to use convincing and positive language.
   - Refuse clearly yet positively.
   - Use a compromise when practical.
   - Close with appropriate, friendly talk that does not recall the bad news.

4 Write adjustment refusals that minimize the negative and overcome bad impressions.

4. Refusals of adjustments follow a similar pattern.
   - First, determine your explanation (reasoning) for refusing.
   - Begin with neutral words that set up your reasoning and do not give away the refusal.
   - Then present your reasoning, building your case convincingly.
   - Refuse clearly and positively.
   - Close with appropriate friendly talk that does not recall the refusal.

5 Compose tactful, yet clear, credit refusals that foster goodwill.

5. Messages refusing credit are more negative than most other types of refusals, for the refusal is tied to personal things.
   - As with other types of refusals, begin by thinking through a strategy.
   - If you are refusing because of the applicant's bad credit character, use a roundabout approach.
   - If you are refusing because of the applicant's weak finances, be more direct.

- In either case, choose opening words that set up your strategy, are neutral, and tie in with the request being answered.
- To the bad character risk, imply the facts rather than stating them bluntly.
- In refusals because of weak finances, look hopefully to credit in the future.
- End all credit refusals with appropriate positive words, perhaps suggesting cash buying, customer services, or other appropriate topics.

6. Sometimes businesses must announce bad news to their customers or employees.
- Indirect organization usually is better for these announcements.
- This means that convincing explanation precedes the bad news.
- And positive words are used to cover the bad news.
- Sometimes directness is appropriate.
- This is the case when the news is expected or will have little negative impact.
- Even so, handle the negative with positive wording.

6 Write negative announcements that maintain goodwill.

1 Give examples of times (or situations) when directness is appropriate for responses giving negative (bad-news) information.

2 Writing in the indirect order usually requires more words than does writing in the direct order. Since conciseness is a virtue in writing, how can the indirect order be justified?

3 What strategy is best in a message refusing a request when the reasons for the refusal are strictly in the writer's best interests?

4 Apologies in refusals are negative for they call attention to what you are refusing. Thus, you should avoid using them. Discuss.

5 An adjustment correspondent explained the refusal of an adjustment request by saying that company policy did not permit granting claims in such cases. Was this explanation adequate? Discuss.

6 Is there justification for positive writing in a message refusing credit? You are not going to sell to the reader, so why try to maintain goodwill?

7 Discuss the difference between refusing credit to a good risk with bad finances or in a poor economic environment and refusing credit to one with character problems.

8 Negative announcements usually need to include much more than the announcement. Explain.

9 Give examples of negative announcements that appropriately are written in direct order.

1 Point out the shortcomings in the following email message from a sports celebrity declining an invitation to speak at the kickoff meeting for workers in a fund-raising campaign for a charity.

Subject: Your request for free lecture

Ms. Chung:

As much as I would like to, I must decline your request that I give your membership a free lecture next month. I receive many requests to give free lectures. I grant some of them, but I simply cannot do them all. Unfortunately, yours is one that I must decline.

I regret that I cannot serve you this time. If I can be of further service in the future, please call on me.

Sincerely yours,

2 Criticize the following message refusing the claim for a defective riding lawn mower. The mower was purchased 15 months earlier. The purchaser has had difficulties with it for some time and submitted with the claim a statement from a local repair service verifying the difficulties. The writer's reason for refusing is evident from the email.

Subject: Your May 12 claim

Mr. Skinner:

Your May 12 claim of defective workmanship in your Model 227 Dandy Klipper riding mower has been reviewed. After considering the information received, I regret to report that we cannot refund the purchase price.

You have had the mower for 15 months, which is well beyond our one-year guarantee. Even though your repair person says that you had problems earlier, he is not one of our authorized repair people. If you will read the warranty you refer to in your letter, you will see that we honor the warranty only when our authorized repair people find defects. I think you will understand why we must follow this procedure.

If you will take the machine to the authorized service center in your area (La Rue Lawn and Garden Center), I am confident they can correct the defect at a reasonable charge.

If I can be of additional service, please contact me.

Sincerely,

Refused Requests

1 As director of Eastern State University's Executive Development Program, you are pleased that your three-week program is off to a good start, except for two no-shows. The two missing people are executives with Middleton Oil and Gas, Inc. Today, the fourth day of the program, you learn why.

From Stephanie Matocha, the Middleton training director, you receive an email message announcing that the two executives asked to be excused from attending, citing unexpected heavy work demands. The company has honored their request. Now Ms. Matocha brazenly requests that you refund the money Middleton has paid—all $27,000 of it ($13,500 each).

You have a problem. Eastern State University runs this program as a service to the area. It sets prices designed to break even, not to make a profit. There is absolutely no room for a loss. You cannot refund the money. You think your decision is justified for another reason. You limit each class to the optimum size of 20 students. Demand has been good for some time. In fact, you turned down seven for this class.

Now you must write an email message to this training director giving her the bad news. You will work hard to convince her that yours is a fair and reasonable decision. And you'll do what you can to maintain goodwill.

---

2 Play the role of a distinguished professor of business communication and assume that you have received an invitation to present the keynote address at the international meeting of the Association for Business Communication next June 14. It is a fitting reward for your professional development over the past years, and you are greatly honored. The meeting will be in Singapore, and this adds to the excitement. Your excitement and happiness are dashed, however, when you check the date on your calendar. This is the date of your family reunion. For the past two years, your Aunt Mildred and Uncle Tony have been arranging this reunion in your old hometown. You will see kinfolk you have not seen in years. Out of love and loyalty you must attend the reunion. In fact, you have promised to attend and have made a generous contribution to the expenses of the event.

Much as you regret it, you will have to refuse the speaking engagement. But you'll try to make the refusal so agreeable that you might be recommended for another such assignment in the future. Send your message by email to Professor Diana Chan of Singapore University, the program chairperson. She is the one who extended the invitation.

---

3 You, the owner of Data Management, Inc., have just received a persuasive message from Ms. Claudine Kennedy, president of Concerned Citizens, a powerful local political action organization. She wants you to buy advertising space in Concerned Citizens' annual election publication, *Vigilance.* As she worded her request, "A $250 contribution would display your company's name prominently in a 2-column, 4-inch space and would mark you as one who stands up for good government."

Your political sympathies lie with Concerned Citizens. You know that many of your customers also sympathize with the organization. But you also know that many of your customers do not. As you see it, you cannot afford to take a stand publicly. It would be bad for business.

So you must refuse the request—politely and with convincing explanation. The organization may get your support at the polls, but not in print. Write the email message to Ms. Kennedy that will courteously refuse her request using logical reasoning.

---

4 For this assignment play the role of manager of the underwriting department of the Sentinel Insurance Company. You must write Wilbur McDonald telling him that Sentinel is canceling his homeowner's insurance policy when it comes up for renewal next month.

Three months ago Mr. McDonald submitted a claim for $3,417 for rain damage to the Sheetrock in his living room. It was a legitimate claim, and you paid it. Your investigator reported that the cause was a leaking skylight in the living room. Five inches of rain had fallen. After the $500 deductible, Sentinel paid Mr. McDonald $2,917.

In the letter that accompanied his check you mentioned the cancellation clause in your contract with him: "Should proximate causes create excessive costs, policies are subject to cancellation." You assumed that Mr. McDonald would read and understand these words.

Yesterday you received another claim, this one for $2,990 for damages to the Sheetrock in the same room. Your investigator reported that another big rain had caused damage through the same skylight. You are obligated to pay for this loss, but under conditions of the contract you will cancel his policy when it comes up for renewal at the end of next month.

Now write him a tactful message giving him the bad news. What you are doing is well within the law and is sound policy. You can't keep him as a customer, but you can try to make him see the logic of Sentinel's decision.

---

5 You have been hired as a screener in the Office of Human Resources at the main office of [you decide what kind of company]. Your job is to check submitted résumés against posted job openings, screen out those with insufficient qualifications, rank the ones that are left, and pass these on to the hiring manager for the opening. You are also expected to take part in job fairs at colleges, do some preliminary interviewing, write routine job-related communications, and offer any suggestions you may have on the company's hiring procedures.

Your company regularly interviews students at the local university for jobs. The student first signs up for an on-campus interview time slot and sends his or her résumé electronically to the campus recruiter. If this stage goes well, the student is invited to the company to take several tests, including a personality test, a writing test, and a test in the given functional area (accounting, economics, finance, information systems, management, marketing, and the like). These take about three hours. If the student does well on this part, he or she is invited back to the company for an in-depth interview with the hiring manager. After this step, the manager either hires the student or informs him or her that he or she did not get the job.

Here's the email template that the company uses to tell all rejected candidates who interviewed with the company—whether on campus or at the main office—that they didn't get the job:

Subject line: [name of your company] Employment Results

Dear [candidate's first and last name]:

Thank you for interviewing with us for the position listed below: [title of the position]

We have identified other candidates with backgrounds that more closely match our specific needs. As a result, we are unable to move your candidacy forward at this time.

[Name of company] sincerely appreciates your interest, and we wish you the best in your career.

If you have any questions, please contact your recruiter.

[Signed, the company]

As the person who sends out these emails, you are troubled by their impersonal quality. They seem particularly bad for those who made it all the way to the in-depth interview at the main office. After all, these people will have spent about five hours on the hiring process, and to brush them off with such hastily written boilerplate seems rude. It also isn't likely to generate a good buzz on campus about your company—and you're sure it wouldn't be wise to alienate this huge pool of well-trained job applicants.

You know that it's relatively easy to create different fields on a form letter that you can fill in with specifics from the candidate's online file. With this knowledge, write a special template for rejecting the candidates who made it to the last stage of the process. At the next staff meeting, you'll share your new template and make your case for using it.

---

6 You own and run a small business [you decide what kind] in your town. You've just received a letter from the Boys and Girls League that you suspect has gone to many local business owners. The letter describes the organization's athletic program for underprivileged youth and asks if you can help them out by sponsoring a spring soccer team for $500. The money would go toward uniforms, equipment, transportation, and hiring referees. Because sponsors' names will be on the jerseys, helping out the kids would also give your company positive PR. The letter ends with a form for you to complete, tear off, and send in with your check.

While you wish you could accommodate the request, $500 is a lot of money—and you had already planned to sponsor your own son's baseball team this year. You have to say no, and you're not confident that you can say yes any time in the near future. However, you would like to help out in some way, and you would like to be included among the League's supporters (the organization surely provides other forms of PR, too, even if it's just listing their sponsors in their newsletter). Do some checking around, think about what might be a feasible alternative to offer, and write the League informing them of your decision.

---

7 As President and CEO of a small _____ company [you choose it], you've just received an email from an employee, Jake Rehnquist. He is currently a volunteer for the Peace Collaborative, a program that brings trained volunteers into the schools to teach conflict-resolution strategies. He would like to use one of your company's monthly lunch meetings to tell others about the program and encourage them to volunteer as well.

You admire Jake for his altruism, you appreciate the work of the Collaborative, and you do want to encourage volunteerism in the company. But you really don't want to set this

kind of precedent for your lunch meetings. You instituted these as a way for employees and managers at all levels to share their work-related concerns and ideas, not to promote special interests. If you let Jake use this forum in this way, who knows how many others would also want to talk about their favorite causes at these meetings? You have to write Jake a refusal—but in such a way that he feels supported in his efforts to contribute to the community. Think of good reasons why it is important to continue to focus these meetings on company matters, and also of how you might accommodate Jake's request in some way.

8 Today you received an email request from one of your employees, Kate McPhee, for immersion language training in Spain. As one of your top domestic marketing executives, Kate has accepted a new position with you in South America to get exposure to your international marketing program there. She is very excited about the move; in fact, she and her husband, Rob, have decided to move their whole family there. Her email request that the company fund her language training is clearly related to this upcoming move, and her enthusiasm to do well in her new assignment is clear.

The program she identified was recommended to her by a friend who had participated in it several years ago. She reported that in just four weeks the friend felt competent enough to speak fluently with native speakers and comprehend them easily. She was convinced that the $15,000 fee, which included airfare, room and board, and training, would be a good investment for the company.

While you agree that some immersion training in Spanish is a good idea for her, going to Spain for it is not something you can agree to since you believe there are other equally effective and less expensive alternatives. One particularly good new program some other employees have attended is at BridgeLinguatec in Denver, a safe, friendly, and beautiful city. In addition to Kate's receiving immersion training with native speakers from a variety of Spanish-speaking countries, her husband could attend for free. And this program is also just four weeks long. Its cost is less than half the cost of the program she suggested.

So while you'll refuse her request to participate in the immersion program in Spain, you want to help her keep her enthusiasm for her new position by offering the alternative program in Denver.

9 Today's email brought a request from Lisa Miller, one of your outstanding new hires. She is requesting to be allowed to choose her own mentor, but your company's practice has been to assign them. You realize that some companies permit new employees to choose, but your company prefers assignment. You believe you can make better matches on objective criteria that are important to your company rather than on subjective ones that naive new employees often use. You have designed a program that gives all new hires a rich resource for well-rounded training. You know the backgrounds and expertise of your employees as well as their current workloads, enabling you to make good matches. You also know the desired outcome of mentoring, which isn't always clear to new hires.

However, you have recently learned that programs at Citigroup, Motorola, and the U.S. Air Force seem to be setting a new trend where both mentors and protégés can choose each other. Companies determine which employees would be good mentors for particular new hires; then both are given the option to choose. However, the company makes the final match. While you haven't tried it yet, you might offer it as an alternative to Lisa when you refuse her request to choose a mentor.

10 As Ryan Penne, director of your school's career center, you received an email today with a good suggestion from a second-term junior, Stephanie Chang. In fact, from her extremely clear, persuasive message, you could tell she had carefully thought through the benefits of her idea of implementing text messaging in the center's on-campus interview program.

She mentioned that since nearly all students have cell phones, you could text message those students on waiting lists to see recruiters when there were last-minute schedule openings—either because of no-shows or revised schedules. She reasoned that texting would be a way to reach students without interrupting classes. And by filling in the schedule gaps, your school would be better serving both the students and the companies recruiting there. And she is right. However, there some drawbacks, too.

The biggest drawback is funding. You are on a shoestring budget as is, and a program like this is likely to be costly. If you did have such a program, you would have to find a way to offer it to everyone, even those without their own cell phones. Furthermore, you would have to offer some staff training and develop some text message templates that were clear. You also wonder how receptive faculty would be to such a program, especially since some have no cell phone rules and many already strictly forbid text messaging during class.

So while Stephanie's suggestion is an interesting one, you'll have to refuse it at this time. However, once you can get answers to your questions about cost, availability, and faculty receptiveness, you would be willing to reconsider it. If she'd like to take that project on, you'd be glad to work with her on it.

Adjustment Refusals

11 As the regional sales manager for EZL, Inc., you have just received an email message from Sebastian Coco, manager of the Central States Seed and Feed Company of Kansas City. Mr. Coco says that your EZL #449 grease is responsible for $3,855 of damage to his conveyor system, and he insists that you pay for the repairs. As he explains the problem, "your grease has resulted in the gumming and jamming of the conveyor system." You have evidence to the contrary.

Four months ago Soledad Garcia, your salesperson for the Kansas City area, acquired the account of the Central States organization. In selling to this account, she had your technical assistance people perform numerous tests for the lubricating needs of Central States. They recommended that the conveyor be lubricated every 12 hours with EZL #449 and not every 8 hours, as was the case with the other grease they were using. Overlubricating, they explained, would lead to "gumming and jamming" of the system. Even though your EZL #449 was a little higher priced than the other grease, your people believed that EZL would save money for Central States.

From Ms. Garcia you learned that Tyrone Capaccio, the maintenance supervisor at Central States, openly rejected

EZL's advice, citing his 30 years of experience in running this equipment. She warned him about the potential problem on two occasions, but to no avail. And now the "gumming and jamming" has occurred. And they want to be reimbursed for their loss?

You will refuse, of course, but you will do it tactfully and courteously. You will try to make your explanation so positive and clear that it will be accepted. Even though you must decline this unjustified claim, you would like to keep the account.

---

12 Today's mail brings you, the owner/manager of Green Thumb Nurseries, a claim from Amelia Placky of Mission Valley, Texas. You remember Ms. Placky well. A few months ago she emailed an order for 50 dozen assorted annual spring bulbs (tulips, daffodils, irises, and the like). You sent them to her without delay, and she promptly paid the $405 she owed for them. In today's message Ms. Placky notes that she planted the bulbs right after she received them (early September) and that they didn't come up in the spring. She also says she followed your planting instructions and included the recommended fertilizer with each bulb.

In checking into the situation, you confirm most of what Ms. Placky says. But she didn't follow the most important

instructions of all. The instruction booklet clearly gives this warning, boxed and in bold type: "Plant bulbs one month before the average frost date in the fall. Keep refrigerated until planting." If she planted them soon after receiving them, she planted them too early. She received the bulbs in early September, and September is a hot month in Texas (average highs of around 85 degrees). November 15 is the average first frost date for the area. It is no wonder the bulbs did not survive.

Because your printed instructions are crystal clear, you are going to refuse her claim. But you don't want to belittle or embarrass her in the process. She is a good customer, and you want to keep her. So you'll explain why you can't give her money back in a way that will keep her doing business with you.

---

13 You are the director of convention services for the Pickins House, a large and prestigious hotel. The National Association of Appraisers met at your hotel last month. All told, almost 1,300 appraisers met for three days to exchange ideas and receive industry information about their work. The meeting was a profitable one for your hotel. You want these people back for another convention, and you want them to tell their friends about your competence, hospitality, and excellent facilities.

Today you received a letter from Roberta Alvarez, who is executive director for the organization. She reports that many of the members did not get the convention rates they had been promised. As she stated the problem, "You'll remember that we have a contract for $105 single rooms and $125 doubles. Many of our participants have reported that when they checked out they were charged your usual rates of $140 for a single and $175 for a double. Attached is a list

of 131 members who have reported to me their overpayment. Please check your records and refund the difference. You have their addresses in your registration information. Please send me verification that you have made the refunds."

You go back to your files to find your information on the meeting. Yes, you did agree to the rates Ms. Alvarez mentioned. But to get them the attendees had to reserve their rooms 15 days prior to the meeting. And those arriving after 6:00 P.M. had to guarantee their registrations through prepayment by credit card. Your check of the 131 people indicates that none of them met these requirements. Experience has convinced you that if you don't use these restrictions you often end up with empty rooms. These requirements are standard in the industry.

You cannot grant this claim. But you want to retain the goodwill of Ms. Alvarez and her large group. And you want a shot at future meetings. Write the message that will accomplish these goals. You'll send it by email.

---

14 You've just received a package in the mail from one Laketa Young, from a small town in North Carolina. In it is the leather jacket that she purchased from the up-scale women's clothing store where you work, Elaine's, in Laguna Beach, California. With the jacket is a request that you refund her money for the jacket, as well as for the cost of shipping the jacket back to you (she had also purchased insurance and delivery confirmation for the package).

You remember this customer. She was on her first trip to California, and she was enchanted with your stylish, if expensive, clothes. As luck would have it, all your leather goods were on sale when she visited your store. It was the end of the winter season, and this was your last effort to sell the season's leather goods before getting in your spring line. And high-quality goods they were, too—all made by Angaro's of Italy. Ms. Young had gotten a $700 jacket for $379. And it had looked great on her. All in all, you remember feeling pleased by the experience.

But now Ms. Young reports that the jacket turned out to be defective. When she got it home and into the daylight, she noticed that one panel of the jacket was a somewhat different color than the other panels. You take it over to a window to look, and while you think you see what she means, the jacket looks fine to your experienced eye. As a tag on the jacket had said, leather is a natural material and, as such, will contain subtle variations in coloring and texture. The panel fits well into the overall look of the jacket. You, therefore, do not want to refund Ms. Young's money. Moreover, many signs above the sale racks had proclaimed "All sales final," and you had brought this fact to Ms. Young's attention as well before you rang up the sale. If you were to take the jacket back now, how would you sell it? All your winter merchandise has been bought up by a discount house, so you don't even have an appropriate rack to display the jacket on. You can't ship the coat back to Angaro's for a refund, because they won't agree that the jacket is defective, and they don't want to get stuck with last season's goods either.

Write Ms. Young to refuse her request while convincing her that your decision is fair and that she has a high-quality garment. Unfortunately, you will also have to ask her in what form she wants to pay the $18 that it will cost to ship the jacket, insured and with delivery confirmation, back to her. You'll include a form with the letter that will allow her to resubmit her credit card information if she would like to pay for the shipping this way.

---

15 You're the service manager for IT Solutions, an on-call PC repair and troubleshooting company. Today you received an email from Susan Patel, whose laptop your company recently serviced (see problem 48 in Chapter 6). She does not want to pay the $510 bill for the service. Yes, Ray Stampe, the service person assigned to this job, did recover most of the files from the damaged hard drive, but Ms. Patel discovered after he left that the recovery was not complete. She is still missing some important customer and business information. Also, she complains that the internal and external drives that Ray provided were too expensive. She found out that she could have gotten these more cheaply online or at a PC center. She would like Ray to return, at no charge, to try to recover the missing files, and she wants you to match the price for the two drives that she would pay if ordering them online.

You discuss the situation with Ray and find out several important things. First, he had asked Ms. Patel before he left to check the recovered files, and she had told him that they looked fine. Also, he had asked her if she wanted the two drives immediately, and she had said yes. True, he hadn't pointed out the prices to her, but he had certainly been willing to tell her had she asked. He did tell her that the drives were, in IT Solution's opinion, the most reliable on the market and that IT Solutions would guarantee them for three years, which is two years and nine months longer than she could get from any dealer unless she paid for the extra coverage.

All in all, you think that what you are charging is fair. Ray saved Ms. Patel a good bit of trouble and delay by providing the hardware on the spot, and it came with a great warranty. As for the unrecovered files, you doubt that there's anything you can do, but you'd be willing to have one of your service people try again. But you won't come to her house—at least, not without a fee. She'll need to bring the laptop in, and she may need to leave it for a day. Write her to let her know that this is the best you can do while also making her feel that she got fair treatment and a good deal overall.

---

16 As owner of Clark's Tree Service, you've just received the kind of letter you always hate to get. A customer whose tree you serviced last fall angrily reports that much of the tree appears to have died over the winter. He wants you to refund his money for the tree trimming, pay for the removal of the tree, and compensate him for the loss of the tree. You drive by his house to take a look, and there's no doubt about it—the tree is so severely compromised that it really should be removed. But you are sure that your people did a good job. In fact, you supervised them yourself, and you are a certified arborist. You had advised the customer that the tree, a variety of birch, was very old, and you had recommended such measures as cabling the weak stems together, ample fertilizing and watering, protecting the tree from severe weather with burlap screens, and keeping deicing salt away from the roots of the tree. But it looks as if the severe winter took its toll, breaking off a couple of major stems and killing most of what remained. You knock on the customer's door to discuss the matter with him, but no one is home. You'll just have to respond to his letter—which isn't all bad, since, if things do get ugly, you'll want your reply to be on record.

Write the customer to convey your refusal. Tell him that your service people followed accepted procedures for trimming the tree, including performing the service in the optimum season for this kind of tree and removing a conservative amount of the tree's crown. Tell him what, in your estimation, caused the demise of the tree (you can consult an Internet source such as the University of Minnesota's Extension Service at <http://www.extension.umn.edu/distribution/horticulture/DG1411.html> for additional logical details). Then tell him what you could do to help him solve his problem—namely, remove the dead tree and replace it with another, hardier type of tree. You would need to talk with him about his preferences in order to work up an estimate for these additional services.

17 As Manny Konedeng, customer relations manager for American Family Insurance, you were surprised to get the following email from one of your long-time customers, David Seaton. He sent the following claim arguing for coverage of medical expenses related to a dog bite. You thought he clearly understood his homeowner's coverage after nearly 11 years with you.

Manny,

I was extremely disappointed to get the rejection of a claim I submitted to you last week to cover the medical expenses for my neighbor who was bitten by my dog. I believe I am covered by my homeowner's policy, which has $300,000 in liability coverage.

While this bill was for nearly $30,000, it doesn't come close to the limit. And the care my neighbor got wasn't excessive since both her arm and shoulder were torn. Additionally, she's being a very good neighbor, stating that accidents can happen and not suing for pain and suffering or anything else.

Five years ago, you covered the expenses when Prince, our old collie, gave a friendly bite in the rear to a neighborhood child not even on our property. This time it occurred in our own home. I believe you should pay it immediately both to keep her goodwill and because it is the right thing to do.

Sincerely,

David Seaton

As you can tell from David's letter, he doesn't understand his policy thoroughly. Your job is to educate him while keeping his goodwill, too.

The primary reason his claim was denied was that it includes an exclusion for dogs with a history of biting. You have this exclusion because dog bites account for nearly one-quarter of homeowner's insurance liability claims, costing the industry over $300 million with the average claim over $16,000. To keep the cost of insurance reasonable for all, the policy has this exclusion. In fact, some companies are even asking all homeowners to sign liability waivers for dog bites while others are offering discounts for not owning dogs. Furthermore, according to the Centers for Disease Control, dog bite fatalities are the highest for pit bulls followed by rottweilers, German shepherds, huskies, and malamutes. David's pit bull is in this group of dogs with long histories of biting.

Although your company doesn't write special policies for pit bulls because it would just be too expensive, you might suggest other things he could do to prevent future incidents. He could have his dog spayed or neutered, reducing the likelihood of biting. Or he could also get special training for the dog that teaches it how to interact with other people and animals. And he could help modify aggressive behavior by playing only nonaggressive games with it, such as fetch rather than tug-of-war.

Feel free to add anything else you think would help retain your customer's goodwill but clearly refuse the adjustment.

---

18 As Sara Meersman, customer service representative for LuggageFree, your job is usually a pleasant one. Most customers report that they are delighted with your competent service, which typically exceeds what they're promised. Today's email, however, brought a claim from Lee McLaughlin, an executive with Bee Line Trucking, requesting reimbursement for lost business potential based on a delayed shipment of products to a trade show in Miami last August.

Mr. McLaughlin's message is polite and even mentions that he has used your service many times for personal trips for golf outings where his golf clubs arrived in a timely fashion every time. Based on this good experience, he decided to use your service to ship some of his new wheel service and frame products to exhibit at a trade show.

He reported that this trade show is the key one his company representatives attend, and they were extremely disappointed that the products did not arrive until the second day of the show. In fact, one of their potential customers came by the company's booth the first day when they were without anything to show and demonstrate. He is convinced this lost business cost the company at least $50,000 in net profits.

He is requesting full reimbursement of his $2,500 shipping fees and $5,000 as a penalty for the lost sales. His message said that this payment is the only way you can keep him as a satisfied customer, so you know you will have to work hard to keep his business when you refuse his claim.

You believe you have sound legal and ethical grounds to stand on when refusing. On your website at <http://www.luggagefree.com> where he completed the request for service form, the limitation of your company's liability is clearly stated. While you will cover physical damage of luggage up to $1,000, your policy clearly states you will not cover "additional costs incurred by the customer if a shipment is late or any other costs outside the cash value." Furthermore, your website presents this paragraph in bold and in a very readable font size. And in checking your records of this shipment, you learned that air traffic all over the Southern Florida area was delayed that day due to the activity of tropical storm Rebekah.

You do want to keep Mr. McLaughlin's business and goodwill, so you'll give him the choice of 50 percent off his next personal use of your service or 10 percent off the next business use.

---

19 As Owen Smith, manager of customer service for Verizon in your city, you received a request that you hadn't encountered before to return a phone. The customer, Colin Deftos, wants to cancel his service and return a phone he has had nearly 18 months. Colin claims his phone caught a virus when he accidentally answered an incoming call labeled "UNAVAILABLE." He was so shocked he dropped the phone, and it hasn't worked right ever since. He wants to change to a safer network even though he has six months left on his contract with you.

While you will refuse this adjustment, you understand that a big part of your job in keeping Colin's business and goodwill is one of educating him. There has been a rumor going around for a couple of years now about a virus being caught when one is answering a call; however, it cannot happen this way. In fact, Verizon has had no reports of people getting phone viruses through daily use. As of today, there are only five known viruses for phones, and usually only security experts are interested in them. Additionally, these viruses do little damage and can be easily removed.

You do believe that eventually as more phones become more like minicomputers, they will become more susceptible to virus attacks. In fact, at this time Bluetooth technology as well as other enhancements such as ring tones, cameras, and other additions do make phones more vulnerable to viruses. But the discoverable feature on a Bluetooth phone can be turned off, and virus software is already available from both McAfee and Norton and a few other companies to protect these phones from being infected. To keep his goodwill, you may want to offer Colin a new basic phone (similar to his old one without enhancements) or $50 off any phone of his choice over $100 with a two-year renewable service contract.

Credit Refusals

20 Kim Gao is opening a ladies' shoe store in a new shopping mall in her home town, and apparently she wants suppliers to finance her. Today, as credit manager for Fifth Avenue Shoes, Inc., you received her application for credit. From the information she supplies you, it is evident that she has everything she needs except money.

The financial information she sent with her credit application does not justify credit. She has very little cash and apparently plans to finance her business mainly through her suppliers. Your company simply does not do business that way. She should get local financing first. After all, her home-town bankers are in a position to understand her situation and take care of her needs better than a distant supplier.

Your information doesn't tell you much about Ms. Gao. Your sales representative in the area tells you that she knows the woman casually. She reports also that Ms. Gao appears to be competent and that she has a good reputation. But she also believes that although the new store is in a good location, there is no shortage of ladies' shoe stores in the area.

Now you must write Ms. Gao, refusing credit. In time you hope to be able to grant it. Meanwhile, you'd like to get her cash business.

21 Assume that you are the credit manager for Duby's, an importer and wholesaler of Asian china and glassware. The business is conscious of its impact in the industry. Its past credit policy has tended to be quite liberal; but this policy has increased the need for collection efforts, some of which have been unsuccessful. As a result of these past policies, delinquent accounts have increased to a danger point. Something must be done about it. And it has been.

Today the store's management informed you that from now on, credit will be tighter. You will have to screen new applicants closely. This means that you will be turning down more of the new applicants. You will need some new credit-refusal model messages to guide you.

You remember from your college training that most credit refusals must be made to two types of applicants: people with inadequate capital and people with character shortcomings. You will need a model refusal message for each. Now you will write one of these (your instructor will determine which). In either case you will be courteous and specific. You will watch out for needless negatives, trite wordings, and anything brusque. And you'll try to keep the reader a friend of the company.

22 For this assignment assume that you are just beginning your working career with Chargit, a credit-card company. The company is national and international in scope and a widely accepted symbol of credit buying. The company differs from other such companies in that it offers credit only to top-rated applicants. It favors young professionals—people on the way up the success ladder.

Today your boss gives you your first major assignment. "I want you to revise our standard refusal message," she tells you. "It was written years ago, and just doesn't project the image we want." Here is the old message:

Dear _____:

We at Chargit were pleased to receive your recent application. Based on the information we have received about you, however, we respectfully regret that we must deny your request.

We trust that you will understand our position and hope you continue to progress in your career.

Sincerely

So now you must rewrite this form message. It's your first chance to show your new employer what you can do. Be sure to include all the information that is legally required where you live.

23 You work in the business office for a Home Bodies store, part of a large national chain that sells home furnishings, maintenance supplies, and light-construction materials to do-it-yourself home decorators and remodelers. The chain has its own credit program. LeeAnn Thomas recently submitted an application to open a Home Bodies account with a $3,000 line of credit. You hate to say no, but you're going to have to.

While headquarters gives each store some latitude for accepting or rejecting such applications, it has the following general guidelines: applicants must have lived at the current address for at least six months, have moved not more than twice in the previous three years, have a steady job with a stable company, and earn an income of at least eight times the credit line they're requesting.

According to her application, Ms. Thomas has lived in your city only four months, and she moved three times over the last three years. She lists her occupation as "Freelance Interior Designer," so she works for herself. She estimates her annual income at $30,000, but there's no one who can confirm or dispute this figure (your company is not authorized to access personal income tax information). You suspect that it is not a reliable indicator of her current income anyway since she just moved here and probably has not yet generated many clients.

Your company's practice is to write each credit applicant a letter, conveying the good or bad news. Write to Ms. Thomas to explain why she cannot be granted the line of credit she seeks. Offer her $500 credit for now (at 10.5 percent interest) and tell her what she needs to do to increase her chances of a higher limit in the future. Try to win her business even though you cannot approve her request at this time. Your boss, the accounts manager for your store, will sign the letter.

---

24 As office manager for a large dental clinic, you sometimes purchase credit checks on patients with little or no dental insurance who nevertheless need expensive work done. These checks, perfomed by major credit bureaus, tell you the patient's bill and loan payment history and current degree of debt, as well as whether or not the patient has ever declared bankruptcy, been sued, or been convicted of a crime. This information is useful in the case of new patients who have not yet built up a strong record of paying their bills.

Today you ordered such a check on Sushil Gami, a new patient who needs to have work done that will cost $2,500. He indicated on your financing request form that he makes a good salary, but from a company that offers no dental insurance. As with all new patients requesting financing, you ordered a credit check on Mr. Gami from a credit bureau, and the news wasn't good. He recently defaulted on a car loan and the car was repossessed. He also has a poor record of paying his other bills. While you wish you could set up a payment plan for him, you do not have any confidence that he would abide by the terms of the plan.

Send Mr. Gami a letter telling him of your decision. Fortunately, not all his dental work needs to be done right away. If he will return for a free follow-up to his first diagnostic appointment, the doctor can work out a treatment plan for him that will stagger the work over several months. You can also point him in the direction of several websites that describe dental "credit cards" and other options for those with little or no dental insurance. Make your decision and the reasons behind it clear while demonstrating genuine interest in helping Mr. Gami get the dental care he needs.

---

25 As Sharon Garbett, owner and operator of a private, local software applications training company, Garbett and Associates, you review all student applications. In most cases you are looking to see whether or not the prospective students are ready for your training, but an application you reviewed today from Matt Gregory was his financial application.

After graduating from college five years ago with a degree in fine arts, Matt has been working in theater and is interested in moving into the business side of theater. His theater experience is well rounded, which when combined with some business skills should prepare him well for this kind of work. However, at the moment he is unable to get any kind of financial aid. He has tried numerous public and private sources, including both scholarships and loans. His persuasive message to you asked you to extend him full credit for his tuition and books at your school; he promises to pay you on a regular schedule once he finishes the program and begins working.

While you admire his initiative, you are not a bank. And plenty of them turned him down for lack of collateral or a co-signer. Since you think he's capable, you don't want to discourage him even though you will refuse credit. You can offer him part-time assistant work during the afternoon to cover the cost of books and class materials. That would allow him to take day classes and work nights in the theater business office, earning the money he need is for tuition as well as giving him the experience he needs to get an even better position once he finishes your program. Furthermore, he could start his new career path debt free.

---

26 As Don Price, owner of Price Acura, you received from one of your young new sales staff, Carol Weissmann, an email concerning a transaction she closed on a lease agreement for your new MDX. She's asking that the contract be amended to allow the client to prepay for 10,000 additional miles on credit. Apparently the client recomputed his average weekly driving miles and discovered that if he drove at that rate for the length of the lease he'd run over his limit by 10,000–15,000 miles. So he has asked her to modify the lease terms to include 10,000 prepaid miles. He realizes that this change will raise his monthly payment a bit, but he'd rather pay the higher rate than be hit with a large fee at the end of the lease.

On checking the client's credit record, you learned he is a recent college graduate with only part-time work in his job history. While his new employer has verified his employment, the client told Carol that he has steep college bills to pay, which is the reason for his decision to lease rather than buy a new car. At this point his credit score is very low; in fact, in most cases you would not have leased to him. But with a new job and college behind him, he looks like a good risk to you. But pushing his credit line further at this time is too risky. So while you will refuse her client the credit now, you can suggest that he consider renegotiating the terms after one year of prompt payments. Or he could be reminded that he can always purchase the car at the end of the lease.

Negative Announcements

27 For this assignment you are the executive assistant to Pierre Delaware, president of EconoAir Airlines. EconoAir began operations only two years ago and has made great strides in its short existence. At the beginning, it offered various incentives to lure passengers to its airplanes. Apparently, the incentives worked since currently the company is solidly entrenched in the travel business. In spite of its solid growth, however, EconoAir is beginning to experience the effects of competition in the industry. Profits have begun to decline. President Delaware is determined to turn things around by taking steps to avoid the problems experienced by some of the other airlines.

One of the incentives EconoAir used at the beginning was a "double mileage" award in its frequent-flyer program. Specifically, this meant that it gave two points rather than the conventional one for every mile flown with EconoAir. "It's time for us to get back to reality," President Delaware tells you. "We must reduce this award to one point for one mile of travel. That's what the other airlines do. This two-for-one plan is costing us too much."

President Delaware then assigned you the task of writing members, announcing the decision to reduce the mileage given in its frequent flyer program. You see your problem as a difficult one. EconoAir is reducing its rewards primarily because of its need to save money. The members of the plan have nothing to gain from the change. So how will you explain the change to their satisfaction? Will you appeal to the members' reason? Their sense of fair play? You will have to think through the situation carefully before selecting a strategy. Then you will write the announcement.

28 You are secretary to the board of regents of Central State University. At today's meeting, the board approved a plan to build new parking lots and generally to better control the parking situation. As a means of paying for a part of the construction costs, the board approved a plan to charge faculty for parking privileges. For parking in the interior streets and small interior lots, the charge will be $40 a month. The charge for parking in the streets and small lots in the perimeter areas will be $25 a month. No charge will be made for parking in the large lots adjacent to the campus.

Knowing that charging for the privilege of parking would be protested vigorously, the board debated the matter long and hard. They concluded that given the university's financial status, this was the only feasible route. Anyway, as one board member put it, "We don't have to face the faculty. Our trusty secretary will write the announcement that will inform them. He/she is gifted with words. I'm sure he/she will make them understand."

Using your imagination logically to fill in any missing information, now prove that the regent is right. (In using your imagination, be guided by what you can see at your university. Your may want to include a map with your message showing the parking areas.)

29 For this assignment you are assistant to the president of Beckwith Manufacturing Company, Inc. For more than 30 years Beckwith has been manufacturing replacement parts for the automobile industry in two plants—the original one in Flint and a relatively new one in Detroit. You have known for some time that things haven't been going well in the old Flint plant—that it was becoming obsolete. You have also known that it would have to be either renovated extensively or abandoned. Today you receive the news you have been anticipating from your boss, Amos T. Beckwith.

President Beckwith explains the matter to you in these words: "We are going to leave this old plant. Just too obsolete and too expensive to renovate. In the future, we'll do all our manufacturing in Detroit. We have sufficient unused capacity there. As you know, sales have declined significantly anyway. Too much competition. Now we'll have to break the news to our employees here in Flint. As well as we can, we will transfer to Detroit those who choose to go there. We will do this based on our need for their skills and their seniority. We cannot guarantee everybody the level of employment they have now, but we'll do the best we can. For those approaching retirement age, we'll work out an early retirement package. And for those who don't choose to transfer or whom we just can't use, we'll give three months' terminal pay. No, we cannot afford to pay any moving expenses, but this isn't a long move."

After giving you some additional information (which you may construct from your logical imagination), Mr. Beckwith assigns you the task of writing the announcement for his signature that will go to all employees at the Flint plant. Another announcement, which you will write later, will inform the Detroit employees of what is happening.

30 The Brothers Club is a not-for-profit organization in your city. It is loosely affiliated with the Catholic Church, but its primary mission is social, not religious. It runs many programs for disadvantaged youth, including teen discussion groups, basketball tournaments, summer camps, and the like. The club is funded largely by the United Way and by corporate and individual donations, but it has also been operating as a private athletic club, whose members have been paying a fee (anywhere from $300 to $450 per year, depending on the level of membership) for use of the facilities.

The board of directors for the Club recently met and decided to discontinue the athletic-club part of the operation as well as to move the organization to a new location. Two factors influenced this decision. First, there have been too few paying customers over the last several years. The facilities are functional but not terribly attractive, and the equipment is not as high-tech as that of the nearby YMCA. Customers have tended to gravitate toward the more upscale, expensive club. As a result of this lost business, it has become too costly to maintain the exercise rooms and equipment at the club. Also, upkeep on the club's extensive facilities has been a drain on money that the board feels would have been better spent on the youth whom the Club is intended to serve. Moving to a smaller location with more limited facilities reserved for the youth alone would make the club more financially viable and also more focused on its central mission.

Your boss, the executive director of the Brothers Club, has asked you, the assistant director, to write a letter announcing these changes to the athletic-club members. She has also discussed with you how the members will be reimbursed for the time remaining on their yearly memberships, so you will give the members this important information as well. Write the letter for your boss's signature, and see if you can minimize your readers' disappointment while also keeping them interested in supporting the club.

31 As Customer Service Supervisor at Billing Software, Inc., you need to send an email to your staff announcing a new policy affecting them. Specifically, the company is going to begin randomly monitoring its help-desk representatives' telephone calls. This monitoring will give you a more dependable way to evaluate trainees, but the main reason for the new policy is that your people are spending too much time on the phone with the callers. You routinely ask your clients—businesses that use your software for their billing procedures—to evaluate your services, and lately these evaluations have included some complaints about being put on hold too much and too long. There's no good reason for the clogged phone lines; you have sufficient staff for the number of clients you have, your software is not that complicated, and all help-desk staff are thoroughly trained on the software. To find out the cause of the problem, you hung around the help-desk area more than usual over the last couple of weeks (often without being noticed), and you learned that your people often talk with clients too long and about matters not related to business. You discussed your findings with your boss, one of the owners of the company, and he agreed that it's time to monitor service calls, as so many companies already do.

What makes the situation complex is that you do want your staff to continue to be cordial on the phone and generous with their time and information. Quality customer service is one edge you have over the competition, and you don't want to do anything that will turn your helpful, friendly staff into impersonal automatons who don't fully solve the callers' problems. You also realize that an occasional off-topic discussion can relieve the tedium of answering calls all day. Still, staying too long on the phone with one caller can keep the next one from getting the help he or she needs in timely fashion. And your company promotes efficiency as one of the main benefits of its software.

Write your staff an email that will help them receive the news of the policy as positively as possible so that you will get the reactions you want, not the ones you don't.

32 The employees of [you decide] have been making good use of one of your most attractive company benefits—namely, tuition reimbursement for college coursework. For courses approved by the company (that is, courses that are related to employees' current or likely future positions in the company), employees have been paying only 33 percent of tuition costs. But this generous benefit is about to be cut back. The cost of tuition has risen dramatically nationwide (think of your own tuition bills, or check the Internet for facts about other schools). The costs of running a business keep rising, too, as energy bills increase, technology has to be updated, and health coverage takes bigger and bigger bites out of revenue. At a recent meeting, the executives of the company targeted tuition coverage as part of a general cost-cutting campaign. Your boss, the VP of human resources, has asked you to write an announcement to the employees regarding the tuition cutbacks.

In the message, you will need to state that the company will now cover only 40 percent of the tuition for approved courses. You know that this will be particularly bad news for those who are in the middle of a degree program, but there were never any guarantees that the coverage would remain at its current level, and the change simply can't be helped. You will also need to inform the employees that there will be more rigorous screening of tuition-reimbursement requests. You should probably give examples of the kinds of courses that are likely to be approved under the new policy. On the other hand, at least some tuition coverage does remain, and—at least for now—none of the other benefits are being affected. Plus, online courses are often cheaper than those offered on-site, so maybe employees can find ways to offset the increased costs of taking courses.

Figure out how to write this message so that you give employees a clear sense of the facts and their options. Help them to feel positive about the company and encouraged to continue to seek out relevant college coursework—which, after all, does save the company in-house training costs and results in a better qualified workforce. Your boss has left it to you to decide the best way to distribute this announcement.

---

33 As your workplace is becoming more diverse in race, religion, and culture, you are beginning to realize that in order for employees to work together more effectively you are going to have to stress similarities rather than differences in all your business practices. And just as English has been a unifying aspect throughout United States history as well as in the world of business, it should help unite your company's staff as well. You believe an English-only policy would help improve the morale of those who speak only English while making all transactions transparent as well. And it would greatly improve the collaborations that go on daily in the workplace.

You know that courts have traditionally upheld English-only workplace policies because they are not seen as discriminatory. So write the announcement of an English-only policy in a way that bilingual speakers will not find offensive.

---

34 Your employees have always searched for Internet content useful to your business, and they seem both to enjoy doing it and to be the first to use what they find. This practice has helped give your business a reputation for innovative work, easily responsible for generating over half your new business this year. But lately many of your employees have consumed hours of valuable time in bad experiences with new beta versions of Web 2.0 applications.

While some of these applications work beautifully from the start, others crash and freeze the users' computers on a regular basis, requiring hours of troubleshooting to get back in business. And there seems to be no consistent guideline to follow in determining which ones work well and which ones don't. Big companies like Microsoft and Google release betas that range from raw to polished, and small companies also release beta products that vary widely in quality. Therefore, you have decided to implement a new policy restricting the use of web-based beta applications. However, you do not want to discourage forward-looking work, so you are setting up a system in which those testing particular beta applications regularly can record their experience with them on a blog you have set up for this purpose. Employees will be required to check this blog of users of these applications before deciding to use these new applications.

While this announcement will mean users of these new applications need to be a bit more proactive in assuring the safety of their computers, the new policy is aimed at saving the user time in the long run by learning from others' firsthand experiences. Write the announcement so it will have the desired effect while continuing to encourge employee innovation.

---

35 Today's mail brought an anonymous note tattling on staff who use the new color copier to make personal wrapping paper for their holiday gifts. Apparently, the Gap published a gift guide on its website outlining how to create wrapping paper on color copiers. It took only one employee doing it and showing others the beautiful result to have others follow.

At first it seemed clever, and the cost could probably be absorbed without much trouble. But the precedent it sets isn't sitting well with you. Letting people use small supplies for personal use might suggest it's OK to appropriate other items as well. So you need to let your staff know that personal use of the copier is not appropriate. You can remind them of both the business and ethical reasons for refraining from the practice. But you don't want to be viewed as miserly at this time of the year, so you'll include a $10 gift card for the neighborhood copy center to send along with the bad news.

chapter eight

Indirectness in Persuasive Messages

LEARNING OBJECTIVES

Upon completing this chapter, you will be able to use persuasion effectively, especially when making requests and composing sales messages. To reach this goal, you should be able to

1   Describe important strategies for writing any persuasive message.

2   Write skillful persuasive requests that begin indirectly, develop convincing reasoning, and close with goodwill and action.

3   Discuss ethical concerns regarding sales messages.

4   Describe the planning steps for direct mail or email sales messages.

5   Compose sales messages that gain attention, persuasively present appeals, and effectively drive for action.

Persuasive messages generally are written in the indirect order. While they do not necessarily involve bad news, their goals often run contrary to the reader's current wishes. The mind-set of the resistant reader must be changed before they can be successful. Achieving this change requires indirectness.

In the following pages we first provide some general advice for effective persuasion. We then explain how the indirect order is used in two kinds of persuasive messages. One is the persuasive request—for situations in which the reader would likely reject the request without convincing explanation. The other is the sales message. As you will see, this latter type involves a highly specialized form of writing.

GENERAL ADVICE ABOUT PERSUASION

All our previous advice about adapting your messages to your readers comes into play with persuasive messages—only more so. Moving your reader from an uninterested or even antagonistic position to an interested, cooperative one is a major accomplishment. To achieve it, keep the following advice in mind.

Know Your Readers

For any kind of persuasive message, thinking about your subject from your readers' point of view is critical. To know what kind of appeals will succeed with your readers, you need to know as much as you can about their values, interests, and needs. Companies specializing in direct-mail campaigns spend a great deal of money to acquire this kind of information. Using a variety of research techniques, they gather demographic information (such as age, gender, income, and geographic location) and psychographic information (such as social, political, and personal preferences) on their target audience. They also develop mailing lists based on prior shows of interest from consumers and purchase mailing lists from other organizations that have had success with certain audiences. But even an individual charged with writing an internal or external persuasive message can increase the chances for success by learning as much as possible about the intended readers. He or she can talk with the customer service people about the kinds of calls they're getting, study the company's customer database, chat with people around the water cooler or online, and run ideas past colleagues. Good persuasion depends on knowledge as well as on imagination and logic.

Choose and Develop Targeted Reader Benefits

No one is persuaded to do something for no reason. Sometimes their reasons for acting are related to tangible or measurable rewards. For example, they will save money, save time, or acquire some kind of desired object. But often, the rewards that persuade are intangible. People may want to make their work lives easier, gain prestige, or have more freedom. Or perhaps they want to identify with a larger cause, feel that they are helping others, or do the right thing. In your quest for the appeals that will win your readers over, do not underestimate the power of intangible benefits, especially when you can pair them with tangible rewards. Take care, too, not to imply in your messages that your audience is motivated only by money. While the emphasis on financial benefit is warranted in some cases—for example, when trying to win clients for your financial consulting business or get them to open an account with your credit card company—people generally do not like the implication that they are motivated only by money. True, it may be the financial benefit that actually gets them to act, but unduly emphasizing the monetary benefit can backfire if you imply that your readers care about no other goals.

When selecting the reader benefits to feature in your persuasive messages, bear in mind that such benefits can be intrinsic, extrinsic, or something in between. Intrinsic benefits are benefits that readers will get automatically by complying with your request. For example, if you are trying to persuade people to attend your company's awards dinner, the pleasure of sharing in their colleagues' successes will be intrinsic to the event. Door prizes would be an extrinsic benefit. We might classify the meal itself

- Persuasive messages are appropriately written in indirect order.

- Following are words of advice for persuasion in general and then for two specific types of messages: persuasive requests and sales.

- Adaptation is especially important in persuasive messages.

- Understanding your readers is critical.

- People can be motivated by tangible or intangible rewards.

- Prefer intrinsic benefits over extrinsic benefits.

as something of a combination—not really the main feature of the event but definitely central to it. Intrinsic benefits are tightly linked to what you're asking people to do, while extrinsic ones are added on and more short-lived. Let intrinsic benefits do the main work of your persuasive effort. Focusing too much on extrinsic benefits can actually cheapen your main cause in the readers' eyes.

When presenting your reader benefits, be sure the readers can see exactly how the benefits will help them. The literature on selling makes a useful distinction between product features and reader benefits. If you say that a wireless service uses a certain kind of technology, you're describing a feature. If you say that the technology results in fewer missed or dropped calls, you're describing a benefit. Benefits persuade by enabling readers to envision the features of the recommended product or action in their own worlds.

One common technique for achieving this goal is to use what we call *scenario painting,* or a description that pictures the reader in a sample situation enjoying the promised benefits. Here is an example of scenario painting written by well-known copywriter Morris Massey, promoting a tour to New Orleans:

> Saturday morning dawns bright and crisp—perfect for casual browsing through the "treasure" shops of the Quarter—where a world of artists, antiques, and astonishing sights awaits you. From noon, you are escorted through some of the famous areas of the city: the Garden District (where the elegance of the past lives on), the lake area, and the most famous historical sites of the Quarter. Late afternoon finds you approaching famed Commander's Palace for an exclusive cocktail party and dinner. You'll practically hear the moan of ol' river steamers on the mighty Mississippi as you dine.

Scenario painting is very common in sales messages, but you can also use it to good advantage in other persuasive messages, even internal ones. Whatever your persuasive situation or strategy, be sure to provide enough detail for readers to see how they will benefit from what you are asking them to do.

Make Good Use of Three Kinds of Appeals

The first acknowledged expert on persuasion, the Greek philosopher Aristotle, lived almost 2,500 years ago, but many of his core concepts are still widely taught and used. Of particular value is his famous categorizing of persuasive appeals into three kinds: those based on logic (logos), those based on emotion (pathos), and those based on the character of the speaker (ethos). All three kinds come into play in every persuasive message—in fact, one might say, in every kind of message. But as the writer of a persuasive message, you will need to think especially carefully about how to manage these appeals and which ones to emphasize given your intended audience.

In practice, these three kinds of appeals often cannot be neatly separated, but to get a sense of your options, you might benefit from thinking about each in turn. What kind of logical appeals might you use—saved money? Saved time? A more dependable or effective product? How about emotional appeals? Higher status? More sex appeal? Increased popularity? And don't neglect appeals based on character. What kind of image of yourself and your company will resonate with the reader? Should you get a celebrity or expert to endorse your product or to serve as the spokesperson? Not only when planning but also when revising your persuasive message, assess your appeals. Be sure to choose and develop the ones most likely to persuade your audience.

Make It Easy for Your Readers to Comply

Sometimes writers focus so much on creating persuasive appeals that they put insufficient thought into making the requested action as clear and easy to perform as possible. If you want people to give money or buy your product, tell them where and how to do it, and supply a preaddressed mailing envelope or a web address if applicable. If you want employees to give suggestions for improving products or operations, tell them exactly where and how to submit their ideas and make it easy for them to do so. If you want people to remember to work more safely or conserve on supplies, give them

- Turn your product features into reader benefits.

- Use scenario painting to help readers visualize themselves enjoying the benefits of the product.

- Aristotle identified three kinds of persuasive appeals: logic based, emotion based, and character based.

- Be sure to make the requested action clear and easy.

specific techniques for achieving these goals and include auxiliary reminders at the actual locations where they need to remember what to do. Making the desired action specific and easy to perform is a key part of moving your readers from resistance to compliance with your request.

With this general advice in mind, we now turn to the two main types of persuasive messages in business: persuasive requests and sales messages.

PERSUASIVE REQUESTS

INTRODUCTORY SITUATION

Persuasive Requests

Introduce yourself to the next business message situation by returning to your hypothetical position at Pinnacle. As a potential executive, you spend some time working for the community. Pinnacle wants you to do this volunteer work for the sake of good public relations. You want to do it because it is personally rewarding.

Currently, as chair of the fund-raising committee of the city's Junior Achievement program, you head all efforts to get financial support for the program from local businesspeople. You have a group of workers who will call on businesspeople. But personal calls take time, and there are many people to call on.

At its meeting today, the Junior Achievement board of directors discussed the problem of contacting businesspeople. One director suggested using a letter to sell them on giving money. The board accepted the idea with enthusiasm. With just as much enthusiasm, it gave you the assignment of writing the letter (for the president's signature).

As you view the assignment, it is not a routine letter-writing problem. Although the local businesspeople are probably generous, they are not likely to part with money without good reason. In fact, their first reaction to a request for money is likely to be negative. So you will need to overcome their resistance in order to persuade them. Your task is indeed challenging.

There will be many times in your work life when you will need to make persuasive requests. Perhaps, as in the scenario above, you will be asked to write a fund-raising message. Perhaps you will need to ask your management for another staff position or for special equipment. You may need to persuade a potential client to join you in a meeting so that you can demonstrate the benefits of your products. Or maybe you will be trying to persuade your employees to change their behavior in some way.

Whether written to internal or external readers, requests that are likely to be resisted require a slow, deliberate approach. You must persuade the reader that he or she should grant the request before making the request. More specifically, you must present facts and logical reasoning that support your case. And you must do it convincingly. Such a presentation requires that you begin by developing a plan.

Determining the Persuasion

Developing your persuasive plan involves three interrelated tasks: determining what you want, figuring out your readers' likely reactions, and deciding upon a persuasive strategy that will overcome reader objections and evoke a positive response.

Think carefully about your actual goals for your persuasive requests. A request for a one-time-only donation might be written very differently from the kind of request that is intended to create a long-time, multiple donor. If you were convincing employees to leave the parking places next to the building for customers' use, you would write a very different message if you cared about maintaining the employees' goodwill than you would if you simply wanted to order them to comply. Your goals, considered in the context of your organization's goals and your relationship with your readers, are key shapers of your persuasive message.

- Planning your strategy involves three interrelated tasks:

- considering your own goals for the message,

• considering your readers' needs and interests,

As we have said, thinking about your readers' needs and interests is paramount when planning any persuasive message. Considering everything you know about your readers, put yourself in their shoes. Look at the request as they are likely to see it. Figure out what's in it for them, and anticipate their likely objections. From this thinking and imagining, your plan should emerge.

• and deciding upon a persuasive plan.

The specific plan you develop will depend on the facts of the case. You may be able to show that your reader stands to gain in time, money, or the like. Or you may be able to show that your reader will benefit in goodwill or prestige. In some cases, you may persuade readers by appealing to their love of beauty, excitement, serenity, or the like. In other cases, you may be able to persuade readers by appealing to the pleasant feeling that comes from doing a good turn. You decide on the benefits that will be most likely to win over your readers.

• A special persuasive plan is the problem-solution strategy, which uses the *common-ground* technique.

A special kind of persuasive request is one that casts the request as a problem–solution message. With this strategy, you first present a problem that you and the readers share—a form of the *common-ground* persuasion technique—and then show how doing as you propose will solve the problem for all concerned. Many fund-raising letters start with this ploy, giving us striking facts about the current political climate, the environment, or living conditions in a certain area of the world. But this strategy can also be a powerful one for internal audiences who might not be receptive to a straightforward proposal for action but who share your opinion that something needs to be done.

A persuasive request situation is a special opportunity for analysis, creativity, and judgment. With careful use of all three, you can plan messages that will change your readers' minds and move them to action.

Gaining Attention in the Opening

In the indirect messages discussed in Chapter 7, the goal of the opening is to set up the explanation. The same goal exists in persuasion messages. Your beginning should lead to your central strategy. But the opening of a persuasive message has an additional goal: to gain attention.

● The opening sets the strategy and gains attention.

The need to draw your reader in with the opening of your persuasive message is obvious. You are writing to a person who has not invited your message and probably does not agree with your goal. So you need to get that person into a receptive mood. An interesting beginning is a good step in this direction.

● Attention is needed to get the reader in a mood to receive the persuasion.

Determine what your reader will find compelling. It might be some statement that arouses curiosity, or it might be a statement offering or implying a reader benefit. Because questions get people thinking, they are often effective openings. The following examples indicate the possibilities.

● What you write to gain attention is limited only by your imagination.

From the cover letter of a questionnaire seeking the opinions of medical doctors:

> What, in your opinion as a medical doctor, is the future of the private practice of medicine?

From a message requesting contributions for orphaned children:

> While you and I dined heartily last night, 31 orphans at San Pablo Mission had only dried beans to eat.

From a message seeking the cooperation of business leaders in promoting a fair:

> What would your profits be if 300,000 free-spending visitors came to our town during a single week?

If writing your proposal in the form of a problem–solution message, you should start with a goal that you and the readers share. For example, let's say that a project manager in your company has retired and that, as one of your company's executive committee, you want a certain member of the office staff to be promoted into the position. The challenge is that no office person in your company has ever broken into the managerial ranks, so any direct proposal to promote your candidate will, you feel sure, be met with this objection. To get readers on your side from the beginning, you could start your message with facts that everyone can agree upon: that someone has retired, that his or her duties are important, that someone capable needs to be found, and fast. Your subject line for an email along these lines might be something like, "Reassigning Jim Martin's Duties" (which everyone supports), not "Promoting Kathy Pearson" (which your readers will resist unless you have prepared them for the idea).

● The opening of a problem-solution message describes a problem that you and your readers share.

Whatever the case, the form of indirectness that you choose for your opening should engage your readers right away and get them thinking along the lines that will lead to their approval of your request.

Presenting the Persuasion

Following the opening, you should proceed with your goal of persuading. Your task here is a logical and orderly presentation of the reasoning you have selected.

● Your persuasion follows.

As with any argument intended to convince, you should do more than merely list points. You should help convey the points with convincing details. Since you are trying to penetrate a neutral or resistant mind, you need to make good use of the you-viewpoint. You need to pay careful attention to the meanings of your words and the clarity of your expression. You need to use logic and emotion appropriately and project an appealing image. And, because your reader may become impatient if you delay your objective, you need to make every word count.

● Present the points convincingly (selecting words for effect, using you-viewpoint, and the like).

Making the Request Clearly and Positively

- Follow the persuasion with the request.

- Word the request for best effect.

After you have done your persuading, move to the action you seek. You have prepared the reader for what you want. If you have done that well, the reader should be ready to accept your proposal.

As with negative points, your request requires care in word choice. You should avoid words that detract from the request. You also should avoid words that bring to mind images and ideas that might work against you. Words that bring to mind reasons for refusing are especially harmful, as in this example:

- Do not use a negative tone.

I am aware that businesspeople in your position have little free time to give, but will you please consider accepting an assignment to the board of directors of the Children's Fund?

The following positive tie-in with a major point in the persuasion strategy does a much better job:

- Be positive.

Because your organizing skills are so desperately needed, will you please serve on the board of directors of the Children's Fund?

- The request can end the message or be followed by more persuasion.

Whether your request should end your message will depend on the needs of the case. In some cases, you will profit by following the request with words of explanation. This procedure is especially effective when a long persuasion effort is needed. In such cases, you simply cannot present all your reasoning before stating your goal. On the other hand, you may end less involved presentations with the request. Even in this case, however, you may want to follow the request with a reminder of the appeal. As illustrated in the example message (on p. 208), this strategy associates the request with the advantage that saying yes will give the reader.

- Ending with a reminder of the appeal is also good.

Summarizing the General Plan for Requests

- Follow this general plan when writing persuasive requests.

From the preceding discussion, the following general plan for the persuasive request message is apparent:

- Open with words that (1) set up the strategy and (2) gain attention.
- Present the strategy (the persuasion) using persuasive language and you-viewpoint.
- Make the request clearly and without negatives (1) either at the end of the message or (2) followed by words that recall the persuasive appeal.

Contrasting Persuasive Requests

- The following messages illustrate bad and good persuasion efforts.

The persuasive request is illustrated by contrasting letters that ask businesspeople to donate to Junior Achievement. The first message is direct and weak in persuasion; the second is indirect and persuasive. The second message, which follows the approach described above, produced better results.

Obvious Failure in Directness. The weaker letter begins with the request. Because the request is opposed to the reader's wishes, the direct beginning is likely to get a negative reaction. In addition, the comments about how much to give tend to lecture rather than suggest. Some explanation follows, but it is weak and scant. In general, the letter is poorly written. It makes little use of the you-viewpoint. Perhaps its greatest fault is that the persuasion comes too late. The selfish close is a weak reminder of the action requested.

Dear Mr. Williams:

Will you please donate to the local Junior Achievement program? We have set $50 as a fair minimum for businesses to give. But larger amounts would be appreciated.

The organization badly needs your support. Currently, about 900 young people will not get to participate in Junior Achievement activities unless more money is raised. Junior Achievement is a most worthwhile organization. As a business leader, you should be willing to support it.

If you do not already know about Junior Achievement, let me explain. Junior Achievement is an organization for high school youngsters. They work with local business executives to form small businesses. They operate the businesses. In the process, they learn about our economic system. This is a good thing, and it deserves our help.

Hoping to receive your generous donation,

This weak letter has no persuasion strategy.

Skillful Persuasion in an Indirect Order. The next message shows good imagination. It follows the recommended indirect pattern. Its opening has strong interest appeal and sets up the persuasion strategy. Notice the effective use of the you-viewpoint throughout. Not until the reader has been sold on the merits of the request does the message ask the question. It does this clearly and directly. The final words leave the reader thinking about a major benefit that a yes answer will give.

Dear Mr. Williams:

Right now—right here in our city—620 teenage youngsters are running 37 corporations. The kids run the whole show, their only adult help being advice from some of your business associates who work with them. Last September they applied for charters and elected officers. They created plans for business operations. For example, one group planned to build websites for local businesses. Another elected to conduct a rock concert. Yet another planned to publish newsletters for area corporations. After determining their plans, the kids issued stock—and sold it, too. With the proceeds from stock sales, they began their operations. Now they are operating. This May they will liquidate their companies and account to their stockholders for their profits or losses.

I am sure you will quickly see the merits of the Junior Achievement program. You know the value of such realistic experience to the kids—how it teaches them the operations of business and how it sells them on the merits of the free enterprise system. You can see, also, that it's an exciting and wholesome program, the kind we need more of to combat economic illiteracy. After you have considered these points and others you will find at <http://www.ja.org/>, I know you will see that Junior Achievement is a good thing.

To continue to succeed, Junior Achievement needs all of us behind it. During the 13 years the program has been in our city, it has had enthusiastic support from local business leaders. But with over 900 students on the waiting list, our plans for next year call for expansion. That's why, as a volunteer myself, I ask that you help make the program available to more youngsters by contributing $50 (it's deductible). Please make your donation now by completing our online contribution form at <www.juniorachievement. org>. You will be doing a good service for the kids in our community.

Sincerely,

This better letter uses good persuasion strategy.

Persuasive Request Letter (A Request for Information about Employment Applicants). In this letter a trade publication editor seeks information from an executive for an article on desirable job application procedures. The request involves time and effort for the executive. Thus, persuasion is necessary.

the OFFICE ADMINISTRATOR

November 20, 2007

Ms. Adelade O. Romano
Director of Human Resources
Chalmers-DeLouche, Inc.
17117 Proden Road
St. Paul, MN 55108

Dear Ms. Romano:

Question opening gets attention

What clues have you found in employment applications that help you estimate a person's character and desirability to your firm?

Opening topic sets up explanation

Explanation follows logically

Young people entering business are eager for any clue that will put them on the other side of the fence. They want to know what goes on in your mind when you are judging the people behind the letters. In our column, "Applications That Talk," we want to send a message especially to those people. To make the article as practical as possible, we are drawing our information from people in the field who really know.

Explanation is straight-forward—appeals subtly to good feeling from helping others

Request evolves from presentation of appeal

A mutual friend of ours, Max Mullins, told me of your recent problem of finding the most desirable person behind 250 applications. What specific points did you look for in these applications? What clues distinguished some people from the others? When the going got hard, what fine points enabled you to make your final choice? The young people of today are eager for you to answer these questions.

Final words recall basic appeal

You can help solve their problem if you will jot down your personal comments on these applications and allow me to study them in confidence as the basis for an article. <u>Will you do that for us and them?</u> It is just possible, you know, that through this article to young businesspeople you may contribute to the success of a future leader in your own company. At least, you will be of service to the mass of young people who are trying to get "that" job that is so important to them right now.

Clear and direct request

Sincerely,

Charlotte C. Clayton

Charlotte C. Clayton
Associate Editor

enclosures

405 Perrin Ave.
Austin, TX 78716
512-437-7080
FAX: 512-437-7081
Clayton@officea.com

A Persuasive Internal Request (Using a Central Emotional Appeal Supported by Logical and Character-Based Appeals).* The writer wants employees to participate in the company's annual blood drive. He needs to convince them of the importance of the drive and overcome their likely objections. This message will be distributed to employees' mailboxes.

AMBERLY
Engineering & Construction

Department of Community Relations
Mail Location 12
123 Jackson Street
Edison, Colorado 80864
(719) 777-4444
CommunityRelations@Amberly.com

February 27, 2006

Opens with an attention-getting, you-focused question

Did you help save Brad Meyer's life?

Tells an engaging story with specific details

A few years ago, an employee of Amberly was driving to a friend's wedding when an oncoming car, operated by a drunk driver, swerved across the center line. Brad doesn't remember the crash. But he does remember two months spent in the hospital, two months of surgery and therapy.

Uses a character-based appeal; invites the reader to identify with these "lifesavers"

Without the help of people like us, Brad would not have lived. Some Amberly employees save lives regularly. We're blood donors. Please be a lifesaver and join us on Friday, March 19th, for Amberly's annual blood drive.

Your help is needed for a successful drive.

Avoids words such as "draw blood" or "needle" that would bring unpleasant parts of the procedure to mind

Giving blood is simple. The entire process will take less than 45 minutes.

Giving blood is safe. Experienced health professionals from the Steinmetz Blood Center will be on-site to conduct the procedure exactly as they would in a clinic setting.

Giving blood is convenient. The Steinmetz staff will be in Room 401, Building B, between 9:00 A.M. and 3:00 P.M. To save time, make an appointment to donate. Call the Steinmetz Blood Center at 569-1170.

Addresses likely reader objections

Giving blood is important. Nobody knows who will need blood next, but one thing is certain—it will be available only if healthy, caring people take time to give it. Brad's accident required 110 units—more than 12 gallons—of blood. Because 110 people set aside 45 minutes, Brad Meyer has a lifetime of minutes to be grateful.

Recalls the emotion-based opening and links it to a logical appeal: you or someone in your family might benefit

Take a few moments now to make your pledge on the reverse side of this letter. Then return it to the Community Relations department, Mail Location 12, by March 15th. For more information about the drive, call the Steinmetz Center at 552-7116.

Makes the requested action clear and easy

From Brad and from other families—like yours and mine—who might need it in the days to come,

Thank you,

John M. Piper

John M. Piper
Director, Community Relations

*Revised and printed with permission from Dr. Joseph A. Steger, President Emeritus, University of Cincinnati.

Words of Wisdom

Organizations have obligations to customers that are not to be taken lightly. Presenting information in a positive light is an acceptable, even desirable, business practice and should be encouraged. However, when companies emphasize the positive aspects of their product to the extent that truth is distorted, and the product is misrepresented, they have acted unethically.

Betsy Stevens, Cornell University

Betsy Stevens, "Persuasion, Probity, and Paltering: The Prudential Crisis," *Journal of Business Communication* 36 (1999): 331.

SALES MESSAGES

INTRODUCTORY SITUATION

Sales Messages

Introduce yourself to the next message type by assuming the role of Anthony A. Killshaw, a successful restaurant consultant. Over the past 28 years, you have acquired an expert knowledge of restaurant operations. You have made a science of virtually every area of restaurant activity: menu design, food control, purchasing, kitchen organization, service. You also have perfected a simple system for data gathering and analysis that quickly gets to the heart of most operations' problems. Testimonials from a number of satisfied clients prove that the system works.

Knowing that your system works is one thing. Getting this knowledge to enough prospective clients is another. So you have decided to publicize your work by writing restaurant managers and telling them about what you have to offer.

At the moment your plan for selling your services is hazy. But you think you will do it by email. It's a fast and easy way to reach your potential customers, you think. They will be more likely to read your message than if you used direct mail. Probably you will use a basic message that will invite the readers to look at your website. The website conveys the details—much more than you could get into the message.

Because sales writing requires special skills, you have decided to use the help of a local advertising agency—one with good experience with this type of selling. However, you have a pretty good idea of what you want, so you will not leave the work entirely up to the agency's personnel. You will tell them what you want included, and you will have the final word on what is acceptable.

• Professionals usually do the sales writing, so why study the subject?

One of the most widely disseminated forms of business communication is the sales message. It is such an important component of most businesses' sales strategies that it has become an elaborate, highly professionalized class, backed by extensive consumer research. Think about the typical sales letter that you receive. Careful attention has been paid to the message on the envelope, to the kinds of pieces inside, and to the visual appeal of those pieces, as well as to the text of the letter itself. Clearly, advertising professionals produce many of these mailings, as well as much of the fundraising literature that we receive. You can also see a professional's hand in many of the sales emails that appear in your in-box. Why, then, you might ask, should you study sales writing?

• You need to be able to share your insider knowledge and judgment with sales-writing professionals.

As a businessperson, you will often find yourself in the position of helping to shape a major sales campaign. You may well have valuable insight into your product's benefits and your potential customers. You need to be familiar with the conventions for sales messages and to be able to offer your own good ideas for their success.

In addition, knowledge of selling techniques can help you in many of your other activities, especially the writing of other kinds of business messages, for in a sense most of them involve selling something—an idea, a line of reasoning, your company, yourself. Sales techniques are more valuable to you than you might think. After you have studied the remainder of this chapter, you should see why.

Questioning the Acceptability of Sales Messages

We begin our discussion of sales messages by noting that they are a controversial area of business communication, for two main reasons: they are often unwanted, and they sometimes use ethically dubious persuasive tactics. Probably you know from your own experience that direct-mail sales literature is not always received happily. Called "junk" mail, these mailings often go into the wastebasket without being read. Even so, they must be successful, for the direct-mail business has survived for over a century.

Sales messages sent by email appear to be creating even more hostility among intended customers. Angrily referred to as "spam," unsolicited email sales messages have generated strong resistance among email users. Perhaps it is because these messages clutter up in-boxes. Maybe the rage results from the fact that mass mailings place a heavy burden on Internet providers, driving up costs to the users. Or perhaps the fact that they invade the reader's privacy is to blame. There are the downright unethical practices of some email advertisers who use "misleading subject lines and invalid email addresses to thwart filtering attempts and get respondents to open them."[1] Whatever the explanation, the resistance is real. You will need to consider these objections any time you use this sales medium.

Fortunately, a more acceptable form of email selling has developed. Called *permission email* or *opt-in email marketing,* it permits potential customers to sign on a company's website or offer their email addresses to a catalog, phone marketer, or other recipient. The potential customers may be asked to indicate the products, services, and specific topics of their interest. Thus the marketers can tailor their messages to the customer, and the customer receives only what he or she wants. According to a recent white paper by eMarketer, building permission-based email distribution lists is one of the most important steps in waging successful emarketing campaigns.[2] Such practices can help address the problem of unwanted sales messages.

As for the charge that persuasive messages use unfair persuasive tactics, this is, unfortunately, sometimes the case. The unfair tactics could range from deceptive wording and visuals to the omission of important information to the use of emotional elements that impair good judgment. In a Missouri court case, Publishers Clearing House was found guilty of deception for direct mail stating that the recipients were already winners, when in fact they were not.[3] To consider a different example, one linen supply company sent a letter to parents of first-year students at a certain university telling them that the students would need to purchase extra-long sheets, offered by this company, to fit the extra-long beds on campus—but omitted the information that only one dorm out of four had such beds. And it is well documented that images, because they work on a visceral level, persuade in ways that tend to bypasses the viewers' reasoned judgment, leading some to question the ethics of such elements.[4]

Any persuasive message is, by its very nature, biased. The writer has a favored point of view and wants to persuade the reader to adopt it. Therefore, considering the ethical dimension of your communication, while important for all types of messages, is especially critical for persuasive messages. Let your conscience and your ability to put

---

[1] Rich Gray, "Spamitize Your Inbox," *Guide to E-Mail and More* 8.7 (2000): 66.

[2] eMarketer, "Effective E-Mail: The Seven Golden Rules You Know (But May Forget to Follow)," 21 Mar. 2006 <http://www.emarketer.com>.

[3] See Helen Rothschild Ewald and Roberta Vann, " 'You're a Guranteed Winner': Composing 'You' in a Consumer Culture," *Journal of Business Communication* 40 (2003): 98–117.

[4] Charles A. Hill, "The Psychology of Rhetorical Images," *Defining Visual Rhetorics,* ed. Charles A. Hill and Marguerite Helmers (Mahwah, NJ: Lawrence Erlbaum, 2004) 30–38.

yourself in the readers' shoes guide you as you consider how to represent your subject and win others to your cause.

Preparing to Write a Sales Message

Before you can begin writing a sales message, you must know all you can about the product or service you are selling. You simply cannot sell most goods and services unless you know them and can tell the prospects what they need to know. Before prospects buy a product, they may want to know how it is made, how it works, what it will do, and what it will not do. Clearly, a first step in sales writing is careful study of your product or service.

In addition, you should know your readers. In particular, you should know about their needs for the product or service. Anything else you know about them can help: their economic status, age, nationality, education, and culture. The more you know about your readers, the better you will be able to adapt your sales message.

In large businesses, a marketing research department or agency typically gathers information about prospective customers. If you do not have such help, you will need to gather this information on your own. If time does not permit you to do the necessary research, you may have to follow your best logic. For example, the nature of a product can tell you something about its likely buyers. Industrial equipment would probably be bought by people with technical backgrounds. Expensive French perfumes and cosmetics would probably be bought by people in high-income brackets. Burial insurance would appeal to older members of the lower economic strata. If you are purchasing a mailing list, you usually receive basic demographics such as age, sex, race, education, income, and marital status of those on the list. Sometimes you know more—interests, spending range, consumption patterns, and such.

Determining the Central Appeal

With your product or service and your prospects in mind, you are ready to create the sales message. This involves selecting and presenting your persuasive appeals, whether emotional, logical, character based, or a combination. But for most sales messages, one appeal should stand out as the main one—mentioned in the beginning, recalled in the middle, and reiterated at the end. While other benefits can be brought in as appropriate, the message should emphasize your central, best appeal.

Emotional appeals—those based on our senses and emotions—can be found in almost any sales message, but they predominate in messages for goods and services that do not perform any discernable rational function. Illustrating emotional appeal is the following example from a message that attempts to sell perfume by linking the romance of faraway places with the product's exotic scent:

> Linger in castle corridors on court nights in London. Dance on a Budapest balcony high above the blue Danube. Seek romance and youth and laughter in charming capitals on five continents. And there you'll find the beguiling perfume that is fragrance Jamais.

Logical appeals are more rational. These include strategies based on saving money, making money, doing a job better, and getting better use from a product. Illustrating a rational appeal (saving money) are these words from a message selling magazine subscriptions:

> I am going to slash the regular rate of $36 a year down to only $28, saving you a full 22 percent. That means you get 12 information-filled new issues of Science Digest for only $2.33 a copy. You save even more by subscribing for 2 or 3 years.

Appeals based on character persuade by implying such arguments as "I use this product, so you should, too" or "I am an authority, so you should do what I recommend." Ads that employ sports figures, film stars, or experts to sell their products are relying heavily on character-based appeals. Companies themselves can often take on an appealing "character" in their sales campaigns. Note how the following excerpt

- Begin work on a sales message by studying the product or service to be sold.

- Also, study your readers.

- Research can help you learn about prospective customers. If research is not possible, use your best logic.

- Next, decide on what appeals and strategies to use, and pick a central selling point.

- Appeals may be emotional (to the feelings),

- or they may be rational (to the reason),

- or they may be based on the projected character of the seller.

from a sales letter for *Consumer Reports* magazine uses the company's identity to persuade:

> *Consumer Reports* is on your side. We're a nonprofit consumer protection organization with no commercial interests whatsoever. To put it bluntly, we don't sell out to big companies and private interest groups—we're accountable to no one except to consumers. And when you're not beholden to advertisers (like other so-called consumer protection publications), you can tell it like it is.

People may also buy a certain product because they want to identify with, and be identified with, a certain successful, socially responsible, or "cool" company as projected in the company's sales messages.

In any given case, many appeals are available to you. You should consider those that fit your product or service and those that fit your readers best. Such products as perfume, style merchandise, candy, and fine food lend themselves to emotional appeals. On the other hand, such products as automobile tires, tools, and industrial equipment are best sold through rational appeals. And almost any product could be promoted through a character-based appeal. Often a combination of appeals is your best strategy, but be sure that they work together to create a coherent effect.

• Select the appeals that fit the product and the prospects.

How the buyer will use the product may be a major basis for selecting a sales strategy. Cosmetics might well be sold to the final user through emotional appeals. Selling cosmetics to a retailer (who is primarily interested in reselling them) would require rational appeals. A retailer would be interested in their emotional qualities only to the extent that these make customers buy. A retailer's main questions about the product are: Will it sell? What turnover can I expect? How much money will it make for me?

• The prospects' uses of the product often determine which appeal is best.

Determining the Makeup of the Mailing

When you write a sales message to be sent by mail, a part of your effort is in determining the make-up of the mailing. To know what you want to say in your main message,

• To know what to say in your sales message, you will need to decide what the auxiliary pieces, if any, will be.

you'll need to decide what kinds of additional pieces will be included and how they will support the main piece.

Consider, for example, a recent mailing by Scotts LawnService (see the case illustration on p. 217). The mailing comes in a 9-inch by 12-inch white envelope with the words "LAWN ANALYSIS ENCLOSED FOR (the recipient's address)" on the front, as well as the words "(recipient's city) RESIDENTS: PLEASE TAKE NOTICE." Both the kind of envelope used and the wording on it convey the image of an official, personalized document.

Inside are three 7½-inch by 10½-inch pages. The top page includes the main sales letter on the front, with bold letters in the top right corner advertising a **"FREE No-Obligation Lawn Analysis for (the resident's address)."** On the back are six testimonials under the heading **"Here's what our customers say about Scotts LawnService."**

The second page, on glossy paper, has "before" and "after" pictures of a lawn under the heading **"Now you can enjoy a thick, green, beautiful lawn . . . *and Scotts Lawn-Service will do the work!*"** On the back are various character appeals for the company, under the heading **"Here's why you can expect more from Scotts LawnService than any other lawn service."**

The third page is a replica of a "FREE LAWN ANALYSIS" form "TO BE COMPLETED FOR (the recipient's) FAMILY at (the recipient's address)," with "SAMPLE" stamped (or appearing to be stamped) across the form.

The last piece is a return envelope with a detachable form to fill out and return. Both parts advertise again the "FREE No-obligation Lawn Analysis."

The author of these documents determined that the free lawn analysis for each individual customer address would be the immediate selling point, with the main reader benefit being the beautiful lawn that the analysis would lead to. With these decisions made, the writer could then decide what to place in the foreground of the letter, what to put into the other pieces, and how to coordinate the letter with the other pieces. Even if someone else, such as a graphic artist or desktop publishing expert, will be designing the pieces of your mailing, you need to plan how all parts of the sales package will work together.

As the Scotts letter shows, the letter itself can include creative elements, such as the attention-getter in boldface in the upper right corner, the tagline before the salutation ("You'll be seeing our truck on [your street] a lot this year!"), and special use of typography and indention. Or, to consider another example, one sales letter eliminated the salutation and inside address, using engaging statements in the place of these standard letter components:

IT'S GREAT FOR PENICILLIN.

BUT YOU CAN DO WITHOUT IT

ON YOUR ROOF . . .

We're referring to roof fungus, which, like penicillin, is a moldlike growth. However, the similarity ends there. Unlike penicillin, roof fungus serves . . .

Email sales messages can use all the publishing features available on the computer. The message can be presented creatively with color, font variations, box arrangements, artwork, and such. It may include links to support material as well as to the ordering procedure. And it may have attachments. Just as with a direct-mail package, the email sales package uses many elements to persuade and to make available all the information a reader needs to complete the sale.

Gaining Attention

The beginnings of all sales messages have one basic requirement. They must gain attention. If they do not, they fail. The reason is apparent. Because sales messages are sent without invitation, they are not likely to be received favorably. In fact, they even may be unwanted. Unless they gain attention early, the messages will not be read.

- Direct mail can contain many kinds of creative components.

- Sales messages may use innovative salutations, headlines, and other attention-gaining devices.

- Email sales messages can use all the creativity that computers allow.

- The basic requirement of the beginning is to gain attention.

With direct mail, the envelope containing the message is the first attention getter. All too often the reader recognizes the mailing as an uninvited sales message and promptly discards it. For this reason many direct-mail writers place an attention getter on the envelope. It may be the offer of a gift ("Free gift inside"). It may present a brief sales message ("12 months of *Time* at 60% off the newsstand price"). It may present a picture and a message (a picture of a cruise ship and "Tahiti and more at 2-for-1 prices"). An official-appearing envelope sometimes is used. So are brief and simple messages such as "Personal," "Sensitive material enclosed," and "May we have the courtesy of a reply." The possibilities are limited only by the imagination.

- With direct mail, attention begins with the envelope.

With email, of course, there is no envelope. The attention begins with the from, to, and subject fields. As one authority explains, you should clearly tell who you are and identify your company.[5] Many "spam" messages disguise these identities, and you hope your readers will not regard your message as spam. You should also address the reader by name. Though some readers will delete the message even with this clear identification, the honesty conveyed will induce some to read on.

- With email, it begins with the from, to, and subject fields. Be honest.

The subject line in email messages is the main place for getting attention. Here honesty and simplicity should be your guide. The subject line should tell clearly what your message is about, and it should be short. It should avoid sensationalism such as "How to earn $60,000 the first month." In addition, avoiding sensationalism involves limiting the use of solid caps, exclamation points, dollar signs, "free" offers, and such. In fact, you risk having spam filters block your message or put it into the junk folder of your readers' computers if you use "free" or other words and phrases commonly used by spam writers. An email with the subject line "Making your restaurant more profitable" that is sent to a researched list of restaurant managers and owners is much more likely to be opened and read than a message with the subject line "You have to read this!" that is sent to thousands of readers indiscriminately.

- Make the subject line clear and short. Avoid sensationalism.

Holding Attention in the Opening

The first words of your message also have a major need to gain attention. The reader must be moved to read on. What you do here is a part of your creative effort. But the method you use should assist in presenting the sales message. That is, it should help set up your strategy. It should not just gain attention for attention's sake. Attention is easy to gain if nothing else is needed. In a sales letter, a small explosion set off when the reader opens the envelope would gain attention. So would an electric shock or a miniature stink bomb. But these methods would not be likely to assist in selling your product or service.

- The opening sentence should hold attention and set up the strategy.

One of the most effective attention-gaining techniques is a statement or question that introduces a need that the product will satisfy. For example, a rational-appeal message to a retailer would clearly tap his or her strong needs with these opening words:

- It can use logic,

> Here is a proven best-seller—and with a 12 percent greater profit.

Another rational-appeal attention getter is this beginning of an email sales message from eFax.com:

> Never type a fax again!

This paragraph of a message selling a fishing vacation at a lake resort illustrates a need-fulfilling beginning of an emotional-appeal approach:

- emotion,

> Your line hums as it whirs through the air. Your line splashes and dances across the smooth surface of the clear water as you reel. From the depth you see the silver streak of a striking bass. You feel a sharp tug. The battle is on!

---

[5] Jim Sterne and Anthony Priore, *Email Marketing: Using Email to Reach Your Target Audience and Build Customer Relationships* (New York: John Wiley & Sons, 2000) 143.

As you can see, the paragraph casts an emotional spell, which is what emotional selling should do. A different tack is illustrated by the following example. It attracts interest by telling a story and using character-based appeal:

> It was in 1984 that three enterprising women met to do something about the lack of accessible health information for women.

As mentioned previously, gimmicks are sometimes used to gain attention in direct-mail sales. But a gimmick is effective only if it supports the theme of the message. One company made effective use of a penny affixed to the top of a letter with these words:

> Most pennies won't buy much today, but this penny can save you untold worry and money—and bring you new peace of mind.

A paper manufacturer fastened small samples of sandpaper, corrugated aluminum, and smooth glossy paper to the top of a letter that began with these words:

> You've seen the ads—
> You've heard the talk—
> Now feel for yourself what we mean by level-smooth.

Thus far, the attention-gaining techniques illustrated have been short. But longer ones have been used—and used effectively. In fact, a technique currently popular in direct-mail selling is to place a digest of the sales message at the beginning—usually before the salutation. The strategy is to quickly communicate the full impact of the sales message before the reader loses interest. If any of the points presented arouse interest, the reader is likely to continue reading.

Illustrating this technique is the beginning of a letter selling subscriptions to *Change*. These lines appeared before the salutation, which was followed by four pages of text.

> A quick way to determine whether you should read this letter:
>
> If you are involved in or influenced by higher education—and you simply don't have the time to read copiously in order to "keep up"—this letter is important. Because it offers you a money-shortcut (plus a *free gift* and a money-back guarantee).
>
> As a subscriber to *CHANGE,* the leading magazine of higher learning, you'll have facts and feelings at your fingertips—to help *you* form opinions on today's topics: tenure, professors' unions, open admissions, the outlook for new PhDs . . . On just about any subject that concerns academe and you.
>
> *CHANGE* has the largest readership of any journal among academic people. To find out why 100,000 people now read *CHANGE* every month, take three minutes to read the following letter.

Building a Persuasive Case

With the reader's attention gained, you proceed with the sales strategy that you have developed. In general, you establish a need. Then you present your product or service as fulfilling that need.

The plan of your sales message will vary with your imagination. But it is likely to follow certain general patterns determined by your choice of appeals. If your main appeal is emotional, for example, your opening has probably established an emotional atmosphere that you will continue to develop. Thus, you will sell your product based on its effects on your reader's senses. You will describe the appearance, texture, aroma, and taste of your product so vividly that your reader will mentally see it, feel it—and want it. In general, you will seek to create an emotional need for your product.

If you select a rational appeal as your central theme, your sales description is likely to be based on factual material. You should describe your product based on what it can do for your reader rather than how it appeals to the senses. You should write matter-of-factly about such qualities as durability, savings, profits, and ease of operation.

When using character-based appeals, you will emphasize comments from a well-known, carefully selected spokesperson. Or, if the character being promoted is that of

A Sales Letter Using All Three Appeals (Logical, Emotional, and Character Based). This letter for a lawn care service comes with several other pieces—including "before" and "after" pictures, customer testimonials, and a sample "free lawn analysis" form with the customer's name and address printed on it.

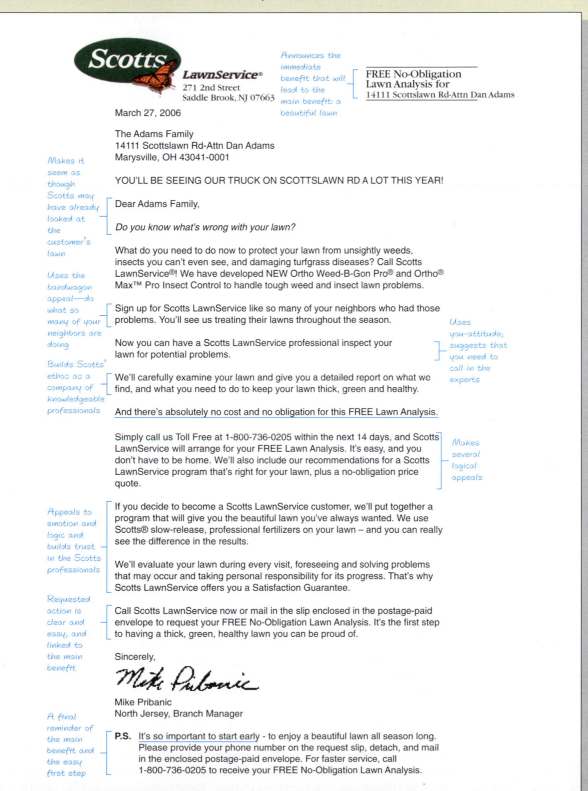

Scotts
LawnService®
271 2nd Street
Saddle Brook, NJ 07663

Announces the immediate benefit that will lead to the main benefit: a beautiful lawn

FREE No-Obligation
Lawn Analysis for
14111 Scottslawn Rd-Attn Dan Adams

March 27, 2006

The Adams Family
14111 Scottslawn Rd-Attn Dan Adams
Marysville, OH 43041-0001

YOU'LL BE SEEING OUR TRUCK ON SCOTTSLAWN RD A LOT THIS YEAR!

Makes it seem as though Scotts may have already looked at the customer's lawn

Dear Adams Family,

Do you know what's wrong with your lawn?

What do you need to do now to protect your lawn from unsightly weeds, insects you can't even see, and damaging turfgrass diseases? Call Scotts LawnService®! We have developed NEW Ortho Weed-B-Gon Pro® and Ortho® Max™ Pro Insect Control to handle tough weed and insect lawn problems.

Uses the bandwagon appeal—do what so many of your neighbors are doing

Sign up for Scotts LawnService like so many of your neighbors who had those problems. You'll see us treating their lawns throughout the season.

Now you can have a Scotts LawnService professional inspect your lawn for potential problems.

Uses you-attitude; suggests that you need to call in the experts

Builds Scotts' ethos as a company of knowledgeable professionals

We'll carefully examine your lawn and give you a detailed report on what we find, and what you need to do to keep your lawn thick, green and healthy.

And there's absolutely no cost and no obligation for this FREE Lawn Analysis.

Simply call us Toll Free at 1-800-736-0205 within the next 14 days, and Scotts LawnService will arrange for your FREE Lawn Analysis. It's easy, and you don't have to be home. We'll also include our recommendations for a Scotts LawnService program that's right for your lawn, plus a no-obligation price quote.

Makes several logical appeals

Appeals to emotion and logic and builds trust in the Scotts professionals

If you decide to become a Scotts LawnService customer, we'll put together a program that will give you the beautiful lawn you've always wanted. We use Scotts® slow-release, professional fertilizers on your lawn – and you can really see the difference in the results.

We'll evaluate your lawn during every visit, foreseeing and solving problems that may occur and taking personal responsibility for its progress. That's why Scotts LawnService offers you a Satisfaction Guarantee.

Requested action is clear and easy, and linked to the main benefit

Call Scotts LawnService now or mail in the slip enclosed in the postage-paid envelope to request your FREE No-Obligation Lawn Analysis. It's the first step to having a thick, green, healthy lawn you can be proud of.

Sincerely,

Mike Pribanic
North Jersey, Branch Manager

A final reminder of the main benefit and the easy first step

P.S. It's so important to start early - to enjoy a beautiful lawn all season long. Please provide your phone number on the request slip, detach, and mail in the enclosed postage-paid envelope. For faster service, call 1-800-736-0205 to receive your FREE No-Obligation Lawn Analysis.

the company itself, you will provide evidence that your company is expert and dependable, understands customers like "you," and stands behind its service or product.

The writing that carries your sales message can be quite different from your normal business writing. Sales writing usually is highly conversational, fast moving, and aggressive. It even uses techniques that are incorrect or inappropriate in other forms of business writing: sentence fragments, one-sentence paragraphs, folksy language, and such. As the case illustrations show, it also uses mechanical emphasis devices (underscore, capitalization, boldface, italics, exclamation marks, color) to a high degree. It can use all kinds of graphics and graphic devices as well as a variety of type sizes and fonts. And its paragraphing often appears choppy. Any sales message is competing with many other messages for the intended reader's attention. In this environment of information overload, punchy writing and visual effects that enable quick processing of the message's main points have become the norm in professional sales writing.

Stressing the You-Viewpoint

In no area of business communication is the use of the you-viewpoint more important than in sales writing. A successful sales message bases its sales points on reader interest. You should liberally use and imply the pronoun *you* throughout the sales message as you present your well-chosen reader benefits.

The techniques of you-viewpoint writing in sales messages are best described through illustration. For example, assume you are writing a sales message to a retailer. One point you want to make is that the manufacturer will help sell the product with an advertising campaign. You could write this information in a matter-of-fact way: "HomeHealth products will be advertised in *Self* magazine for the next three issues." Or you could write it based on what the advertising means to the reader: "Your customers will read about HomeHealth products in the next three issues of *Self* magazine." Viewing things from the reader's perspective will strengthen your persuasiveness. The following examples further illustrate the value of presenting facts as reader benefits:

Facts	You-Viewpoint Statements
We make Aristocrat hosiery in three colors.	You may choose from three lovely shades.
The Regal weighs only a few ounces.	You'll like Regal's featherlight touch.
Lime-Fizz is a lime flavored carbonated beverage.	You'll enjoy the refreshing citrus taste of Lime-Fizz.
Baker's Dozen is packaged in a rectangular box with a bright bull's-eye design.	Baker's Dozen's new rectangular package fits compactly on your shelf, and its bright bull's-eye design is sure to catch the eyes of your customers.

You may also want to make use of scenario painting, putting the reader in a simulated context that brings out the product's appeal. The J. Peterman clothing company is famous for this technique, exemplified in the following excerpt from an advertisement for a men's silk sweater:

> Your P-38 has lost a wing in a dogfight somewhere over France.
>   You eject seconds before it turns into a fireball.
>   Newton was right, those trees down there are getting close fast.
>   Hard pull on the ripcord, a loud "whump," a bone-jarring shock . . . you look up and hallelujah, there it is:
>   The silk.
>   Can you think of a single good reason why a man shouldn't have a sweater made of this same terrific stuff?

Choosing Words Carefully

In persuasive messages, your attention to word choice is extremely important, for it can influence whether the reader acts on your request. Try putting yourself in your reader's place as you select words for your message. Some words, while closely related in meaning, have clearly different emotional effects. For example, the word *selection* implies a

An Email Sales Message (Using Rational Appeal). Note now complete coverage is made easier by using short paragraphs, bold text, and underlining.

From: NextStudent <ven@mailsubs.com>
To: marie.flatley@sdsu.edu
Subject: Urgent news regarding your student loans

Subject line identifies the nature of the message while luring the reader to open it immediately

Can't see any images? Click to view!

Colorful headline draws reader's attention

URGENT NEWS REGARDING YOUR STUDENT LOANS

Quick Links:
Student Loan
Consolidation
Application
Rates and Terms
Private Student Loans
www.nextstudent.com

Places important links at the top of email message for easy access

Dear Marie Flatley,

Opens with attention getter that offers reader benefit

Currently, you may be eligible to consolidate your student loans at a fixed rate as low as 2.75% through NextStudent. Consolidation prevents payment increases.

Background details help build interest

However, the U.S. Department of Education has just announced two HUGE changes to the federal student loan consolidation and reconsolidation programs. Starting April 1, the government will require most borrowers to consolidate through their current lender only – even if they can get a better deal elsewhere. In addition, most borrowers will be permitted to consolidate one time only (right now you can consolidate whenever you find a better deal).

If you have already consolidated, you may save thousands of dollars over the life of your loans by reconsolidating with NextStudent before March 29, 2006 and taking advantage of special borrower-incentive interest rate reductions to reduce your rate to as low as 2.75%! By taking action now, the average student can save up to 60% on their payments! Even if you have already consolidated, you can slash your interest rate if you act immediately!

Use of you -viewpoint while providing details creates desire. Bolding emphasizes key ideas

If you have not yet consolidated your student loans, it is essential that you do so immediately! Interest rates on federal student loans **will be rising July 1, 2006**. Consolidation is a *free* federal program that can **save you thousands** by locking in the current low rates for the life of your loan.

Link here makes action easy to take

APPLY ONLINE – It's FAST, easy and FREE.

There will be a mad dash to consolidate and reconsolidate – last year at this time, procrastinators missed out on the lowest rates ever! Reconsolidation or consolidation can be done online in a matter of minutes. These programs are FREE - they cost nothing and can save you thousands of dollars!

(concluded)

NextStudent's *online application is quick, easy, and secure. If you have any questions about consolidation or reconsolidation, give us a call; our Education Finance Advisors are here to help you.*

Again, we cannot stress enough the urgency of this news to everyone who holds student loans. *Consolidating or reconsolidating before it is too late will mean thousands of extra dollars in your pocket over the term of your student loans!* Call NextStudent immediately at 800-778-0882 or apply online at www.NextStudent.com

Urges immediate action through choice of channel—online or toll-free call

Sincerely,

NextStudent Inc.
www.NextStudent.com
(800) 778-0882
11225 N. 28th Drive, Suite A-202
Phoenix, AZ 85029
Hours of Operation
Monday – Friday 8 a.m. to 11 p.m. EST

Provides physical address and phone as required by the can spam legislation

To unsubscribe, please click here.

Provides reader with an opt-out choice

P.S. You must act immediately to take advantage of these programs that cost nothing. Apply online now – less than 60 seconds can save you thousands of dollars!

Gives an added punch, equating seconds with dollars

Copyright © 2006 NextStudent Inc., All rights reserved.

All trademarks and registered trademarks are property of their respective owners.

You have received this offer because you have elected to receive these notices from office.com. To edit your subscriptions, please click here.

Use of a seal often gives reader the assurance needed to respond.

The Importance of Vividness in Sales Messages

In reviewing the research on visual persuasion, Charles A. Hill identifies *vividness* as a key element in persuasive messages, whether verbal or visual.*

Research has shown that readers are more persuaded by one vivid picture or story than they are by statistics. For example, the picture of a hungry child or a detailed story about the child can persuade more successfully than the statistic that thousands of children are hungry. This finding seems illogical because many cases should logically outweigh one case. But as Hill points out, reactions to vividness are not logic based. They tend to elicit immediate, emotional responses, not reasoned ones, and emotion often persuades more powerfully than reason.

Hill offers the following hierarchy of vividness, with the most vivid information at the top and the least at the bottom:

Actual experience

Moving images with sound

Static photograph

Realistic painting

Line drawing

Narrative, descriptive account

Abstract, impersonal analysis

Statistics

Look for ways to include vivid, attractive detail—whether in the form of words or graphics—at key points in your persuasive message.

*Charles A. Hill, "The Psychology of Rhetorical Images," *Defining Visual Rhetorics*, ed. Charles A. Hill and Marguerite Helmers (Mahwah, NJ: Lawrence Erlbaum, 2004) 25–40.

choice while the word *preference* implies a first choice. Here are some examples where a single adjective changes the effect of a sentence:

> You'll enjoy our hot salsa.
> You'll enjoy our fiery salsa.
> You'll enjoy our spicy salsa.

Framing your requests in the positive is also a proven persuasive technique. Readers will clearly opt for solutions to problems that avoid negatives. Here are some examples:

Original Wording	Positive Wording
Tastee ice cream has nine grams of fat per serving.	Tastee ice cream is 95 percent fat free.
Our new laser paper keeps the wasted paper from smudged copies to less than 2 percent.	Our new laser paper provides smudge-free copies more than 98 percent of the time.

Including All Necessary Information

Of course, the information you present and how you present it are matters for your best judgment. But you must make sure that you present enough information to complete the sale. You should leave none of your readers' questions unanswered. Nor should you fail to overcome any likely objections. You must work to include all such basic information in your message, and you should make it clear and convincing.

As we say, you will also need to decide how to apportion your information across all the pieces in your mailing or the layout of a screen. With direct mail, you should use your letter to do most of the persuading, with any enclosures, attachments, or links

- Give enough information to sell. Answer all questions; overcome all objections.

- Make the letter carry the main sales message. Enclosures should serve as supplements.

As in this Habitat for Humanity example, most sales mailings consist of a letter and a coordinated group of support pieces.

providing supplementary information. These supplements might provide in-depth descriptions, price lists, diagrams, and pictures—in short, all the helpful information that does not fit easily into the letter. You may want to direct your readers' attention to these other pieces with such comments as "you'll find comments from your satisfied neighbors in the enclosed brochure," "as shown on page 7 of the enclosed catalog," or "you'll see testimonials of satisfied customers in the blue shaded boxes."

- In email sales messages, the supporting information can be accessed through links or attachments.

When you send the sales message by email, the supporting information must be worked into the message or presented in links or attachments that you invite the reader to view. You must take care to avoid the appearance of too much length or clutter when working this material into the message. By skillfully cutting up the message visually (see Next Student case illustration, pp. 219–220), you can reduce the effect of excessive length. And by making the boxes attractive with imaginative use of color, font selection, and formatting, you can enhance the effectiveness of the presentation. In either mail or email selling, your goal is to give the readers all they need to know to complete a sale, while allowing them the option of reading only as much as they desire.

Driving for the Sale

- End with a drive for the sale.

After you have caught your reader's interest in your product or service, the next logical step is to drive for the sale. After all, this is what you have been working for all along. It is a natural conclusion to the sales effort you have made.

- In strong selling efforts, a command is effective. For milder efforts, a request is appropriate. Take the reader through the motions.

How to word your drive for the sale depends on your strategy. If your selling effort is strong, your drive for action also may be strong. It may even be worded as a command. ("Order your copy today—while it's on your mind.") If you use a milder selling effort, you could use a direct question ("May we send you your copy today?"). In any event, the drive for action should be specific and clear. In no way should it resemble a hint. For best effect, it should take the reader through the motions of whatever he or she must do. Here are some examples:

> "Just check your preferences on the enclosed order form. Then fax it to us today at 888.755.5265!"

> "Mail the enclosed card today—and see how right *Fast Company* is for you!"

Similarly, in email selling you will need to make the action easy. Make it a simple click—a click to an order form, to order instructions, or such. Words such as these do the job well: "Just click on the button below to order your customized iPod case now!" and "You can download our free new catalog of business gifts at <http://thankyoutoo.com>."

Urging the Action

Because readers who have been persuaded sometimes put things off, you should urge immediate action. "Do it now" and "Act today" are versions of this technique, although some people dislike the commanding tone of such words. Even so, this type of action is widely used. A milder and generally more acceptable way of urging action is to tie it in with a practical reason for doing it now. Here are some examples:

> . . . to take advantage of this three-day offer.
>
> . . . so that you can be ready for the Christmas rush.
>
> . . . so that you will be the first in your community.

● Urge action now.

Recalling the Appeal

Yet another effective technique for the close of a sales message is to use a few words that recall the main appeal. Associating the action with the benefits that the reader will gain by taking it adds strength to your sales effort. Illustrating this technique is a message selling Maxell DVDs to retailers. After building its sales effort, the message asks for action and then follows the action request with these words:

> . . . and start taking your profits from the fast-selling Maxell DVDs.

Another illustration is a message selling a fishing resort vacation that follows its action words with a reminder of the joys described earlier.

> It's your reservation for a week of battle with the fightingest bass in the Southland.

● Recalling the appeal in the final words is good technique.

Adding a Postscript

Unlike other business messages where a postscript (P.S.) appears to be an afterthought, a sales message can use a postscript as a part of its design. It can be used effectively in a number of ways: to urge the reader to act, to emphasize the major appeal, to invite attention to other enclosures, to suggest that the reader pass along the sales message, and so on. Postscripts effectively used by professionals include the following:

> PS: Don't forget! If ever you think that *Action* is not for you, we'll give you every cent of your money back. We are that confident that *Action* will become one of your favorite magazines.
>
> PS: Hurry! Save while this special money-saving offer lasts.
>
> PS: Our little magazine makes a distinctive and appreciated gift. Know someone who's having a birthday soon?
>
> PS: Click now to order and automatically enter our contest for a Motorola Q smartphone.

● Postscripts are acceptable and effective.

Offering Name Removal to Email Readers

Until January 1, 2004, it was a courtesy to offer the recipients of commercial email the option of receiving no further emails from the sender. Now, thanks to the so-called CAN-SPAM Act, it is a legal requirement as well.[6] Consider placing this invitation in a prominent place—perhaps even before the message text. According to one authority, "This is the equivalent of asking, 'Is it OK if we come in?'"[7]

● Offer to remove readers from your email list—it's the law.

Reviewing the General Sales Plan

From the preceding discussion, a general plan for the sales message emerges. This plan is similar to the classic AIDA (attention, interest, desire, action) model developed almost a century ago. It should be noted, however, that in actual practice, sales

● Sales messages vary in practice, but this plan is used most often.

---

[6] For further information, visit the Federal Trade Commission's website at <http://www.ftc.gov/bcp/conline/pubs/buspubs/canspam.htm>.

[7] Nick Usbornn, as quoted in Sterne and Priore, *Email Marketing*, 151.

messages vary widely. Creativity and imagination are continually leading to innovative techniques. Even so, the general prevailing plan is the following:

- Gain favorable attention.
- Create desire by presenting the appeal, emphasizing supporting facts, and emphasizing reader viewpoint.
- Include all necessary information—using a coordinated sales package (brochures, leaflets, links, appended parts, and such).
- Drive for the sale by urging action now and recalling the main appeal.
- Possibly add a postscript.
- In email writing, offer to remove name from your email list to comply with new legal requirements.

Evaluating Contrasting Examples

The following two email sales messages show bad and good efforts to sell Killshaw's restaurant consulting services. Clearly, the weak message is the work of an amateur and the better one was written by a professional.

Weakness in an Illogical Plan. Although the subject line of the amateur's sales message presents the main appeal, it is dull and general. The opening statement is little more than an announcement of what the consultant does. Then, as a continuation of the opening, it offers the services to the reader. Such openings do little to gain attention or build desire. Next comes a routine, I-viewpoint review of the consultant's services. The explanation of the specific services offered is little better. Although the message tells what the consultant can do, it is dull. The drive for action is more a hint than a request. The closing words do suggest a benefit for the reader, but the effort is too little too late.

The weak email is amateurish. It does little more than announce that services are available.

Subject: A plan to increase profits

Ms. Collins,

You have probably heard in the trade about the services I provide to restaurant management. I am now pleased to be able to offer these services to you.

From 28 years of experience, I have learned the details of restaurant management. I know what food costs should be. I know how to find other cost problems, be they the buying end or the selling end. I know how to design menu offerings for the most profitability. I have studied kitchen operations and organization. And I know how the service must be conducted for best results.

From all this knowledge, I have perfected a simple system for analyzing a restaurant and finding its weaknesses. This I do primarily from guest checks, invoices, and a few other records. As explained on my website (<http://www.restaurantimp.com>), my system finds the trouble spots. It shows exactly where to correct all problems.

I can provide you with the benefits of my system for only $1,500—$700 now and $800 when you receive my final report on your operations. If you will fill out and return by email the information requested below, I will show you how to make more money.

Larry Kopel, Consultant

Skillful Presentation of a Rational Appeal. The better message follows the conventional sales pattern described in the preceding pages. Its main appeal is rational, which is justified in this case. Its subject line gains interest with a claim of the main message presented in you-viewpoint language. The beginning sentence continues this appeal with an attention-holding testimonial. The following sentences explain the service quickly—and interestingly. Then, in good you-viewpoint writing, the reader learns what he or she will get from the service. This part is loaded with reader benefits (profits, efficiency, cost cutting). Next, after the selling has been done, the message drives for action. The last sentence ties in the action with its main benefit—making money. A post note about how to "unsubscribe" meets the legal requirements and uses a courteous tone.

Subject: A proven plan that guarantees you more profits

Ms. Collins,

"Killshaw is adding $15,000 a year to my restaurant's profits!"

With these words, Bill Summers, owner of Boston's famed Pirate's Cove, joined the hundreds of restaurant owners who will point to proof in dollars in assuring you that I have a plan that can add to your profits.

My time-proven plan to help you add to your profits is a product of 28 years of intensive research, study, and consulting work with restaurants all over the nation. I found that where food costs exceed 40 percent, staggering amounts slip through restaurant managers' fingers. Then I tracked down the causes of these losses. I can find these trouble spots in your business—and I'll prove this to you in extra income dollars!

To make these extra profits, all you do is send me, for a 30-day period, your guest checks, bills, and a few other items. After analyzing these items using my proven method, I will write you an eye-opening report that will tell you how much money your restaurant should make and how to make it.

From the report, you will learn in detail just what items are causing your higher food costs. And you will learn how to correct them. Even your menu will receive thorough treatment. You will know what "best-sellers" are paying their way—what "poor movers" are eating into your profits. All in all, you'll get practical suggestions that will show you how to cut costs, build volume, and pocket a net 10 to 20 percent of sales.

For a more detailed explanation of this service, review the information presented at my website (<http://www.restaurantimp.com/>). Then let me prove to you, as I have to so many others, that I can add money to your income this year. This added profit can be yours for the modest investment of $1,500 ($700 now and the other $800 when our profit plan report is submitted). Just email the information requested below and I'll do the rest.

That extra $25,000 or more will make you glad you did!

Larry Kopel, Consultant

You were sent this message because of your status in the restaurant field. If you wish to be removed from our list, please send an email with the word "unsubscribe" in the subject line.

Following the conventional plan, the better email uses good strategy and technique.

SUMMARY BY LEARNING OBJECTIVES

1 Describe important strategies for writing any persuasive message.

1. Certain advice applies to all persuasive messages:
   - Know your readers—well.
   - Choose and develop targeted reader benefits.
     — Both tangible and intangible benefits can be persuasive.
     — Prefer intrinsic to extrinsic benefits.
     — Express product features as reader benefits.
     — Use scenario painting to help your readers experience the product's appeal.
   - Make good use of three kinds of appeals.
     — Emotional appeals play on our senses (taste, hearing, and so on) and our feelings (love, anger, and the like).
     — Rational appeals appeal to logic (with a focus on thrift, durability, efficiency, and such).
     — Character-based appeals use an appealing spokesperson or an attractive image of the company to help sell the product.
   - Make it easy for your readers to comply.

2 Write skillful persuasive requests that begin indirectly, use convincing reasoning, and close with goodwill and action.

2. Requests that are likely to be resisted require an indirect, persuasive approach.
   - Such an approach involves developing a strategy—a plan for persuading.
   - Your opening words should set up this strategy and gain attention.
   - Follow with convincing persuasion.

- Then make the request—clearly yet positively.
- The request can end the message, or more persuasion can follow (whichever you think is appropriate).

3. Sales messages are a controversial area of business communication.

3 Discuss ethical concerns regarding sales messages.

- Many sales messages are unwanted.
  — "Junk" mail clutters people's mailboxes.
  — "Spam" clutters their in-boxes.
- Some sales messages use unethical tactics.
  — They may make deceptive claims.
  — They may omit important information.
  — They may rely heavily on visuals that trigger a visceral response.
- Use your conscience and your ability to put yourself in the readers' shoes to create ethical persuasive messages.

4. A sales message requires special planning.

4 Describe the planning steps for direct mail or email sales messages.

- Learn all you can about your service or product and your intended readers.
- Then select an appropriate central appeal and supporting appeals.
- Determine the makeup of the mailing.
  — Decide what you will include in the letter and what you will put in auxiliary pieces.
  — Consider a creative approach to the letter format itself.
  — Email sales messages can also have auxiliary pieces and innovative format.

5. Although innovations are frequently used, the basic sales message generally follows this traditional plan:

5 Compose sales messages that gain attention, persuasively present appeals, and effectively drive for action.

- The opening seeks to gain attention and set up the sales presentation.
- The body makes your persuasive case.
  — It develops the appeals you have chosen.
  — It uses punchy writing and techniques for visual emphasis (typography, white space, color, and other visual elements).
- In emotional selling, the words establish an emotional atmosphere and build an emotional need for the product or service.
- Character-based appeals build trust and invite identification with the company.
- In rational selling, the appeal is to the thinking mind, using facts and logical reasoning.
- Throughout the message, emphasis is on good sales language and the you-viewpoint.
- All the information necessary for a sale (prices, terms, choices, and the like) is included in the message, though references are made to supporting information.
- Next comes a drive for a sale.
  — It may be a strong drive, even a command, if a strong sales effort is used.
  — It may be a direct question if a milder effort is desired.
  — In either case, the action words are specific and clear, frequently urging action *now*.
  — Taking the action may be associated with the benefits to be gained.
  — Postscripts often are included to convey a final sales message.
  — In email messages, opt-out links are often provided as a professional courtesy, and to comply with new laws.

1 Explain why a persuasive request is usually written in the indirect order. Could the direct order ever be used for such messages? Discuss.

2 What is the role of the you-viewpoint in persuasive requests?

3 Compare persuasive requests and sales messages. What traits do they share? How are they different?

4 Consider ads that you have seen on television. Which ones rely heavily on emotional appeals? Which on logical appeals? Which on character-based appeals? Do the chosen appeals seem appropriate given the product, service, or cause that is being promoted?

5 Think of a television, radio, print, email, or Internet sales message or persuasive request that you regard as especially effective. Explain why you think it was well designed.

6 What appeals would be appropriate for the following products when they are being sold to consumers?

  a. Shaving cream.   b. Carpenter's tools.
  c. Fresh vegetables.   d. Software.

  e. Lubricating oil.   f. Women's dresses.
  g. Perfume.   h. Fancy candy.
  i. CD players.   j. Hand soap.

7 When could you justify addressing sales letters to "occupant"? When to each reader by name?

8 Rarely should a sales letter exceed a page in length. Discuss this statement.

9 Should the traditional sales-message organization discussed in the text ever be altered? Discuss.

10 Discuss the relationship between the sales message and its accompanying support information in an example you've seen. What was the purpose of each piece?

11 When do you think a strong drive for action is appropriate in a sales message? When do you think a weak drive is appropriate?

12 Think of a sample persuasive request or sales message that you regard as ethically questionable. Discuss the nature of the ethical problems.

1 Assume that, as a volunteer for a nonprofit organization in your town, you have been asked to write the next fundraising letter for the organization. In what ways might you gather enough information about the intended readers to write a successful message?

2 List the tangible and intangible benefits that you might describe when promoting the following items or services:

  a. Membership in a health club

  b. High-speed Internet service or digital cable service

  c. A certain line of clothing

3 List some extrinsic benefits you might use as an extra push if you were promoting the items in number 2.

4 For each item in number 2, list two likely product features and then turn them into reader benefits.

5 Choose one of the items in number 2 and write a paragraph that uses scenario painting to promote the item.

6 Criticize the persuasive request message below. It was written by the membership chairperson of a chapter of the Service Corps of Retired Executives (SCORE), a service organization consisting of retired executives who donate their managerial talents to small businesses in the area. The recipients of the message are recently retired executives.

> Dear Ms. Petersen:
>
> As membership chair it is my privilege to invite you to join the Bay City chapter of the Service Corps of Retired Executives. We need you, and you need us.
>
> We are a volunteer, not-for-profit organization. We are retired business executives who give free advice and assistance to struggling small businesses. There is a great demand for our services in Bay City, which is why we are conducting this special membership drive. As I said before, we need you. The work is hard and the hours can be long, but it is satisfying.
>
> Please find enclosed a self-addressed envelope and a membership card. Fill out the card and return it to me in the envelope. We meet the first Monday of every month (8:30 at the Chamber of Commerce office). This is the fun part—strictly social. A lot of nice people belong.
>
> I'll see you there Monday!
>
> Sincerely yours,

7 Evaluate the following sales message. It was written to people on a mailing list of fishing enthusiasts. The writer, a professional game fisher, is selling his book by direct mail. The nature of the book is evident from the letter.

Have you ever thought

why the pros catch fish

and you can't?

They have secrets. I am a pro, and I know these secrets. I have written them and published them in my book, *The Bible of Fishing*.

This 240-page book sells for only $29.95, including shipping costs, and it is worth every penny of the price. It tells where to fish in all kinds of weather and how the seasons affect fishing. It tells about which lures to use under every condition. I describe how to improve casting and how to set the hook and reel them in. There is even a chapter on night fishing.

I have personally fished just about every lake and stream in this area for over forty years and I tell the secrets of each. I have one chapter on how to find fish without expensive fish-finding equipment. In the book I also explain how to determine how deep to fish and how water temperature affects where the fish are. I also have a chapter on selecting the contents of your tackle box.

The book also has an extensive appendix. Included in it is a description of all the game fish in the area—with color photographs. Also in the appendix is a glossary that covers the most common lures, rods, reels, and other fishing equipment.

The book lives up to its name. It is a bible for fishing. You must have it! Fill out the enclosed card and send it to me in the enclosed stamped and addressed envelope. Include your check for $29.95 (no cash or credit cards, please). Do it today! Sincerely yours,

8 Criticize each of the following parts of sales messages. The product or service being sold and the part identification are indicated in the headings.

Email Subject Lines

a. Earn BIG profits NOW!!!

b. Reduce expenses with an experienced consultant's help.

c. Free trial offer ends this week!

Openings

Product or Service: A Color Fax Machine

a. Now you can fax in color!

b. Here is a full-color fax that will revolutionize the industry.

c. If you are a manufacturer, ad agency, architect, designer, engineer, or anyone who works with color images, the Statz Color Fax can improve the way you do business.

Product or Service: A Financial Consulting Service

d. Would you hire yourself to manage your portfolio?

e. Are you satisfied with the income your portfolio earned last year?

f. Dimmitt-Hawes Financial Services has helped its clients make money for over a half century.

Parts of Sales Presentations

Product or Service: A Paging Service

a. Span-Comm Messaging is the only paging service that provides service coast to coast.

b. Span-Comm Messaging is the only paging service that gives you the freedom to go coast to coast and still receive text messages.

c. Span-Comm Messaging gives you coast-to-coast service.

Product or Service: A Color Fax Machine

d. The Statz Color Fax is extraordinary. It produces copies that are indistinguishable from the originals.

e. The extraordinary Statz Color Fax produces copies identical to the originals.

f. Every image the Statz Color Fax produces is so extraordinary you may not be able to tell a fax from an original.

Product or Service: Vermont Smoked Hams

g. You won't find a better-tasting ham than the old-fashioned Corncob Smoked Ham we make up here on the farm in Vermont.

h. Our Corncob Smoked Ham is tender and delicious.

i. You'll love this smoky-delicious Corncob Smoked Ham.

Product or Service: A Unique Mattress

j. Control Comfort's unique air support system lets you control the feel and firmness of your bed simply by pushing a button.

k. The button control adjusts the feel and firmness of Control Comfort's air support system.

l. Just by pushing a button you can get your choice of feel and firmness in Control Comfort's air support system.

Action Endings

Product or Service: An Innovative Writing Instrument

a. To receive your personal Airflo pen, you have but to sign the enclosed card and return it to us.

b. You can experience the writing satisfaction of this remarkable writing instrument by just filling out and returning the enclosed card.

c. Don't put it off! Now, while it's on your mind, sign and return the enclosed card.

Product or Service: A News Magazine

    d. To begin receiving your copies of *Today's World*, simply fill out and return the enclosed card.

    e. For your convenience, a subscription card is enclosed. It is your ticket to receiving *Today's World*.

    f. If you agree that *Today's World* is the best of the news magazines, just sign and return the enclosed card.

Postscripts

    a. You can also monogram items you order before November 1.

    b. If you order before November 1, you can monogram your items.

    c. Items ordered before November 1 can be monogrammed.

CRITICAL THINKING PROBLEMS

Persuasive Requests

1 As manager of the Little City Chamber of Commerce, your current assignment is to sell the area's business leaders on the need to construct a Teen Recreation Center. This would be a place where the local teenagers could go on weekends and evenings to have good and safe recreation.

The need for the project should be apparent to all Little City residents. Particularly on weekends, the teenagers "cruise" the city's main thoroughfare for hours. Traffic becomes so snarled that a "stop-and-go" pace is normal for miles. Teenagers yell to one another and even hang out of their cars to visit with those in other cars. Traffic control by the local police has been ineffective. The problem has become so severe that emergency vehicles have had serious problems getting to their destinations.

It has become apparent to you and a few of the city leaders that a solution is needed. A place for the teenagers to meet and socialize appears to be the answer. But the project will need money, and this is where you come in. The Chamber of Commerce will spearhead the effort to raise the funds needed from local businesses. And you have been assigned the task of writing the message that will explain the problem and solution so clearly and persuasively that the money will come in.

You and your small group of business leaders have located a vacant building in the warehouse district, although it is in need of repair. The owner, Jim Falkenstein, has agreed to donate the structure if the funds for renovating it can be raised. Fortunately, the building has an abundance of parking space around it, and its size is adequate. Anna Frisch, a Chamber member and local architect, estimates that $92,000 would do the initial renovation work. The center would need $60,000 annually for operating expenses. Thus your appeal will be for up-front money to get the project going and a pledge for continuing support to keep the project going. Your persuasive request will be in letter form and will include a return card that will suggest initial donations in $100 increments—$100, $200, $300, $400, $500, and "other." The card will also include an annual support pledge section in the same increments.

Now use your best imagination and thinking to construct the persuasive message that will show how this center will benefit Little City's citizenry and businesses—and, of course, bring in the money.

2 Assume that you are the placement and career planning director at your university. One of your many tasks is publishing the annual report of the current year's employment of graduating seniors. The report consists of beginning salary data for each degree with highs, lows, averages, and total number of job offers made through your office.

Unfortunately, over the past few years you have noticed that the number of students reporting their beginning salaries to you is slipping. Most probably, the new graduates are so enthusiastic that they forget to fill out the salary information sheet you include with all applications for graduation packets. You have asked professors to announce the need for returning the forms to you in their classes, and you placed such a request in the student newspaper. But your efforts have been in vain. Presently your records indicate that about

60 percent of the graduating students get initial job contacts through your office, but only 36 percent report their salary data to you.

You believe that the report you publish yearly is useful on a number of counts. First, it can help you assess the marketability of the university's products—its graduates. Second, it can be useful in determining which majors are in most demand. Third, the report can serve as a career-counseling guide for students just beginning their academic programs. But the quality of the report depends on having complete and current data from the students.

Thus, you decide to write a persuasive message to this year's spring graduates requesting that they return the salary information sheet to you. The information will remain anonymous and will be compiled into summary statistics by major field of study. However, you depend on each student to provide accurate and complete information.

What will motivate the students to comply with your request? Pride in their university? Providing help for other students? General cooperativeness? Perhaps there are other possibilities. Select the appeal(s) that is (are) most appropriate, and write the message.

---

3 For this assignment you are human resources manager for Toby's, a manufacturer of medium-priced women's dresses, skirts, and blouses. You are going to have to persuade your labor force to follow safety rules more closely in their production work.

Over the past year, you have noticed that on-the-job injuries have increased—particularly ones involving the stitching assemblers. It appears that the assemblers have had numerous claims for emergency room treatment for injuries to their fingers and hands from the sewing machines. From one view, these injuries are increasing your insurance cost (you pay for the coverage under the garment workers' union contract). From another, lost days by experienced workers mean less productivity for you. Thus, you decide to investigate the situation further.

Your informal investigation reveals the primary source of the problem. The union contract that you negotiate every three years stipulates that management take every precaution for worker safety. Federal law specifies that sewing machine needle guards (to prevent fingers from getting too close to stitching needles) must be installed on all machines.

While the machines are safer this way, the workers cannot produce as many assembled garments. According to the time and motion studies conducted by your industrial engineers, output with the safety guards is restricted by about 15 percent. Thus, the workers remove the guards to make more money based on the piece-rate incentive program you use for compensation. The risk they take for more money is the chance of increased accidents.

You have alerted your supervisors to the problem. But the informal norms of making more money at any risk have overridden the supervisors' formal efforts to keep the safety guards in place. Thus, you have decided to write a message to the entire union labor force at your company persuading them to follow the safety rules. In the long run, it will be better for everyone involved, For you, as a representative of the company, it will follow the union contract, increase safety, and lower insurance costs.

Think through the situation from the reader's view and construct a persuasive reasoning approach to precede your request. Then write the message.

---

4 A year ago you, the training director of Shehan-Welch Industries, got management approval to offer an extensive training program for employees. The program consisted of a variety of course offerings. For those whose basic knowledge of mathematics, English, and science is weak, courses were offered after work hours in the company training center. Qualified public school teachers were brought in to teach these courses. For those desiring college course work, Shehan-Welch offered to pay all costs for one course a semester at the local university. And for those merely wanting to study interesting and exciting topics, Shehan-Welch offered a variety of short courses at its training center. To date these have included ceramics, music appreciation, video editing, and interior decorating. Clearly, the plan had something for everyone.

In spite of your best efforts to promote the program, however, few have taken advantage of it. As you see it, the program has been a miserable failure.

Before writing off the program, you will make one last effort to increase participation. Up to this point, bulletin-board announcements and publicity on the company portal have been the primary means of promoting the courses. Now you will use a persuasive message sent to each worker. Those with computer accessibility will receive your message as email. Those without computer accessibility will get the message by mail. You will write the message.

In your message, you will present your most persuasive arguments for taking advantage of the educational opportunities being offered. You will enclose a brochure describing the courses scheduled for the coming months and giving the details of the program.

If you need additional facts, you may supply them as long as they are consistent with the information given.

---

5 Assume that you are a member of your student government. From time to time the organization has tried to get faculty members to deposit their old examinations in the library so that all students could have access to them before tests. In general, these efforts have met with little success.

Looking over the messages used in the past to persuade faculty members to cooperate, you conclude that they just might be an explanation of the failure. The messages are poorly written—blunt, tactless, and without convincing argument. Obviously they were not written by people who had taken the communication course in which you now are enrolled.

After you point out some of the obvious shortcomings of these messages to other members of the student government, they call your hand. "If you think you can do better," they tell you, "you are welcome to it!" You know that you can, so you accept the challenge. Think out the most effective appeal you can, then write the message that will be sent to all faculty members. You'll send the message by email.

---

6 To hear Dallas Williams say it, Micah Wong is the best consultant there is. She connected with Micah through the local chapter of SCORE, Service Corp of Retired Executives. She credits him with much of the early success of her local importing business specializing in high-quality Indian rugs.

While she got the idea for the business and made the connection for the product with an Indian student while in college majoring in business, much of her time the first two years was consumed with just running the business on a day-to-day basis. However, after reading a story in the local paper about SCORE, she decided to check out their website (<www.score.org>) to see if tax help was available for businesses like hers.

She learned not only that SCORE offers free workshops and personalized counseling locally, but also that it has 389 chapters nationally. Its website alone is a rich resource for small businesses getting off the ground, offering templates for business planning, financial guides, and marketing workbooks. It even has an online quiz to help users determine if they have entrepreneurial potential. In fact, SCORE is funded by a $5 million dollar grant from Congress, but most of the consultants are retired executives who want to share their business know-how. It was at a tax workshop that Dallas Williams learned about Micah.

So far Dallas's business had been profitable even though she was competing in a highly competitive niche market; her competitive advantage was that she had the best product. But with Micah's help, she learned how to manage her inventory better and promote the store more effectively. Both Micah's extensive retail background and his exceptional ability to read financial statements and interpret them in terms of what needed to be done helped increase sales and profits. Dallas's enthusiasm for both Micah and SCORE is so contagious, you are convinced he's the one to contact with your new idea for [you supply an idea for a retail store].

However, Micah's time is in high demand. He already schedules appointments five days a week and is always booked a couple of months ahead. But Dallas suggested you might be able to talk with him by scheduling a lunch meeting. Since you know that he often works out of the downtown office of the Small Business Administration (SBA), you want to persuade him to join you for lunch somewhere near the SBA office. Your message should get him interested in your idea as well as convince him to accept your invitation for lunch sometime next week.

---

7 You have been friends with Ashley Gonzales ever since you worked with her on team projects in college. When she graduated, she moved to Galveston, Texas, where she has held various jobs in the hospitality management field. So she has both had broad experience and begun to establish a good network of people in the industry.

You, on the other hand, have been growing a business you started in San Diego to train workers for various types of hospitality jobs. In fact, in the last five years, you have grown from serving 5 to 12 cities in the Southwest. And you're about ready to break into the Hawaii market, a potentially lucrative one. So you recruited Ashley to open up the market, beginning in Honolulu.

You cannot be happier having both a friend and a talented worker join you. In fact, you have tremendously enjoyed the emails and phone conversations you have been having with her in the preliminary planning of the expansion. As a result of your exchanges, Ashley has a long list of things to do in addition to organizing her own relocation to Hawaii.

However, this morning one more task occurred to you—getting a local phone number for the business in Hawaii. You are a believer in the value of vanity numbers. You would like one that is memorable, easily recognizable, and convenient. It should be personalized for your company. A good number would also assist in marketing, helping to increase sales and expand referrals. Finally, it would be a facilitator in creating an image for your company.

While it's yet another task for Ashley, it's clearly one with a lot of value. So you'll need to persuade her to add it to her list and to make it a high priority.

You might want to remind her that there is a web-based tool she can use to try out various combinations. She will find it on the Verizon website, <http://www22.verizon.com/Vanity/>. Be sure to ask her to run her choices by you before she takes off for Hawaii this Friday; you would like to have the weekend to think them through. Send this message as soon as you can.

---

8 You recently read in *BusinessWeek* of a company that is helping the environment and its employees at the same time. Hyperion Solutions of Sunnyvale, California, is offering its 2,500 employees $5,000 toward the purchase of a "green" car, a car that gets over 45 miles per gallon. What a great idea! You wish your company would do that, too.

So when the announcement went up on your company's portal today calling for suggestions for improving company morale and motivation, you thought this would be a good idea to propose. But because of the expense, you know you need to be persuasive. You believe it is a win-win-win idea: a win for the environment, the employees, and the company. Your message has to show how it is good for company morale and motivation. Use some specific examples to illustrate how it might be used as a reward or an incentive for meeting goals at your company. It could also be used to help reduce turnover as well as building company loyalty. While its cost is high, it can be expensed. And it definitely makes company values clear.

Write a persuasive message to Mike McLaughlin, CEO of your company, suggesting your company adopt this practice.

---

9 You work in a research center on your campus that has partnered with one of your center's sponsors in a clothing drive. It is for the nonprofit Dress for Success program that helps women enter the workplace and stay there. One aspect of its work is providing business clothing for low-income women. These women need the suits when they go to interview for jobs, and they get a week's worth of working clothes when they are hired.

While the organization relies on cash donations, volunteers, and in-kind donations, one of your center's sponsors has asked you to help them collect in-kind donations of business clothing. They need new or nearly new suits (pants or skirts), blouses, shoes, and accessories. All items should be clean and stylish, and they should be turned in on hangers or in boxes. Let them know when and where locally they can drop off their donations. You'll get the most current information from the Dress for Success website at <http://www.dressforsuccess.org>. Additionally, you'll tell them where to find a donation bin on your campus. Volunteers will be on hand at all collection sites this week to accept their donations and give receipts for them.

Your job is to write a persuasive message to send to all campus faculty and staff soliciting their donations of clothing that is appropriate to wear to work. Use your creativity and an appeal that will generate lots of donations. You can give them an alternative of making a cash donation.

---

10 You work in the Investor Relations department of Wise Real Estate Funds, Inc., a real-estate-based mutual fund that many financial advisors and brokerage houses offer for inclusion in investment portfolios.

Periodically, the firm sends informational/promotional mailings to your clients, updating them on facts about the firm (for example, how many clients it has, how its assets are diversified, and what new property it has acquired). An accountant for the firm recently calculated that it spends approximately $6 per investor on client mailings—not counting such confidential mailings as quarterly statements, tax information, and confirmations of transactions. If your firm could send your general communications out by email, it would save a lot of money, which would increase the money available to invest in property and thus, in all likelihood, the return on investment for your clients.

Your boss, the director of investor relations, wants you to draft a letter from the president for the next informational mailing that will persuade clients to sign up for email delivery of these mailings. Sure, the firm could simply announce that information would be sent electronically from now on, but some clients would not approve, and others would not take the trouble to read the material if it meant reading it on-screen. So you will try to persuade people to choose email delivery by going to a special screen on your website or by calling your company. You'll reassure them that all materials including personal information will still be sent by mail.

Everyone involved agrees that getting people to take the trouble to perform this action will require special motivating. So the company has decided to add an extrinsic benefit to the appeal—namely, that for each investor who signs up for email delivery, Wise will have a tree planted in the Gulf Coast areas that have been hit by hurricanes. Your company will partner with American Forests, a conservation group based in Washington, D.C., to plant the trees.

The letter will be on the front page of the next newsletter-type mailing. Give the letter your best shot, and consider using visual elements to enhance its appeal.

---

11 You are the recently hired marketing director for Webwaves Conferencing, a small teleconferencing firm, and you've just gotten great news: You have received a request for a proposal (RFP) from a giant corporation, General Machines, to bid on providing its teleconferencing services. You have worked for this RFP for three months, ever since coming on board with Webwaves. You repeatedly met with, emailed, and called their operations people, describing the advantages of your technology and services. Lo and behold, you succeeded. You have now been asked, along with the biggest players in the web-conferencing industry, to submit a bid for becoming General Machines' web-conferencing provider. This contract, if you win it, will mean over $1.3 million a year for your company for the next three years. Your company has never before had an opportunity to bid on this large a contract.

But reality sinks in: Now you have to prepare the proposal. And you cannot do it alone. You can write the overall narrative for the proposal and be responsible for putting it together, but you need the subject matter experts in the other departments to give you the specific pieces. You are going to need the help of your colleagues in the technology architecture department to match up your products' features with General Machines' needs and technological capabilities. You are going to need the accounting department to price the products for General Machines and work up the proposed budget. You will need the sales and training department to develop a plan for training the General Machines employees on the new services. And the legal department will need to work out the terms and conditions for the proposed contract between Webwaves and General Machines.

In other words, you're going to need a lot of good help, fast, from a lot of busy people. And they are not used to putting their own work aside for a collaborative project like this. Before you came, your company essentially had no marketing department. But as the teleconferencing industry began to take off, the company executives realized that they needed to hire someone to get them a bigger piece of the action. You were this someone. And now, your first major opportunity to achieve the goal you were hired for has arrived. To turn this opportunity into a contract, you're going to have to have the help of people who hardly know you, who do not work under you, who have plenty of other work to do, and who probably have heard very little, if anything, about the work you've been doing. In other words, you're going to have to persuade them to cooperate.

Write an email addressed to all the heads of the relevant departments to share the good news and persuade them to give you what you need. You would like each department head to designate a person who will be in charge of that department's piece and to let you know who this person is. You will also describe the collaborative process for the participants: the department representatives will meet with you early next week for further direction from you; they'll send their pieces to you within two weeks after that; you'll put the proposal together, send it out to all the collaborators for review, and then meet again to discuss any necessary revisions; you'll revise the proposal and send it out for one last review by the parties involved; and then you'll submit the proposal one month from today—the deadline for the RFP. To avoid the appearance of strong-arming people into cooperation, you will not copy the CEO on this email. But you plan to announce your news at next week's executive staff meeting and to invite the CEO to the second meeting of the collaborators.

---

12 You are the assistant manager of Randolph's Grocery, a midsized grocery store in an eclectic urban neighborhood. Your store offers all the important staples, a fairly wide variety of brands, and some specialty items requested by your clientele (such as international packaged foods, vegetarian entrees, organic produce, and fresh sushi). But it doesn't offer as many different kinds of items or brands as the superstore that just opened about a mile from your store. Nor does it offer a pharmacy, flower shop, and bakery, as the superstore does. And, when you factor in the discounts that the superstore offers on its house brand and special purchases, it probably saves customers about 10 percent on what a cart of groceries at your store would cost. There's no doubt about it: The new store is a major threat to the livelihood of your store.

Fortunately, price and size aren't everything when it comes to determining people's shopping preferences. You've spoken to a lot of your regular customers about their views on the new store, and while they agree that the other store has advantages, they praise three things in particular about your store: They can easily find what they want, they like the specialty items and the management's willingness to respond to customers' requests, and—most importantly—they like the way your people treat them.

To try to keep this critical competitive edge, you have decided to write a message to all the employees of the store persuading them to go out of their way to deliver exceptional customer service. You will include this message with their paychecks at the end of the week. And, since you have primary responsibility for personnel issues and have a closer relationship with the employees than the manager does, you will sign it yourself. Let the employees know what the situation is and what you'd like them to do to help keep your store—which has been serving this neighborhood since 1923—in business. Put some careful thought into both your appeals and your requests for action.

---

13 Assume that your business communication class has been asked by a nonprofit organization in your area to help with its mission by writing a fundraising letter. As your instructor directs, either individuals or the class as a whole should pick an existing nonprofit, and the class can write the letter either as an assignment only or for actual use by the organization. Find out all you can about the organization from its website (if there is one), its current materials, interviews, and news articles. And find out about its different supporters and audiences. Who usually gives, and why? Is there a group that doesn't usually give but that might be persuaded to do so in response to the right kind of letter? Work hard to develop a clear sense of your intended audience. Note that all three kinds of appeals—logic, emotion, and character—are likely to be important. And don't forget the power of specific details and stories. Make your letter look official by using the organization's logo, if possible. Your instructor may also ask you to design additional pieces for this mailing.

14 Since your graduation five years ago, you've been working for a medium-sized company in your area [you choose which one]. You love your work and have learned a great deal about your company's business and industry in five years. But somehow, you don't wake up each day looking forward to your day. And when you read an article in *BusinessWeek* about several companies offering a variety of sabbatical plans to their employees, you begin to think that some of the plans would interest you.

In researching it further, you find that companies as varied as Nike, Pfizer, PricewaterhouseCoopers, Cisco, and Patagonia offer sabbaticals. But you also learned that only 2 percent of U.S. companies offer them, most stating they would not be able to replace the worker. But you think there are benefits that might outweigh some of the drawbacks as well as a variety of plans and lengths.

Not only do employees get to relieve pent-up frustrations through travel, sports, or spas, but they usually return refreshed, recharged, and more productive. Some report that they are more creative, their sabbaticals contributing to their growth and new perspectives. Others, like the Cisco employees who set up wireless networks in Southeast Asia to aid the tsunami disaster relief, provided favorable publicity for their companies.

Use these benefits and others to help persuade your employer to provide sabbaticals for employees. You might suggest that the program could start small with five-week paid sabbaticals for employees who have worked at least five years, or perhaps short sabbaticals for those volunteering their skills in nonprofits that the company supports.

Sales

15 You are now the director of the Chamber of Commerce of _____ (a city of your instructor's choice with good convention facilities). Next week the site selection committee of the State Teachers Association will meet to determine where their group will meet in August two years from now. You will try to sell them on meeting in your city.

You would like to make a personal presentation, but your request to do so was denied. "The meeting will be behind closed doors," the committee chair told you. "Just send us the information." So you will have to sell the committee members by mail. Your plan is to gather all the facts that convention planners need (hotel capacities, meeting rooms, rates, transportation service, and such). Then you will mold it into a well-organized sales presentation. You may assume that your message will be accompanied by a collection of brochures that the Chamber typically hands out for publicity purposes, but your message will be the primary selling piece.

As you plan the mailing, keep in mind that the members will do more than just attend meetings. Some will bring spouses and children. Most will want to dine at good restaurants. And some will want to take in the scenic, historic, and recreational places in the area. You will send the message to all members of the organization's site selection committee. You have their names and addresses.

16 As a freelance copywriter you must now write a sales message for the Memory Preservation Studio, specialists in children's photographs. Jan Chambers, the owner, wants to offer new parents a contract whereby the studio agrees to take 8- by 10-inch color pictures of their babies at one month, six months, one year, two years, and three years of age for a total of $120. At each session the parents will have four proofs from which to make their selection. The studio will keep a file and notify parents of the dates when each picture should be taken. The contract requires a payment of $60 up front and $15 at each of the four following sessions.

You may assume that your sales message will be accompanied by a brochure showing in miniature three sequences of photographs of the type that will be taken. There will also be a contract form to be signed and returned, with payment, of course. Or if they prefer, new parents can call the studio and sign the contract and pay at the first session. Your mailing list will be constructed from referrals and birth announcements in the local newspaper. Now think through the situation, select the appeal (or appeals) that will make new parents want to preserve memories of their new babies, and write the message.

17 Play the role of the new advertising manager for Davenport's Department Store. Each year before Mother' Day (or Valentine's Day, if your instructor prefers), your predecessor wrote a sales message to all the store's charge customers. The objective of the message was to get the recipients to do their shopping for this special day at Davenport's. You have decided to carry on this practice.

As you review the messages written in past years, you conclude that they were not very persuasive. They are unimaginative, dull, and flat. You can do better. And you will. So you begin the task by thinking through the situation. What appeals can you use? What can you say that will make the readers want to buy for this holiday—and to buy at Davenport's? Can you suggest certain products? You will try to answer many more such questions before you begin writing. But the end result will be a well-designed and effective sales message.

18 Select from a current magazine or newspaper an advertisement of a product that could be sold profitably by direct mail to business executives. Preferably select an advertisement that presents a thorough description of the product. Then write a sales message for this product. As you write it, be careful not to borrow the wording in the advertisement. In other words, make your message's wording original from start to finish. Also, assume that you are including a descriptive brochure and an order card in the mailing. The messages will be individually processed and made to appear as if written to the one reader. Address the one to be submitted for class purposes to the first executive on your list, Abby Lee Abbot, Director of Human Resources, Global Insurance Company. (You supply the remainder of the address.)

---

19 You are finally making your dream come true. You and two friends have recently opened an arts and crafts store in the small city where you live (you can decide the geographical location). It's in a one-story building with about 3,500 square feet of floor space, divided up into 11 small, attractively decorated rooms that help focus customers' attention on the displayed works.

The works themselves come from artists all across your geographical region, and you sell them on commission. The artists rent display space from you, whether a bookshelf (the smallest unit available), a wall (the largest), or something in between. They then provide you with the works they want to sell, tell you what to charge for each, and get paid 80 percent of the selling price. You make money on the rent and the 20 percent commission. Everybody wins, and the arts and crafts industry in your region gets a boost. In fact, with its unique and eclectic wares, your store is getting quite a bit of notice in the local and regional press, as well as considerable word-of-mouth promotion. Customers can find many kinds of interesting handmade items here that they cannot find in galleries or in other stores.

Though things have started well, you need to keep building the business, and an important part of achieving this goal is to attract more artists and more kinds of art. Over the last several years you have been compiling a list of artists' names and addresses that you've gathered from talking to people at craft fairs and art shows, from taking notes on items sold by other stores, from talking to your current group of artists, and from reading magazines and newsletters in the trade. It's time to write these potential clients to sell them on selling their works through you.

There is just one problem: your store is in a less-than-ideal location. It is far from the downtown area, on the outskirts of town. Worse yet, it is in a building next to the recycling center for your city—which is clean but industrial looking. It is because of the location, in fact, that you were able to rent the space cheaply and get your dream business off the ground. Of course, it is also because your rent is cheap that you're able to keep the rent cheap for the artists.

Using your analytical skills and creativity—as well as any helpful facts about arts and crafts in a particular region—write a message that will appeal to your readers and have them calling you for further details. (At your instructor's discretion, you may substitute another type of goods for the arts and crafts.)

---

20 Write an email message promoting your services as a(n) _____ consultant (you pick the type). Assume that your company—which can consist solely of yourself, if you like—has compiled a distribution list of recipients who would be likely to be interested in your services, and that your message will be targeted toward these people.

In planning your sales message, figure out what it is exactly that you have to offer, who the recipients are (other businesses of some kind? individuals with certain needs and interests?), how your expertise can benefit them, and what you want them to do. Decide, also, how you will handle the cost issue. (Will you include the cost in this message or deliver it another way? If in this message, what will the cost be, and how can you present it as positively as possible?) You can get ideas for your business from websites, textbooks, promotional material you've received, your acquaintances and classmates, or any other useful source.

Remember that an email message can take many forms and contain many kinds of attachments. Use your creativity and logic to design the message that will get a favorable response from your readers. Keep in mind that character appeals, designed to build your readers' confidence in you and your services, will be important in this kind of message. And don't forget to put careful thought into the subject line—the feature of your message that will determine whether or not your recipients will even see your hard work.

---

21 You are chair of the Residence Hall Association's fund-raising committee for your college or university. The association, made up of students who serve as residence hall advisors, needs money to buy special items that the residence hall fees don't cover. For example, you have used such money in the past to buy soccer balls and other light sports equipment, to liven up the drab walls of the dorms' common areas with movie posters, and to deliver little treats to the residents on certain special days. The fund-raising committee's latest idea is to sell final exam care packages, to be delivered to the students during exam week. Your task is to write the students' parents or guardians to persuade them to buy the packages.

The packages will cost $20 each. Parents/guardians can choose from two packages. One has Teddy Grahams, peanut butter crackers, cookies, cereal, a bag of chips, hot chocolate mix, popcorn, trail mix, a granola bar, candy, ramen noodles, goldfish-shaped crackers, and gum. The other (healthier) package has low-fat Ritz Bits, Teddy Grahams, low-fat chocolate chip cookies, a granola bar, low-sugar cereal, lite popcorn, reduced-fat Pringles, a Special K bar, a fruit snack, tea bags, goldfish-shaped crackers, dry roasted peanuts, and sugarless gum.

On the order form, which you will design, people need to indicate which package they want; supply the student's name, dorm name, and room number; and add any brief message that they'd like to have delivered with the package. They need to return the form along with a check, made out to the name of your school, to you at your school mailing address within three weeks. You will include a phone number and email address in case they have any questions. They will have to supply their own return envelopes and stamps.

22 You work as the office manager for one of the most popular places in town, a local veterinary clinic. It is popular because the owners and their pets always get the best treatment from the vet, Dr. Marina Munson, and her staff. Not only are they extremely competent in handling and taking care of a variety of pets, but they also have great empathy with their owners.

One area both owners and the veterinary group agree on is that pets should get the best care whenever possible. However, sometimes the tests and treatments are available but the costs are prohibitive. This not only puts the clinic in a bad light; it also makes the owners feel terribly guilty for not being able to give their pets the best medical care available. One solution to this problem is pet insurance.

Dr. Munson realizes that just like people, pets with good medical care are living longer and more subject to age-related diseases. While most insurance policies do not cover routine office visits for checkups and shots, they do cover over 50 percent of the cost of major procedures. She wants you to create a message she can send to all the cat and dog owners with pets over five years old that the clinic serves. Your message should persuade them to purchase pet insurance for their pets.

While Dr. Munson has no financial interest in any of the pet insurance providers, she believes three have good track records: Veterinary Pet Insurance Superior, PetCare Pals QuickCare Gold, and Petshealth Care Plan's Basic Care. The plans offer a variety of benefits and a range of deductibles, so most owners should be able to find one that would fit their circumstances. All have websites for further explanations and contact information. Your job is to persuade the readers to enroll their pet in a plan of their choice.

23 Your company, Sustained Fitness, Inc., believes its new products are a logical extension of today's fitness videos distributed on DVDs. These three- to five-minute video clips take the form of a personal trainer sent to the customer's cell phone on demand or on your preselected schedule. The complete set of video programs helps users integrate exercise into their daily schedule in small chunks that are customized to the needs of the user.

By integrating exercise into daily activities in short spurts during the day, users will become fit quickly and without big changes in their daily routines and be able to maintain their fitness. Additionally, you have a website where users can keep track of their progress and a virtual fitness center (an online blog) where users can exchange ideas about fitness, food, and other products. The virtual fitness center also offers a free regularly updated newsletter with information for using seasonal produce.

You want to create a message that will draw customers to your website to sign up for a program. Your prices start at $49 for a basic 12-week program and extend to $120 for yearly subscriptions.

24 You were just elected to the position of promotions chair for your campus ambassador program. The campus ambassadors represent the university in a variety of ways, including going to community events, talking to high school students about your school, and giving tours to campus visitors. Your job is to build the school spirit of new incoming students between the time they are accepted and when they arrive on campus.

Since you were not given a big promotional budget line, you have decided to try to do this efficiently using technology and the help of a small focus group. With the group's help you have designed a website with some download "goodies" such as the school logo for their cell phones, a school fight song ringtone, computer wallpaper featuring campus photos, animated screensavers with newcomer info tidbits, and some mobile video-like games relating to campus sports and other activities. You might even want to include downloadable coupons from the stores and businesses in the campus area as well as anything else that might build their goodwill and school spirit.

Write a message to draw these future students to the website and prompt them to download the goodies they want.

chapter nine

Strategies in the Job-Search Process

LEARNING OBJECTIVES

Upon completing this chapter, you will be able to conduct an effective job search; compose effective cover messages, résumés, and follow-ups; and prepare for interviews. To reach these goals, you should be able to

1   Develop and use a network of contacts in your job search.

2   Assemble and evaluate information that will help you select a job.

3   Identify the sources that can lead you to an employer.

4   Compile print and digital résumés that are strong, complete, and organized.

5   Write targeted cover messages that skillfully sell your abilities.

6   Explain how you can participate effectively in an interview.

7   Write application follow-up messages that are appropriate, friendly, and positive.

8   Maintain your job-search activities.

The Job-Search Process

Introduce yourself to this chapter by assuming a role similar to one you are now playing. You are Jason Andrews, a student at Olympia University. In a few months, you will complete your studies for work in marketing.

You believe that it is time to begin seeking the job for which those studies have been preparing you. But how do you do this? Where do you look? What does the search involve? How should you present yourself for the best results? The answers to these and related questions are reviewed in the following pages.

THE JOB SEARCH

Of all the things you do in life, few are more important than getting a job. Whether it involves your first job or one further down your career path, job seeking is directly related to your success and your happiness. It is vital that you conduct the job search properly—that you prepare wisely and carefully and proceed diligently. The following review of job-search strategies should help you succeed.

- For success in job seeking, use the following procedures.

Building a Network of Contacts

You can begin the job search long before you are ready to find employment. In fact, you can do it now by building a network of contacts. More specifically, you can build relationships with people who can help you find work when you need it. Such people include classmates, professors, and businesspeople.

- Begin the job search by building a network of contacts in this way:

At present, your classmates are not likely to be holding positions in which they make or influence hiring decisions. But in the future, when you may want to make a career change, they may hold such positions. Right now, some of them may know people who can help you. The wider your circle of friends and acquaintances, the more likely you are to make employment contacts.

- (1) Broaden your circle of friends.

Knowing your professors and making sure that they know you also can lead to employment contacts. Because professors often consult for business, they may know key executives and be able to help you contact them. Professors sometimes hear of position openings, and in such cases they can refer you to the hiring executives. Demonstrating your work ethic and your ability in the classroom is probably the best way to get your professors to know you and help you. Take advantage of opportunities to meet your professors outside the classroom, especially the professors in your major field.

- (2) Know your professors.

Obviously, meeting key business executives also can lead to employment contacts. You already may know some through family and friends. But broadening your relationships among businesspeople would be helpful. You can do this in various ways, but especially through college professional groups such as the Association for Information Technology Professionals, Delta Sigma Pi, and the Society for the Advancement of Management. By taking an active role in the organizations in your field of study, especially by working on program committees and by becoming an officer, you can get to know the executives who serve as guest speakers. You also might meet businesspeople online. If you share a particular interest on a blog or are known as one who contributes valuable comments to others' blogs, you may get some good job leads there.

- (3) Meet executives.

If your school offers internships, you can make good career contacts through them. But you should find the one that is best for you, that offers you the best training for your career objective. And by all means, do not regard an internship as just a job. Regard it as a foundation step in your career plan. The experience you gain and the

- (4) Make contacts through internships.

contacts you make in an internship might lead to your first career position. In fact, if you perform well, your internship could turn into full-time employment.

In addition to these more common ways of making contacts, you can use some less common ones. By working in community organizations (charities, community improvement groups, fund-raising groups), you can meet community leaders. By attending meetings of professional associations (every field has them), you can meet the leaders in your field. In fact, participation in virtually any activity that provides contacts with business leaders can be mutually beneficial, both now and in the future.

- (5) Work with community organizations.

Identifying Appropriate Jobs

To find the right job, you need to investigate both internal and external factors. The best fit occurs when you have carefully looked at yourself: your education, personal qualities, experience, and any special qualifications. However, to be realistic, these internal qualities need to be analyzed in light of the external factors. Some of these factors may include the current and projected job market, economic needs, location preferences, and family needs.

- Look at both your internal and external factors.

Analyzing Yourself. When you are ready to search for a job, you should begin the effort by analyzing yourself. In a sense, you should look at yourself much as you would look at a product or service that is for sale. After all, when you seek employment, you are really selling your ability to work—to do things for an employer. A job is more than something that brings you money. It is something that gives equal benefits to both parties—you and your employer. Thus, you should think about the qualities you have that enable you to be an accountable and productive worker that an employer needs. This self-analysis should cover the following categories.

- Begin with a self-analysis covering these background areas:

Education. The analysis might well begin with education. Perhaps you have already selected your career area such as accounting, economics, finance, information systems, international business, management, or marketing. If you have, your task is simplified,

- (1) Education. For specialized curricula, the career path is clear.

STEIN

THE CHRONICLE OF HIGHER EDUCATION

"Do you have any other references besides these people in your chat room?"

SOURCE: © 2000 by Eli Stein. Reprinted with permission.

for your specialized curriculum has prepared you for your goal. Even so, you may be able to note special points—for example, electives that have given you special skills or that show something special about you (such as psychology courses that have improved your human-relations skills, communication courses that have improved your writing and speaking skills, or foreign language courses that have prepared you for international assignments).

If you have pursued a more general curriculum (general business, liberal arts, or such), you will need to look at your studies closely to see what they have prepared you to do. Perhaps you will find an emphasis on computers, written communication, human relations, foreign languages—all of which are sorely needed by some businesses. Or perhaps you will conclude that your training has given you a strong general base from which to learn specific business skills.

- For general curricula, a career choice must be made.

In analyzing your education, you should look at the quality of your record—grades, projects honors, special recognitions. If your record is good, you can emphasize it. But what if your work was only mediocre? As we will point out later, you will need to shift the emphasis to your stronger sales points—your willingness to work, your personality, your experience. Or perhaps you can explain, for example, by noting that while working your way through school may have limited your academic performance, it gave you valuable business qualities such as initiative, collaboration, and risk-taking.

- Consider quality of educational record (grades, honors, courses taken).

Personal Qualities. Your self-analysis also should cover your personal qualities. Employers often use personality tests such as the Myers-Briggs to screen new hires, and you can take them online as well as at most campus career centers. Qualities that relate to working with people are especially important. Qualities that show leadership or teamwork ability are also important. And if you express yourself well in writing or speaking, note this, for good communication skills are valuable in most jobs.

- (2) Personal qualities (people skills, leadership, and such).

Of course, you may not be the best judge of your personal qualities, for we do not always see ourselves as others see us. You may need to check with friends to see whether they agree with your assessments. You also may need to check your record for evidence supporting your assessments. For example, organization membership and participation in community activities are evidence of people and teamwork skills. Holding office in an organization is evidence of leadership ability. Participation on a debate team, college bowl, or collegiate business policy team is evidence of communication skills.

Work Experience. If you have work experience, you should analyze it. Work experience in your major deserves emphasis. In fact, such work experience becomes more and more important as you move along in your career. Work experience not related to the job you seek also can tell something important about you—even if the work was part-time. Part-time work can show willingness and determination, especially if you have done it to finance your education. And almost any work experience can help develop your skills in dealing with people and taking responsibility.

- (3) Work experience (with interpretations).

Special Qualifications. Your self-analysis also should include special qualifications that might be valuable to an employer. The ability to speak a foreign language can be very helpful for certain business environments. Athletic participation, hobbies, and interests also may be helpful. To illustrate, athletic experience might be helpful for work for a sporting goods distributor, a hobby of automobile mechanics might be helpful for work with an automotive service company, and an interest in music might be helpful for work with a piano manufacturer or an online music website. An interest in or skills with computers would be valuable across a broad range of businesses.

- (4) Special qualities (languages, communication skills, and such).

You also might take an interest inventory such as the Strong Campbell Interest Inventory or the Minnesota Vocational Interest Inventory. These tests help match your interests to those of others successful in their careers. Most college counseling and

career centers make these tests available to their students, and some are available online. Getting good help in interpreting the results is critical to providing you with valuable information.

- Also consider external factors.

Analyzing Outside Factors. After you have analyzed yourself, you need to combine this information with the work needs of business and other external influences. Your goal in this process is to give realistic direction to your search for employment. Where is the kind of work you are seeking available? Are you willing to move? Is such a move compatible with others in your life—your partner, your children, your parents? Does the location meet with your lifestyle needs? Although the availability of work may drive the answer to some of these questions, you should answer them as well as you can on the basis of what you know now and then conduct your job search accordingly. Finding just the right job should be one of your most important goals.

Finding Your Employer

- Search for potential employers by using these sources:

You can use a number of sources in your search for an employer with whom you will begin or continue your career. Your choice of sources will probably be influenced by the stage of your career.

- (1) your school's career center,

Career Centers. If you are just beginning your career, one good possibility is the career center at your school. Most large schools have career centers, and these attract employers who are looking for suitable applicants. Many centers offer excellent job-search counseling and maintain databases on registrants containing school records, résumés, and recommendations for review by prospective employers. Most have directories listing the major companies with contact names and addresses. And most provide interviewing opportunities. Campus career centers often hold career fairs. They are an excellent place to find employers who are looking for new graduates as well as to gather information about the kinds of jobs different companies offer. By attending them early, you often find out about internships and summer jobs as well as gather ideas for selecting courses that might give you a competitive advantage when you do begin your career search.

- (2) your network of personal contacts,

Network of Personal Contacts. As has been noted, the personal contacts you make can be extremely helpful in your job search. In fact, according to some employment reports, personal contacts are the leading means of finding employees. Obviously, personal contacts are more likely to be a source of employment opportunities later in your career—when you may need to change jobs. Acquaintances, may provide job leads outside those known to your friends.

Classified Advertisements. Help-wanted advertisements in newspapers and professional journals, whether online or in print, provide good sources of employment opportunities for many kinds of work. Many are limited, however, in the opportunities they provide for new college graduates. Classified ads are good sources for experienced workers who are seeking to improve their positions, and they are especially good sources for people who are conducting a major search for high-level positions. However, they are only a partial list of jobs available.

- (3) classified advertisements,

Online Sources. In addition to finding opportunities in classifieds, you also will find them in online databases. Monster.com, for example, lists jobs available throughout the country, with new opportunities posted regularly. Many companies even post job openings on the Web, some with areas dedicated to new college graduates. If you are working now, you may want to check the company's intranet or portal for positions there, too. And professional associations often maintain job databanks. Furthermore, you could use blogs to post queries about job openings that readers might have information. All these online systems are sources for job opportunities. See the textbook website for links to many useful websites.

- (4) online sources,

Employment Agencies. Companies that specialize in finding jobs for employees can be useful. Of course, such companies charge for their services. The employer sometimes pays the charges, usually if qualified applicants are scarce. Executive search consultants (headhunters) are commonly used to place experienced people in executive positions. Employment agencies also can help job seekers gain temporary employment.

- (5) employment agencies,

Temping can lead to permanent employment with a good fit. It allows the worker to get a feel for the company and the company to observe the worker before making a job commitment.

Personal Search Agents. In addition to searching online sources, you can request that job notices be sent to you automatically by websites. These sites use tools called personal search agents or job agents. Using a filter based on a confidential profile you have completed for the site, these tools find jobs that match your profile and send you an email messages about these jobs. Starting with a very precise or narrow profile first is wise. You can always modify your profile to something broader later if you find the number or nature of the job leads isn't what you expected. If you learn of a job listing that interests you for a company recruiting at your school, you should ask the recruiter about it. Not only will it show the employer you have done your homework, but it will also show that you have a sincere interest in working for the company.

- (6) personal search agents,

Web Page Profiles. To make yourself more visible to potential employers, you may want to consider posting your résumé to the Web. Some employers actively search for new employees on university websites. Posting a web page profile is not difficult. Today's word processors let you save your documents in hypertext markup language (HTML), creating a basic web page for you. Additionally, easy-to-use web page building and generating tools are available on the Web to help novices create personal web profiles. Once posted, it is a good idea to link your web page to your major department or to a business student club, allowing more potential employers to find your résumé. With a little extra effort, you can create a web page that greatly expands on the printed résumé. You will want to put your web page address on your printed résumé.

- (7) web page profiles,

Posting a web page profile is another way of showcasing yourself and your communication skills. Not only can you add much more detail than on a print résumé, but you can also use colorful photos, videos, and sounds. You can show examples of real projects, documents, and presentations you have created as well as demonstrate your skills and creativity. A web page profile can range from the simple one you see here, created by completing an online form, to the mailable one you see in Figure 9–6, to a sophisticated one that uses a full range of media and interaction.

Today, creating a simple web page profile is pretty easy, even for the beginner. In fact, you may already have a web page authoring tool if you have FrontPage or access to website builders. Some of these web-based applications let you create for free and for a small fee will host your web page profile, too. You can find links to some of these sites on your textbook website. And once you have posted your web page profile, you will want to be sure to include its URL on your print résumé as well as on any business cards you use in the job search.

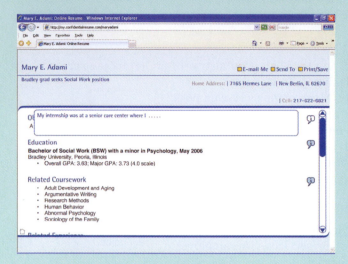

- (8) prospecting techniques.

Prospecting. Some job seekers approach prospective employers directly, either by personal visit, mail, or email. Personal visits are effective if the company has an employment office or if a personal contact can set up a visit. Mail contacts typically include a résumé and a cover letter. An email contact can include a variety of documents and be sent in various forms. The construction of these messages is covered later in the chapter.

PREPARING THE APPLICATION DOCUMENTS

INTRODUCTORY SITUATION

Résumés and Applications

In your role as Jason Andrews, you consider yourself well qualified for a career in marketing. You know the field from both personal experience and classroom study. You grew up in a working-class neighborhood. From an early age, you worked at a variety of jobs, the most important of which was a job as a pollster. You were a restaurant host and a food server for two years. Your college studies were especially designed to prepare you for a career in marketing. You studied Olympia University's curriculum in marketing, and you carefully chose the electives that would give you the best possible preparation for this career. As evidenced by your grades, your preparation was good.

Now it is time to begin your career. Over the past weeks you followed good procedures in looking for employment (as reviewed in the preceding pages). Unfortunately, you had no success with the recruiters who visited your campus. Now you will send written applications to a select group of companies that you think might use a person with your knowledge and skills. You have obtained the names of the executives you should contact at these companies. You will send them the application documents—résumé and cover message. The following discussion shows you how to prepare these documents for best results, both in print and digital form.

After your search has uncovered a job possibility, you pursue it. How you pursue it depends on the circumstances of the case. When it is convenient and appropriate to do so, you make contact in person. It is convenient when the distance is not great, and it is appropriate when the employer has invited such a contact. When a personal visit is not convenient and appropriate, you apply online or by mail, email, or fax.

Whether or not you apply in person, you are likely to use some written material. If you apply in person, probably you will take a résumé with you to leave as a record of your qualifications. If you do not apply in person, of course, the application is completely in writing. Typically, it consists of a résumé, a cover message, and a reference sheet. At some point in your employment efforts, you are likely to use each of these documents.

Preparing these documents is much like preparing a sales document—both types involve selling. You are selling a product or services—your ability to do work. The résumé and reference sheet are much like the supporting material that accompanies the sales message. The cover message is much like the sales message. These similarities should become obvious to you as you read the following pages.

As in preparing a sales campaign, you begin work on a written application for a job by studying what you are selling, and what you are selling is you. Then you study the work. Studying yourself involves taking personal inventory—the self-analysis discussed earlier in the chapter. You should begin by listing all the information about you that you believe an employer would want to know. Studying the work means learning as much as you can about the company—its plans, its policies, its operations. You can study the company's website, read its annual report and other publications, find any recent news articles about the company, and consult a variety of business databases. (See Chapter 19 for a more detailed list of resources for company information.) You can also learn the requirements of the work the company wants done. Today, campus career centers and student organizations often invite employers to give information sessions. Reading about various careers in the *Opportunity Outlook Handbook* at <http://www.bls.gov/oco/> will tell you about the nature of the work as well as salary range and demand. Sometimes you can get this information through personal investigation. More often, you will have to develop it through logical thinking.

With this preliminary information assembled, you are ready to plan the application. First, you need to decide just what your application will consist of. Will it be just a cover message, a cover message and a résumé (also called a *vita, curriculum vita, qualifications brief,* or *data sheet*), or a cover message, résumé, and reference sheet? The résumé is a summary of background facts in list form. You will probably select the combination of cover message and résumé, for this arrangement is likely to do the best job. Some people prefer to use the cover message alone. When you send a print cover message, it usually contains substantial detail, for it must do the whole sales job. When you send a digital message, it can be adapted to the channel chosen. You will include the reference sheet when asked or when it supports your case.

- Pursue job openings by personal visit, online, mail, email, or fax.

- You are likely to use résumés, cover messages, and reference sheets in your job search.

- Prepare them as you would prepare a sales mailing.

- Study the product (you) and the work.

- Next, decide on whether to send a message alone, with a résumé, or with a résumé, and a reference sheet.

CONSTRUCTING THE RÉSUMÉ

After you have decided to use the résumé, you must decide whether to use a print or a digital format. The traditional print format is used in face-to-face interviews where you know it will be used exclusively there. If you have reason to believe the company will store your résumé digitally, you should use a scannable print format. Constructing these forms is similar, but they differ in some very important ways.

A digital format, on the other hand, is used when sending your application document by email or submitting or posting it via the Web. Depending on the capabilities of the recipient's system and any forms an employer may specify, the documents can range from a low-end ASCII or text form to midrange attached files, to high-end, full-featured web pages. In both the print and digital formats, you set up the documents to present your credentials in the most favorable way.

- Choose the print or digital format.

After deciding what your format will be, you construct the parts. In selecting these parts you not only choose how to present them, but you also tailor the content and order to the specific job you are applying for. While the print résumé you will use now when just coming out of school will generally be one page long, after you've worked several years it may grow to a couple of pages. However, the digital version has no physical page limitation, so you should include all that is relevant to the particular job.

TRADITIONAL PRINT RÉSUMÉ

You will want to include in the résumé all background information you think the reader should have about you. This means including all the information that a cover letter reviews plus supporting and incidental details. Designed for quick reading, the résumé lists facts that have been arranged for the best possible appearance. Rarely does it use sentences.

The arrangements of résumés differ widely, but the following procedures generally describe how most are written:

- Logically arrange information on education (institutions, dates, degrees, major field); information on employment (dates, places, firms, and accomplishments); personal details (memberships, interests, achievements, and such—but not religion, race, and sex); and special information derived from other information (achievements, qualifications, capabilities). Add a reference sheet as needed.
- Construct a heading for the entire résumé and subheadings for the parts.
- Include other vital information such as objectives and contact information.
- Arrange the data for best eye appeal, making the résumé balanced—not crowded and not strung out.

Selecting the Background Facts. Your first step in preparing the résumé is to review the background facts you have assembled about yourself and then to select the facts you think will help your reader evaluate you. You should include all the information covered in the accompanying cover message, for this is the most important information. In addition, you should include significant supporting details not covered in the accompanying cover message to avoid making that message too cluttered.

Arranging the Facts into Groups. After selecting the facts you want to include, you should sort them into logical groups. Many grouping arrangements are possible. The most conventional is the three-part grouping of *Education, Experience,* and *Skills* or *Interests*. Another possibility is a grouping by job functions or skills, such as *Selling, Communicating,* and *Managing.* You may be able to work out other logical groups.

You also can derive additional groups from the four conventional groups mentioned above. For example, you can have a group of *Achievements*. Such a group would consist of special accomplishments taken from your experience and education information. Another possibility is to have a group consisting of information highlighting your major *Qualifications*. Here you would include information drawn from the areas of experience, education, and skills or personal qualities. Illustrations of and instructions for constructing groups such as these appear later in the chapter.

Constructing the Headings. With your information organized, a logical next step is to construct the headings for the résumé. Probably you will begin by constructing the main head—the one that covers the entire document.

The most widely used form of main head is the topic, which consists only of words that describe what follows. Your name is usually the main heading. It should be presented clearly; usually this means using larger and bolder type so that the name stands out from the rest of the résumé. If an employer remembers only one fact from your résumé, that fact should be your name. It can be presented in all caps or caps and lowercase, as in this example:

Terrence P. Lenaghan

The next level of headings might be *Objective, Education, Experience,* and *Skills.* These headings can be placed to the left or centered above the text that follows.

A second and less widely used form is the talking head. This form uses words that tell the nature of what follows. For example, instead of the topic head, *Education,* a talking head might read *Specialized Training in Accounting* or *Computer Software Application Skills Acquired.* Obviously, these heads add to the information covered. They help the reader interpret the facts that follow.

• Talking heads interpret for the reader.

As you can see from the illustrations in the chapter, the headings are distinguished from the other information in the résumé by the use of different sizes and styles of type. The main head should appear to be the most important of all (larger and heavier). Headings for the groups of information should appear to be more important than the information under them. Courtesy requires that you choose heading forms carefully, making sure they are neither so heavy and large that they offend nor so light and small that they show no distinctions. Your goal is to choose forms that properly show the relative importance of the information and are pleasing to the eye.

• Distinguish the headings from the other information by font selection.

Including Contact Information. Your address, telephone number, and email address are the most likely means of contacting you. Most authorities recommend that you display them prominently somewhere in the résumé. You also may want to display your fax number or web page address. The most common location for displaying contact information is at the top, under the main head.

• Display your contact information prominently.

When it is likely that your address or telephone number will change before the job search ends, you would be wise to include two addresses and numbers: one current and the other permanent. If you are a student, for example, your address at the time of applying for a job may change before the employer decides to contact you. Therefore, you may want to consider using the voice-mail on your cell phone or an Internet-based voice message service so that you can receive your messages wherever you go.

• Anticipate changes in contact information.

The purpose of making the contact information prominent and inclusive has been to make it easy for the employer to reach you. However, recently, in the interest of privacy, some schools have begun advising their students to include only their names, phone numbers, and an innocuous email address created specifically for job searches. For business use, a professional email address is always preferable to an informal one such as surferchick@hotmail.com. However, you will likely still need to include complete information on application forms provided by employers.

Including a Statement of Objective. Although not a category of background information, a statement of your objective is appropriate in the résumé. Headings such as *Career Objective, Job Objective,* or just *Objective* usually appear at the beginning.

• Consider a statement of your objective.

Not all authorities agree on the value of including the objective, however. Recommending that they be omitted from today's résumés, some authorities suggest that the résumé should concentrate instead on skills, experience, and credentials. They argue that the objective includes only obvious information that is clearly suggested by the remainder of the résumé. Moreover, they point out that an objective limits the applicant to a single position and eliminates consideration for other jobs that may be available.

• However, note that some authorities oppose it.

Those favoring the use of a statement of objective reason that it helps the recruiter see quickly where the applicant might fit into the company. Since this argument appears

• Even so, probably you should use it.

to have greater support, at least for the moment, probably you should include the objective. When your career goal is unclear, you may use broad, general terms. And when you are considering a variety of employment possibilities, you may want to have different versions of your résumé for each possibility.

Primarily, your statement of objective should describe the work you seek. When you know the exact job title of a position you want at the targeted company, use it.

Objective: Marketing Research Intern

Another technique includes using words that convey a long-term interest in the targeted company, as in this example. However, using this form may limit you if the company does not have the career path you specify.

Objective: Sales Representative for McGraw-Hill leading to sales management.

Also, wording the objective to point out your major strengths can be very effective. It also can help set up the organization of the résumé.

Objective: To apply three years of successful ecommerce accounting experience at a small startup to a larger company with a need for careful attention to transaction management and analysis.

Presenting the Information. The information you present under each heading will depend on your good judgment. You should list all the facts that you think are relevant. You will want to include enough information to enable the reader to judge your ability to do the work you seek.

Your coverage of work experience should identify completely the jobs you have held. Minimum coverage would include dates, places, firms, and responsibilities. If the work was part-time or volunteer, you should say so without demeaning the skills you developed on the job. In describing your duties, you should select words that highlight what you did, especially the parts of this experience that qualify you for the work you seek. Such a description will reflect your practice of good business ethics. For example, in describing a job as credit manager, you could write "Credit Analyst for Federated Stores, St. Petersburg, Florida, 2005–08." But it would be more meaningful to give this fuller description: "Credit Analyst for Federated Stores, St. Petersburg, Florida, 2005–08, supervising a staff of seven in processing credit applications and communications."

If your performance on a job shows your ability to do the work you seek, you should consider emphasizing your accomplishments in your job description. For example, an experienced marketer might write this description: "Marketing Specialist for Colgate-Palmolive, 2005–2008. Served in advisory role to company management. Developed marketing plan that increased profits 24 percent in two years." Or a successful advertising account executive might write this description: "Phillips-Ramsey Inc., San Diego, 2005–08. As account executive, developed successful campaigns for nine accounts and led development team in increasing agency volume 18 percent."

As you can see from the previous examples, the use of action verbs strengthens job descriptions. Verbs are the strongest of all words. If you choose them well, they will do much to sell your ability to do work. One strategy is to choose verbs that describe both the work you want to do as well as the work you have done, making it easier for the reader to see how you have transferable skills. A list of the more widely used action verbs appears in Figure 9–1.

Because your education is likely to be your strongest selling point for your first job after college, you will probably cover it in some detail. (Unless it adds something unique, you usually do not include your high school education once you have finished a college degree. Similarly, you also minimize the emphasis on all your education as you gain experience.) At a minimum, your coverage of education should include institutions, dates, degrees, and areas of study. For some jobs, you may want to list and even describe specific courses, especially if you have little other information to present or if your coursework has uniquely prepared you for those jobs. If

----

Marginal notes (left column):

- The statement should cover the job you seek and more, as in these examples.

- List the facts under the headings.

- When covering work experience, at a minimum include dates, places, firms, and responsibilities.

- When appropriate, show achievements.

- Use action verbs to strengthen the appeal.

- For education, include institutions, dates, degrees, and areas of study.

Figure 9–1

A List of Action Verbs That Add Strength to Your Résumé

The underlined words are especially good for pointing out **accomplishments**.

Clerical/Detail Skills

approved
arranged
catalogued
checked
classified
collected
compiled
confirmed
copied
detected
dissected
executed
generated
implemented
inspected
monitored
operated
organized
prepared
processed
purchased
recorded
retrieved
scheduled
screened
specified
systematized
tabulated
validated

Communication Skills

addressed
arbitrated
arranged
articulated
authored
collaborated
composed
convinced
corresponded
developed
directed
drafted
edited
enlisted
formulated

influenced
interpreted
lectured
mediated
moderated
negotiated
persuaded
presented
promoted
publicized
reconciled
recruited
reported
spoke
translated
wrote

Creative Skills

acted
built
conceived
conceptualized
created
customized
designed
developed
devised
directed
established
fabricated
fashioned
founded
illustrated
initiated
instituted
integrated
introduced
invented
originated
performed
planned
revitalized
shaped

Financial Skills

administered
allocated
analyzed
appraised

audited
balanced
budgeted
calculated
computed
consolidated
converted
developed
dispensed (financial)
forecast
managed
marketed
planned
projected
researched

Helping Skills

advised
assessed
assisted
challenged
clarified
coached
counseled
demonstrated
diagnosed
educated
expedited
facilitated
guided
motivated
referred
rehabilitated
represented

Management Skills

accomplished
addressed
administered
allocated
analyzed
anticipated
approved
assigned
attained
chaired
completed

conserved
consolidated
contracted
controlled
coordinated
critiqued
decided
defined
delegated
delivered
developed
directed
evaluated
executed
guided
hired
implemented
improved
increased
initiated
led
organized
oversaw
planned
prioritized
produced
recommended
reviewed
scheduled
strengthened
supervised

Research Skills

analyzed
clarified
collected
compiled
conducted
critiqued
detected
diagnosed
discovered
evaluated
examined
experimented
extracted
gathered

identified
inspected
interpreted
interviewed
investigated
organized
reviewed
sampled
summarized
surveyed
systematized

Teamwork/Interpersonal Skills

clarified
collaborated
coordinated
facilitated
harmonized
negotiated
networked

Technical Skills

accessed
assembled
built
calculated
charted
computed
configured
designed
devised
diagnosed
engineered
fabricated
installed
maintained
operated
overhauled
performed troubleshooting
programmed
remodeled
repaired
retrieved
solved
upgraded

Training/Supervision Skills

adapted
advised
assembled
clarified
coached
communicated
conducted
coordinated
demonstrated
demystified
developed
enabled
encouraged
evaluated
explained
facilitated
guided
informed
instructed
lectured
persuaded
set goals
stimulated
trained
tutored

More Accomplishment Verbs

achieved
acquired
earned
eliminated (waste)
expanded
founded
improved
pioneered
reduced (losses)
resolved (problems)
restored
revamped
solved
spearheaded
transformed

Revised and updated from Yana Parker, *The Damn Good Résumé Guide* (Berkeley, CA: Ten Speed Press, 2002).

your grade-point average (GPA) is good, you may want to include it. Remember, for your résumé, you can compute your GPA in a way that works best for you as long as you label it accurately. For example, you may want to select just those courses in your major, labeling it Major GPA. Or if your last few years were your best ones, you may want to present your GPA for just that period. In any case, include GPA when it works favorably for you.

• For legal reasons, some personal information (on race, religion, sex) should probably not be listed.

What personal information to list is a matter for your best judgment. In fact, the trend appears to be toward eliminating such information. If you do include personal information, you should probably omit race, religion, sex, age, and marital status because current laws prohibit hiring based on them. But not everyone agrees on this matter. Some authorities believe that at least some of these items should be included. They argue that the law only prohibits employers from considering such information in hiring—that it does not prohibit applicants from presenting the information. They reason that if such information helps you, you should use it. The illustrations shown in this chapter support both viewpoints.

• Information on activities and interests tells about one's personal qualities.

Personal information that is generally appropriate includes all items that tell about your personal qualities. Information on your organization memberships, civic involvement, and social activities is evidence of experience and interest in working with people. Hobbies and athletic participation tell of your balance of interests. Such information can be quite useful to some employers, especially when personal qualities are important to the work involved.

• Consider listing references, but know that some authorities favor postponing using them.

Authorities disagree on whether to list references on the résumé. Some think that references should not be contacted until negotiations are further along. Others think that references should be listed because some employers want to check them early in the screening process. One recent study by the Society for Human Resource Management of 2,500 human resource professionals said 96 percent of their companies always check references.[1] Therefore, including them on the résumé would make it easier for the company to proceed through the background check process. Clearly, both views have substantial support. You will have to make the choice based on your best knowledge of the situation.

• Good etiquette requires that you get permission.

When you do list someone as a reference, good business etiquette requires that you ask for permission first. Although you will use only those who can speak highly of you, sometimes asking for your reference's permission beforehand helps that person prepare better. And, of course, it saves you from unexpected embarrassment such as a reference not remembering you, being out of town, or, worse yet, not having anything to say.

• Consider using a separate sheet for references.

A commonly used tool is a separate reference sheet. When you use it, you close the résumé with a statement indicating references are available. Later, when the reader wants to check references, you give her or him this sheet. The type size and style of the main heading of this sheet should match that used in your résumé. It may say something like "References for [your name]." Below this heading is a listing of your references, beginning with the strongest one. In addition to solving the reference dilemma, use of this separate reference sheet allows you to change both the references and their order for each job. A sample reference sheet is shown in the example in Figure 9–4.

Sometimes you may have good reason not to list references, as when you are employed and want to keep the job search secret. If you choose not to list them, you should explain their absence. You can do this in the accompanying cover message, or you can do it on the résumé by following the heading "References" with an explanation, such as "Will be furnished on request."

• Select references that cover your background.

How many and what kinds of references to include will depend on your background. If you have an employment record, you should include one for every major job you have held—at least for recent years. You should include references related to the work

---

[1] Cheryl Soltis, "Eagle-Eyed Employers Scour Résumé for Little White Lies," *The Wall Street Journal* 21 Mar. 2006: B7.

you seek. If you base your application heavily on your education or your personal qualities, or both, you should include references who can vouch for these areas: professors, clergy, community leaders, and the like. Your goal is to list those people who can verify the points on which your appeal for the job is based. At a minimum, you should list three references. Five is a good maximum.

Your list of references should include accurate mailing addresses, with appropriate job titles. Accurate addresses are important so the reader can easily contact the references. Also useful are telephone and fax numbers as well as email addresses. Job titles (officer, manager, president, supervisor) are helpful because they show what the references are able to tell about you. It is appropriate to include forms of address: Mr., Mrs., Ms., Dr., and so on. Do get permission from your references to include the contact information.

- Include accurate mailing and email addresses and job titles.

Organizing for Strength. After you have identified the information you want to include on your résumé, you will want to organize or group items to present yourself in the best possible light. Three strategies for organizing this information are the *reverse chronological approach,* the *functional* or *skills approach,* and the *accomplishments/ achievements* or *highlights approach.*

- Choose an organizational strategy that best presents your case.

The *reverse chronological* organizational layout (Figures 9–5 and 9–6) presents your education and work experience from the most recent to oldest. It emphasizes the order and time frame in which you have participated in these activities. It is particularly good for those who have progressed in an orderly and timely fashion through school and work.

- The reverse chronological approach is orderly.

A *functional* or *skills* layout (Figure 9–7) organizes around three to five areas particularly important to the job you want. Rather than forcing an employer to determine that you developed one skill on one job and another skill on another job, this organizational plan groups related skills together. It is particularly good for those who have had many jobs, for those who have taken nontraditional career paths, and for those who are changing fields. Creating this kind of résumé takes much work and careful analysis of both jobs and skills to show the reader that you are a good match for the position. If you use a functional résumé, be sure that readers can see from the other sections—such as employment and education—where you likely developed the skills that you are emphasizing. Enabling your readers to make these connections lends credibility to your claims to have such skills.

- The functional or skills approach emphasizes relevant skills.

An *accomplishments/achievements* layout (Figure 9–8) presents a picture of you as a competent worker. It puts hard numbers and precise facts behind skills and traits you have. Refer back to Figure 9–1 for some good verb choices to use in describing accomplishments. Here is an example illustrating this arrangement in describing work done at a particular company:

- The accomplishments/ achievements approach shows you can perform.

> Successfully managed the Austin store for two years in a period of low unemployment with these results:
>
> - Reduced employee turnover 55 percent.
> - Increased profits 37 percent.
> - Grew sales volume 12 percent.

Information covered under a *Highlights* or *Summary* heading may include key points from the three conventional information groups: education, experience, and personal qualities. Typically, this layout emphasizes the applicant's most impressive background facts that pertain to the work sought, as in this example:

- The highlights or summary approach shows you are a good fit for the position.

> ### Highlights
>
> - **Experienced:** three years of practical work as programmer/analyst in designing and developing financial databases for the banking industry.
> - **Highly trained:** B.S. degree with honors in management information systems.
> - **Self-motivated:** proven record of successful completion of three online courses.

Although such items will overlap others in the résumé, using them in a separate group emphasizes strengths while showing where they were obtained. See an example of an accomplishments layout in Figure 9–8.

Writing Impersonally and Consistently. Because the résumé is a listing of information, you should write without personal pronouns (no *I*'s, *we*'s, *you*'s). You should also write all equal-level headings and the parts under each heading in the same (parallel) grammatical form. For example, if one major heading in the résumé is a noun phrase, all the other major headings should be noun phrases. The following four headings illustrate the point. All but the third (an adjective form) are noun phrases. The error can be corrected by making the third a noun phrase, as in the examples to the right:

- List the information without use of personal pronouns (I, we, you).

- Use the same (parallel) grammatical form for all equal-level headings and for the parts listed under each heading.

Not Parallel	**Parallel**
Specialized study	Specialized study
Experience in promotion work	Experience in promotion work
Personal and physical	Personal and physical qualities
Qualified references	Qualified references

The following items illustrate grammatical inconsistency in the parts of a group:

Have good health

Active in sports

Ambitious

Inspection of these items shows that they do not fit the same understood words. The understood word for the first item is *I* and for the second and third, the understood words are *I am*. Any changes that make all three items fit the same understood words would correct the error.

Making the Form Attractive. The attractiveness of your résumé will say as much about you as the words. The appearance of the information that the reader sees plays a part in forming his or her judgment. While using a template is one solution, it will make you look like many other applicants. A layout designed with your reader and your unique data in mind will probably do a better job for you. Not only will your résumé have a distinctive appearance, but the design should sell you more effectively than one where you must fit your data to the design. A sloppy, poorly designed presentation, on the other hand, may even ruin your chances of getting the job. Thus, you have no choice but to give your résumé and your cover message an attractive physical arrangement.

Designing the résumé for eye appeal is no routine matter. There is no one best arrangement, but a good procedure is to approach the task as a graphic designer would. Your objective is to design an arrangement of type and space that appeals to the eye. You would do well to use the following general advice for arranging the résumé.

Margins look better if at least an inch of space is left at the top of the page and on the left and right sides of the page and if at least 1½ inches of space are left at the bottom of the page. Your listing of items by rows and columns appears best if the items are short and if they can be set up in two uncrowded columns, one on the left side of the page and one on the right side. Longer items of information are more appropriately set up in lines extending across the page. In any event, you would do well to avoid long and narrow columns of data with large sections of wasted space on either side. Arrangements that give a heavy crowded effect also offend the eye. Extra spacing between subdivisions and indented patterns for subparts are especially pleasing to the eye.

- Make the résumé attractive.

- Design it as a graphic designer would. Use balance and space for eye appeal.

- Here are some suggestions on form.

While layout is important in showing your ability to organize and good spacing increases readability, other design considerations such as font and paper selection affect attractiveness almost as much. Commercial designers say that type size for headings should be at least 14 points and for body text, 10 to 12 points. They also recommend using fewer than four font styles on a page. Some word processing programs have a "shrink to fit" feature that allows the user to fit information on one page. It will automatically adjust font sizes to fit the page. Be sure the resulting type size is both appropriate and readable.

- Choose fonts carefully.

Another factor affecting the appearance of your application documents is the paper you select. The paper should be appropriate for the job you seek. In business, erring on the conservative side is usually better; you do not want to be eliminated from consideration simply because the reader did not like the quality or color of the paper. The most traditional choice is white, 100 percent cotton, 20- to 28-lb. paper. Of course, reasonable variations can be appropriate.

- Conservative paper usually is best.

Contrasting Bad and Good Examples. The résumés in Figures 9–2 and 9–3 are at opposing ends of the quality scale. The first one, scant in coverage and poorly arranged, does little to help the applicant. Clearly, the second one is more complete and better arranged.

- Figures 9–2 and 9–3 show bad and good form.

Weakness in Bad Arrangement and Incompleteness. Shortcomings in the first example (Figure 9–2) are obvious. First, the form is not pleasing to the eye. The weight of the type is heavy on the left side of the page. Failure to indent wrapped lines makes reading difficult.

This résumé also contains numerous errors in wording. Information headings are not parallel in grammatical form. All are in topic form except the first one. The items listed under *Personal* are not parallel either. Throughout, the résumé coverage is scant, leaving out many of the details needed to present the best impression of the applicant. Under *Experience,* little is said about specific tasks and skills in each job; and under *Education,* high school work is listed needlessly. The references are incomplete, omitting street addresses and job titles.

Strength through Good Arrangement and Completeness. The next résumé (Figure 9–3) appears better at first glance, and it gets even better as you read it. It is attractively arranged. The information is neither crowded nor strung out. The balance is good. Its content is also superior to that of the other example. Additional words show the quality of Mr. Andrews's work experience and education, and they emphasize points that make him suited for the work he seeks. This résumé excludes trivial personal information and has only the facts that tell something about Andrews's personal qualities. Complete contact information permits the reader to contact the references easily. Job titles tell how each is qualified to evaluate the subject.

Scannable Print Résumé

Although paper résumés are not obsolete, a recent addition to the job-search process is the scannable résumé. This résumé bridges the print-to-digital gap. It is simply one that can be scanned into a database and retrieved when a position is being filled. Since the objective is getting your résumé reviewed in order to be interviewed, you should use the following strategies to improve your chances of having it retrieved by the computer.

- The scannable résumé should be constructed to be read accurately by a computer and retrieved when an appropriate position is being filled.

Include Keywords. One strategy, using keywords, is often recommended for use with electronic scanning software. These keywords are usually nouns or

- Use keywords that describe precisely what you can do.

Figure 9–2

Incompleteness and Bad Arrangement in a Traditional Print Résumé. This résumé presents Jason Andrews ineffectively (see "Introductory Situation for Résumés and Applications"). It is scant and poorly arranged.

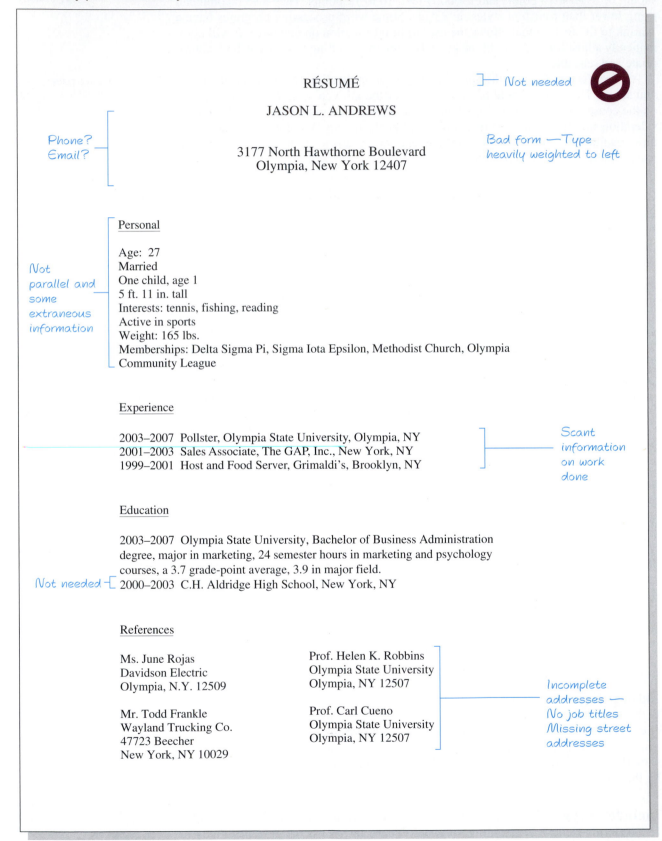

RÉSUMÉ ── Not needed

JASON L. ANDREWS

3177 North Hawthorne Boulevard
Olympia, New York 12407

Phone?
Email?

Bad form — Type
heavily weighted to left

Not
parallel and
some
extraneous
information

Personal

Age: 27
Married
One child, age 1
5 ft. 11 in. tall
Interests: tennis, fishing, reading
Active in sports
Weight: 165 lbs.
Memberships: Delta Sigma Pi, Sigma Iota Epsilon, Methodist Church, Olympia
Community League

Experience

2003–2007 Pollster, Olympia State University, Olympia, NY
2001–2003 Sales Associate, The GAP, Inc., New York, NY
1999–2001 Host and Food Server, Grimaldi's, Brooklyn, NY

Scant
information
on work
done

Education

2003–2007 Olympia State University, Bachelor of Business Administration
degree, major in marketing, 24 semester hours in marketing and psychology
courses, a 3.7 grade-point average, 3.9 in major field.

Not needed ─ 2000–2003 C.H. Aldridge High School, New York, NY

References

Ms. June Rojas
Davidson Electric
Olympia, N.Y. 12509

Mr. Todd Frankle
Wayland Trucking Co.
47723 Beecher
New York, NY 10029

Prof. Helen K. Robbins
Olympia State University
Olympia, NY 12507

Prof. Carl Cueno
Olympia State University
Olympia, NY 12507

Incomplete
addresses —
No job titles
Missing street
addresses

Figure 9–3

Thoroughness and Good Arrangement in a Traditional Print Résumé. This complete and reverse chronologically organized résumé presents Jason Andrews's case effectively (see "Introductory Situation" for "Résumés and Applications").

Jason L. Andrews

3177 North Hawthorne Boulevard
Olympia, NY 12407-3278
914.967.3117 (Voice/Message)
jandrews@hotmail.com

Presents contact data clearly

Objective

A position in marketing that will lead to work as a marketing manager for an ebusiness.

Education

Bachelor of Business Administration
Olympia State University—May 2008
GPA: 3.7/4.0

Major: Marketing
Minor: Psychology
Dean's List

Emphasizes education by position

Related Coursework:

Highlights most relevant courses and subjects

- Strategic Marketing
- Marketing Research
- Marketing Communications & Promotion
- Global Marketing

- Interpersonal Communication
- Statistical Analysis
- Consumer and Buyer Behavior
- Social Psychology

- Research Projects: Cultural Influence on Purchasing, Customer Brand Preference, and Motivating Subordinates with Effective Performance Appraisals.

Experience

Pollster, Olympia State University, Olympia, NY, 2007–present (internship)

Sales Associate, The Gap, Inc., New York, NY (named top store sales associate four of eight quarters), 2005–2007

Host and Food Server, Grimaldi's, Brooklyn, NY (part-time), 2003–2005

Emphasizes positions; de-emphasizes dates

Personal Qualities

Includes only most relevant information

Interests: tennis, blogging, reading, and jogging
Memberships: Delta Sigma Pi (professional); Sigma Iota Epsilon (honorary), served as treasurer and president; Board of Stewards for church; League of Olympia, served as registration leader

References

Personal and professional references gladly furnished upon request.

Tells reader someone will speak for him

Figure 9–4

Thoroughness and Good Arrangement for a Reference Sheet. This reference sheet presents Jason Andrews's references completely.

Jason L. Andrews
3177 North Hawthorne Boulevard
Olympia, NY 12407-3278
914.967.3117 (Voice/ Message)
jandrews@hotmail.com

Heading format matches résumé

Ms. June Rojas, Polling Supervisor
Olympia State University
7114 East 71st Street
Olympia, NY 12509-4572
Telephone: 518.342.1171
Fax: 518.342.1200
Email: June.Rojas@osu.edu

Mr. Todd E. Frankle, Store Manager
The Gap, Inc.
Lincoln Square
New York, NY 10023-0007
Telephone: 212.466.9101
Fax: 212.468.9100
Email: tfrankle@gap.com

Professor Helen K. Robbins
Department of Marketing
Olympia State University
Olympia, NY 12507-0182
Telephone: 518.392.6673
Fax: 518.392.3675
Email: Helen.Robbins@osu.edu

Professor Carol A. Cueno
Department of Psychology
Olympia State University
Olympia, NY 12507-0234
Telephone: 518.392.0723
Fax: 518.392.7542
Email: Carol.Cueno@osu.edu

Complete information and balanced arrangement

Figure 9–5

Traditional Print Résumé Organized in Reverse Chronological Format.

Large size emphasizes name

Manny Konedeng
5602 Montezuma Road • Apartment 413 • San Diego • California • 92115
Phone: (619) 578-8508 • Email: mkonedeng@yahoo.com

Includes complete contact information

OBJECTIVE | A financial analyst internship with a broker-dealer where both analytical and interpersonal communication skills and knowledge are valued

Uses descriptive statement with two highly important qualities

EDUCATION | **Bachelor of Science Degree in Business Administration**, May 2007, San Diego State University, Finance Major

Expands and emphasizes strongest points through precise detail

Dean's List
Current GPA: 3.32/4.00
Accomplishments:
- Published in *Fast Company Magazine* and the *San Diego Union Tribune*
- Won Greek Scholarship
- Finished in top five in mathematics competition

Related Courses:
- Business Communication, A
- Investments, A
- Tax Planning, A–
- Estate Planning, A
- Risk Management, A
- Business Law, B+

Computer Skills:
- Microsoft Office—Excel, Word, PowerPoint, and Access
- Web-based Applications—Surveymonkey, Blogger, GoToMeeting
- Research Tools—SPSS, Internet Explorer, Google Advanced Search

WORK EXPERIENCE | *Sales and Front Desk*, Powerhouse Gym, Modesto, CA 95355   Summer 2005
- Sold memberships and facilitated tours for the fitness center
- Listened to, analyzed, and answered customers' inquires
- Accounted for membership payments and constructed sales reports
- Trained new employees to understand company procedures and safety policies

Emphasizes position held rather than place or date

Relay Operator, MCI, Riverbank, CA 95367   Summers 2003 & 2004
- Assisted over 100 callers daily who were deaf, hard of hearing, or speech disabled to place calls
- Exceeded the required data input of 60 wpm with accuracy
- Multitasked with typing and listening to phone conversations
- Was offered a promotion as a Lead Operator

Uses descriptive action verbs

Co-founder and owner, Fo Sho Entertainment, Modesto, CA 95355   2003
- Led promotions for musical events in the Central Valley
- Managed and hosted live concerts
- Created and wrote proposals to work with local businesses
- Collaborated with team members to design advertisements

UNIVERSITY INVOLVEMENT | *Communications Tutor*, San Diego State University,   Spring 2006
San Diego, CA 92182
- Critiqued and evaluated the written work for a business communication course
- Set up and maintained blog for business communication research

Includes items that will set him apart from other applicants

Recruitment Chairman, Kappa Alpha Order Fraternity,   Fall 2005
San Diego, CA 92115
- Supervised the selection process for chapter membership
- Individually raised nearly $1,000 for chapter finances
- Organized recruitment events with business sponsors, radio stations, and special guests

REFERENCES | *Will gladly furnish personal and professional references on request*

Provides closure and says someone will speak for him

Figure 9–6

Digital HTML Résumé Organized in Reverse Chronological Format and Sent as Rich Email. Presents the applicant's education and experience and highlights career-related experience. Links help provide detailed support. See this résumé on the textbook web page and explore its links.

Large purple heading attracts attention

Colorful menu links allow the reader to navigate the document easily

Other links showcase research, writing, and presentation skills

Reference information can be provided in full here

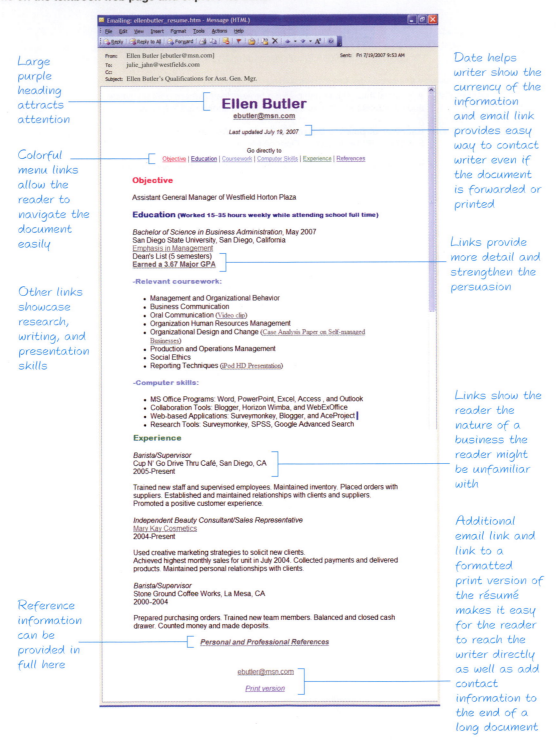

Date helps writer show the currency of the information and email link provides easy way to contact writer even if the document is forwarded or printed

Links provide more detail and strengthen the persuasion

Links show the reader the nature of a business the reader might be unfamiliar with

Additional email link and link to a formatted print version of the résumé makes it easy for the reader to reach the writer directly as well as add contact information to the end of a long document

Figure 9–7

Carolynn W. Workman

12271 69th Terrace North
Seminole, FL 33772
727.399.2569 (Voice/Message)
cworkman@msn.com

Emphasizes tight organization through use of horizontal ruled lines

Objective	An accounting position with a CPA firm

Education

Emphasizes degree and GPA through placement

Bachelor of Science: University of South Florida, December 2007
Major: Business Administration
Emphasis: Accounting
GPA: 3.42 with Honors

Uses internal bullets to increase readability

Accounting-Related Course Work:
Financial Accounting ❖ Cost Accounting and Control ❖ Accounting Information Systems ❖ Auditing ❖ Concepts of Federal Income Taxation ❖ Financial Policy ❖ Communications for Business and Professions

Activities:
Vice-President of Finance, Beta Alpha Psi
Editor, Student Newsletter for Beta Alpha Psi
Member, Golden Key National Honors Society

Emphasizes key skills relevant to objective

Skills

Computer

- ▶ Assisted in installation of small business computerized accounting system using QuickBooks Pro.
- ▶ Prepared tax returns for individuals in the VITA program using specialty tax software.
- ▶ Mastered Excel, designing data input forms, analyzing and interpreting results of most functions, generating graphs, and creating and using macros.

Accounting

- ▶ Experienced with financial statements and general ledger.
- ▶ Reconciled accounts for center serving over 1300 clients.
- ▶ Experienced in preparing income, gift, and estate tax returns.
- ▶ Processed expense reports for twenty professional staff.
- ▶ Experienced in using Great Plains and Solomon IV.

Varies use of action verbs

Business Communication

- ▶ Conducted client interviews and researched tax issues.
- ▶ Communicated both in written and verbal form with clients.
- ▶ Delivered several individual and team presentations on business cases, projects, and reports to business students.

Work History

Administrative Assistant

Office of Student Disability Services, University of South Florida
Tampa, FL. Spring 2007.

Tax Assistant

Rosemary Lenaghan, Certified Public Accountant. Seminole, FL 2006.

References available upon request

Figure 9–8

Traditional Print Résumé Using Highlights of Qualifications and Accomplishments Sections.

Kimberly M. VanLerBerghe

2411 27th Street
Moline, IL 61265
309.764.0017 (Mobile)
kmv@yahoo.com

JOB TARGET	TRAINER/TRANSLATOR for a large, worldwide industrial company

HIGHLIGHTS OF QUALIFICATIONS

Emphasizes those qualifications most relevant to position sought

- Experienced in creating and delivering multimedia PowerPoint presentations.
- Enthusiastic team member/leader whose participation brings out the best in others.
- Proficient in analytical ability.
- Skilled in gathering and interpreting data.
- Bilingual—English/Spanish.

EDUCATION

Presents the most important items here

DEGREE	B.S. English—June 2007—Western Illinois University	
EMPHASIS	Education	MAJOR GPA—3.87/4.00
HONORS	Dean's List, four semesters Chevron Scholarship, Fall 2006	
MEMBER	Mortar Board, Women's Golf Team	

EMPLOYMENT

Identifies most significant places of work and de-emphasizes less important work

DEERE & COMPANY, INC. Student Intern, Summer 2006	CONGRESSMAN J. DENNIS HASTERT Volunteer in Computer Services, Fall 2005

Several years' experience in the restaurant business including supervisory positions.

ACCOMPLISHMENTS

Presents only selected accomplishments from various work and volunteer experience that relate to position sought

- ► Trained executives to create effective cross-cultural presentations.
- ► Developed online training program for executive use of GoToMeeting.
- ► Designed and developed a database to keep track of financial donations.
- ► Coded new screens and reports; debugged and revised screen forms for easier data entry.
- ► Provided computer support to virtual volunteers on election committee.

REFERENCES

Will gladly furnish personal and professional references on request.

concrete words that describe skills and accomplishments precisely. Instead of listing a course in comparative programming, you would list the precise languages compared, such as PHP, C#, and Java. Instead of saying you would like a job in information systems, you would name specific job titles such as systems analyst, network specialist, or application specialist. Using industry-specific terminology is highly recommended.

One way to identify the keywords in your field is by reading ads, listening to recruiters, and listening to your professors. Start building a list of words you find used repeatedly. From this list, choose those words most appropriate for the kind of work you want to do. Amplify your use of abbreviations, acronyms, and jargon appropriate to the work you want to do. In the early days of preparing scannable résumés, some experts recommended using a separate keyword section at the beginning of the résumé, loading it with all the relevant terms. Reportedly this technique improved the odds of the résumé being retrieved. If this helps you ensure that your résumé includes all the appropriate terms, you might still use it. However, today most résumé writers are well aware of the importance of using keywords and consciously work to integrate them into their résumés. This is especially true of those who use the hybrid résumés to cover both the face-to-face and scanning purposes in one document.

Choose Words Carefully. Unlike the traditional résumé, the scannable résumé is strengthened not by the use of action verbs but rather by the use of nouns. Informal studies have shown that those retrieving résumés from such databases tend to use precise nouns.

For the hybrid résumé, one you use in both face-to-face and scanning situations, you can combine the use of precise nouns with strong action verbs. The nouns will help ensure that the résumé gets pulled from the database, and the verbs help the face-to-face recruiter see the link to the kind of work you want to do.

Present the Information. Since you want your résumé to be read accurately, you will use a font most scanners can read without problem. Some of these fonts include Helvetica, Arial, Garamond, and Times Roman. Most scanners can easily handle fonts between 10 and 14 points. Although many handle bold, when in doubt use all caps for emphasis rather than bold. Also, because italics often confuse scanners, avoid them. Underlining is best left out as well. It creates trouble with descending letters such as *g* or *y* when the line cuts through the letter. In fact, you should use all lines sparingly. Also, avoid graphics and shading wherever possible; they just confuse the software. Use white paper to maximize the contrast, and always print in the portrait mode. The Manny Konedeng résumé in Figure 9–9 is a scannable résumé employing these guidelines.

Today companies accept résumés by mail, fax, and email. Be sure to choose the channel that serves you best. If a company asks for résumés by fax and email, it may prefer to capture them electronically. Others still prefer to see an applicant's ability to organize and lay out a printed page. Some employers give the option to the sender. Obviously, when speed gives you a competitive advantage, you'll choose the fax or email options. However, you do lose some control over the quality of the document. If you elect to print and send a scannable résumé, it is best not to fold it. Just mail it in a 9 × 12 envelope. For a little extra cost, you will help ensure that your résumé gets scanned accurately rather than wondering if your keywords were on a fold that a scanner might have had difficulty reading.

Digital Résumé

Transmitting a digital résumé involves making decisions about the receiver's preferences and capabilities for receiving them as well as leveraging the technology to present you in the best possible light. These documents range from low-end plain text

- Use keywords common to those an employer would use to retrieve your résumé.

- Use precise nouns on the scannable résumé.

- Use both precise nouns and action verbs in the hybrid résumé.

- Be sure the font you use can be read easily by scanners.

- Send your résumé by the channel that serves you best.

- Digital résumés enable you to leverage the technology.

Figure 9–9

Digital ASCII/Text Résumé for Use with Online Databases and Requests from Employers. Notice how the writer has expanded the length through some added text when no longer confined to one physical page.

Manny Konedeng
5602 Montezuma Road
Apartment 413
San Diego, California 92115
Phone: (619) 578-8058
Email: mkonedeng@yahoo.com

Avoids italics and underlines yet is arranged for both scanner and human readability

OBJECTIVE

A financial analyst internship with a broker-dealer where both analytical and interpersonal communication skills and knowledge are
valued

Uses all caps and spacing for enhanced human readability

EDUCATION

Bachelor of Science Degree in Business Administration, May 2007
San Diego State University, Finance Major

Deanís List
Current GPA: 3.32/4.00

Related Courses

Business Communication A
Investments A
Tax planning A-
Estate Planning A
Risk Management A
Business Law B+

All items are on one line and tabs avoided for improved comprehension

Computer Skills

Microsoft Office: Excel, Word, PowerPoint, Access
Web-based Applications: Surveymonkey, Blogger, GoToMeeting
Research Tools: SPSS, Internet Explorer

Accomplishments

Published in Fast Company Magazine and the San Diego Union Tribune
Won Greek scholarship
Finished in top five mathematics competition

WORK EXPERIENCE

Powerhouse Gym, Sales and Front Desk, Summer 2005 Modesto,
CA 95355

Sold memberships and facilitated tours for the fitness center
Listened to, analyzed, and answered customers inquires
Accounted for membership payments and constructed sales reports
Trained new employees to understand company procedures and safety
policies

Integrates precise nouns and industry-specific jargon as keywords

MCI, Relay Operator, Summer 2004 & 2003, Riverbank, CA 95367

Assisted over 100 callers daily who were deaf, hard of hearing, or
speech disabled to place calls
Exceeded the required data input of 60wpm with accuracy
Multitasked with typing and listening to phone conversations
Was Offered a promotion as a Lead Operator

Figure 9–9

Continued

Fo Sho Entertainment, Co-founder and Owner, Modesto, CA 95355

Led promotions for musical events in the Central Valley
Managed and hosted live concerts
Created and wrote proposals to work with local businesses
Collaborated with team members to design advertisements

UNIVERSITY EXPERIENCE

Information Decision Systems, Communications Tutor, Spring 2006,
San Diego, CA 92182
Critiqued and evaluated the written work for a business communica-
tion course
Set up and maintained blog for business communication research

Avoids graphics and extra lines

Kappa Alpha Order Fraternity, Recruitment Chairman, Fall 2005,
San Diego, CA 92115

Supervised the selection process for chapter membership
Individually raised nearly $1,000 for chapter finances
Organized recruitment events with business sponsors, radio sta-
tions, and special guests

ACTIVITIES AND SERVICE

Campus Leadership

Adds other relevant information since there is no physical page limit

Recruitment Chairman, Kappa Alpha Order Fraternity
Supervised all new member recruitment
Coordinated fundraisers for chapter finances
Organized recruitment events with business sponsors, radio sta-
tions, and special guests
Advocated Freshmen Summer Orientation and Greek life

Correspondent for External Chapter Affairs, Kappa Alpha Order
Fraternity

Communicated with chapter alumni and National Office to fulfill
chapter obligations

Upsilon Class Treasurer, Kappa Alpha Order Fraternity

Managed chapter budgets and expenditures

Several Interfraternity Council Roles

Member, Fraternity Men against Negative Environments and Rape
Situations
Co-chairman, Greek Week Fundraiser
Candidate, IFC Treasurer

Professional and Community Service

Member, Finance & Investment Society
Presenter, Peer Health Education
Marshal, SDSU New Student & Family Convocation
Sponsor, Muscular Dystrophy national philanthropy
Sponsor, Service for Sight philanthropy
Sponsor, Victims of Domestic Violence philanthropy
Sponsor, Camp Able philanthropy
Associated Studentsí Good Neighbor Program volunteer
Volunteer, Designated Driver Association
Volunteer, Beach Recovery Project

REFERENCES

Available upon request

Uses black on white contrast for improved scanning accuracy

files, to formatted word processor files, to full-blown multimedia documents and web pages.

While much of the content of a digital résumé is similar to that of the print résumé, two important changes should be made. The first is to delete all contact information except your email address. Not only can you lose control over the distribution of the document since digital files can be passed along easily and quickly, but your information could be added to databases and sold. Many experts recommend setting up a web-based email account that you use solely for your job search. Second, you should date the résumé. That way when an unscrupulous recruiter pulls it from a database and presents it to your boss two years later, you will be able to explain that you are truly happy working there and that the résumé is clearly dated before you went to work for your employer. These content changes should be made to all forms of the digital résumé.

The low-end digital résumé is usually a document saved as a plain (unformatted) ASCII or text file. You will use it when an employer requests that form. Sometimes you will send it as an attached file and other times you will place it inside your email. Since you can create it in your word processor and run a spell checker on it, you will probably want to cut and paste from it when you are completing online applications. It is also a good idea to test it out by sending it to yourself and viewing it with as many different email programs as you can. Then you will know if you need to shorten lines, add spacing, or make other changes to improve its readability.

To help ensure readability, you may want to send your résumé as a formatted attached file. Of course, you would only send it this way when you know the receiver welcomes getting résumés this way. You have a couple of choices of file format with attached files. You could send it in a standard word processing file format, one that is widely read by a variety of programs. Or you could send it as an RTF (rich text format) or PDF (portable document file). All these formats attempt to preserve the layout of your document. You also can help by using standard fonts most readers are likely to have installed or by embedding your font, so that the receiver's view is the one you intended.

The multimedia format can be a dramatic extension of the print résumé. Not only can you add links, color, and graphics, but you can also add sound, animation, and even video. If your receiver is like many others today, he or she is likely able to receive HTM files within the email program. You could use the email as a cover message with a link to a web page profile (an example is shown in the technology box in this chapter), or you could put the HTM résumé file inside the email. An HTM file allows you to display links to supporting files as well as include color, graphics, photos, and so on in your résumé. If used effectively, it could enhance your strengths and showcase your knowledge, creativity, and skills.

Since length is not the issue it is with the print résumé, the digital résumé should include all the detail needed to support your case. You also should take care to use the terms and keywords on which the document is likely to be searched, including nouns, buzzwords, jargon, and even acronyms commonly used in the field. You want your résumé retrieved when an appropriate position is available.

WRITING THE COVER MESSAGE

You should begin work on the cover message by fitting the facts from your background to the work you seek and arranging those facts in a logical order. Then you present them in much the same way that a sales writer would present the features of a product or service, carefully managing the appeal. Wherever possible, you adapt the points you make to the reader's needs. Like those of sales messages, the organizational plans of cover messages vary depending on whether the print or digital channel is chosen.

- Digital résumés are used in three basic file formats.

- (1) ASCII or text files;

- (2) word processor, RTF, and PDF files;

- (3) multimedia HTM files.

- Digital résumés are not constrained in length by a page size.

- Writing the cover message involves matching your qualifications with the job.

We can see, then, that using the Internet to recruit for managerial and non-managerial jobs offers many benefits. For example, turnaround times are considerably shorter than they are for traditional recruiting techniques. Also, the recruiters are sometimes able to recruit passive job candidates. Those who are not looking for another position are often more highly qualified than those who are. Furthermore, using Websites has turned out to be less expensive than other forms of job advertising.

C. Glenn Pearce, Virginia Commonwealth University

Tracy L. Tuten, Longwood College

C. Glenn Pearce and Tracy L. Tuten, "Internet Recruiting in the Banking Industry," *Business Communication Quarterly* 64. 1 (2001): 17.

Print Cover Letters

The following procedure (discussed in detail below) is used in most successful print efforts:

- Begin with words selected to gain attention appropriately and to set up the review of information.
- Present your qualifications, keeping like information together and adapting to the company and the job.
- Use good sales strategy, especially you-viewpoint and positive language.
- Drive for the appropriate action (request for interview, reference check, further correspondence).

- This plan for writing the letter has proved to be effective.

Gaining Attention in the Opening. As in sales writing, the opening of the cover message has two requirements: It must gain attention and it must set up the review of information that follows.

- Gain attention and set up the information review in the opening.

Gaining attention is especially important in prospecting messages (cover messages that are not invited). Such letters are likely to reach busy executives who have many things to do other than read cover messages. Unless the writing gains favorable attention right away, the executives probably will not read them. Even invited messages must gain attention because they will compete with other invited messages. Invited messages that stand out favorably from the beginning have a competitive advantage.

- Gaining attention in the opening makes the letter stand out.

As the cover message is a creative effort, you should use your imagination in writing the opening. But the work you seek should guide your imagination. Take, for example, work that requires an outgoing personality and a vivid imagination such as sales or public relations. In such cases, you would do well to show these qualities in your opening words. At the opposite extreme is work of a conservative nature, such as accounting or banking. Openings in such cases should normally be more restrained.

- Use your imagination in writing the opening. Make the opening fit the job.

In choosing the best opening for your case, you should consider whether you are writing a prospecting or an invited message. If the message has been invited, your opening words should begin qualifying you for the work to be done. They also should refer incidentally to the invitation, as in this example:

- An invited application might refer to the job and the source of the invitation.

Will an honors graduate in accounting, with experience in tax accounting, qualify for the work you listed in today's *Times*?

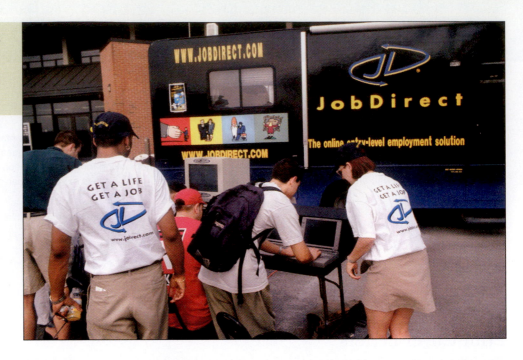

In addition to fitting the work sought, your opening words should set up the review of qualifications. The preceding example meets this requirement well. It structures the review of qualifications around two areas: education and experience.

- **You can gain attention by showing an understanding of the reader's operations.**

You can gain attention in the opening in many ways. One way is to use a topic that shows understanding of the reader's operation or of the work to be done. Employers are likely to be impressed by applicants who have made the effort to learn something about the company, as in this example:

> Now that Taggart, Inc., has expanded operations to Central America, can you use a broadly trained international business major who knows the language and culture of the region?

Another way is to make a statement or ask a question that focuses attention on a need of the reader that the writer seeks to fill. The following opening illustrates this approach:

- **You can stress a need of the reader that you can fill.**

> How would you like to hire a University of Cincinnati business major to fill in for your vacationing summer employees?

If you seek more conservative work, you should use less imaginative openings. For example, a message answering an advertisement for a beginning accountant might open with this sentence:

- **Use conservative openings for applications in a conservative field.**

> Because of my specialized training in accounting at State University and my practical experience in cost-based accounting, I believe I have the qualifications you described in your *Journal* advertisement.

- **Using an employee's name gains attention.**

Sometimes one learns of a job possibility through a company employee. Mentioning the employee's name can gain attention, as in this opening sentence:

> At the suggestion of Mr. Michael McLaughlin of your staff, I am sending the following summary of my qualifications for work as your loan supervisor.

- **Many opening possibilities exist, but avoid the old-style ones.**

Many other possibilities exist. In the final analysis, you will have to use what you think will be best for the one case. But you should avoid the overworked beginnings that were popular a generation or two ago such as "This is to apply for . . ." and "Please

Choice Lines Gleaned from Application Letters

consider this my application for . . ." Although the direct application these words make may be effective in some cases (as when answering an advertisement), the words are timeworn and dull.

Selecting Content. Following the opening, you should present the information about your qualifications for the work. Begin this task by reviewing the job requirements. Then select the facts about you that qualify you for the job.

- Present your qualifications. Fit them to the job.

If your application has been invited, you may learn about the job requirements from the source of the invitation. If you are answering an advertisement, study it for the employer's requirements. If you are following up an interview, review the interview for information about job requirements. If you are prospecting, your research and your logical analysis should guide you.

- You do this by studying the job. Use all available information sources.

In any event, you are likely to present facts from three background areas: education, experience, and skills and/or personal details. You also may include a fourth—references. But references are not exactly background information. If you include references, they will probably go on a separate reference sheet.

- Include education, experience, personal qualities, references.

How much you include from each of these areas and how much you emphasize each area should depend on the job and on your background. Most of the jobs you will seek as a new college graduate will have strong educational requirements. Thus, you should stress your education. When you apply for work after you have accumulated experience, you will probably need to stress experience. As the years go by, experience becomes more and more important—education, less and less important. Your personal characteristics are of some importance for some jobs, especially jobs that involve working with people.

- The emphasis each of these areas deserves varies by job. So consider the job in determining emphasis.

If a résumé accompanies the cover message, your message may rely on it too much. Remember that the message does the selling and the résumé summarizes the significant details. Thus, the message should contain the major points around which you build your case, and the résumé should include these points plus supporting details. As the two are parts of a team effort, somewhere in the message you should refer the reader to the résumé.

- Do not rely too heavily on the résumé. The cover message should carry all the major selling points.

Organizing for Persuasion. You will want to present the information about yourself in the order that is best for you. In general, the plan you select is likely to follow one of three general orders. The most common order is a logical grouping of the information, such as education, experience, and skills and/or personal details. A second possibility is a time order. For example, you could present the information to show

- In organizing the background facts, select the best of these orders: logical grouping, time, job requirements.

Figure 9–10

Cover Letter (A Conservative Request for Work). Using a company executive's name to gain attention, this message is conservative in style and tone.

Mildred E. Culpepper

2707 Green Street
Lincoln, NE 68505
Voice/Message: 402-786-2575
Fax: 402-594-3675
Email: mculpepper@credighton.edu

April 22, 2008

Ms. Marlene O'Daniel
Vice President for Administration
Continental Insurance Company
3717 Saylor Road
Des Moines, IA 50313-5033

Dear Ms. O'Daniel:

One of your employees, Victor Krause, suggested that I apply for the communications specialist position you have open. Here are a summary of my qualifications and a resume for your review. *(Gains attention with associate's name—opens door)*

Presently, I am in my fifth year as a communications specialist for Atlas Insurance. My work consists primarily of writing a wide variety of documents for Atlas policyholders. This work has made me a convert of business communication, and it has sharpened my writing skills. And, more importantly, it has taught me how to get and keep customers for my company through writing well. *(Employs conservative style and tone)*

(Shows the writer knows the skills needed for the job) Additional experience working with businesspeople has given me an insight into the communication needs of business. This experience includes planning and presenting a communication improvement course for local civil service workers, a course in business writing for area executives, and an online course in financial communication for employees of Columbia National Bank. *(Uses subtle you-viewpoint—implied from writer's understanding of work)*

My college training provided a solid foundation for work in business communication. Advertising and public relations were my areas of concentration for my B.S. degree from Creighton University. As you will see on the enclosed résumé, I studied all available writing courses in my degree plan. I also studied writing through English and journalism. *(References résumé)*

(Brings review to a conclusion—fits qualifications presented to the job) In summary, Ms. O'Daniel, both my education and experience have prepared me for work as your communication specialist. I know business writing, and I know how it can be used to your company's advantage. May we discuss this in person? You can reach me at 402-786-2575 to arrange a convenient time and place to meet. *(Moves appropriately for action)*

Sincerely,

Mildred Culpepper

Mildred E. Culpepper

Enc.

Figure 9–11

Cover Letter (Interest and Good Organization in a Response to an Advertisement). Three job requirements listed in an advertisement determined the plan used in this letter.

4407 Sunland Avenue
Phoenix, AZ 85040-9321
July 8, 2008

Ms. Anita O. Alderson, Manager
Tompkins-Oderson Agency, Inc.
3901 Tampico Avenue
Los Angeles, CA 90032-1614

Dear Ms. Alderson:

Uses reader's words for good attention gainer

Sound background in advertising ... well trained ... works well with others....

Demonstrates ability to write advertising copy through writing style used

These key words in your July 6 advertisement in the *Times* describe the person you want, and I believe I am that person.

Shows clearly what the writer can do on the job through interpretation

I have gained experience in every area of retail advertising while working for the *Lancer*, our college newspaper. I sold advertising, planned layouts, and wrote copy. During the last two summers, I gained firsthand experience working in the advertising department of Wunder & Son. I wrote a lot of copy for Wunder, some of which I am enclosing for your inspection; you will find numerous other examples on my blog at <http://janekbits.blogspot.com>. I also did just about everything else there is to do in advertising work. I enjoyed it, and I learned from it. This experience clearly will help me contribute to the work in your office.

Shows strong determination through good interpretation

In my major, I studied marketing with a specialization in advertising and integrated marketing communications. I completed every course offered in both areas. My honor grades show that I worked hard, especially on a project using a variety of media raising money for schools in Louisiana, Texas, and Mississippi's hurricane damaged areas. Understanding the importance of being able to get along well with people, I actively participated in Sigma Chi (social fraternity), the Race for the Cure (breast cancer), and Pi Tau Pi (honorary business fraternity). From the experience gained in these associations, I am confident that I can fit in well at Tompkins-Oderson.

Provides good evidence of social skills

Leads smoothly to action

As you can see from this description and the enclosed résumé, I am well qualified for your position in advertising. You can email me at janek@hotmail.com or call and text message me at 602-713-2199 to arrange a convenient time to talk about my joining your team.

Uses a clear and strong drive

Sincerely,

Michael S. Janek

Michael S. Janek

enclosures

Figure 9–12

Cover Letter. Straightforward prospecting letter targeted and sent as an attached file to a particular receiver.

12712 Sanchez Drive
San Bernadino, CA 92405
April 9, 2008

Mr. Conrad W. Butler
Office Manager
Darden, Inc.
14326 Butterfield Road
San Francisco, CA 94129

Dear Mr. Butler:

Gains attention with question

Can Darden, Inc., use a hardworking Grossmont College business administration major who wants a career in today's technology-intensive office? My experience, education, and personal qualities qualify me well for this work.

Sets up rest of letter tightly

My five years of work experience (see attached résumé) have taught me the major aspects of office work. For the past two years I have been in charge of payroll at Gynes Manufacturing Company. As the administrator of payroll, I have had to handle all types of office operations, including records management and general communication. Although I am happy at this job, it does not offer the career opportunity I see at Darden.

Justifies job search

Brings out highlights with review of experience

Complementing my work experience are my studies at Grossmont College. In addition to studying the prescribed courses in my major field of business office technology, I selected electives in Dreamweaver, QuickBooks, and professional speaking to help me in my career objective. And I believe I have succeeded. In spite of full-time employment through most of my time in college, I was awarded the Associate of Arts degree last May with a 3.3 grade point average (4.0 basis). But most important of all, I learned from my studies how office work should be done efficiently.

Interprets positively

In addition, I have the personal qualities that would enable me to fit smoothly into your organization. I like people, and through experience I have learned how to work with them as both a team player and a leader.

Sets up action and uses adaptation in concluding statement

I am well prepared for work in office administration, Mr. Butler. May I meet with you to talk about working for Darden? Please call me at 714-399-2569 or email me at jgoetz@gmail.com to arrange an interview.

Requests action clearly and appropriately

Sincerely,

Jimmy I. Goetz

Jimmy I. Goetz

Enc.

Figure 9–13

Cover Letter. (Persuasion in a Form Prospecting Letter). Written by a recent college graduate seeking her first job, this letter was prepared for use with a number of different types of companies.

MARY O. MAHONEY

May 17, 2008

Mr. Nevil S. Shannon
Director of Personnel
Snowdon Industries, Inc.
1103 Boswell Circle
Baltimore, MD 21202

Dear Mr. Shannon:

Effective attention-getting question

Will you please review my qualifications for work in your management trainee program? My education, work attitude, and personal skills qualify me for this program.

Good organization plan set-up

Good interpretation of education

My education for administration consists primarily of four years of business administration study at State University. The Bachelor of Business Administration degree I will receive in June has given me a broad foundation of business knowledge. As a general business major, I studied all the functional fields (management, marketing, information systems, finance, accounting) as well as the other core business subjects (communications, statistics, law, economics, production, and human resources). I have the knowledge base that will enable me to be productive now. And I can build upon this base through practical experience.

Skillfully handles lack of experience

As I am seeking my first full-time job, I must use means other than work experience to prove my work attitude. My grade point record at State is evidence that I took my studies seriously and that I worked hard. My 3.8 overall average (4.0 basis) placed me in the top 10 percent of the graduating class. I also worked diligently in student associations. My efforts were recognized by the special assignments and leadership roles you see listed in the enclosed résumé. I assure you that I would bring these work habits with me to Snowdon Industries.

Individually adapted

Good use of fact to back up personal qualities

Throughout college, I devoted time to the development of my personal skills. As an active member of the student chapter of the Society for the Advancement of Management, I served as treasurer and program chairperson. I participated in intramural golf and volleyball. And I was an active worker in the Young Republicans, serving as publicity chairperson for three years. All this experience has helped me to have the balance you seek in your administrative trainees.

Good ending message

These highlights and the additional evidence presented in the enclosed résumé present my case for a career in management. May I have an interview to continue my presentation? You can reach me at 301.594.6942 or marymahoney@yahoo.com. I could be in your office at your convenience to talk about working for Snowdon.

Clear request for action — flows logically from preceding presentation

Sincerely,

Mary O Mahoney

Mary O. Mahoney

Enclosure

1718 CRANFORD AVENUE • ROCKWELL, MD • 20854
VOICE/MESSAGE/FAX: 301.594.6942 • EMAIL: MARYMAHONEY@YAHOO.COM

a year-by-year preparation for the work. A third possibility is an order based on the job requirements. For example, selling, communicating, and managing might be the requirements listed in an advertised job.

● Use words that present your qualifications most favorably.

Merely presenting facts does not ensure conviction. You also will need to present the facts in words that make the most of your assets. You could say, for example, that you "held a position" as sales manager; but it is much more convincing to say that you "supervised a sales force of 14." Likewise, you do more for yourself by writing that you "earned a degree in business administration" than by writing that you "spent four years in college." And it is more effective to say that you "learned tax accounting" than to say that you "took a course in tax accounting."

● Use the you-viewpoint wherever practical.

You also can help your case by presenting your facts in reader-viewpoint language wherever this is practical. More specifically, you should work to interpret the facts based on their meaning for your reader and for the work to be done. For example, you could present a cold recital like this one:

> I am 21 years old and have an interest in mechanical operations and processes. Last summer I worked in the production department of a container plant.

Or you could interpret the facts, fitting them to the one job:

> The interest I have held in things mechanical over most of my 21 years would help me fit into one of your technical manufacturing operations. And last summer's experience in the production department of Miller Container Company is evidence that I can and will work hard.

● Avoid the tendency to overuse *I*'s, but use some.

Since you will be writing about yourself, you may find it difficult to avoid overusing I-references. But you should try. An overuse of *I*'s sounds egotistical and places too much attention on the often repeated word. Some *I*'s, however, should be used. The message is personal. Stripping it of all I-references would rob it of its personal warmth. Thus, you should be concerned about the number of I-references. You want neither too many nor too few.

Overall, you are putting your best foot forward, not only as a prospective employee but also as a person. Carefully shaping the character you are projecting is arguably just as important to the success of your cover message as using convincing logic.

● In the close, drive for whatever action is appropriate.

Driving for Action in the Close. The presentation of your qualifications should lead logically to the action that the close proposes. You should drive for whatever action is appropriate in your case. It could be a request for an interview, an invitation to engage in further communication (perhaps to answer the reader's questions), or an invitation to contact references. Rarely would you want to ask for the job in a first message. You are concerned mainly with opening the door to further negotiations.

● Make the action words clear and direct.

Your action words should be clear and direct. As in the sales message, the request for action may be made more effective if it is followed by words recalling a benefit that the reader will get from taking the action. The following closes illustrate this technique, although some may think the second may be overly aggressive in some circumstances:

> The highlights of my education and experience show that I have been preparing for a career in human resources. May I now discuss beginning this career with you? You can reach me at 727-921-4113 or by email at owensmith@att.com to talk about how I can help in your human resource work.

> I am very much interested in discussing with you how my skills will contribute to your company's mission. If I do not hear from you by Friday, April 22, I'll call on Monday to arrange a time for a mutually convenient meeting.

● The following two messages show bad and good application techniques.

Contrasting Cover Messages. Illustrating bad and good techniques, the following two cover messages present the qualifications of Jason L. Andrews, the job seeker described in the introductory situation at the beginning of the chapter. The first message follows few of the suggestions given in the preceding pages, whereas the second message is in general accord with these suggestions.

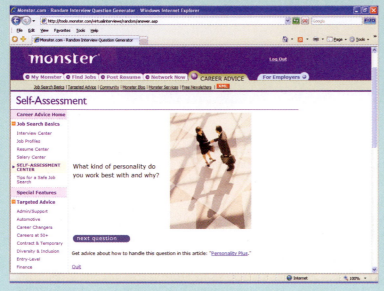

Used with permission of Monster.com.

The Web is a rich resource for help with interviewing. Your school's career center may have a website with interview schedules. Sites such as Monster.com and many of the other online job database sites offer tips on all aspects of interviewing. You can get ideas for questions to ask interviewers, techniques for staying calm, and methods of handling the telephone screening interview. They even include practice interactive virtual interviews with immediate feedback on your answers to questions as well as suggestions and strategies for handling difficult questions. The Monster site includes a planner listing a host of good common-sense tips from polishing your shoes to keeping an interview folder to keeping track of all written and verbal communication. Using these sites to help you prepare for interviews not only will help you feel more confident and interview more effectively, but also can help you evaluate the company as well.

A Bland and Artless Presentation of Information. The bad message begins with an old-style opening. The first words stating that this is an application are obvious and of little interest. The following presentation of qualifications is a matter-of-fact, uninterpreted review of information. Little you-viewpoint is evident. In fact, most of the message emphasizes the writer (note the *I*'s), who comes across as bored and selfish. The information presented is scant. The closing action is little more than an I-viewpoint statement of the writer's availability.

Dear Mr. Stark:

This is to apply for a position in marketing with your company.

At present, I am completing my studies in marketing at Olympia State University and will graduate with a Bachelor of Business Administration degree with an emphasis in marketing this May. I have taken all the courses in marketing available to me as well as other helpful courses such as statistics, organizational psychology, and ecommerce.

I have had good working experience as a host and food server, sales associate, and pollster. Please see details on the enclosed résumé. I believe that I am well qualified for a position in marketing and am considering working for a company of your size and description.

Because I must make a decision on my career soon, I request that you write me soon. For your information, I will be available for an interview on March 17 and 18.

Sincerely,

This cover message is dull and poorly written.

Skillful Selling of One's Ability to Work. The better message begins with an interesting question that sets the stage for the following presentation. The review of experience is interpreted by showing how the experience would help in performing the job sought. The review of education is similarly covered. Notice how the interpretations show that the writer knows what the job requires. Notice also that reader-viewpoint is stressed throughout. Even so, a moderate use of *I*'s gives the letter a personal quality and the details show the writer to be a thoughtful, engaged person. The closing request for action is a clear, direct, and courteous question. The final words recall a main appeal of the letter.

This better cover message follows textbook instructions.

Dear Mr. Stark:

Is there a place in your marketing department for someone who is well trained in the field and can talk easily and competently with clients? My background, experience, and education have given me these special qualifications.

All my life I have lived and worked with a wide variety of people. I was born and reared by working parents in a poor section of New York City. While in high school, I worked mornings and evenings in New York's garment district, primarily as a host and food server. For two years, between high school and college, I worked full time as a pollster for Olympia State University. Throughout my four years of college, I worked half time as a sales associate for The Gap. From these experiences, I have learned to understand marketing. I speak marketing's language and listen carefully to people.

My studies at Olympia State University were specially planned to prepare me for a career in marketing. I studied courses in advertising, marketing communication, marketing research, and ecommerce. In addition, I studied a wide assortment of supporting subjects: economics, business communication, information systems, psychology, interpersonal communication, and operations management. My studies have given me the foundation to learn an even more challenging practical side of marketing work. I plan to begin working in June after I receive the Bachelor of Business Administration degree with honors (3.7 grade point average on a basis of 4.0).

These brief facts and the information in my résumé describe my diligent efforts to prepare for a position in marketing. May I now talk with you about beginning that position? You can reach me at 917.938.4449 to arrange an interview to talk about how I could help in your marketing department.

Sincerely,

Email Cover Message

An email cover message can take different forms depending on the document file format it introduces. Like other email messages, it needs a clear subject line; like print cover messages, it needs a formal salutation and closing. And its purpose is still to highlight your qualifications for the particular job you are applying for. While it could be identical to one you might create for print, most readers prefer shorter documents onscreen. And since the length of the résumé is not limited by page size, much of the supporting detail could be included there. The primary job of the email cover message is to identify the job, highlight the applicant's strengths, and invite the reader to review the résumé.

Notice how the solicited cover message below quickly gains the reader's attention in the opening, highlights the skills in the body, and calls for action in the close.

To: Kate Troy <kate_troy@thankyoutoo.com>
From: Megan Adami <mmadami@msn.com>
Date: October 1, 2008
Subject: Web Design Intern Position

Dear Ms. Troy:

Yesterday my advisor here at Brown University, Dr. Payton Kubicek, suggested that I contact you about the summer intern position in web design you recently announced.

At Brown I have taken courses that have given me a good understanding of both the design aspects as well as the marketing functions that a good website needs. Additionally, several of my course projects involved working with successful web-based businesses, analyzing the strengths and weaknesses of their business models.

I would enjoy applying some of these skills in a successful site targeted at the high-end retail customers that Thankyoutoo.com attracts. You will see from my web page profile at http://www.meganadami.com/ that my design skills complement those on your company's website, allowing me to contribute almost immediately. Please let me know as soon as possible when we can talk further about this summer position.

Sincerely,

Megan Adami
mmadami@msn.com

HANDLING THE INTERVIEW

Your initial contact with a prospective employer can be by mail, email, phone, or a personal (face-to-face) visit. Even if you contact the employer by mail, a successful application will eventually involve a personal visit—or an *interview*, as we will call it. Sometimes, before inviting candidates to a formal interview session, recruiters use phone interviews for preliminary screening. Much of the preceding parts of this chapter concerned the mail contact. Now our interest centers on the interview.

- Apply for the job—by mail, email, phone, or visit.

In a sense, the interview is the key to the success of the application—the "final examination," so to speak. You should carefully prepare for the interview, as the job may be lost or won in it. The following review of employment interview highlights should help you understand how to deal with the interview in your job search. You will find additional information about interviewing in the resource links on the textbook website.

- The interview is essential. For it, follow these procedures:

Investigating the Company

Before arriving for an interview, you should learn what you can about the company: its products or services, its personnel, its business practices, its current activities, its management. Such knowledge will help you talk knowingly with the interviewer. And perhaps more important, the interviewer is likely to be impressed by the fact that you took the time to investigate the company. That effort might even give you a competitive advantage.

- (1) Find out what you can about the employer.

Making a Good Appearance

How you look to the interviewer is a part of your message. Thus, you should work to present just the right image. Interviewers differ to some extent on what that image is, but you would be wise to present a conservative appearance. This means avoiding faddish, offbeat styles, preferring the conservative, conventional business colors such as black, brown, navy, and gray. Remember that the interviewer wants to know whether you fit into the role you are seeking. You should appear to look like you want the job.

- (2) Make a good appearance (conservative dress and grooming).

Some may argue that such an insistence on conformity in dress and grooming infringes on one's personal freedom. Perhaps it does. We will even concede that employers should not force such biases on you. But you will have to be realistic if you want a successful career. If the people who can determine your future have fixed views on matters of dress and grooming, it is good business sense to respect those views.

Anticipating Questions and Preparing Answers

- (3) Anticipate the questions; plan the answers.

You should be able to anticipate some of the questions the interviewer will ask. Questions about your education (courses, grades, honors, and such) are usually asked. So are questions about work experience, interests, career goals, location preferences, and activities in organizations. You should prepare answers to these questions in advance. Your answers will then be thorough and correct, and your words will display poise and confidence. Your preparation will also reflect your interest.

"You walk the walk and talk the talk. We need someone who can also blog the blog!"

In addition to general questions, interviewers often ask more complicated ones. Some of these are designed to test you—to learn your views, your interests, and your ability to deal with difficult problems. Others seek more specific information about your ability to handle the job in question. Although such questions are difficult to anticipate, you should be aware that they are likely to be asked. Following are questions of this kind that one experienced interviewer asks:

What can you do for us?

Would you be willing to relocate? To travel?

Do you prefer to work with people or alone?

How well has your performance in the classroom prepared you for this job?

What do you expect to be doing in 10 years? In 20 years?

What income goals do you have for those years (10 and 20 years ahead)?

Why should I rank you above the others I am interviewing?

Why did you choose _____ for your career?

How do you feel about working overtime? Nights? Weekends?

Did you do the best work you are capable of in college?

Is your college record a good measure of how you will perform on the job?

What are the qualities of the ideal boss?

What have you done that shows leadership potential? Teamwork potential?

What are your beginning salary expectations?

Sometimes interviewers will throw in tough or illegal questions to test your poise. These are naturally stressful, but being prepared for these kinds of questions will keep you cool and collected.[2] Here are some examples:

● tough questions,

What is your greatest weakness?

With hindsight, how could you have improved your progress?

What kind of decisions are most difficult for you?

What is the worst thing you have heard about this company?

See this pen I'm holding? Sell it to me.

Tell me about a time when you put your foot in your mouth.

What kinds of people do you find it difficult to deal with?

What religion do you practice?

● illegal questions,

How old are you?

Are you married?

Do you plan to have children?

If you get through these types of questions, some brainteasers or puzzles may be thrown your way. Microsoft often gets credit for starting this trend because the company used it extensively in attempting to hire only the best and brightest employees. Other companies soon followed, often creating their own versions of some of these questions or creating some tougher ones of their own. Many of these questions do not have a right answer; rather, they are designed to elicit an applicant's thinking, logic, and creativity skills. In answering them, be sure that you reason aloud rather than sitting there silently so that you can show you are thinking. Feel free to make assumptions as well as to supply needed information. Giving a good answer the interviewer has not heard before is often a good strategy. Here are some real questions that have been asked in interviews by Microsoft and other companies:[3]

● brainteaser or critical thinking questions,

---

[2] Martin Yate, *Knock'em Dead 2006* (Avon, MA: Adams Media Corp., 2006) 205–32.

[3] William Poundstone, *How Would You Move Mount Fuji?: Microsoft's Cult of the Puzzle: How the World's Smartest Companies Select the Most Creative Thinkers* (Boston, MA: Little, Brown and Company, 2003) 80–6, 118–20.

Why are manhole covers round?

Why do mirrors reverse right and left instead of up and down?

How many piano tuners are there in the world?

How many times a day do a clock's hands overlap?

Design a spice rack for a blind person.

Why are beer cans tapered at the top and bottom?

You have eight coins, and one of them is lighter than the others. Find the light coin in two weighings of a pan balance.

- and behavioral questions.

Recently, the behavioral interview style has become popular with campus recruiters. Rather than just determining your qualifications for the job, interviewers are attempting to verify if you can do the work. They ask questions about current situations because how you behave now is likely to transfer to similar situations in another job. Here are a few examples of behavioral questions:

What major problem have you faced in group projects and how have you dealt with it?

Do you tend more toward following the rules or toward stretching them?

What do you think your performance review will say one year from now?

For more practice preparing for questions, check the resource links on the textbook website.

Putting Yourself at Ease

- (4) Be at ease—calm, collected, confident.

Perhaps it is easier to say than to do, but you should be at ease throughout the interview. Remember that you are being inspected and that the interviewer should see a calm and collected person. How to appear calm and collected is not easy to explain. Certainly, it involves talking in a clear and strong voice. It also involves controlling your facial expressions and body movements. Developing such controls requires self-discipline—working at it. You may find it helpful to convince yourself that the stress experienced during an interview is normal. Or you may find it helpful to look at the situation realistically—as merely a conversation between two human beings. Other approaches may work better for you. Use whatever approaches work. Your goal is to control your emotions so that you present the best possible appearance to the interviewer.

Helping to Control the Dialogue

- (5) Help bring out the questions that show your qualifications.

Just answering the questions asked is often not enough. Not only are you being evaluated, but you are evaluating others as well. The questions you ask and the comments you play off them should bring up what you want the interviewer to know about you. Your self-analysis revealed the strong points in your background. Now you should make certain that those points come out in the interview.

- Here are some examples of how to do it.

How to bring up points about you that the interviewer does not ask is a matter for your imagination. For example, a student seeking a job in advertising believed that a certain class project should be brought to the interviewer's attention. So she asked, "Do you attach any importance to business plans written as class projects in your evaluation?" The anticipated affirmative answer allowed her to show her successful project. For another example, a student who wanted to bring out his knowledge of the prospective employer's operations did so with this question: "Will your company's expansion in the Bakersfield area create new job opportunities there?" How many questions of this sort you should ask will depend on your need to supplement your interviewer's questioning. You might also want to ask questions to determine if the company is a good fit for you such as "How would you describe the work environment?" Your goal should be to make certain that both the interviewer and you get all the information you consider important.

Some Quotes on Thank-you Notes by Today's Businesspeople

Technology has changed many aspects of communication in the business world today. Email, voicemail and the Internet have reduced the amount of personal interaction among professionals in the business environment. Writing a personal "thank you" note is an effective way to differentiate yourself and make a positive impact with your supervisors, co-workers and clients.

Pam Bettencourt, Regional Human Resources Manager
Moore Wallace, Inc.

Sending thank-you notes to each person a student interviews with is very important. It demonstrates appreciation and consideration for the hospitality extended to the student and is also an indication of how he or she will treat the employer's customers, if hired. The interviewer is most likely to remember such candidates for not only current opportunities, but for future opportunities as well, even if no offer is extended at that time.

Dee Thomas, College Relations & Diversity/Outreach
Administrator
Science Applications International Corporation (SAIC)

When you're serious about pursuing a career, your attention to the little things can make the difference in being perceived as a quality candidate. It can separate you from the crowd, elevating you from "good" to "great." For me, thank-you notes have always made the difference. I always appreciate receiving a thank-you card; it's a personal touch, a one-to-one acknowledgement above and beyond the rote. That attention usually carries over into a sales career, making the difference with customers. The little things mean everything.

Eric Mason, District Marketing Manager
Federated Insurance Company

FOLLOWING UP AND ENDING THE APPLICATION

The interview is only an early step in the application process. A variety of other steps can follow. Conveying a brief thank-you message by letter, email, or telephone is an appropriate follow-up step. It not only shows courtesy but also it can give you an advantage because some of your competitors will not do it. If you do not hear from the prospective employer within a reasonable time, it is appropriate to inquire by telephone, email, or letter about the status of your application. You should certainly do this if you are under a time limit on another employer's offer. The application process may end with no offer (frequently with no notification at all—a most discourteous way of handling applicants), with a rejection notice, or with an offer. How to handle these situations is reviewed in the following paragraphs.

- Follow up the interview with thank-you, status-inquiry, job-acceptance, and job-rejection messages.

Other Job-Search Messages

Writing a Thank-you Message. After an interview it is courteous to write a thank-you message, whether or not you are interested in the job. If you are interested, the message can help your case. It singles you out from the competition and shows your interest in the job.

Such messages are usually short. They begin with an expression of gratefulness. They say something about the interview, the job, or such. They take care of any additional business (such as submitting information requested). And they end on a goodwill note—perhaps a hopeful look to the next step in the negotiations. The following message does these things:

- Common courtesy requires that you write a thank-you message following an interview.

- The typical order for such a message is as follows: (1) expression of gratefulness, (2) appropriate comments fitting the situation, (3) any additional information needed, and (4) a goodwill close.

Dear Mr. Woods:

I genuinely appreciate the time you gave me yesterday. You were most helpful. And you did a good job of selling me on Sony Corporation of America.

As you requested, I have enclosed samples of the financial analysis I developed as a class project. If you need anything more, please let me know.

I look forward to the possibility of discussing employment with you soon.

Sincerely,

● When employers do not respond, you may write a follow-up message. It is ordered like the routine inquiry.

Constructing a Follow-up to an Application. When a prospective employer is late in responding or you receive another offer with a time deadline, you may need to write a follow-up message. Employers are often just slow, but sometimes they lose the application. Whatever the explanation, a follow-up message may help to produce action.

Such a message is a form of routine inquiry. As a reason for writing, it can use the need to make a job decision or some other good explanation. The following message is an example:

Dear Ms. Yang:

Because the time is approaching when I must make a job decision, will you please tell me the status of my application with you?

You may recall that you interviewed me in your office November 7. You wrote me November 12 indicating that I was among those you had selected for further consideration.

SAIC remains one of the organizations I would like to consider in making my career decision. I will very much appreciate hearing from you by December 3.

Sincerely,

● You may need to write to accept a job. Write it as you would a favorable response.

Planning the Job Acceptance. Job acceptances in writing are merely favorable response messages with an extra amount of goodwill. Because the message should begin directly, a yes answer in the beginning is appropriate. The remainder of the message should contain a confirmation of the starting date and place and comments about the work, the company, the interview—whatever you would say if you were face to face with the reader. The message need not be long. This one does the job well:

Dear Ms. Garcia:

Yes, I accept your offer of employment. After my first interview with you, I was convinced that Allison-Caldwell was the organization for me. It is good to know that you think I am right for Allison-Caldwell.

Following your instructions, I will be in your Toronto headquarters on May 28 at 8:30 AM ready to work for you.

Sincerely,

● To refuse a job offer, use the normal refusal pattern (indirect).

Writing a Message Refusing a Job. Messages refusing a job offer follow the indirect refusal pattern. One good technique is to begin with a friendly comment—perhaps something about past relations with the company. Next, explain and present the refusal in clear yet positive words. Then end with a more friendly comment. This example illustrates the plan:

Dear Mr. Chen:

Meeting you and the other people at Northern was a genuine pleasure. All that I saw and heard impressed me most favorably. I was especially impressed to receive the generous job offer that followed.

In considering the offer, I naturally gave some weight to these favorable impressions. Even though I have accepted a job with another firm, they remain strong in my mind.

Thank you for the time and the courteous treatment you gave me.

Sincerely,

Writing a Resignation. At some point in your career you are likely to resign from one job to take another. When this happens, probably you will inform your employer of your resignation orally. But when you find it more practical or comfortable, you may choose to resign in writing. In some cases, you may do it both ways. As a matter of policy, some companies require a written resignation even after an oral resignation has been made. Or you may prefer to give a written resignation following your oral announcement of it.

- Job resignations are made in person, by letter, or both.

Your resignation should be as positive as the circumstances permit. Even if your work experiences have not been pleasant, you will be wise to depart without a final display of anger. As an anonymous philosopher once explained, "When you write a resignation in anger, you write the best letter you will ever regret."

- Make the letter as positive as circumstances permit.

The indirect order is usually the best strategy for negative messages like a resignation. But many are written in the direct order. They present the resignation right away, following it with expressions of gratitude, favorable comments about past working experiences, and the like. Either approach is acceptable. Even so, you would do well to use the indirect order, for it is more likely to build the goodwill and favorable thinking you want to leave behind you.

- Preferably use indirect order, for the situation is negative.

The example below shows the indirect order, which is well known to you. It begins with a positive point—one that sets up the negative message. The negative message follows, clearly yet positively stated. The ending returns to positive words chosen to build goodwill and fit the case.

Dear Ms. Shuster:

Working as your assistant for the past five years has been a genuinely rewarding experience. Under your direction I have grown as an administrator. And I know you have given me a practical education in retailing.

- This illustration begins and ends positively.

As you may recall from our past discussions, I have been pursuing the same career goals that you held early in your career. So you will understand why I am now resigning to accept a store management position with Lawson's in Belle River. I would like my employment to end on the 31st, but I could stay a week or two longer if needed to help train my replacement.

I leave with only good memories of you and the other people with whom I worked. Thanks to all of you for a valuable contribution to my career.

Sincerely,

Continuing Job-Search Activities

Some authorities recommend continuing your job search two weeks into a new job. It provides insurance if you should discover the new job isn't what you expected. In any case, continuously keeping your finger on the pulse of the job market is a good idea. Not only does it provide you with information about changes occurring in your field, but it also keeps you alert to better job opportunities as soon as they are announced.

- Keeping your attention on the job market alerts you to changes and opportunities in the field.

- Update your résumé regularly to reflect new accomplishments and skills.

Maintaining Your Résumé. While many people intend to keep their résumés up to date, they just do not make it a priority. Some others make it easy by updating as changes occur. And a few update their résumés at regularly designated times such as a birthday, New Year's Day, or even the anniversary of their employment. No matter what works best for you, updating your résumé as you gain new accomplishments and skills is important. Otherwise, you will be surprised to find how easily you can lose track of important details.

- Keeping current in your professional reading brings many benefits.

Reading Job Ads/Professional Journals. Nearly as important as keeping your résumé updated is keeping up on your professional reading. Most trade or professional journals have job notices or bulletin boards you should check regularly. These ads give you insight into what skills are in demand, perhaps helping you choose assignments where you get the opportunity to develop new skills. Staying up to date in your field can be stimulating; it can provide both challenges and opportunities.

SUMMARY BY LEARNING OBJECTIVES

1 Develop and use a network of contacts in your job search.

1. A good first step in your job search is to build a network of contacts.
   - Get to know people who might help you later: classmates, professors, business leaders, and such.
   - Use them to help you find a job.

2 Assemble and evaluate information that will help you select a job.

2. When you are ready to find work, analyze yourself and outside factors.
   - Look at your education, personal qualities, and work experience.
   - From this review, determine what work you are qualified to do.
   - Then select the career that is right for you.

3 Identify the sources that can lead you to an employer.

3. When you are ready to find a job, use the contact sources available to you.
   - Check university career centers, personal contacts, advertisements, online sources, employment agencies, personal search agents, and web page profiles.
   - If these do not produce results, prospect by mail.

4 Compile print and electronic résumés that are strong, complete, and organized.

4. In your application efforts, you are likely to use résumés and cover messages. Prepare them as you would written sales material.
   - First, study your product—you.
   - Then study your prospect—the employer.
   - From the information gained, construct the résumé, cover message, and reference sheet.

   In writing the résumé (a listing of your major background facts), you can choose from two types.
   - The *print résumé*—traditional and scannable.
   - The *digital résumé*—ASCII, attached file, and HTM file.

   In preparing the traditional résumé, follow this procedure:
   - List all the facts about you that an employer might want to know.
   - Sort these facts into logical groups: *experience, education, personal qualities, references, achievements, highlights.*
   - Put these facts in writing. As a minimum, include job experience (dates, places, firms, duties) and education (degrees, dates, fields of study). Use some personal information, but omit race, religion, sex, marital status, and age.
   - Authorities disagree on whether to list references. If you list them, use complete mailing addresses and have one for each major job.
   - Include other helpful information: address, telephone number, email address, web page address, and career objective.

- Write headings for the résumé and for each group of information; use either topic or talking headings.
- Organize for strength in reverse chronological, functional/skills, or accomplishment/highlights approach.
- Preferably write the résumé without personal pronouns, make the parts parallel grammatically, and use words that help sell your abilities.
- Present the information for good eye appeal, selecting fonts that show the importance of the headings and the information.

In preparing the scannable résumé, follow these procedures:

- Include industry-specific keywords.
- Choose precise nouns over action verbs.
- Present the information in a form read accurately by scanners.

In preparing the electronic résumé, follow these procedures:

- Use the electronic format the receiver specifies or prefers.
- Remove all contact information except your email address.
- Consider adding a last updated notation.
- Extend the HTML format to include colors, graphics, video, and sound as appropriate.

5. As the cover message is a form of sales message, plan it as you would a sales message.

5 Write targeted cover messages that skillfully sell your abilities.

- Study your product (you) and your prospect (the employer) and think out a strategy for presentation.
- Begin with words that gain attention, begin applying for the job, and set up the presentation of your sales points.
- Adapt the tone and content to the job you seek.
- Present your qualifications, fitting them to the job you seek.
- Choose words that enhance the information presented.
- Drive for an appropriate action—an interview, further communication, reference checks.

6. Your major contact with a prospective employer is the interview. For best results, you should do the following:

6 Explain how you can participate effectively in an interview.

- Research the employer in advance so you can impress the interviewer.
- Present a good appearance through appropriate dress and grooming.
- Try to anticipate the interviewer's questions and to plan your answers.
- Make a good impression by being at ease.
- Help the interviewer establish a dialogue with questions and comments that enable you to present the best information about you.

7. You may need to write other messages in your search for a job.

7 Write application follow-up messages that are appropriate, friendly, and positive.

- Following the interview, a thank-you message is appropriate.
- Also appropriate is an inquiry about the status of an application.
- You also may need to write messages accepting, rejecting, or resigning a job.
- Write these messages much as you would the messages reviewed in preceding chapters: direct order for good news, indirect order for bad.

8. To learn information about the changes occurring in their field and to be aware of better job opportunities, you should

8 Maintain your job-search skills.

- Maintain their résumés.
- Read both job ads and professional journals.

1 "Building a network of contacts to help one find jobs appears to be selfish. It involves acquiring friendships just to use them for one's personal benefit." Discuss this view.

2 Maryann Brennan followed a broad program of study in college and received a degree in general studies. She did her best work in English, especially in the writing courses. She also did well in history, sociology, and psychology. As much as she could, she avoided math and computer courses.

　　Her overall grade point average of 3.7 (4.0 basis) placed her in the top 10 percent of her class. What advice would you give her as she begins her search for a career job?

3 Discuss the value of each of the sources for finding jobs to a finance major (*a*) right after graduation and (*b*) after 20 years of work in his or her specialty.

4 Assume that in an interview for the job you want, you are asked the questions listed in the text under the heading "Anticipating Questions and Preparing Answers." Answer these questions.

5 The most popular arrangement of résumé information is the three-part grouping: education, experience, and personal details. Describe two other arrangements. When would each be used?

6 Distinguish between the print résumé and the electronic résumé. When would each be most appropriate?

7 What is meant by *parallelism of headings?*

8 Describe the cover message and résumé you would write (*a*) immediately after graduation, (*b*) 10 years later, and (*c*) 25 years later. Point out similarities and differences, and defend your decisions.

9 What differences would you suggest in writing cover messages for jobs in (*a*) accounting, (*b*) banking, (*c*) advertising copy writing, (*d*) management, (*e*) sales, (*f*) consulting, and (*g*) information systems?

10 Discuss the logic of beginning a cover message with these words: "This is to apply for . . ." and "Please consider this my application for the position of . . ."

11 "In writing cover messages, just present the facts clearly and without analysis and interpretation. The facts alone will tell the employer whether he or she wants you." Discuss this viewpoint.

12 When should the drive for action in a cover message (*a*) request the job, (*b*) request an interview, and (*c*) request a reference check?

13 Discuss some of the advantages that writing a thank-you note to the interviewer gives the writer.

14 Identify some of benefits one gains from continuing to read professional journals for job information after one is employed.

1 Criticize the following résumé parts. (They are not from the same résumé.)

　a. Work Experience

2005–2008	Employed as sales rep for Lloyd-Shanks Tool Company
2002–2005	Office manager, Drago Plumbing Supply, Toronto
1999–2002	Matson's Super Stores. I worked part time as sales clerk while attending college.

　b. References

　　Mr. Carl T. Whitesides
　　Sunrise Insurance, Inc.
　　317 Forrest Lane
　　Dover, DE 19901-6452

Patricia Cullen
Cullen and Cullen Realtors
2001 Bowman
Dr. Wilmington, DE 19804

Rev. Troy A. Graham
Asbury Methodist Church
Hyattsville, MD 20783

D. W. Boozer
Boozer Industries
Baltimore, MD 21202

　c. Education

2004	Graduated from Tippen H.S. (I was in top 10 percent of class.)
2008	B.S. from Bradley University with major in marketing
2008 to present	Enrolled part time in M.B.A. program at the University of Phoenix

d. Qualifications

Know how to motivate a sales force. I have done it. Experienced in screening applicants and selecting salespeople.

Know the pharmaceutical business from 11 years of experience.

Knowledgeable of realistic quota setting and incentives.

Proven leadership ability.

2 Criticize these sentences from cover messages:

Beginning Sentences

a. Please consider this my application for any position for which my training and experience qualify me.

b. Mr. Jerry Bono of your staff has told me about a vacancy in your loan department for which I would like to apply.

c. I am that accountant you described in your advertisement in today's *Times-Record*.

d. I want to work for you!

Sentences Presenting Selling Points

e. From 2004 to 2008 I attended Bradley University where I took courses leading to a B.S. degree with a major in finance.

f. I am highly skilled in trading corporate bonds as a result of three years spent in the New York office of Collins, Bragg, and Weaver.

g. For three years (2005–2008) I was in the loan department at Bank One.

h. My two strongest qualifications for this job are my personality and gift of conversation.

Sentences from Action Endings

i. I will call you on the 12th to arrange an interview.

j. If my qualifications meet your requirements it would be greatly appreciated if you would schedule an interview for me.

k. Please call to set up an interview. Do it now—while it is on your mind.

CRITICAL THINKING PROBLEMS

Applications

1 You have successfully prepared yourself for the career of your choice, but the recruiters visiting your school have not yet offered you a job. Now you must look on your own. So by searching newspapers, online job databases, and company website announcements, find the best job for which you believe you are qualified. Write two cover messages that you might use to present your qualifications for this job: one for print presentation and one for email. Attach a copy of the job description to the messages. (Assume that a résumé accompanies the cover message.)

2 Write the résumé and reference sheet to accompany the message for Problem 1.

3 Project yourself three years past your graduation date. During those years, you have had good experience working for the company of your choice in the field of your choice. (Use your imagination to supply this information.)

Unfortunately, your progress hasn't been what you had expected. You think that you must look around for a better opportunity. Your search through the classified advertisements in your area newspapers, online, and in *The Wall Street Journal* turns up one promising possibility (you find it). Write a cover message that skillfully presents your qualifications for this job. (You may make logical assumptions about your experience over the three-year period.) For class purposes, attach the advertisement to your message.

4 Write the résumé and reference sheet to accompany the message in Problem 3.

5 Assume you are in your last term of school and graduation is just around the corner. Your greatest interest is in finding work that you like and that would enable you to support yourself now and to support a family as you win promotions.

No job of your choice is revealed in the want ads of newspapers and trade magazines. No career center has provided anything to your liking. So you decide to do what any good salesperson does: survey the product (yourself) and the market (companies that could use a person who can do what you are prepared to do) and then advertise (send each of these companies a résumé with a cover message). This procedure sometimes creates a job where none existed before; and sometimes it establishes a basis for negotiations for the "big job" two, three, or five years after graduation. And very frequently, it puts you on the list for the good job that is not filled through advertising or from the company staff. Write the cover message.

6 Write the résumé and reference sheet to accompany the message for Problem 5.

7 Move the calendar to your graduation date so that you are now ready to sell your working ability in the job market for as much as you can get and still hold your own. Besides canvassing likely firms with the help of prospecting messages and diligently following up family contacts, you have decided to look into anything that appears especially good in the ads of newspapers, online sources, and magazines. The latest available issues of large city publications and online services list the following jobs that you think you could handle.

Concentrate on the ad describing the job you would like most or could do best—and then write a cover message that will get you that job. Your message will first have to survive the filtering that eliminates dozens (sometimes hundreds) of applicants who lack the expected qualifications. Toward the end you will be getting into strong competition in which small details may give you the little extra margin of superiority that will get you an interview and a chance to campaign further.

Study your ad for what it says and even more for what it implies. Weigh your own preparation even more thoroughly than you weigh the ad. You may imagine far enough ahead to assure completion of all the courses that are planned for your degree. You may build up your case a bit on what you actually have. Sort out the things that line you up for the one job, organize them strategically, and then present them. Assume that you have attached a résumé.

a. *Office manager.* Currently seeking an office manager with initiative and flexibility for work in a fast-paced environment. Must have an outgoing personality and excellent communication skills and be a team player. Must be a "power user" of Word and Excel and have excellent Internet Search Skills. Knowledge of PowerPoint a plus. Some overtime expected during crunch periods. Send application materials to Chris Eveland at ceveland@qconline.com.

b. *Assistant webmaster.* Outstanding information technology, organizational, and interpersonal skills are needed for work on a company portal. Mastery of HTML and PHP, website design including graphic design, and client server technology is vital. Candidates also must possess excellent writing skills and the ability to effectively manage multiple projects while interfacing with company employees. A bachelor's degree with a background in information systems, marketing, or communications is required. Please send résumé to Megan Adami in Human Resources, 7165 North Main Street, (your city) , or fax it to 1-888-444-5047, or email it to megan_adami@cnet.com.

c. *Management trainee.* Named by *Fortune* magazine as one of the best places to work, this constantly expanding international company uses shared decision making and clear career paths so that employees can be productive and well rewarded. The challenging management training program requires candidates with good communications skills and high energy levels to be successful. Applicants must be computer literate and possess good interpersonal skills. Fax résumé to Don Zatyko at 1-888-399-2569.

d. *Staff accountant—payroll specialist.* We are looking for an accountant who desires to grow and move up the ladder. One should be motivated and willing to work in a fast-paced, multitasking environment. An associate's degree in accounting or finance is required. Additionally, the ideal candidate will be detail-oriented and able to meet deadlines. The job involves coordinating transfers of time worked data from time collection systems to payroll systems. Must have extended knowledge of Excel to compute withholdings and deductions, and must stay up to date on multiple state laws regarding payroll. Excellent compensation package and benefits. Apply to Carolynn Workman, accounting director, at carolynn_workman@adelphia.net.

e. *Staff accountant.* Successful candidate should have a B.S. in accounting and be proficient in QuickBooks and/or Excel. Would be responsible for performing account analysis for corporate accounts, assisting in consolidation of subsidiaries, and assisting in the preparation of annual and quarterly financial statements and financial reports for certain subsidiaries. Experience in the local environment of small business is desirable. If you are concerned with order, quality, and accuracy, please contact us by mail at Administrative Partner, Winship and Acord, P.C., 3013 Stonybrook Drive, (your city) , or by email at CWA@msn.com, or by fax at 1-217-399-2569.

f. *Network specialist.* We seek someone who can help deliver reliable, secure, and integrated networks. Must be able to bring together data and voice, WAN and LAN, fiber optics and wireless. Opportunity to learn newest technologies. Must have network certification such as MCP, MSCE, CNA, or CNE as well as a college degree or the equivalent experience. Requires excellent interpersonal and problem-solving skills. Experience with multiplatform computing is preferred. Will be expected to develop technical documentation and help establish network policies, procedures, and standards to ensure conformance with information systems and client objectives and strategy. Qualified applicants should send application documents to Robert Edwards at redwards@tyt.com.

g. *Technology analyst/consultant.* A fast-growing, highly regarded information technology assessment/consulting firm has a position for someone with expertise in client/server technology and Access. Must have excellent written communications and interpersonal skills. Vendor or user organization experience is highly desirable. Position is in the Bay Area. Send or fax your résumé to director of human resources at 500 Airport Road, Suite 100, (your city) , or 415-579-1022.

h. *Financial analyst.* An eastern-based investment firm is seeking an analyst to help with the evaluation of potential private equity investments and marketing of an existing and a new leveraged buyout fund. Should have a bachelor's degree from a good school and some experience in banking. Ideal candidates will have strong analytical capabilities and excellent computer skills, particularly spreadsheet, statistics, and database. Please fax résumé and cover letter to 203-869-1022 or send an email file to andrewwinston@fidelity.com.

i. *Trade show exhibits coordinator.* Position reports to the national sales manager and requires an individual who can work independently as well as part of a team. Professional telephone and computer skills are essential. Coordinator will maintain exhibitor contact databases, serve as an internal liaison to accounting and as an external liaison to vendors, and assist the on-site floor managers with various exhibitor-related responsibilities. Also must create exhibitor and attendee pre- and post-show surveys, collect data, and compile results. Trade show, association, or convention services experience is a plus. Some limited travel is expected. Send your résumé to lmiller@aol.com.

j. *Sales representative.* Major pharmaceutical company is expanding and looking for a sales representative in your area. Ideal candidate will have a successful record of sales experience, preferably in a business-to-business environment. Candidate must be well-versed in science and willing to continually learn about new products. Good knowledge of your area is highly desirable. Send your résumé to Jane_Adami@pfizer.com.

k. *Internet programmer.* Seeking a professional individual with experience in complex HTML/DHTML, strong web development, and a thorough understanding of ajax and PHP. Will design, write, modify, test, and maintain programs and scripts for a suite of server applications. Must be comfortable in a UNIX environment and possess some competency in SQL. Any experience with data warehousing would be a plus. Additionally, a qualified candidate should be a team player and self-motivated and possess excellent speaking and writing skills. Send all application documents to James.Andrews@menshealth.com.

l. *Marketing professional.* An international, rapidly growing consumer and trade publisher is seeking a self-motivated individual to help us reach our goal of doubling revenues by the year 2015. Ideal candidate will be an innovative, results-oriented professional willing to take the challenge of developing new markets. Should be good at packaging and repackaging information products for a large and expanding customer base. We are looking for those with some experience, creative writing talent, leadership skills, good communications skills, and strong interpersonal skills. Sell yourself through your cover message and résumé. Send a rich media text to Thomas McLaughlin, corporate vice president, Blackhawk Publishing at tjmclaughlin@blackhawk.com.

m. *Executive administrative assistant.* Vice president of a Fortune 500 manufacturing company seeks a highly competent, personable, organized, and dependable executive assistant. College degree desired. Must have excellent communication skills and thorough command of Internet navigation as well as word processing and presentation programs. In addition to basic business knowledge in accounting, economics, computer systems, finance, marketing, and management, an understanding of manufacturing in a global market would be desirable. Apply to director of human resources, P.O. Box 3733, (your city) .

n. *Graphic artist.* An employee-owned systems integration firm has an immediate need for a graphic artist. A bachelor's degree or an associate's degree with some experience desired. Must be proficient in PhotoShop and Illustrator, preferably in a Windows environment. Will prepare presentation and curriculum support graphics for government customer. Knowledge of project management software is a plus. Must have a work portfolio. Send résumé to the attention of KML, P.O. Box 900, (your city) .

o. *MIS specialist.* A local medical clinic is seeking an individual to manage a multisite, multiplatform computer system. Will be responsible for troubleshooting and coordinating problems in a Windows Vista environment and writing reports for management. A background in the health care/medical field combined with a good knowledge of computing is highly desirable.

Send résumé to (your city's name) Community Clinic, 1113 Henderson, (your city) or fax to 888-316-1026.

p. *Financial manager.* Multispecialty medical group (60 doctors) needs dedicated professional to work in providing financial planning and control in a growing organization. Join a team of financial specialists who bear responsibility for budgeting, general accounting, reimbursement, billing processes, and external reporting. Also responsible for development of long- and short-range financial goals and evaluation of their impact on strategic objectives and service mission. Degree in accounting/finance. Technical and team skills needed. Competitive salary and benefits package. Send letter and résumé to Mount Renault Medical Group, Box 14871, New York, NY 00146.

q. *Accountant.* A major real estate developer and property management company seeks an accountant. Must have a bachelor's degree in accounting. Will assist in financial reporting, tax preparation, cash flow projections, and year-end audit workpaper preparation. Mastery of Excel is required as are good communication skills. Some work experience in accounting is desirable; internship experience in an accounting or real estate environment is also desirable. Send your résumé and cover letter to TPL, P.O. Box 613, (your city) or email it to tpl@hotmail.com.

r. *Accounting majors.* Multinational consumer electronics firm seeks entry-level accountant for work in its controller's division. This person must be knowledgeable in financial and managerial accounting, internal auditing, budgeting, and capital investments. A multinational orientation, degree in accounting, and progress toward completion of CPA or CMA are a plus. Good communication skills (written and oral) and computer applications are required. Interested applicants should send letter and résumé to hrdirector@circuitcity.com.

s. *Bank examiner.* Federal Reserve Bank (nearest to your location) seeks career-oriented individuals. Persons hired will conduct on-site examinations of foreign banks operating in the U.S. in their lending activities, derivative products, bank operations, and financial information. Applicants must possess a bachelor's degree in accounting, finance, or economics. Evidence of cross-cultural sensitivity and foreign language proficiency is preferred. Travel 30–50 percent of the time. Excellent oral/written skills and U.S. citizenship required. Apply with letter, résumé, and reference sheets to Federal Reserve Board, Human Resources Department, (your region) .

t. *Proposal writer.* Global leader in high-technology asset management needs individual to prepare proposals for clients. Person selected must be a team player, thrive on high-tech challenges in fast-paced environment, and possess a state-of-the-art solution orientation. Excellent writing skills essential, along with BBA degree and experience with various hardware/software technologies. Job includes coordinating appropriate persons to define solutions and preparing program plans with cost estimation for clients. Send letter, résumé, and writing sample to Department SAS, (your city) .

u. *Assistant to operations manager.* Proven leader in the insurance industry seeks a highly motivated assistant to the operations manager of regional service center. Technical skills include proficiency in Internet use and Microsoft Word, Excel, PowerPoint, Access, and other database applications. College training preferred with good people skills. Person selected must be able to develop and maintain effective working relationships with internal and external customers. Apply to H R Department, Box 7438, (your city) or email to hrdirector@statefarm.com.

v. *Environmental safety and health assistant.* World leader in battery manufacturing is looking for an individual to work in safety and health area of production plant and distribution center. The successful candidate will need to have a business or environmental engineering degree and possess excellent organizational and people skills. Job duties involve administering health/safety programs, conducting training, and working with governmental agencies and regulatory personnel. Excellent opportunity for results-oriented individual seeking to work for a safe, attractive, and sanitary environment. Send cover message and résumé to Box SH, (your city) .

w. *Account executive for display advertising.* State business journal invites applications for career-oriented individuals. Qualified candidates must be college graduates (business preferred) and have work background to demonstrate reliability and commitment. Job scope involves selling display advertising in creative ways for specialized business print and online publications. Applicants should be of high energy, aggressive, and creative. Send applications to Drawer HBD, (your city) or salesmgr@busjrnl.com.

x. *Financial consultant.* Large communications services company needs qualified person to provide communication-based utility automation consulting to electric utilities. Must have comprehensive financial management knowledge. Perform economic analyses on current and proposed projects; assist in development of budgets; evaluate budget to actual performance; prepare monthly reports. Demonstrated knowledge of strategic planning, valuation techniques, accounting principles, and economic forecasts. Must communicate well orally and in writing. Email letter, résumé, and references to applications@alc.com.

y. *SEO Blogger.* New website is seeking a writer/intern for its search engine optimization (SEO) blog. This new site, which has free SEO tools, is attracting a growing worldwide interest. We are seeking two writers for three to five posts per week. Must have a background in SEO and be abreast of the field in order to write on current topics. Telecommuting is OK. Please send samples of your work or links to it along with your SEO credentials to jobs@nonbot.com.

z. *Corporate trainer.* Exciting opportunity is available for a professional with strong presentation skills, good organizational skills, and excellent written and oral communication skills. Successful trainer will be able to effectively communicate technical information to both technical and nontechnical users. Should be able to design classroom training modules and measure their effectiveness. Good time management and use of Outlook is required. Some travel to clients' sites may be required. Application documents including a sample PowerPoint presentation should be sent to Sharon Garbett, President, Sedona Training, P.O. Box 1308, Moline, Illinois 61266.

---

8 Write the résumé and reference sheet to accompany the message for Problem 7.

---

9 You are looking ahead to your graduation soon. You've decided to begin to look for jobs online. Tap into a system that you know posts jobs in your major or a corporate website that posts job openings. (See textbook website for links to some of these sites.) Browse through the jobs until you see one that appeals to you and for which you will be qualified when you graduate. Print (or save) a copy of the ad so you will have it handy when you write your résumé and cover messages. Address the points covered in the ad and explain that you learned about the position from a particular online system. Plan to send your résumé digitally, creating both an ASCII text and an HTM file.

---

10 Create a web page profile complete with links that provide supporting details. Take care that your design is easy to navigate as well as pleasing to view.

Anne Sweeney, President of Disney Channel Worldwide and President of ABC Cable Networks Group, began her television career at age 19 as a network page and as a researcher studying children who liked *Sesame Street* magazine. The research led her to enroll in Harvard's School of Education, where she learned the benefits of investigation for shaping both television programming and business strategy. Named by *Fortune* magazine as one of the most powerful women in business in 2005, Sweeney considers curiosity to be the most important factor in her success.

Research of "tween" viewers helped Disney add one million new subscribers per month for five years.

"We had been hearing from kids from the research we were conducting that there was an age group of kids that felt too old for Nickelodeon and too young for MTV. I'm always really interested in what's missing, so we probed deeper. We looked at a lot of lifestyle information, we looked at how kids spent their days, and at what time they came home from school. We took a very hard look at who they are and what was going on in their lives. [That research] really launched our live-action programming strategy."

Anne Sweeney, President of Disney Channel Worldwide and
President of ABC Cable Networks Group

chapter ten

Basics of Report Writing

LEARNING OBJECTIVES

Upon completing this chapter, you will be able to prepare well-organized, objective reports. To reach this goal, you should be able to

1   State a problem clearly in writing.

2   List the factors involved in a problem.

3   Explain the common errors in interpreting and develop attitudes and practices conducive to good interpreting.

4   Organize information in outline form, using time, place, quantity, factor, or a combination of these as bases for division.

5   Turn an outline into a table of contents whose format and wording are logical and meaningful.

6   Write reports that are focused, objective, consistent in time viewpoint, smoothly connected, and interesting.

7   Prepare reports collaboratively.

Report Writing

Introduce yourself to the subject of report writing by assuming the role of administrative assistant to the president of Technisoft, Inc. Much of your work at this large software company involves getting information for your boss. Yesterday, for example, you looked into the question of excessive time spent by office workers web surfing. A few days earlier, you worked on an assignment to determine the causes of unrest in one of the local branches. Before that assignment you investigated a supervisor's recommendation to change an evaluation process. You could continue the list indefinitely, for investigating problems is a part of your work.

So is report writing, for you must write a report on each of your investigations. You write these reports for good reasons. Written reports make permanent records. Thus, those who need the information contained in these reports can review and study them at their convenience. Written reports also can be routed to a number of readers with a minimum of effort. Unquestionably, such reports are a convenient and efficient means of transmitting information.

Your report-writing work is not unique to your job. In fact, report writing is common throughout the company. For example, the engineers often report on the technical problems they encounter. The accountants regularly report to management on the company's financial operations. From time to time, production people report on various aspects of operations. The salespeople regularly report on marketing matters. And so it is throughout the company. Such reporting is vital to your company's operations—as it is to the operations of all companies.

Writing to external audiences can also be critical to an organization's success. If the organization is a consulting firm, reports to the client may be its primary deliverable. If the company is publicly traded, it is required by law to publish financial reports to the government and to shareholders. Depending on the nature of its business, a company may have to write reports to various agencies about its impact on the environment, its hiring practices, or its compliance with quality standards.

Sometimes reports are written by individuals. Increasingly, however, they are prepared in collaboration with others. Even if one person has primary responsibility for a report, he or she will often need contributions from many people. Indeed, report writing draws on a wide variety of communication skills, from getting information to presenting it clearly.

This chapter and the following two chapters describe the structure and writing of this vital form of business communication.

How often you write reports in the years ahead will depend on the size and nature of the organization you work for. If you work for a very small organization (say, one with fewer than 10 employees), you will probably write only a few. But if you work for a midsize or larger organization, you are likely to write many. In fact, the larger the organization, the more reports you are likely to write. The explanation is obvious. The larger the organization, the greater is its complexity; and the greater the complexity, the greater is the need for information to manage the organization.

- Reports are vital to larger organizations.

The nature of the business can also influence the number and type of reports you will write. The Securities and Exchange Commission requires all publicly traded businesses to write certain financial reports at regular intervals. A consulting firm's whole business effort may be directed toward informational and advisory reports to its clients. A business performing work under government contracts will also have special reporting needs. The frequency with which you will write reports, and the kinds you will write, will depend on your employer. But you can be fairly certain that report writing will figure significantly in your business career.

- The nature of the business also determines how many and what kinds of reports are needed.

- Report writing is likely to be important in your career.

DEFINING REPORTS

You probably have a good idea of what reports are. Even so, you would be likely to have a hard time defining them. Even scholars of the subject cannot agree, for their definitions range from one extreme to the other. Some define reports to include almost any presentation of information; others limit reports to only the most formal presentations.

- A business report is an orderly and objective communication of factual information that serves a business purpose.

For our purposes, this middle-ground definition is best: *A business report is an orderly and objective communication of factual information that serves a business purpose.*

The key words in this definition deserve emphasis. As an *orderly* communication, a report is prepared carefully. Thus, care in preparation distinguishes reports from casual exchanges of information. The *objective* quality of a report is its unbiased approach. Reports seek to present facts. They avoid human biases as much as possible. The word *communication* is broad in meaning. It covers all ways of transmitting meaning: speaking, writing, drawing, and such. The basic ingredient of reports is *factual information.* Factual information is based on events, records, data, and the like. Not all reports are business reports. Research scientists, medical doctors, ministers, students, and many others write them. To be classified as a business report, a report must *serve a business purpose*.

This definition is specific enough to be meaningful, yet broad enough to take into account the variations in reports. For example, some reports (information reports) do nothing more than present facts. Others (analytical reports) go a step further by including interpretations, sometimes accompanied by conclusions. Recommendation reports go further yet, presenting advice for future action. There are reports that are highly formal both in writing style and in physical appearance. And there are reports that show a high degree of informality. Our definition permits all of these variations.

DETERMINING THE REPORT PURPOSE

Your work on a report logically begins with a need, which we refer to generally as the *problem* in the following discussion. Someone or some group (usually your superiors) needs information for a business purpose. Perhaps the need is for information only; perhaps it is for information and analysis; or perhaps it is for information, analysis, and recommendations. Whatever the case, someone with a need (problem) will authorize you to do the work. Usually the work will be authorized orally. But it could be authorized in a written message.

After you have been assigned a report problem, your first task should be to get your problem clearly in mind. Elementary and basic as this task may appear, all too often it is done haphazardly. And all too often a report fails to reach its goal because of such haphazardness.

The Preliminary Investigation

Getting your problem clearly in mind is largely a matter of gathering all the information needed to understand it and then applying your best logic to it. Gathering the right information can involve many tasks, depending on the problem. It may mean gathering material from company files, talking over the problem with experts, searching through print and electronic sources, and discussing the problem with those who authorized the report. In general, you should continue this preliminary investigation until you have the information you need to understand your problem.

Need for a Clear Statement of the Problem

After you understand your problem, your next step is to state it clearly. Writing the problem statement is good practice for several reasons. A written statement serves as a helpful touchstone, keeping you on track as you continue through the project. In addition, a written statement can be reviewed, approved, and evaluated by people whose assistance may be valuable. Most important of all, putting the problem in writing forces you to think it through.

The problem statement normally takes one of three forms: infinitive phrase, question, or declarative statement. To illustrate each, we will use the problem of determining why sales at a certain store have declined:

1. *Infinitive phrase:* "To determine the causes of decreasing sales at Store X."
2. *Question:* "What are the causes of decreasing sales at Store X?"

Report-Writing Practices and the Sarbanes-Oxley Act

Changes in the regulatory environment can have a significant impact on the kinds of reporting that companies must do. One of the most major changes in recent history was the adoption of the Sarbanes-Oxley Act in 2002.* The law, which applies to all publicly traded companies, is intended to prevent financial scandals like those involving Enron, Arthur Andersen, Tyco, and WorldCom and to restore investor confidence. It requires companies to submit periodic reports on their financial practices to outside audit committees and assessments of those practices to the Securities and Exchange Commission (SEC), beyond the financial reports they were already submitting (such as their annual 10-K reports). But chief financial officers are not the only ones writing more reports. Managers, office personnel, and information technology professionals also must do much more reporting on procedures and controls involving financial transactions and record keeping. And the process of bringing these companies into compliance has generated thousands of internal directives and reports.

You will not be able to predict all the kinds of reports you may be asked to write. At any moment, your company, its needs, or its environment may change. You must be ready to adapt with your problem-analysis, data-gathering, interpreting, and writing skills.

*For further information, see the Securities and Exchange Commission website at <http://www.sec.gov/about/laws.shtml#sox2002> and the Beginner's Guide website at <http://beginnersguide.com/accounting/sarbanesoxley/>.

---

3. *Declarative statement:* "Store X sales are decreasing, and management wants to know why."

You may use any of the three forms for stating the report problem. All of them should give a problem statement with equal clarity and with the same intended meaning.

- One form is not superior to the others.

One way to make sure you have the problem clearly in mind is to state it in one form (say the infinitive phrase) and then state it again in another form (say the question form). No differences in meanings should exist between the two problem statements. If there are differences, you should rethink the report problem for clarity before you proceed further in the report process.

- State the problem in several forms. The meaning should be the same.

Understand, though, that no matter how earnestly you've tried to frame the problem correctly, your conception of it may change as you continue with your research. As Chapters 1 and 5 point out, effective writing often involves a certain amount of revisiting earlier steps (*recursivity*). You may need to revise your conception of the problem as you gather more information. But a clear statement of your problem-solving purpose at any given point is essential, both to guide your research and to let others know where you are headed. It will also be an essential component of the introduction for your finished report and of other front matter intended to orient your readers (for example, the letter of transmittal and executive summary).

- You may need to revise your problem statement as you continue your research.

DETERMINING THE FACTORS

After stating the problem, you determine what needs to be done to solve it. Specifically, you look for the factors of the problem. That is, you determine what subject areas you must look into to solve the problem.

- Next, you should determine the factors of the problem.

Problem factors may be of three types. First, they may be subtopics of the overall topic about which the report is concerned. Second, they may be hypotheses that must be tested. Third, in problems that involve comparisons, they may be the bases on which the comparisons are made.

- The factors may be subtopics of the overall topic, hypotheses, or bases for comparison.

Use of Subtopics in Information Reports

If the problem concerns a need for information, your mental effort should produce the main areas about which information is needed. Illustrating this type of situation is

- Subtopics of the overall topic are the factors in information reports.

the problem of preparing a report that reviews Company X's activities during the past quarter. Clearly, this is an informational report problem—that is, it requires no analysis, no conclusion, no recommendation. It requires only that information be presented. The mental effort in this case is concerned simply with determining which subdivisions of the overall topic should be covered. After thoroughly evaluating the possibilities, you might come up with something like this analysis:

Problem statement: To review operations of Company X from January 1 through March 31.

Subtopics:

1. Production
2. Sales and promotion
3. Financial status
4. Computer systems
5. Product development
6. Human resources

Hypotheses for Problems Requiring Solution

- Hypotheses (possible explanations of the problem) may be the factors in problems requiring solution.

Some problems concern why something bad is happening and perhaps how to correct it. In analyzing problems of this kind, you should seek explanations or solutions. Such explanations or solutions are termed *hypotheses*. Once formulated, hypotheses are tested, and their applicability to the problem is either proved or disproved.

To illustrate, assume that you have the problem of determining why sales at a certain store have declined. In preparing to investigate this problem, you would think of the possible explanations (hypotheses) for the decline. Your task would be one of studying, weighing, and selecting, and you would brainstorm such explanations as these:

- For example, these hypotheses could be suggested to explain a store's loss in sales.

Problem statement: Sales at the Springfield store have declined, and management wants to know why.

Hypotheses:

1. Activities of the competition have caused the decline.
2. Changes in the economy of the area have caused the decline.
3. Merchandising deficiencies have caused the decline.
4. Changes in the environment (population shifts, political actions, etc.) have caused the decline.

In the investigation that follows, you would test these hypotheses. You might find that one, two, or all apply. Or you might find that none is valid. If so, you would have to advance additional hypotheses for further evaluation.

Bases of Comparison in Evaluation Studies

- For evaluation problems, the bases for evaluating are the factors.

When the problem concerns evaluating something, either singularly or in comparison with other things, you should look for the bases for the evaluation. That is, you should determine what characteristics you will evaluate. In some cases, the procedure may concern more than naming the characteristics. It also may include the criteria to be used in evaluating them.

- This illustration shows the bases for comparing possible sites for expansion.

Illustrating this technique is the problem of a company that seeks to determine which of three cities would be best for expansion. Such a problem obviously involves a comparison of the cities. The bases for comparison are the factors that determine success for the type of work involved. After careful mental search for these factors, you might come up with a plan such as this:

Problem statement: To determine whether Y Company's new location should be built in City A, City B, or City C.

Report writing requires hard work and clear thinking in every stage of the process. To determine the problem and to gather facts, you will need to consult many sources of information.

Comparison bases:

1. Availability of skilled workers
2. Tax structure
3. Community attitude
4. Transportation facilities
5. Nearness to markets

Each of the factors selected for investigation may have factors of its own. In the last illustration, for example, the comparison of transportation in the three cities may well be covered by such subdivisions as water, rail, truck, and air. Workers may be compared by using such categories as skilled workers and unskilled workers. Breakdowns of this kind may go still further. Skilled workers may be broken down by specific skills: engineers, programmers, technical writers, graphic designers, and such. The subdivisions could go on and on. Make them as long as they are helpful.

- The factors sometimes have factors of their own. That is, they also may be broken down.

GATHERING THE INFORMATION NEEDED

For most business problems, you will need to investigate personally. A production problem, for example, might require gathering and reviewing the company's production records. A sales problem might require collecting information through discussions with customers and sales personnel. A computer problem might require talking to both end users and programmers. A purchasing problem might require getting product information, finding prices, compiling performance statistics, and so on. Such a personal investigation usually requires knowledge of your field of work, which is probably why you were assigned the problem.

- The next step is to conduct the research needed. A personal investigation is usually appropriate.

Some business problems require a more formal type of research, such as an experiment or a survey. The experiment is the basic technique of the sciences. Business uses experiments primarily in the laboratory, although experiments have some nonlaboratory

- Experiments or surveys are sometimes needed.

OneNote Helps Writers Integrate Ideas from Diverse Sources

Microsoft's recently introduced OneNote brings the flexibility of a paper pad and the power of digital technology together. It allows writers to use pages as blank sheets, typing or writing on them, drawing or doodling on them, and pasting graphics, photos, text, and even sounds on them. Additionally, users can also open the new research tool introduced with Office 2003. This tool gives users access to a variety of standard and subscription reference services. Furthermore, it allows users to combine information from its new sticky note application, Side Step.

In the example you see here, the writer is beginning to compile a list of resources on graphics. The notes are on a page titled Resources in a Uses section within a Graphics folder. It reveals a photo and some text describing an upcoming publication by Edward Tufte that was pasted from a website, which the software documented with the pasting. The writer noted in digital ink that the publication date needs to be checked. Additionally, the writer is using the Research tool to search for information on JASC, a major graphics software company. OneNote allows writers to integrate easily a

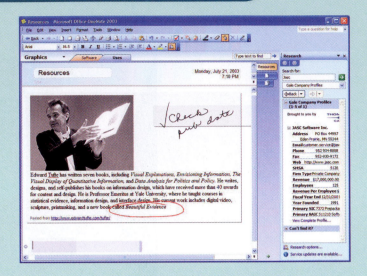

variety of information formats. Once data are in place, writers can grab chunks of information and reorganize them as needed. By giving writers a tool to integrate these diverse technologies, OneNote can help improve both a writer's efficiency and the quality of the end document.

---

applications in marketing. Surveys are more likely to be used in business, especially in marketing problems. If you are called on to use experiments or surveys, it will probably be because your training has prepared you to use them. If you should need these techniques in this course, you will find them summarized in Chapter 19.

- **Sometimes library research is used.**

In some cases, you may use library and online research to find the information you need. Perhaps you have a good working knowledge of the techniques of research. If you do not, you will find these techniques also summarized in Chapter 19. To present facts from published sources in reports, you will need to use still other techniques: constructing a bibliography, citing references, quoting, paraphrasing, and so on. These techniques are covered in Appendix E.

- **The Internet gives you access to many information sources. Quality may vary.**

With the computer, you can search for electronically stored information. By using the Internet, a worldwide collection of networks, you can connect to information sources throughout the world. For example, you can work with others at different locations, you can access databases, you can use larger computers to help in your research, or you can browse any number of library catalogs. As noted in Chapter 19, the Internet is a vital source for information gathering in business reports. Information quality varies widely on the Internet, however. You should make sure the sources you consult are reliable. You will find more information on evaluating sources in Chapter 19.

- **Apply the research techniques needed for the problem.**

In any event, your task is to apply whatever research techniques are required to get the information you need for your problem.

INTERPRETING THE FINDINGS

- **Next, interpret the information in light of your problem and your readers' needs.**

The next major stage of the report-writing process is to interpret the information you've gathered. Actually, you will have done a good bit of interpreting already by the time you reach this stage. You had to interpret the elements of the situation to come

Interpreting facts requires not only analytical skills and objective judgment but consideration for ethical issues as well.

up with your conception of the problem. You also had to interpret your data as you were gathering them to make sure that you were getting appropriate and sufficient information. But when your research is finished, you will need to come up with the interpretations that will guide the shape and contents of your report. To do this, keep both your problem and your readers in mind. Your findings will need to apply clearly to the given problem in order to be viewed as logical solutions. But they will also need to meet the readers' needs in order to be viewed as relevant and helpful. If you have kept your reader-based problem statement in mind while doing your research, making logical, reader-based analyses of your data should follow naturally.

Interpretation is obviously a mental process, and how you interpret your data will vary from case to case. Still, the following general advice can help you with this process.

Advice for Avoiding Human Error

The first advice is to avoid certain human tendencies that lead to error in interpretation. Foremost among these are the following:

1. *Report the facts as they are*. Do nothing to make them more or less exciting. Adding color to interpretations to make the report more interesting amounts to bias.

2. *Do not think that conclusions are always necessary*. When the facts do not support a conclusion, you should just summarize your findings and conclude that there is no conclusion. All too often report writers think that if they do not conclude, they have failed in their investigation.

3. *Do not interpret a lack of evidence as proof to the contrary*. The fact that you cannot prove something is true does not mean that it is false.

4. *Do not compare noncomparable data*. When you look for relationships between sets of data, make sure they have similarities—that you do not have apples and oranges.

- How you will interpret your data will vary specifically from case to case, but you can benefit from the following advice.

- Avoid human error by remembering these fundamentals:

- 1. Report the facts as they are.

- 2. Do not think that conclusions are always necessary.

- 3. Do not interpret a lack of evidence as proof to the contrary.

- 4. Do not compare noncomparable data.

You're right. This report does make you look like a fool.

SOURCE: Copyright, *USA Today*. Reprinted with permission.

5. Do not draw illogical cause–effect conclusions.

5. *Do not draw illogical cause–effect conclusions.* The fact that two sets of data appear to affect each other does not mean they actually do. Use your good logic to determine whether a cause–effect relationship is likely.

6. Beware of unreliable and unrepresentative data.

6. *Beware of unreliable and unrepresentative data.* Much of the information to be found in secondary sources is incorrect to some extent. The causes are many: collection error, biased research, recording mistakes. Beware especially of data collected by groups that advocate a position (political organizations, groups supporting social issues, and other special interest groups). Make sure the sources you uncover are reliable. And remember that the interpretations you make are no better than the data you interpret.

7. Do not oversimplify.

7. *Do not oversimplify.* Most business problems are complex, and all too often we neglect some important parts of them.

8. Make only those claims that your evidence can support.

8. *Tailor your claims to your data.* There's a tendency among inexperienced report writers to use too few facts to generalize far too much. If you have learned about a certain phenomenon, do not assume that your interpretations can automatically be applied to similar phenomena. Or if your research has revealed the source of a problem, do not assume that you can also propose solutions. Finding solutions can be a separate research project altogether. Make only those claims that are well supported by your evidence, and when you are not sure how strong to make them, use such qualified language as "may be," "could be," and "suggest."

Appropriate Attitudes and Practices

Adopt the following attitudes and practices:

In addition to being alert to the most likely causes of error, you can improve your interpretation of findings by adopting the following attitudes and practices:

1. Maintain a judicial attitude.

1. *Maintain a judicial attitude.* Play the role of a judge as you interpret. Look at all sides of every issue without emotion or prejudice. Your primary objective is to form the most reliable interpretations of the situation.

2. Consult with others.

2. *Consult with others.* It is rare indeed when one mind is better than two or more. Thus, you can profit by talking over your interpretations with others.

3. Test your interpretations.

3. *Test your interpretations.* While the ultimate test of your interpretations' validity will be how well they hold up in their actual application to a company problem, you can perform two tests to help you make reasonable inferences from your data.

Use the test of experience—reason.

First is the test of experience. In applying this test, you use the underlying theme in all scientific methods—reason. You ponder each interpretation you make, asking yourself, "Does this appear reasonable in light of all I know or have experienced?"

Second is the negative test, which is an application of the critical viewpoint. You begin by making the interpretation that is directly opposite your initial one. Next, you examine the opposite interpretation carefully in light of all available evidence, perhaps even building a case for it. Then you compare the two interpretations and retain the one that is more strongly supported.

Statistical Tools in Interpretation

In many cases, the information you gather is quantitative—that is, expressed in numbers. Such data in their raw form usually are voluminous, consisting of tens, hundreds, even thousands of figures. To use these figures intelligently, you first must find ways of simplifying them so that your reader can grasp their general meaning. Statistical techniques provide many methods for analyzing data. By knowing them, you can improve your ability to interpret. Although a thorough review of statistical techniques is beyond the scope of this book, you should know the more commonly used methods described in the following paragraphs.

Possibly of greatest use to you in writing reports are *descriptive statistics*—measures of central tendency, dispersion, ratios, and probability. Measures of central tendency—the mean, median, and mode—will help you find a common value of a series that appropriately describes a whole. The measures of dispersion—ranges, variances, and standard deviations—should help you describe the spread of a series. Ratios (which express one quantity as a multiple of another) and probabilities (which determine how many times something will likely occur out of the total number of possibilities) also can help you convey common meaning in data analysis. Inferential and other statistical approaches are also useful but go beyond these basic elements. You will find descriptions of these and other useful techniques in the help documentation of your spreadsheet and statistics software as well as in any standard statistics textbook.

A word of caution, however: Your job as a writer is to help your reader interpret the information. Sometimes unexplained statistical calculations—even if elementary to you—may confuse the reader. Thus, you must explain your statistical techniques explicitly with words and visuals when needed. You must remember that statistics are a help to interpretation, not a replacement for it. Whatever you do to reduce the volume of data deserves careful explanation so that the reader will receive the intended meaning.

ORGANIZING THE REPORT INFORMATION

When you have interpreted your information, you know the message of your report. Now you are ready to organize this message for presentation. Your goal here is to arrange the information in a logical order that meets your reader's needs.

The Nature and Benefits of Outlining

An invaluable aid at this stage of the process is an outline. A good one will show what things go together (grouping), what order they should be in (ordering), and how the ideas relate in terms of levels of generality (hierarchy). Although you can outline mentally, a written plan is advisable for all but the shortest reports. Time spent on outlining at this stage is time well spent, because it will make your drafting process more efficient and orderly. For longer reports, your outline will also form the basis for the table of contents.

If you have proceeded methodically thus far, you probably already have a rough outline. It is the list of topics that you drew up when planning how to research your problem. You may also have added to this list the findings that you developed when interpreting your data. But when it's time to turn your research plan into a report plan, you need to outline more deliberately. Your goal is to create the most logical, helpful pattern of organization for your readers.

- Use the negative test—question your interpretations.

- Statistics permit you to examine a set of facts.

- Descriptive statistics should help the most.

- Do not allow statistical calculations to confuse; they should help the reader interpret.

- After you know what your findings mean, you are ready to construct an outline.

- An outline helps you group and order the information and distinguish main from supporting points.

- When you reach the main organizing stage, you will probably have already done some of the work.

Software Tools Assist the Writer in Both Identifying Factors and Outlining

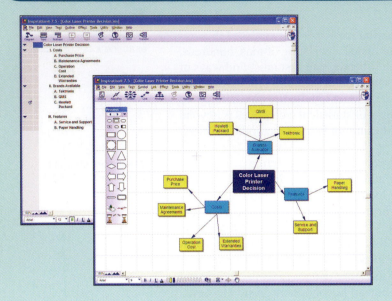

Inspiration is a conceptmapping tool aimed at helping business executives create and outline business documents. The example shown here demonstrates how individuals or groups can brainstorm the factors of a report that investigates which color laser printer a product design department should purchase. Using either the diagram or outline view (or both), a report writer would list as many ideas as possible. Later the items and relationships can be rearranged by dragging and moving pointers.

The software will update the outline symbols as changes are made. Users can toggle between the different views to work with the mode that works best for them. When ready to write, users can export the outline or diagram to Word or RTF format.

- Your outline should usually be written. It can later provide your headings and table of contents.

In constructing your outline, you can use any system of numbering or formatting that will help you see the logical structure of your planned contents. If it will help, you can use the conventional or the decimal symbol system to mark the levels. The conventional system uses Roman numerals to show the major headings and letters of the alphabet and Arabic numbers to show the lesser headings, as illustrated here:

Conventional System

- This conventional symbol system is used in marking the levels of an outline.

    I. First-level heading
      A. Second level, first part
      B. Second level, second part
        1. Third level, first part
        2. Third level, second part
          a. Fourth level, first part
            (1) Fifth level, first part
              (a) Sixth level, first part
    II. First-level heading
      A. Second level, first part
      B. Second level, second part
        Etc.

The decimal system uses whole numbers to show the major sections. Whole numbers followed by decimals and additional digits show subsections. That is, the digits to the right of the decimal show each successive step in the outline. Illustration best explains this system:

Decimal System

- This decimal system is also used.

    1.0 First-level heading
      1.1 Second level, first part
      1.2 Second level, second part
        1.2.1 Third level, first part

```
        1.2.2  Third level, second part
            1.2.2.1  Fourth level, first part
                1.2.2.1.1  Fifth level, first part
                    1.2.2.1.1.1  Sixth level, first part
    2.0  First-level heading
        2.1  Second level, first part
        2.2  Second level, second part
        Etc.
```

Bear in mind that the outline is a tool for you, even though it is geared toward your reader. Unless others will want to see an updated outline as you work, spend minimal time on its appearance. Allow yourself to change it, scribble on it, depart from it—whatever seems appropriate as your report develops. For example, you might want to note on your outline which sections will contain visuals, or to jot down a particularly good transition between sections that came to mind. The time to sweat over the outline's format and exact wording will be when you use it to create the headings and the table of contents for your finished report.

- The outline is a tool for you. Use it in any way that will help you write a good report.

Organization by Division

One methodical way to create an outline is to use the process of dividing the contents into smaller and smaller sections. With this method, you begin by looking over all your information. You then identify its major parts. This first level of division gives you the major outline parts indicated in Figure 10–1 by the Roman numerals (I, II, III, and so on).

- You may view organizing as a process of division. First, you divide the whole into parts.

Next, you find ways to subdivide the contents in each major section, yielding the second-level information (indicated by A, B, C). If practical, you keep dividing the contents, generating more levels. This method helps you divide your report into digestible chunks while also creating a logical and clear structural hierarchy.

- Then you divide the parts into subparts. You may subdivide further.

Division by Conventional Relationships

In dividing your information into subparts, you have to find a way of dividing that will produce approximately equal parts. Time, place, quantity, and factor are the general bases for these divisions.

- Time, place, quantity, and factor are the bases for the process of division.

Whenever the information you have to present has some time aspect, consider organizing it by *time*. In such an organization, the divisions are periods of time. These time periods usually follow a sequence. Although a past-to-present or present-to-past sequence is the rule, variations are possible. The periods you select need not be equal in duration, but they should be about equal in importance.

- When the information has a time basis, division by time is possible.

A report on the progress of a research committee illustrates this possibility. The period covered by this report might be broken down into the following comparable subperiods:

The period of orientation, May–July

Planning the project, August

Implementation of the research plan, September–November

The happenings within each period might next be arranged in order of occurrence. Close inspection might reveal additional division possibilities.

If the information you have collected has some relation to geographic location, you may use a *place* division. Ideally, this division would be such that the areas are nearly equal in importance.

- When the information is related to geographic location, a place division is possible.

A report on the U.S. sales program of a national manufacturer illustrates a division by place. The information in this problem might be broken down by these major geographic areas:

New England

Atlantic Seaboard

Figure 10–1

Procedure for Constructing an Outline by Process of Division

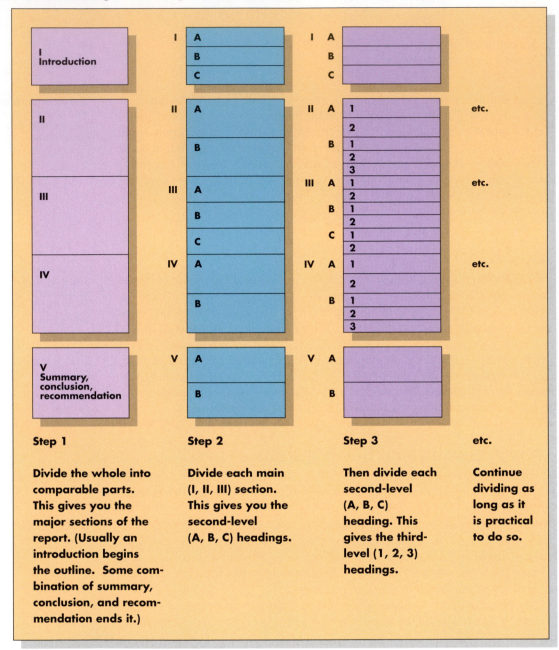

Step 1	Step 2	Step 3	etc.
Divide the whole into comparable parts. This gives you the major sections of the report. (Usually an introduction begins the outline. Some combination of summary, conclusion, and recommendation ends it.)	Divide each main (I, II, III) section. This gives you the second-level (A, B, C) headings.	Then divide each second-level (A, B, C) heading. This gives the third-level (1, 2, 3) headings.	Continue dividing as long as it is practical to do so.

South

Southwest

Midwest

Rocky Mountains

Pacific Coast

Another illustration of organization by place is a report on the productivity of a company with a number of customer service branches. A major division of the report might be devoted to each of the branches. The information for each branch might be broken down further, this time by sections, departments, divisions, or the like.

Quantity divisions are possible for information that has quantitative values. To illustrate, an analysis of the buying habits of potential customers could be divided by such income groups as the following:

- Division based on quantity is possible when the information has a number base.

Under $30,000
$30,000 to under $45,000
$45,000 to under $60,000
$60,000 to under $85,000
$85,000 to under $100,000
$100,000 and over

Another example of division on a quantitative basis is a report of a survey of men's preferences for shoes, in which an organization by age groups might be used to show variations in preference by ages. Perhaps the following divisions would be appropriate:

Youths, under 18
Young adults, 18–30
Adults, 31–50
Senior adults, 51–70
Elder adults, over 70

Factor breakdowns are less easily seen than the preceding three possibilities. Problems often have few or no time, place, or quantity aspects. Instead, they require that certain information areas be investigated. Such areas may consist of questions that must be answered in solving a problem, or of subjects that must be investigated and applied to the problem.

- Factors (areas to be investigated) are a fourth basis for dividing information.

An example of a division by factors is a report that seeks to determine which of three locations is the best for a new office for property management. In arriving at this decision, one would need to compare the three locations based on the factors affecting the office location. Thus, the following organization of this problem would be a possibility:

Location accessibility
Rent
Parking
Convenience to current and new customers
Facilities

Another illustration of organization by factors is a report advising a manufacturer whether to begin production of a new product. The solution of this problem will be reached by careful consideration of the factors involved. Among the more likely factors are these:

Production feasibility
Financial considerations
Strength of competition
Consumer demand
Marketing considerations

Combination and Multiple Division Possibilities

Not all division possibilities are clearly time, place, quantity, or factor. In some instances, combinations of these bases of division are possible. In a report on the progress of a sales organization, for example, the information collected could be arranged by a combination of quantity and place:

- Combinations of time, place, quantity, and factor are sometimes logical.

Areas of high sales activity
Areas of moderate sales activity
Areas of low sales activity

Some reports on sales of cyclical products might use the following combination of time and quantity:

Periods of low sales
Periods of moderate sales
Periods of high sales

- Multiple organization possibilities can occur.

Some problems can be organized in more than one way. For example, take the problem of determining the best of three locations for an annual sales meeting. It could be organized by site or by the bases of comparison. Organized by sites, the bases of comparison would probably be the second-level headings:

- This meeting problem is organized by place.

> Site A
> > Airport accessibility
> > Hotel accommodations
> > Meeting facilities
> > Favorable weather
> > Costs
> > Restaurant/entertainment options
> Site B
> > Airport accessibility
> > And so on
> Site C
> > Airport accessibility
> > And so on

Organized by bases of comparison, cities would probably be the second-level headings:

- Here, it is organized by factors (the bases of comparison).

> Airport accessibility
> > Site A
> > Site B
> > Site C
> Hotel accommodations
> > Site A
> > Site B
> > Site C
> Meeting facilities
> > Site A
> > Site B
> > Site C

- The second plan is better because it makes comparison easy.

At first glance, both plans appear logical. Close inspection, however, shows that organization by cities separates information that has to be compared. For example, you must examine three different parts of the report to find out which city has the best hotel accommodations. In the second outline, the information that has to be compared is close together. You can determine which city has the best hotel accommodations after reading only one section of the report.

Nevertheless, these two plans show that some problems can be organized in more than one way. In such cases, you must compare the possibilities carefully to find the one that best presents the report information.

From Outline to Table of Contents

- A table of contents requires rigorous attention to detail.

When you are ready to prepare the table of contents for your report, you will be, in essence, turning the outline that helped you write into an aid for the reader. Because it will be your public outline, the table of contents needs to be carefully formatted and worded.

True, you will probably design the table of contents late in the report-writing process. We discuss it here as a logical conclusion to our discussion of outlining. But in the event that others involved in the project want to see a well-prepared outline before your report is done, you can use the following advice to prepare that outline. Note also that what we say about preparing the headings for the table of contents also applies to writing the headings for the report sections. The two sets of headings, those in the table of contents and those in the report itself, should match exactly. Using the

Outline view in Word with the Table of Contents generator will assure that these are exact matches.

Formatting Decisions. Whatever format you used for your outline, you now need to choose a format that your reader will find instructive, readable, and appropriate. An *instructive* format is one that clearly indicates the hierarchy of the information. Rely mostly on form (font selection, size, style, and color as well as on effects) and placement to distinguish among the levels of your contents, as the sample in Chapter 12 shows. A *readable* format is one that uses ample vertical white space between topics and enables readers to see at a glance how the report is organized. Using leaders (dots with intervening spaces) between your topics and your page numbers can also enhance readability. An *appropriate* format is one that your reader expects. Most business readers nowadays view the conventional outlining system (Roman numerals, letters, and Arabic numbers) and the decimal system (as in 1.2.1) as adding unnecessary clutter to the table of contents. Instead, they prefer the use of form and placement to show them how the parts relate to each other. However, in the military and some technical environments, the decimal system is expected, and in other contexts, your readers may want the full numerals and letters of the conventional system. In our examples, we use format rather than numbering to indicate levels of information, but be sure to get a sense of what your particular readers will prefer.

- Make your format instructive, readable, and appropriate.

Topic or Talking Headings. In selecting the wording for your table of contents headings, you have a choice of two general forms: topic headings and talking headings. *Topic headings* are short constructions, frequently consisting of one or two words. They merely identify the topic of discussion. Here is a segment of a topic-heading table of contents:

- You may use topic or talking headings. Topic headings give only the subject of discussion.

Present armor unit
    Description and output
    Cost
    Deficiencies
Replacement effects
    Space
    Boiler setting
    Additional accessories
    Fuel

Like topic headings, *talking headings* (or *popular headings* as they are sometimes called) identify the subject matter covered. But they go a step further. They also indicate what is said about the subject. In other words, talking headings summarize the material they cover, as in this illustration:

- Talking headings identify the subject and tell what is said about it.

Operation analyses of armor unit
    Recent lag in overall output
    Increase in cost of operation
    Inability to deliver necessary steam
Consideration of replacement effects
    Greater space requirements
    Need for higher boiler setting
    Efficiency possibilities of accessories
    Practicability of firing two fuels

The following table of contents excerpt is made up of headings that talk:

Orientation to the problem
    Authorization by board action
    Problem of locating a woolen mill
    Use of miscellaneous government data
    Factors as bases of problem solution

Community attitudes toward the woolen industry
    Favorable reaction of all towns to new mill
    Mixed attitudes of all towns toward labor policy
Labor supply and prevailing wage rates
    Lead of San Marcos in unskilled labor
    Concentration of skilled workers in San Marcos
    Generally confused pattern of wage rates
Nearness to the raw wool supply
    Location of Ballinger, Coleman, and San Marcos in the wool area
    Relatively low production near Big Spring and Littlefield
Availability of utilities
    Inadequate water supply for all towns but San Marcos
    Unlimited supply of natural gas for all towns
    Electric rate advantage of San Marcos and Coleman
    General adequacy of all towns for waste disposal
Adequacy of existing transportation systems
    Surface transportation advantages of San Marcos and Ballinger
    General equality of airway connections
A final weighting of the factors
    Selection of San Marcos as first choice
    Recommendation of Ballinger as second choice
    Lack of advantages in Big Spring, Coleman, and Littlefield

This contrasting version uses topic headings:

Introduction
    Authorization
    Purpose
    Sources
    Preview
Community attitudes
    Plant location
    Labor policy
Factors of labor
    Unskilled workers
    Skilled workers
    Wage rates
Raw wool supply
    Adequate areas
    Inadequate areas
Utilities
    Water
    Natural gas
    Electricity
    Waste disposal
Transportation
    Surface
    Air
Conclusions
    First choice
    Alternative choice
    Other possibilities

● Headings making up a level of division should be parallel grammatically.

Parallelism of Construction. As a general rule, you should write headings at each level of the table of contents in the same grammatical form. In other words, equal-level headings should be parallel in structure. This rule is not just an exercise in grammar; its purpose is to show similarity. As you will recall from the discussion of conventional relationships of data, equal-level headings are divided consistently using time, place, quantity, factor, or combinations. You want to show consistently such equal-level divisions through parallel headings. For example, if the first major heading is a noun phrase, all other major headings should be noun phrases. If the first second-level heading under a major head is an *-ing* phrase, all second-level headings in this section should be *-ing* phrases. However, authorities also permit varying the form from one section and level to another; that is, the second-level heads in one section need to match, but they do not need to match the second-level heads in the other sections, and the third-level heads do not need to match the second-level heads.

The following headings illustrate violations of parallelism:

Programmer output is lagging (sentence).

Increase in cost of labor (noun phrase)

Unable to deliver necessary results (decapitated sentence)

You may correct this violation in any of three ways: by making the headings all sentences, all noun phrases, or all decapitated sentences. If you desire all noun phrases, you could construct such headings as these:

Lag in programmer output

Increase in cost of labor

Inability to deliver necessary results

Or you could make all the headings sentences, like this:

Programmer output is lagging.

Cost of labor is increasing.

Information systems cannot deliver necessary results.

Conciseness in Wording. Your talking headings should be the shortest possible word arrangement that also can meet the talking requirement. Although the following headings talk well, their excessive lengths obviously affect their roles in communicating the report information:

- Make the talking headings concise.

Personal appearance enhancement is the most desirable feature of contact lenses that wearers report.

The drawback of contacts mentioned by most people who can't wear them is that they are difficult to put in.

More comfort is the most desired improvement suggested by wearers and nonwearers of contact lenses.

Obviously, the headings contain too much information. Just what should be left out, however, is not easily determined. Much depends on the analysis the writers have performed on the material and what they have determined to be most significant. One analysis, for example, would support these revised headings:

Personal appearance most desirable feature

Difficulty of insertion prime criticism

Comfort most desired improvement

Variety of Expression. In wording of headings, as in all other forms of writing, you should use a variety of expressions. You should not overwork words, for repeating words too frequently makes for monotonous writing, and monotonous writing is not pleasing to the reader. The following outline excerpt illustrates this point:

- Repeating words in headings can be monotonous.

Oil production in Texas

Oil production in California

Oil production in Louisiana

As a rule, if you make the headings talk well, there is little chance of monotonous repetition. Since your successive sections would probably not be presenting similar

- Talking headings are not likely to be monotonous.

or identical information, headings really descriptive of the material they cover would not be likely to use the same words. The headings in the preceding example can be improved simply by making them talk:

Texas leads in oil production.
California holds runner-up position.
Rapidly gaining Louisiana ranks third.

As we say, the same guidelines that make for an informative, logical, and interesting table of contents also apply to the headings for your report.

WRITING THE REPORT

- You will already have done a lot of writing when you "start to write" your report.

When you write your report, you will have already done a good deal of writing. You will have written—and probably rewritten—a problem statement to guide you through your research. You will have collected written data or recorded your findings in notes, and you will have organized your interpretations of the data into a logical, reader-centered structure. Now it is time to flesh out your outline with clearly expressed facts and observations.

- In writing the report, communicate clearly and quickly.

- When drafting, get the right things in the right order. Do not strive for a perfect first draft.

When you draft your report, your first priority is to get the right things said in the right order. As Chapter 5 advises, you do not need to strive for a perfect draft the first time around. Understand that some pieces will seem to write themselves, while others will be much more difficult. Allow yourself to move along, stitching together the pieces. Once you have a draft to work with, you can perfect it later.

- Your finished report should communicate clearly and quickly.

When revising, let the advice in the previous chapters be your guide. As with all the business messages previously discussed, reports should communicate as clearly and quickly as possible. Your readers' time is valuable, and you risk having your report misread or even ignored if you do not keep a healthy respect for this fact in mind. Use both words and formatting to get your contents across efficiently.

- Also give it these characteristics: objectivity, time consistency, transition, and interest.

You can help your reader receive the report's message clearly by giving your report some specific qualities of well-written reports. Two critical ingredients are a reader-centered beginning and ending. Such characteristics as objectivity, consistency in time viewpoint, transition, and interest can also enhance the reception of your report. We review these topics in the following pages.

Beginning and Ending

- The beginning and ending of your report will probably be the most important and most frequently read parts.

Arguably the most critical parts of your report will be the beginning and ending. In fact, researchers agree that these are the most frequently read parts of report. Chapters 11 and 12 go into detail about beginnings and endings, but some general advice is in order here.

- Early on, your report should convey what you studied, how you studied it, and what you found out.

Whatever other goals it may achieve, the opening of your report should convey what problem you studied, how you studied it, and (at least generally) what you found out. Why? Because these are the facts that the reader most wants to know when he or she first looks at your report.

Here is a simple introduction that follows this pattern:

In order to find out why sales were down at the Salisbury store, I interviewed the manager, observed the operations, and assessed the environment. A high rate of employee turnover appears to have resulted in a loss of customers, though the deteriorating neighborhood also seems to be a contributing factor.

In a formal report, some brief sections may precede this statement of purpose (for example, facts about the authorization of the study), and there might be extensive front matter (for example, a title page, letter of transmittal, table of contents, and executive summary). What follows the core problem statement can also vary depending on the size and complexity of the report (for example, it may or may not be appropriate to go into more detail about the research methods and limitations, or to announce specifically how the following sections will be organized). But whatever kind of report you are writing, make sure that the beginning gets across the subject of the report, what kind of data it is based upon, and its likely significance to the reader.

Your ending will provide a concise statement of the report's main payoff—whether facts, interpretations, or recommendations. In a short report, you may simply summarize your findings with a brief paragraph, since the specific findings will be easy to see in the body of the report. In a longer report, you should make this section a more thorough restatement of your main findings, formatted in an easy-to-digest way. The gist ("so what did you find out?") and significance ("and why should I care?") of your report should come through loud and clear.

● Make sure the ending of your report provides efficient answers to the reader questions "what did you find out?" and "why should I care?"

Requirement of Objectivity

Good report writing presents facts and interprets them logically. It avoids presenting the writer's opinions, biases, and attitudes. In other words, it is objective. You can make your report objective by putting aside your prejudices and biases, by approaching the problem with an open mind and looking at all sides of every issue, and by fairly reviewing and interpreting the information you have uncovered. Your role should be much like that of a fair-minded judge presiding over a court of law. You will leave no stone unturned in your search for the best information and the most reasonable interpretations.

● Good report writing is objective.

Objectivity as a Basis for Believability. An objective report has an ingredient that is essential to good report writing—believability. Biased writing in artfully deceptive language may at first glance be believable. But if bias is evident at any place in a report, the reader will be suspicious of the entire report. Maintaining objectivity is, therefore, the only sure way to make report writing believable.

● Objective writing is believable.

Objectivity and the Question of Impersonal versus Personal Writing. Recognizing the need for objectivity, the early report writers worked to develop an objective style of writing. Since the source of bias in reports was people, they reasoned that objectivity was best attained by emphasizing facts rather than the people involved in writing and reading reports. So they tried to take the human beings out of their reports. The result was impersonal writing, that is, writing in the third person—without *I*'s, *we*'s, or *you*'s.

● Historically, objective writing has meant writing impersonally (no I's, we's, you's).

In recent years, some writers have questioned impersonal report writing. They argue that personal writing is more forceful and direct than impersonal writing. They point out that writing is more conversational and, therefore, more interesting if it brings both the reader and the writer into the picture. They contend that objectivity is an attitude—not a matter of person—and that a report written in personal style can be just as objective as a report written in impersonal style. These writers argue that impersonal writing frequently leads to an overuse of the passive voice and a dull writing style. While this last claim may be true, impersonal writing need not be boring. Any dullness that impersonal writing may have is the fault of the writer. As proof, one has only to look at the lively style of writers for newspapers, newsmagazines, and journals. Most of this writing is impersonal—but it is usually not dull.

● Recently, some writers have argued that personal writing is more interesting than impersonal writing and just as objective.

As in most controversies, the arguments of both sides have merit. In some situations, personal writing is better. In other situations, impersonal writing is better. And in still other situations, either type of writing is good.

● There is merit to both sides. You would be wise to do what your reader expects of you.

Your decision should be based on the facts of each report situation. First, you should consider the expectations of those for whom you are preparing the report. More than likely, you will find a preference for impersonal writing, for businesspeople have been slow to break tradition. Then you should consider the formality of the situation. You should use personal writing for informal situations and impersonal writing for formal situations.

● Good advice is to use personal style for routine reports and impersonal style for more formal reports.

An Example of Objective Reporting?

The story is told of the sea captain who once found his first mate drunk on duty. A man of the old school, the captain dutifully recorded the incident in his daily report to the ship's owners. He wrote: "Today First Mate Carlos E. Sperry was drunk on duty."

The first mate, unhappy about the incident, was determined to get revenge at the first opportunity. Some days later, his chance came. The captain was so ill that he could not leave his quarters, and First Mate Sperry was now in charge. At the end of the day it was Sperry's duty to write the daily report. This is what he wrote: "Today Captain Eli A. Dunn was sober."

The words were literally true, of course. But what a second meaning they carried!

Perhaps the distinction between impersonal and personal writing is best made by illustration.

Personal

Having studied the advantages and disadvantages of using coupons, I conclude that your company should not adopt this practice. If you use the coupons, you would have to pay out money for them. You also would have to hire additional employees to take care of the increase in sales volume.

Impersonal

A study of the advantages and disadvantages of using coupons supports the conclusion that the Mills Company should not adopt this practice. The coupons themselves would cost extra money. Also, use of coupons would require additional personnel to take care of the increase in sales volume.

Consistency in Time Viewpoint

- Keep a consistent time viewpoint throughout the report.

- There are two time viewpoints: past and present. Select one, and do not change.

- The past-time viewpoint views the research and the findings as past, and prevailing concepts and proven conclusions as present.

- The present-time viewpoint presents as current all information that can be assumed to be current at the time of writing.

Presenting information in the right place in time is essential to your report's clarity. Not doing so confuses the reader. Thus, it is important that you maintain a proper time viewpoint.

You have two choices of time viewpoint: past and present. Although some authorities favor one or the other, either viewpoint can produce a good report. The important thing is to be consistent—to select one time viewpoint and stay with it. In other words, you should view all similar information in the report from the same position in time.

If you adopt the past-time viewpoint, you treat the research, the findings, and the writing of the report as past. Thus, you would report the results of a recent survey in past tense: "Twenty-two percent of the managers *favored* a change." You would write a reference to another part of the report this way: "In Part III, this conclusion *was reached*." Your use of the past-time viewpoint would have no effect on references to future happenings. It would be proper to write a sentence like this: "If the current trend continues, 30 percent *will favor* a change by 2009." Prevailing concepts and proven conclusions are also exceptions. You would present them in present tense. For examples, you would write: "Solar energy *is* a major potential source of energy" and "The findings *show* conclusively that managers are not adequately trained."

Writing in the present-time viewpoint presents as current all information that can logically be assumed to be current at the time of writing. All other information is presented in its proper place in the past or future. Thus, you would report the results of a recent survey in these words: "Twenty-two percent of the managers *favor* a change." You would refer to another part of the text like this: "In Part III, this conclusion *is reached*." In referring to an old survey, you would write: "In 2003 only 12 percent *held* this opinion." And in making a future reference, you would write: "If this trend continues, 30 percent *will hold* this opinion by 2009."

Need for Transition

A well-written report reads as one continuous story. The parts connect smoothly. Much of this smoothness is the result of good, logical organization. But more than logical order is needed in long reports. As you will see in Chapter 12, a special coherence plan may be needed in such reports. In all reports, however, lesser transitional techniques are useful to connect information.

By *transition* we mean a "bridging across." Transitions are words or sentences that show the relationships of succeeding parts. They may appear at the beginning of a part as a way of relating this part to the preceding part. They may appear at the end of a part as a forward look. Or they may appear within a part as words or phrases that help move the flow of information.

Whether you use transitional words or a transitional sentence in a particular place depends on need. If there is a need to relate parts, you should use a transition. Because good, logical organization frequently clarifies the relationships of the parts in a short report, such reports may need only a few transitional words or sentences. Longer and more involved reports, on the other hand, usually require more.

Before we comment more specifically on transitions, we should make one point clear. You should not use transitions mechanically. You should use them only when they are needed—when leaving them out would produce abruptness. Transitions should not appear to be stuck in. They should blend naturally with the surrounding writing. For example, avoid transitions of this mechanical form: "The last section discussed Topic X. In the next section, Y will be analyzed."

Sentence Transitions. Throughout the report you can improve the connecting network of thought by the wise use of sentence transitions. You can use them especially to connect parts of the report. The following example shows how a sentence can explain the relationship between Sections A and B of a report. Note that the first words draw a conclusion for Section B. Then, with smooth tie-in, the next words introduce Section C and relate this part to the report plan. The words in brackets explain the pattern of the thought connections.

> [Section B, concluded] . . . Thus, the data show only negligible differences in the cost for oil consumption [subject of Section B] for the three models of cars.

> [Section C] Even though the costs of gasoline [subject of Section A] and oil [subject of Section B] are the more consistent factors of operation expense, the picture is not complete until the costs of repairs and maintenance [subject of Section C] are considered.

In the following examples, succeeding parts are connected by sentences that make a forward-looking reference and thus set up the next subject. As a result, the shift of subject matter is smooth and logical.

> These data show clearly that alternative fuel cars are the most economical. Unquestionably, their operation by gas and hydrogen and their record for low-cost maintenance give them a decided edge over gas-fueled cars. *Before a definite conclusion about their merit is reached, however, one more vital comparison should be made.*

(The final sentence clearly introduces the subsequent discussion of an additional comparison.)

> *. . . At first glance the data appear convincing, but a closer observation reveals a number of discrepancies.*

(Discussion of the discrepancies is logically set up by this sentence.)

Placing topic sentences at key points of emphasis is another way of using sentences to link the various parts of the report. Usually the topic sentence is best placed at the paragraph beginning. Note in the following example how topic sentences maintain the flow of thought by emphasizing key information.

- You should use transitions to connect the parts of the report.

- *Transition* means a "bridging across."

- Transitions should be used where there is a need to connect the parts of the report.

- They should be made naturally, not mechanically.

- For connecting large parts, transition sentences may be used.

- Use of topic sentences also helps improve thought flow.

Choice Lines Gleaned from Accident Reports Submitted to Insurance Companies

- Coming home, I drove into the wrong house and collided with a tree I don't have.
- The other car collided with mine without giving warning of its intentions.
- I thought my window was down, but found it was up when I put my hand through it.
- I collided with a stationary truck coming the other way.
- A pedestrian hit me and went under my car.
- The guy was all over the road. I had to swerve a number of times before I hit him.
- I pulled away from the side of the road, glanced at my mother-in-law, and headed over the embankment.
- I was having rear-end trouble when my universal joint gave way, causing me to have this accident.
- My car was legally parked as it backed into the other car.
- I told police that I was not injured, but on removing my hat, I found that I had a fractured skull.
- I was sure the old fellow would never make it to the other side of the road when I struck him.
- The pedestrian had no idea which direction to run, so I ran over him.
- The indirect cause of this accident was a little guy in a small car with a big mouth.
- The telephone pole was approaching. I was attempting to swerve out of the way when it struck my front end.
- I saw the slow-moving, sad-faced old gentleman as he bounced off the hood of my car.

The Acura accelerates faster than the other two brands, both on a level road and on a 9 percent grade. According to a test conducted by *Consumer Reports*, Acura reaches a speed of 60 miles per hour in 13.2 seconds. To reach the same speed, Toyota requires 13.6 seconds, and Volkswagen requires 14.4 seconds. On a 9 percent grade, Acura reaches the 60-miles-per-hour speed in 29.4 seconds, and Toyota reaches it in 43.3 seconds. Volkswagen is unable to reach this speed.

Because it carries more weight on its rear wheels than the others, Acura has the best traction of the three. Traction, which means a minimum of sliding on wet or icy roads, is important to safe driving, particularly during the cold, wet winter months. Since traction is directly related to the weight carried by the rear wheels, a comparison of these weights should give some measure of the safety of the three cars. According to data released by the Automobile Bureau of Standards, Acura carries 47 percent of its weight on its rear wheels. Nissan and Toyota carry 44 and 42 percent, respectively.

• Transitional words show relationships between lesser parts.

Transitional Words. Although the most important transition problems concern connection between the major parts of the report, transitions are needed between the lesser parts. If the writing is to flow smoothly, you will need to connect clause to clause, sentence to sentence, and paragraph to paragraph. Transitional words and phrases generally serve to make such connections.

Numerous transitional words are available. The following list shows such words and how you can use them. With a little imagination to supply the context, you can easily see how these words relate ideas. For better understanding, the words are grouped by the relationships they show between what comes before and what follows.

Relationship	Word Examples
Listing or enumeration of subjects	In addition
	First, second, and so on
	Besides
	Moreover
Contrast	On the contrary
	In spite of
	On the other hand
	In contrast
	However
Likeness	In a like manner
	Likewise
	Similarly
Cause–result	Thus
	Because of
	Therefore
	Consequently
	For this reason
Explanation or elaboration	For example
	To illustrate
	For instance
	Also
	Too

- This partial list shows how words explain relationships.

Maintaining Interest

Like any other form of writing, report writing should be interesting. Actually, interest is as important as the facts of the report, for communication is not likely to occur without interest. Readers cannot help missing parts of the message if their interest is not held—if their minds are allowed to stray. Interest in the content is not enough to ensure communication. The writing itself must be interesting. This should be evident to you if you have ever tried to read dull writing in studying for an examination. How desperately you wanted to learn the subject, but how often your mind strayed!

Perhaps writing interestingly is an art. But if so, it is an art you can develop by working at it. To develop this ability, you need to avoid the rubber-stamp jargon so often used in business and instead work to make your words build concrete pictures. You need to cultivate a feeling for the rhythmic flow of words and sentences. You need to remember that in back of every fact and figure there is life—people doing things, machines operating, a commodity being marketed. A technique of good report writing is to bring that life to the surface by using concrete words and active-voice verbs as much as possible. You also should work to achieve interest without using more words than are necessary.

Here a word of caution should be injected. You can overdo efforts to make report writing interesting. Such is the case whenever your reader's attention is attracted to how something has been said rather than to what has been said. Effective report writing simply presents information in a clear, concise, and interesting manner. Perhaps the purpose and definition of report-writing style are best summarized in this way: Report-writing style is at its best when the readers are prompted to say "Here are some interesting facts" rather than "Here is some beautiful writing."

- Report writing should be interesting. Interesting writing is necessary for good communication.

- Interesting writing is the result of careful word choice, rhythm, concreteness—in fact, all the good writing techniques.

- But efforts to make writing interesting can be overdone. The writing style should never draw attention away from the information.

The first benefit of group work in the classroom is that it teaches students how to work collaboratively in the business environment. Business organizations repeatedly indicate that the increased use of teams in the real world has increased students' need for exposure and experience with teams. Companies that use teams creatively spend many hours and dollars training individuals to work in teams and training managers to manage teams.

Jacqueline K. Eastman, Valdosta State University
Cathy Owens Swift, Georgia Southern University

Jacqueline K. Eastman and Cathy Owens Swift, "Enhancing Collaborative Learning: Discussion Boards and Chat Rooms as Project Communication Tools," *Business Communication Quarterly* 65. 3 (2002): 30.

COLLABORATIVE REPORT WRITING

- Collaborative report preparation is common for good reasons.

In your business career, you are likely to participate in collaborative writing projects. That is, you will work on a report with others. Group involvement in report preparation is becoming increasingly significant for a number of reasons. For one, the specialized knowledge of different people can improve the quality of the work. For another, the combined talents of the members are likely to produce a document better than any one of the members could produce alone. A third reason is that dividing the work can reduce the time needed for the project. And fourth, new software tools allow groups to collaborate from different places.

Determination of Group Makeup

- Groups should have five or fewer members and include all pertinent specialization areas.

As a beginning step, the membership of the group should be determined. In this determination, the availability and competencies of the people in the work situation involved are likely to be the major considerations. As a minimum, the group will consist of two. The maximum will depend on the number actually needed to do the project. As a practical matter, however, a maximum of five is a good rule, for larger groups tend to lose efficiency. More important than size, however, is the need to include all major areas of specialization involved in the work to be done.

- Preferably, the group has a leader, but there are exceptions.

In most business situations the highest ranking administrator in the group serves as leader. In groups made up of equals, a leader usually is appointed or elected. When no leader is so designated, the group works together informally. In such cases, however, an informal leader usually emerges.

Techniques of Participation

- Leaders and participants have clear duties to make the procedure work.

The group's work should be conducted much the way a meeting should be conducted. As described in Chapter 14, leaders and members of meetings have clear roles and duties. Leaders must plan the sessions and follow the plan. They must move the work along. They must control the discussion, limiting those who talk too much and encouraging input from those who are reluctant to participate. Group members should actively participate, taking care not to monopolize. They should be both cooperative and courteous in their work with the group.

- Groups often experience results that are less than ideal. Consult references on effective groups.

All too often, groups experience results that vary from these patterns. Although a discussion of group development and processes is beyond the scope of this book, you

might want to consult one of the many references on the subject.[1] Group members should recognize that effective groups do not just happen. They have unique characteristics and processes that are planned for and managed explicitly.

Procedure of the Work

As a general rule, groups working together on report projects need a minimum of two meetings with a work period between meetings. But the number of meetings required will vary with the needs of the project. For a project in which data gathering and other preliminary work must be done, additional meetings may be necessary. On the other hand, if only the writing of the report is needed, two meetings may be adequate.

- At least two meetings and a work period are needed.

Activities Involved

Whatever number of meetings is scheduled, the following activities typically occur, usually in the sequence shown. As you review them, it should be apparent that because of the differences in report projects, these activities vary in their implementation.

- The following activities normally occur, usually in this sequence.

Determine the Purpose. As in all report projects, the participants must determine just what the report must do. Thus, the group should follow the preliminary steps of problem determination discussed previously. They also need to develop a coherent, shared sense of the report's intended readers and their needs.

- First, determine the report purpose.

---

[1] Two especially good resources are Allan R. Cohen and Stephen L. Fink, *Effective Behavior in Organizations,* 7th ed. (New York: McGraw-Hill/Irwin, 2001) and Gerald L. Wilson, *Groups in Context: Leadership and Participation in Small Groups,* 6th ed. (New York:McGraw-Hill, 2001).

Comment and Review Tools Help Track Others' Changes to Your Documents

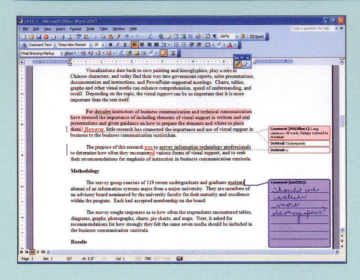

The commenting and reviewing tools in most word processors help people work together on documents asynchronously. When others review content and edit your document electronically, the commenting tool allows them to express opinions and concerns while the tracking tool makes their editing changes clearly visible. In fact, the tools allow you to accept or reject their suggestions individually or en masse.

In the example shown here, the reviewer turned on the reviewing toolbar to put frequently used tools at hand. Using this tool on a Tablet PC enabled the reviewer to choose from a variety of input methods—keyboard, digital ink, or voice. The tracking system allows reviewers to use a variety of colors, so that others can easily determine whom in the changes belong to. The commenting tool inserts identifying information, too. If a reviewer had entered a voice comment, the user would have simply clicked on the speaker icon to listen to the comment.

- Next, derive the factors involved.

Identify the Factors. The group next determines what is needed to achieve the purpose. This step involves determining the factors of the problem, as described earlier in the chapter. An advantage of collaboration is that several minds are available for the critical thinking that is so necessary for identifying the factors of the problem.

- If necessary, make a plan for gathering the information needed.

Gather the Information Needed. Before the group can begin work on the report, it must get the information needed. This activity could involve conducting any of the research designs mentioned earlier in this chapter and in Chapter 19. In some cases, group work begins after the information has been assembled, thus eliminating this step.

- The members interpret the information, applying it to the problem.

Interpret the Information. Determining the meaning of the information gathered is the next logical step for the group. In this step, the participants apply the findings to the problem, thereby selecting the information to be used in the report. In applying the findings to the problem, they also give meaning to the facts collected. The facts do not speak for themselves. Rather, group participants must think through the facts, apply the facts to the problem, derive logical meaning from the facts, and see them from the readers' points of view. Interpretations are no better than the thinking of the people in the group.

- They organize the information for presentation in the report.

Organize the Material. Just as in any other report-writing project, the group next organizes the material selected for presentation. They will base the report's structure on the time, place, quantity, factor, or other relationships in the data.

- They plan the writing of the report.

Plan the Writing. A next logical step is that of planning the makeup of the report. In this step the formality of the situation and the audience involved determine the decision. In addition, matters of writing such as tone, style, and formality are addressed. Needs for coherence, time consistency, and interesting writing are usually reinforced.

Assign Parts to Be Written. After the planning has been done, the group next turns its attention to the writing. The usual practice is to assign each person a part of the report.

• They assign themselves report parts to write.

Write Parts Assigned. Following comes a period of individual work. Each participant writes his or her part. Each will apply the ideas in Chapters 2 and 3 about word selection, sentence design, and paragraph construction to writing the assigned parts.

• The members then write their parts.

Revise Collaboratively. The group meets and reviews each person's contribution and the full report. This should be a give-and-take session with each person actively participating. It requires that every person give keen attention to the work of each participant, making constructive suggestions wherever appropriate. It requires courteous but meaningful criticisms. It also requires that the participants be open-minded, remembering that the goal is to construct the best possible document. In no case should the group merely give automatic approval to the work submitted. In cases of controversy, the majority views of the group should prevail.

• The group members collaboratively review the writing.

Edit the Final Draft. After the group has done its work, one member usually is assigned the task of editing the final draft. This gives the document consistency. In addition, the editor serves as a final proofreader. Probably the editor should be the most competent writer in the group.

• A selected member edits the final draft.

If all the work has been done with care and diligence, this final draft should be a report better than anyone in the group could have prepared alone. Those who study groups use the word *synergistic* to refer to groups that function this way. The final report is better than the sum of the individual parts.

SUMMARY BY LEARNING OBJECTIVES

1. Your work on a report begins with a problem (purpose, goal, objective).
   - Get the problem in mind by gathering all the information you need about it.
   - Then develop a problem statement from the information.
   - Phrase this statement as an infinitive phrase, a question, or a declarative statement.
   - Understand that you may need to revise your problem definition as you proceed with your research.

1 State a problem clearly in writing.

2. From the problem statement, determine the factors involved.
   - These may be subtopics in information reports.
   - They may be hypotheses (possible explanations) in problems requiring a solution.
   - They may be bases of comparison in problems requiring evaluations.

2 List the factors involved in a problem.

3. After you have gathered the information needed, interpret it as it applies to the problem.
   - Interpret the information in light of your problem and your readers' needs.
   - Heed this advice for avoiding human error:
     — Report the facts as they are.
     — Do not think that conclusions are always necessary.
     — Do not interpret a lack of evidence as proof to the contrary.
     — Do not compare noncomparable data.
     — Do not draw illogical cause–effect conclusions.
     — Beware of unreliable and unrepresentative data.
     — Do not oversimplify.
     — Tailor your claims to your data.

3 Explain the common errors in interpreting and develop attitudes and practices conducive to good interpreting.

- Adopt these attitudes and practices:
  - — Maintain a judicial attitude.
  - — Consult with others.
  - — Test your interpretations by applying the test of experience (reason) and the negative test (question them).
  - — Use statistical analysis to help you interpret numerical data.

4. Next, organize the information (construct an outline).

4 Organize information in outline form, using time, place, quantity, factor, or a combination of these as bases for division.

- An outline helps you group and order the information and create an information hierarchy.
  - — Your research plan and interpretation notes can help you make your report outline.
  - — You may choose to use conventional outline symbols (I, A, 1, a) or numeric symbols (1, 1.1, 1.1.1), but any outline format is fine if it helps you write a well-organized draft.
  - — The outline is a tool to help you—feel free to mark it up and revise it.
- Organize the report body (the part between the introduction and the ending section) by a process of division.
  - — Look over the findings for ways of dividing on the basis of time, place, quantity, factor, or combinations.
  - — Then divide, forming the major parts of the report.
  - — Next, look at these divisions for ways of dividing them.
  - — Continue to subdivide as far as necessary.
  - — The end result is your outline.

5. Turn your outline into a table of contents.

5 Turn an outline into a table of contents whose format and wording are logical and meaningful.

- Use a format that your reader will find instructive, readable, and appropriate.
- Use the topic form (identifies topic).
- Or use the talking form (identifies topic and says something about it).
- Make the wording of comparable parts parallel grammatically.
- Prune each heading for conciseness.
- Avoid excessive repetition of words.

6. From the outline, write the report.

6 Write reports that are focused, objective, consistent in time viewpoint, smoothly connected, and interesting.

- Draft to get the right information in the right order; then revise for perfection.
- Make your beginning and ending reader centered.
  - — Write a beginning that tells what problem you studied, how you studied it, and what you found out.
  - — Write an ending that summarizes the main findings and their significance to the readers.
- Maintain objectivity (no bias).
  - — An impersonal writing style (third person) has long been associated with objectivity.
  - — But some authorities question this style, saying that a personal style is more interesting.
  - — The argument continues, although most formal reports are written in the impersonal style.
- Be consistent in time viewpoint—either past or present.
  - — Past-time viewpoint views the research and findings as past and prevailing concepts and conclusions as present.

- — Present-time viewpoint presents as current all that is current at the time of writing.
- Use transitions to make the report parts flow smoothly.
  - — Between large parts, you may need to use full sentences to make connections.
  - — Topic sentences also can help the flow of thought.
  - — Use transitional words and phrases to connect the lesser parts.
- Work to make the writing interesting.
  - — Select words carefully for best effect.
  - — Follow techniques of good writing (correctness, rhythmic flow of words, vigorous words, and such).
  - — Do not overdo these efforts by drawing attention to how you write rather than what you say.

7. Expect that you will sometimes prepare reports collaboratively in groups.

7 Prepare reports collaboratively.

- Groups (two to five members) may produce better reports than individuals if all things go well.
- Members of groups (leaders and participants) should have clear roles.
- Groups should plan two or more meetings with a work period.
- Groups should follow this procedure in writing reports collaboratively:
  - — Determine report purpose.
  - — Identify factors.
  - — Collect facts for the report.
  - — Interpret the facts.
  - — Organize the facts.
  - — Plan for writing.
  - — Assign parts to members.
  - — Write assigned parts.
  - — Revise members' contributions collaboratively.
  - — Edit the final draft.

CRITICAL THINKING QUESTIONS

1 What kinds of reports do you expect to write in your chosen profession? Why?

2 Explain the concept of outlining as a division process.

3 In what ways can the format of the table of contents aid in reader comprehension? Find some examples of helpfully formatted tables of contents.

4 You are writing a report on the progress of your local cable company's efforts to increase sales of five of its products through extensive advertising in print and online newspapers and magazines and on television and radio. Discuss the possibilities for major headings. Evaluate each possibility.

5 Not all business reports are written objectively. In fact, many are deliberately biased. Why, then, should we stress objectivity in a college course that includes report writing?

6 Explain the difference between personal and impersonal writing. Which is "better"? Argue both sides.

7 Explain the differences between the present-time viewpoint and the past-time viewpoint.

8 Is it incorrect to have present, past, and future tense in the same report? In the same paragraph? In the same sentence? Discuss.

9 "Transitional sentences are unnecessary. They merely add length to a report and thus are contrary to the established rules of conciseness." Discuss.

10 "Reports are written for business executives who want them. Thus, you don't have to be concerned about holding your reader's interest." Discuss.

11 Collaborative reports are better than reports written by an individual because they use many minds rather than one. Discuss.

CRITICAL THINKING EXERCISES

1 For each of the following problem situations, write a clear statement of the problem and list the factors involved. When necessary, you may use your imagination logically to supply any additional information needed.

   a. A manufacturer of breakfast cereals wants to determine the characteristics of its consumers.

   b. The manufacturer of a toothpaste wants to learn what the buying public thinks of its product in relation to competing products.

   c. Wal-Mart wants to give its stockholders a summary of its operations for the past calendar year.

   d. A building contractor engaged to build a new office for Company X submits a report summarizing its monthly progress.

   e. The Able Wholesale Company must prepare a report on its credit relations with the Crystal City Hardware Company.

   f. The supervisor of Department X must prepare a report evaluating the performance of a secretary.

   g. Baker, Inc., wants a study made to determine why its employee turnover is high.

   h. An executive must rank three subordinates on the basis of their suitability for promotion to a particular job.

   i. The supervisor of production must compare three competing machines that are being considered for use in a particular production job.

   j. An investment consultant must advise a client on whether to invest in the development of a lake resort.

   k. A consultant seeks to learn how a restaurant can improve its profits.

2 Select a hypothetical problem with a time division possibility. What other division possibilities does it have? Compare the two possibilities as the main bases for organizing the report.

3 Assume that you are writing the results of a survey conducted to determine what styles of shoes are worn throughout the country on various occasions by women of all ages. What division possibilities exist here? Which would you recommend?

4 For the problem described in the preceding exercise, use your imagination to construct topic headings for the outline.

5 Point out any violations of grammatical parallelism in these headings:

   a. Region I sales lagging.

   b. Moderate increase seen for Region II.

   c. Region III sales remain strong.

6 Point out any error in grammatical parallelism in these headings:

   a. High cost of operation.

   b. Slight improvement in production efficiency.

   c. Maintenance cost is low.

7 Which of the following headings is logically inconsistent with the others?

   a. Agricultural production continues to increase.

   b. Slight increase is made by manufacturing.

   c. Salaries remain high.

   d. Service industries show no change.

8 Select an editorial, feature article, book chapter, or the like that has no headings. Write talking headings for it.

9 Assume that you are writing a report that summarizes a survey you have conducted. Write a paragraph of the report using the present-time viewpoint; then write the paragraph using the past-time viewpoint. The paragraph will be based on the following information:

   Answers to the question about how students view the proposed Aid to Education Bill in this survey and in a survey taken a year earlier (in parentheses).

   For, 39 percent (21); Against, 17 percent (43).

   No answer, undecided, etc., 44 percent (36).

chapter eleven

Short Reports and Proposals

LEARNING OBJECTIVES

Upon completing this chapter, you will be able to write well-structured short reports. To reach this goal, you should be able to

1   Explain the structure of reports relative to length and formality.

2   Discuss the four major differences involved in writing short and long reports.

3   Choose an appropriate form for short reports.

4   Adapt the procedures for writing short reports to routine operational, progress, problem-solving, and audit reports as well as minutes of meetings.

5   Write adapted, well-organized, and persuasive proposals.

Short Reports and Proposals

Assume again the position of assistant to the president of Technisoft and the report-writing work necessary in this position. Most of the time, your assignments concern routine, everyday problems: human resource policies, administrative procedures, work flow, and the like. Following what appears to be established company practice, you write the reports on these problems in simple email form.

Occasionally, however, you have a more involved assignment. Last week, for example, you investigated a union charge that favoritism was shown to the nonunion workers on certain production jobs. As your report on this very formal investigation was written for the benefit of ranking company administrators as well as union leaders, you dressed it up.

Then there was the report you had helped prepare for the board of directors last fall. That report summarized pressing needs for capital improvements. A number of executives contributed to this project, but you were the coordinator. Because the report was important and was written for the board, you made it as formal as possible.

Clearly, reports vary widely. How their structures vary is the first topic of this chapter. Because short reports are critical to your daily work, they are discussed next. The chapter concludes with a discussion of proposals, which have report-like traits but differ in their fundamental purpose.

- You can use your general understanding of report writing to tackle many varieties of reports.

- Here we focus on short reports and proposals.

With a general understanding of what reports do and how to write them, you are ready to consider the many varieties of reports. We focus in this chapter on the shorter forms—the reports that enable much of any organization's work. We also include an analysis of proposals, which resemble reports but differ from them in significant ways.

AN OVERVIEW OF REPORT STRUCTURE

As you prepare to write a report, you will need to decide on its structure. Will it be a simple email? Will it be a long, complex, and formal report? Or will it fall between these extremes?

- Length and formality determine report structure.

Your decision about report structure will be based on the needs of your situation. Those needs are related to report length and the formality of the situation. The longer the problem and the more formal the situation, the more involved the report structure is likely to be. The shorter the problem and the more informal the situation, the less involved the report structure is likely to be. Such adjustments of report structure to length and formality help meet the reader's needs in each situation.

- The following classification plan provides a general picture of report structure.

To help you understand the various report structures, we will review the possibilities. The following classification plan provides a very general picture of how reports are structured. This plan does not account for all the possible variations, but it does acquaint you with the general structure of reports. It should help you construct reports that fit your specific need.

- It pictures report structure as a stairway (Figure 11–1). Long, formal reports are at the top. Prefatory pages dress up these reports.

The classification plan arranges all business reports as a stairway, as illustrated by the diagram in Figure 11–1. At the top of the stairway are the most formal, full-dress reports. Such reports have a number of pages that come before the text material, just as this book has pages that come before the first chapter. These pages serve useful purposes, but they also dress up the report. Typically, these *prefatory pages,* as they are called, are included when the problem situation is formal and the report is long. The exact makeup of the prefatory pages may vary, but the most common arrangement includes these parts: title fly, title page, letter of transmittal, table of contents, and executive summary. Flyleaves (blank pages at the beginning and end that protect the report) also may be included.

- Prefatory pages consist of the title fly, title page, letter of transmittal, table of contents, and executive summary.

These parts are explained in Chapter 12, but a brief description of them at this point should help you understand their roles. The first two pages (title fly and title page) contain identification information. The *title fly* carries only the report title. The *title*

Figure 11–1

Progression of Change in Report Makeup as Formality Requirements and Length of the Problem Decrease

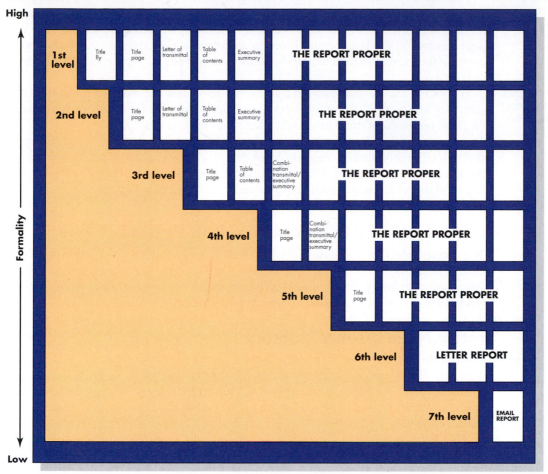

page typically contains the title, identification of the writer and reader, and usually the date. As the words imply, the *letter of transmittal* is a letter that transmits the report. It is a personal message from the writer to the reader. The *table of contents,* of course, is a listing of the report contents. It is the report outline in finished form, with page numbers to indicate where the parts begin. It also may include a list of illustrations (tables, figures, diagrams), which may be a separate part. The *executive summary* summarizes whatever is important in the report—the major facts and analyses, conclusions, and recommendations.

As the need for formality decreases and the problem becomes smaller, the makeup of the report changes. The changes primarily occur in the prefatory pages. As we have noted, these pages give the report a formal appearance. So it is not surprising that they change as the report situation becomes less formal. Usually, such reports are shorter.

Although the changes that occur are far from standardized, they follow a general order. First, the title fly drops out. This page contains only the report title, which also appears on the next page. Obviously, the title fly is used primarily for reasons of formality.

Next in the progression, the executive summary and the letter of transmittal are combined. When this stage is reached, the report problem is short enough to be summarized in a short space. As shown in Figure 11–1, the report at this stage has three prefatory parts: title page, table of contents, and combination transmittal letter and executive summary.

At the fourth step, the table of contents drops out. The table of contents is a guide to the report text, and a guide has limited value in a short report. Certainly, a guide to a 100-page report is necessary. But a guide to a one-page report is not. Somewhere

- As reports become shorter and less formal, changes occur in this general order.

- The title fly drops out.

- The executive summary and the letter of transmittal are combined.

- Next, the table of contents is omitted.

CHAPTER 11   Short Reports and Proposals   325

between these extremes a dividing point exists. You should follow the general guide of including a table of contents whenever it appears to be of some value to the reader.

- The combined letter of transmittal and executive summary drops out, and what is left forms the popular short report.

Another step down, as formality and length requirements continue to decrease, the combined letter of transmittal and executive summary drops out. Thus, the report commonly called the *short report* now has only a title page and the report text. The title page remains to the last because it serves as a very useful cover page. In addition, it contains the most important identifying information. The short report is a popular form in business.

- The next step is the letter report, and the step after that is the email report.
- This progression of structure is general.

Below the short-report form is a form that reinstates the letter of transmittal and summary and presents the entire report as a letter—*thus, the letter report*. And finally, for short problems of more informality, the *email* form is used.

As mentioned earlier, this is a general analysis of report change; it probably oversimplifies the structure of reports. Most reports, however, fit generally within the framework of the diagram. Knowledge of the general relationship of formality and length to report makeup should help you understand and plan reports.

CHARACTERISTICS OF SHORTER REPORTS

- The shorter report forms are the most common in business.

The shorter report forms (those at the bottom of the stairway) are by far the most common in business. These are the everyday working reports—those used for the routine information reporting that is vital to an organization's communication. Because these reports are so common, our study of report types begins with them.

Little Need for Introductory Information

- Shorter reports have little need for introductory material.

Most of the shorter, more informal reports require little (sometimes no) introductory material. These reports typically concern day-to-day problems. Their lives are short; that is, they are not likely to be kept on file for future readers. They are intended for only a few readers, and these readers know the problem. They are likely to need little introduction to it.

This is not to say that all shorter reports have no need for introductory material. Some do need it. In general, however, the need is likely to be small.

- Some shorter reports need introductory material. Include as much introductory material as is necessary to prepare the reader for the report.

Determining what introductory material is needed is simply a matter of answering one question: What does my reader need to know before receiving the information in this report? In very short reports, sufficient introductory material is provided by an incidental reference to the problem, authorization of the investigation, or the like. In extreme cases, however, you may need a detailed introduction comparable to that of the more formal reports.

Reports need no introductory material if their very nature explains their purpose. This holds true for personnel actions. It also holds true for weekly sales reports, inventory reports, and some progress reports.

Predominance of the Direct Order

- The shorter reports usually begin directly—with conclusions and recommendations.

Because the shorter reports usually solve routine problems, they are likely to be written in the direct order. By *direct order* we mean that the report begins with its most important information—usually the conclusion and perhaps a recommendation. Business writers use this order because they know that their readers' main concern is to get the information needed to make a decision. So they present this information right away.

- Longer reports are often indirect, but that is because such front matter as the letter of transmittal and executive summary can foreground the findings.

As you will see in Chapter 12, the form that the direct order takes in longer reports is somewhat different. The main findings will be somewhere up front—either in the letter of transmittal, executive summary, or both—but the report itself may be organized indirectly. The introduction will present the topic and purpose of the report, but the actual findings may not come out until the body sections, and their most succinct statement will usually appear in the conclusions or recommendations section. As one moves down the structural ladder toward the more informal and shorter reports, however, the need for the direct order in the report itself increases. At the bottom of the ladder, the direct order is more the rule than the exception.

Deciding whether to use the direct order is best based on a consideration of your readers' likely use of the report. If your readers need the report conclusion or recommendation as a basis for an action that they must take, directness will speed their effort by enabling them to quickly receive the most important information. If they have confidence in your work, they may choose not to read beyond this point and to proceed with the action that the report supports. Should they desire to question any part of the report, however, the material is there for their inspection.

- Use the direct order when the conclusion or recommendation will serve as a basis for action.

On the other hand, if there is reason to believe that your readers will want to arrive at the conclusion or recommendation only after a logical review of the analysis, you should organize your report in the indirect order. This arrangement is especially preferable when your readers do not have reason to place their full confidence in your work. If you are a novice working on a new assignment, for example, you would be wise to lead them to your recommendation or conclusion by using the indirect order. As you can see, the indirect and direct orders are ways of relating to the information needs of the reader.

- Use the indirect order when you need to take the readers through the analysis.

Because order is so vital a part of constructing the shorter reports, let us be certain that the difference between the direct arrangement and the indirect arrangement is clear. To make it clear, we will go through each, step by step.

The direct arrangement presents right away the most important part of the report. This is the answer—the achievement of the report's goal. Depending on the problem, the direct beginning could consist of a summary of facts, a conclusion, a recommendation, or some combination of summary, conclusion, and recommendation.

- The direct order gives the main message first.

FRANK & ERNEST©
SOURCE: Reprinted by permission of *United Features Syndicate, Inc.*

There are specific concepts that the students should learn and skills that they should improve by completing the business report assignment. These include organizing, writing, editing, revising, formatting, data gathering and evaluation, audience analysis, understanding how the report will be used for decision-making, and the need to pay careful attention to detail when writing so that their report is mechanically correct.

Kathleen M. Hiemstra, John Carroll University

Kathleen M. Hiemstra, "Instructor and Student Perceptions of What Is Learned by Writing the Business Report," *Business Communication Quarterly* 64. 2 (2002): 50.

- Then it covers introductory material (if any), findings and analyses, conclusions, and recommendations.

Whatever background information is needed usually follows the direct opening. As noted previously, sometimes little or none is needed in the everyday, routine reports. Next come the report findings, organized in good order (as described in Chapter 10). From these facts and analyses comes the conclusion, and perhaps a recommendation.

Illustrating this arrangement is the following report of a short and simple personnel problem. For reasons of space economy, only the key parts of the report are shown here.

> Clifford A. Knudson, administrative assistant in the accounting department, should be fired. This conclusion has been reached after a thorough investigation brought about by numerous incidents during the past two months. . . .
>
> The recommended action is supported by this information from his work record for the past two months:
>
> - He has been late to work seven times.
> - He has been absent without acceptable excuse for seven days.
> - Twice he reported to work in a drunken and disorderly condition.
> - [And so on].

- The indirect order has this sequence: introduction, facts and analyses, conclusions, and recommendations.

The indirect arrangement begins with whatever introductory material is needed to prepare the reader for the report. Then comes the presentation of facts, with analyses when needed. Next comes the part that accomplishes the goal of the report. If the goal is to present information, this part summarizes the information. If the goal is to reach a conclusion, this part reviews the analyses and draws a conclusion from them. And if the goal is to recommend an action, this part reviews the analyses, draws a conclusion, and, on the basis of the conclusion, makes a recommendation.

Using the simple personnel problem from the last example, the indirect arrangement would appear like this:

> Numerous incidents during the past two months appear to justify an investigation of the work record of Clifford A. Knudson, administrative assistant in the accounting department.
>
> The investigation of his work record for the past two months reveals these points:
>
> - He has been late to work seven times.
> - He has been absent without acceptable excuse for seven days.
> - Twice he reported to work in a drunken and disorderly condition.
> - [And so on to the conclusion that Knudson should be fired].

More Personal Writing Style

- Personal writing is common in the shorter reports.

Although the writing for all reports is much the same, the writing in shorter reports tends to be more personal. That is, the shorter reports are likely to use the personal pronouns *I, we,* and *you* rather than only the third person.

Templates Help Writers Format Reports

Templates for word processors help report writers format reports easily and consistently. Once a template is selected, report writers can concentrate on the report message and let the software create a professional-looking document.

These templates contain margin settings, font type and size for headings and text, and even graphic layouts. Most are designed to help the writer present a report that communicates its message with a professional look. Although standard templates can be used, some companies design their own templates to give their reports consistent and distinct images.

Word and WordPerfect have templates that set up both short and long reports. In addition to the standard templates, you can find more on the web. Here you see a list of templates found in Microsoft's Template Gallery after a search on *reports* followed by view of the template before downloading. Finally, you see the template loaded in Word.

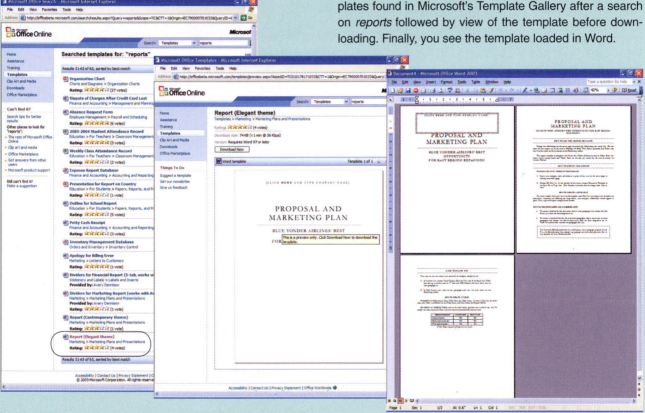

The reasons for this tendency toward personal writing in shorter reports should be obvious. In the first place, short-report situations usually involve personal relationships. Such reports tend to be from and to people who know each other and who normally address each other informally when they meet. In addition, shorter reports are apt to involve personal investigations and to represent the observations, evaluations, and analyses of their writers. Finally, shorter reports tend to deal with day-to-day, routine problems. These problems are by their very nature informal. It is logical to report them informally, and personal writing tends to produce this informal effect.

- The reasons are that the shorter reports usually (1) involve personal relationships, (2) concern a personal investigation, and (3) are routine.

As explained in Chapter 10, your decision about whether to write a report in personal or impersonal style should be based on the situation. You should consider the expectations of those who will receive the report. If they expect formality, you should write impersonally. If they expect informality, you should write personally. If you do not know their preferences, you should consider the formality of the situation. Convention favors impersonal writing for the most formal situations. Like the direct and indirect

- Write impersonally (1) when your reader prefers it and (2) when the situation is formal.

order, the question of personal versus impersonal style involves the matter of relating to the reader in ways that he or she prefers.

From this analysis, it should be clear that either personal or impersonal writing can be appropriate for reports ranging from the shortest to the longest types. The point is, however, that short-report situations are most likely to justify personal writing.

Less Need for a Structured Coherence Plan

As you will see in Chapter 12, long and formal reports usually require a structured coherence plan. Short reports do not. This is not to say that coherence is not essential to short reports. It is. The point is that a *structured* plan is not needed. By structured coherence plan we mean an arrangement of summarizing, forward looking, and backward looking parts that tie together the report presentation. When you study this plan, you will understand why it has little use in short reports. We mention it now primarily for the sake of completeness in covering differences between long and short reports.

FORMS OF SHORTER REPORTS

- Following is a review of the more popular shorter reports.

As noted earlier, the shorter report forms are by far the most numerous and important in business. In fact, the three forms represented by the bottom three steps of the stairway (Figure 11–1) make up the bulk of the reports written. Thus, a review of each of these three types is in order.

The Short Report

- The short report consists of a title page and the report text.

One of the more popular of the less formal report forms is the short report. Representing the fifth step in the diagram of report progression, this report consists of only a title page and text. Its popularity may be explained by the middle-ground impression of formality that it conveys. Including the most important prefatory part gives the report at least some appearance of formality. And it does this without the tedious work of preparing the other prefatory pages. The short report is ideally suited for the short but somewhat formal problem.

- It is usually in the direct order, beginning with the conclusion.

Like most of the less formal report forms, the short report may be organized in either the direct or indirect order. But the direct order is far more common. As illustrated by Figure 11–2, this plan begins with a quick summary of the report, including and emphasizing conclusions and recommendations. Such a beginning serves much the same function as the executive summary (described in Chapter 12) of a long, formal report.

- The introduction comes next, then the findings and analyses, and finally the conclusions.

Following the summary come whatever introductory remarks are needed. (See Chapter 12 for a more detailed discussion of the introduction.) Sometimes this part is

Figure 11–2

Illustration of a Short Report. Designed for the busy reader who wants the main message quickly, this report begins with the recommendations. Then it presents the report in logical order, following a brief introduction with a comparison of three methods of depreciation for delivery trucks (the subject of the investigation). The somewhat formal style is appropriate for reports of this nature.

743 Beaux Avenue
New Orleans, LA 70118-4913

Brewington and Karnes, CPAs

*5 Ws and
1 H produce
complete title*

Recommendations for Depreciating Delivery Trucks

An Analysis of Three Plans Proposed for the Bagget Laundry Company

*Use of
three-spot title
page gives good
emphasis to
writer–reader
relationship and
balances page*

April 16, 2008

Figure 11–2

Continued

Topic-sentenc—first paragraph designs and transition words give emphasis and forward movement to ideas.

Recommendations for Depreciating Delivery Trucks

An Analysis of Three Plans Proposed for the Bagget Laundry Company

Direct order accents report solution.

Recommendation of Reducing Charge Method

The Reducing Charge method appears to be the best method to depreciate Bagget Laundry Company delivery trucks. The relative equality of cost allocation for depreciation and maintenance over the useful life of the trucks is the prime advantage under this method. Computation of depreciation charges is relatively simple by the Reducing Charge plan but not quite so simple as computation under the second best method considered.

The second best method considered is the Straight-Line depreciation plan. It is the simplest to compute of the plans considered, and it results in yearly charges equal to those under the Reducing Charge method. The unequal cost allocation resulting from increasing maintenance costs in successive years, however, is a disadvantage that far outweighs the method's ease of computation.

Third among the plans considered is the Service Hours method. This plan is not satisfactory for depreciating delivery trucks primarily because it combines a number of undesirable features. Prime among these is the complexity and cost of computing yearly charges under the plan. Also significant is the likelihood of poor cost allocation under this plan. An additional drawback is the possibility of variations in the estimates of the service life of company trucks.

The Whats and Whys of the Problem

Authorization by President Bagget. This report on depreciation methods for delivery trucks of the Bagget Laundry Company is submitted on April 16, 2008, to Mr. Ralph P. Bagget, President of the Company. Mr. Bagget orally authorized Brewington and Karnes, Certified Public Accountants, to conduct the study on March 15, 2008.

Problem of Selecting Best Depreciation Method. Having decided to establish branch agencies, the Bagget Laundry Company has purchased delivery trucks to transport laundry back and forth from the central cleaning plant in downtown New Orleans. The Company's problem is to select from three alternatives the most advantageous method to depreciate the trucks. The three methods concerned are the Reducing Charge, Straight-Line, and Service-Hours. The trucks have an original cost of $25,000, a five-year life, and trade-in value of $10,000.

1

Figure 11–2

Continued

Preview paragraph gives sequence of body divisions and justifies it.

Use of Company Records to Solve Problem. In seeking an optimum solution to the Company's problem, we studied Company records and reviewed authoritative literature on the subject. We also applied our best judgment and our experience in analyzing the alternative methods. We based all conclusions on the generally accepted business principles in the field.

Presentation of Analysis. In the following analysis, our evaluations of the three depreciation methods appear in the order in which we rank the methods. Since these methods involve different factors, direct comparison by factors is meaningless. Thus our plan is that we evaluate each method in turn.

Marked Advantages of the Reducing Charge Method

Sometimes called Sum-of-the-Years'-Digits, the Reducing Charge method consists of applying a series of decreasing fractions over the life of the property. To determine the fraction, first compute the sum of years of use for the property. This number becomes the denominator. Then determine the position number (first, second, etc.) of the year. This number is the numerator. Then apply the resulting fractions to the depreciable values for the life of the property. In the case of the trucks, the depreciable value is $15,000 ($25,000 – $10,000).

Sub-ordinate reference to graphic allows main sentence to begin interpretation.

As shown in Table I, this method results in large depreciation costs for the early years and decreasing costs in later years. But since maintenance and repair costs for trucks are higher in the later years, this method provides a relatively stable charge over the life of the property. In actual practice, however, the sums will not be as stable as illustrated, for maintenance and repair costs will vary from those used in the computation.

Table I			
Depreciation and Maintenance Costs for Delivery Trucks of Bagget Laundry for 2004–2008 Using Reducing Charge Depreciation			
End of Year	Depreciation	Maintenance	Sum
1	5/15 ($15,000) = $ 5,000	$ 200	$ 5,200
2	4/15 ($15,000) = 4,000	1,000	5,000
3	3/15 ($15,000) = 3,000	1,800	4,800
4	2/15 ($15,000) = 2,000	2,600	4,600
5	1/15 ($15,000) = 1,000	3,400	4,400
Totals	$15,000	$9,000	$24,000

In summary, the Reducing Charge method uses the most desirable combination of factors to depreciate trucks. It equalizes periodic charges, and it is easy to compute. It is our first choice for Bagget Laundry Company.

2

Figure 11–2

Continued

Incidental reference to graphic ties text and illustration together.

Runner-up Position of Straight-Line Method

The Straight-Line depreciation method is easiest of all to compute. It involves merely taking the depreciable value of the trucks ($15,000) and dividing it by the life of the trucks (5 years). The depreciation in this case is $3,000 for each year.

As shown in Table II, however, the increase in maintenance costs in later years results in much greater periodic charges in later years. The method is not usually recommended in cases such as this.

Table II				
Depreciation and Maintenance Costs for Delivery Trucks of Bagget Laundry for 2004–2008 Using Straight-Line Depreciation				
End of Year	Depreciation		Maintenance	Sum
1	1/5 ($15,000) =	$ 3,000	$ 200	$ 3,200
2	1/5 ($15,000) =	3,000	1,000	4,000
3	1/5 ($15,000) =	3,000	1,800	4,800
4	1/5 ($15,000) =	3,000	2,600	5,600
5	1/5 ($15,000) =	3,000	3,400	6,400
	Totals	$15,000	$9,000	$24,000

Summary statements at section endings provide reader with time to see solution unfold.

In addition, the Straight-Line method generally is best when the properties involved are accumulated over a period of years. When this is done, the total of depreciation and maintenance costs will be about even. But Bagget Company has not purchased its trucks over a period of years. Nor is it likely to do so in the years ahead. Thus, Straight-Line depreciation will not result in equal periodic charges for maintenance and depreciation over the long run.

Poor Rank of Service-Hours Depreciation

The Service-Hours method of depreciation combines the major disadvantages of the other ways discussed. It is based on the principle that a truck is bought for the direct hours of service that it will give. The estimated number of hours that a delivery truck can be used efficiently according to automotive engineers is computed from a service total of 100,000 miles. The depreciable cost ($15,000) for each truck is allocated pro rata according to the number of service hours used.

Completeness and detail in analysis give objectivity.

The difficulty and expense of maintaining additional records of service hours is a major disadvantage of this method. The depreciation cost for the delivery trucks under this method will fluctuate widely between the first and last years. It is reasonable to assume that as the trucks get older more time will be spent on maintenance. Consequently, the larger depreciation costs will occur in the initial years. As can be seen in Table III, the periodic

3

Figure 11–2

Continued

charges for depreciation and maintenance hover between the two previously discussed methods.

Table III				
Depreciation and Maintenance Costs for Delivery Trucks of Bagget Laundry for 2004–2008 Using Service-Hours Depreciation				
End of Year	Estimated Service Miles	Depreciation	Maintenance	Sum
1	30,000	$ 4,500	$ 200	$ 4,700
2	25,000	3,750	1,000	4,750
3	20,000	3,000	1,800	4,800
4	15,000	2,250	2,600	4,850
5	10,000	1,500	3,400	4,950
	100,000	$15,000	$9,000	$24,000

The periodic charge for depreciation and maintenance increases in the later years of ownership. Another difficulty encountered is the possibility of a variance between estimated service hours and the actual service hours. The wide fluctuation possible makes it impractical to use this method for depreciating the delivery truck.

The difficulty of maintaining adequate records and increasing costs in the later years are the major disadvantages of this method. Since it combines the major disadvantages of both the Reducing Charge and Straight-Line methods, it is not satisfactory for depreciating the delivery trucks.

The disadvantages of this method, together with those of the straight-line method, make the reducing charge method the best method of depreciation for Bagget's delivery trucks.

Completeness and detail in analysis give objectivity.

4

not needed. Usually, however, a single paragraph covers the facts of authorization and a brief statement of the problem and its scope. After the introductory words come the findings of the investigation. As in the longer report forms, the findings are presented, analyzed, and applied to the problem. From all this comes a conclusion and, if needed, a recommendation. These last two elements—conclusions and recommendations—may come at the end even though they also appear in the beginning summary. Omitting a summary or a conclusion would sometimes end the report abruptly. It would stop the flow of reasoning before reaching the logical goal.

● See Figure 11–2 for this report form.

The mechanics of constructing the short report are much the same as the mechanics of constructing the more formal, longer types. The short report uses the same form of title page and page layout. Like the longer reports, it uses headings. But because of the short report's brevity, the headings rarely go beyond the two-division level. In fact, one level of division is most common. Like any other report, the short report uses graphics, an appendix, and a bibliography when these are needed.

Letter Reports

● Letter reports are reports in letter form.

The second of the more common shorter report forms is the letter report, that is, a report in letter form. Letter reports are used primarily to present information to persons outside the organization, especially when the information is to be sent by mail or fax. For example, a company's written evaluation of its experience with a particular product may be presented in letter form and sent to the person who requests it. An outside consultant may write a report of analyses and recommendations in letter form. Or the officer of an organization may report certain information to the membership in a letter.

● They usually cover short problems.

Typically, the length of letter reports is three or four pages or less. But no hard-and-fast rule exists on this point.

● They are usually written in personal style.

As a general rule, letter reports are written personally, using *I*, *you*, and *we* references (see Figure 11–3). Exceptions exist, of course, such as letter reports for very important readers—for example, a company's board of directors. Otherwise, the writing style recommended for letter reports is much the same as that recommended for any other reports. Certainly, clear and meaningful expression is a requirement for all reports.

● Most of them begin indirectly.

Letter reports may be in either the direct order or the indirect order. If such a report is to be mailed, there is some justification for using the indirect order. Because such reports arrive unannounced, it is logical to begin with a reminder of what they are, how they originated, and the like. A letter report written to the membership of an organization, for example, might appropriately begin as follows:

> As authorized by your board of directors last January 6, this report reviews member company expenditures for travel.

● Subject lines are appropriate to begin them.

If a letter report is begun in the direct order, a subject line is appropriate. The subject line consists of identifying words appearing at the top of the letter, usually right after the salutation. Another common practice is to omit the word *subject* and the colon and to type the entire subject description in capital letters. Although subject lines may be formed in many ways, one acceptable version begins with the word *subject* and follows it with words that identify the situation. As the following example illustrates, this identifying device helps overcome any confusion that the direct beginning might otherwise create.

> Subject: Travel Expenditures of Association Members, Authorized by Board of Directors, January 2005
>
> Association members are spending 11 percent more on travel this year than they did the year before. Current plans call for a 10 percent increase for next year.

● The organizational plans of letter reports are much like those of longer reports.

Regardless of which type of beginning is used, the organizational plans for letter reports correspond to those of longer, more formal types. Thus, the indirect-order letter report follows its introduction with a logical presentation and analysis of the information gathered. From this presentation, it develops a conclusion or recommendation, or both, in the end. The direct-order letter report follows the initial summary-conclusion-recommendation

Figure 11–3

Illustration of a Letter Report. This direct-order letter report compares two hotels for a meeting site. Organized by the bases used in determining the choice, it evaluates the pertinent information and reaches a decision. The personal style is appropriate.

INTERNATIONAL COMMUNICATION ASSOCIATION

314 N Capitol St. NW • Washington, DC 20001 • 202.624.2411

October 26, 2008

Professor Helen Toohey
Board of Directors
International Communication Association
Thunderbird American Graduate School of International Management
15249 N. 59th Ave.
Glendale, AZ 85306-6000

Dear Professor Toohey:

Subject: Recommendation of Convention Hotel for the 2009 Meeting

Direct order emphasizes decision.

The Hyatt Hotel is my recommendation for the International Communication Association meeting next October. The Hyatt has significant advantages over the Marriott, the other potential site for the meeting.

First, the Hyatt has a definite downtown location advantage, and this is important to convention goers and their spouses. Second, accommodations, including meeting rooms, are adequate in both places, although the Marriott's rooms are more modern. Third, Hyatt room costs are approximately 15 percent lower than those at the Marriott. The Hyatt, however, would charge $500 for a room for the opening session. Although both hotels are adequate, because of location and cost advantages the Hyatt appears to be the better choice from the members' viewpoint.

Preview gives transition lead.

ORIGIN AND PLAN OF THE INVESTIGATION

In investigating these two hotels, as was my charge from you at our October 7 board meeting, I collected information on what I believed to be the three major factors of consideration in the problem. First is location. Second is adequacy of accommodations. And third is cost. The following findings and evaluations form the basis of my recommendation.

Bases of comparison (factors) permit hotels (units) to be compared logically.

THE HYATT'S FAVORABLE DOWNTOWN LOCATION

The older of the two hotels, the Hyatt is located in the heart of the downtown business district. Thus it is convenient to the area's major mall as well as the other downtown shops. The Marriott, on the other hand, is approximately nine blocks from the major shopping area. Located in the periphery of the business and residential area, it provides little location advantage for those wanting to shop. It does, however, have shops within its walls that provide for virtually all of the guests' normal needs. Because many members will bring spouses, however, the downtown location does give the Hyatt an advantage.

Short sentences and transitional words increase readability and move ideas forward.

Figure 11–3

Continued

Alternate placement of topic sentences offers pattern variety.

Board of Directors   -2-   October 26, 2008

ADEQUATE ACCOMMODATIONS AT BOTH HOTELS

Talking captions (all noun phrases) help interpretation.

Both hotels can guarantee the 600 rooms we will require. Because the Marriott is newer (built 2004), its rooms are more modern and, therefore, more appealing. The 9-year-old Hyatt, however, is well preserved and comfortable. Its rooms are all in good condition, and the equipment is up-to-date.

The Marriott has 11 small meeting rooms and the Hyatt has 13. All are adequate for our purposes. Both hotels can provide the 10 we need. For our opening session, the Hyatt would make available its Capri Ballroom, which can easily seat our membership. It would also serve as the site of our presidential luncheon. The assembly facilities at the Marriott appear to be somewhat crowded, although the management assures me that their largest meeting room can hold 600. Pillars in the room, however, would make some seats undesirable. In spite of the limitations mentioned, both hotels appear to have adequate facilities for our meeting.

Paragraph length shows good organization.

LOWER COSTS AT THE HYATT

Text analysis relates facts to problem.

Both the Hyatt and the Marriott would provide nine rooms for meetings on a complimentary basis. Both would provide complimentary suites for our president and our executive director. The Hyatt, however, would charge $500 for use of the room for the opening session. The Marriott would provide this room without charge.

Convention rates at the Hyatt are $169 for singles, $179 for double-bedded rooms, and $229 for suites. Comparable rates of the Marriott are $189, $199, and $350. Thus, the savings at the Hyatt would be approximately 15 percent per member.

Cost of the dinner selected would be $35 per person, including gratuities, at the Hyatt. The Marriott would meet this price if we would guarantee 600 plates. Otherwise, they would charge $38. Considering all of these figures, the total cost picture at the Hyatt is the more favorable one.

Sincerely,

Willard K Mitchell

Willard K. Mitchell
Executive Secretary

section with whatever introduction is appropriate. For example, the direct beginning illustrated previously could be followed with these introductory sentences:

> These are the primary findings of a study authorized by your board of directors last January. Because they concern information vital to all of us in the Association, they are presented here for your confidential use.

Following such an introduction, the report would present the supporting facts and their analyses. The writer would systematically build up the case supporting the opening comment. With either the direct or indirect order, a letter report may close with whatever friendly, goodwill comment fits the occasion.

- Supporting facts and analyses follow an appropriate introduction.

Email Reports

As we noted in Chapter 5, email is the most widely used form of written communication in business. Although heavily used for communicating with outside parties, email dominates internal written communication. That is, email is written by and to people in an organization, as Figure 11–4 illustrates.

- Email (internal written messages) is widely used.

Figure 11–4

Illustration of a Progress Report in Email Form. This email report summarizes a sales manager's progress in opening a new district. It begins with highlight information—all a busy reader may need to know. Organized by three categories of activity, the factual information follows. The writer–reader relationship justifies personal style.

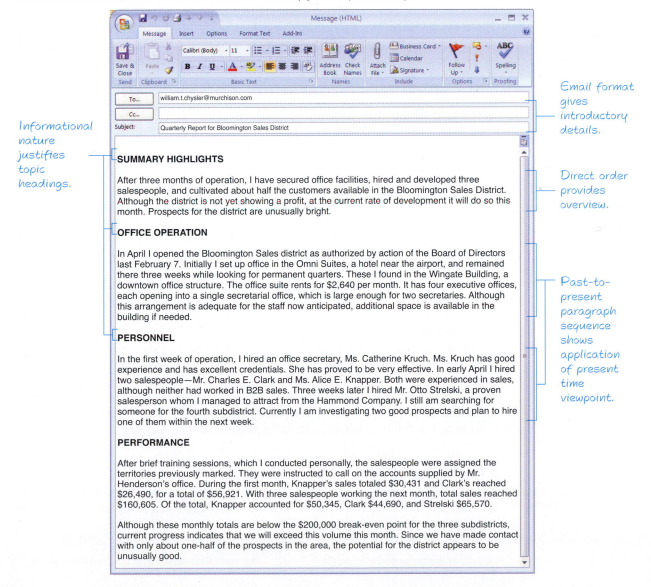

Informational nature justifies topic headings.

Email format gives introductory details.

Direct order provides overview.

Past-to-present paragraph sequence shows application of present time viewpoint.

To... william.t.chysler@murchison.com
Cc...
Subject: Quarterly Report for Bloomington Sales District

SUMMARY HIGHLIGHTS

After three months of operation, I have secured office facilities, hired and developed three salespeople, and cultivated about half the customers available in the Bloomington Sales District. Although the district is not yet showing a profit, at the current rate of development it will do so this month. Prospects for the district are unusually bright.

OFFICE OPERATION

In April I opened the Bloomington Sales district as authorized by action of the Board of Directors last February 7. Initially I set up office in the Omni Suites, a hotel near the airport, and remained there three weeks while looking for permanent quarters. These I found in the Wingate Building, a downtown office structure. The office suite rents for $2,640 per month. It has four executive offices, each opening into a single secretarial office, which is large enough for two secretaries. Although this arrangement is adequate for the staff now anticipated, additional space is available in the building if needed.

PERSONNEL

In the first week of operation, I hired an office secretary, Ms. Catherine Kruch. Ms. Kruch has good experience and has excellent credentials. She has proved to be very effective. In early April I hired two salespeople—Mr. Charles E. Clark and Ms. Alice E. Knapper. Both were experienced in sales, although neither had worked in B2B sales. Three weeks later I hired Mr. Otto Strelski, a proven salesperson whom I managed to attract from the Hammond Company. I still am searching for someone for the fourth subdistrict. Currently I am investigating two good prospects and plan to hire one of them within the next week.

PERFORMANCE

After brief training sessions, which I conducted personally, the salespeople were assigned the territories previously marked. They were instructed to call on the accounts supplied by Mr. Henderson's office. During the first month, Knapper's sales totaled $30,431 and Clark's reached $26,490, for a total of $56,921. With three salespeople working the next month, total sales reached $160,605. Of the total, Knapper accounted for $50,345, Clark $44,690, and Strelski $65,570.

Although these monthly totals are below the $200,000 break-even point for the three subdistricts, current progress indicates that we will exceed this volume this month. Since we have made contact with only about one-half of the prospects in the area, the potential for the district appears to be unusually good.

- Most email messages are written informally.

- Some resemble letters and follow letter form.
- Some are reports. Such email reports tend to be formal, factual, and problem related.

- There are many types of short reports. Here we cover five common types.

- Routine operational reports keep others informed about company operations.

- The form and content will vary, depending on the company.

- These reports should deliver the required information efficiently, clearly, and on time.

- Your word-processing program's template macro or merge feature can save you time on routine reports.

- Progress reports review progress on an activity.

Because email is primarily communication between people who know each other, it is usually informal. In fact, many are hurried, casual messages. Some email, however, is formal, especially reports directed to readers high in the administration of the organization.

As indicated in Chapter 5, some email messages resemble letters. Others, however, are more appropriately classified as reports. Most email reports tend to be more formal and factual. In fact, some email reports rival the longer forms in formality. Like the longer forms, they may use headings to display content and graphics to support the text. Email reports tend to be problem related.

TYPES OF SHORT REPORTS

Because organizations depend heavily on short reports, there are many varieties, written for many different purposes. We cover some of the most common types here, but the form they take will vary from company to company. Also, most companies will have developed certain unique report forms for their special purposes. Always study your company's ways of reporting before contributing a report yourself.

Routine Operational Reports

The majority of the reports written within companies are routine reports that keep supervisors, managers, and team members informed about the company's operations. These can be daily, weekly, monthly, or quarterly reports on the work of each department or even each employee. They can relate production data, information on visits to customers, issues that have arisen, or any kind of information that others in the organization need on a routine basis.

The form and contents of these reports will vary from company to company and manager to manager. Many will be submitted on predesigned forms. Others may not use forms but will follow a prescribed format. Still others will be shaped by the writer's own judgment about what to include and how to present it. The nature and culture of the organization can heavily influence the forms taken by these reports. One innovative format for weekly reporting is the 5-15 report.[1]

The name comes from the fact that it is intended to be read in 5 and written in 15 minutes. Its typical three-part contents are a description of what the employee did that week, a statement about the employee's morale and that of others he or she worked with, and one idea for how to improve operations. Clearly, this format would work best in an organization where employees have nonroutinized jobs and the management values the employees' opinions.

Whatever the form, the routine operational report should convey clearly and quickly what readers most need and want to know about the time period in question. It is also an opportunity for you, the writer, to showcase your ability to gather needed information on deadline.

When using standardized forms for periodic reports, you should consider developing a template macro or merge document with your word processing software. A macro would fill in all the standard parts for you, pausing to let you fill in the variable information. A template merge document would prompt you for the variables first, merging them with the primary document later. However standardized the process, you will still need to be careful to gather accurate information and state it clearly.

Progress Reports

You can think of an internal progress report as a routine operational report except that it tends to be submitted on an as-needed basis and, as its name implies, it focuses on

---

[1] For a fuller description and history, see Joyce Wycoff, "5-15 Reports: Communication for Dispersed Organizations," 2001, InnovationNetwork, 8 May 2006 <http://www.thinksmart.com/articles/515_reports.html>.

progress toward a specific goal. If you are working on a project for an external client, you may also need to submit progress reports to show that your work is on track. For example, a fund-raising organization might prepare weekly summaries of its efforts to achieve its goal. Or a building contractor might prepare a report on progress toward completing a building for a customer. Typically, the contents of these reports concern progress made, but they also may include such related topics as problems encountered or anticipated and projections of future progress.

Progress reports follow no set form. They can be quite formal, as when a contractor building a large manufacturing plant reports to the company for whom the plant is being built. Or they can be very informal, as in the case of a worker reporting by email to his or her supervisor on the progress of a task being performed. Some progress reports are quite routine and structured, sometimes involving filling in blanks on forms devised for the purpose. Most, however, are informal, narrative reports, as illustrated by the example in Figure 11–4.

● Most are informal and narrative; some are formal.

As with most reports, you have some choice about the tone to use when presenting your information. With progress reports, you want to emphasis the positive if possible. The overall message should be "I (or we) have made progress." The best way to convey this message confidently, of course, is to be sure that you or your team has in fact made some progress on the issue at hand.

● With progress reports, you want to emphasize the positive.

Problem-Solving Reports

Many short reports are *problem-solving reports*. These reports help decision makers figure out what to do any time a problem arises within an organization—which is often. For example, a piece of equipment may have broken down, causing mayhem on the production line. Or employees may have gotten hurt on the job. Or, less dramatically, a company procedure may have become outdated, or a client company may want to know why it's losing money. If we define *problem* as an issue facing the company, we could include many other scenarios as well—for example, whether or not a company should adopt flextime scheduling or what location it should choose for a new store. Whatever the context, the writer of a problem-solving report needs to gather facts about the problem or issue, define it clearly, research solutions, and recommend a course of action.

● Problem-solving reports help decision makers choose a course of action.

Like progress reports, problem-solving reports can be internal or external. Internal problem-solving reports are usually assigned, but sometimes employees may need to write unsolicited problem-solving reports—for example, if they must recommend that a subordinate be fired or if they feel that a change in procedures is necessary. External problem-solving reports are most often written by consulting companies for their clients. In these cases, the report is the main product that the client is paying for.

● These reports can be internal or external.

A type of problem-solving report that deserves special attention is a *feasibility study*. For these reports, writers study several courses of action and then propose the most feasible, desirable one. For instance, you might be asked to compare Internet service providers and recommend the one that suits the company's needs and budget best. Or you might investigate what type of onsite childcare center, if any, is feasible for your organization. Sometimes feasibility studies are not full-blown problem-solving reports. They may offer detailed analysis but stop short of making a recommendation. The analysis they provide nevertheless helps decision makers decide what to do.

● A special type of problem-solving report is a feasibility study.

In fact, many short reports that help solve company problems may not be complete problem-solving reports. Decision makers who assign research reports may not want recommendations. They may want only good data and careful analysis so that they can formulate a course of action themselves. Whether you are preparing an internal or external report, it is important to understand how far your readers want you to go toward proposing solutions.

● Whether or not you should make a recommendation will depend on the situation.

You have some latitude when deciding how direct to make your opening in a problem-solving report. If you believe that your readers will be open to any reasonable

● You will need to decide whether to use a direct or indirect approach.

Figure 11–5

Military Form For Problem-Solving Report

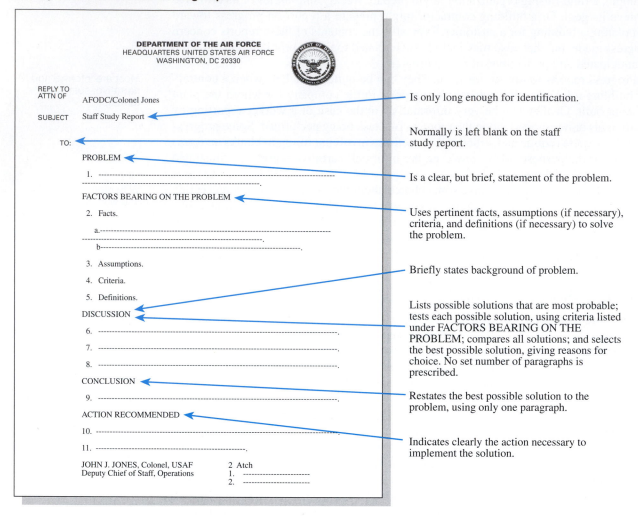

DEPARTMENT OF THE AIR FORCE
HEADQUARTERS UNITED STATES AIR FORCE
WASHINGTON, DC 20330

REPLY TO
ATTN OF   AFODC/Colonel Jones

SUBJECT   Staff Study Report — Is only long enough for identification.

TO: — Normally is left blank on the staff study report.

PROBLEM — Is a clear, but brief, statement of the problem.

1. --
---.

FACTORS BEARING ON THE PROBLEM — Uses pertinent facts, assumptions (if necessary), criteria, and definitions (if necessary) to solve the problem.

  2. Facts.
    a.---
    ----
    b--.

  3. Assumptions.
  4. Criteria.
  5. Definitions. — Briefly states background of problem.

DISCUSSION — Lists possible solutions that are most probable; tests each possible solution, using criteria listed under FACTORS BEARING ON THE PROBLEM; compares all solutions; and selects the best possible solution, giving reasons for choice. No set number of paragraphs is prescribed.

  6. --
  7. --
  8. --

CONCLUSION — Restates the best possible solution to the problem, using only one paragraph.

  9. --.

ACTION RECOMMENDED — Indicates clearly the action necessary to implement the solution.

  10. --
  11. ---.

JOHN J. JONES, Colonel, USAF   2 Atch
Deputy Chief of Staff, Operations   1. ----------------------
                                     2. ----------------------

findings or recommendations, you should state those up front. If you think your conclusions will be unexpected or your readers will be skeptical, you should still state your report's purpose and topic clearly at the beginning but save the conclusions and recommendations until the end, after leading your readers through the details. Figure 11–5, a pattern for a problem-solving report used by the U.S. military, follows this more indirect route. As always, try to find out which method of organization your readers prefer.

- Even though they are not overtly persuasive, problem-solving reports still need to be convincing.

While they usually propose action, problem-solving reports are not true persuasive messages. Because they have either been assigned or fall within an employee's assigned duties, the writer already has a willing reader. Furthermore, the writer has no obvious personal stake in the outcome the way he or she does with a persuasive message. However, when writing a problem-solving report, especially one that makes recommendations, you do need to show that your study was thorough and your reasoning sound. The decision makers may not choose to follow your advice, but your work, if it is carefully performed, still helps them decide what to do and reflects positively on you.

Audit Reports

- Audit reports hold organizations accountable to certain standards.

A specialized type of report is the audit report. This type is written to hold an organization accountable to certain standards that they are required to meet. While audit reports

A successful businessman fell in love with a woman who he felt might not meet the requirements of a person in his position. So he hired a detective agency to investigate her background.

After weeks of intensive checking, the detective agency submitted this report:

Ms. Stoner has an excellent reputation. She has high morals, lives within her means, and is well respected in the community. The only blemish on her record is that in recent months she has been seen repeatedly in the company of a business executive of doubtful repute.

---

can be assessments of an organization's finances, operations, or compliance with the terms of a contract, and while they can be written by internal or external auditors, the most common type of audit report is that written by a accounting firm to verify the truthfulness of a company's financial reports. These reports are short and standardized. You can find such reports in almost any corporate annual report. But accounting firms are also contracted to write longer, less standardized reports that help the company assess its financial health and adopt better accounting practices. Long-form audit reports vary greatly in their makeup, but, like other reports, they tend to include an executive summary followed by an introduction, methodology and standards used, findings, discussion, and conclusions or recommendations.

- The most common type is the financial audit written by accounting firms.

- Short financial audits follow a standardized format.

- Longer audit reports vary in form and contents.

As Chapter 10 notes, the Sarbanes-Oxley Act of 2002 has had an enormous impact on financial recordkeeping and reporting. This new set of federal regulations was prompted by the financial scandals of Enron, WorldCom, and other publicly traded companies. To restore and maintain investor confidence in companies' financial reports, Sarbanes-Oxley requires companies to have not only their financial records but also their financial reporting practices audited by external parties. As an employee, you may find yourself having to write reports related to this kind of audit. If you are an accountant working for an independent accounting firm, you may well find yourself involved in writing such audit reports.

- The Sarbanes-Oxley Act has increased the need for audit reports.

Meeting Minutes

Many short reports in business, especially internal ones, do not recommend or even analyze. Instead, they describe. Trip reports, incident reports, and the like are meant to provide a written record of something that happened. Whatever their type and specific purpose, they all share the need to be well organized, easy to read, and factual. Perhaps the most common of these reports is minutes for meetings. We thus single them out for special emphasis.

- Meeting minutes are a common type of descriptive report.

Minutes provide a written record of a group's activities and decisions, a history that includes announcements, reports, significant discussions, and decisions. Minutes might report who will do what and when, but they are primarily a summary that reports the gist of what happened, not a verbatim transcript. Minutes include only objective data; their writer carefully avoids using descriptive adjectives such as *brilliant, intelligent, reasonable,* and so on. However, if the group passes a resolution that specific wording be officially recorded, a writer would then include it. Accurate minutes are important because they can have some legal significance as to whether decisions are binding.

- Minutes provide a written record of a group's activities

The physical form is typically a memo or email, but the layout varies among organizations. Basically, it should enable the reader to easily focus on the content as well as easily retrieve it. Some writers find that numbering items in the minutes to

- Most are distributed by memo or email, but their layout varies among organizations.

Figure 11–6

Illustration of Meeting Minutes.

Minutes of the Policy Committee
Semiannual Meeting
November 21, 2007, 9:30–11:30 A.M., Conference Room A

Present: Megan Adami (chair), D'Marie Simon, DeAnne Overholt, Michelle Lum, Joel Zwanziger, Rebecca Shuster, Jeff Merrill, Donna Wingler, Chris Woods, Tim Lebold (corporate attorney, guest).

Absent: Joan Marian, Jeff Horen (excused), Leonna Plummer (excused)

Complete preliminary information provides a good record.

Minutes

Minutes from the May 5, 2007, meeting were read and approved.

Subheads help readers retrieve information.

Announcements

Chris Woods invited the committee to a reception for Milton Chen, Director in our Asia region. It'll be held in the executive dining room at 3:00 P.M. tomorrow. Chris reminded us that Asia is ahead of the United States in its use of wireless technology. He suggested that perhaps we can get some idea of good policies to implement now.

Old Business—Email Policy

Joel Zwanziger reported the results of his survey on the proposed new email policy. While 16 percent of the employees approved implementing the policy, 84 percent were not opposed. The committee approved a January 1, 2008, implementation subject to its distribution to all employees before the Christmas break.

Discussions are summarized and actions taken are included.

Web Surfing Policy

D'Marie Simon reported on the preliminary findings of other companies in the industry. Most have informal guides but no official policies. The guidelines generally are that all surfing must be related to the job and that personal surfing should be done on breaks. The committee discussed the issue at length. It approved a policy that reflects the current general guidelines.

Temp Policy

Tim Lebold presented the legal steps we need to take to get our old and new temporary employees to sign a nondisclosure agreement prior to working here as we've been discussing in relation to a new temp policy. The committee directed Tim to begin the process so that the policy could be put in force as soon as possible.

New Business—Resolution

Resolutions often include descriptive language.

Michelle Lum proposed that a resolution of thanks be added to the record recognizing Megan for her terrific attention to detail as well her clear focus on keeping the committee abreast of policy issues. It was unanimously approved.

Next Meeting

The next meeting of the committee will be May 3, 2008, from 9:30–11:30 A.M. in Conference Room A.

Closing gives reader complete needed facts.

Adjournment

The meeting was adjourned at 11:25 A.M.

Respectfully submitted,

Megan Adami
Megan Adami

Signing signifies the minutes are official records.

agree with the numbering of a meeting's agenda helps in retrieving and reviewing specific discussions. Subheads are often useful, especially if they are bold, italicized, or underlined to make them stand out. Most important, minutes should provide an adequate record.

Figure 11–6 illustrates typical minutes. The following preliminary, body, and closing items may be included.

● Typical minutes include common preliminary, body, and closing items.

Preliminary Items

- Name of the group.
- Name of document.
- Type of meeting (monthly, emergency, special).
- Place, date, and time called to order.
- Names of those attending including guests (used to determine if a quorum is present).
- Names of those absent and reasons for absence.

Body Items

- Approval of minutes of previous meeting.
- Meeting announcements.
- Old business—Reports on matters previously presented.
- New business—Reports on matters presented to the group.

Closing Items

- Place and time of next meeting.
- Notation of the meeting's ending time.
- Name and signature of the person responsible for preparing the minutes.

When you are responsible for preparing the minutes of a meeting, you can take several steps to make the task easier. First, get an agenda in advance. Use it to complete as much of the preliminary information as possible, including the names of those expected to attend. If someone is not present, you can easily move that person's name to the absentee list. You might even set up a table in advance with the following column headings to encourage you to take complete notes.

● Preparing ahead of time makes the job easier and encourages more complete notes.

Topic	Summary of Discussion	Action/Resolution

Bear in mind that meeting minutes, while they look innocent enough, almost always have political implications. Because minutes are the only tangible record of what happened, meeting participants will want their contributions included and cast in a positive light. Since you cannot record every comment made, you will need to decide which ones to include, whether or not to credit a particular speaker, how to capture the group's reaction, and so forth. Use your good judgment when translating a rich oral event into a written summary.

● Be aware of the political dimension of minutes.

PROPOSALS

We include proposals in this chapter because they share certain characteristics with reports. Both forms (genres) require careful gathering and presenting of facts. And both tend to use a direct pattern of organization. But proposals differ from reports in one essential way: proposals are intentionally *persuasive*. Proposal writers are not just providing information in an orderly, useful way. They are writing to get a particular result, and they have a vested interest in that result. The following sections provide an introduction to the main types of proposals and offer guidelines for preparing them. As you read this advice, bear in mind the general advice on persuasion in Chapter 8. Also,

● Proposals resemble reports but differ in their fundamental purpose.

● Proposals are intentionally persuasive.

while we focus on shorter, less formal proposals in this chapter, understand that you can use many of the guidelines presented in Chapter 12 when preparing longer, more formal proposals.

Types of Proposals

- There are many kinds of proposals.

Proposals can vary widely in purpose, length, and format. Their purpose can be anything from acquiring a major client to getting a new copier for your department. They can range from one page to hundreds of pages. They are usually written, but they can be presented orally or delivered in oral and written form. As with other kinds of business communication, the context will determine the specific traits of a given proposal. But all proposals can be categorized as either internal or external, and either solicited or unsolicited.

- Proposals can be either internal or external.

Internal or External. Proposals can be either *internal* or *external*. That is, they may be written for others within your organization or for readers outside your organization.

- Internal proposals help you get what you need for you or your department to do your work.

The reasons for internal proposals differ, but you will almost surely find yourself having to write them. They are a major means by which you will get what you need in order to do or enhance your job, or to effect an important change in your organization. Whether you want a computer upgrade, an improved physical environment, specialized training, travel money, or additional staff members, you will usually need to make your case to management. Of course, much of what you need as an employee will already be provided by your company. But when resources are tight, as they almost always are, you will have to persuade your superiors to give you the money rather than allocating it to another employee or department. Even if your idea is to enhance company operations in some way—for example, to make a procedure more efficient or cost effective—you may find yourself having to persuade. Companies tend to be conservative in terms of change. The management wants good evidence that the trouble and expense of making a change will pay off.

In addition, as the practice of outsourcing has grown, many companies have adopted a system in which departments have to compete with external vendors for projects. As the director of technical publications for a company, for example, you may find yourself bidding against a technical-writing consulting firm for the opportunity, and the funding, to write the company's online documentation. If you are not persuasive, you may find yourself with a smaller and smaller staff and, eventually, no job yourself. Clearly, the ability to write a persuasive internal proposal is an important skill.

External proposals are also written for a variety of reasons, but the most common purpose is to acquire business for a company or money from a grant-awarding organization. Every consulting firm—whether in training, financial services, information technology, or virtually any other business specialty—depends upon external proposals for its livelihood. If such firms cannot persuade companies to choose their services, they will not be in business for long. Companies that supply other companies with goods they need, such as uniforms, computers, or raw materials, may also need to prepare proposals to win clients. Business-to-business selling is a major arena for external proposals.

- External proposals acquire business for the company or external funding for a project.

But external proposals are also central to other efforts. A company might propose to merge with another company; a city government might propose that a major department store choose the city for its new location; a university professor might write a proposal to acquire research funding. Many nonprofit and community organizations depend upon proposals for the grant money to support their work. They might write such proposals to philanthropic foundations, to wealthy individuals, to businesses, or to government funding agencies. Depending on the nature of the organization that you work for, proficiency in external proposal writing could be critical.

Solicited or Unsolicited. Another way to categorize proposals is *solicited* versus *unsolicited*. A solicited proposal is written in response to an explicit invitation tendered by a company, foundation, or government agency that has certain needs to meet or goals to fulfill. An unsolicited proposal, as you can probably guess, is one that you submit without an official invitation to do so.

- Proposals can be either solicited or unsolicited.

The primary means by which organizations solicit proposals is the request for proposals, or RFP (variations are requests for quotes—RFQs—and invitations for/to bid—IFBs or ITBs—both of which tend to focus only on price). These can range from brief announcements to documents of 50, 100, or more pages, depending upon the scope and complexity of the given project. As you might expect, their contents can also vary. But a lot of thought and research go into a good RFP. In fact, some RFPs—for instance, a company's request for proposals from IT firms to design and implement their technology infrastructure—need to be just as elaborately researched as the proposals being requested. Whatever the originating organization, the RFP needs to include a clear statement of the organization's need, the proposal guidelines (due date and time, submission process, and proposal format and contents), and the approval process, in addition to such helpful information as background about the organization.

- Organizations use requests for proposals—RFPs—to solicit proposals.

- Writing a good RFP requires considerable research itself.

When responding to an RFP, you should be careful to heed its guidelines. With some firms, your proposal goes into the trash if it arrives even one minute late or omits a required section. This is particularly true for proposals to the federal government, whose proposal guidelines are notoriously, and perhaps understandably, regimented. On the other hand, most RFPs give you some latitude to craft your proposal in such a way that your organization can put its best foot forward. You will want to take advantage of this maneuvering room to make your proposal the most persuasive of those submitted. Of course, you will decide in the first place to respond only to those RFPs that give your organization (or, if it is an internal RFP, your department) a fighting chance to win.

- When responding to a solicited proposal, carefully follow the RFP guidelines.

In business situations, solicited proposals usually follow preliminary meetings between the parties involved. For example, if a business has a need for certain production equipment, its buyers might first identify likely suppliers by considering those they already know, by looking at industry material, or by asking around in their professional

- The response to an RFP should be part of a larger business relationship.

networks. Next they would initiate meetings with these potential suppliers to discuss the business's needs. Some or all of these suppliers would then be invited to submit a proposal for filling the need with its particular equipment. As you can see, the more relationships you have with companies that might use your goods or services, the more likely it is that they will invite you to a preliminary meeting and then invite you to bid. One expert, in fact, asserts that the success of a proposal depends even more on the conversations and relationships that led to the proposal than on the proposal itself.[2] Another advises that "proposals can be won (or lost) before the RFP hits the streets."[3]

- Making contact with the granter can lead to stronger proposals for grants.

Even if you are preparing a proposal for a government or foundation grant, it is wise—unless the RFP specifically forbids it—to call the funding source's office and discuss your ideas with a representative.

- Unsolicited proposals are like sales messages.

When writing unsolicited proposals, your job is harder than with solicited proposals. After all, in these scenarios, the intended reader has not asked for your ideas or services. For this reason, your proposal should resemble a sales message. It should quickly get the readers' attention, bring a need of theirs vividly to mind, and show how your product or services will answer the need. And from beginning to end, it should build your credibility. For example, if you want to provide training for a company's workforce or persuade a company to replace their current insurance provider with your company, you will need to target your readers' need in the opening, use further details to prepare them to receive your plan, lay out the benefits of your proposal quickly and clearly, and get the readers to believe that yours is the best company for the job. Careful and strategic preparation of unsolicited proposals can result in much success.

- Prior contact with your recipient, if possible, is desirable for unsolicited proposals as well.

As with solicited proposals, you should try, if at all possible, to make prior contact with a person in the organization who has some power to initiate your plan. All other things being equal, a proposal to someone you know is preferable to a "cold" proposal. It is best to view the unsolicited proposal as part of a larger relationship that you are trying to create or maintain.

Proposal Format and Contents

- As with reports, proposal format and formality can vary.

Every proposal is unique, but some generalizations can be made. To succeed, proposals must be designed with the key decision makers in mind, emphasize the most persuasive elements, and present the contents in a readable format and style.

- Their formats vary from short emails to long, elaborate proposals.

Format and Formality. The physical arrangement and formality of proposals vary widely. The simplest proposals resemble formal email reports. Internal proposals (those written for and by people in the same organization) usually fall into this category, though exceptions exist. The more complex proposals may take the form of full-dress, long reports, including prefatory pages (title pages, letter of transmittal, table of contents, executive summary), text, and an assortment of appended parts. Most proposals have arrangements that fall somewhere between these extremes.

- Select the format appropriate for your one case.

Because of the wide variations in the makeup of proposals, you would be wise to investigate carefully before designing a particular proposal. In your investigation, try to determine what format is conventional among those who will read it. Look to see what others have done in similar situations. In the case of an invited proposal, review the request thoroughly, looking for clues concerning the preferences of the inviting organization. If you are unable to follow any of these courses, design a format based on your analysis of the audience and your knowledge of formatting strategies. Your design should be the one that you think is best for the one situation.

- The formality requirements of proposals vary. Do what is appropriate.

The same advice applies to your decisions about formality. Let your reader and the circumstances be your guide. Internal proposals tend to be less formal than external ones because the parties are often familiar with each other and because internal

---

[2] Alan Weiss, *How to Write a Proposal That's Accepted Every Time,* expanded 2nd ed. (Peterborough, NH: Kennedy Information, Inc., 2003) 13.

3 "What a Private Sector Company Can Learn From Government Proposals," 2001, CapturePlanning.com, 5 May 2006 <http://captureplanning.com/articles/12548.cfm>.

The Seven Deadly Sins of Proposal Writing

1. Failure to focus on the client's business problems and payoffs—the content sounds generic.
2. No persuasive structure—the proposal is an "information dump."
3. No clear differentiation of this vendor compared to others.
4. Failure to offer a compelling value proposition.
5. Buried key points—no impact, no highlighting.
6. Lack of readability because content is full of jargon, too long, or too technical.
7. Credibility killers—misspellings, grammar and punctuation errors, use of the wrong client's name, inconsistent formats, and similar mistakes.

SOURCE: Tom Sant, *Persuasive Business Proposals* (New York: American Management Association, 2004) 11.

documents, in general, are less formal than external ones. If you are proposing a major initiative or change, however, using a formal presentation—whether oral, written, or both—may be in order. Contrarily, external proposals, while they tend to be formal, can be quite informal if they are short and the two parties know each other well. Many successful business proposals are pitched in letter format. As with every other kind of message, knowledge of and adaptation to your reader are key.

Content. Whether you are writing an external or internal proposal or a solicited or unsolicited one, your primary goal is the same: to make a persuasive argument. Every element of your proposal—from the title to the cover letter to the headings and organization of your content to the way you say things—needs to be informed by your central argument.

- The primary objective of your content is to make a persuasive argument.

To be able to design your proposal according to this principle, you need to know your readers and their needs (which may be represented in an RFP). You also need to know how you can meet those needs. From these two kinds of knowledge you can develop your central argument. What is your competitive edge? Value for the money? Convenience? Reliability? Congruence of your reader's needs or mission and what you have to offer? Some or all of the above? How you frame your argument will depend on how you think your proposal will be evaluated.

- First, review the readers' needs and your own ability to meet them.
- Then develop your central argument.

The reader of a business proposal will bring three basic criteria to the evaluation process:

- Readers of business proposals bring three main criteria to the evaluation process.

- Desirability of the solution (Do we need this? Will it solve our problem?)
- Qualifications of the proposer (Can the author of the proposal, whether an individual or company, really deliver, and on time and on budget?)
- Return on investment (Is the expense, whether time or money, justified?)

If you can answer these three questions affirmatively from the point of view of your intended recipient, you have a good chance of winning the contract or your management's approval.

When you have figured out what to propose and why, you need to figure out how to propose it. If the RFP provides strict guidelines for contents and organization, follow them. Otherwise, you have considerable discretion when determining your proposal's components. Although the number of content possibilities is great, you should consider including the eight topics listed below. They are broad and general, and you can combine or subdivide them as needed to fit the facts of your case. (See Figures 11–7 and 11–8 for two examples.)

- Consider including these eight topics:

Figure 11–7

Illustration of a Short Internal Proposal. This simple proposal seeks organization membership for its writer. It begins with a quick introduction that recalls the reader's invitation for the proposal. Then it presents the case, logically proceeding from background information to advantages of membership, to costs. It concludes with the recommendation to sponsor membership.

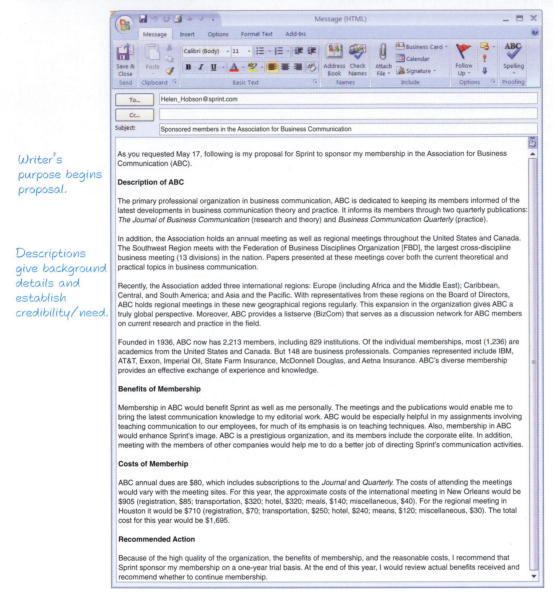

Writer's purpose begins proposal.

Descriptions give background details and establish credibility/need.

Membership advantages to company and to individual add connection.

Particulars reinforce persuasive effort.

Specified action completes the plan.

- 1. Writer's purpose and the reader's need (good beginning topics).

1. *Writer's purpose and the reader's need.* An appropriate beginning is a statement of the writer's purpose (to present a proposal) and the reader's need (such as reducing turnover of field representatives). If the report is in response to an invitation, that statement should tie in with the invitation (for example, as described in the July 10 announcement). The problem should be stated clearly, in the way described in Chapter 10. This proposal beginning illustrates these recommendations:

   As requested at the July 10 meeting with Alice Burton, Thomas Cheny, and Victor Petrui in your Calgary office, Murchison and Associates present the following proposal for studying the high rate of turnover among your field representatives. We will assess the job satisfaction of the current sales force, analyze exit interview records, and compare company compensation and human resource practices with industry norms to identify the causes of this drain on your resources.

Figure 11–8

Solicited External Proposal. A design and manufacturing company has invited research firms to propose plans for tracking its implementation of an enterprise resource planning (ERP) system—information technology that integrates all functions of the company, from job orders to delivery and from accounting to customer management. The midlevel formality of this proposal responding to the RFP is appropriate given the proposal's relative brevity and the two parties' prior meeting.

WHITFIELD
Organizational Research

7 Research Parkway, Columbus, OH 45319 614-772-4000 Fax: 614-772-4001

February 3, 2007

Janice Spears
Chief Operations Officer
RT Industries
200 Midland Highway
Columbus, OH 45327

Dear Janice:

Identifies the context for the proposal and shows appreciation for being invited to submit.

Reinforces the need for the study.

Thank you for inviting Whitfield Organizational Research to bid on RFP 046, "Study of InfoStream Implementation at RT Industries." Attached is our response. We enjoyed meeting with you to learn about your goals for this research. All expert advice supports the wisdom of your decision to track InfoStream's implementation. As you know, the road of ERP adoption is littered with failed, chaotic, or financially bloated implementations. Accurate and timely research will help make yours a success story.

Reminds the reader of the previous, pleasant meeting.

Whitfield Organizational Research is well qualified to assist you with this project. Our experienced staff can draw upon a variety of minimally invasive, cost-effective research techniques to acquire reliable information on your employees' reception and use of InfoStream. We are also well acquainted with ERP systems and can get a fast start on collecting the data you need. And, because Whitfield is a local firm, we will save you travel and lodging costs.

Summarizes the proposing company's advantages.

Compliments the receiving company, shows the writer's knowledge of the company, and states the benefits of choosing the writer's company.

RT's culture of employee involvement has earned you a persistent presence on *Business Ohio*'s list of the Best Ohio Workplaces. The research we propose, performed by Whitfield's knowledgeable and respectful researchers, will help you maintain your productive culture through this period of dramatic change. It will also help you reap the full benefits of your investment.

We would welcome the opportunity to work with RT Industries on this exciting initiative.

Indirectly asks the reader for the desired action.

Sincerely yours,

Evan Lockley

Evan Lockley
Vice President, Account Management

Figure 11–8

Continued

Response to RFP 046:
Study of InfoStream Implementation at RT Industries

Proposed by
Whitfield Organizational Research
February 3, 2007

I. Executive Summary

Provides a clear overview of the problem, purpose, and benefits.

RT Industries has begun a major organizational change with its purchase of InfoStream enterprise resource planning (ERP) software. To track the effect of this change on personnel attitudes and work processes in the company, RT seeks the assistance of a research firm with expertise in organizational studies. Whitfield Organizational Research has extensive experience with personnel-based research and familiarity with ERP software. We propose a four-part plan that will take place across the first year of implementation. It will yield three major deliverables: an initial, a midyear, and a year-end report. Our methodology will be multifaceted, minimally disruptive, and cost effective. The results will yield a reliable picture of how InfoStream is being received and used among RT's workforce. Whitfield can also advise RT management on appropriate interventions during the process to enhance the success of this companywide innovation.

II. Project Goals

RT Industries has so far invested over $1.6 million and over 1,000 employee hours in the purchase of and management's training on InfoStream's ERP system. As RT integrates the system fully into its company of 800+ employees over the next 12 months, it will invest many additional dollars and hours in the project, with the total investment likely to top $2 million. Adopting such a system is one of the most wide-ranging and expensive changes a company can make.

Shows knowledge of the company; reminds readers of the investment they want to protect.

Reinforces the need for the study.

As Jeri Dunn, Chief Information Officer of Nestle USA, commented in *CIO Magazine* about her company's well-publicized troubles with their ERP software, "No major software implementation is really about the software. It's about change management." An ERP system affects the daily work of virtually everyone in the company. The most common theme in ERP-adoption failure stories—of which there are many—is lack of attention to the employees' experience of the transition. Keeping a finger on the pulse of the organization during this profound organizational change is critical to maximizing the return on your investment.

Our research will determine

Statement of benefits, supported by clear logic.

- How well employees are integrating InfoStream into their jobs.
- How the new system is changing employees' work processes.
- How the system is affecting the general environment or "culture" in the company.

Whitfield has designed a four-part, multimethod research plan to gather these data. Through our periodic reports, you will be able to see how InfoStream is being integrated into the working life of the company. As a result, you will be

Figure 11–8

Continued

2   **Whitfield Organizational Research**

able to make, and budget for, such interventions as strategic communications and additional training. You will also find out where employee work processes need to be adjusted to accommodate the new system.

Instituting a change of this magnitude *will* generate feedback, whether it is employee grumbling or constructive criticism. Whitfield associates will gather this feedback in a positive, orderly way and compile it into a usable format. The findings will enable RT's management to address initial problems and ward off future problems. The research itself will also contribute to the change management efforts of the company by giving RT's employee stakeholders a voice in the process and allowing their feedback to contribute to the initiative's success.

III. Deliverables

Readers can see the products of the proposed research up front.

The information you need will be delivered as shown below. All dates assume a project start date of July 1, 2007.

Approximate Date:	Deliverable:
October 1, 2007	Written report on **initial** study of 12–14 employees' work processes and attitudes and on companywide survey.
February 1, 2008	Written report at **midyear** on employees' work processes and attitudes and on companywide survey.
June 30, 2008	**Year-end** report (written and oral) on employees' work processes and attitudes and on companywide survey.

IV. Anticipated Schedule/Methods

The research will take place from July 1, 2007, the anticipated go-live date for InfoStream at RT, to approximately June 30, 2008, a year later. As shown below, there will be four main components to this research, with Part III forming the major part of the project.

Gives details of the project in a readable format.

Research Part and Time Frame	Purpose	Methods
Part I (July '07)	Gather background information; recruit research participants	Gather data on RT (history, products/mission, organizational structure/culture, etc.). Interview personnel at RT and at InfoStream about why RT considered adopting an ERP system, why RT bought InfoStream, and how employees at RT have been informed about InfoStream. During this period we will also work with the COO's staff to recruit participants for the main part of the study (Part III).

Figure 11–8

Continued

Whitfield Organizational Research 3

Research Part and Time Frame	Purpose	Methods
Part II (July '07):	Obtain the perspective of the launch team on InfoStream	Focus-group interview with RT's launch team for InfoStream, with particular emphasis on their goals for and concerns about the implementation. Anticipated duration of this interview would be one hour, with participants invited to share any additional feedback afterward in person or by email.
Part III (July–Sept. '07; Nov. '07–Jan. '08; Mar.–June '08):	Assess the impact of InfoStream on employee work processes and attitudes	Conduct three rounds of 1–2 hour interviews with approximately 12–14 RT employees to track their use of InfoStream. Ideally, we will have one or two participants from each main functional area of the company, with multiple levels of the company represented.
Part IV (September '07, January '08, May '08)	Assess companywide reception of InfoStream	Conduct three web-based surveys during the year to track general attitudes about the implementation of InfoStream.

This plan yields the following time line:

	7/07	8/07	9/07	10/07	11/07	12/07	1/08	2/08	3/08	4/08	5/08	6/08
Initial research	■											
Focus group	■											
1st round of interviews	■	■	■									
1st web survey			■									
Initial report				■								
2nd round of interviews					■	■	■					
2nd web survey								■				
Mid-year report									■			
3rd round of interviews										■	■	■
3rd web survey											■	
Year-end report												■

Time line makes it easy to see what will happen at each point.

Figure 11–8

Continued

4	**Whitfield Organizational Research**

V. Interview Structure and Benefits

While Parts I, II, and IV will provide essential information about the project and its reception, the most valuable data will come from Part III, the periodic on-site interviews with selected RT employees. Gathering data in and about the subject's own work context is the only reliable way to learn what is really happening in terms of the employees' daily experience. Following is a description of our methodology for gathering these kinds of data:

Initial interview:

- Gather background information about the participants (how long they have worked at RT, what their jobs consist of, what kind of computer experience they've had, how they were trained on InfoStream).
- Ask them to show us, by walking us through sample tasks, how they use InfoStream.
- Ask them to fill out a questionnaire pertaining to their use of InfoStream.
- Go back over their answers, asking them to explain orally why they chose the answers they did.
- Ask them either to keep notes on or email us about any notable experiences they have with InfoStream.
- Take notes on any interruption, interactions, and other activities that occur during the interview.

From data gained in these interviews, we will assess how well the participants' current work processes are meshing with InfoStream. We will also document how use of InfoStream is affecting the participants' attitudes and their interactions with other employees and departments. We will check our findings with the participants for accuracy before including these data in the initial report.

Midyear interview:

- Ask the participants if they have any notable experiences to relate about InfoStream and/or if any changes have occurred in the tasks they perform using InfoStream.
- Have the participants fill out the same questionnaire as in the first interviews.
- Discuss with participants the reasons for any changes in their answers since the first questionnaire.
- Observe any interactions or other activities that occur during the interview.
- Check our findings with the participants for accuracy before including these data in the midyear report.

Year-end interviews:

- Will be conducted in the same fashion as the second interviews.
- Will also include questions allowing participants to debrief about the project and about InfoStream in general.

Benefits of this interview method:

- Because researchers will be physically present in the employees' work contexts, they **can gather a great deal of information,** whether observed or reported by the employee, **in a short amount of time.**
- Because employees will be asked to elaborate on their written answers, the researcher **can learn the true meaning of the employee's responses.**

Figure 11–8

Continued

Whitfield Organizational Research   5

- Asking employees to verify the researcher's findings **will add another validity check and encourage honest, thorough answers.**

VI. Specific Knowledge Goals

We will design the interviews and the companywide surveys to find out the extent to which

- InfoStream is making participants' jobs easier or harder, or easier in some ways and harder in others.
- InfoStream is making their work more or less efficient.
- InfoStream is making their work more or less effective.
- They believe InfoStream is helping the company overall.
- They are satisfied with the instruction they have received about the system.
- InfoStream is changing their interactions with other employees.
- InfoStream is changing their relations with their supervisors.
- InfoStream is affecting their overall attitude toward their work.

The result will be a detailed, reliable picture of how InfoStream is playing out at multiple levels and in every functional area of RT Industries, enabling timely intervention by RT management.

VII. Cost

Because we are a local firm, no travel or lodging expenses will be involved.

Research Component	Estimated Hours	Cost
Part I (background fact finding)	6 hours	$300
Part II (focus group with launch team)	3 hours (includes preparation and analysis)	$300
Part III (3 rounds of on-site interviews)	474 hours	$18,960
Part IV (3 rounds of web-based surveys)	48 hours	$1,920
Preparation of Reports	90 hours	$3,600
		Total: $25,080

VIII. Credentials

Whitfield Organizational Research has been recognized by the American Society for Training and Development as a regional leader in organizational consulting. We have extensive education and experience in change management, organizational psychology, quantitative and qualitative research methods, and team building. Our familiarity with ERP software, developed through projects with such clients as Orsys and PRX Manufacturing, makes us well suited to serve RT's needs. Résumés and references will be mailed upon request or can be downloaded from <www.whitfieldorganizationalresearch.com>.

If a proposal is submitted without invitation, its beginning has an additional requirement: it must gain attention. As noted previously, uninvited proposals are much like sales messages. Their intended readers are not likely to be eager to read them. Thus, their beginnings must overcome the readers' reluctance. An effective way of doing this is to begin by briefly summarizing the highlights of the proposal with emphasis on its benefits. This technique is illustrated by the beginning of an unsolicited proposal that a restaurant consultant sent to prospective clients:

> The following pages present a proven plan for operations review that will (1) reduce food costs, (2) evaluate menu offerings for maximum profitability, (3) increase kitchen efficiency, (4) improve service, and (5) increase profits. Mattox and Associates proposes to achieve these results through its highly successful procedures, which involve analysis of guest checks and invoices and observational studies of kitchen and service work.

Your clear statement of the purpose and problem may be the most important aspect of the proposal. If you do not show right away that you understand what needs to be done and have a good plan for doing it, you may well have written the rest of your proposal in vain.

2. *Background*. A review of background information promotes an understanding of the problem. Thus, a college's proposal for an educational grant might benefit from a review of the college's involvement in the area to which the grant would be applied. A company's proposal of a merger with another company might review industry developments that make the merger desirable. Or a chief executive officer's proposal to the board of directors that a company's administration be reorganized might present the background information that justifies the proposal.

- 2. Background.

3. *Need*. Closely related to the background information is the need for what is being proposed. In fact, background information may well be used to establish need. But because need can be presented without such support, we list it separately. You might wonder if this section applies in situations where an RFP has been issued. In such cases, won't readers already know what they need? In many cases the answer is no, not exactly. They may think they know, but you may see factors that they've overlooked. Plus, recasting their problem in ways that lead to your proposed solution helps your persuasive effort. And whatever the situation, elaborating on the receiving organization's needs enables your readers to see that *you* understand their needs.

- 3. Need.

4. *Description of plan*. The heart of a proposal is the description of what the writer proposes to do. This is the primary message of the proposal. It should be concisely presented in a clear and orderly manner, but it should give sufficient detail to convince the reader of the plan's logic, feasibility, and appropriateness. It should also identify the "deliverables," or tangible products, of the proposal.

- 4. Plan description.

5. *Benefits of the proposal*. Your proposal should make it easy for your readers to see how your proposed action will benefit them. A brief statement of the benefits should appear at the front of your proposal, whether in the letter of transmittal, executive summary, opening paragraph, or all of the above. But you should elaborate on those benefits in the body of your proposal. You might do so in the section describing your plan, showing how each part will yield a benefit. Or, you might have a separate section detailing the benefits. As with sales writing, the greater the need to persuade, the more you should stress the benefits.

- 5. Benefits of the proposal (especially if selling is needed).

As an example of benefits logically covered in proposals, a college's request for funding to establish a program for retaining the older worker could point to the profitability that such funding would give local businesses. And a proposal offering a consulting service to restaurants could stress such benefits as improved work efficiency, reduced employee theft, savings in food costs, and increased profits.

6. *Particulars*. Although the particulars of the proposal are really a part of your plan, they are often discussed separately. By *particulars* we mean the specifics: time schedules, costs, performance standards, means of appraising performance, equipment and supplies needed, guarantees, personnel requirements, and such.

- 6. Particulars (time schedules, costs, performance standards, equipment and supplies needed, and such).

What is needed in a given case depends on its unique requirements. But in any event, the particulars should anticipate and answer the readers' questions and be presented in the most positive light.

7. Ability to deliver.

7. *Evidence of ability to deliver.* The proposing organization must sometimes establish its ability to perform. This means presenting information on such matters as the qualifications of personnel, success in similar cases, the adequacy of equipment and facilities, operating procedures, and financial status. Whatever information will serve as evidence of the organization's ability to carry out what it proposes should be used. With an external proposal, resist the temptation to throw long, generic résumés at the readers. The best approach is to select only the most persuasive details about your personnel. If you do include résumés, tailor them to the situation.

8. Concluding comments (words directed toward the next step).

8. *Concluding comments.* In most proposals you should urge or suggest the desired action. This statement often occurs in a letter to the readers, but if there is no cover letter or the proposal itself is not a letter, it can form the conclusion of your proposal. You might also include a summary of your proposal's highlights or provide one final persuasive push in a concluding section.

In Chapter 12, you will see how to adapt this chapter's guidelines for short reports and proposals to longer, more formal documents. As you might expect, these too will be shaped by the readers' needs and expectations.

SUMMARY BY LEARNING OBJECTIVES

1 Explain the structure of reports relative to length and formality.

1. Length and formality determine the following general progression of report structure:
   - The very long ones have prefatory pages (title fly, title page, letter of transmittal, table of contents, executive summary).
   - As reports become shorter and less formal, the composition of the prefatory parts section changes, generally in this order:
     — First, the title fly drops out.
     — Then, in succession, the executive summary and letter of transmittal are combined,
     — The table of contents is omitted, and
     — The combined letter of transmittal and executive summary is dropped.
   - Even less elaborate are the letter report and the email report.

2 Discuss the four major differences involved in writing short and long reports.

2. The shorter and by far the most common reports are much like the longer ones except for these four differences:
   - They have less need for introductory material.
   - They are more likely to begin directly (conclusion and recommendation first).
   - They are more likely to use personal style.
   - They have less need for a formal coherence plan.

3 Choose an appropriate form for short reports.

3. The shorter reports come in three main forms.
   - The report form has these traits:
     — It consists of a title page and report text.
     — Usually it begins with a summary or conclusion.
     — Then it presents findings and analyses.
   - Letter reports are also popular.
     — Usually they are written in the indirect order.
     — They are organized much like longer reports.
   - Email reports are like letter reports.
     — They are usually written for and by people within an organization.
     — They are the most common report form.

4. Among the varieties of short reports, five types stand out.

- Routine operational reports keep others informed about company operations.
  - Their form and content will vary, depending on the organization.
  - They should deliver the required information efficiently, clearly, and on time.
  - Special word-processing features can assist you with standardized reports.
- Progress reports review progress on an activity.
  - Most are informal and in narrative form, but some are formal.
  - They should emphasize the positive.
- Problem-solving reports help decision makers choose a course of action.
  - They can be internal or external.
  - You will need to decide whether or not to make recommendations.
  - You will need to decide whether to take a direct or indirect approach.
  - Though not persuasive per se, these reports do need to convince with their good data and analysis.
- Audit reports hold organizations accountable to certain standards.
  - The most common type is the financial audit prepared by an accounting firm.
  - Short financial audits follow a standardized format.
  - Longer audit reports vary in form and content.
  - The Sarbanes-Oxley Act has increased the need for audit reports.
- Meeting minutes, a type of descriptive report, provide a written record of a group's activities and decisions.
  - Most are distributed by memo or email, but their layout varies.
  - Typical minutes include common preliminary, body, and closing items.
  - Minutes have political implications. Use good judgment when preparing them.

4 Adapt the procedures for writing short reports to routine operational, progress, problem-solving, and audit reports as well as minutes of meetings.

5. Proposals resemble reports but differ in their fundamental purpose.

- They are intentionally persuasive.
- They can be categorized in two ways:
  - Internal or external.
  - Solicited or unsolicited.
- They vary widely in terms of format and formality.
  - As with reports, proposal formats can range from short emails to long, elaborate documents.
  - Their levels of formality vary as well.
- The goal for your content is to make a persuasive argument.
  - Review your readers' needs and your ability to address them.
  - Then develop your central argument.
  - Bear in mind the main criteria that evaluators use.
- The contents of proposals vary with need, but one should consider these topics:
  - Writer's purpose and reader's need.
  - Background.
  - Need.
  - Plan description.
  - Benefits.
  - Particulars (time, schedule, costs, performance standards, and such).
  - Ability to deliver.
  - Concluding comments.

5 Write adapted, well-organized, and persuasive proposals.

1 Discuss the effects of formality and problem length on report makeup as described in the chapter.

2 Which of the prefatory pages of reports appear to be related primarily to the length of the report? Which to the need for formality?

3 Explain why some routine report problems require little or no introduction.

4 Why is the direct order generally used in the shorter reports? When is the indirect order desirable for such reports?

5 Describe the organization of the conventional short report.

6 What types of problems are written up as letter reports? As email reports? Explain the differences.

7 What kinds of information might go into routine operational reports for different kinds of organizations? Why would these organizations need this information regularly?

8 Given what you've learned about progress reports, suggest an appropriate structure for these reports. What might go into the beginning? What might the middle parts be? What would the conclusion do?

9 How might an internal problem-solving report that has been assigned differ from one on the same subject that an employee generated on his or her own?

10 Study the audit reports in several companies' annual reports. What seem to be the common features of such audit reports?

11 Discuss the pros and cons of including a list of absentees in meeting minutes.

12 "To be successful, a proposal must be persuasive. This quality makes the proposal different from most short reports (which stress objectivity)." Discuss.

13 Discuss the differences between solicited and unsolicited proposals.

14 For what kinds of situations might you select email format for your proposal? Letter format? A longer, report-like format?

15 "I don't need to discuss my readers' needs in my proposal. They know what their needs are and don't want to waste time reading about them." Discuss.

1 Review the following report situations and determine for each the makeup of the report you would recommend for it:

a. A professional research organization has completed a survey of consumer attitudes toward BankOne. The survey results will be presented to the bank president in a 28-page report, including seven charts and three tables.

b. Joan Marion was asked by her department head to inspect the work area and report on safety conditions. Her report is two pages long and written in personal style.

c. Bill Wingler has an idea for improving a work procedure in his department at McLaughlin Body Company. His department head suggested that Bill present his idea in a report to the production superintendent. The report is almost five pages long, including a full-page diagram. It is written in the personal style.

d. Karen Canady, a worker in the corporate library of Accenture, was asked by Doug Edmunds, its president, for current inventory information on a number of subscriptions. Her report is less than a full page and consists mostly of a list of items and numbers.

e. Bryan Toups, a sales manager for Johnson and Johnson, was asked by the vice president of marketing to prepare an analysis of the results of a promotional campaign conducted in Toups's district. The report is six pages long (including one chart) and is written in the personal style.

2 Following is a report that was written for the manager of a large furniture retail store by the manager's assistant. The manager was concerned about customer complaints of late deliveries of furniture purchased and wanted to know the cause of the delays. Critique this report.

11-17-04

TO: Martina Kalavoda

FROM: Anthony Dudrow

SUBJECT: Investigation requested 11-17-04

This morning at staff meeting it was requested that an investigation be made of the status of home deliveries and of the causes of the delays that have occurred. The investigation has been made with findings as follows.

Now that a new driver's helper, Morris Tunney, has been hired, there should be no more delays. This was the cause of the problem.

Over the past two weeks (10 working days), a total of 143 deliveries were made; and of these, 107 were made on or before the date promised. But

some of the deliveries were late because of the departure two weeks ago of the driver's helper, Sean Toulouse, who had to be fired because of dishonesty and could not be replaced quickly with a permanent, qualified helper. Now that a permanent, qualified helper has been hired, there should be no more delays in delivery as this was the cause of the problem.

The driver was able to find a temporary helper, a man by the name of Rusty Sellers, for some help in the unloading work, but he got behind and couldn't seem to catch up. He could have caught up by working overtime, in the opinion of the writer, but he refused to do so. Of the 36 deliveries that were late, all were completed within two days. The problem is over now that the driver has a helper, so there should be no additional delays.

CRITICAL THINKING PROBLEMS

Short-Length Reports

1 *Reporting damage by vandals to the home office.* For this assignment, you are the manager of the Bigg City branch of Heartland Department Stores, Inc. Last night your store was attacked by vandals. Bricks were thrown through two display windows at the main entrance, graffiti (seventeen impressions) were painted on the north and west walls of the building, and fires were set in two dumpsters at the service entrance. Fortunately, the police night patrol noticed the fires and called the fire department before major fire damage was done. And they began investigating the other malicious damage done immediately. Other than the likely identity of the gang involved (suggested by the graffiti), they found no clues.

When you arrived at the store this morning your attention immediately turned to cleaning up the mess so that business

could go on as usual. You called the Stubbs Glass Company and got their promise to have the windows fixed today. Then you called Perez the Painters and got their promise to begin work on eradicating the graffiti tomorrow. This work, however, will take three or four days. The glass replacement will cost $720 and the graffiti removal $680. The dumpsters suffered only cosmetic damage, which your janitorial staff can handle.

Now you must report the damage and your remedial actions to the home office. In your report you may assume additional necessary facts as long as they are consistent with the information given. Address your memorandum report to Sylvia Dark, who is operations manager for the chain.

---

2 *Writing an evaluation report on Leon Parma.* Assume that you are the sales manager for Land Rodgers Investments, a major brokerage firm. You are in the process of writing annual evaluation reports on your subordinates. At the moment, you are working on the report for Leon Parma. Your garbled notes are as follows:

Great personality. A tireless worker. Has acquired and cultivated 18 new accounts in past year—well above company average of 7. Has lost 4 accounts—but all small ones. Follow-up indicates that these accounts lost because of lack of attention. Sales and purchase records suggest that he has been

overly aggressive—more interested in turnover (and resulting sales commissions) than customer service. No record of community service or membership in local business organizations (considered important by Land-Rodgers).

Obviously, Leon has great potential but needs direction in ethics and service. As these are delicate matters, you will need to work with care. Prepare the report in the memorandum form used by Land-Rodgers for this purpose. Send it to Boudreaux by email and prepare a hard copy for his personnel file.

---

3 *Evaluating effects of a promotion on your department's sales.* You are manager of the athletics department of Midville's Recreation Warehouse. This chain conducts a major promotion every July in all its stores. As in past years, you were asked to select seven products to feature in the store's local television and newspaper advertising. The plan was to

select items that would appeal to a wide range of customers, get them into the store, and sell to them.

Now that the promotion is over, Oscar Sladczyk, store manager, is assessing results. He has asked each department manager to gather the information on sales of the products advertised as well as on overall sales. Specifically, he wants to know how well the advertised products did—that is, how much did their sales increase as a result of the promotion. Also, since customers brought in by the advertising often buy other products, Mr. Sladczyk wants a comparison of total sales volume for the department during the week of the promotion with past weekly sales volume totals.

Your computations for this report produce the following information concerning sales of the advertised products:

Advertised Product	Average Number Sold Weekly Preceding Weeks	Number Sold During Promotion
World Cup tennis racquets, Model A-13	3	8
Silky Spinning reels, Master	11	39
Straight Arrow golf balls, 3-packs	14	93
Alpha-Beta jogging shoes	4	13
Mountaineer backpack	2	7
Little Devil camp stoves	2	11
Classic athletic socks, 3-packs	11	27

Sales for the department for the week of the promotion totaled $43,885. The weekly sales average during the preceding four weeks was $7,488.

Now present this information with your interpretations in a memorandum report addressed to Mr. Sladczyk. You may supply price and/or date for the products advertised if you think they are needed.

4 *Recommending that an erring subordinate be terminated.* You don't like to do such things, but you have no choice. You must write a report recommending that Brad C. Trigg be fired.

You are the sales manager for Caldwell Plumbing Wholesalers, Inc. Three months ago you transferred Mr. Trigg , a fifteen-year Caldwell veteran, from his job as order taker in the Dallas home office to the position of traveling salesperson for the five-state area. His new job involved calling on large contractors in the area with the goal of getting them to buy in quantity from Caldwell. You thought you had made a good decision. Brad appeared to have all the qualifications needed for the job—good people skills, excellent communication abilities, and a strong work ethic. But you didn't know about his dishonesty.

For the first two months his sales were disappointing, but you concluded that he needed time to adjust to the new job. In the third month some improvement occurred, but not enough to cover his expenses and salary. Throughout this time you noticed that his expenses were rather high. In Corpus Christi, for example, there was a $485 charge for fishing boat rental, guide service, and dinners. His expense form indicated he was entertaining Carlton DeLeon, a major plumbing contractor in the area. Then in Houston there was a claim for $185 for dinner with Dennis Hrozek of Hrozek and Son Plumbers as

guest. Similar claims were made in other cities—Oklahoma City, New Orleans, Little Rock. All were well supported by receipts and listed major contractors as guests.

Yesterday, by chance, you ran into Carlton DeLeon, whom you know well. In your conversation with Carlton you asked about his success on the fishing trip he made with Trigg. Carlton was surprised. "What fishing trip?" he responded. After returning to the office you checked the most recent expense claims submitted by Trigg. You found that many of the receipts were forgeries—and not very good ones, at that. Obviously, the man is dishonest.

This morning you confronted Trigg with the evidence. He admitted that he had submitted false claims with the explanation that he had given Caldwell fifteen years of his life "at slave wages" and was merely getting back what was due him. He ended the conversation abruptly and walked out. You find his attitude intolerable. He must be terminated.

Termination requires the approval of Amos T. Caldwell, the company president and your boss. In addition to recommending Trigg's termination, you will suggest that no legal action be taken against the man, although you have a good case. In your report you may assume additional details as long as they are consistent with the information given above.

5 *Determining the effects on sales of an in-store promotion.* Play the role of advertising manager for the Emperor Penguin Ice Cream Company. You have conducted an experiment to find out whether an in-store promotion can increase sales of

your super deluxe ice cream. The design of your experiment was as follows.

First, you selected two comparable cities—Middleton (population 744,000) and River Bend (population 828,000).

The two cities are about as alike as two cities could be, even in their sales of Emperor Penguin products. Eight Super Saver grocery stores in Middleton were your test stores. Eight comparable Super Saver stores in River Bend were your control stores. Prior to the experiment, sales of Emperor Penguin were about the same in the two groups. For one week in the Middleton stores you set up stands where employees gave away small samples of your deluxe ice cream to shoppers passing by. The shoppers also received a $1 discount store coupon good on the purchase of a gallon of any Emperor Penguin deluxe ice cream. No stand was set up in the River Bend stores.

Sales of Emperor Penguin deluxe ice cream were recorded for both groups of stores for the week prior to the experiment and for the week of the experiment. Then to determine whether the experiment had any lasting effect, you recorded sales for both groups of stores for a week one month after the experiment and a week two months after the experiment. No other promotion of the product was conducted at either store or in the shopping areas during this time.

Now you have your results. In summary fashion, they are as follows:

	Gallons Sold in Middleton Stores	Gallons Sold in River City Stores
One week before promotion	777	803
Week of the promotion	1,317	844
One week a month after promotion	1,219	832
One week two months after promotion	979	798

Your task is now to analyze these results and report them in your analysis to Reba Vorman, vice president of marketing for Emperor Penguin. Ms. Vorman authorized the experiment and is anxiously waiting for the results. You will limit your analysis to sales effects. The matter of cost is another problem—one that you will take up later. Send this memo report by company email.

6 *Recommending a dress and grooming code for a pharmaceutical company.* For this assignment you are the assistant to William D. Kidd, President and CEO of Kidd Pharmaceuticals. For years the company representatives who call on medical doctors have followed a very strict dress and grooming code, including for men such requirements as coat and tie, no facial hair, and no visible tattoos. Mr. Kidd's view was that the representatives should project a picture of dignity. But now his view has softened. As Mr. Kidd explained to you, "Perhaps I have been too strict in our dress code. Some of our board members think that I represent the distant past and that we should relax the code a bit."

President Kidd has instructed you to work up a new code—"one that fits both today's world and our male and female representatives." But he makes it clear that nothing should change unless there is good reason for change. "Think of how today's doctors view propriety, and develop a code that fits their views. Be sure to cover all areas that involve dress and grooming: clothing, hair (including facial), body piercing, tattoos, jewelry—the works."

Now you must write the report using the company's memorandum form. Address it to Mr. Kidd.

7 *Recommending a scholarship recipient.* Assume the role of executive secretary at the Abernathy Foundation. It is your job to recommend to the foundation's board a recipient for the Abernathy Scholarship at your school. This scholarship is one of the better ones: It pays all tuition plus a stipend of $500 a month while the recipient is enrolled for classes, and covers the remaining years of his or her undergraduate education.

Following the announcement of the scholarship award two months ago, 24 applications came in. You carefully evaluated all of them, and you narrowed the selection to two applicants: Eileen Whiteside and Timothy Valdez. You will present these two students to the board, along with a comparative review of their background facts and your recommendation. In summary form, the facts you have assembled in your notes are as follows:

Eileen Whiteside. Age 19. Second semester sophomore. Grade point average, 3.6. Memberships: YMCA Fellowship Club (past president), Accounting Club (secretary-treasurer), Afro-American Society (current president), University Methodist Church. Dean's list all semesters. Major in accounting. Father employed as construction laborer. Mother an invalid. Three younger siblings at home. Parents unable to give any financial assistance. Eileen works 16 hours a week as sales clerk at Econo-Mart. Her professors give high praise of her intelligence and work ethic. Very personable. Her character references all report favorably.

Timothy Valdez. First-semester junior. Grade-point average 3.9. Memberships: University Choral. Major in Finance. Mother works as maid at Northside Marriott Hotel, father in prison, six siblings at home. No financial support from parents. Appears to be timid. Professors all report favorably: hard-working, intelligent, a loner. Works 24 hours a week at University McDonald's. Character references all excellent.

Using your best objectivity, now you will evaluate the two people. You will present your evaluations and recommendation in a memorandum report addressed to Marybell Schmidt, the foundation's current president.

8 *Writing a personnel action report on an erring subordinate.* As department head of the purchasing department at the Los Angeles plant of the Blue Sky Aviation Company, you must recommend termination of one of your subordinates.

For the past eight months you have been putting up with the antics of Cyrus T. Lohmann. Cyrus came to the company eight months ago. From the beginning his work was questionable. Your first quarterly report on him rated his work as "inferior." His second report was no better. Both of these evaluations were supported by Inez Gohmert, his immediate supervisor.

In recent weeks his work has gotten progressively worse. He has made numerous costly errors. One involved a $2,346 overpayment, and three of his orders involved delays that affected work on the production line. In the past six weeks he has been absent from work a total of 12 days, only one with an acceptable explanation (illness). On three occasions he reported to work in a drunken condition and had to be sent home. You talked with him after each of these events. He placed the blame on marital problems and said he now had matters under control—that there would be no recurrence. But after the last of these incidents you have no more hope for him. You will have to recommend his termination.

Now you must write a personnel-action report on the man recommending that he be fired. You will use Blue Sky's memorandum form and will address your report to Topaz Drury, Director of Human Relations. Standard practice at Blue Sky is to write such reports in the direct form with the conclusion-recommendation first and then to justify with facts and analyses. You may create any of the specific facts you need that support the information above.

9 *Should the Hill Country National Bank use a janitorial service?* As assistant to the president of the Hill Country National Bank, you have been asked to look into the possibility of using a janitorial service instead of the two full-time janitors employed by the bank. In recent years the firm has had much difficultly keeping janitors. In fact, seven people have filled the two $360-a-week positions within the past two years, the longest lasting 10 months. The two janitors currently employed have been with the bank for only three and five weeks, respectively.

As you gather the facts, you learn that, in addition to the two salaries, the bank must pay about $22 a week for janitorial supplies. Then, of course, there are the workers' fringe benefits, which amount to an extra 20 percent. And once each year for major housecleaning, extra help costing about $2,000 has to be hired. The Pinkerton Janitorial Service has offered to do all of the bank's janitorial work for $1,800 a week.

Your job is to analyze all these facts and arrive at a decision. You will give the cost factors heavy weight, but you must remember that there are other less tangible reasons that should be considered. Write up your analysis and recommendation in the bank's standard memo report form. Address it to your boss, Kevin P. Rodgers, who is the president.

Middle-Length Reports

10 *Recommending a current business book for executives of Zorro Computers.* As administrative assistant to Anthony Zorro, CEO and founder of Zorro Computers, you have been assigned the task of helping your boss select a current business book as a personal Christmas gift for the company's top 144 executives. (Of course, they will also receive their usual bonuses.) Mr. Zorro wants a book that will be most likely to help the executives improve their management skills as well as one that will be well received. "Go to *The Wall Street Journal*," he suggests, "or perhaps *BusinessWeek*. They list the top-selling business books periodically. Check them out. Then recommend the top three or so. Tell me what they are about and why you selected them."

You welcome the assignment, for it is a good opportunity to display your intellect and business acumen. You don't have to read the books (although it wouldn't be a bad idea to do so), for you can find reviews on the Internet and in the business publications. After you have completed your research, you will present your findings in appropriate report form. How well you do this assignment might determine your future with this company.

11 *Recommending a purchase for Goliath Chemical Company.* Goliath Chemical needs to purchase a given quantity of _____ (desktop computers, copiers, shredders, or such—as determined by your instructor). You, assistant to the director of purchasing, have the assignment of helping to determine the model and brand to buy.

Your plan for completing this assignment is as follows. Using the Internet as well as the literature available from local distributors and other sources, you will collect the pertinent information (prices, features, maintenance problems, reliability, and the like) on three competing products. Then you will compare the three on the basis of the appropriate factors to be considered in making a choice. While price is important, it will be negotiated after a preference has been determined. Even so, you will compare the price information you collect to serve as a general guideline. You will, of course, evaluate the information in terms of Goliath's unique needs (which you or your instructor may determine). Finally,

you will reach your conclusion. You will write up your conclusion and supporting analyses in appropriate report format. You will address the report to Emily Polansky, director of purchasing. You know she will take copies of the report with her when she seeks approval of this major purchase from top management.

12 *Evaluating your team for next year.* Assume that you are employed by a rival school (you name it) as assistant to the athletic director. You have been assigned the task of collecting and analyzing information on this school's opponents (football, baseball, basketball, soccer, or whatever—male or female) for next year. One of these opponents, of course, is your school's team. It is the one you will work on first.

You will begin your work by collecting all information available on who will be the likely players—who is returning, who is coming in, and such. Then you will gather all available information on abilities and performance records.

With this information available, you will systematically analyze it. From your analysis you will lead to conclusions concerning the team's strengths and weaknesses.

Of course, such a report could be quite long, but you recall the words of your boss: "I am interested primarily in highlights—not the minute details. At the same time, I want your report to be thorough. Use good judgment here." You are determined to please. You will present your work in appropriate short-report format. Address it to the athletic director (find his or her name if you don't know it).

13 *Recommending an automobile rental company.* For years the executives and salespeople of Westmoreland Pharmaceuticals, Inc. have rented automobiles from a leading national company (your instructor will determine which one) whenever they needed out-of-town automobile transportation. Generally, Westmoreland has been satisfied with the equipment and service they have received. But recent advertising of a number of competing rental companies has prompted the administration to take a comparative look at what the other rental companies have to offer—especially the newer, smaller ones. You, an executive trainee working

under the vice president for administration, Chad Capaccio, have been assigned the task of taking this look.

Specifically, Mr. Capaccio has asked you to use the Internet and other appropriate information sources to gather the pertinent facts on two smaller, newer rental companies and the company Westmoreland is now using. Then he wants you to evaluate what you find in terms of Westmoreland's needs. The result of your evaluations should be a recommendation as to which best serves the needs of the company. You will present the information, analyses, and recommendation in a report form that this situation justifies.

14 *Recommending a meeting on your campus.* For this assignment you are a member of the site selection committee of the Future Business Leaders of America. Every summer this association of university business students meets on a college campus. The meetings are held on a campus in late August, between semesters for most schools. About 140 members usually attend the one-week program. They meet in classrooms, union facilities, and such. They stay in vacant dormitories and eat in campus cafeterias and restaurants, although sometimes they use off-campus lodging and eating facilities.

For next year the committee is considering meeting on your campus. The members have asked you to gather the pertinent information for them. Of primary importance are such vital matters as the availability and costs of meeting rooms, dormitory rooms, and meals. The group needs one large meeting room with a capacity of 150 and five small

rooms with a capacity of 30. Seventy-five dormitory rooms will be adequate (two to a room). Men and women will be about equally represented. Meals usually are bought individually, but a weekly rate would be considered. (You need not get actual cost information from your university officials but may make reasonable estimates with the advice and approval of your instructor.)

In addition to these basic needs, organization members are interested in information on after-hours activities. So you will report on the recreational, sightseeing, and cultural attractions of the area. Of course, you will emphasize the attractions that are likely to interest college students.

After you have gathered the information, you will organize it and present it in appropriate report form. Because the committee members must make a decision, you will help them by making your recommendation. Try hard to be objective.

15 *Determining consumer attitudes toward fraudulent practices.* For this assignment, you are a research specialist in the public relations department in the home office of

Econo-Mart Stores. Econo-Mart is a major chain selling a wide variety of merchandise, including food, clothing, automotive items, and garden supplies. Your current task is to investigate a problem that affects this chain's relations with its customers: the fraudulent behavior of customers (shoplifting, altering price tags, returning worn clothing, and such).

Econo-Mart management is well aware that some of its customers deal fraudulently with company stores. Ideas on how to handle this problem have been numerous, but all involve possible negative results. In fact, it could be that some solutions would produce results worse than the fraud. Before Econo-Mart management takes any action, it believes that it should know more about the attitudes of consumers toward fraud and how it should be combated. So management has asked you to gather and analyze this information.

You began the task by surveying 300 Econo-Mart customers (you may fill in the details of your research procedure). To each of the 300 you presented 14 fraud situations. Then you asked the interviewees for their personal viewpoints of each situation You asked, also, for an indication of how their friends would react to each situation—a subtle way of learning the recipients' true thinking. The information in Tables 1, 2, and 3 summarize your findings. You will present your finding in appropriate report form. Address it to Ms. Geraldine Fornier, director of public relations. In general, your report will present and interpret the data you collected. Your goal is to guide management in forming policies regarding fraudulent practices.

Table 1   **Personal Attitudes of Consumers toward Fraudulent Practices (percent)**

Fraudulent Practice	Very Wrong	Not Serious	Understandable	Not Wrong
Shoplifting	97.0	0.3	2.7	0.0
Returning worn clothing	93.7	2.3	3.3	0.7
Changing or switching price tags	96.7	1.3	2.0	0.0
Writing bad checks	82.3	15.3	2.4	0.0
Eating food in store without paying	77.7	18.3	4.0	0.0
Ignoring change error at checkout	76.0	16.7	7.3	0.0
Dishonest use of coupons	64.3	27.7	2.7	5.3
Making invalid warranty claim	53.0	35.3	10.0	1.7
Ignoring undercharge	49.3	37.7	8.7	4.3
Ignoring billing error	52.3	35.3	8.7	3.7

Table 2   **Percent of Customers Whose Friends Would Engage in Fraudulent Practices When Opportunity Occurs**

Fraudulent Practice	Most of Time	Occasionally	Rarely	Never
Shoplifting	10.3	2.3	22.0	65.4
Returning worn clothing	21.0	2.0	4.3	72.7
Changing or switching price tag	12.7	3.7	22.3	67.3
Writing bad checks	5.3	12.0	26.7	56.0
Eating food in store without paying	25.7	5.0	37.0	32.3
Ignoring change error at checkout	33.0	17.3	30.7	19.0
Dishonest use of coupons	8.0	21.0	35.3	35.7
Making invalid warranty claim	24.7	36.3	22.3	16.7
Ignoring undercharge	39.3	37.0	15.7	8.0
Ignoring billing error	21.0	20.7	31.3	27.0

Table 3   **Customers' Viewpoints of Appropriate Actions for Certain Fraudulent Practices**

Fraudulent Practice	Do Nothing	Take Preventive Action	Give Warning	Take Drastic Action
Shoplifting	1.3	.3	58.7	39.7*
Returning worn clothing	3.0	7.7	11.0	78.3**
Changing or switching price tag	.7	3.7	70.3	25.3*

PART 4   Fundamentals of Report Writing

Table 3   continued

Fraudulent Practice	Do Nothing	Take Preventive Action	Give Warning	Take Drastic Action
Writing bad checks	1.0	7.3	59.3	32.3*
Eating food in store without paying	4.7	32.3	63.7	.3
Ignoring change error at checkout	1.7	37.0	60.3	1.0*
Dishonest use of coupons	2.7***	7.0	27.0	63.3**
Making invalid warranty claim	3.0***	14.3	28.7	54.0*
Ignoring undercharge	5.7	76.3	18.0	0
Ignoring billing error	5.0	31.3	63.7	0

*Notify authorities
**Refuse
***Accept coupon or claim

16 *Advising a client on how to invest $1.4 million.* Tingbi Wang has come to your financial consulting service for advice. He has just inherited $1.4 million and is eager to invest it. "I am 64 years old—almost ready to retire," he tells you. "I will have a fair pension, but not enough to support my wife and me in the style I would like. So I will want a reasonably good income flow. Of course, I want diversity—with little downside risk."

After surveying the market carefully, you come up with what you think he wants. Of course, you have concrete reasoning to support your selections. Mr. Wong is bright and is not interested in just hunches. You will write up your recommendations and the supporting information in appropriate report form. Your company is _____ (your name) Financial Planners, Inc.

17 *An impersonal analysis of yourself as a prospect for a job.* Assume that you have your degree in hand and are searching for the job of your choice with the company of your choice. You have just completed a long interview with a recruiter whom you think can provide you with what you seek. You think the interview went very well.

Now change roles with this recruiter. You liked the person you just interviewed. And you will recommend her or him for the position. As your recommendation will have to be approved by the department head involved, you will make your recommendation thorough. It will describe the applicant, covering all the pertinent categories—academic record, personal qualities, work experience, and such. (You will use the true information about you, although you may project your accomplishments to the date of your graduation.) You will need to work hard to maintain objectivity, so strive to view yourself as others see you. If you have weaknesses, you may include explanations that would persuade the reader to overlook them.

You will present your recommendation in appropriate report form. Address it to a person who might be your first boss at the company of your choice.

18 *Determining whether your prices are in line with the competition.* Assume that you, an independent research specialist, are employed by one of your local grocery stores (you choose one) to compare the store's prices with the prices of its primary competitor. For some time now, the management has been hearing comments about how much lower the prices of this and that product are at other stores in town. Much of this talk, of course, could be the result of advertised loss leaders—that is, goods advertised at low prices merely to attract customers. But one can't be too sure. Anyway, the fact that sales have dropped recently makes the manager want to investigate the question. And he or she wants you to make this investigation.

To get the information you need, you plan to construct a diversified shopping basket of grocery items and then to check the prices of each item at the two stores. Specifically, you will first select a group of items from each department (meats, canned goods, fresh vegetables, etc.). You will take care to select items that can be checked easily—that is, your selections will be carefully specified by grade, quantity, and brand. Also, the items you select will adequately represent the goods in each department. Once you have selected the items, you will visit each of the stores and record the prices of each item. Because you are concerned primarily with normal prices, you will take care to note any prices that are "specials." (In order to simplify this work, your instructor may permit you to work in teams to gather prices and determine the shopping basket.)

With these data collected, your next chore will be to evaluate them and write your results in appropriate report form. Because management wants to be able to pinpoint the departments and items that may be in or out of line, your report will present your findings in some detail.

Proposals

19 *Competing for travel-abroad funding.* A generous alum has established a Fund for International Learning at your school. Every fall term, the director of the fund issues a request for proposals to all juniors inviting them to apply for money to study abroad during the upcoming summer months.

Prepare a proposal that will earn you the money to travel to a country of your choice to undertake a particular learning project. Keep in mind these guidelines:

- Only six recipients are chosen each year.
- The maximum award is $5,000. It can be used for travel, lodging, meals, and expenses related to the educational project.
- The trips can vary in duration. Propose a time frame well suited to the project and to the amount of money you are requesting.
- Be sure you provide details that show your project to be well researched and thought out. (For example, will you study at a library with a unique collection? Take a course at a local university? Do research on the country's citizens, business, art, history, or social life?)
- The purpose of the project and its anticipated benefits to your professional/educational development need to be clear and convincing. The more closely you can tie the project to your specific career or learning goals, the better.

- You will be acting, to some extent, as a representative of your country and your school. Be sure you display the kind of character that would be appropriate in this role.

Assume that the request for proposals will be issued with a cover sheet that you will need to fill out and include with your proposal. It will ask you to supply your name, your major, the number of credit hours you have completed, the title of your project, the amount of money you are requesting, and the date. The format of the rest of the proposal is up to you.

You may need to do considerable research to develop a winning proposal. Consult such resources as the U.S. government's *World Factbook,* the *World Almanac Reference Database*, news sources such as LexisNexis and Facts on File, and other countries' websites to gather information about your chosen country and develop your project. If your instructor permits, you can make up some of the details (for example, that the project grew out of a course you took, that a certain professor is advising you on the project, or that you have a contact in the chosen country), as long as they are realistic. It will take hard work to interest and persuade the selection committee—but given the anticipated benefits to you and your career, it will be worth it.

20 *Educating employees about identity theft.* You work in the sales department of the Great Northern Insurance Company, a provider of auto, home, and life insurance. Part of your job is to give educational (which are also promotional) seminars on topics related to your employer's products. You give the seminars at universities, corporations, and other types of organizations. With many of these, Great Northern has struck up partnerships: the organizations' employees get a discount on Great Northern insurance, and, in return, Great Northern is allowed to promote its products among the employees. Educational seminars are an important part of these promotional efforts. You help develop, schedule, and deliver the seminars, not only to provide helpful advice but also to inform the employees about any new products that your company has developed. But sometimes you give these seminars to prospective organizational partners, hoping to create significant new streams of income for your company.

In fact, there is a lull in your seminar schedule just now, so you have decided to write an unsolicited proposal to certain new organizations to see if you can get your foot in the door. You will offer to conduct a free seminar for their em-

ployees on an important, timely topic: identity theft. Specifically, you will describe the forms that identity theft can take, how to avoid it, and what to do if one becomes a victim. Your company did a great deal of research on this topic in order to develop a new policy to cover the costs of identity theft—whether incurred by purchases the thief made, court costs related to crimes committed in the victim's name, or the effort to get one's credit record cleared. In the process, several in the company, including you, have become quite expert on the subject. (The new identity-theft policy, by the way, has to be purchased as an add-on to a basic Great Northern policy. People cannot buy only the identity-theft coverage.)

One might think that any organization would jump at a free seminar on this important topic, but you know that you face a couple of obstacles. One is that these potential clients don't know you and may not know much about your company. For all they know, you won't know what you're talking about, or you'll turn the event into a big sales spiel. Your proposal will need to gain your readers' trust that you are in fact knowledgeable and that you will focus on the promised topic with only brief comments about your company. Another hurdle is getting organizations to allow employees to attend a seminar rather than do their scheduled work. The management will need to be convinced that your seminar will be worth the loss of work time. The more you can show how the organization can benefit from this seminar, the better.

Write a letter proposal customized to Sujata Jafrez, Director of Human Resources for Children's Hospital. Get her to contact you for further details about setting up an identity theft seminar. (Of course, you should do some research on identity theft to come up with convincing details for your proposal.) Persuade Ms. Jafrez to take the next step—which will be, you hope, the first step toward Children's developing a relationship with Great Northern. Who knows? Maybe your goodwill-building gesture will result in the hospital's becoming one of Great Northern's organizational partners.

---

21 *Growing business with CRM software.* You take a deep breath and get ready to write a proposal to the owners of Lakeside Fitness Club. You're the manager of the facility, and you think the time has come for the owners to spring for a customer relationship management (CRM) system. You hope to convince them that the set-up fee of $1,500, the $30-a-month service fee, and the $550 for training on the application you've selected will be worth the gain in business.

The CRM product that you have in mind, e-Customer, is actually a hosted application. That is, the software itself resides on e-Customer's web server. You enter all the data about your customers into your computer using e-Customer's web interface, and the information is stored on e-Customer's server in a secure, searchable database. When you need to find out something about your customers—for example, which ones live in a certain neighborhood, bought a certain kind of membership, or came to a certain event—you can query the database and instantly retrieve the information. You can also have e-Customer send you "tickle" notices on customers whose memberships are about to expire. And because it is compatible with your email program, you can set it up to send customers emails at certain times. If you want to do a special mailing to particular groups, e-Customer makes that easy, too. In short, e-Customer will enable you to keep and retrieve much more information on your customers, and communicate with them much more extensively, than your current system—a simple database program—will allow. But that's not all. You can add an e-Customer web page to the club's website so that customers can purchase memberships and other services online. And as they enter their information, it will go directly into the database on e-Customer's server. Plus, e-Customer is compatible with the club's accounting software. Customers' financial information in e-Customer can be extracted and uploaded to the accounting database, and e-Customer will even alert you when there are updates for the accounting records. It's a modern, integrated approach that really does enable a company to manage its customers effectively.

It comes at a price, however, involving a one-time set-up fee and a monthly service fee. And you and your assistant really need to be trained on the product so that you can learn its full capabilities and start reaping the benefits fast. But the owners will be hesitant to take on a new expense. The club's business has expanded so much over the last eight years, as the surrounding community has grown, that the owners are building a new wing for the facility. This giant investment is not likely to make them receptive to a request for money. But it's because of the increased business that, in your view, the club needs a much more robust customer-records system. And with better access to better customer information, the club can be more strategic in its promotions and services.

You have a few persuasive statistics. Lakeside currently pays $30 a month for its basic Internet service. If it were to add on $30 a month for e-Customer, the total cost would be about equal to what the company would pay for an e-commerce service (that is, a secure website that enables people to purchase things online)—and an e-commerce service wouldn't bring the customer-management benefits that e-Customer would. Also, you read online that, according to a study of 448 companies conducted by an independent research group, 51 percent of the companies reported that their CRM systems had paid for themselves within a year, and 76 percent of the companies' systems had paid for themselves within 18 months. (Of course, these companies were of all sizes and in various industries, but the findings are still a good sign.) Research also shows that customers like CRM. They feel that they get more individualized attention and information.

You have occasionally mentioned a CRM system to your bosses when they drop by, but they seem to listen politely and then move on to more pressing concerns. You don't think that just sharing your idea orally with them is going to work. Instead, you will carefully lay out your plan—complete with the details that will help your bosses visualize what can be done with the new system—and present it in the form of an attractive, persuasive proposal.

---

22 *Getting reimbursed for an online course.* You work for the _____ company (you decide what kind) as a _____ (you decide what position). You want to take an online course on _____ (you decide what topic) and have the company cover the cost.

You've run the idea past your supervisor, who is basically supportive but will need to get the OK from the boss. For this you'll need to make your case in writing, and persuasively.

Write an email proposal to your supervisor requesting that the company cover the cost of the course. Convince the decision makers that the course is worth the money. Be sure to tie it to your current or likely future job responsibilities and explain how the company will benefit from your training.

---

23 *Learning how to maintain good credit scores.* As Director of Human Resources for your medium-sized business (you name it), you often hire new college graduates in a variety of positions. As a part of your screening process, you check credit scores. While a low credit score alone will not eliminate a job candidate from consideration, you have noticed that many of these new grads, your new hires, are unaware of the importance of good credit. Although you are more concerned about hiring competent workers, you also want employees who are not unnecessarily burdened by financial concerns.

A recent story in *The Wall Street Journal* stressed the importance of good credit. It talked about some of the advantages of good credit, including lower rates on home mortgages and car loans. In addition, not only are employers checking credit scores, but landlords and auto insurers are also checking them. Furthermore, more and more of them are using expansion scores, scores that include payment histories for apartment rentals, utility bills, and book and music clubs. The story also gave some pointers for improving one's credit score.

You believe your employees would benefit greatly from learning how to get and maintain good credit, and the basics could probably be covered in a couple of hours. Even employees with good credit already will benefit by learning new tips about credit lines, number and age of accounts, and the like. So you'd like to bring in a local independent certified financial planner to both talk about the topic and answer employees' questions. Since employees will be getting this instruction on company time for information not directly tied to their work, you realize you will need to be persuasive in your proposal to company president, Sydney Meersman. You can tell her that you plan to create a video from the session, so both current and future employees can review it later from the company intranet. Be sure to include some costs estimates in addition to citing benefits to the employees and the company in your proposal.

---

24 *Using product placement in videos to complement your online marketing strategy.* As Assistant Market Research Director at PhotoSmarts, you help determine the best ways to let the market know about your company's products and services. Your business caters to those who take and edit videos, and you sell a wide variety of cameras, software, and accessories. The rapid growth of this industry is often credited to the availability of high-speed broadband access to a critical mass of households. Combining this factor with new software tools for compressing video easily and efficiently, cheap storage for the large files video creates, and excellent, easy-to-use video cameras, it is easy to understand the explosive growth of this industry.

Until recently, you have been promoting your business both in print and online. And business has been good, very good. But you also recognize that as people shift their time spent to viewing more video, you need to be promoting your business there, too. But the cost for dedicated video time slots is prohibitive since you are competing with large Fortune 500 companies such as Coca-Cola and the Gap for those slots. So product placement in the videos themselves makes sense to you. And by going to sites where you already advertise such as vMix and YouTube that target the technologically savvy 18- to 30-year old market, you can learn which videos have large audiences. You believe it is critical if you want to expand your business that the company use this channel to reach potential customers.

Write a proposal to Marketing Director Colin Deftos, seeking time and an assistant to help you gather information needed to determine the cost and payback of employing this product placement advertising strategy at PhotoSmarts.

---

25 *Using gyms while traveling.* Lately you feel like you have been inundated by reports about obesity among Americans, a problem that can lead to a variety of diseases and even an impending epidemic of diabetes. While unhealthy lifestyles have contributed to this state, they also run up the costs of healthcare programs for employers. As a result, many companies, including your employer, have set up a variety of programs for their employees. In addition to installing walking paths around their buildings and onsite gyms, they have also offered programs for smoking cessation, dieting, and healthy cooking. Some are even giving financial incentives for succeeding in these programs.

While these are good first steps, you'd like your employer to extend it even further to cover encouraging healthy lifestyles while traveling. Because traveling breaks an employee's normal routine, it is easy to lapse into unhealthy behaviors such as eating and drinking in airport restaurants. Additionally, travel can be very stressful and unproductive. However, by paying employee expenses for using gyms in airports, airport hotels, or nearby health clubs for $10 or so per visit, an employer can continue to promote a healthy life-style as well as help reduce an employee's stress.

At the website Airport Gyms <http://www.airportgyms. com/>, a listing of onsite as well as nearby gyms and their costs is available for the United States and Canada. You are proposing that your employer pay all reasonable expenses associated with using these facilities while traveling. Write the proposal and send copies to your boss and the company president.

TOPICS FOR REPORT PROBLEMS

Following are topics that may be developed into reports of varying length and difficulty. In each case, you will need to create the facts of the situation through your (or the instructor's) imagination to indicate that a business-type problem exists. The information needed in most cases should be available on the Internet or in the library.

1 Recommend for X Company a city and hotel for holding its annual meeting of sales representatives.

2 Determine the problem areas and develop a set of policies for employees who work at home during business hours for X Company.

3 For an investment service, determine which mutual funds do better: those that invest for the long run or those that emphasize market timing.

4 What can X Company (you choose the name and industry) do to improve the quality of its product or service?

5 Investigate the problem of employee absenteeism and recommend ways to decrease it.

6 Using the data found at three major reporting agencies, evaluate your own credit for the ability to get a new car once you graduate.

7 Determine the problems of recycling and recommend ways to overcome them.

8 Investigate the advantages and disadvantages of requiring workers to wear uniforms and recommend whether X Company should require them.

9 Advise X Company on the advantages and disadvantages of hiring student interns from the local college.

10 Evaluate and compare the economic forecasts of three leading forecasters over the past five years.

11 Advise Company X on the desirability of establishing a child care center for the children of its employees.

12 Report to Company X management what other leading companies are doing to increase ethics consciousness among employees.

13 Report to a large ecommerce site on current means of reducing online fraud.

14 Determine the effects of fitness programs on worker health and/or productivity.

15 Determine whether Company X should ban personal web surfing in the workplace.

16 Advise your student government association on whether a social-norm marketing campaign to curb drinking would be effective on your campus.

17 Report on the office design of the future for Company X.

18 What can Company X (you choose the type of company) do to improve employee retention?

19 Determine how Company X should cope with the problem of an aging workforce.

20 Evaluate the advantages and disadvantages of flextime.

21 Determine the advantages and disadvantages of fixed-rate and variable-rate mortgages.

22 Study the benefits and problems of adding a competitive intelligence division, and draw conclusions on the matter.

23 Study and report on the more popular forms of creative financing being used in real estate today.

24 Review the literature to determine the nature and causes of executive burnout and remedies for it.

25 What should Company X do about employees who have been made obsolete by technological change?

26 Your company (to be specified by your instructor) is considering the purchase of _____ (number) smart phones for its sales representatives. Evaluate three brands, and recommend one for purchase.

27 Evaluate the use of the Tablet PC's handwriting input for use by sales reps in completing sales reports for Company X.

28 Advise Company X (a national grocery chain) on whether to add online shopping.

29 Investigate and report on the demand for college-trained people in the coming years in _____ (a major of your choice).

30 Report to Company X which major hotel chain offers the best value in Internet access for your employees when they travel domestically.

31 Determine the recent developments in, current status of, and outlook for _____ industry.

32 Investigate and report on the criminal liability of corporate executives.

33 Investigate whether hiring physically challenged workers is charity or good business for Company X.

34 Assess the status of pollution control in _____ industry for an association of firms in that industry.

35 Review the status of consumer protection laws, and recommend policies for Company X.

36 Review current developments in technology and determine whether we are truly moving toward the "paperless office."

37 Advise Company X (your choice of a specific manufacturer) on the problems and procedures involved in exporting its products to _____ (country or countries of your choice).

38 Report to Company X on the quality of life in your city. The company may open an office there and would move some executives to it.

39 Report to Company X on the ethics and effectiveness of product placement in movies and television shows.

40 Compare the costs, services, and other relevant factors of the major automobile rental firms, and recommend which of these firms Company X should use.

41 Survey the franchise possibilities for _____ (fast foods, automotive services, or such), and select one of these possibilities for a business client.

42 Advise Company X on developing a wellness (preventive health) program.

Additional topics are listed at the end of the long-length problem section following Chapter 12. Many of these topics are suitable for intermediate-length reports, just as some of the topics above are suitable for long reports.

chapter twelve

Long, Formal Reports

LEARNING OBJECTIVES

Upon completing this chapter, you will be able to construct long, formal reports for important projects. To reach this goal, you should be able to

1 Describe the roles and contents and construct the prefatory parts of a long, formal report.

2 Organize the introduction of a long report by considering the likely readers and selecting the appropriate contents.

3 Prepare the body of a long, formal report by applying the advice in Chapter 10 and in other chapters.

4 Determine, based on the report's purpose, the most effective way to end a report: a summary, a conclusion, a recommendation, or a combination of the three.

5 Describe the role and content of the appendix and bibliography of a report.

6 Prepare a structural coherence plan for a long, formal report.

Long, Formal Reports

Assume the role of associate director of research, Midwestern Research, Inc. As your title indicates, research is your business. Perhaps it would be more accurate to say that research and reports are your business. Research is your primary activity, of course. But you must present your findings to your customers. The most efficient way of doing so is through reports.

Typical of your work is your current assignment with Nokia, a manufacturer of mobile phones. The sales division of Nokia wants information that will help improve the effectiveness of its salespeople. Specifically, it wants answers to the question of what its salespeople can do to improve their performance. The information gathered will be used in revising the curriculum of Nokia's sales training program.

To find the answer to the basic question, you plan to investigate three areas of sales activities: how salespeople use their time, how they find prospects, and how they make sales presentations. You will get this information for two groups of Nokia salespeople: the successful and the unsuccessful. Next, you will compare the information you get from these two groups. You will compare the groups on the three areas of sales activity (the bases of comparison). The differences you detect in these comparisons should identify the effective and the ineffective sales practices.

Your next task will be to determine what your findings mean. When you have done this, you will present your findings, analyses, conclusions, and recommendations in a report to Nokia. Because Nokia executives will see the report as evidence of the work you did for the company, you will dress the report up. You know that what Nokia sees will affect what it thinks of your work.

So you will use the formal arrangement that is traditional for reports of this importance. You will include the conventional prefatory pages. You will use headings to guide the readers through the text. And you will use graphics liberally to help tell the report story. If the situation calls for them, you may use appended parts. In other words, you will construct a report that matches the formality and importance of the situation. How to construct such reports is the subject of this chapter.

- Long, formal reports are important but not numerous in business.

- See Chapters 10 and 11 for advice about developing the contents and structure of reports and proposals.

Although not numerous, long, formal reports are highly important in business. They usually concern major investigations, which explains their length. They are usually prepared for high-level executives, which explains their formality.

The advice in Chapter 10 about creating reports—determining the purpose, gathering information, and choosing a logical structure adapted to the readers—applies to long, formal reports as well. And much of the advice in Chapter 11 about proposals can apply to long, formal proposals. We will not repeat this advice here. Instead, this chapter will focus on the special components of formal reports, emphasizing their purpose and design. For any given case, you will need to decide which of these components to use and whether or not your report or proposal needs different special elements. As always, the facts of the situation and your readers' preferences should be your guide.

ORGANIZATION AND CONTENT OF LONGER REPORTS

- Needs should determine the structure of long, formal reports.

- The need for the prefatory parts decreases as reports become shorter and less formal.

In determining the structure of longer, more formal reports, you should view your work much as architects view theirs. You have a number of parts to work with. Your task is to design from those parts a report that meets your reader's needs.

The first parts in your case are the prefatory pages. As noted in Chapter 11, the longest, most formal reports contain all of these. As the length of the report and the formality of the situation decrease, certain changes occur. As the report architect, you must decide which arrangement of prefatory parts meets the length and formality requirements of your situation.

To make this decision, you need to know these parts. Thus, we will describe them in the following pages. In addition, we will describe the remaining structure of the longest, most formal report. As you proceed through these descriptions, it will be helpful to trace the parts through the illustration report at the end of this chapter. In addition, it will help to consult Appendix B for illustrations of page form.

For convenience in the following discussion, the report parts are organized by groups. The first group comprises the prefatory parts, the parts that are most closely related to the formality and length of the report. Then comes the report proper, which, of course, is the meat of all reports. It is the report story. The final group comprises the appended parts. These parts contain supplementary materials, information that is not essential to the report but may be helpful to some readers. In summary, the presentation follows this pattern:

Prefatory parts: Title fly. Title page. Authorization message. Transmittal message, preface, or foreword. Table of contents and list of illustrations. Executive summary.

The report proper: Introduction. The report findings (presented in two or more divisions). Summary, conclusion, or recommendation.

Appended parts: Appendix. Bibliography.

THE PREFATORY PARTS

As you know from preceding discussion, there may be many variations in the prefatory parts of a formal report. Even so, the six parts covered in the following pages are generally included in longer reports.

Title Fly

The first of the possible prefatory report pages is the title fly (see page 387). It contains only the report title, and it is included solely for reasons of formality. Since the title appears again on the following page, the title fly is somewhat repetitive. But most books have one, and so do most formal reports.

Although constructing the title fly is simple, composing the title is not. In fact, on a per-word basis, the title requires more time than any other part of the report. This is as it should be, for titles should be carefully worded. Their goal is to tell the reader at a glance what the report does and does not cover. A good title fits the report like a glove. It covers all the report information tightly.

- In determining which prefatory parts to include, you should know their roles and contents.

- Thus, they are reviewed in the following pages.

- The title fly contains only the report title.

- Construct titles to make them describe the report precisely.

For completeness of coverage, you should build your titles around the five Ws: *who, what, where, when, why*. Sometimes *how* may be important. In some problems, you will not need to use all the Ws. Nevertheless, they serve as a good checklist for completeness. For example, you might construct a title for the report described at the chapter beginning as follows:

Who:	Nokia
What:	Sales training recommendations
Where:	Implied (Nokia regional offices)
When:	2008
Why:	Understood (to improve sales training)
How:	Based on a 2008 study of company sales activities

From this analysis comes this title: "Sales Training Recommendations for Nokia Based on a 2008 Study of Company Sales Activities."

For another example, take a report analyzing Petco's 2008 advertising campaigns. This analysis would be appropriate:

Who:	Petco
What:	Analysis of advertising campaigns
Where:	Not essential
When:	2008
Why:	Implied
How:	Not essential

Thus, this title emerges: "Analysis of Petco's 2008 Advertising Campaigns."

Obviously, you cannot write a completely descriptive title in a word or two. Extremely short titles tend to be broad and general. They cover everything; they touch nothing. Even so, your goal is to be concise as well as complete. So you must seek the most economical word pattern consistent with completeness. In your effort to be concise and complete, you may want to use subtitles. Here is an example: "A 2007 Measure of Employee Morale at Florida Human Resource Offices: A Study Based on a Survey Using the Semantic Differential."

Title Page

Like the title fly, the title page presents the report title. In addition, it displays information essential to identification of the report. In constructing your title page, you should include your complete identification and that of the authorizer or recipient of the report. You also may include the date of writing, particularly if the date is not in the title. An example of a three-spot title page appears in the report at the end of the chapter. You can see a four-spot arrangement (used when writer and reader are within the same organization) in Appendix B.

Authorization Message

Although not illustrated in the diagram of report structure in Chapter 11 or in the report at the end of this chapter, an authorization message can be a prefatory part. It was not shown in the diagram (Figure 11–1) because its presence in a report is not determined by formality or length but by whether the report was authorized in writing. A report authorized in writing should include a copy of the written authorization. This part usually follows the title page.

As the report writer, you would not write the authorization message. But if you ever have to write one, handle it as you would a direct-order message. In the opening, authorize the research. Then cover the specific information that the reader needs in order to conduct it. This might include a clear description of the problem, time and money limitations, special instructions, and the due date. Close the message with an appropriate goodwill comment.

Transmittal Message, Foreword, Preface

Most formal reports contain a personal message of some kind from the writer to the reader. In most business reports, the transmittal message performs this function. In some cases, particularly where the report is written for a group of readers, a foreword or preface is used instead.

The transmittal message transmits the report to the reader. In less formal situations, the report is transmitted orally or by email. In more formal situations, a letter does the job. But keep in mind that a written message merely substitutes for a face-to-face meeting. What you write in it is much like what you would say if you were face to face with the reader. This personal touch enhances the communication effect of your report.

Because the goal of transmitting the report is positive, you should begin the transmittal message directly, without explanation or other delaying information. Your opening words should say, in effect, "Here is the report." Tied to or following the transmittal of the report, you should briefly identify the report goal, and you can refer to the authorization (who assigned the report, when, why).

What else you include in the transmittal message depends on the situation. In general, you should include anything that would be appropriate in a face-to-face presentation. What would you say if you were handing the report to the reader? It would probably be something about the report—how to understand, use, or appreciate it. You might make suggestions about follow-up studies, advise about limitations of the report, or comments about side issues. In fact, you might include anything that helps the reader understand and value the report. Typically, the transmittal message ends with an appropriate goodwill comment. An expression of gratefulness for the assignment or an offer to do additional research if necessary makes good closing material.

When you combine the transmittal message with the executive summary (an acceptable arrangement), you follow the opening transmittal statement with a summary of the report highlights. In general, you follow the procedure for summarizing described in the discussion of the executive summary. Following the summary, you include appropriate talk about the report. Then you end with a goodwill comment.

Because the transmittal message is a personal note to the reader, you may write in a personal style. In other words, you may use personal pronouns (*you, I, we*). In addition, you may write the message in conversational language that reflects your personality. You may not want to use the personal style in very formal cases, however. For example, if you were writing a report for a committee of senators or for other high-ranking dignitaries, you might elect to write the transmittal message impersonally. But such instances are rare. In whatever style, you should convey genuine warmth to the contact with another human being.

- The transmittal message is a personal message from the writer to the reader.

- It substitutes for a face-to-face meeting.

- Its main goal is to transmit the report.

- In addition, it includes helpful comments about the report. The close is goodwill.

- A summary follows the opening when the executive summary and the transmittal message are combined.

- The transmittal message is usually in personal style.

Playing possum doesn't work anymore, Stephmeyer! I want that report by 5 P.M. or else!

A Questionable Example of Effective Reporting

"How could I have hired this fellow Glutz?" the sales manager moaned as he read this first report from his new salesperson: "I have arrive in Detroit. Tomorry I will try to sell them companys here what ain't never bought nothing from us."

Before the sales manager could fire this stupid fellow, Glutz's second report arrived: "I done good here. Sold them bout haff a millun dollars wirth. Tomorry I try to sell to them there Smith Company folks what threw out that last feller what sold for us."

Imagine how the sales manager's viewpoint changed when he read Glutz's third report: "Today I seen them Smith folks and sole them bout a millun dollars wirth. Also after dinner I got too little sails mountin to bout half a millun dollars. Tomorry I going to do better."

The sales manager was so moved that he tacked Glutz's reports on the company bulletin board. Below them he posted his note to all the salespeople: "I want all you should reed these reports wrote by Glutz who are on the road doin a grate job. Then you should go out and do like he done."

- For broad audiences, a foreword (or preface) is used. Forewords do not transmit the report—they comment about it.

As noted previously, you may transmit reports to broad audiences in a foreword or a preface. Minor distinctions are sometimes drawn between forewords and prefaces. But for all practical purposes, they are the same. Both are preliminary messages from the writer to the reader. Although forewords and prefaces usually do not formally transmit the report, they do many of the other things transmittal messages do. Like transmittal messages, they seek to help the reader appreciate and understand the report. They may, for example, include helpful comments about the report—its use, interpretation, follow-up, and the like. In addition, they frequently contain expressions of indebtedness to those helpful in the research. Like transmittal messages, they are usually written in the first person. But they are seldom as informal as some transmittal messages. There is no established pattern for arranging the contents of forewords and prefaces.

Table of Contents, List of Illustrations

- Include a table of contents when the report is long enough to need a guide to its contents.

If your report is long enough to need a guide to its contents, you should include a table of contents. This table is the report outline in finished form with page numbers. It previews the structure and contents of the report and helps readers find what they most want to read. It is especially helpful to those readers who want to read only a few selected parts of the report—and there can be many such readers for a given report or proposal.

- Follow the guidelines in Chapter 10 for preparing a table of contents.

Because the table of contents is such an important reading support, be sure to follow the specific guidelines in Chapter 10 for preparing one.

- The table of contents lists text headings, prefatory parts, appended parts, and figures and tables. It gives page numbers.

In addition to listing the text headings, the table of contents lists the parts of the report that appear before and after the report proper. Thus, it lists the prefatory parts (though not the title fly or title page), the appended parts (bibliography, appendix), and the figures and tables that illustrate the report. Typically, the figures and tables appear as separate listings following the listings reviewed above. See the textbook website for instructions on how to generate a table of contents easily using Word.

Executive Summary

- The executive summary summarizes the report.

The executive summary (also called *synopsis, abstract, epitome, précis, digest*) is the report in miniature. It concisely summarizes whatever is important in the report. For some readers, the executive summary serves as a preview to the report. But it is written primarily for busy executives who may not have time to read the whole report. Perhaps they can get all they need to know by reading the executive summary. If they need to know more about any part, they can find that part through the table of contents. Thus, they can find out whatever they need to know quickly and easily.

You construct the executive summary by reducing the parts of the report in order and in proportion. More specifically, you go through the report, selecting whatever is essential. You should include the basic information about the report, such as its origin and purpose. You should include the key facts and all the major analyses of the information presented. And you should include all the conclusions and recommendations derived from these analyses. The finished product should be a miniature of the whole, with all the important ingredients. As a general rule, the executive summary is less than an eighth as long as the writing it summarizes.

- It includes the report purpose, highlights of the facts, analyses, conclusions, and recommendations—in proportion.

Because your goal is to cut the report to a fraction of its length, much of your success will depend on your skill in word economy. Loose writing is costly. But in your efforts to be concise, you are more likely to write in a dull style. You will need to avoid this tendency.

- Work on writing style in this part.

The traditional executive summary reviews the report in the indirect order (introduction, body, conclusion). In recent years, however, the direct order has gained in popularity. This order shifts the conclusions and/or recommendations (as the case may be) to the major position of emphasis at the beginning. Direct-order executive summaries resemble the short reports described in Chapter 11. From this direct beginning, the summary moves to the introductory parts and then through the major highlights of the report in normal order.

- Either direct or indirect order is appropriate.

Diagrams of both arrangements appear in Figure 12–1. Whichever arrangement you choose, you will write the executive summary after the report proper is complete.

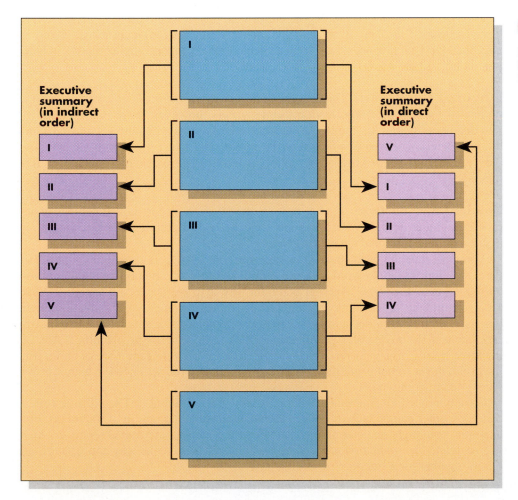

Figure 12–1

Diagram of the Executive Summary in Indirect and Direct Order

THE REPORT PROPER

Arrangements of the report proper may vary, but the following review of the indirect order should be helpful.

As noted in Chapter 11, the body of most longer reports is written in the indirect order (introduction, body, conclusion). But there are exceptions. Some longer reports are in the direct order—with summaries, conclusions, or recommendations at the beginning. And some are in an order prescribed by your company or the client. Even though the orders of longer reports may vary, the ingredients of all these reports are similar. Thus, the following review of the makeup of a report in the indirect order should help you in writing any report.

Introduction

The introduction should prepare the readers.

The purpose of the introduction of a report is to prepare the readers to receive the report. Whatever will help achieve this goal is appropriate content. Giving your readers what they need makes a good first impression and displays good you-viewpoint.

In deciding what to include, consider all likely readers.

In determining what content is appropriate, consider all the likely readers of your report. As we noted earlier, the readers of many shorter reports are likely to know the problem well and have little or no need for an introduction. But such is not often the case for longer reports. Many of these reports are prepared for a large number of readers, some of whom know little about the problem. These reports often have long lives and are kept on file to be read in future years. Clearly, they require some introductory explanation to prepare the readers.

Then determine what those readers need to know. Use the following checklist.

Determining what should be included is a matter of judgment. You should ask yourself what you would need or want to know about the problem if you were in your readers' shoes. As the report's author, you know more about the report than anyone else. So you will work hard not to assume that readers have the same knowledge of the problem that you do. In selecting the appropriate information, you would do well to use the following checklist of likely introduction contents. Remember, though, that it is only a checklist. Only on rare occasions, such as in the longest, most complex reports, would you include all the items.

1. Origin—the facts of authorization.

Origin of the Report. The first part of your introduction might well include a review of the facts of authorization. Some writers, however, leave this part out. If you decide to include it, you should present such facts as when, how, and by whom the report was authorized; who wrote the report; and when the report was submitted. Information of this kind is particularly useful in reports that have no transmittal message.

2. Problem—what prompted the report.

Problem and Purpose. A vital part of almost every report is a statement of its problem. The *problem* is what the report seeks to do, the situation that it addresses. It is the need that prompted the investigation.

The problem is commonly stated in infinitive, question, or declarative form.

You may state the problem of your report in three ways, as shown in Chapter 10. One common way is to word it in the infinitive form: "To determine standards for corporate annual reports." Another common way is to word it as a question: "What retail advertising practices do Springfield consumers disapprove of?" Still another way is to word it as a declarative statement: "Company X wants to know the characteristics of the buyers of Y perfume as a guide to its advertising planning." Any of the three should give your reader a clear picture of what your report seeks to do. But the problem statement is not the only item you include. You will need to elaborate on what you are going to do.

The purpose is the reason for the report.

Closely related to *what* you are doing is *why* you are doing it. The *purpose* (often called by other names such as *objective, aim, goal*) tells the reason of the report. For example, you might be determining standards for the corporate annual report *in order to streamline the production process*. You will need to weave the why and what of the report together for a smooth flow of thoughts.

Using a Table of Contents Generator for Speed and Accuracy

The table of contents generator tool in today's word processors frees writers from both the physical formatting and the accuracy tasks. Just a few clicks produces and formats the table of contents, along with leaders and page numbers. Additionally, today's generators add links so that those reading the report on the screen rather than on paper can easily navigate to a particular section or page by simply clicking on it in the table of contents.

The table of contents generator works with styles, using them as tags for marking items to include in the table of contents. If you are using a standard report template, styles are already incorporated in it. If you are creating your own report from a blank document, you could use predefined styles or define your own styles to create titles, headings, and subheads. Styles provide consistency so that headings at certain levels always appear the same, helping the reader see the relationship of the parts of your report.

Furthermore, if you decide to change the material in your report after you have generated the table of contents, you simply regenerate it to update page numbers with only a few clicks.

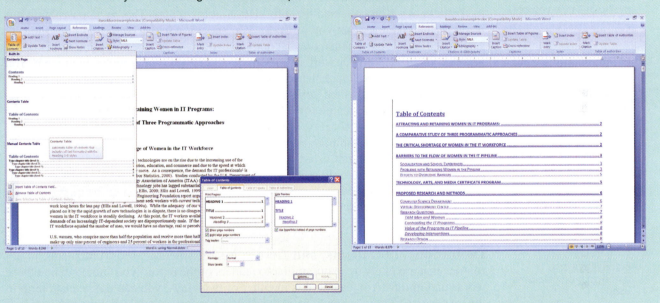

Scope. If the scope of the problem is not clearly covered in any of the other introductory parts, you may need to include it in a separate part. By *scope* we mean the boundaries of the problem. In this part of the introduction—in plain, clear language—you should describe what is included in the problem. You also should identify the limitations—what you have not included.

- 3. Scope—the boundaries of the problem.

Limitations. In some reports, you will need to explain limitations. By *limitations* we mean things that keep your report from being an ideal treatment of the problem. Of course, in reality there is no such thing as an ideal treatment. No real-world problem can be completely explored, and because different writers will approach the same problem differently, what seems complete to one person may not seem complete to another. Everyone understands that no report can provide coverage of a given topic in an absolute sense. But in certain cases, you will want to state explicitly what forms of research were not employed so that your readers will know how to evaluate your information. For example, if time constraints permitted only a quick email survey rather than in-depth interviews of your sources, you would say so. Or if a major source of

- 4. Limitations—anything that limits the report's treatment of the problem.

information was unavailable (perhaps a key informant had left the company or relevant industry reports were too expensive), you would note this limitation in your report. Be frank in this section but not too negative. State clearly what was not done and why, but do so without apology or such negative wording as "impair" or "compromised the validity of our findings." If you have done a good job with the resources at your disposal, this section of the report can use a directness that shows confidence in the report's usefulness despite its limitations.

- 5. History—how the problem developed and what is known about it.

Historical Background. Knowledge of the history of the problem is sometimes essential to understanding the report. Thus, you may need to cover that history in your introduction. You will need to do more than merely list and present facts. You will need to organize and interpret them for the readers. Your general aim in this part is to acquaint the readers with how the problem developed and what has been done about it. Your discussion here should bring out the main issues. It should review what past investigations have determined about the problem, and it should lead to what still needs to be done.

- 6. Sources and methods—how you got the information.

Sources and Methods of Collecting Information. You usually need to tell the readers how you collected the information in the report. That is, you explain your research methodology and you justify it. You specify whether you used published research, surveys, experiments, or what not. And you describe the steps you followed. In general, you describe your work in enough detail to allow your readers to judge it. You tell them enough to convince them that your work was done competently.

- Sometimes it is necessary to cite sources.

In a simple case in which you gathered published research, you need to say little. If most of your findings came from a few sources, you could name the sources. If you used a large number of sources, you would be wise to note that you used secondary research and refer to the bibliography in the report appendix.

- More complex research requires thorough description.

More complex research usually requires a more detailed description. If you conducted a survey, for example, you probably would need to explain all parts of the investigation. You would cover sample determination, construction of the questionnaire, interview procedure, and checking techniques. In fact, you would include as much detail as is needed to gain the readers' confidence in your work.

- 7. Definitions of unfamiliar words, acronyms, or initialisms used.

Definitions, Initialisms, and Acronyms. If you use words, initialisms, or acronyms that are likely to be unfamiliar to readers of the report, you should define these words and initials. You can do this in either of two ways: you can define each term in the text or as a footnote when it is first used in the report, or you can define all unfamiliar terms in a separate part of the introduction. This part begins with an introductory statement and then lists the terms with their definitions. If the list is long, you may choose to arrange the terms alphabetically.

- 8. Preview—a description of the route ahead.

Report Preview. In very long reports, a final part of the introduction should preview the report presentation. In this part you tell the readers how the report will be presented—what topics will be taken up first, second, third, and so on. Of even greater importance, you give your reasons for following this plan. That is, you explain the *strategy* of your report. In short, you give your readers a clear picture of the road ahead. As you will see later in the chapter, this part of the introduction is a basic ingredient of the coherence plan of the long report. Illustrations of report previews appear in the discussion of this plan (page 385) and in the report at the end of the chapter (see Figure 12–3, page 387).

The Report Body

- The report body presents and analyzes the information gathered.

In the report body, the information collected is presented and related to the problem. Normally, this part of the report comprises most of its content. In a sense, the report body is the report. With the exception of the conclusion or recommendation part, the other parts of the report are attached parts.

Technical Writer's Report on Humpty Dumpty

A 72-gram brown Rhode Island Red country-fresh candled egg was secured and washed free of feathers, blood, dirt, and grit. Held between thumb and index finger, about 3 ft. or more from an electric fan (GE Model No. MC-2404, Serial No. JC23023, nonoscillating, rotating on "Hi" speed at approximately 1045.23 plus or minus 0.02 rpm), the egg was suspended on a pendulum (string) so that it arrived at the fan with essentially zero velocity normal to the fan rotation plane. The product adhered strongly to the walls and ceiling and was difficult to recover. However, using putty knives a total of 13 grams was obtained and put in a skillet with 11.2 grams of hickory-smoked Armour's old-style bacon and heated over a low Bunsen flame for 7 min. 32 sec. What there was of it was of excellent quality.

"The DP Report," Du Pont Explosives Department, Atomic Energy Division, Savannah River Laboratories, 12 July 1954.

Advice presented throughout this book will help you prepare this part of the report. Its organization was discussed extensively in Chapter 10. It is written in accord with the instructions on style presented in Chapter 10 and with the general principles for clear writing presented in the early chapters. It may use the components of shorter reports and proposals discussed in Chapter 11. Any sources used must be appropriately noted and documented as illustrated in Appendix E. It uses good presentation form as discussed in Appendix B and elsewhere, and it follows the guidelines for use of figures and tables discussed in Chapter 13. In short, writing this major section of the long, formal report will require virtually all your organizing, writing, and formatting skills.

- Preparing this part will employ much of the advice in this book.

The Ending of the Report

You can end your report in any of a number of ways: with a summary, a conclusion, a recommendation, or a combination of the three. Your choice depends on the purpose of your report. You should choose the way that enables you to satisfy that purpose.

- Reports can end in various ways.

Ending Summary. When the purpose of the report is to present information, the ending is logically a summary of the major findings. There is no attempt to interpret at this point. Any interpretations of the information in the report occur on the reader's part at this point, but not the writer's. Such reports usually have minor summaries at the end of the major sections. When this arrangement is followed, the ending summary recapitulates these summaries.

- Informational reports usually end with a summary of the major findings.

You should not confuse the ending summary with the executive summary. The executive summary is a prefatory part of the report; the ending summary is a part of the report text. Also, the executive summary is more complete than the ending summary. The executive summary reviews the entire report, usually from the beginning to the end. The ending summary reviews only the highlights of the report.

- The ending summary is not as complete as the executive summary.

Conclusions. Some reports must do more than just present information. They must analyze the information in light of the problem; and from this analysis, they must reach a conclusion. Such reports typically end with this conclusion.

- Reports that seek an answer end with a conclusion.

The make-up of the conclusion section varies from case to case. In problems for which a single answer is sought, the conclusion section normally reviews the preceding information and analyses and, from this review, arrives at the answer. In problems with more than one goal, the report plan may treat each goal in a separate section and draw conclusions in each section. The conclusion section of such a report might well summarize the conclusions previously drawn. There are other arrangements. In fact, almost any plan that brings the analyses together to reach the goals of the report is appropriate.

- The structure of the conclusion varies by problem.

Recommendations. When the goal of the report is not only to draw conclusions but also to present a course of action, a recommendation is in order. You may organize it as a separate section following the conclusion section. Or you may include it in the conclusion section. In some problems, the conclusion is the recommendation—or at least a logical interpretation of it. Whether you include a recommendation should be determined by whether the readers want or expect one.

Appended Parts

Sometimes you will need to include an appendix, a bibliography, or both at the end of the report. Whether you include these parts should be determined by need.

Appendix. The appendix, as its name implies, is a tacked-on part. You use it for supplementary information that supports the body of the report but has no logical place within the body. Possible appendix contents are questionnaires, working papers, summary tables, additional references, and other reports.

As a rule, the appendix should not include the charts, graphs, and tables that directly support the report. These should be placed in the body of the report, where they support the findings. Reports should be designed for the convenience of the readers. Obviously, it is not convenient for readers to look to the appendix for illustrations of the facts they read in the report body. They would have to thumb back and forth in the report, thus losing their concentration. Such a practice would not help the reader.

Bibliography. When your investigation makes heavy use of published sources, you normally include a bibliography (a list of the publications used). The construction of this list is described in Appendix E of this book.

THE STRUCTURAL COHERENCE PLAN

As we have noted, the writing in the longer reports is much like the writing in the shorter ones. In general, the instructions given in earlier chapters apply to the longer reports. But the longer reports have one writing need that is not present in the shorter ones—the need for a structural coherence plan.

By *structural coherence plan* we mean a network of explanations, introductions, summaries, and conclusions that guide the reader through the report. Of course, you will also employ the devices for coherent writing discussed in Chapters 3 and 4. But because of the formal report's length, your reader will probably need additional help relating the parts of the report to each other or keeping track of where he or she is in the report. A structural coherence plan provides this extra help. Although you should not use its components mechanically, it is likely to follow the general plan illustrated in Figure 12–2.

The coherence plan begins with the report preview in the introduction. As you will recall, the preview tells the readers what lies ahead. It covers three things: the topics to be discussed, their order, and the logic of that order. With this information in mind, the readers know how the parts of the report relate to one another. They know the overall strategy of the presentation. The following paragraphs do a good job of previewing a report comparing four automobiles to determine which is the best for a company's sales fleet.

> To identify which light car Allied Distributors should buy, this report compares the cars under consideration on the basis of three factors: cost, safety, and performance. Each of these factors is broken down into its component parts, which are applied to the specific models being considered.
>
> Because cost is the most tangible factor, it is examined in the first major section. In this section, the four automobiles are compared for initial and trade-in values. Then they are compared for operating costs, as determined by mileage, oil use, repair expense, and the like. In the second major section, the safety of the four makes is compared. Driver visibility, special safety features, brakes, steering quality,

Include recommenda-
tions when the readers
want or expect them.

Add an appendix or
a bibliography when
needed.

The appendix contains
information that indirectly
supports the report.

Information that directly
supports the report
belongs in the text of the
report.

Include a bibliography if
you make heavy use of
published sources.

Longer reports need
extra structural
coherence devices.

These are a network
of explanations,
introductions,
summaries, and
conclusions.

The coherence plan
begins with the preview,
which describes the
route ahead.

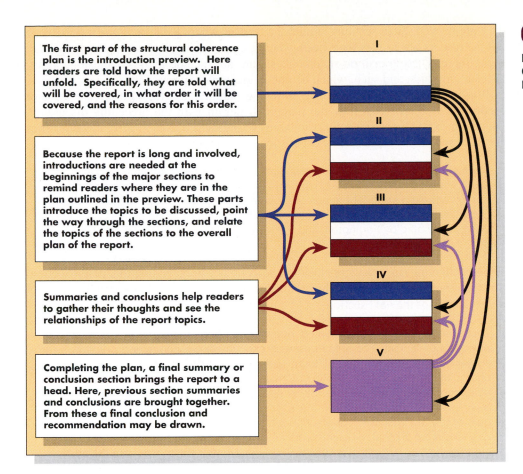

The first part of the structural coherence plan is the introduction preview. Here readers are told how the report will unfold. Specifically, they are told what will be covered, in what order it will be covered, and the reasons for this order.

Because the report is long and involved, introductions are needed at the beginnings of the major sections to remind readers where they are in the plan outlined in the preview. These parts introduce the topics to be discussed, point the way through the sections, and relate the topics of the sections to the overall plan of the report.

Summaries and conclusions help readers to gather their thoughts and see the relationships of the report topics.

Completing the plan, a final summary or conclusion section brings the report to a head. Here, previous section summaries and conclusions are brought together. From these a final conclusion and recommendation may be drawn.

acceleration rate, and traction are the main considerations here. In the third major section, the dependability of the four makes is compared on the basis of repair records and salespersons' time lost because of automobile failure. In the final major section, weights are assigned to the foregoing comparisons, and the automobile that is best suited to the company's needs is recommended.

In addition to the preview in the introduction, the plan uses introductory and summary sections at convenient places throughout the report. Typically, these sections are at the beginning and end of major divisions, but you should use them wherever

• Introductions to and summaries of the report sections keep readers informed of where they are in the report.

Structural coherence helpers guide readers through the report. Helpers are similar to today's car navigational systems. Readers can clearly see where they have been, where they are, and where they will go next. By constructing paragraphs, sentences, and words at important positions throughout the report, readers can be guided skillfully to the report's ending.

they are needed. Such sections remind the readers where they are in the report. They tell the readers where they have been, where they are going, and perhaps why they are going there. These transition statements should not include facts, conclusions, references to graphics, and such, which belong in the content paragraphs.

Illustrating this technique is the following paragraph, which introduces a major section of a report. Note how the paragraph ties in with the preceding discussion, which concerned industrial activity in three geographic areas. Note also how it justifies covering secondary areas in the next section of the report.

> Although the great bulk of industry is concentrated in three areas (Grand City, Milltown, and Port Starr), a thorough industrial survey needs to consider the secondary, but nevertheless important, areas of the state. In the rank of their current industrial potential, these areas are the Southeast, with Hartsburg as its center; the Central West, dominated by Parrington; and the North Central, where Pineview is the center of activities.

The following summary-conclusion paragraph is a good ending to a major section. The paragraph brings to a head the findings presented in the section and points the way to the subject of the next section.

> These findings and those pointed out in preceding paragraphs all lead to one obvious conclusion. The small-business executives are concerned primarily with subject matter that will assist them directly in their work. That is, they favor a curriculum slanted in favor of the practical subjects. They insist, however, on some coverage of the liberal arts, and they also are convinced of the value of studying business administration. On all these points, they are clearly *out of tune* with the bulk of the big-business leaders who have voiced their positions on this question. Even the most dedicated business administration professors would find it difficult to support such an extremely practical approach. Nevertheless, these are the opinions of the small-business executives. Because they are the consumers of the business-education product, their opinions should at least be considered. Likewise, their specific recommendations on courses (the subject of the following section) deserve careful review.

- The final major section of the report brings together the preceding information and applies it to the goal.

Completing the coherence plan is the final major section of the report. In this section, you achieve the goal of the report. Here you recall from the preceding section summaries all the major findings and analyses. Then you apply them to the problem and present the conclusion. Sometimes you will make recommendations. Thus, you complete the strategy explained in the introduction preview and recalled at convenient places throughout the report.

- Use coherence helpers naturally—when they are needed.

Wisely used coherence helpers can form a network of connections throughout the report. You should keep in mind, however, that these helpers should be used only when they are needed. That is, you should use them when your readers need help in seeing relationships and in knowing where they are and where they are going. If you use them well, they will appear as natural parts of the report story. They should never appear to be mechanical additions. When paragraphs are combined with sentence and word transitions, as discussed in Chapters 3, 4, and 10, the total plan should guide your readers smoothly and naturally through the report.

THE LONG ANALYTICAL REPORT ILLUSTRATED

- Figure 12–3 is an illustration of a long, formal report.

Illustrating the long analytical report is the report presented at the end of this chapter (Figure 12–3). The report's structure includes the formal elements described in the preceding pages.

Figure 12–3

Illustration of a Long, Formal Report. This long, formal report presents the findings of an observational study of successful and unsuccessful salespeople to determine the differences in how each group works. The results will be used to revise the content of the company's sales training program. Because the report is extensive and the situation formal, the report has all the major prefatory parts. The significant statistical findings are effectively emphasized by graphics. Whenever secondary sources are used, they are appropriately noted and listed in the bibliography. Its physical presentation uses Word's contemporary report template. Its documentation uses MLA style.

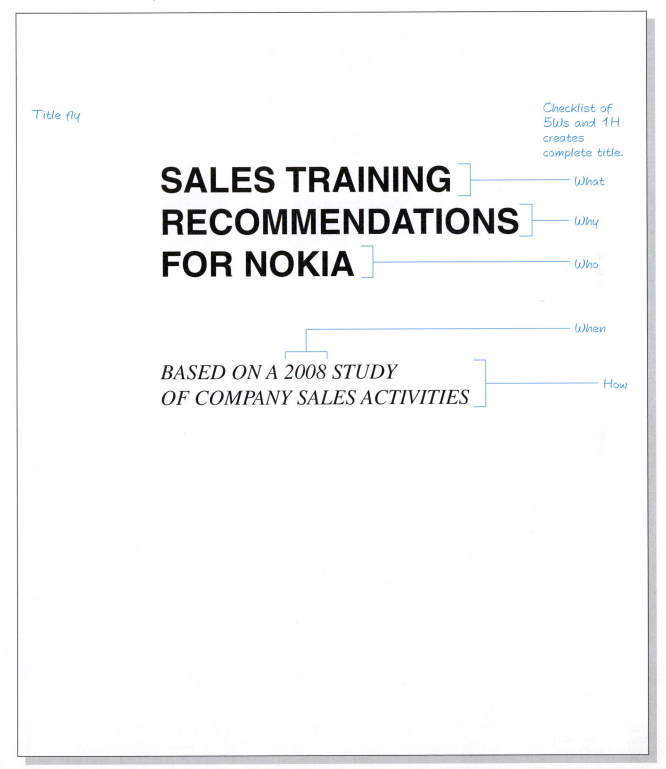

Title fly

Checklist of 5Ws and 1H creates complete title.

SALES TRAINING RECOMMENDATIONS FOR NOKIA

What

Why

Who

When

How

BASED ON A 2008 STUDY OF COMPANY SALES ACTIVITIES

Figure 12–3

Continued

Three-spot title page

SALES TRAINING RECOMMENDATIONS FOR NOKIA

BASED ON A 2008 STUDY OF COMPANY SALES ACTIVITIES

Recipient of report receives prime position on page.

Prepared for
Mr. Peter R. Simpson, Vice President for Sales
Nokia Inc.
72117 North Musselman Road
Dearborn, MI 48126-2351

Writer receives subordinate page position.

Prepared by
Ashlee P. Callahan
Midwestern Research Associates
Suite D, Brownfield Towers
212 North Bedford Avenue
Detroit, MI 48219-6708

November 17, 2008

Figure 12–3

Continued

Transmittal message

Midwestern Research Associates

Suite D, Brownfield Towers
212 North Bedford Avenue
Detroit, MI 48219-6708
312-222-2575 research@midwestern.com

November 17, 2008

Mr. Peter R. Simpson
Vice President for Sales
Nokia Inc.
72117 North Musselman Road
Dearborn, MI 48126-2351

Dear Mr. Simpson:

Begins directly, with the transmittal.

Here is the report on the observational study of your salespeople that you asked us to conduct on August 28.

Brief summary helps the reader understand and appreciate the research.

Our study of two groups of salespeople—20 top performers and 20 low performers—revealed significant differences in three areas: use of work time, ability to generate prospects, and quality of sales presentations. The resulting recommendations for your sales training program should help you correct the shortcomings in your sales force.

Goodwill comment ends letter.

We appreciate your choosing Midwestern for this assignment. If you should need any additional research or assistance in implementing our recommendations, please contact us at acallahan@midwestern.com or 312-222-2575.

Sincerely yours,

Ashlee P. Callahan

Ashlee P. Callahan
Senior Research Associate

Figure 12–3

Continued

Table of contents

TABLE OF CONTENTS

Background details of the problem prepare the reader to receive the report.

Three areas of sales work investigated logically form main headings.

Subfactors of the work areas make logical second-level headings.

First- and second-level headings are parallel.

Conciseness in headings improves readability.

Divisions of main body parts by factors (and subdivisions) show good thought and logical solution to problem.

Talking captions avoid monotonous repetition in wording.

iv

Figure 12–3

Continued

*List of figures
(a continuation
of the table of
contents)*

LIST OF FIGURES

*Titles use 5
Ws and 1H in
title
construction.*

v

Figure 12–3

Continued

Executive summary

EXECUTIVE SUMMARY

To enhance the performance of Nokia's salespeople, this report recommends adding the following topics to Nokia's sales training program:

- Negative effects of idle time
- Techniques of cultivating prospects
- Development of bird dog networks
- Cultivation of repeat sales
- Projection of integrity image
- Use of moderate persuasion
- Value of product knowledge

Following the direct-order plan, this executive summary places the recommendations first. Highlights of the supporting findings follow.

Supporting these recommendations are the following findings and conclusions drawn from an observational study of 20 productive and 20 marginal salespeople. The two groups were compared on three types of sales activities.

Remaining paragraphs summarize the major findings in the order presented in the report.

The data show that the productive salespeople used their time more effectively than did the marginal salespeople. Compared with marginal salespeople, the productive salespeople spent less time in idleness (28% vs. 53%). They also spent more time in contact with prospects (31.3% vs. 19.8%) and more time developing prospects (10.4% vs. 4.4%).

Investigation of how the salespeople got their prospects showed that because field assignments were about equal, both groups profited about the same from unsolicited web inquiries. The productive group got 282; the marginal group got 274. The productive group used bird dogs more extensively, having 64 contacts derived from this source during the observation period. The marginal group had 8. Productive salespeople also were more successful in turning these contacts into sales.

Significant comparisons and conclusions are emphasized throughout.

Observations of sales presentations revealed that productive salespeople displayed higher integrity, used pressure more reasonably, and knew the product better than marginal salespeople. Of the 20 productive salespeople, 16 displayed images of moderately high integrity (Group II). Marginal group members ranged widely with 7 in Group III (questionable) and 5 each in Group II (moderately high integrity) and Group IV (deceitful). Most (15) of the productive salespeople used moderate pressure, whereas the marginal salespeople tended toward extremes (10 high pressure, 7 low pressure). On the product knowledge test, 17 of the productive salespeople scored excellent and 3 fair. Of the marginal members, 5 scored excellent, 6 fair, and 9 inadequate.

vi

Figure 12–3

Continued

Report proper
(introduction)

SALES TRAINING RECOMMENDATIONS FOR NOKIA

BASED ON A 2008 STUDY OF COMPANY SALES ACTIVITIES

INTRODUCTION

Incidentals of Authorization and Submittal

Authorization
facts identify
participants in
the report.

This study of Nokia salespeople's sales activities is submitted to Mr. Peter R. Simpson, Vice President for Sales, on November 17, 2008. As authorized on August 28, the investigation was conducted under the direction of Ashlee P. Callahan of Midwestern Research Associates.

Objective of the Study

Purpose section
explains the
problem clearly
and precisely.

There is a significant performance gap between Nokia's top salespeople and its lowest performers. The objective of this study was to discover the reasons for this disparity and, given these findings, to recommend changes in Nokia's sales training program.

Use of Observational Techniques

The methodology used in this investigation was an observational study of Nokia salespeople. Specifically, the study employed the contrived observation technique, which is a unique means of observing work performance under real conditions.[1] A detailed description of this technique is a part of the proposal approved at the August meeting and is not repeated here. Specific items relative to the application of this method in this case are summarized below.

Thorough
review of
methodology
permits reader
to judge
credibility of
research.

Two groups of 20 Nokia salespeople were selected for the observation—a productive and a marginal group. The productive group was made up of the company's top producers for the past year; the marginal group comprised the lowest producers. Only salespeople with three years or more of experience were eligible.

A team of two highly trained observers observed each of the salespeople selected for a continuous period of five working days. Using specially designed forms, the observers recorded the work activities of the salespeople. At the end of the observation period, the

---

[1] William G. Zikmund, *Business Research Methods,* 7th ed. (Cincinnati, OH: South-Western, 2003) 240.

All sources used are
appropriately credited and
thoroughly documented.

1

Figure 12–3

Continued

2

observers conducted an exit interview, recording certain demographic data and administering a test of the salesperson's knowledge of Nokia 's mobile phones.

A Preview of the Presentation

Preview prepares reader for what follows in body sections.

In the following pages, the findings and analysis appear in the arrangement discussed at the August meeting. First comes a comparison of how the productive and the marginal salespeople spend their work time. Second is an analysis of how the productive and the marginal salespeople find their prospects. Third is a comparative analysis of the observable differences in sales presentations of the two groups. Conclusions drawn from these comparisons form the bases for recommendations regarding the content in Nokia's sales training program.

ANALYSIS OF WORK TIME USE

Body sections contain facts, interpretations, and solutions to report problems.

The time-duty observation records were examined to determine whether differences exist between the productive and marginal salespeople in their use of work time. Activities were grouped into four general categories: (1) idleness, (2) contacting prospects, (3) finding prospects, and (4) miscellaneous activities. This examination revealed the followingresults.

Section introductions tell what follows in subdivisions.

Negative Effect of Idle Time

Subordinate reference to figure ties text and graphic together and allows interpretation to begin in main sentence.

As shown in Figure 1, the productive salespeople spent less work time in idleness (28%) than did the marginal salespeople (53%). Further examination of the observations reveals that the top five of the 20 productive salespeople spent even less time in idleness (13%), and the bottom five of the marginal salespeople spent more time in idleness (67%). Clearly, these observations suggest the predictable conclusion that successful salespeople work more than their less productive counterparts.

Sentence conclusions complement formal coherence plan.

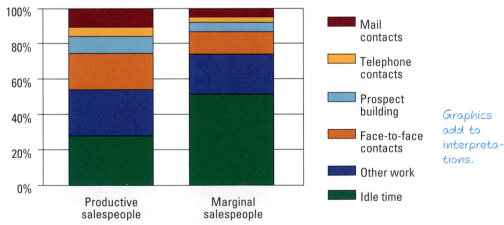

Graphics add to interpretations.

Figure 1. How productive and marginal salespeople use work time.

Figure 12–3

Continued

3

Correlation of Prospect Contacting and Success

Productive salespeople spent more time contacting prospects face to face, by telephone, and by mail (31.3%) than did marginal salespeople (19.8%). The specific means of making these contacts show similar differences. Productive and marginal salespeople spent their work time, respectively, 23.2% and 13.5% in face-to-face contacts, 4.8% and 2.0% in mail contacts, and 8.3% and 4.6% in telephone contacts. These data lend additional support to the conclusion that work explains sales success.

Vital Role of Prospect Building

During the observation period, productive salespeople spent more than twice as much time (10.5%) as marginal salespeople (4.4%) in building prospects. Activities observed in this category include contacting bird dogs (people who give sales leads) and other lead sources and mailing literature to established and prospective customers.

Necessity of Miscellaneous Activities

Both productive and marginal salespeople spent about a fourth of their work time in miscellaneous activities (tending to personal affairs, studying sales literature, attending sales meetings, sending and responding to email, and such). The productive group averaged 25.2%; the marginal group averaged 22.5%. As some of this time is related to mobile phone sales, productive salespeople would be expected to spend more time in this category.

The preceding data reveal that the way salespeople spend their time affects their productivity. Productive salespeople work at selling. In sharp contrast with the marginal salespeople, they spend little time in idleness. They work hard to contact prospects and to build prospect lists. Like all mobile phone salespeople, they spend some time in performing miscellaneous duties.

DIFFERENCES IN FINDING PROSPECTS

A comparison of how productive and marginal salespeople find prospects and the productivity of these methods were a second area of investigation. For this study, the observations were classified by the four primary sources of prospects: (1) unsolicited web inquiries, (2) bird dogs and other referrals, (3) repeat customers, and (4) other. Only prospects that were contacted in person or by telephone during the observation period were included. Prospects were counted only once, even though some were contacted more than once.

Near Equal Distribution of Web Inquiries

As expected, most of the contacts of both productive and marginal salespeople were web inquiries. Because both groups had about equal field assignments, they got about the same number of prospects from this source. As illustrated in Figure 2, productive members got 282 (an average of 14.1 each) and marginal members got 274 (an average of 13.7 each).

Although both groups got about the same number of prospects from web inquiries, productive salespeople got better results. A review of sales records shows that productive salespeople averaged 260 units per week from web inquiries; marginal salespeople averaged 220 units. The difference, although appearing slight, represents roughly 40 mobile phones per week.

Report text presents data thoroughly yet concisely — and with appropriate comparisons.

Section summary helps the reader identify and remember the major findings.

Section introduction continues formal coherence plan.

Variety in sentence design helps maintain reader interest.

Report length and situation formality justify third-person writing.

Tense consistency places concepts in appropriate time frames and gives a present time viewpoint.

Key transitional words used in emphasis positions keep ideas moving.

Figure 12–3

Continued

4

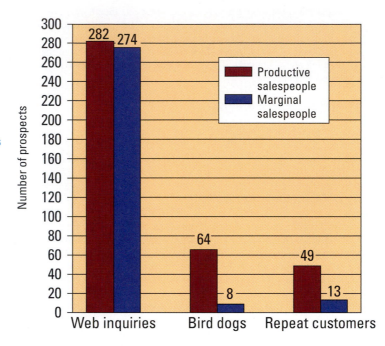

Figure 2. Prospects contacted during observation period by productive and marginal salespeople by method of obtaining them.

Color adds interest and helps reader visualize comparisons in graphics.

Use of graphics allows only important details to be emphasized in report text.

Value of Cultivating Repeat Customers

Predominance of active voice verbs provide flow and concreteness in text.

Repeat customers and friends referred by them constitute the second most productive source of prospects. During the observation period, productive salespeople had contacts with 49 such prospects; marginal salespeople had 13. Productive salespeople also had better sales success with these prospects, turning 40 of them into sales—an average of two per week. Marginal group members made sales to seven of these prospects—an average of 0.35 per person. These findings agree with those of a recent study reported in the *American Salesman*.[2] These differences appear to be a direct result of effort (or lack of it) in maintaining contacts with customers after the sale.

[2] Alex Hatzivassilis and Igor Kotlyar, "Increase the Number of Top Performers on Your Team," *American Salesman* 48.7 (2003): 17.

Figure 12–3

Continued

5

Limited Effectiveness of Using Bird Dogs

Interweaving facts and interpretations gives good emphasis.

Contacts from bird dogs comprise the third largest group, producing 64 total contacts for the productive and 8 for the marginal salespeople. Sales from this source totaled 9 for productive salespeople and 2 for marginal salespeople—an average of 0.45 and 0.1 sales per person, respectively. Although not large in terms of volume, these data explain much of the difference between the two groups. The use of bird dogs involves work,[3] and the willingness to work varies sharply between the two groups.

Scant Use of Other Techniques

Talking headings help emphasize the major findings.

Other prospect-gaining techniques were little used among the salespeople observed. Techniques long discussed in industry sales literature such as cold spearing, placing written messages on automobile windshields, and random telephoning produced no prospects for either group during the observation period.[4] All of the salespeople observed noted that they had used these techniques in the past, but with little success. The lack of evidence in this study leaves unanswered the question of the effectiveness of these techniques.

Word choice and sentence length contribute to readability.

Sectional summary draws ideas together before report moves to next section.

The obvious conclusion drawn from the preceding review of how prospects are found is that the productive salespeople work harder to get them. Although both groups get about the same number of web inquiries, the successful ones work harder at maintaining contacts with past customers and at getting contacts from a network of bird dogs and friends.

OBSERVABLE VARIATIONS IN PRESENTATIONS

Differences in the sales presentations used constituted the third area of study. Criteria used in this investigation were (1) integrity, (2) pressure, and (3) product knowledge. Obviously, the first two of these criteria had to be evaluated subjectively. Even so, highly trained observers who used comprehensive guidelines made the evaluations. These guidelines are described in detail in the approved observation plan.

Formal coherence pattern continues with sectional introduction.

Positive Effect of Integrity

Evaluations of the salespeople's integrity primarily measured the apparent degree of truthfulness of the sales presentations. The observers classified the images of integrity they perceived during the sales presentations into four groups: Group I—Impeccable (displayed the highest degree of truthfulness), Group II—Moderately High (generally truthful, some exaggeration), Group III—Questionable (mildly deceitful and tricky); and Group IV—Deceitful (untruthful and tricky).

Of the 20 productive salespeople observed, 16 were classified in Group II, as shown in Figure 3. Of the remaining four, 2 were in Group I and 2 in Group III.

---

[3] Julie Jahn, "Big Business Encourages Effective Use of Bird Dogs throughout Their Organizations," *BusinessWeek* 22 April 2003, 22 Oct. 2007 <http://:www.businessweek.com/bwdaily/dnflash/ap203126__085.htm>.

[4] James Poon Teng Fatt, "Criteria Used for Evaluating Sales Persons," *Management Research News* 23.1 (2000): 27.

Figure 12–3

Continued

6

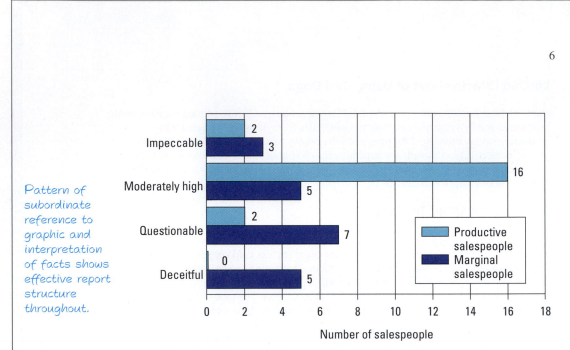

Pattern of subordinate reference to graphic and interpretation of facts shows effective report structure throughout.

Figure 3. Observed images of integrity in sales presentations of productive and marginal salespeople.

Distribution of the marginal salespeople was markedly different: 3 in Group I, 5 in Group II, 7 in Group III, and 5 in Group IV. Clearly, integrity was more apparent among the productive salespeople.

Apparent Value of Moderate Pressure

Measurements (by observation) of pressure used in the sales presentations were made in order to determine the relationship of pressure to sales success. Using the guidelines approved at the August meeting, the observers classified each salesperson's presentations into three categories: (1) high pressure, (2) moderate pressure, and (3) low pressure. Observers reported difficulties in making some borderline decisions, but they felt that most of the presentations were easily classified.

Of the 20 productive salespeople, 15 used moderate pressure, 3 used low pressure, and 2 used high pressure, as depicted in Figure 4. The 20 marginal salespeople presented a different picture. Only 3 of them used moderate pressure. Of the remainder, 10 used high pressure and 7 used low pressure. The evidence suggests that moderate pressure is most effective.

Interpretation of significant report facts follows subordinate reference to graphic.

Figure 12–3

Continued

7

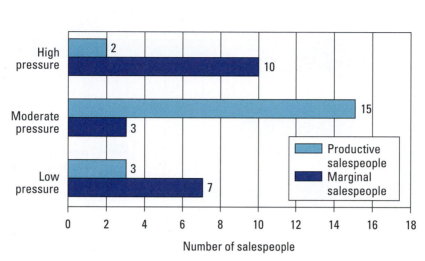

Figure 4. Observed use of pressure in sales presentations of productive and marginal salespeople.

Graphic placement amplifies text analysis.

The facts are not just presented. They are compared and conclusions are drawn from them.

Central idea and factual support demonstrate paragraph unity.

Necessity of Product Knowledge

Product knowledge, a widely accepted requirement for successful selling, was determined during the exit interview.[5] Using the 30 basic questions developed by Nokia management from sales literature, observers measured the salespeople's product knowledge. Correct responses to 27 or more of the questions was determined to be excellent, 24 through 26 was fair, and below 24 was classified as inadequate.

Productive salespeople displayed superior knowledge of the product with 17 of the 20 scoring excellent. As shown in Figure 5, the remaining 3 scored fair.

Balanced, short paragraphs indicate good organization of thought and improve readability.

[5] Barton Weitz, Stephen B. Castleberry, and John F. Tanner, *Selling: Building Partnerships,* 5th ed. (New York: McGraw-Hill, 2004) 247.

Figure 12–3

Continued

8

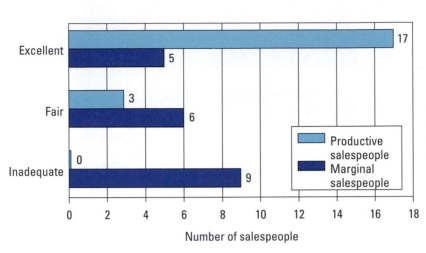

Clustered bar chart is appropriate for presenting information.

Text and graphics work closely together to present the information.

Figure 5. Product knowledge ratings of productive and marginal salespeople.

Scores for product knowledge were sharply different in the marginal salesperson group. Although 5 of them scored excellent, 6 scored fair, and 9 scored inadequate. These data point to an apparent weakness in training or a lack of individual preparation.

Another summary-conclusion brings section to a close.

The preceding presentation reveals some basic differences in the sales presentations of the productive and marginal salespeople. The productive salespeople displayed higher integrity (though not the highest). They used moderate pressure, whereas the marginal people tended toward high or low extremes. Also, the productive people knew their products better.

RECOMMENDATIONS FOR TRAINING

The conclusions reached in the preceding sections suggest certain actions that Nokia Inc. should take in training its sales force. Specifically, the instruction should be altered to include the following topics:

From the summary-conclusions of the preceding three sections the recommendations are derived.

- Importance of minimizing idle time.
- Sales rewards from productive work (mailing literature, telephoning, cultivating prospects, etc.).
- Significance of creating a network of bird dogs and friends in building prospects.
- Value of maintaining contacts with past customers.
- Need for integrity, within reasonable limits.
- Use of moderate pressure, avoiding extremes in either direction.
- Need for a thorough knowledge of the product.

Bulleting shows the reader recommendations are unordered and equally weighted.

Figure 12–3

Continued

9

BIBLIOGRAPHY

Fatt, James Poon Teng. "Criteria Used for Evaluating Sales Persons." *Management Research News* 23.1 (2000): 27–32.

Hatzivassilis, Alex, and Igor Kotlyar. "Increase the Number of Top Performers on Your Team." *American Salesman* 48.7 (2003): 17.

Jahn, Julie. "Big Business Encourages Effective Use of Bird Dogs throughout Their Organizations." *BusinessWeek* 22 April 2003. 22 Oct. 2007 <http://:www.businessweek.com/ bwdaily/dnflash/ap203126__085.htm>.

Weitz, Barton, Stephen B. Castleberry, and John F. Tanner. *Selling: Building Partnerships.* 5th ed. New York: McGraw-Hill, 2004.

Zikmund, William G. *Business Research Methods.* 7th ed. Cincinnati, OH: South-Western, 2003.

Bibliography sources are presented alphabetically and completely. They present last name first and use the hanging indent format.

SUMMARY BY LEARNING OBJECTIVES

1 Describe the roles and contents and construct the prefatory parts of a long, formal report.

1. The prefatory section of the long, formal report consists of these conventional parts:
   - Title fly—a page displaying only the title.
     - As a checklist for constructing the title, use the 5 Ws (*who, what, where, when, why*).
     - Sometimes *how* is important.
   - Title page—a page displaying the title, identification of writer and recipient, and date.
   - Authorization message—included only when a message authorized the report.
   - Transmittal message—a message transmitting the report (a *foreword* or *preface* in very long and highly formal papers).
     - This part takes the place of a face-to-face presentation.
     - Begin it with a presentation of the report.
     - Include comments about the report you would have made in a face-to-face presentation.
     - In some cases you may combine it with the executive summary.
     - Write the message in personal style (first and second person).
   - Table of contents, list of illustrations—a listing of the report parts and illustrations with page numbers.
   - Executive summary—the report in miniature.
     - Include, in proportion, everything that is important—all the major facts, analyses, and conclusions.
     - Write it in either direct or indirect order.

2 Organize each introduction of a long report by considering the likely readers and selecting the appropriate contents.

2. The report introduction prepares the readers to follow and interpret the report.
   - Include whatever helps reach this goal.
   - Use these items as a checklist for content: purpose, scope, limitations, problem history, methodology, definitions, preview.
   - A preview telling the order and reasoning for the order is useful in longer, more involved reports.

3 Prepare the body of a long, formal report by applying the advice in Chapter 10 and in other chapters.

3. Preparing the body of a long, formal report will require virtually all your organizing, writing, and formatting skills.

4 Determine, based on the report's purpose, the most effective way to end a report: a summary, a conclusion, a recommendation, or a combination of the three.

4. The ending of the report achieves the report purpose.
   - Use a summary if the purpose is to review information.
   - Use a conclusion if the purpose is to reach an answer.
   - Use a recommendation if the purpose is to determine a desirable action.

5 Describe the role and content of the appendix and bibliography of a report.

5. An appendix and/or bibliography can follow the report text.
   - The appendix contains items that support the text but have no specific place in the text (such as questionnaires, working papers, summary tables).
   - The bibliography is a descriptive list of the secondary sources that were used in the investigation.

6 Prepare a structural coherence plan for a long, formal report.

6. The longer reports need various structural devices to give them coherence.
   - These devices consist of a network of explanations, introductions, summaries, and conclusions that guide the reader through the report.
   - Begin the coherence plan with the introduction preview, which tells the structure of the report.
   - Then use the introductions and summaries in following parts to tell readers where they are in this structure.

- At the end, bring together the preceding information, analyses, and conclusions to reach the report goal.
- Make these coherence helpers inconspicuous—that is, make them appear to be a natural part of the message.

CRITICAL THINKING QUESTIONS

1 Long, formal reports are not often written in business. So why should you know how to write them?

2 A good title should be complete and concise. Are not these requirements contradictory? Explain.

3 Discuss the relative importance of the title fly and the title page in a report.

4 Distinguish among the transmittal message, the foreword, and the preface.

5 Describe the role and content of a transmittal message.

6 Why is personal style typically used in the transmittal message?

7 What is the basis for determining whether a report should have a table of contents?

8 Explain how to write the executive summary of a report.

9 Why does the executive summary include key facts and figures in addition to the analyses and conclusions drawn from them?

10 Some reports need little or no introduction; others need a very long introduction. Why is this so?

11 Give examples of report problems whose introduction could require coverage of methods of collecting data, historical background, and limitations.

12 Explain how the advice in Chapter 10 can help you prepare the body of a long report.

13 Give examples of report problems that would require, respectively, (a) an ending summary, (b) an ending conclusion, and (c) an ending recommendation.

14 Using as a guide the diagram in Figure 12–2, summarize the coherence plan of the long, formal report.

CRITICAL THINKING EXERCISES

1 Making any assumptions needed, construct complete yet concise titles for the reports described below:

a. A report writer reviewed records of exit interviews of employees at Marvel-Floyd Manufacturing Company who quit their jobs voluntarily. The objective of the investigation was to determine the reasons for leaving.

b. A researcher studied data from employee personnel records at Magna-Tech, Inc., to determine whether permanent (long-term) employees differ from short-term employees. Any differences found would be used in hiring employees in the future. The data studied included age, education, experience, sex, marital status, test scores, and such.

c. A report writer compared historical financial records (1935 to the present) of Super Saver Foods to determine whether this grocery chain should own or rent store buildings. In the past it did both.

2 Criticize the following beginning sentences of transmittal messages:

a. "In your hands is the report you requested January 7 concerning . . ."

b. "As you will recall, last January 7 you requested a report on . . ."

c. "That we should open a new outlet in Bragg City is the conclusion of this report, which you authorized January 7."

3 In a report comparing four automobiles (Alpha, Beta, Gamma, and Delta) to determine which one is the best buy for a company, section II of the report body covered these cost data: (a) initial costs, (b) trade-in values, and (c) operating expenses. Section III presented a comparison of these safety features of the automobiles: (a) standard safety features, (b) acceleration data, (c) weight distribution, and (d) braking quality.

a. Criticize this introductory paragraph at the beginning of section III:

In the preceding section was presented a thorough analysis of the cost data. Now safety of the cars will be compared. Although costs are important, Warren-Burke also is concerned about the safety of its salespeople, who spend almost half their work time driving.

b. Write a more appropriate introductory paragraph.

4 The next section of the report (section IV) covered these topics: (*a*) handling, (*b*) quality of ride, and (*c*) durability.

a. Criticize this introductory paragraph for the section:

This section of the report presents a comparison of the overall construction of the four automobiles. These considerations also are important because they affect how a car rides, and this is important. Thus, we will take up in this order: handling, general riding quality, and construction qualities.

b. Write a more appropriate introductory paragraph.

5 Criticize this final paragraph (a preview) of the introduction of the report described above:

This report compares the automobiles by three factors. These are costs, safety, and comfort and construction, in that order. Costs include initial expenditure, trade-in value, and operating expense. Safety covers safety devices, acceleration, weight distribution, and braking. Comfort and construction includes handling, ride quality, and durability. A ranking is derived from this comparison.

CRITICAL THINKING PROBLEMS

Long Report Problems

1 *Selecting a university for a scholarship.* In your role as training officer for Galloway Manufacturing, Inc., a manufacturer of kitchenware, you have been asked by your president to select a university to receive a scholarship. President Blake W. Reddoch wants to establish the scholarship in the hope that the recipient will consider signing on after graduation. But there would be no legal obligation to do so.

The scholarship will be in _____ (accounting, marketing, information systems, etc., as determined by your instructor). It will cover all expenses: tuition, fees, supplies, incidentals, room, and board. It will be awarded to a beginning student selected on the basis of academic ability. And it will continue for four years as long as the student maintains a minimum grade-point average of 3.0 and makes satisfactory progress toward graduation.

Your role now is to find the university that will receive this scholarship. President Reddoch explains his instructions to you in these words: "I want you to help me select the school that will give us the very best training in this curriculum. Find three leading schools in this general geographic area. Review their curricula. Evaluate their offerings, their facilities, their reputation, their standards, their students—everything that will help us select the best one. Find out what it costs to go there. This includes tuition, fees, living cost estimates—all we need to know in determining the amount to put in to the scholarship. But cost is not the only consideration. Equally important is the quality of the education obtained. You might help me if you ranked the three schools. Of course, there is no guarantee I'll follow your rankings."

You will get most of what you need on the websites of the schools. But you may use other sources as well: opinions of knowledgeable people, catalogs, brochures, and such. When you have the information you need, you'll study it, make comparisons, and organize your findings and analyses in appropriate report form. You will address the report to Mr. Reddoch. Probably he will want additional copies for the other executives who will be in on the decision.

2 *Determining what business will be like in the months ahead.* Nicole Garza, president of Bon Marche Department Stores, Inc., has assigned you, her assistant, the task of writing a consensus business forecast for presentation at the next board of directors meeting. Bon Marche does not have an economist. "Why should we pay for one?" Ms. Garza reasons. "We can't afford such frills. We can get all we need from current business periodicals, newspapers, and the Internet."

Since Ms. Garza's instructions were—as usual—quite vague, much of what you do will depend on your good judgment. All she said was that she wanted you to survey the predictions of the leading economic forecasters for the months ahead and to present your finding in a clear and meaningful report to herself and the board. She wants the forecasts consolidated—that is, she does not want a mere succession of individual forecasts. Your report, covering the entire economy, will be largely general in nature. But you will give special emphasis to forecasts pertaining to retailing.

Of course, your report will be in a form appropriate for the board. Because the members will want to get at the most important material quickly, be sure to include a fast-moving executive summary. Address the report to the board. Ms. Garza chairs the board.

3 *Recommending a resort for Sterling Pharmaceutical's annual sales meeting.* As assistant to Felix W. Baskin, national sales manager for Sterling Pharmaceuticals, Inc., you have just concluded a meeting with your boss. He wants you to help him select a resort for Sterling's annual sales meeting.

Mr. Baskin explained your assignment in these words: "As you know, we hold our annual sales meeting at a resort—a place where we can work and play a little. The meeting is scheduled for five days in late August. As you can imagine, I have had many suggestions about where we should meet. My three favorites are the Grand Hotel Marriott Resort and Golf Club in Alabama, the PGA National Resort and Spa in Florida, and the Horseshoe Bay Resort and Conference Center in Texas. (Your instructor may choose to change these selections.) I want you to investigate these three, evaluate them, and recommend one of them."

"I may not go along with your recommendation," he added, "so give me sufficient information to permit me to make my decision. Cost is important, but not the major factor. We will negotiate price after we have a final selection.

But give me the prospects' listed cost information, and make it a part of your evaluation. As you know, we hold sales meeting in the mornings. For this we'll need a meeting room that holds 56 people. The afternoons and evenings will be fun times. We want to reward our people for their hard work throughout the year. So they may do whatever they like after lunch. I know we have a good number of golfers and some tennis players. Some like swimming. Of course, they all like to eat and party. If you can think of anything else to include, do so. I want a thorough report. I am pretty sure you can get what you need from their websites."

After gathering the information available, you will evaluate it, make comparisons, and reach a decision. Probably you will rank the three. Of course, you will present all this to Mr. Baskin in appropriate report form.

---

4 *Evaluating the quality of life in a selected city.* Cutting-Edge Technology, Inc., is considering moving its headquarters to _____ (a city selected by your instructor). The company has completed a study considering the economic advantages of relocating, and this study was positive. But before finally deciding, the company's leaders want to know more about the quality of life that they and their employees could expect there. They have hired your research organization to get the information they need.

Although *quality of life* is a very general term, you and the company's top executives have agreed that housing, educational institutions, recreational and cultural facilities, and climate would be considered. You may think of other factors as you get into the problem.

Your first step is to gather the information available for the factors involved. Some of it you can get from Internet

sources—the website of the Chamber of Commerce in particular. More may come from local libraries, the telephone directory, travel brochures, and such. Some you may get by personal observation and knowledge.

After you have gathered, assembled, and analyzed the information you need, you will organize it for presentation in a formal report. You will present the information and interpret it objectively. In the end, you will arrive at a recommendation on whether this city would offer a good quality of life for the 227 employees and their families who would move there.

Address the report to Geraldine Probst, the CEO of Cutting-Edge Technologies, and to the members of her board of directors. Give your report the formality expected at this level of administration.

---

5 *Evaluating three charities for a philanthropist.* You are the business manager for Elise M. Fahrendorf, a multimillionaire, successful business leader, and philanthropist of the first order. Today she gave you a challenging assignment.

"As you know," she explained to you, "I make substantial contributions to what I think are worthy causes every year. But I really don't know whether my selections are the most worthy ones. I want my money to go to the most deserving groups. I want it to do the most good for the most people. I hear horror stories about how some of them are run—especially how high their administrative costs are. And I hear reports that much of the money some charities raise goes to the people who solicit it. So I want you to check out my three favorites—the three that have received most of my money in recent years. They are the Alzheimer's Association, National

Multiple Sclerosis Society, and Memorial Sloan-Kettering Cancer Center. (Your instructor may choose to change this selection.) I want you to find out what good they do, how efficient they are—and anything else that will help me decide on whether to favor them. Your objective will be to determine how deserving they are. When you have gathered all this information, analyze it, compare, and conclude. You might even rank these three. I might decide to give only to one, give to all equally, or vary among them. I'll do whatever appears to be right."

Now you must follow your boss's instructions. You will present the results of your work in a formal report (she likes formality). As usual, you will include a fast-moving executive summary that will give her the answers right away.

---

6 *Investigating the outlook for investments in an industry.* Assume you are employed in the Investments Research Department of the Warneke Foundation, a philanthropic trust with over $550 million of invested funds. You have been

assigned the task of determining the general outlook for investments in the _____ industry. (Choose one from this list or another with your instructor's approval:)

Aircraft	Electronics (technology)	Chemicals
Aluminum	Steel	Textiles
Shoes	Pharmaceuticals	Tobacco
Paper	Food processing	Automotive
Petroleum	Publishing	Clothing
Mining	Utilities	

Using the Internet as well as the leading business databases and publications, you will review the past and present status of the industry's profits, sales, production, and the like. From these reviews you will look for trends that will suggest the industry's future. Also, you will gather all facts and authoritative opinions relating to future growth. From all of this you hope to be able to make a recommendation about investments in the industry in general.

Although your report will concern the industry rather than a specific company (or companies), you are likely to refer frequently to the major firms in the industry. And your recommendation might point out the industry leaders. Write your report in a form appropriate for the formality of this situation. Submit it to Theodore M. McMichael, Chair, The Investment Board, The Warneke Foundation.

---

7 *Presenting the pros and cons of gun control to an arms manufacturer.* Assume the position of a research associate employed by the Abraham-Doral Company, manufacturers of a full line of rifles, shotguns, and handguns. In recent years advocates of gun control have exerted increasing pressure on the company. Until now, the management of Abraham-Doral has ignored them. But now it believes that their position must be given due consideration. As a result, you were called into a long executive staff meeting, in which President Samuel T. Abraham's final words summarized your instructions.

"As you can see, we are disturbed. We think we should know more about this matter. So we're asking you to get for us the principal arguments for and against gun control and the supporting evidence for those arguments. This should lead to recommendations concerning what our stand should be, what messages we should communicate, what actions we should take, and so on. Of course, we're biased—guns are our livelihood. But we want your report to look at this question objectively. Please have your research in our hands for the board meeting one month from today."

---

8 *Determining the best Internet source for buying _____.* Play the role of assistant to the purchasing manager for Sentinel Insurance, Inc. In response to criticisms that the company's current source of _____ (office supplies, furniture, or such to be determined by your instructor) is not giving the company the best deals, you have been asked to help correct the situation. Specifically, you have been asked to "survey the major outlets on the Internet, get their prices on the items Sentinel buys as well as their return policies, and recommend a source for us." Currently, Sentinel gets its _____ from _____ (to be determined by your instructor).

You will begin your effort by making a list of the items Sentinel typically purchases. Use your best judgment here, but certainly the list will include all those items common to most offices. But since these items vary in quality and style, select only items that are comparable to items carried by most of the outlets. That is, you will want to be certain that you are not comparing apples to oranges.

With your list completed, you will then search for these items on the Internet. Then you will record the prices for the items on your list. As you will see, there are many outlets, but make certain that you find at least two. Of course, in addition you will include Sentinel's current supplier.

After you have gathered the information you need and made comparisons, you will make your recommendation. (Sentinel prefers to do business primarily with one supplier.) Because the report will be read by various top management people, you will dress it up with the trappings suitable for a report of this nature. If they will help, you will use appropriate graphics.

---

9 *Determining how prices at near-campus stores compare with prices away from campus.* As a member of your student government, you have heard many complaints about the high prices students must pay at stores in the campus area. Many of the complaints you heard suggest that the local stores are gouging students—that prices at stores off campus are much lower. After long debate, the student government members agreed that they needed specific information, and they formed a special committee to study and report on the question. You were chosen to serve as chairperson of this committee.

Working with your committee members, you selected a few campus stores and some comparable off-campus stores (in a mall or shopping district some distance away). You then worked out a student's market basket—products frequently bought by students. Next, you got prices for these items at the two groups of stores. Of course, you ignored special promotions and the like. (Your instructor may permit you to collect this information in teams, but of course the writing will be done individually.)

When you have gathered this information, you are ready to give it meaning. You will carefully analyze it and organize it for presentation. Then you will present it in the formal report form you learned in your business communication course. As the information is largely statistical, you will present the major facts in graphic form. Your conclusion will determine whether there is truth to the complaint that campus stores have higher prices. You will not only address the general question but also look into differences in the major categories of items in your shopping basket. Address the report to your student-body president.

---

10 *Solving a problem on your campus.* Certain problems exist on most college campuses. At least, they exist in the minds of many of the faculty, students, and staff. From the following list of such problems, you (or your instructor) will select one that needs attention on your campus.

Library operation	Cultural atmosphere on campus
Campus security	
Policies on sales of tickets to athletic events	Class attendance policies
	Scholastic probation policies
Regulation of social activities	Parking, traffic control
Faculty–student relations	Grade inflation
	Student government
Orientation program for beginning students	Emphasis on athletics
Curriculum improvement	Campus beautification
Increasing (or decreasing) enrollments	Fire prevention
	Admission policies (including diversification practices)
Scholastic honesty	
Campus crime	

You will first gather all the significant facts regarding the problem you select. When you are thoroughly acquainted with them, you will gather authoritative opinions concerning the solution.

Obtaining such information may involve looking through bibliographic sources as well as the Internet to find out what has been done on other campuses. It may involve interviewing people on campus who are attempting to deal with the problem. Next you will carefully analyze your problem in light of all you have learned about it. Then you will develop a solution.

To make the situation appear realistic, place yourself in the proper role at your school to handle such a problem. Then write your work in a report appropriate for the situation. Address it to the person or persons at your school who would be likely to handle such matters.

TOPIC SUGGESTIONS FOR INTERMEDIATE-LENGTH AND LONG REPORTS

Following are suggestions for additional report problems ranging from the simple to the highly complex. You can convert them into realistic business problems by supplying details and/or adapting them to real-life business situations. For most of these problems, you can obtain the needed information through secondary research. The topics are arranged by business field, although many of them cross fields.

Accounting

1 Report on current depreciation accounting practices, and recommend depreciation accounting procedures for Company X.

2 Design an inventory control system for X Company.

3 Report to Company X executives on how tax court decisions handed down over the past six months will affect their firm.

4 What security measures should Company X take regarding access to its accounting data online?

5 Advise the managers of X Company on the accounting problems that they can anticipate when the company begins overseas operations.

6 Analyze break-even analysis as a decision-making tool for X Company.

7 Explain to potential investors which sections in Company X's most recent annual report they should review most carefully.

8 Analyze the relative effects on income of the first-in, first-out (FIFO) and last-in, first-out (LIFO) methods of inventory valuation during a prolonged period of inflation.

9 Write a report for the American Accounting Association on the demand for accountants with computer systems training.

10 Develop information for accounting students at your college that will help them choose between careers in public accounting and careers in private accounting.

11 Advise the management of X Company on the validity of return on investment as a measure of performance.

12 Report on operations research as a decision-making tool for accountants and managers.

13 Report to the management of X Company on trends in the content and design of corporate annual reports.

14 Report to an association of accountants the status of professional ethics in accounting.

15 Report to management of X Company on the communication skills important to accounting.

16 Investigate the matching principle and its effects on financial statements for Company X.

17 Report to the board of directors at X on Company whether the balance sheet fails to recognize important intangible assets.

18 Explain the extent to which accounting reflects the intent of Company X's business decisions.

19 Review for Company X whether disclosure could be an effective substitute for recognition in financial statements.

20 Report to the management of Company X on whether intangible assets have finite or infinite lives.

21 Advise the founders of new Company X on income tax considerations in the selection of a form of business organization.

22 Review for Company X the pros and cons of current methods of securities evaluation.

General Business

23 Evaluate the adequacy of current college programs for developing business leadership.

24 Which business skills should schools and colleges teach, and which should companies teach?

25 What should be the role of business leaders in developing courses and curricula for business schools?

26 Report on ways to build and use good teams in the workplace.

27 Identify the criteria Company X should use in selecting a public relations firm.

28 Report on the advisability of including business internships in a business degree program.

29 Investigate the impact of electronic signatures on the business community.

30 How does today's business community regard the master of business administration (MBA) degree?

31 Evaluate the contribution that campus business and professional clubs make to business education.

32 How effective is online training in education for business?

33 Should education for business be specialized, or should it provide a generalized, well-rounded education?

34 Determine how to get and use permission for music added to business presentations.

35 Determine which of three franchises (your instructor will select) offer the best opportunity for investment.

36 Determine guidelines for avoiding sexual harassment for Company X.

37 Determine cultural problems likely to be encountered by employees going to work in _____ (a foreign country).

38 Investigate the pros and cons of international business majors studying abroad for one term.

39 Should Company X use the U.S. Postal Service or a private courier (Federal Express, United Parcel Service)?

40 For an instructor, answer the question of whether IM should be used as a class teaching tool.

41 Advise a client on whether to invest in a company producing renewable energy (wind, solar, etc.).

Labor

42 For the executives of the National Association of Manufacturers (or some such group), report on the outlook for labor–management relations in the next 12 months.

43 For the officers of a major labor union, research and report progress toward decreasing job discrimination against minorities.

44 For X Union, project the effects that a particular technology (you choose) will have on traditionally unionized industries by the year 2012.

45 Advise the management of X Company on how to deal with Y Union, which is attempting to organize the employees of X Company.

46 Interpret the change in the number of union members over the past _____ years.

47 Report on the successes and failures of employee-run businesses.

48 Report on the status and effects of "right to work" laws.

49 Evaluate the effects of a particular strike (your choice) on the union, the company, the stockholders, and the public. Write the report for a government investigating committee.

50 For Union X, prepare an objective report on union leadership in the nation during the past decade.

51 Layoffs based on seniority are causing a disproportionate reduction in the number of women and minority workers at Company X. Investigate alternatives that the company can present to the union.

52 Investigate recent trends relative to the older worker and the stands that unions have taken in this area.

53 Review the appropriateness of unionizing government workers, and recommend to a body of government leaders the stand they should take on this issue.

54 Report on the role of unions (or management) in politics, and recommend a course for them to follow.

55 Reevaluate _____ (unions or employment relations—your instructor will specify) for the management of X Company.

56 Analyze the changing nature of work for the leaders of _____ union (your instructor will designate).

57 Report on the blending of work and family issues for X Union.

Finance

58 As a financial consultant, evaluate a specific form of tax shelter for a client.

59 Review the customer-relations practices of banks and recommend customer relations procedures for Bank X.

60 Review current employee loan practices and recommend whether Company X should make employee loans.

61 Report on what Company X needs to know about financial matters in doing business with _____ (foreign country).

62 Give estate planning advice to a client with a unique personal situation.

63 Advise X Company on whether it should lease capital equipment or buy it.

64 Advise Company X on whether it should engage in a joint venture with a company overseas or establish a wholly owned foreign subsidiary.

65 Compare the costs for X Company of offering its workers child care or elder care benefits.

66 Should Company X accept national credit cards or set up its own credit card system?

67 Advise Company X on how to avoid a hostile takeover.

68 Which will be the better investment in the next three years: stocks or bonds?

69 Advise Company X on whether it should list its stock on a major stock exchange.

70 Advise Company X, which is having problems with liquidity, on the pros and cons of factoring accounts receivable.

71 Recommend the most feasible way to finance a start-up restaurant.

Management

72 Develop for Company X a guide to ethics in its highly competitive business situation.

73 After reviewing pertinent literature and experiences of other companies, develop a plan for selecting and training administrators for an overseas operation for Company X.

74 Survey the current literature and advise Company X on whether its management should become politically active.

75 After reviewing the pros and cons, advise X Company on whether it should begin a program of hiring individuals with disabilities or the disadvantaged.

76 Report on the behavioral and psychological effects of introducing wellness programs to Company X.

77 The executives of X Company (a manufacturer of automobile and truck tires) want a report on recent court decisions relating to warranties. Include any recommendations that your report justifies.

78 Report on the problems involved in moving Company X headquarters from _____ (city) to _____ (city).

79 After reviewing current practices with regard to worker participation in management, advise Company X on whether it should permit such participation.

80 Should Company X outsource for _____ (service) or establish its own department?

81 Review the advantages and disadvantages of rotating executive jobs at Company X, and then make a recommendation.

82 What should be Company X's policy on office romances?

83 Develop an energy conservation or recycling plan for X Company.

84 Evaluate the effectiveness of a portal for handling internal communications for Company X.

85 Design a security system for preventing computer espionage at Company X, a leader in the highly competitive _____ industry.

86 Evaluate the various methods for determining corporate performance and select the one most appropriate for Company X.

87 Advise X Company on the procedures for incorporating in _____ (state or province).

88 Report to Company X on the civil and criminal liabilities of its corporate executives.

89 Report on the quality awards being given to businesses.

90 Determine how diversity enrichment is addressed at Company X.

91 Determine for a legislative committee the extent of minority recruiting, hiring, and training in the industry.

92 As a consultant for an association of farmers, evaluate the recent past and project the future of growing, raising, or bioengineering _____ (your choice—cattle, poultry, wheat, soybeans, or the like).

93 Develop a plan for reducing employee turnover for Company X.

94 Report to a labor union on recent evidence of sexual harassment, and recommend steps that the union should take to correct any problems you find.

95 Investigate the feasibility of hiring older workers for part-time work for Company X.

Personnel/Human Resource Administration

96 Report on and interpret for Company X the effects of recent court decisions on the testing and hiring of employees.

97 Survey company retirement practices and recommend retirement policies for Company X.

98 Report on practices in compensating key personnel in overseas assignments and recommend for Company X policies for the compensation of such personnel.

99 Report on what human resource executives look for in application documents.

100 Report on the advantages and disadvantages of Company X's providing on-site day care for children of employees.

101 After reviewing the legal and ethical questions involved, recommend whether Company X should use integrity tests in employee hiring.

102 Review what other companies are doing about employees suffering from drug or alcohol abuse, and recommend a policy on the matter for Company X.

103 Report on effective interviewing techniques used to identify the best people to hire.

104 Investigate the impact of the Family Leave Act on Company X.

105 Compare the pros and cons of alternative methods of dispute resolution.

106 Report on ways Company X can link performance improvement plans to discipline and pay.

107 Investigate the impact of the legal aspects of human resource management (EEO, ADA, wrongful termination, harassment, family care and medical leave, workplace violence—your instructor will select one or several) on Company X.

108 Analyze the impact of changing work priorities in a culturally diverse workplace for Company X.

109 Report on recent issues in employee communication for Company X.

Marketing

110 Review the available literature and advise Company X on whether it should franchise its _____ business.

111 Select a recent national marketing program and analyze why it succeeded or failed.

112 Advise the advertising vice president of Company X on whether the company should respond to or ignore a competitor's direct attack on the quality of its product.

113 Review the ethical considerations involved in advertising to children and advise Company X on the matter.

114 Determine for Company X the social and ethical aspects of pricing for the market.

115 Explore the possibilities of trade with _____ (a foreign country) for Company X.

116 Determine for a national department store chain changing trends in the services that customers expect when shopping online.

117 Prepare a report to help a contingent of your legislature decide whether current regulation of advertising should be changed.

118 Determine the problems X Company will encounter in introducing a new product to its line.

119 Report on the success of rebates as a sales stimulator and advise Company X on whether it should use rebates.

120 Should Company X buy or lease minivans for distributing its products?

121 Determine the trends in packaging in the _____ industry.

122 Should X Company establish its own sales force, use manufacturer's agents, or use selling agents?

123 How should Company X evaluate the performance of its salespeople?

124 Determine for X Company how it can evaluate the effectiveness of its (online, print, or radio) advertising.

125 Select the best channel of distribution for new product Y and justify your choice.

126 Should X Company establish its own advertising department or use an advertising agency?

127 Conduct a market study of _____ (city) to determine whether it is a suitable location for _____ (a type of business).

128 Report to X Company on drip marketing and recommend whether it should use drip marketing to increase sales.

129 Investigate the factors to consider when marketing online through the Internet to children.

130 Compare the effectiveness of three different types of online advertising and recommend one for Company X.

131 Determine whether any of the products of Company X are good candidates for infomercials.

Computer Applications

132 Recommend a handheld computer for use by the salespeople of Company X.

133 Advise Company X about the steps it can take to protect its computer files from internal sabotage.

134 Determine whether Company X should purchase or lease its computer equipment.

135 Report to the president of Company X the copyright and contract laws that apply to the use of computer programs.

136 Investigate the possibility of using the majority of office applications from the Internet rather than continually purchasing and upgrading programs.

137 Determine which positions Company X should designate as possible telecommuting candidates.

138 Report to the CIO on the impact of wireless technology on Company X.

139 Report on the future developments of robotics in the _____ industry.

140 Review and rank for possible adoption three software programs that Company X might use for its _____ work (name the field of operations).

141 Determine for Company X the factors it should consider in selecting computer insurance.

142 Compare three online programs for training your employees on _____ (name the software application) and recommend one.

143 Report on the collaborative web-based meeting tools used in businesses similar to Company X.

144 Explore the procedures and methods for measuring information system effectiveness and productivity for Company X.

145 Investigate how to improve information security and control for Company X.

146 Identify and recommend web-based survey tools that would be appropriate for Company X.

147 Should _____ (a small company) use blogs as a marketing tool?

Business Education

148 Evaluate the effect of remodeling your new office site using both ergonomic and feng shui principles.

149 Report on ways companies now use and plan to use desktop meeting applications.

150 Analyze the possibility of instituting companywide training on etiquette, covering everything from handling telephone calls, to sexual harassment, to dining out.

151 Advise management on the importance of the air quality in its offices.

152 Investigate ways to complete and submit company forms on the web or the company portal.

153 Evaluate the reprographic services and practices at your school from an environmental perspective.

154 Report on ways to hire and keep the best employees in the computer support center.

155 Report on ways to improve literacy in the workplace.

156 Report on the availability and quality of online training programs.

157 Report on ways to improve the communication of cross-cultural work groups.

158 Analyze the possibility of using voice-recognition software with the products available today.

159 Determine for Company X whether it should replace the laptop computers of its sales reps with tablet PCs.

160 Evaluate at least three data visualization programs and recommend one for use at Company X.

chapter thirteen

Graphics

LEARNING OBJECTIVES

Upon completing this chapter, you will be able to use graphics effectively in business reports. To reach this goal, you should be able to

1   Plan which parts of your report should be communicated by graphics.

2   Explain the general mechanics of constructing graphics—size, layout, type, rules and borders, color and cross-hatching, clip art, background, numbering, titles, title placement, and footnotes and acknowledgments.

3   Construct textual graphics such as tables, pull quotes, flowcharts, and process charts.

4   Construct and use visual graphics such as bar charts, pie charts, line charts, scatter diagrams, and maps.

5   Avoid common errors and ethical problems when constructing and using graphics.

6   Place and interpret graphics effectively.

Graphics

In your management job at Pinnacle, you proofread reports prepared by your co-workers. Because Pinnacle uses chemicals in its products, many of the reports are highly technical and complex. Many others, especially those coming from finance and sales, are filled with facts and figures. In your judgment, most of the reports you have proofread are hard to understand.

The one you are looking at now is packed with page after page of sales statistics. Your mind quickly gets lost in the mass of details. Why didn't the writer take the time to summarize the more important figures in a chart? And why didn't the writer put some of the details in tables? Many of the other reports you have been reading, especially the technical ones, are in equal need of graphics. Bar charts, pie charts, and maps would certainly help explain some of the concepts discussed. If only report writers would understand that words alone sometimes cannot communicate clearly—that words sometimes need to be supplemented with visual communication techniques. If the writers of your reports studied the following review of graphics, your job would be easier and more enjoyable. So would the jobs of the readers of those reports.

In many of your reports you will need to use graphics to help convey information quickly and accurately. Graphics both grab attention and are retained longer. By *graphics* we mean any form of illustration: charts, pictures, diagrams, maps. Although tables and bulleted lists are predominantly text, their format permits us to include them here. Also, most computer presentation programs include these formats.

- A graphic is any form of illustration.

PLANNING THE GRAPHICS

You should plan the graphics for a report soon after you organize your findings. Your planning of graphics should be based on the need to communicate. Graphics serve one main purpose—to communicate—and you should use them primarily for that purpose. Graphics can clarify complex or difficult information, emphasize facts, add coherence, summarize data, and provide interest. Additionally, today's data mining and visualization tools help writers filter the vast amount of data that are gathered and stored regularly. Of course, well-constructed graphics also enhance the appearance of a report.

- You should plan the use of graphics as you plan your report.

In selecting graphics, you should review the information that your report will contain, looking for any possibility of improving communication of the report through the use of graphics. Specifically, you should look for complex information that visual presentation can make clear, for information too detailed to be covered in words, and for information that deserves special emphasis.

- In planning their use, look for information that they can help communicate.

Of course, you will want to plan with your reader in mind. You will choose graphics appropriate to both the content and context where they are presented. The time and money you spend on gathering information or creating a graphic should be balanced in terms of the importance of the message you want to convey. Thus, you construct graphics to help the reader understand the report more quickly, easily, and completely.

- Plan graphics with your reader in mind.

As you plan the graphics, remember that unlike info graphics that stand alone, report graphics should supplement the writing or speaking—not take its place. They should help the wording by covering the more difficult parts, emphasizing the important points, and presenting details. But the words should carry the main message—all of it.

- But remember that graphics supplement and do not replace the writing

DETERMINING THE GENERAL MECHANICS OF CONSTRUCTION

In constructing graphics, you will be concerned with various mechanical matters. The most common are summarized in the following paragraphs.

Size Determination

- Make each graphic the size that its contents justify.

One of the first decisions you must make in constructing a graphic is determining its size. This decision should not be arbitrary, and it should not be based on convenience. You should give the graphic the size that its contents and importance justify. If a graphic is simple (with only two or three quantities), a quarter page might be more than enough and a full page would be too much unless its importance needed emphasis. But if a graphic must display complex or detailed information, a full page might be justified.

- Graphics larger than a page are justified if they contain enough information.

With extremely complex, involved information, you may need to use more than a full page. When you do, make certain that this large page is inserted and folded so that the readers can open it easily. The fold you select will be determined by the size of the page. You simply have to experiment until you find a convenient fold.

Layout Arrangement

- Size and contents determine the shape of graphics.

You should determine the layout (shape) of the graphic by size and content requirements. Sometimes a tall, narrow rectangle (portrait) is the answer; sometimes the answer is a short, wide rectangle or a full-page rectangle (landscape). You simply consider the logical possibilities and select the one that appears best.

Type

- Choose a type to help convey the message clearly.

Type used in graphics throughout a report is generally consistent in both style and font. Style refers to the look of the type such as bold or italics; font refers to the look of the letters such as with or without feet (*serif* or *sans serif*). Occasionally you may want to vary the type, but do so by design for some special reason. Be aware that even the design of the font you choose will convey a message, a message that should work with the text content and design. If your reader will be viewing the document on screen in Word 2007 or on a Vista computer with ClearType, be sure to use one of the fonts optimized for use with ClearType such as Cambria or Calibri. They were designed to render well on the screen, and Microsoft's research has confirmed that they enable people to read faster and more accurately, leading to a 7 percent average increase in productivity.[1]

- Choose a type size that is readable.

Size is another variable to watch. The size you choose should look appropriate in the context in which it is used. Your top priority in choosing type style, font, and size should be readability.

Rules and Borders

- Use rules and borders when they help appearance.

You should use rules and borders when they help the appearance of the graphic. Rules help distinguish one section or graphic from another, while borders help separate graphics from the text. In general, you should place borders around graphics that

"This is where we added high-caffeine cappuccino in our office coffee machines."

[1] Bill Hill, Microsoft Project Manager, video interview, 29 May 2006 <http://download.microsoft.com/download/8/1/c/81cdb151-0aae-4f50-ab44-654b5f7ae0db/cleartype_2005.wmv>.

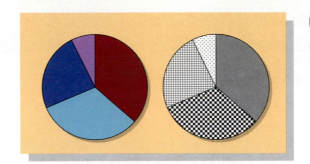

Figure 13–1

Color versus Cross-hatched Pie

occupy less than a full page. You also can place borders around full-page graphics, but such borders serve little practical value. Except in cases in which graphics simply will not fit into the normal page layout, you should not extend the borders of graphics beyond the normal page margins.

Color and Cross-Hatching

Color and cross-hatching, appropriately used, help readers see comparisons and distinctions (see Figure 13–1). In fact, research has found that color in graphics improves the comprehension, retention, and ease of extracting information. Also, both color and cross-hatching add to the attractiveness of the report. Because color is especially effective for this purpose, you should use it whenever practical and appropriate.

- Color and cross-hatching can improve graphics.

Clip Art

Today you can get good-looking clip art easily—so easily in fact that some writers often overuse it. Although clip art can add interest and bring the reader into a graphic effectively, it also can overpower and distract the reader. The general rule is to keep in mind the purpose your clip art is serving: to help the reader understand the content. It should be appropriate in both its nature and size. It also should be appropriate in its representation of gender, race, and age. Also, if it is copyrighted, you need permission to use it.

- Use clip art to help your reader understand your message.

Background

Background colors, photos, and art for your graphics should be chosen carefully. The color should provide high contrast with the data and not distract from the main message. Photos, especially faded photos, that are well chosen can add interest and draw the reader in. However, photos as well as other art can send other messages and evoke emotions not appropriate or desirable for the message the graphic conveys. Additionally, when graphics are used cross-culturally, you will want to be sure the message your background sends is the one you intended by testing or reviewing it with the intended receivers.

- Background color, photos, and art should enhance the message of the graphic.

Numbering

Except for minor tabular displays, pull quotes, and clip art, you should number all the graphics in the report. Many schemes of numbering are available to you, depending on the make-up of the graphics.

If you have many graphics that fall into two or more categories, you may number each of the categories consecutively. For example, if your report is illustrated by six tables, five charts, and six maps, you may number these graphics Table I, Table II, . . . Table VI; Chart 1, Chart 2, . . . Chart 5; and Map 1, Map 2, . . . Map 6.

But if your graphics comprise a wide mixture of types, you may number them in two groups: tables and figures. Figures, a miscellaneous grouping, may include all types other than tables. To illustrate, consider a report containing three tables, two maps, three

- Number graphics consecutively by type.

- Figures are a miscellaneous grouping of types. Number tables separately.

Clear Evidence of the Value of Accurate Charts

"To what do you attribute your company's success?" asked the interviewer.

"A line chart," replied the executive. "In the early years of our company, we had some real problems. Productivity was low, and we were losing money. So to impress our problem on our workers, I had a line chart painted on the wall of our main building. Every day, when the workers arrived, they saw our profit picture. Well, the profit line kept going down. It went from the third floor, to the second, to the first, to ground level. Then we had to bring in digging equipment to keep the line going. But keep it going we did—until the line dramatically reversed direction."

"The workers finally got the message?" asked the interviewer.

"No," replied the executive, "the digger struck oil."

charts, one diagram, and one photograph. You could number these graphics Table I, Table II, and Table III and Figure 1, Figure 2, . . . Figure 7. By convention, tables are not grouped with other types of graphics. But it would not be wrong to group and number as figures all graphics other than tables even if the group contained sufficient subgroups (charts, maps, and the like) to permit separate numbering of each of them.

Construction of Titles and Captions

> The titles should describe content clearly (consider the five Ws: *who, what, where, when, why*).

Every graphic should have a title or caption that adequately describes its contents. A title is used with graphics displayed in oral presentations; a caption is used with graphics included in print documents. Like the headings used in other parts of the report, the title or caption of the graphic has the objective of concisely covering the contents. As a check of content coverage, you might well use the journalist's five Ws: *who, what, where, when,* and *why,* and sometimes you also might use *how*. But because conciseness also is desired, it is not always necessary to include all the Ws in the title. The title or caption of a chart comparing the annual sales volume of the Texas and California territories of the Dell Company for the years 2006–07 might be constructed as follows:

Who: Dell Company
What: Annual sales
Where: Texas and California branches
When: 2006–07
Why: For comparison

The title or caption might read, "Comparative Annual Sales of Texas and California Territories of the Dell Company, 2006–07." For even more conciseness, you could use a major title and subtitle. The major title might read, "A Texas and California Sales Comparison"; the subtitle might read, "Dell Company 2006–07." Similarly, the caption might read "A Texas and California Sales Comparison: Dell Company 2006–2007."

An alternative to this kind of topic heading is a talking heading. As you learned in Chapter 10, the talking heading tells the reader the nature of what is to follow. The same holds true for a graphic. In this case a talking heading might read, "Texas Leads California in Total Annual Sales for 2006." In a sense, it gives the reader the main message of the graphic. You'll see another example of a talking heading in Figure 13–8, Illustration of a Bi-lateral Column Chart, which reads, "NASCAR Leads in Fan Base Growth."

Placement of Titles and Captions

> The conventional placement of titles is at the top for tables and at the bottom for charts. But many place all titles at the top.

In documents, titles of tables conventionally appear above the tabular display; captions of all other types of graphics conventionally appear below it. In presentations, titles of both tables and other charts and illustrations are usually placed above the graphic. There has been a trend toward using title case type for all illustration titles and placing the titles of both tables and figures at the top. In fact, most presentation programs default to the top. These practices are simple and logical; yet you should follow the conventional practices for the more formal reports.

Footnotes and Acknowledgments

Parts of a graphic sometimes require special explanation or elaboration. When this happens, as when similar situations arise in connection with the text of the report, you should use footnotes. Such footnotes are concise explanations placed below the illustration and keyed to the part explained by means of a superscript (raised) number or symbol (asterisk, dagger, double dagger, and so on). Footnotes for tables are best placed immediately below the graphic presentation. Footnotes for other graphic forms follow the illustration when the title or caption is placed at the bottom of the graphic.

- Use footnotes to explain or elaborate.

Usually, a source acknowledgment is the bottom entry made in the graphic context. By *source acknowledgment* we mean a reference to the body or authority that deserves the credit for gathering the data used in the illustration. The entry consists simply of the word *Source* followed by a colon and the source name. A source note for data based on information gathered by the U.S. Department of Commerce might read like this:

- Acknowledge the source of data with note below.

Source: U.S. Department of Commerce

If you or your staff collected the data, you may either omit the source note or give the source as "Primary," in which case the note would read like this:

- "Source: Primary" is the proper note for data you gathered.

Source: Primary

CONSTRUCTING TEXTUAL GRAPHICS

Graphics for communicating report information fall into two general categories: those that communicate primarily by their textual content (words and numerals) and those that communicate primarily by some form of picture. Included in the textual group are tables, pull quotes, and a variety of flow and process charts (Gantt, flow, organization, and such).

- Graphics fall into two general categories: (1) textual (words and numerals) and (2) visual (pictures).

Tables

A *table* is an orderly arrangement of information in rows and columns. As we have noted, tables are not truly graphic (not really pictures). But they communicate like graphics, and they have many of the characteristics of graphics.

- A table is an orderly arrangement of information.

Two basic types of tables are available to you: the general-purpose table and the special-purpose table. General-purpose tables cover a broad area of information. For example, a table reviewing the answers to all the questions in a survey is a general-purpose table. Such tables usually belong in the appendix.

- You may use general-purpose tables (those containing broad information),

Special-purpose tables are prepared for one special purpose: to illustrate a particular part of the report. They contain information that could be included with related information in a general-purpose table. For example, a table presenting the answer to one of the questions in a survey is a special-purpose table. Such tables belong in the report text near the discussion of their contents.

- or you may use special-purpose tables (those covering a specific area of information).

Aside from the title, footnotes, and source designation previously discussed, a table contains heads, columns, and rows of data, as shown in Figure 13–2. Row heads are the titles of the rows of data, and spanner heads are the titles of the columns. The spanner heads, however, may be divided into column heads, as they are often called.

- See Figure 13–2 for details of table arrangement.

The construction of text tables is largely influenced by their purpose. Nevertheless, a few general construction rules may be listed:

- If rows are long, the row heads may be repeated at the right.

Figure 13–2   Good Arrangement of the Parts of a Typical Table

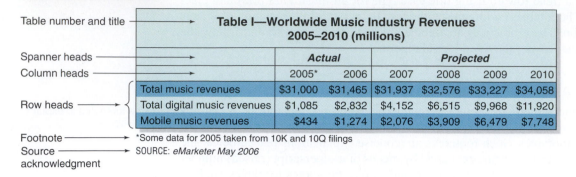

Table number and title → | Spanner heads → | Column heads → | Row heads → | Footnote → | Source acknowledgment →

Table I—Worldwide Music Industry Revenues 2005–2010 (millions)					
	Actual		*Projected*			
	2005*	2006	2007	2008	2009	2010
Total music revenues	$31,000	$31,465	$31,937	$32,576	$33,227	$34,058
Total digital music revenues	$1,085	$2,832	$4,152	$6,515	$9,968	$11,920
Mobile music revenues	$434	$1,274	$2,076	$3,909	$6,479	$7,748

*Some data for 2005 taken from 10K and 10Q filings
SOURCE: *eMarketer May 2006*

- The em dash (—) or the abbreviation *n.a.* (or *N.A.* or *NA*), but not the zero, is used to indicate data not available.
- Footnote references to numbers in the table should be keyed with asterisks, daggers, double daggers, and such. Numbers followed by footnote reference numbers may cause confusion. Small letters of the alphabet can be used when many references are made.
- Totals and subtotals should appear whenever they help the purpose of the table. The totals may be for each column and sometimes for each row. Row totals are usually placed at the right; but when they need emphasis, they may be placed at the left. Likewise, column totals are generally placed at the bottom of the column, but they may be placed at the top when the writer wants to emphasize them. A ruled line (usually a double one) separates the totals from their components.
- The units in which the data are recorded must be clear. Unit descriptions (bushels, acres, pounds, and the like) appropriately appear above the columns, as part of the headings or subheadings. If the data are in dollars, however, placing the dollar mark ($) before the first entry in each column is sufficient.

- Tabular information also can be presented as (1) leaderwork (as illustrated here), or

Tabular information need not always be presented in formal tables. In fact, short arrangements of data may be presented more effectively as parts of the text. Such arrangements are generally made as either leaderwork or text tabulations.

Leaderwork is the presentation of tabular material in the text without titles or rules. (*Leaders* are the repeated dots with intervening spaces.) Typically, a colon precedes the tabulation, as in this illustration:

The August sales of the representatives in the Western Region were as follows:

Charles B. Brown $33,517
Thelma Capp 39,703
Bill E. Knauth 38,198

Text tabulations are simple tables, usually with column heads and some rules. But they are not numbered, and they have no titles. They are made to read with the text, as in this example:

- (2) text tabulations (as illustrated here).

In August the sales of the representatives in the Western Region increased sharply from those for the preceding month, as these figures show:

Representative	July Sales	August Sales	Increase
Charles B. Brown	$32,819	$33,517	$ 698
Thelma Capp	37,225	39,703	2,478
Bill E. Knauth	36,838	38,198	1,360

Figure 13–3

Illustration of a Pull Quote

Managing Authenticity: The Paradox of Great Leadership

of the mountaineer because water and the environment are emotional issues for many people. But the photo is not artificial. That's what I wear on weekends. I'm a climber. In the mountaineering picture, it's a human being talking. In the [other picture], I am talking for the institution. The photographs are different, but they both capture something essential about me."

A long-successful music industry executive we'll call Dick is also a careful communicator of his multiple selves. Dick is from the Caribbean, and on many occasions in the rough-and-tumble of the music business, we have seen him switch from corporate-speak to an island patois liberally sprinkled with expletives. He is absolutely at home in the cutthroat environment that recording artists and their agents operate in. But, at the same time, Dick's parents are affluent, well-established members of Caribbean society, and, on the occasions that require it, Dick can play up this aspect of himself to create a rapport with the media moguls and celebrities with whom he must also deal. All these facets of his personality ring true; his skill is in deciding which to reveal to whom and when.

Playing multiple roles usually demands a lot of thought and work. "Before I go into a situation, I try to understand

But it is one thing to develop this complexity and another thing entirely to wield it effectively. Using your complex self (or, rather, selves) requires a degree of *self-knowledge* and the willingness to share that self-knowledge with others, what we call *self-disclosure*. This is not to say that authentic leaders spend a lot of time exploring their inner lives through meditation or therapy. They may be profoundly self-aware and essentially authentic (in the sense that we are giving the term here), but not because of contemplation or analysis; they are not characters in some Woody Allen film. Few authentic leaders will even be conscious that they are engaged in self-expression and self-disclosure, which is probably why they are so hard to imitate.

So how do authentic leaders acquire these attributes? The relative simplicity of their goals often helps. A great leader is usually trying to accomplish no more than three or four big goals at a time. He is unwavering about these goals; he doesn't question them any more than he questions himself. That's because the goals are usually connected in some way to one or another of the leader's authentic selves. His pursuit of the goals, and the way he communicates them to followers, is intense—which natu-

If a leader is playing a role that isn't a TRUE EXPRESSION OF HIS AUTHENTIC SELF, followers will sooner or later feel like they've been tricked.

what it is [people] will be thinking. I prepare what I am going to say and who I am going to be in that context," explains Jean Tomlin, former HR director at Marks & Spencer and one of the most influential black businesswomen in Britain. "I want to be me, but I am channeling parts of me to context. What you get is a segment of me. It is not a fabrication or a facade—just the bits that are relevant for that situation."

Let's look more closely at just what makes it possible for Brabeck-Letmathe, Tomlin, and executives like them to present fragments of themselves – without seeming inauthentic.

Know Yourself and Others

It goes almost without saying that the exercise of leadership is complex and requires both skills and practice. Over time, and through various life experiences, a leader develops an extensive repertoire of roles, which can make her seem very different to different people in different situations. Indeed, if a leader doesn't acquire this complexity, she will be able to recruit as followers only those people with whom she already shares some common ground.

rally promotes the kind of self-disclosure we are talking about and educates him further about his various selves.

We have also found that great leaders keep close to them people who will give them honest feedback. As Roche Pharmaceuticals head Bill Burns told us, "You have to keep your feet on the ground when others want to put you on a pedestal. After a while on a pedestal, you stop hearing the truth. It's filtered by the henchmen, and they read you so well they know what you want to hear. You end up as the queen bee in the hive, with no relationships with the worker bees. My wife and secretary are fully empowered, if they ever see me getting a bit uppity, to give me a thumping great hit over the head."

As consultants, we often have been called in to do precisely that for senior executives, acting both as priests and spies as we try to make leaders more open to truths about themselves and their relationships with others. This does not necessarily mean helping these leaders develop more of what psychologist Dan Goleman calls emotional intelligence; rather, it means helping them to sharpen their skills in disclosing the emotional intelligence they already have so they can give better performances for their followers.

90

HARVARD BUSINESS REVIEW

SOURCE: *Harvard Business Review* Dec. 2005: 90.

Pull Quotes

The pull quote is a textual visual that is often overlooked yet extremely useful in emphasizing key points. It is also useful when the text or content of the report does not lend itself naturally or easily to other graphics. By selecting a key sentence, copying it to a text box, enlarging it, and perhaps even enhancing it with a new font, style, or color, a writer can break up the visual boredom of a full page or screen of text. Drawing software lets users easily wrap text around shapes as well as along curves and irregular lines. Figure 13–3 shows an example that is simple yet effective in both drawing the reader's attention to a key point and adding visual interest to a page.

- Pull quotes emphasize key concepts.

Bullet Lists

Bullet lists are listings of points arranged with bullets (•) to set them off. These lists can have a title that covers all the points, or they can appear without titles, as they appear at various places in this book. When you use this arrangement, make the points grammatically parallel. If the points have subparts, use sub-bullets for them. Make the sub-bullets different by color, size, shape, or weight. Darts, check marks, squares, or triangles can be used for the secondary bullets.

- Bullet lists show points set off by a bullet symbol.

Flowcharts and Process Charts

If you have studied business management, you know that administrators use a variety of specialized charts in their work. Often these charts are a part of the information presented in reports. Perhaps the most common of these is the *organization chart* (see Figure 13–4). These charts show hierarchy of positions, divisions, departments, and such in an organization. *Gantt charts* are graphic presentations that show planning and

- Various specialized management charts are useful in reports—for example, organization charts, Gantt charts, and flowcharts.

Figure 13–4   **Illustration of an Organization Chart**

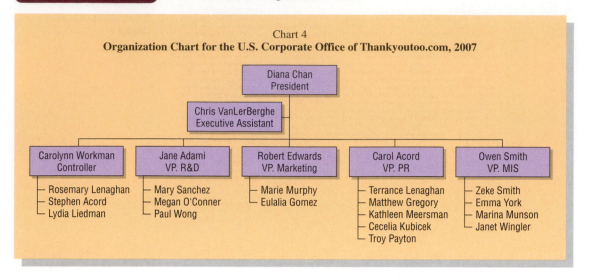

Chart 4
Organization Chart for the U.S. Corporate Office of Thankyoutoo.com, 2007

Figure 13–5   **Illustration of a Flowchart**

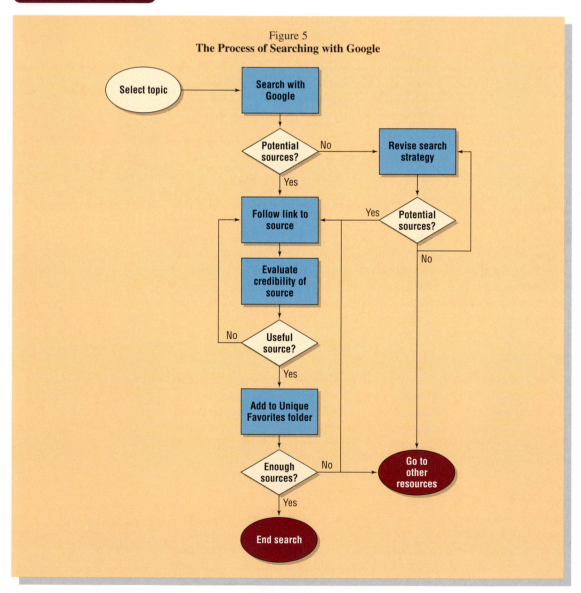

Figure 5
The Process of Searching with Google

scheduling activities. As the word implies, a *flowchart* (see Figure 13–5) shows the sequence of activities in a process. Traditionally, flowcharts use specific designs and symbols to show process variations. A variation of the organization and flowchart is the *decision tree*. This chart helps one follow a path to an appropriate decision. You can easily construct these charts with presentation and drawing software.

CONSTRUCTING VISUAL GRAPHICS

The truly visual types of graphics include a variety of forms: charts and illustrations. Charts are graphics built with raw data and include bar, pie, and line charts and all their variations and combinations. Illustrations includes maps, diagrams, drawings, photos, cartoons, and such.

- Visual graphics include data-generated charts, photographs, and artwork.

Bar and Column Charts

Simple bar and *column charts* compare differences in quantities by differences in the lengths of the bars representing those quantities. You should use them primarily to show comparisons of quantity changes at a moment in time.

- Simple bar and column charts compare differences in quantities by varying bar lengths.

As shown in Figure 13–6, the main parts of the bar chart are the bars and the grid (the field on which the bars are placed). The bars, which may be arranged horizontally or vertically (also called a column chart), should be of equal width. You should identify each bar or column, usually with a caption at the left or bottom. The grid (field) on which the bars are placed is usually needed to show the magnitudes of the bars, and the units (dollars, pounds, miles, and such) are identified by the scale caption below.

When you need to compare quantities of two or three different values in one chart, you can use a *clustered* (or *multiple*) *bar chart*. Cross-hatching, colors, or the like on the bars distinguish the different kinds of information (see Figure 13–7). Somewhere within the chart, a legend (explanation) gives a key to the differences in the bars. Because clustered bar charts can become cluttered, usually you should limit comparisons to three to five kinds of information in one of them.

- Clustered bar charts are useful in comparing two or three kinds of quantities.

When you need to show plus and minus differences, you can use *bilateral column charts*. The columns of these charts begin at a central point of reference and may go either up or down, as illustrated in Figure 13–8. Bar titles appear either within, above, or below the bars, depending on which placement fits best. Bilateral column charts are especially good for showing percentage changes, but you may use them for any series in which plus and minus quantities are present.

- When you need to show plus and minus differences, bilateral column charts are useful.

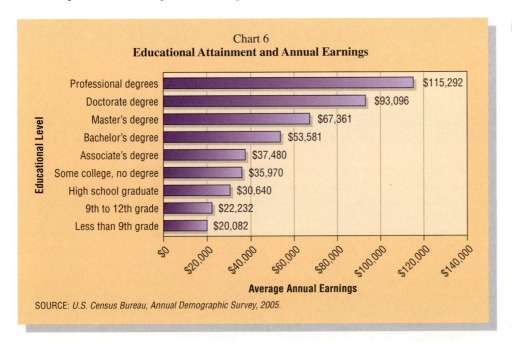

Figure 13–6

Illustration of a Bar Chart

Chart 6
Educational Attainment and Annual Earnings

Professional degrees — $115,292
Doctorate degree — $93,096
Master's degree — $67,361
Bachelor's degree — $53,581
Associate's degree — $37,480
Some college, no degree — $35,970
High school graduate — $30,640
9th to 12th grade — $22,232
Less than 9th grade — $20,082

Educational Level

$0 $20,000 $40,000 $60,000 $80,000 $100,000 $120,000 $140,000

Average Annual Earnings

SOURCE: *U.S. Census Bureau, Annual Demographic Survey, 2005.*

Figure 13–7

Illustration of a Clustered
Bar Chart

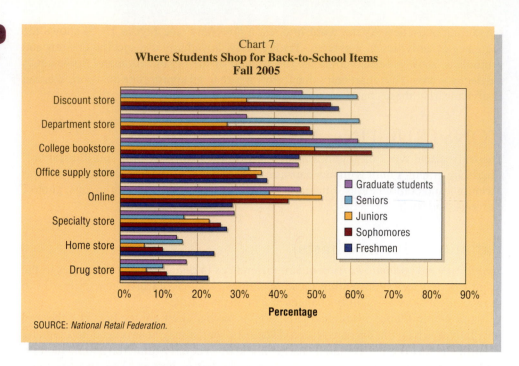

Chart 7
**Where Students Shop for Back-to-School Items
Fall 2005**

SOURCE: *National Retail Federation.*

Figure 13–8

Illustration of a Bilateral
Column Chart

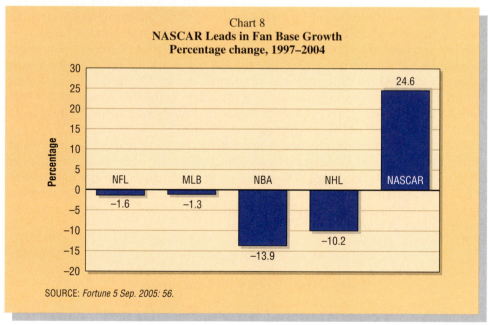

Chart 8
**NASCAR Leads in Fan Base Growth
Percentage change, 1997–2004**

SOURCE: *Fortune 5 Sep. 2005: 56.*

• To compare subdivisions of columns, use a stacked bar chart.

If you need to compare subdivisions of columns, you can use a *stacked* (*subdivided*) *column chart*. As shown in Figure 13–9, such a chart divides each column into its parts. It distinguishes these parts by color, cross-hatching, or the like; and it explains these differences in a legend. Subdivided columns may be difficult for your reader to interpret since both the beginning and ending points need to be found. Then the reader has to subtract to find the size of the column component. Clustered column charts or pie charts do not introduce this possibility for error.

• Two-dimensional columns on two-dimensional axes are easiest for readers to use.

Another feature that can lead to reader error in interpreting bar and column chart data is the use of three dimensions when only two variables are being compared. One study evaluated the speed and accuracy of readers' interpretation of two-dimensional columns on two-dimensional axes with three-dimensional columns on two-dimensional axes and three-dimensional columns on three-dimensional axes. The results showed that readers were able to extract information from the column chart fastest and most accurately when it was presented in the simple two-dimensional

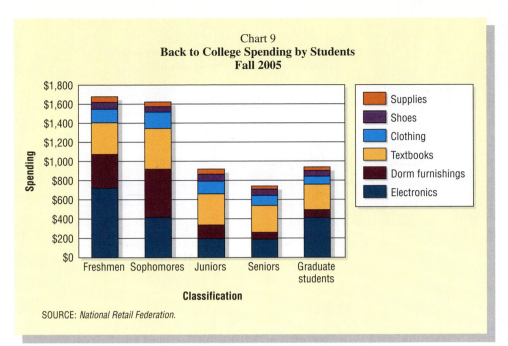

Figure 13–9

Illustration of a Stacked Column Chart

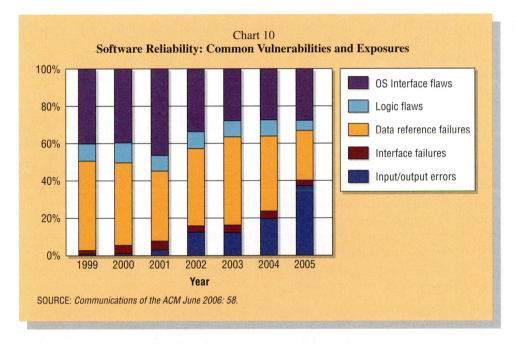

Figure 13–10

Illustration of a 100 Percent Stacked Column Chart

column on the two-dimensional axis.[2] Therefore, unless more than two variables are used, choosing the two-dimensional presentation over the three-dimensional form is usually better.

A special form of stacked (subdivided) column chart is used to compare the subdivisions of percentages. In this form, all the bars are equal in length, for each represents 100 percent. Only the subdivisions within the bars vary. The objective of this form is to compare differences in how wholes are divided. The component parts may be labeled, as shown in Figure 13–10, but they also may be explained in a legend.

● You also can use such a chart for comparing subdivisions of percentages.

_____

[2] Theophilus B. A. Addo, "The Effects of Dimensionality in Computer Graphics," *Journal of Business Communication* 31 (1994): 253.

Figure 13–11

Illustration of a Pictograph

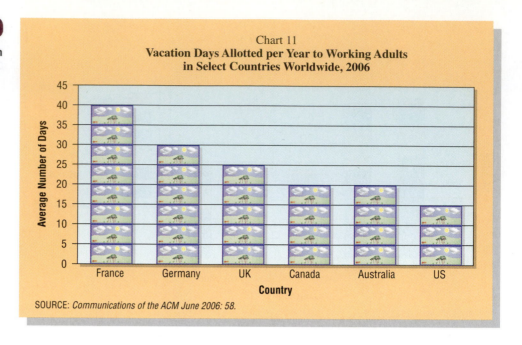

Chart 11
**Vacation Days Allotted per Year to Working Adults
in Select Countries Worldwide, 2006**

SOURCE: *Communications of the ACM June 2006: 58.*

Pictographs

- Pictographs are bar or column charts made with pictures.

A *pictograph* is a bar or column chart that uses bars made of pictures. The pictures are typically drawings of the items being compared. For example, the number of vacation days in selected countries, instead of being shown by ordinary bars (formed by straight lines), could be shown by bar drawings of harmrmocks. This type of column chart is a pictograph (see Figure 13–11).

- In constructing pictographs, follow the procedure for making bar and column charts, plus two special rules.

In constructing a pictograph, you should follow the procedures you used in constructing bar and column charts and two special rules. First, you must make all the picture units equal in size. That is, you must base the comparisons wholly on the number of picture units used and never on variation in the areas of the units. The reason for this rule is obvious. The human eye is grossly inadequate when comparing geometric designs that vary in more than one dimension. Second, you should select pictures or symbols that fit the information to be illustrated. In comparing the cruise lines of the world, for example, you might use ships. In comparing computers used in the world's major countries, you might use computers. The meaning of the drawings you use must be immediately clear to the readers.

Pie Charts

- Pie charts show subdivisions of a whole.

The most frequently used chart in comparing the subdivisions of wholes is the *pie chart* (see Figure 13–12). As the name implies, pie charts show the whole of the information being studied as a pie (circle), and the parts of this whole as slices of the pie. The slices may be distinguished by labeling and color or cross-hatching. A single slice can be emphasized by exploding—pulling out—a piece. Because it is hard to judge the values of the slices with the naked eye, it is good to include the percentage values within or near each slice. Also, placing a label near each slice makes it quicker for the reader to understand the items being compared than using a legend to identify components. A good rule to follow is to begin slicing the pie at the 12 o'clock position and then to move around clockwise. It is also good to arrange the slices in descending order from largest to smallest.

Line Charts

- Line charts show changes over time.

Line charts are useful in showing changes of information over time. For example, changes in prices, sales totals, employment, or production over a period of years can be shown well in a line chart.

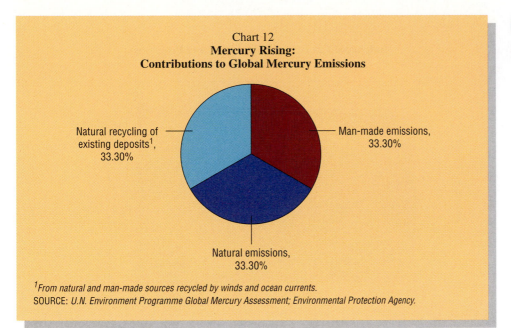

Chart 12
Mercury Rising:
Contributions to Global Mercury Emissions

Natural recycling of existing deposits[1], 33.30%

Man-made emissions, 33.30%

Natural emissions, 33.30%

[1]*From natural and man-made sources recycled by winds and ocean currents.*
SOURCE: *U.N. Environment Programme Global Mercury Assessment; Environmental Protection Agency.*

Footnote: *The Wall Street Journal, 20 April 2006: A10.*

Figure 13–12

Illustration of a Pie Chart

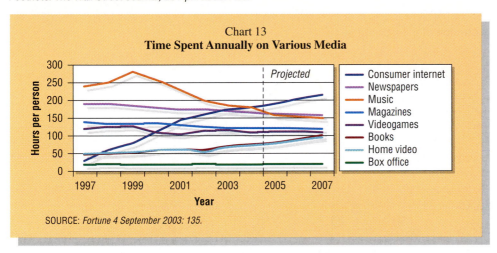

Chart 13
Time Spent Annually on Various Media

Projected

Legend:
- Consumer internet
- Newspapers
- Music
- Magazines
- Videogames
- Books
- Home video
- Box office

Hours per person

Year

SOURCE: *Fortune 4 September 2003: 135.*

Figure 13–13

Illustration of a Line Chart

In constructing a line chart, you draw the information to be illustrated as a continuous line on a grid. The grid is the area in which the line is displayed. It is scaled to show time changes from left to right across the chart (X-axis) and quantity changes from bottom to top (Y-axis). You should mark clearly the scale values and the time periods. They should be in equal increments.

You also may compare two or more series on the same line chart (see Figure 13–13). In such a comparison, you should clearly distinguish the lines by color or form (dots, dashes, dots and dashes, and the like). You should clearly label them on the chart or by a legend somewhere in the chart. But the number of series that you may compare on one line chart is limited. As a practical guide, the maximum number is five to eight.

It is also possible to show parts of a series by use of an *area* chart. Such a chart, however, can show only one series. You should construct this type of chart, as shown in Figure 13–14, with a top line representing the total of the series. Then, starting from the base, you should cumulate the parts, beginning with the largest and ending with the smallest. You may use cross-hatching or coloring to distinguish the parts.

Line charts that show a range of data for particular times are called *variance* or *hi-lo* charts. Some variance charts show high and low points as well as the mean, median, or mode. When used to chart daily stock prices, they typically include closing price in addition to the high and low. When you use points other than high and low, be sure to make it clear what these points are.

- The line appears on a grid (a scaled area) and is continuous.

- Two or more lines may appear on one chart.

- Area charts show the makeup of a series.

- Variance charts show high and low points—sometimes more.

Figure 13–14

Illustration of an Area Chart

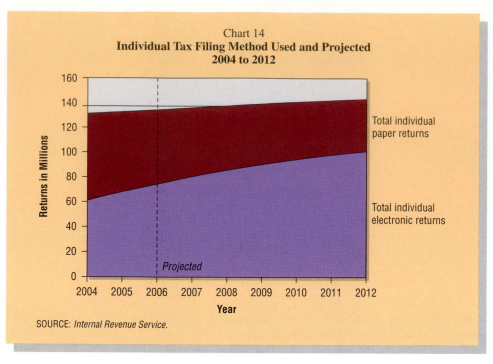

Chart 14
Individual Tax Filing Method Used and Projected
2004 to 2012

SOURCE: *Internal Revenue Service.*

Figure 13–15   Illustration of a Scatter Diagram

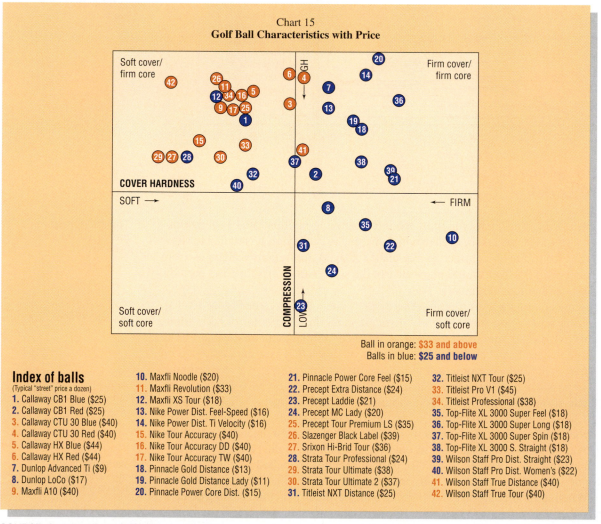

Chart 15
Golf Ball Characteristics with Price

Ball in orange: **$33 and above**
Balls in blue: **$25 and below**

Index of balls
(Typical "street" price a dozen)

1. Callaway CB1 Blue ($25)
2. Callaway CB1 Red ($25)
3. Callaway CTU 30 Blue ($40)
4. Callaway CTU 30 Red ($40)
5. Callaway HX Blue ($44)
6. Callaway HX Red ($44)
7. Dunlop Advanced Ti ($9)
8. Dunlop LoCo ($17)
9. Maxfli A10 ($40)
10. Maxfli Noodle ($20)
11. Maxfli Revolution ($33)
12. Maxfli XS Tour ($18)
13. Nike Power Dist. Feel-Speed ($16)
14. Nike Power Dist. Ti Velocity ($16)
15. Nike Tour Accuracy ($40)
16. Nike Tour Accuracy DD ($40)
17. Nike Tour Accuracy TW ($40)
18. Pinnacle Gold Distance ($13)
19. Pinnacle Gold Distance Lady ($11)
20. Pinnacle Power Core Dist. ($15)
21. Pinnacle Power Core Feel ($15)
22. Precept Extra Distance ($24)
23. Precept Laddie ($21)
24. Precept MC Lady ($20)
25. Precept Tour Premium LS ($35)
26. Slazenger Black Label ($39)
27. Srixon Hi-Brid Tour ($36)
28. Strata Tour Professional ($24)
29. Strata Tour Ultimate ($38)
30. Strata Tour Ultimate 2 ($37)
31. Titleist NXT Distance ($25)
32. Titleist NXT Tour ($25)
33. Titleist Pro V1 ($45)
34. Titleist Professional ($38)
35. Top-Flite XL 3000 Super Feel ($18)
36. Top-Flite XL 3000 Super Long ($18)
37. Top-Flite XL 3000 Super Spin ($18)
38. Top-Flite XL 3000 S. Straight ($18)
39. Wilson Staff Pro Dist. Straight ($23)
40. Wilson Staff Pro Dist. Women's ($22)
41. Wilson Staff True Distance ($40)
42. Wilson Staff True Tour ($40)

SOURCE: *Golf Digest* July 2002: 61.

Scatter Diagrams

Scatter diagrams are often considered another variation of the line chart. Although they do use X and Y axes to plot paired values, the points stand alone without a line drawn through them. For example, a writer might use a scatter diagram in a report on digital cameras to plot values for price and resolution of several cameras. While clustering the points allows users to validate hunches about cause and effect, they can only be interpreted for correlation—the direction and strength relationships. The points can reveal positive, negative, or no relationships. Additionally, by examining the tightness of the points, the user can see the strength of the relationship. The closer the points are to a straight line, the stronger the relationship. In Figure 13–15, the paired values are *Cover Hardness* and *Compression*.

● Scatter diagrams show direction and strength of paired values.

Maps

You also may use *maps* to communicate quantitative as well as physical (or geographic) information. Statistical maps are useful primarily when quantitative information is to be compared by geographic areas. On such maps, the geographic areas are clearly outlined, and some graphic technique is used to show the differences between areas (see Figure 13–16). Quantitative maps are particularly useful in illustrating and analyzing complex data. Traffic patterns on a website could be mapped as well as patterns in a retail store. Physical or geographic maps (see Figure 13–17) can show distributions as

● Maps show quantitative and geographic information.

Figure 13–16   **Illustration of a Map (quantitative)**

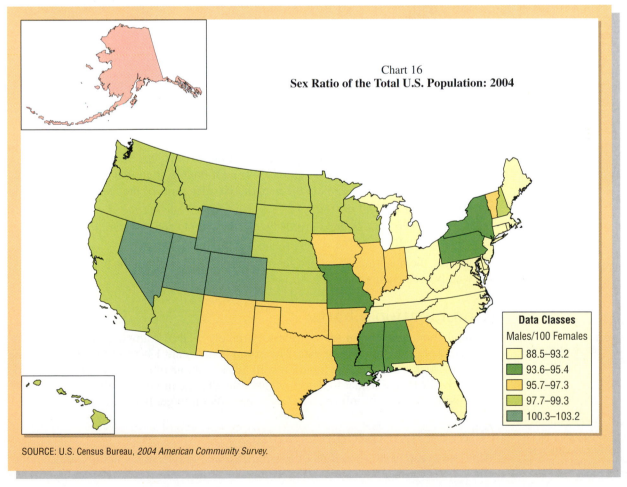

Chart 16
Sex Ratio of the Total U.S. Population: 2004

Data Classes
Males/100 Females
- 88.5–93.2
- 93.6–95.4
- 95.7–97.3
- 97.7–99.3
- 100.3–103.2

SOURCE: U.S. Census Bureau, *2004 American Community Survey.*

Figure 13–17   Illustration of a Map (Physical)

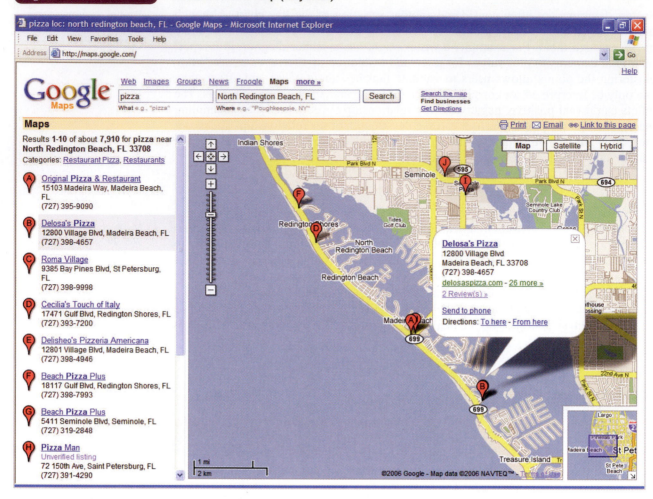

well as specific locations. Of the numerous techniques available to you, these are the most common:

- Here are some specific instructions for statistical maps.

- Showing differences of areas by color, shading, or cross-hatching is perhaps the most popular technique (see Figure 13–16). Of course, maps using this technique must have a legend to explain the quantitative meanings of the various colors, cross-hatchings, and so forth.
- Graphics, symbols, or clip art may be placed within each geographic area to depict the quantity for that area or geographic location.
- Placing the quantities in numerical form within each geographic area is another widely used technique.

Combination Charts

- Sometimes a combination of chart types is effective.

Combination charts often serve readers extremely well by allowing them to see relationships of different kinds of data. The example in Figure 13–18 shows the reader the price of stock over time (the trend) as well as the volume of sales over time (comparisons). It allows the reader to detect whether the change in volume affects the price of the stock. This kind of information would be difficult to get from raw data.

Three-Dimensional Graphics

- With multiple variables, 3D graphics can help readers understand the data better.

Until now you have learned that three-dimensional graphs are generally undesirable. However, we have mostly been referring to the three-dimensional effect applied to

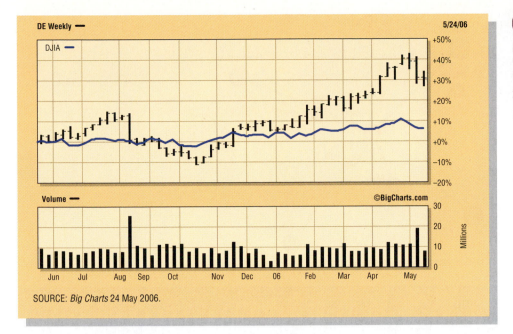

Figure 13–18

Illustration of a
Combination Chart,
Comparing the Dow Jones
Average to the volume and
Weekly Change Range of
Deere Common Stock

graphics with two variables. But when you actually have three or more variables, presenting them in three dimensions is an option. It is the difference between the raised pie chart versus the ball. Adding a third dimension to a pie chart by "raising" it (including a shadow) will not enhance its information value, but if you actually have three-dimensional data, putting it in the form of a ball will enable your readers to see it from multiple perspectives and gain additional information. In fact, Francis Crick, a Nobel prize-winner for discovering the structure of DNA, once revealed it was not until he and his collaborators took a sheet of paper, cut it, and twisted it that they understood the configuration of DNA. Today we have sophisticated statistics, graphics, and data mining tools to help us filter and see our data from multiple perspectives.

These three-dimensional tools are beginning to make their way from science labs into business settings. Several factors seem to be driving the trend. Businesses large and small are collecting and attempting to analyze extremely large amounts of detailed data. They are analyzing not only their own data but also data on their competitors. And advances in hardware, software, and web-based applications are making it easier to graphically represent both quantitative and qualitative data.

- 3D graphics facilitate analyzing large data sets.

Although 3D graphics help writers display the results of their data analysis, they change how readers look at information and may take some time getting used to. These tools enable users both to see data from new perspectives and to interact with it. They allow users to free themselves from two dimensions and give them ways to stretch their insights and see new possibilities. These graphics can help businesses make timely decisions through leveraging their corporate information assets.

- 3D graphics facilitate seeing data from a new perspective.

Figure 13–19 shows a three-dimensional visual thesaurus for the word *graph*. The color of its node and the distance of the node from the centroid reflect the degree of similarity between the node and the centroid, something you cannot get from a traditional thesaurus. Here the closer the synonym to *graph*, the redder or hotter it is and the more similar to the word. In this case *chart* is hotter than drawing, and *drawing* is hotter than *outline*.

- Tools allow users to interact with their data.

Using 3-D graphic tools clearly has a place and use. They are especially good for helping to analyze large data sets with multiple variables, query them, and interpret them. In deciding whether to use a three-dimensional representation such as this one or a two-dimensional one such as one you might see at <http://www.visualthesaurus.com>, you need to consider your audience, the context, and goal of your communication. Overall, multidimensional presentation on paper is difficult; multiple representations can be made from separate two-dimensional views, but not always effectively.

Figure 13–19

Illustration of a Three-Dimensional Graphic

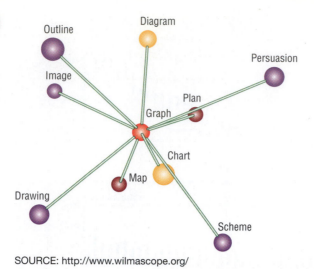

SOURCE: http://www.wilmascope.org/

Figure 13–20

Illustration of a Photo

If the document is being presented online or digitally where the reader can rotate it to see perspectives, it is likely to be much more effective with a larger number of readers. Writers should take care to use three-dimensional graphics appropriately.

Photographs

Cameras are everywhere today. If we do not have them in our phones, we might have them in a credit card size or even smaller. And free and for-fee photos are readily available on the Internet, too. In documents, photos can serve useful communication purposes. They can be used to document things and events as well as show products, processes, or services. You could use the photo in Figure 13–20 as a metaphor for the concept of a hole in a company's computer security (someone getting in) or the loss of corporate intelligence (something getting out). Today photos, like data-generated graphics, can easily be manipulated. A writer's job is to use them ethically, including getting permission when needed and presenting them objectively.

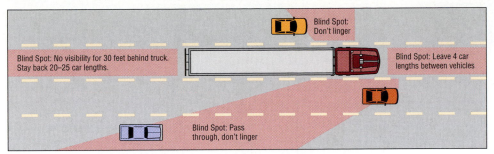

Figure 13–21

Illustration of a Diagram

SOURCE: U.S. Department of Transportation, *Share the Road Safely Program*.

Figure 13–22

Illustration of a Drawing

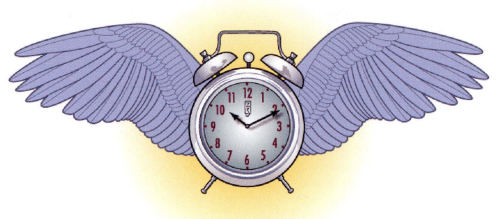

Illustration by Zeke Smith © 2003.

Other Graphics

The types of graphics discussed thus far are the ones most commonly used. Other types also may be helpful. *Diagrams* (see Figure 13–21) and drawings (see Figure 13–22) may help simplify a complicated explanation or description. *Icons* are another useful type of graphic. You can create new icons and use them consistently, or you can draw from an existing body of icons with easily recognized meanings, such as ⊘. Even carefully selected *cartoons* can be used effectively. *Video clips* and *animation* are now used in electronic documents. See the text website for some examples. For all practical purposes, any graphic is acceptable as long as it helps communicate the true story. The possibilities are almost unlimited.

- Other graphics available to you are diagrams, drawings, and even cartoons. *icons, video clips ianimation*

Visual Integrity[3]

In writing an objective report, you are ethically bound to present data and visuals in ways that enable readers to interpret them easily and accurately. By being aware of some of the common errors made in presenting graphics, you learn how to avoid them as well as how to spot them in other documents. Even when errors are not deliberately created to deceive a reader, they cause loss of credibility with the reader—casting doubt on the document as well as on other work you have completed. Both data-generated graphics and visual graphics can misrepresent information. Writers need to be diligent in applying high quality standards when using them.

- Business writers are ethically bound to present data that readers can extract easily and accurately.

---

[3] For an excellent expanded discussion of graphic errors, see Gerald E. Jones, *How to Lie with Charts* (San Jose, CA: iUniverse.com, 2001).

Students must be sensitized in the importance of pictures that accompany written messages to the same extent that they are sensitized to the importance of nonverbal communication that accompanies messages.

Shirley Kuiper, The University of South Carolina
Rosemary Booth, The University of North Carolina at Charlotte
Charles D. Bodkin, The University of North Carolina at Charlotte

Shirley Kuiper, Rosemary Booth, and Charles D. Bodkin, "The Visual Portrayal of Women in IBM's *Think:* A Longitudinal Analysis," *Journal of Business Communication* 35 (1998): 259.

Data-generated Graphs

- Common errors are errors of scale, format, and context presentation.

Two categories of common errors in using graphs are errors of scale and errors of format. Another more difficult category of error is inaccurate or misleading presentation of context.

Errors of scale include problems with uniform scale size, scale distortion, and zero points. You need to be sure that all the dimensions from left to right (X axis) are equal, and the dimensions from the bottom to the top (Y axis) are equal. Otherwise, as you see here, an incorrect picture would be shown.

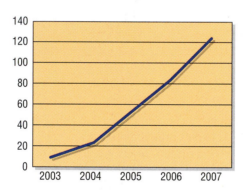
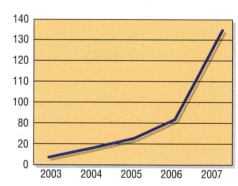

Scale distortion occurs when a graphic is stretched excessively horizontally or vertically to change the meaning it conveys to the reader. Expanding a scale can change the appearance of the line. For example if the values on a chart are plotted one-half unit apart, changes appear much more suddenly. Determining the distances that present the most accurate picture is a matter of judgment. Notice the different looks of the graphic show here when stretched vertically and horizontally.

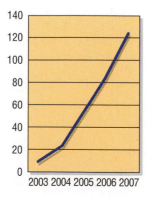
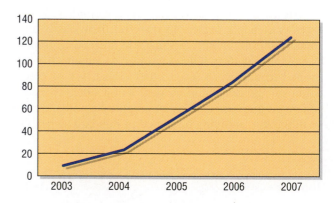

Finally, another type of scale error is violating the zero beginning of the series. For accuracy, you should begin the scale at zero. But when all the information shown in the chart has high values, it is awkward to show the entire scale from zero to the highest value. For example, if the quantities compared range from 1320 to 1350 and the chart shows the entire area from zero to 1350, the line showing these quantities would be almost straight and very high on the chart. Your solution in this case is not to begin the scale at a high number (say 1300), for this would distort the information, but to begin at zero and show a scale break. Realize, however, that while this makes the differences easier to see, it does exaggerate the differences. You can see this here.

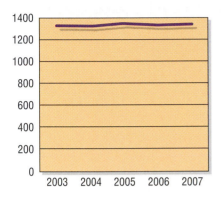
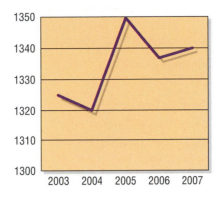
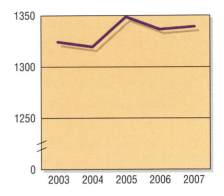

Errors of format come in a wide variety. Some of the more common ones include choice of wrong chart type, distracting use of grids and shading, misuse of typeface, and problems with labels. If a company used pie charts to compare expenses from one year to the next, readers might be tempted to draw conclusions that would be inappropriate because, although the pies both represent 100 percent of the expenses, the size of the business and the expenses may have grown or shrunk drastically in a year's time. If one piece of the pie had been colored or shaded in such a way as to make it stand out from the others, it could mislead readers. And, of course, small type or unlabeled, inconsistently labeled, or inappropriately labeled graphics clearly confuse readers. You need to be careful to present graphics that are both complete and accurate.

Another ethical dilemma is accurately presenting context. Politicians are often deliberately guilty of framing the issue to suit their cause. Business writers can avoid this deception both by attempting to frame the data objectively and by presenting the data

Software programs enable writers to create a wide variety of graphics from small to huge data sets.

Practicing Visual Ethics

As you have learned in this chapter, graphics can serve several useful purposes for the business writer. However, the writer needs to be accountable in using graphics to present images that in the eye and mind of the reader communicate accurately and completely. To do this, the careful writer pays attention to both the design and content of the graphic. These are particularly important, for readers often skim text but read the graphics. Research shows that people remember images much better and longer than text.

The following guides will help you in evaluating the graphics you use:

- Does the visual's design create accurate expectations?
- Does the story told match the data?
- Is the implied message congruent with the actual message?
- Will the impact of the visual on your audience be appropriate?
- Does the visual convey all critical information free of distortion?
- Are the data depicted accurately?

Adapted from Donna S. Kienzler, "Visual Ethics," *Journal of Business Communication* 34 (1997): 171–87.

with the reader in mind. For example, one might look at the cost of attending college for the past 30 years. A line chart of the actual dollar cost over the years would show a clear upward trend. However, to present the costs without factoring in inflation during that 30-year period would distort the results. In Figure 13–23, you can see that the actual cost of college tuition and fees in dollars adjusted for inflation would show costs that are lower or equal to today's costs.

Visual Graphs

Visual graphs, too, need to be used ethically. Writers need to be careful when choosing the information to represent and the visual elements to represent it. One area writers

Figure 13–23

Illustration of Accuracy of Content

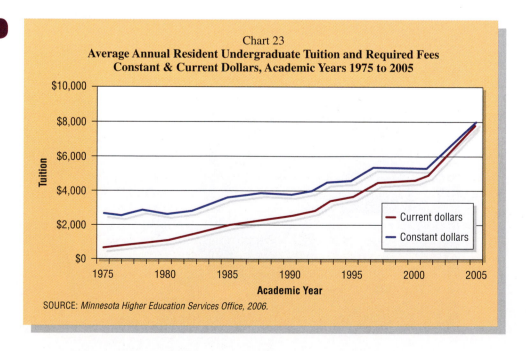

Chart 23
**Average Annual Resident Undergraduate Tuition and Required Fees
Constant & Current Dollars, Academic Years 1975 to 2005**

SOURCE: *Minnesota Higher Education Services Office, 2006.*

need to watch is appropriate selection. Are people or things over- or underrepresented? Are the numbers of men and women appropriate for the context? Are their ages appropriate? Is ethnicity represented appropriately? Have colors been used appropriately and not to evoke or manipulate emotions? What about volume and size? Are the number of visuals and size appropriate for the emphasis the topic deserves? Are visuals presented accurately, free of distortion or alteration? Have photos been cropped to be consistent with the context? Writers need to carefully select and use visual graphs to maintain high integrity.

PLACING AND INTERPRETING THE GRAPHICS

For the best communication effect, you should place each graphic near the place where it is covered in writing. Exactly where on the page you should place it, however, should be determined by its size. If the graphic is small, you should place it within the text that discusses it. If it is a full page, you should place it on the page following the first reference to the information it covers.

- Place the graphics near the first place in the text in which you refer to them.

Some writers like to place all graphics at the end of the report, usually in the appendix. This arrangement may save time in preparing the report, but it does not help the readers. They have to flip through pages every time they want to see a graphic. Common sense requires that you place graphics in such a way as to help readers understand the report.

- Placing graphics at the end of the report does not help the readers.

Sometimes you may need to include graphics that do not fit a specific part of the report. For example, you may have a graphic that is necessary for completeness but is not discussed in the report. Or you may have summary charts or tables that apply to the entire report but to no specific place in it. When such graphics are appropriate, you should place them in the appendix. And you should refer to the appendix somewhere in the report.

- Graphics not discussed in the report belong in the appendix.

Graphics communicate most effectively when the readers see them at the right place in the report. Thus, you should refer the readers to them at the right place. That is, you should tell the readers when to look at a graphic and what to see. Of the many wordings used for this purpose, these are the most common:

- At the right place, incidentally invite the readers to look at the graphics.

> . . . , as shown in Figure 4, ...
> . . . , indicated in Figure 4, ...
> . . . , as a glance at Figure 4 reveals, . . .
> . . . (see Figure 4) . . . .

If your graphic is carrying the primary message, as in a detailed table, you can just make an incidental reference to the information in the graphic, as in "Our increased sales over the last three years . . . ."

However, if the words are carrying the primary message such as in the bar chart in Figure 13–14, you might start with a reference to the chart followed closely by a thorough interpretation. One good mantra to use is GEE, standing for generalization, example, and exception.[4] You'll start with a summary statement that reveals the big picture. In the case of Figure 13–14, you might say, "As Figure 14 shows, the number of individuals filing tax returns electronically will grow from 65 million today to 90 million in 2012." After presenting the figure, you'll give one or more supporting examples that call your readers' attention to key findings. Then you will give the exception to the general trend, if there is one—for example, "In most years the increase is expected to be four million; however, in the first year it will be five million when easy-to-use web-based tax preparation software first becomes available."

- Interpret using a generalization, example, exception (GEE) strategy.

Your readers will appreciate well-chosen, well-designed, and well-explained graphics, and you will achieve powerful communication results.

---

[4] Jane E. Miller, "Implementing 'Generalization, Example, Exceptions (GEE),'" *The Chicago Guide to Writing about Numbers: The Effective Presentation of Quantitative Information* (Chicago: The University of Chicago Press, 2004) 265.

SUMMARY BY LEARNING OBJECTIVES

1 Determine which parts of your report should be communicated by graphics and where in the report the graphics should appear.

1. Because graphics are a part of the communication in a report, you should plan for them.
   - But remember that they supplement the writing; they do not replace it.
   - Use them wherever they help communicate the report information.

2 Explain the general mechanics of constructing graphics—size, layout, type, rules and borders, color and cross-hatching, clip art, background, numbering, titles, title placement, and footnotes and acknowledgments.

2. Construct each graphic carefully, following these general instructions:
   - Give each the size and arrangement that its contents and importance justify.
   - Choose a readable type. New Clear Type fonts such as Calibri or Cambria improve on-screen readability.
   - Use rules, borders, and color when they help.
   - Use clip art and background appropriately.
   - Number the graphics consecutively by type.
   - Construct topic titles for them using the five Ws (*who, what, where, when, why*) and one H (*how*) as a checklist. Alternatively, use the main message as a talking heading.
   - Use footnotes and acknowledgments when needed, placing them below the graphic.

3 Construct textual graphics such as tables, pull quotes, flowcharts, and process charts.

3. Choose textual graphics to display data that are largely text based.
   - Use general-purpose tables for information that is broad in scope.
   - Use special-purpose tables for information that is specific in scope.
   - Use leaderwork or tabulations for short arrangement of data.
   - Use pull quotes to emphasize a key idea.
   - Use bullet lists to set off points.
   - Use flowcharts and process charts to show activity sequences.

4 Construct and use visual graphics such as bar charts, pie charts, scatter diagrams, and maps.

4. In selecting a graphic, consider these primary uses of each:
   - *Simple bar* or *column chart*—shows quantity comparisons over time or over geographic distances.
   - *Clustered bar* or *column chart*—shows two or three quantities on one chart.
   - *Bilateral column chart*—shows plus and minus differences and is especially good for showing percentage changes.
   - *Stacked* or *subdivided bar chart*—used to compare differences in the division of wholes.
   - *Pictograph*—shows quantitative differences in picture form.
   - *Pie chart*—used to show how wholes are divided.
   - *Line chart*—useful in showing changes over time. Variations include belt charts, surface charts, and variance charts.
   - *Scatter diagram*—compares pairs of values.
   - *Map*—shows quantitative and physical differences by area.
   - *Combination chart*—used to show relationships between separate data sets.
   - *Three-dimensional graphic*—used to analyze and interpret large data sets with three or more variables.
   - *Photograph*—used to document things and events or show products, processes, and services.

   Apply other graphics to serve special needs:
   - Diagrams and drawings.
   - Icons.

- Cartoons.
- Video clips and animation.

5. Visual integrity applies to both data-generated graphics and visuals.
   - To present data objectively avoid these common errors :
     — *Errors of scale*—no uniform scale size, scale distortion, missing zero point.
     — *Errors of format*—wrong chart type, distracting use of grids and shading, misuse of typeface, and problems with labels.
     — *Errors of context presentation.*
   - Visuals need special attention to the following:
     — *Selection.*
     — *Color.*
     — *Volume and size.*
     — *Distortion, dropping, and alterations.*

6. Place and interpret graphics effectively.
   - Place graphics near to the text part they illustrate.
   - Place in the appendix those that you do not discuss in the text.
   - Invite the readers to look at them at the appropriate place.
   - Interpret using a generalization, example, exception strategy.

5 Avoid common errors and ethical problems when constructing and using graphics.

6 Place and interpret graphics effectively.

CRITICAL THINKING QUESTIONS

1 For the past 20 years, Professor Clark Kupenheimer has required that his students include five graphics in the long, formal report he assigns them to prepare. Evaluate this requirement.

2 Because it was easier to do, a report writer prepared each of the graphics on a full page. Some of these graphics were extremely complex; some were very simple. Comment on this practice.

3 A report has five maps, four tables, one chart, one diagram, and one photograph. How would you number these graphics?

4 How would you number these graphics in a report: seven tables, six charts, nine maps?

5 Discuss the techniques that may be used to show quantitative differences by area on a statistical map.

6 Select data that are ideally suited for presentation in three dimensions. Explain why use of a data visualization is good for this case.

7 Discuss the advantages and disadvantages of using pictographs.

8 Find a graph that uses scale breaks. Discuss the possible effects of its use on the reader.

9 Find a graphic with errors in format. Tell how you would correct the errors to present the chart's data more clearly to the reader.

10 "I have placed every graphic near the place I write about it. The reader can see the graphic without any *additional* help from me. It just doesn't make sense to direct the reader's attention to the graphics with words." Evaluate this comment.

CRITICAL THINKING EXERCISES

1 Construct a complete, concise title for a bar chart showing annual attendance at home football (or basketball, or soccer) games at your school from 2000 to the present.

2 The chart prepared in Question 1 requires an explanation for the years 2005 to the present. In each of those years, one extra home game was played. Explain how you would provide the necessary explanation.

3 For each of the areas of information described on the following page, which form of graphic would you use? Explain your decision.

a. Record of annual sales for the Kenyon Company for the past 20 years.

b. Comparison of Kenyon Company sales, by product, for this year and last year.

c. Monthly production of the automobile industry in units.

d. Breakdown of how the average middle-income family in your state (or province) disposes of its income dollar.

e. How middle-income families spend their income dollar as compared with how low-income families spend their income dollar.

f. Comparison of sales for the past two years for each of the B&B Company's 14 sales districts. The districts cover all 50 states, Canada, and Puerto Rico.

g. National production of trucks from 1950 to present, broken down by manufacturer.

h. Relationship between list price and gas mileage of alternative and gasoline-fueled cars.

4 For each of the following sets of facts, (*a*) determine the graphic (or graphics) that would be best, (*b*) defend your choice, and (*c*) construct the graphic.

a. Average (mean) amount of life insurance owned by Fidelity Life Insurance Company policyholders. Classification is by annual income.

Income	Average Life Insurance
Under $30,000	$15,245
$30,000–34,999	24,460
$35,000–39,999	36,680
$40,000–44,999	49,875
$45,000–49,999	61,440
$50,000 and over	86,390

b. Profits and losses for Whole Foods Stores, by store, 2003–2007, in dollars.

		Store		
Year	Able City	Baker	Charleston	Total
2003	234,210	132,410	97,660	464,280
2004	229,110	−11,730	218,470	435,850
2005	238,430	−22,410	216,060	432,080
2006	226,730	68,650	235,510	530,890
2007	230,080	91,450	254,820	576,350

c. Share of real estate tax payments by ward for Bigg City, 2002 and 2007, in thousands of dollars.

	2002	2007
Ward 1	17.1	21.3
Ward 2	10.2	31.8
Ward 3	19.5	21.1
Ward 4	7.8	18.2
City total	54.6	92.4

d. Percentage change in sales by employee, 2006–2007, District IV, Abbott, Inc.

Employee	Percentage Change
Joan Abraham	+7.3
Helen Calmes	+2.1
Edward Sanchez	−7.5
Clifton Nevers	+41.6
Wilson Platt	+7.4
Clara Ruiz	+11.5
David Schlimmer	−4.8
Phil Wirks	−3.6

5 The basic blood types are O, A, B, and AB. These can be either positive or negative. With some basic research, determine what percentage of each type people in the United States have. Choose an appropriate graph type and create it to convey the data.

6 Through your research, find the approximate milligrams of caffeine in the following items and create an appropriate graphic for Affiliated Food Products, Inc., to illustrate your findings.

5-oz. cup of coffee (drip brewed)

7-oz. glass of iced tea

6-oz. glass of soda with caffeine

1-oz. dark chocolate, semisweet

7 Choose five or six outdoor summer sport activities. In a graphic identify the activity and whether it affects cardiovascular, arms, legs, back, or abdominals. You can assume these activities can affect more than one fitness zone. You work for the Parks and Recreation Department of a city of your choosing.

Considered one of Fortune 500's "Most Powerful Black Executives" at age 39, Pamela Thomas-Graham was the first black woman to become a partner at management consulting firm McKinsey & Company. Thomas-Graham recognizes the importance of communicating informally to gather information and harvest good ideas.

"It's very important to have a lot of interaction with people at every level of the company. You should spend time walking around talking with people, and have meetings that bring together different groups of people, either from different areas of the company or from different levels within the company. And my basic philosophy is, 'The best idea wins.' It doesn't matter where it comes from."

Pamela Thomas-Graham, Group President, Liz Claiborne Inc.

chapter fourteen

Informal Oral Communication

Upon completing this chapter, you will be able to understand and use good talking techniques, lead and participate in meetings, communicate effectively by telephone, dictate messages effectively, listen well, and understand nonverbal communication. To reach these goals, you should be able to

1 Discuss talking and its key elements.

2 Explain the techniques for conducting and participating in meetings.

3 Describe good telephone and voice mail techniques.

4 Describe the techniques of good voice input.

5 Explain the listening problem and how to solve it.

6 Describe the nature and role of nonverbal communication.

Informal Oral Communication on the Job

Your job as assistant director in the Public Relations Department at Mastadon Chemicals, Inc., seems somewhat different from what you expected. It makes full use of your specialized college training, as you expected; but it also involves duties for which you did not train because you did not expect them. Most of these duties seem to involve some form of oral communication. In fact, you probably spend more of your work time in talking and listening than in any other activity.

To illustrate, take today's activities. Early this morning, you discussed a morale problem with some of your supervisors. You don't think they understood what you said. After that, you conducted a meeting of the special committee to plan the department's annual picnic. As chairperson, you ran the meeting. It was a disaster, you felt—everybody talking at once, interrupting, arguing. It was a wonder that the committee made any progress. It seemed that everybody wanted to talk but nobody wanted to listen.

In the afternoon, you had other job duties involving oral communication. After you returned from lunch, you must have had a phone conversation every 20 minutes or so. You felt comfortable with most of these calls, but you thought some of the callers needed a lesson or two in phone etiquette. Also, using speech recognition in Word, you dictated a few messages and emails between phone calls.

You most certainly do a lot of talking (and listening) on your job, as do most of the people at Mastadon and just about everywhere else. Oral communication is a vital part of your work. Perhaps you can become better at it by studying the following review of oral communication techniques.

As you know, your work will involve oral as well as written communication. The written communication will probably give you more problems, but the oral communication will take up more of your time. In fact, you are likely to spend more time in oral communication than in any other work activity.

Much of the oral communication that goes on in business is the informal, person-to-person communication that occurs whenever people get together. Obviously, we all have experience with this form of communication, and most of us do it reasonably well. But all of us can improve our informal speaking and listening with practice.

In addition to informal talking and listening, various kinds of other more formal oral communication take place in business. Sometimes businesspeople conduct and participate in committee meetings, conferences, and group discussions. Often they call one another on the phone. Even their messages and reports may begin orally as spoken dictation. And frequently, they are called upon to make formal presentations: speeches, lectures, oral reports, and the like. All these kinds of oral communication are a part of the work that businesspeople do.

This and the following chapter cover these kinds of oral communication. This chapter reviews the somewhat less formal kinds: informal talking, listening, participating in meetings, talking by phone, and dictating. The following chapter presents the two most formal kinds: public speaking and oral reporting. Together, the two chapters should give you an understanding of the types of oral communication situations you will encounter in business.

- You will spend more time talking than writing in business.

- Most of your oral communication will be informal.

- But some of it will be formal, as in meetings, phone calls, dictation, speeches, and oral reports.

- This and the following chapter cover these types of oral communication.

INFORMAL TALKING

As noted previously, most of us do a reasonably good job of informal talking. In fact, we do such a good job that we often take talking for granted and overlook the need for improving our talking ability. Most of us could stand to improve. To improve our talking ability, we need to be aware of its nature and qualities. We need to assess our abilities. Then we need to work to overcome our shortcomings.

- Most of us talk reasonably well, but probably we can do better.

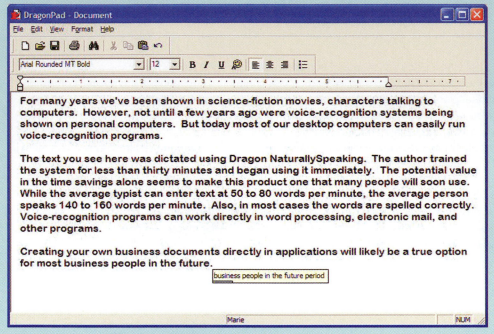

For many years we've been shown in science-fiction movies, characters talking to computers. However, not until a few years ago were voice-recognition systems being shown on personal computers. But today most of our desktop computers can easily run voice-recognition programs.

The text you see here was dictated using Dragon NaturallySpeaking. The author trained the system for less than thirty minutes and began using it immediately. The potential value in the time savings alone seems to make this product one that many people will soon use. While the average typist can enter text at 50 to 80 words per minute, the average person speaks 140 to 160 words per minute. Also, in most cases the words are spelled correctly. Voice-recognition programs can work directly in word processing, electronic mail, and other programs.

Creating your own business documents directly in applications will likely be a true option for most business people in the future.

Created with Dragon Naturally Speaking. Used with permission.

Definition of Talking

- Think about having no words to speak. If you try to express yourself, you probably become frustrated.

Imagine for a few moments what it would be like to have no words. All that you have to express your thoughts are grunts, groans, and other such utterances. Of course, you have various nonverbal symbols such as pointing your fingers, nodding your head, and the like. As you find yourself increasingly in need of expressing yourself, you probably become more and more emotional and frustrated—to the point of exaggerating the nonverbal symbols and experiencing many physical symptoms such as redness of the face, heavy breathing, and an increased heartbeat.

- Thus, we learn words to control ourselves and the world about us.

- Talking, then, is the oral expression of knowledge, viewpoints, and emotions through words.

More than likely, the foregoing analogy describes the way you learned to talk. As a dependent child, you expressed yourself with screams, cries, and nonverbal symbols. But as you matured, you learned words, and the words greatly reduced the frustrations of the past. They enabled you to communicate with others more exactly. They enabled you to relate better to the world about you and to some extent to control it.

The foregoing review of how you learned to talk gives us the basis for defining *talking*. From it we can derive this definition: *Talking* is the oral expression of knowledge, viewpoints, and emotions through words. Also, from this review we can see that talking replaces many of the body movements we made before we were able to talk. And as we will see, it is supplemented by various body movements we have acquired as we learned to talk: gestures, facial expressions, body positions, and such.

- Think about the best and worst speakers you can imagine. This contrast should give you the qualities of good talking: voice quality, speaking style, word choice, adaptation.

As a first step in improving your talking ability, think for a moment about the qualities you like in a good talker—one with whom you would enjoy talking in ordinary conversation. Then think about the opposite—the worst conversationalist you can imagine. If you will get these two images in mind, you can form a good picture of the characteristics of good talking. Probably this mental picture includes good voice

Words of Wisdom

Oral communication was consistently identified as the most important competency in evaluating entry-level candidates. The four oral communication skills identified as most important for entry-level jobs are following instructions, listening, conversing, and giving feedback.

Jeanne D. Maes, University of South Alabama
Teresa G. Weldy, University of South Alabama
Marjorie L. Icenogle, University of South Alabama

Jeanne D. Maes, Teresa G. Weldy, Marjorie L. Icenogle, "A Managerial Perspective: Oral Communication Is Most Important for Business Students in the Workplace," *Journal of Business Communication* 34 (1997): 78.

quality, excellence in talking style, accuracy of word choice, and adaptation. As these elements control the overall quality of oral expression, we will now review them.

Elements of Good Talking

The techniques of good talking use four basic elements: (1) voice quality, (2) style, (3) word choice, and (4) adaptation.

Voice Quality. It should be obvious that good voice quality is central to good talking. By voice quality we mean the vocal sounds one hears when another speaks. Primarily voice quality refers to the pitch and resonance of the sounds made. But for our purposes, speed and volume are included. Because we cover these topics in Chapter 15, our review here is brief. We need only to say that voices vary widely—from the unpleasant to the melodious. Each of us is saddled with the voice given us. But we can work for improvement.

- Good voice quality helps one communicate. It involves pitch, delivery speed, and volume.

Perhaps the best way of improving voice quality is first to refer to your life experiences. From your life experiences you know good voice quality when you hear it. You know bad voice quality when you hear it. You know the effect received from talking that is too fast or too slow. You know the effect of talking in a monotone. You know the effect of a high-pitched voice, a guttural voice, a melodious voice. With this knowledge in mind, you should analyze your own voice, perhaps with the assistance of a recorder. Listen carefully to you. Fit what you hear into impressions you have gained from your life experiences. Then do what you can to improve. It will take conscious effort.

- Study the quality of your voice and compare it with what experience tells you is good. Then correct the shortcomings.

Style. Talking style refers to how the three parts of voice quality—pitch, speed, and volume—blend together. It is the unique way these parts combine to give personality to one's oral expression. As such, style refers to a set of voice behaviors that give uniqueness to a person.

From the self-analysis described in our review of voice quality, you also should have a good idea of your talking style. What is the image your talking projects? Does it project sincerity? Is it polished? Smooth? Rough? Dull? After your honest assessment, you should be able to determine your style deficiencies. Then you should work to improve.

- Style is the blending of pitch, speed, and volume to form a unique talking personality.

- A self-analysis of your talking should show you your talking style and the image it projects.

Word Choice. A third quality of talking is word choice. Of course, word choice is related to one's vocabulary. The larger the vocabulary, the more choices one has. Even so, you should keep in mind the need for the recipient to understand the words you choose. You should choose words you know are in his or her vocabulary. In addition, the words you choose should be appropriate. They should convey the morality and

- Choose words in your listener's vocabulary. Select those that appropriately convey the morality and courtesy you intend and respect the listener's knowledge.

courtesy you desire. And they should respect the listener's knowledge of the subject matter—that is, they should not talk down to or above the listener.

- Adaptation is fitting the message to the listener. It includes word selection, but here we refer to the combined effect of words, voice, and style.

Adaptation. Adaptation is the fourth quality of good talking. It is an extension of our discussion in the paragraphs above. Adaptation means fitting the message to the intended listener. Primarily this means fitting the words to the listener's mind. But it also can include voice and style. To illustrate, the voice, style, and words in an oral message aimed at children would be different for the same message aimed at adults. Similarly, these qualities might vary in messages delivered in different cultures as well as different social situations, work situations, and classrooms.

Courtesy in Talking

- Good talkers are courteous. They don't attempt to dominate.

- They are assertive, but they treat others as they want to be treated.

Our review of talking would not be complete without a comment about the need for courtesy. Good relations between human beings require courtesy. We all know talkers who drown out others with their loud voices, who butt in while others are talking, who attempt to dominate others in conversation. They are universally disliked. Do not be one of them. Good talkers encourage others to make their voices heard. They practice courtesy in their conversations.

This emphasis on courtesy does not suggest that you should be submissive in your conversations—that you should not be aggressive in pressing your points. It means that you should accord others the courtesy that you expect of them. What we are suggesting is simply the Golden Rule applied to conversation.

CONDUCTING AND PARTICIPATING IN MEETINGS

- Meetings involve oral communication.

From time to time, you will participate in business meetings. They will range from extreme formality to extreme informality. On the formal end will be conferences and committee meetings. On the informal end will be discussions with groups of fellow workers. Whether formal or informal, the meetings will involve communication. In fact, the quality of the communication will determine their success. As noted in Chapter 10, collaborative report-writing groups should use the suggestions for conducting effective meetings.

Collaborative Tools Support Virtual Meetings

Virtual meetings are becoming common in small and large business alike. No longer do businesses need sophisticated teleconferencing equipment to work together from different locations. A typical desktop or laptop with an Internet connection will work nicely. With the proper system configuration, meeting participants can both see and hear others as well as see and work with various software applications.

Businesses are using this technology with their employees, their suppliers, and their customers. Some of the uses include training, sales presentations, review meetings, product demonstrations, and much more—sometimes even just-in-time meetings. All uses help the businesspeople do their jobs while saving both time and travel costs.

One such meeting tool is GoTo Meeting, a web-based application, which has won awards for its technology. Because the technology is scalable, meeting size can vary widely. And its cost and ease-of-use make it readily available to large and small businesses alike.

Your role in a meeting will be that of either leader or participant. Of course, the leader's role is the primary one, but good participation is also vital. The following paragraphs review the techniques of performing well in either role.

- In a meeting you will be either a leader or a participant.

Techniques of Conducting Meetings

How you conduct a meeting depends on the formality of the occasion. Meetings of such groups as formal committees, boards of directors, and professional organizations usually follow generally accepted rules of conduct called *parliamentary procedure*. These very specific rules are too detailed for review here. When you are involved in a formal meeting, you would do well to study one of the many books covering parliamentary procedure before the meeting. In addition, you should know and practice the following techniques. For less formal meetings, you can depart somewhat from parliamentary procedure and those techniques. But you should keep in mind that every meeting has goals and that such departures should never hinder you from reaching them.

- To lead some formal meetings, you should know parliamentary procedure. So study the subject.

Plan the Meeting. A key to conducting a successful meeting is to plan it thoroughly. That is, you develop an agenda (a list of topics to be covered) by selecting the items that need to be covered to achieve the goals of the meeting. Then arrange these items in the most logical order. Items that explain or lead to other items should come before the items that they explain or lead to. After preparing the agenda, make it available to those who will attend if the meeting is formal. For informal meetings, you may find keeping the agenda in mind satisfactory.

- In addition, you should do the following: (1) plan the items to be covered (the agenda),

Follow the Plan. You should follow the plan for the meeting item by item. In most meetings the discussion tends to stray and new items tend to come up. As leader, you should keep the discussion on track. If new items come up during the meeting, you can take them up at the end—or perhaps postpone them to a future meeting.

- (2) follow the plan item by item,

Move the Discussion Along. As leader, you should control the agenda. When one item has been covered, bring up the next item. When the discussion moves off

- (3) move the discussion along,

subject, move it back on subject. In general, do what is needed to proceed through the items efficiently. But you should not cut off discussion before all the important points have been made. Thus, you will have to use your good judgment. Your goal is to permit complete discussion on the one hand and to avoid repetition, excessive details, and useless comments on the other.

● (4) allow no one to talk too much,

Control Those Who Talk Too Much. Keeping certain people from talking too much is likely to be one of your harder tasks. A few people usually tend to dominate the discussion. Your task as leader is to control them. Of course, you want the meeting to be democratic, so you will need to let these people talk as long as they are contributing to the goals of the meeting. However, when they begin to stray, duplicate, or bring in useless matter, you should step in. You can do this tactfully and with all the decorum of business etiquette by asking for other viewpoints or by summarizing the discussion and moving on to the next topic.

● (5) encourage everybody to take part,

Encourage Participation from Those Who Talk Too Little. Just as some people talk too much, some talk too little. In business groups, those who say little are often in positions lower than those of other group members. Your job as leader is to encourage these people to participate by asking them for their viewpoints and by showing respect for the comments they make.

● (6) control time when time is limited, and

Control Time. When your meeting time is limited, you need to determine in advance how much time will be needed to cover each item. Then, at the appropriate times, you should end discussion of the items. You may find it helpful to announce the time goals at the beginning of the meeting and to remind the group members of the time status during the meeting.

● (7) at appropriate places, summarize what the group has covered and concluded.

Summarize at Appropriate Places. After a key item has been discussed, you should summarize what the group has covered and concluded. If a group decision is needed, the group's vote will be the conclusion. In any event, you should formally conclude each point and then move on to the next one. At the end of the meeting, you can summarize the progress made. You also should summarize whenever a review will help the group members understand their accomplishments. For some formal meetings, minutes kept by a secretary provide this summary.

Techniques for Participating in a Meeting

From the preceding discussion of the techniques that a leader should use, you know something about the things that a participant should do. The following review emphasizes them.

● As a participant in a meeting you should

● (1) follow the agenda,

Follow the Agenda. When an agenda exists, you should follow it. Specifically, you should not bring up items not on the agenda or comment on such items if others bring them up. When there is no agenda, you should stay within the general limits of the goal for the meeting.

● (2) participate in the meeting,

Participate. The purpose of meetings is to get the input of everybody concerned. Thus, you should participate. Your participation, however, should be meaningful. You should talk only when you have something to contribute, and you should talk whenever you have something to contribute. Practice professional etiquette as you work courteously and cooperatively with others in the group.

● (3) avoid talking too much,

Do Not Talk Too Much. As you participate in the meeting, be aware that other people are attending. You should speak up whenever you have something to say, but do not get carried away. As in all matters of etiquette, always respect the rights of others. As you speak, ask yourself whether what you are saying really contributes to the discussion. Not only is the meeting costing you time, but it is costing other people's time and salaries as well as the opportunity costs of other work they might be doing.

Cooperate. A meeting by its very nature requires cooperation from all the participants. So keep this in mind as you participate. Respect the leader and her or his efforts to make progress. Respect the other participants, and work with them in every practical way.

• (4) cooperate with all concerned, and

Be Courteous. Perhaps being courteous is a part of being cooperative. In any event, you should be courteous to the other group members. Specifically, you should respect their rights and opinions, and you should permit them to speak.

• (5) practice courtesy.

USING THE PHONE

A discussion of business phone techniques may appear trivial at first thought. After all, most of us have had long experience in using the phone and may feel that we have little to learn about it. No doubt, some of us have excellent phone skills. But you have only to call a few randomly selected businesses to learn that not everyone who talks on the phone is proficient in its use. You will get some gruff, cold greetings, and you will be subjected to a variety of discourtesies. And you will find instances of inefficient use of time (which, of course, is costly). This is not to say that the problem is major, for most progressive businesses are aware of the need for good phone habits and do something about it. But poor phone techniques are found often enough to justify reviewing the subject of phone use in a business communication textbook.

• Many businesspeople are discourteous and inefficient in phone communication.

Need for Favorable Voice Quality

In reviewing good phone techniques, keep in mind that a phone conversation is a unique form of oral communication. Only voices are heard; the speakers are not seen. Impressions are received only from the words and the quality of the voices. Thus, when speaking by phone, it is extremely important that you work to make your voice sound pleasant and friendly.

• Because only sound is involved, friendly voices are important.

One often-suggested way of improving your phone voice is to talk as if you were face to face with the other person—even smiling and gesturing as you talk if this helps you be more natural. In addition, you would do well to put into practice the suggestions given earlier in this chapter concerning the use of the voice in speaking (voice quality, variation in pitch, and speed). Perhaps the best instructional device for this problem is to record one of your phone conversations. Then judge for yourself how you come across and what you need to do to improve.

• So talk as if you were in a face-to-face conversation.

Techniques of Courtesy

If you have worked in business for any length of time, you have probably experienced most of the common phone discourtesies. You probably know that most of them are not intended as discourtesies but result from ignorance or unconcern. The following review should help you avoid them and incorporate business etiquette into your phone conversations.

• Be courteous.

The recommended procedure when you are calling is to introduce yourself immediately and then to ask for the person with whom you want to talk:

> "This is Wanda Tidwell of Tioga Milling Company. May I speak with Mr. José Martinez?"

If you are not certain with whom you should talk, explain the purpose of your call:

> "This is Wanda Tidwell of Tioga Milling Company. We have a question about your service warranty. May I talk with the proper executive about it?"

• When calling, immediately introduce yourself and ask for the person you want (or explain your purpose).

When a secretary or someone else who is screening calls answers the phone, the recommended procedure is to first identify the company or office and then to make an offer of assistance:

• When receiving a call, identify your company or office; then offer assistance.

"Rowan Insurance Company. How may I help you?"

"Ms. Santo's office. May I help you?"

When a call goes directly into the office of the executive, the procedure is much the same, except that the executive identifies herself or himself:

"Bartosh Realty. Toby Bartosh speaking. May I help you?"

When an assistant answers for an executive (the usual case), special care should be taken not to offend the caller. Following a question like "Who is calling?" by "I am sorry, but Mr. Gordon is not in" leaves the impression that Gordon may be in but does not want to talk with this particular caller. A better procedure would be to state directly "Mr. Gordon is not in right now. May I ask him to return your call?" Or perhaps "May I tell him who called?" or "Can someone else help you?" could be substituted for the latter sentence.

Especially irritating to callers is being put on hold for unreasonable periods of time. If the person being called is on another line or involved in some other activity, it may be desirable to place the caller on hold or ask if the caller would like to leave a message. But good business etiquette dictates that the choice should be the caller's. If the hold continues for a period longer than anticipated, the assistant should check back with the caller periodically showing concern and offering assistance. Equally irritating is the practice of having an assistant place a call for an executive and then put the person called on hold until the executive is free to talk. Although it may be efficient to use assistants for such work, as a matter of courtesy and etiquette the executive should be ready to talk the moment the call goes through.

Assistants to busy executives often screen incoming calls. In doing so, they should courteously ask the purpose of the calls. The response might prompt the assistant to refer the caller to a more appropriate person in the company. It also might reveal that the executive has no interest in the subject of the call, in which case the assistant should courteously yet clearly explain this to the caller. If the executive is busy at the moment, the assistant should explain this and either suggest a more appropriate time for a call or promise a callback by the executive. But in no case should the assistant promise a callback that will not be made. Such a breach of etiquette would likely destroy any goodwill between the caller and the company.

Effective Phone Procedures

At the beginning of a phone conversation that you have initiated, it is good practice to state the purpose of the call. Then you should cover systematically all the points involved. For really important calls, you should plan your call, even to the point of making notes of the points to cover. Then you should follow your notes to make certain you cover them all.

Courteous procedure is much the same in a telephone conversation as in a face-to-face conversation. You listen when the other person is talking. You refrain from interrupting. You avoid dominating the conversation. And perhaps most important of all, you cover your message quickly, saving time (and money) for all concerned.

Effective Voice Mail Techniques

Sometimes when the person you are calling is not available, you will be able to leave a voice message in an electronic voice mailbox. Not only does this save you the time involved in calling back the person you are trying to reach, but it also allows you to leave a more detailed message than you might leave with an assistant. However, you need to be prepared for this to be sure your message is both complete and concise.

You begin the message nearly the same way you would a telephone call. Be as courteous as you would on the telephone and speak as clearly and distinctly as you can. Tell the listener in a natural way your name and affiliation. Begin with an overview of the message and continue with details. If you want the listener to take action, call for it at the end. If you want the listener to return your call, state that precisely, including when you can be reached. Slowly give the number where your call can be returned. Close with a brief goodwill message. For example, as a program coordinator for a professional training organization, you might leave this message in the voice mailbox of one of your participants:

> This is Ron Ivy from Metroplex Development Institute. I'm calling to remind Ms. Melanie Wilson about the Chief Executive Round Table (CERT) meeting next week (Wednesday, July 20) at the Crescent Hotel in Dallas. Dr. Ken Cooper of the Dallas Aerobics Center will present the program on Executive Health in the 21st Century. We will begin with breakfast at 7:30 AM and conclude with lunch at noon. Some of the CERT members will play golf in the afternoon at Dallas Country Club. If Ms. Wilson would like to join them, I will be glad to make a tee time for her. She can contact me at 940-240-1003 before 5:00 PM this Friday. We look forward to our Chief Executive Round Table meeting next Wednesday.

Cell Phones and Their Courteous Use

In recent years the use of cell phones has become ubiquitous. In fact, according to the Yankee Group, 70 percent of all Americans have a cell phone. To say the least, the benefits of this technology have greatly expanded our ability to communicate. Even so, their use has become an annoyance to 82 percent of Americans and 87 percent of cell phone users.[1] Each of us should be aware of these annoyances and do what we can to reduce them. We can do this by following these suggestions, any one of which can be broken in cases of emergency:

- Cell phones are widely used. Their use can be annoying.

1. Turn off the ringer in meetings and other places where it would be disruptive.
2. Do not use the cell phone at social gatherings.
3. Do not place the phone on the table while eating.
4. Avoid talking whenever it will annoy others. Usually this means when within earshot of others.
5. Avoid discussing personal or confidential matters when others can hear you.
6. Do not talk in an excessively loud voice.
7. Preferably call from a quiet place, away from other people.
8. If you must talk while around people, be conscious of them. Don't hold up lines, obstruct the movements of others, or such.
9. Avoid using the phone while driving (the law in some states).

- You can reduce these annoyances by following these suggestions.

USING SPEECH RECOGNITION FOR MESSAGES AND REPORTS

Dictating messages and reports is probably one of the most underutilized input methods for writers today. Speech recognition software has been improved to allow continuous speech and short setup periods with little training. Additionally, it works with most standard software applications, and it is inexpensive compared to the value it offers writers. Not only does such technology spell correctly, it can quickly learn specialized vocabularies. And it is generally faster for most people than writing by hand or keying information because most people can speak 140 to 160 words per minute. Although proofreading dictated documents is a bit different because it involves looking for homophones (words that sound alike) rather than misspelled or misused words, most programs offer users the ability to play back the dictation, which will help them catch other errors.

- Dictation is an underutilized input method.

- Today's software make the process easy . . .

If you haven't started dictating documents yet, one of the best ways to learn is to use voice recognition software to handle your email. If you are using Office XP or higher, you already have the software; you simply need a microphone and a few minutes

- and inexpensive.

---

[1] Lee Rainie and Scott Keeter, "Cell Phone Use," Pew Internet Project, April 2006, 21 June 2006 <http://www.pewinternet.org/Pds/PIP_cell_phone_study.pdf>.

for training. Two other excellent programs are Dragon NaturallySpeaking and Simply Speaking. Once you have the tools, following the steps below will help you become proficient at dictating.

Techniques of Dictating

You should (1) get all the information you need to avoid interruption later;

Gather the Facts. Your first logical step in dictating is to get all the information you need for the message. This step involves such activities as getting past correspondence from files, consulting with other employees, and ascertaining company policy. Unless you get all the information you need, you will be unable to work without interruption.

(2) plan the message following the procedures described in preceding chapters;

Plan the Message. With the facts of the case before you, you next plan the message. You may prefer to do this step in your mind or to jot down a few notes or an outline. Whatever your preference, your goal in this step is to decide what your message will be and how you will present it. In this step, you apply the procedures covered in our earlier review of message and report writing.

(3) talk through the message,

Make the Words Flow. Your next step is to talk through the message. Simple as this step appears, you are likely to have problems with it. Thinking out loud even to the computer frightens most of us at first. The result is likely to be slow and awkward dictation.

forcing the words to flow if necessary (you can revise later);

Overcoming this problem requires self-discipline and practice. You should force yourself to concentrate and to make the words flow. Your goal should be to get the words out—to talk through the message. You need not be too concerned about producing a polished work on the first effort. You will probably need to revise, perhaps several times. After you have forced your way through several messages, your need to revise will decrease and the speed and quality of your dictation will improve.

(4) speak distinctly for improved accuracy;

Speak Clearly. Because your dictation must be heard clearly by your system, you should speak as distinctly as you can. Even small improvements in accuracy—say from 95 percent to 99 percent—will have big payoffs in the time it takes you to complete documents.

(5) give the paragraphing, punctuation, and other instructions as the system needs;

Give Paragraphing, Punctuation, and Other Instructions as Needed. How much of the paragraphing, spelling, punctuation, and other mechanics you dictate depends on how well trained your system is. The more often you use the software, the more it knows your dictation style and the fewer instructions it will need. If you take care to spell out words unknown to your system in addition to training your system, it will serve you better. You can see how to dictate effectively in the following illustration.

Play Back Intelligently. Although you should try to talk through the message without interruption, you will sometimes need to stop and get a playback of what you have dictated. But do this only when necessary. More than likely, the need for a playback results from confused thinking. When you are learning to dictate, however, some confused thinking is normal. And until you gain experience, you may profit from playbacks.

● (6) play back when necessary; and

Proofread for Accuracy. You will find a playback especially helpful at the end of the message to give you a check on the overall effect of your words. Additionally, conducting playbacks while visually reading your final document will help you proofread your document for homophone errors (for example, using "there" for "their").

● (7) play back to proofread for accuracy, especially checking for homophone errors.

Illustration

Many of the preceding techniques are illustrated in the following transcript of a dictated routine email message. This example shows all the dictator's words, including punctuation, paragraphing, and corrections, that were spoken after the microphone was activated. Note that the dictator spells out words that might not be in the program's vocabulary. However, if the word were the name of a client one expected to have for a long time, the name could be added to the program for future use. Also, note that the program attempts to learn your usage patterns, even the usage of homophones. For example, if most of the time you used the word *sweet* rather than *suite,* the program would first supply *sweet.* As the software improves and as your dictation speed improves, the program may be able to select the correct word forms based on context. At first, though, careful proofreading is essential.

● Here is the exact transcript of a short confirmation message.

> Dear Payton *spell that* p-a-y-t-o-n *cap that comma new paragraph* Three crates of orchard *hyphen* fresh Florida oranges should be in your store sometime Wednesday morning as they were shipped today by Greene *spell that* g-r-e-e-n-e *cap that* motor *cap that* freight *cap that period new paragraph* As you requested in your August 29 order *comma* the three hundred sixty-one dollars and sixty cents *left paren* invoice *cap that* 14721 *right paren* was credited to your account *period new paragraph* Your customers will go for these large *comma* tasty oranges *comma* I am sure *period* They are the best we have handled in months *period new paragraph* Thanks *comma* Payton *comma* for another opportunity to serve you *period new paragraph* Sincerely *comma new line* Alex

LISTENING

Up to this point, our review of oral communication has been about sending information (talking). Certainly, this is an area in which businesspeople need help. But evidence shows that the receiving side (listening) causes more problems.

● Poor listening is a major cause of miscommunication.

The Nature of Listening

When listening is mentioned, we think primarily of the act of sensing sounds. In human communication, of course, the sounds are mainly spoken words. Viewed from a communication standpoint, however, the listening process involves the addition of filtering and remembering.

● Listening involves sensing, filtering, and remembering.

Sensing. How well we sense the words around us is determined by two factors. One factor is our ability to sense sounds—how well our ears can pick them up. As you know, we do not all hear equally well, although mechanical devices (hearing aids) can reduce our differences in this respect.

● How well we sense spoken words is determined by (1) our ability to sense sounds and

The other factor is our attentiveness to listening. More specifically, this is our mental concentration—our will to listen. Our mental concentration on the communication symbols that our senses can detect varies from moment to moment. It can range from almost totally blocking out those symbols to concentrating on them very intensely. From your own experience, you can recall moments when you were oblivious to the words

● (2) our attentiveness.

Listening Error in a Chain of Communication

Colonel to the executive officer:	"As the general feels the soldiers are unaware of the dangers of drinking impure water, he wishes to explain the matter to them. Have all personnel fall out in fatigues at 1400 hours in the battalion area, where the general will address them. In the event of rain, assemble them in the theater."
Executive officer to company commander:	"By order of the colonel, tomorrow at 1400 hours all personnel will fall out in fatigues in the battalion area if it rains to march to the theater. There the general will talk about their unawareness of the dangers of drinking."
Company commander to lieutenant:	"By order of the colonel, in fatigues the personnel will assemble at the theater at 1400 hours. The general will appear if it rains to talk about the dangers of the unawareness of drinking."
Lieutenant to sergeant:	"Tomorrow at 1400 hours the troops will assemble at the theater to hear the general talk about unawareness of drinking dangerously."
Sergeant to the enlisted personnel:	"Tomorrow at 1400 hours the drunken general will be at the theater in his underwear talking dangerously. We have to go and hear him."

spoken around you and moments when you listened with all the intensity you could muster. Most of the time, your listening fell somewhere between these extremes.

- Filtering is the process of giving symbols meanings through the unique contents of each person's mind.

Filtering. From your study of the communication process in Chapter 1, you know that interpretation enables you to give meanings to the symbols you sense. In this process, the contents of your mind serve as a sort of filter through which you give meaning to incoming messages. This filter is formed by the unique contents of your mind: your knowledge, emotions, beliefs, biases, experiences, expectations, and such. Thus, you sometimes give messages meanings different from the meanings that others give them.

- Remembering what we hear is a part of listening.

Remembering. Remembering what we hear is the third activity involved in listening. Unfortunately, we retain little of what we hear. We remember many of the comments we hear in casual conversation for only a short time—perhaps for only a few minutes or hours. Some we forget almost as we hear them. According to authorities, we even quickly forget most of the message in formal oral communications (such as speeches), remembering only a fourth after two days.

Improving Your Listening Ability

- To improve your listening, you must want to improve it.

Improving your listening is largely a matter of mental conditioning—of concentrating on the activity of sensing. You have to want to improve it, for listening is a willful act. If you are like most of us, you are often tempted not to listen or you just find it easier not to listen. We human beings tend to avoid work, and listening may be work.

- Be alert. Force yourself to pay attention.

After you have decided that you want to listen better, you must make an effort to pay attention. How you do this will depend on your mental makeup, for the effort requires disciplining the mind. You must force yourself to be alert, to pay attention to the word spoken. Active listening is one technique individuals can use successfully. It involves focusing on what is being said and reserving judgment. Other components include sitting forward and acknowledging with "um-hm" and nodding. Back-channeling is a variation of this technique that groups can use. Users leverage technologies such as chat and blogs to comment on and enhance presentations in real time, which helps keep a sharp focus on what is being said. Whatever technique you choose, improvement requires hard work.

In addition to working on the improvement of your sensing, you should work on the accuracy of your filtering. To do this, you will need to think in terms of what words mean to the speakers who use them rather than what the dictionary says they mean or what they mean in your mind. You must try to think as the speaker thinks—judging the speaker's words by the speaker's knowledge, experiences, viewpoints, and such. Like improving your sensing, improving your ability to hear what is being said requires conscious effort.

- Concentrate on improving your mental filtering.
- Think from the speaker's viewpoint.

Remembering what you hear also requires conscious effort. Certainly, there are limits to what the mind can retain, but authorities agree that few of us come close to them. By taking care to hear what is said and by working to make your filtering process give more accurate meanings to the words you hear, you add strength to the messages you receive. The result should be improved retention.

- Consciously try to remember.

In addition to the foregoing advice, various practical steps may prove helpful. Assembled in a classic document titled, "The Ten Commandments of Listening,"[2] the following list summarizes the most useful of them:

- In addition, follow these practical guidelines (summarized in italics).

1. *Stop talking.* Unfortunately, most of us prefer talking to listening. Even when we are not talking, we are inclined to concentrate on what to say next rather than on listening to others. So you must stop talking before you can listen.

2. *Put the talker at ease.* If you make the talker feel at ease, he or she will do a better job of talking. Then you will have better input to work with.

3. *Show the talker you want to listen.* If you can convince the talker that you are listening to understand rather than oppose, you will help create a climate for information exchange. You should look and act interested. Doing things like reading, looking at your watch, and looking away distracts the talker.

4. *Remove distractions.* The things you do also can distract the talker. So don't doodle, tap with your pencil, shuffle papers, or the like.

5. *Empathize with the talker.* If you place yourself in the talker's position and look at things from the talker's point of view, you will help create a climate of understanding that can result in a true exchange of information.

6. *Be patient.* You will need to allow the talker plenty of time. Remember that not everyone can get to the point as quickly and clearly as you. And do not interrupt. Interruptions are barriers to the exchange of information.

---

[2] To some anonymous author goes a debt of gratitude for these classic and often-quoted comments about listening.

7. *Hold your temper.* From our knowledge of the workings of our minds, we know that anger impedes communication. Angry people build walls between each other. They harden their positions and block their minds to the words of others.

8. *Go easy on argument and criticism.* Argument and criticism tend to put the talker on the defensive. He or she then tends to "clam up" or get angry. Thus, even if you win the argument, you lose. Rarely does either party benefit from argument and criticism.

9. *Ask questions.* By frequently asking questions, you display an open mind and show that you are listening. And you assist the talker in developing his or her message and in improving the correctness of meaning.

10. *Stop talking!* The last commandment is to stop talking. It was also the first. All the other commandments depend on it.

From the preceding review it should be clear that to improve your listening ability, you must set your mind to the task. Poor listening habits are ingrained in our makeup. We can alter these habits only through conscious effort.

THE REINFORCING ROLE OF NONVERBAL COMMUNICATION

● Nonverbal communication accounts for more of a total message than words do.

In your role of either speaker or listener in oral communication, you will need to be aware of the nonverbal—nonword—part of your communication. In both roles, nonverbal communication accounts for a larger part of the total message than do the words you send or receive. Usually, we use nonverbal communication to supplement and reinforce our words. Sometimes, nonverbal communication communicates by itself. Because it is so important to our communication, we will look at the nature of nonverbal communication and some types of it.

Nature of Nonverbal Communication

● Nonverbal (nonword) communication means all communication without words. It is broad and imprecise.

Nonverbal or nonword communication means all communication that occurs without words. As you can see, the subject is a broad one. And because it is so broad, nonverbal communication is quite vague and imprecise. For instance, a frown on someone's forehead is sometimes interpreted to mean worry. But could it be that the person has a headache? Or is the person in deep thought? No doubt, there could be numerous meanings given to the facial expression.

The number of possible meanings is multiplied even more when we consider the cross-cultural side of communication. As noted in Chapter 16, culture teaches us about body positions, movements, and various factors that affect human relationships (intimacy, space, time, and such). Thus, the meanings we give to nonverbal symbols will vary depending on how our culture has conditioned us.

● Cross-cultural aspects give many meanings to nonverbal communication.

Because of these numerous meanings, you need to be sensitive to what others intend with nonverbal communication. And you need to make some allowance for error in the meanings you receive from nonverbal symbols. As a listener, you need to go beyond the obvious to determine what nonword symbols mean. As we have said about word symbols, you need to see what people intend with their nonverbal symbols as well. Perhaps one good way to grasp the intent of this suggestion is to look at the intended meanings you have for the nonverbal symbols you use.

● Be sensitive to intended nonverbal meanings. Go beyond the obvious.

Think for a few moments about the smile on your face, a gesture, or such. What do you mean by it? What could it mean to others? Is it exactly as you intend? Could it be interpreted differently? Could someone from a different culture give a different meaning to it? Only if you look at nonverbal symbols through the prism of self-analysis and realize their multiple meaning potential can you get some idea of how they might be interpreted differently. And when you become aware of the many differences, you then can become sensitive to the meaning intended by the nonverbal communication.

● Realize that nonverbal symbols can have many meanings.

In order to become sensitive to the myriad of nonverbal symbols, we will look at some types of nonverbal communication. Specifically, we will study four types of communication that occur without words.

Types of Nonverbal Communication

Although there are many ways to classify nonverbal communication, we will examine four of the more common types: body language, space, time, and paralanguage. These four types are especially important to our discussion of speaking and listening.

● Four common types of nonverbal communication are (1) body language, (2) space, (3) time, and (4) paralanguage.

Body Language. Much of what we say to others without using words is sent through the physical movements of our bodies. When we wave our arms and fingers, wrinkle our foreheads, stand erect, smile, gaze at another, wear a coat and tie, and so on, we convey certain meanings; and others convey meanings to us in return. In particular, the face and eyes, gestures, posture, and physical appearance reflect the inner workings of emotions in our bodies.

● Our bodies send nonword messages— through arms, fingers, expressions, posture, and so on.

The face and eyes are by far the most important features of body language. We look to the face and eyes to determine much of the meaning behind body language and nonverbal communication. For example, happiness, surprise, fear, anger, and sadness usually are accompanied by definite facial expressions and eye patterns. You should be aware of these two aspects of body language as you speak and listen to others.

● The face and eyes are the most important.

Gestures are another way we send nonword messages through our body parts. *Gestures* are physical movements of our arms, legs, hands, torsos, and heads. Through the movement of each of these body parts, we can accent and reinforce our verbal messages. And we can observe how others punctuate their verbal efforts with gestures. For example, observe the hand movements of another person while he or she is talking. As you observe these gestures, you will get a good picture of the internal emotional state of the person. Moreover, speaking and gestures appear to be linked. In general, the louder someone speaks, the more emphatic the gestures used, and vice versa.

● Gestures (physical movements of the arms, legs, torso, and head) send nonword messages.

Another area of body language is physical appearance—our clothing, hair, and adornments (jewelry, cosmetics, and such). The appearance of our bodies can affect how our body movements are seen. Consider, for example, how you might perceive a speaker at a formal banquet dressed in faded blue jeans. No doubt, the speaker's gestures, facial features, posture, and such would be perceived in relation to attire. Accordingly, you want to make sure that your appearance fits the situation. And you

● Physical appearance— clothing, hair, jewelry, cosmetics, and so on—also communicates.

want to remember that appearance is an important part of the body messages that are sent and received in oral communication.

Space.

Another type of nonverbal communication involves space and how it communicates meaning in speaking and listening. How we use space and what we do in certain spaces we create tell much about us. Thus, each of us has a space language just as we do a body language. This space language is crafted by our culture.

- Space is another type of nonverbal language.

Authorities tell us that we create four different types of space: intimate (physical contact to 18 inches); personal (18 inches to 4 feet); social (4 to 12 feet); and public (12 feet to range of seeing and hearing). In each of these spaces, our communication behaviors differ and convey different meanings. For example, consider the volume of your voice when someone is 18 inches from you. Do you shout? Whisper? Now contrast the tone of your voice when someone is 12 feet away. Unquestionably, there is a difference, just because of the distance involved.

- Four types of space exist: (1) intimate, (2) personal, (3) social, and (4) public. Communication behavior differs in each.

Our behaviors in each type of space are learned from our cultures. Thus, you will need to be sensitive to the spaces of others—especially those from different cultures. As noted in Chapter 16, when people's attitudes toward space are different, their actions are likely to be misinterpreted.

- Communication behaviors are learned from cultures.

Time.

A third type of nonverbal communication involves time. Just as there are body language and space language, there is also a time language. That is, how we give meaning to time communicates to others. To illustrate, think about how you manage your daily schedule. Do you arrive early for most appointments? Do you prioritize phone calls? Do you prepare agendas for meetings? Your response to time in these ways communicates to others and, of course, others' use of time communicates to you. In terms of nonverbal communication, you should recognize that time orientations are not always the same—especially in the cross-cultural arena—but they do communicate. For Americans, Canadians, and many others from English-speaking countries, time values are monochronic. Monochronic people tend to view time as linear and always moving ahead. They expect events to happen at scheduled times. Polychronic people—such as those from Asian, Arabic, and Spanish-speaking countries—have a more indefinite view of time. Unlike the monochronic person who expects a meeting to start precisely at 9:00 AM, the polychronic person sees a 9:00 AM meeting as an objective to be accomplished if possible. Nevertheless, time orientations become parts of the messages we send to and receive from one another.

- Time is a third type of nonverbal communication.

Paralanguage.

Paralanguage, meaning "like language," is a fourth type of nonverbal communication. Of all the types, it is the closest to communication with word symbols. It has to do with the sound of a speaker's voice, the "how" of it—those hints and signals in the way words are delivered.

- Paralanguage involves *how* we say something.

To illustrate, read the following series of statements, emphasizing the underscored word in each.

I am a good communicator.

I am a good communicator.

I am a good communicator.

I am a good communicator.

I am a good communicator.

By emphasizing the underscored word in each statement, you change the meaning of that statement from the others even though you used the same words. You do so by the way in which the word sequence sounds. As another example, try counting from 1 to 10 a number of times, each time expressing a different emotional state—say anxiety, anger, or happiness. The way you state each sequence of numbers will show what you intend quite accurately.

- You can change the meaning of spoken sentences by accenting different words in each.

Paralanguage is the communication effect of the speed, pitch, volume, and connectivity of spoken words. Are they fast or slow? Are they high pitched or deep? Are they

- Paralanguage creates meanings because of speed, pitch, volume, and connection of words.

PART 5   Other Forms of Business Communication

loud and forceful or barely audible? Are they smooth or disjointed? These questions are examples of the types you would ask to analyze the nonverbal symbols of paralanguage. The symbols become a part of the meaning that is filtered from a spoken message.

Paralanguage meanings also are conveyed by consistencies and inconsistencies in what is said and how it is said. Depending on the circumstance, a person's voice may or may not be consistent with the intended word meanings. But you should make every effort to avoid inconsistencies that will send a confusing message. Consistency between the words you choose and how you deliver them to create clear meaning should be your goal.

Senders and receivers have certain expectancies about how a message should sound. Whether real or imagined, people infer background factors (race, occupation, etc.); physical appearance (age, height, gender); and personality (introversion, social orientation, etc.) when they receive and filter voice patterns. When you speak, you should do whatever you can to influence these expectancies positively. Many of the suggestions in this chapter and the following one should help you deliver a consistent and effective message. Active listeners will also want to listen between the lines of a spoken message to determine the true meaning a speaker is sending.

- Degrees of consistency between what and how someone says something convey meaning.

- Expectancies about background, appearance, and personality are part of paralanguage.

Other Types of Nonverbal Communication. Other types of nonverbal communication exist. But the preceding four types are the primary forms. For example, color communicates different meanings to us. Artists, interior decorators, and "image consultants" believe that different colors project different meanings. What meanings do you get from red, yellow, black, blue? That you can answer at all should prove that colors produce meanings in our minds. Applications of the idea to speaking and listening include visual-aid construction, wardrobe, office decor, and the like. Thus, you should give more than casual attention to color as a type of nonverbal communication. Indeed, you will want to create a specific and intended meaning with it.

- Two other nonverbal types exist, but they are minor. One is color.

Still another type of nonverbal communication involves the structure of our physical context—its layout and design. In an office, the physical arrangements—furniture, carpeting, size, location, and decorations—all communicate meaning to us and to others. These elements provide the context for many of our speaking and listening activities. As such, we should consider them as part of the messages we send and receive.

- Another is physical context—office, carpeting, decorations, and such.

SUMMARY BY LEARNING OBJECTIVES

1. Talking is the oral expression of our knowledge, viewpoints, and emotions. It depends on four critical factors:
   - Voice quality—talking with variations in pitch, delivery, and volume.
   - Speaking style—blending voice quality and personality.
   - Word choice—finding the right word or words for the listener.
   - Adaptation—fitting a message to the mind of a unique listener.

1 Discuss talking and its key elements.

2. In business, you are likely to participate in meetings, some formal and some informal.
   - If you are in charge of a meeting, follow these guidelines.
     — Know parliamentary procedure for formal meetings.
     — Plan the meeting; develop an agenda and circulate it in advance.
     — Follow the plan.
     — Keep the discussion moving.
     — Control those who talk too much.
     — Encourage participation from those who talk too little.
     — Control time, making sure the agenda is covered.
     — Summarize at appropriate times.

2 Explain the techniques for conducting and participating in meetings.

- If you are a participant at a meeting, follow these guidelines:
  — Stay with the agenda; do not stray.
  — Participate fully.
  — But do not talk too much.
  — Cooperate.
  — Be courteous.

3 Describe good phone and voice mail techniques.

3. To improve your phone and voice mail techniques, consider the following:
- Cultivate a pleasant voice.
- Talk as if in a face-to-face conversation.
- Follow courteous procedures.
  — When calling, introduce yourself and ask for the person you want.
  — State your purpose early.
  — Cover points systematically.
  — When receiving a call, identify your company or office and offer assistance.
  — When answering for the boss, do not offend by asking questions or making comments that might give a wrong impression; and do not neglect callers placed on hold.
  — When screening calls for the boss, be courteous and honest.
  — Listen when the other person is talking.
  — Do not interrupt or dominate.
  — Plan long conversations, and follow the plan.
- For good voice mail messages, follow these suggestions:
  — Identify yourself by name and affiliation.
  — Deliver a complete and accurate message.
  — Speak naturally and clearly.
  — Give important information slowly.
  — Close with a brief goodwill message.
- Demonstrate courtesy when using cell phones by following these general guidelines:
  — Turn off the ringer where it could disrupt others.
  — Avoid use at social gatherings.
  — Keep the phone off the table during meals.
  — Talk only in places where others won't be in earshot.
  — Avoid talking about confidential or private business.
  — Keep voice volume down.
  — Initiate calls in quiet places away from others.
  — Be conscious of others when you talk.
  — Avoid talking while driving, especially if it is against the law.

4 Describe the techniques of good voice input.

4. In dictating messages and reports, follow these suggestions.
- First, gather all the information you will need so you will not have to interrupt your dictating to get it.
- Next, plan (think through) the message.
- Until you are experienced, force the words to flow—then revise.
- Remember, also, to speak in a strong, clear voice.
- Give punctuation and paragraphing in the dictation.

- Play back only when necessary.
- Proofread for accuracy.

5. Listening is just as important as talking in oral communication, but it causes more problems.

5 Explain the listening problem and how to solve it.

- Listening involves how we sense, filter, and retain incoming messages.
- Most of us do not listen well because we tend to avoid the hard work that good listening requires.
- You can improve your listening with effort.
- Put your mind to it and discipline yourself to be attentive.
- Make a conscious effort to improve your mental filtering of incoming messages; strive to retain what you hear.
- Follow the practical suggestions offered in "The Ten Commandments of Listening."

6. Nonverbal (nonword) communication is the communication that occurs without words.

6 Describe the nature and role of nonverbal communication.

- One major type is body language—the movements of our arms, fingers, facial muscles, and such.
  — Our face and eyes are the most expressive parts of body language.
  — Gestures also send messages.
  — Our physical appearance (clothing, cosmetics, jewelry, hairstyle) communicates about us.
- Space is a second major type of nonverbal communication.
  — We create four unique types of spaces: (1) intimate, (2) physical, (3) social, and (4) public.
  — We communicate differently in each space, as determined by our culture.
- How we give meaning to time is a third type of nonverbal communication.
- Meanings the sounds of our voices convey (paralanguage) are a fourth type.
- Color and physical context are minor nonverbal forms.
- In our speaking, we should use nonverbal communication to accent our words.
- In listening, we need to "hear" the nonverbal communication of others.

CRITICAL THINKING QUESTIONS

1 Talking is a natural occurrence, so we should give it little attention. Discuss.

2 How do the elements of talking help us communicate better?

3 Being able to start a conversation is especially important when meeting clients in social settings. Discuss the types of topics that would and would not be appropriate.

4 The people attending a meeting—not the leader—should determine the agenda. Discuss.

5 As meetings should be democratic, everyone present should be permitted to talk as much as he or she wants without interference from the leader. Discuss.

6 Describe an annoying phone practice that you have experienced or know about (other than the ones discussed in the chapter). Explain and/or demonstrate how it should be corrected.

7 Describe the strengths and weaknesses of voice mail systems with which you are familiar.

8 Use the Internet to gather information and present a report on recent developments in voice recognition.

9 Discuss why we have difficulty in listening.

10 What can you do to improve your listening?

11 Explain how each type of nonverbal communication relates to speaking and to listening.

CRITICAL THINKING EXERCISES

Meetings

Because group meetings are meaningful only when they concern problems that the participants know about and understand, the following topics for meetings involve campus situations. For one of these topics, develop a specific problem that would warrant a group meeting. (Example: For student government, the problem might be "To determine the weaknesses of student government on this campus and what should be done to correct them.") Then lead the class (or participate) in a meeting on the topic. Class discussion following the meeting should reinforce the text material and bring out the effective and ineffective parts of the meeting.

- a. Student drinking
- b. Scholastic dishonesty
- c. Housing regulations
- d. Student–faculty relations
- e. Student government
- f. Library
- g. Grading standards
- h. Attendance policies
- i. Varsity athletics
- j. Intramural athletics
- k. Degree requirements
- l. Parking
- m. Examination scheduling
- n. Administrative policies
- o. University calendar
- p. Homework requirements
- q. Tuition and fees
- r. Student evaluation of faculty
- s. Community–college relations
- t. Maintaining files of old examinations for students
- u. Wireless Internet availability

Phoning

Make a list of bad phone practices that you have experienced or heard about. With a classmate, first demonstrate the bad practice and then demonstrate how you would handle it. Some possibilities: putting a caller on hold tactlessly, harsh greeting, unfriendly voice quality, insulting comments (unintended), attitude of unconcern, cold and formal treatment.

Dictating

Working with the voice recognition feature in Office XP or higher (or any other your instructor specifies) select a writing case from the problems following the chapters on messages, Chapters 6, 7, and 8. Then dictate a message. You may need to train the software before using it. After you have finished your dictation, proofread it carefully. Then play back the message for, review one final time.

Listening

After the class has been divided into two (or more) teams, the instructor reads some factual information (newspaper article, short story, or the like) to only one member of each team. Each of these team members tells what he or she has heard to a second team member, who in turn tells it to a third team member—and so on until the last member of each team has heard the information. The last person receiving the information reports what she or he has heard to the instructor, who checks it against the original message. The team able to report the information with the greatest accuracy wins.

Nonverbal

Using a digital camera or pictures from magazines, get three to five pictures of men and women with different facial expressions (happiness, sadness, anger, etc.) or gestures. Ask those native to your area to identify the emotions or the meanings of the gestures the pictures convey. Then ask at least three others from different countries (preferably different continents) to identify the emotions. Report your results to the class.

chapter fifteen

Public Speaking and Oral Reporting

LEARNING OBJECTIVES

Upon completing this chapter, you will be able to use good speaking and oral-reporting techniques. To reach this goal, you should be able to

1 Select and organize a subject for effective formal presentation to a specific audience.

2 Describe how personal aspects and audience analysis contribute to formal presentations.

3 Explain the use of voice quality and physical aspects such as posture, walking, facial expression, and gestures in effective oral communication.

4 Plan for visuals (graphics) to support speeches and oral reports.

5 Work effectively with a group in preparing and making a team presentation.

6 Define oral reports and differentiate between them and written reports on the basis of their advantages, disadvantages, and organization.

7 Plan and deliver effective virtual presentations.

Formal Speaking

In addition to your informal speaking and listening activities at Mastadon Chemicals, you have more formal ones involving oral communication.

Take last week, for example. Marla Cody (your boss) asked you to do something very special for the company. It seems that each year Mastadon Chemicals awards a $5,000 scholarship to a deserving business student at State University. The award is presented at the business school's annual Honors Day Convocation, usually by Ms. Cody. To show the business school's appreciation for the award, its administration requested that Ms. Cody be the speaker at this year's convocation. But Ms. Cody has a conflicting engagement, so you got the assignment. You responded to the challenge as well as you could, but you were not pleased with the results.

Then, at last month's meeting, Mastadon's executive committee asked you for a special oral report from your department for about the fifth time. This time the report concerned the results of a survey that your department conducted to determine local opinions about a dispute between Mastadon and its union. You did your best, but you felt uneasy about what you were doing.

Such assignments are becoming more and more a part of your work as you move up the administrative ladder at Mastadon. You must try to do them better, for your future promotions are involved. The following review of formal oral presentations (speeches and reports) should help you in this effort.

MAKING FORMAL SPEECHES

- Speeches are difficult for most of us. The following techniques should help you.

The most difficult kind of oral communication for many people is a formal speech. Most of us do not feel comfortable speaking before others, and we generally do a poor job of it. But it need not be this way. With effort, we can improve our speaking. We can do this by learning what good speaking techniques are and then putting those techniques into practice.

Selection of the Topic

- Your topic may be assigned.

Your first step in formal speechmaking is to determine the topic of your presentation. In some cases, you will be assigned a topic, usually one within your area of specialization. In fact, when you are asked to make a speech on a specified topic, it is likely to be because of your knowledge of the topic. In some cases, your choice of topic will be determined by the purpose of your assignment, as when you are asked to welcome a group or introduce a speaker.

- If you must select a topic, consider (1) your knowledge, (2) your audience, and (3) the occasion.

If you are not assigned a topic, then you must find one on your own. In your search for a suitable topic, you should be guided by three basic factors. The first is your background and knowledge. Any topic you select should be one with which you are comfortable—one within your areas of proficiency. The second basic factor is the interests of your audience. Selecting a topic that your audience can appreciate and understand is vital to the success of your speech. The third basic factor is the occasion of the speech. Is the occasion a meeting commemorating a historic event? A monthly meeting of an executives' club? An annual meeting of a hairstylists' association? Whatever topic you select should fit the occasion. A speech about Japanese management practices might be quite appropriate for the members of the executives' club, but not for the hairstylists. Your selection should be justified by all three factors.

Preparation of the Presentation

- Conduct research to get the information you need.

After you have decided what to talk about, you should gather the information you need for your speech. This step may involve searching through your mind for experiences or ideas, conducting research in a library or in company files, gathering information

Cornered by Mike Baldwin

2-17 © 2004 Mike Baldwin / Dist. by Universal Press Syndicate www.cornered.com
cornered@comic.com

"Which brings us to my next point."

online, or consulting people in your own company or other companies. In short, you do whatever is necessary to get the information you need.

When you have that information, you are ready to begin organizing your speech. Although variations are sometimes appropriate, you should usually follow the time-honored order of a speech: *introduction, body, conclusion*. This is the order described in the following paragraphs.

- Then organize the information.

Although not really a part of the speech, the first words usually spoken are the greeting. Your greeting, of course, should fit the audience. "Ladies and gentlemen" is appropriate for a mixed audience; "gentlemen" fits an all-male audience; and "my fellow Rotarians" fits an audience of Rotary Club members. Some speakers eliminate the greeting and begin with the speech, especially in more informal and technical presentations.

- The greeting usually comes first.

Introduction. The introduction of a speech has much the same goal as the introduction of a written report: to prepare the listeners (or readers) to receive the message. But it usually has the additional goal of arousing interest. Unless you can arouse interest at the beginning, your presentation is likely to fail. The situation is somewhat like that of the sales message. At least some of the people with whom you want to communicate are not likely to be interested in receiving your message. As you will recall from your study of listening, it is easy for a speaker to lose the audience's attention. To prove the point, ask yourself how many times your mind has drifted away from the speaker's words when you have been part of an audience. There is no question about it: You, the speaker, will have to work to gain and hold the attention of your audience.

- Gain attention in the opening.

The techniques of arousing interest are limited only by the imagination. One possibility is a human-interest story, for storytelling has strong appeal. For example, a speaker presenting a message about the opportunities available to people with original ideas might open this way: "Nearly 150 years ago, an immigrant boy of 17 walked the streets of our town. He had no food, no money, no belongings except the shabby clothes he wore. He had only a strong will to work—and an idea."

- There are many opening possibilities: human interest,

Humor, another possibility, is probably the most widely used technique. To illustrate, an investment broker might begin a speech on investment strategy as follows: "What you want me to give you today is some 'tried and trusted' advice on how to make money in the stock market. This reminds me of the proverbial 'tried and trusted' bank teller. He was trusted; and when they caught him, he was tried." Humor works best and is safest when it is closely related to the subject of your presentation.

- humor,

Other effective ways for gaining attention at the opening are by using quotations and questions. By quoting someone the audience would know and view as credible, you build interest in your topic. You also can ask questions. One kind of question is

- quotations, questions, and so on.

A Speaker's Classic Putdown of an Unruly Audience

The speaker had covered his subject carefully and thoroughly. But his conclusion, which followed logically from his presentation, was greeted with loud hisses by some members of his audience. Because hisses leave little trace of their origin, the speaker did not know who the dissenters were and could not respond directly to them. So he skillfully handled the situation by saying: "I know of only three creatures that hiss—snakes, geese, and fools. I will leave it to you to determine which of the three we have here."

the rhetorical question—the one everyone answers the same, such as "Who wants to be freed of burdensome financial responsibilities?" Another kind of question gives you background information on how much to talk about different aspects of your subject. With this kind of question, you must follow through by basing your presentation on the response. If you had asked "How many of you have IRAs?" and nearly everyone put a hand up, you wouldn't want to talk about the importance of IRAs. You could skip that part of your presentation, spending more time on another aspect, such as managing your IRA effectively.

Yet another possibility is the startling statement, which presents facts and ideas that awaken the mind. Illustrating this possibility is the beginning of a speech to an audience of merchants on a plan to reduce shoplifting: "Last year, right here in our city, in your stores, shoplifters stole over $3.5 million of your merchandise! And most of you did nothing about it."

- The opening should set up your subject.

In addition to arousing interest, your opening should lead into the theme of your speech. In other words, it should set up your message as the examples above do.

- Tell the subject of your speech . . .

Following the attention-gaining opening, it is appropriate to tell your audience the subject (theme) for your speech. In fact, in cases where your audience already has an interest in what you have to say, you can begin here and skip the attention-gaining opening. Presentations of technical topics to technical audiences typically begin this way. Whether you lead into a statement of your topic or begin with it, that statement should be clear and complete.

- unless you have reason not to, as when you must persuade.

Because of the nature of your subject, you may find it undesirable to reveal a position early. In such cases, you may prefer to move into your subject indirectly—to build up your case before revealing your position. This inductive pattern may be especially desirable when your goal is to persuade—when you need to move the views of your audience from one position to another. But in most business-related presentations you should make a direct statement of your theme early in the speech.

- Organize most speeches by factors, as you would a report.

Body. Organizing the body of your speech is much like organizing the body of a report (see Chapter 10). You take the whole and divide it into comparable parts. Then you take those parts and divide them. You continue to divide as far as it is practical to do so. In speeches, however, you are more likely to use factors rather than time, place, or quantity as the basis of division because in most speeches your presentation is likely to be built around issues and questions that are subtopics of the subject. Even so, time, place, and quantity subdivisions are possibilities.

- Emphasize transitions between parts.

You need to emphasize the transitions between the divisions because, unlike the reader who can see them, the listener may miss them if they are not stressed adequately. Without clear transitions, you may be talking about one point and your listener may be relating those ideas to your previous point.

- The ending usually (1) restates the subject, (2) summarizes key points, and (3) draws a conclusion.

Conclusion. Like most reports, the speech usually ends by drawing a conclusion. Here you bring all that you have presented to a head and achieve whatever goal the

speech has. You should consider including these three elements in your close: (1) a restatement of the subject, (2) a summary of the key points developed in the presentation, and (3) a statement of the conclusion (or main message). Bringing the speech to a climactic close—that is, making the conclusion the high point of the speech—is usually effective. Present the concluding message in strong language—in words that gain attention and will be remembered. In addition to concluding with a summary, you can give an appropriate quote, use humor, and call for action. The following close of a speech comparing Japanese and American management techniques illustrates this point: "These facts make my conclusion crystal clear. We are not Japanese. We do not have the Japanese culture. Most Japanese management methods have not worked—cannot work—will not work in our society."

Determination of the Presentation Method

With the speech organized, you are ready to prepare its presentation. At this time, you need to decide on your method of presentation—that is, whether to present the speech extemporaneously, to memorize it, or to read it.

Presenting Extemporaneously. Extemporaneous presentation is by far the most popular and effective method. With this method, you first thoroughly prepare your speech, as outlined above. Then you prepare notes and present the speech from them. You usually rehearse, making sure you have all the parts clearly in mind, but you make no attempt to memorize. Extemporaneous presentations generally sound natural to the listeners, yet they are (or should be) the product of careful planning and practice.

Memorizing. The most difficult method is memorizing. If you are like most people, you find it hard to memorize a long succession of words. And when you do memorize, you are likely to memorize words rather than meanings. Thus, when you make the speech, if you miss a word or two, you become confused—and so does your speech. You even may become panic-stricken.

Probably few of the speakers who use this method memorize the entire speech. Instead, they memorize key passages and use notes to help them through the speech. A delivery of this kind is a cross between an extemporaneous presentation and a memorized presentation.

- Choose one of these presentation methods:

- (1) extemporaneous presentation (thorough preparation, uses notes, rehearsed),

- (2) memorizing, or

Presentation Delivery Tools Help You Convey Your Message Effectively

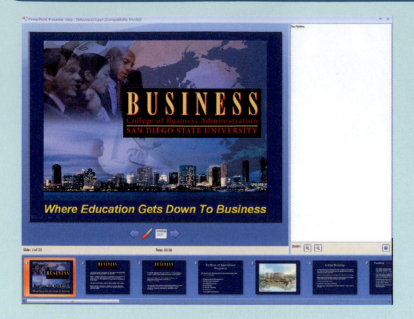

Delivery tools can help you to a better job preparing and delivering oral presentations. One tool within PowerPoint, Presenters View, should help you plan, practice, and deliver good presentations. You can see its major tools in the screenshot here. As your audience sees only the slide, you are seeing the presenter's view. You see the current slide being projected and its slide notes. Additionally, you see the title to the upcoming slide as well as the elapsed time since the beginning of the presentation. Furthermore, along the right column are several buttons that allow you to start or end the show on one click, black out that screen to bring the attention back to you, and perform other actions. As the presenter, you have the flexibility to skip slides or change the ordering on the fly. The slider bar at the bottom enables you easily to pull up slides during question and answer sessions as well.

- (3) reading.

Reading. The third presentation method is reading. Unfortunately, most of us tend to read aloud in a dull monotone. We also miss punctuation marks, fumble over words, lose our place, and so on. Of course, many speakers overcome these problems, and with effort you can, too. One effective way is to practice with a recorder and listen to yourself. Then you can be your own judge of what you must do to improve your delivery. You would be wise not to read speeches until you have mastered this presentation method. In most settings, it is a breach of etiquette to read. Your audience is likely to be insulted, and reading is unlikely to be as well received as an extemporaneous delivery. However, when you are in a position where you will be quoted widely, such as President of the United States or the CEO of a major company, reading from a carefully prepared speech is recommended. Many top executives today use teleprompters when delivering read speeches, and many of these appear well done, especially with practice.

Consideration of Personal Aspects

- A logical preliminary to speechmaking is to analyze yourself as a speaker. You are a part of the message.

A preliminary to good speechmaking is to analyze yourself as a speaker. In oral presentations you, the speaker, are a very real part of the message. The members of your audience take in not only the words you communicate but also what they see in you. And what they see in you can significantly affect the meanings that develop in their minds. Thus, you should carefully evaluate your personal effect on your message. You should do whatever you can to detect and overcome your shortcomings and to sharpen your strengths.

- You should seek the following four characteristics:

The following summary of characteristics that should help you as a speaker may prove useful, but you probably already know what they are. To some extent, the problem is recognizing whether you lack these characteristics. To a greater extent, it is doing something about acquiring them. The following review should help you pinpoint and deal with your problem areas.

Confidence. A primary characteristic of effective oral reporting is confidence—your confidence in yourself and the confidence of your audience in you. The two are complementary, for your confidence in yourself tends to produce an image that gives your audience confidence in you; and your audience's confidence in you can give you a sense of security that increases your confidence in yourself.

Typically, you earn your audience's confidence over periods of association. But there are things you can do to project an image that builds confidence. For example, preparing your presentation diligently and practicing it thoroughly gives you confidence in yourself. That confidence leads to more effective communication, which increases your listeners' confidence in you. Another confidence-building technique is an appropriate physical appearance. Unfair and illogical as it may seem, certain types of dress and hairstyles create strong images in people's minds, ranging from highly favorable to highly unfavorable. Thus, if you want to communicate effectively, you should analyze the audience you seek to reach. And you should work to develop the physical appearance that projects an image in which that audience can have confidence. Yet another confidence-building technique is simply to talk in strong, clear tones. Such tones do much to project an image of confidence. Although most people can do little to change their natural voice, they can use sufficient volume.

Sincerity. Your listeners are quick to detect insincerity. And if they detect it in you, they are likely to give little weight to what you say. On the other hand, sincerity is valuable to conviction, especially if the audience has confidence in your ability. The way to project an image of sincerity is clear and simple: You must *be* sincere. Pretense of sincerity is rarely successful.

Thoroughness. Generally, a thorough presentation is better received than a scanty or hurried presentation. Thorough coverage gives the impression that time and care have been taken, and this tends to make the presentation believable. But thoroughness can be overdone. Too much detail can drown your listeners in a sea of information. The secret is to leave out unimportant information. This, of course, requires good judgment. You must ask yourself just what your listeners need to know and what they do not need to know. Striking such a balance is the secret to achieving integrity in your presentation.

- (1) Having confidence in yourself is important. So is having the confidence of your audience.

- You must earn the confidence of your audience, project the right image, and talk in a strong, clear voice.

- (2) Sincerity is vital. You convey an image of sincerity by being sincere.

- (3) Thoroughness—giving your listeners all they need—helps your image.

Successful oral presentations to large audiences are the result of thorough preparation.

Friendliness. A speaker who projects an image of friendliness has a significant advantage in communicating. People simply like friendly people, and they are generally receptive to what such people say. Like sincerity, friendliness is hard to feign and must be honest to be effective. Most people are genuinely friendly. Some, however, are just not able to project a genuinely friendly image. With a little self-analysis and a little mirror watching as you practice speaking, you can find ways of improving your projection of your friendliness.

These are but a few of the characteristics that should assist you as a speaker. There are others: *interest, enthusiasm, originality, flexibility,* and so on. But the ones discussed are the most significant and the ones that most speakers need to work on. Through self-analysis and dedicated effort, you can improve your speaking ability.

Audience Analysis

One requirement of good speechmaking is to know your audience. You should study your audience both before and during the presentation.

Preliminary Analysis. Analyzing your audience before the presentation requires that you size it up—that you search for audience characteristics that could affect how you should present your speech.

For example, the size of your audience is likely to influence how formal or informal your speech should be. As a rule, large audiences require more formality. Personal characteristics of your audience, such as age, gender, education, experience, and knowledge of subject matter, also should influence how you make your speech—affecting the words, illustrations, and level of detail you use. Like writing, speeches should be adapted to the audience. And the more you know about the audience, the better you will adapt your presentation to them.

Analysis during Presentation. Your audience analysis should continue as you make the speech. *Feedback* is information about how your listeners are receiving your words. Armed with this information, you can adjust your presentation to improve the communication result.

Your eyes and ears will give you feedback information. For example, facial expressions will tell you how your listeners are reacting to your message. Smiles, blank stares, and movements will give you an indication of whether they understand, agree with, or accept it. You can detect from sounds coming (or not coming) from them whether they are listening. If questions are in order, you can learn directly how your message is coming across. In general, you can learn much from your audience by being alert; and what you learn can help you make a better speech.

Appearance and Physical Actions

As your listeners hear your words, they are looking at you. What they see is a part of the message and can affect the success of your speech. What they see, of course, is you and what surrounds you. In your efforts to improve the effects of your oral presentations, you should understand the communication effects of what your listeners see. Some of the effects that were mentioned in Chapter 14 are expanded on here because they are particularly important to speeches and oral reports.

The Communication Environment. Much of what your audience sees is the physical things that surround you as you speak: the stage, lighting, background, and so on. These things tend to create a general impression. Although not visual, outside noises have a related influence. For the best communication results, the factors in your communication environment should contribute to your message, not detract from it. Your own experience as a listener will tell you what factors are important.

Personal Appearance. Your personal appearance is a part of the message your audience receives. Of course, you have to accept the physical traits you have, but most of us do not need to be at a disadvantage in appearance. All that is necessary is to use what you have appropriately. Specifically, you should dress in a manner appropriate for the audience and the occasion. Be clean and well groomed. Use facial expressions and physical movements to your advantage. Just how you should use facial expressions and physical movements is described in the following paragraphs.

Posture. Posture is likely to be the most obvious of the things that your audience sees in you. Even listeners not close enough to detect such things as facial expressions and eye movements can see the general form of the body.

● (3) your posture,

You probably think that no one needs to tell you about good posture. You know it when you see it. The trouble is that you are not likely to see it in yourself. One solution is to have others tell you whether your posture needs improvement. Another is to practice speaking before a mirror or watch yourself on video.

In your efforts to improve your posture, keep in mind what must go on within your body to form a good posture. Your body weight must be distributed in a way consistent with the impression you want to make. You should keep your body erect without appearing stiff and comfortable without appearing limp. You should maintain a poised, alert, and communicative bearing. And you should do all this naturally. The great danger with posture is an appearance of artificiality.

Walking. Your audience also forms an impression from the way you walk before it. A strong, sure walk to the speaker's position conveys an impression of confidence. Hesitant, awkward steps convey the opposite impression. Walking during the presentation can be good or bad, depending on how you do it. Some speakers use steps forward and to the side to emphasize points. Too much walking, however, attracts attention and detracts from the message. You would be wise to walk only when you are reasonably sure that this will have the effect you want. You would not want to walk away from a microphone.

● (4) your manner of walking,

Facial Expression. As noted in Chapter 14, probably the most apparent and communicative physical movements are facial expressions. The problem, however, is that you may unconsciously use facial expressions that convey unintended meanings. For example, if a frightened speaker tightens the jaw unconsciously and begins to grin, the effect may be an ambiguous image that detracts from the entire communication effort. A smile, a grimace, and a puzzled frown all convey clear messages. Of course, you should choose those expressions that best convey your intended meaning.

● (5) facial expressions (smiles, frowns, eye contact), and

Eye contact is important. The eyes, which have long been considered "mirrors of the soul," provide most listeners with information about the speaker's sincerity, goodwill, and flexibility. Some listeners tend to shun speakers who do not look at them. On the other hand, discriminate eye contact tends to show that you have a genuine interest in your audience.

Gestures. Like posture, gestures contribute to the message you communicate. Just what they contribute, however, is hard to say, for they have no definite or clear-cut meanings. A clenched fist, for example, certainly adds emphasis to a strong point. But it also can be used to show defiance, make a threat, or signify respect for a cause. And so it is with other gestures. They register vague meanings, as discussed in Chapter 14.

● (6) gestures.

Even though gestures have vague meanings, they are strong, natural helps to speaking. It appears natural, for example, to emphasize a plea with palms up and to show disagreement with palms down. Raising first one hand and then the other reinforces a division of points. Slicing the air with the hand shows several divisions. Although such gestures are generally clear, we do not all use them in exactly the same way.

● Gestures have vague meanings, but they communicate.

In summary, it should be clear that physical movements can help your speaking. Just which physical movements you should use, however, is hard to say. The appropriateness of physical movements is related to personality, physical makeup, and the size and nature of the audience. A speaker appearing before a formal group should generally use relatively few physical movements. A speaker appearing before an informal

● In summary, your physical movements help your speaking.

group should use more. Which physical movements you should use on a given occasion is a matter for your best judgment.

Use of Voice

● Good voice is a requirement of good speaking. Four faults affect voice:

Good voice is an obvious requirement of good speaking. Like physical movements, the voice should not hinder the listener's concentration on the message. More specifically, it should not detract attention from the message. Voices that cause such difficulties generally fall into these areas of fault: (1) lack of pitch variation, (2) lack of variation in speed, (3) lack of vocal emphasis, and (4) unpleasant voice quality. Although these areas are mentioned in Chapter 14, we will examine them here because of their key significance to formal oral communication.

● (1) lack of variation in pitch (usually a matter of habit),

Lack of Pitch Variation. Speakers who talk in monotones are not likely to hold the interest of their listeners for long. Since most voices are capable of wide variations in pitch, the problem usually can be corrected. The failure to vary pitch generally is a matter of habit—of voice patterns developed over years of talking without being aware of their effect.

● (2) lack of variation in speed (cover the simple quickly, the hard slowly),

Lack of Variation in Speaking Speed. Determining how fast to talk is a major problem. As a general rule, you should present the easy parts of your message at a fairly fast rate and the hard parts and the parts you want to emphasize at a slower rate. The reason for varying the speed of presentation should be apparent: it is more interesting. A slow presentation of easy information is irritating; hard information presented fast may be difficult to understand.

A problem related to the pace of speaking is the incorrect use of pauses. Properly used, pauses emphasize upcoming subject matter and are effective means of gaining attention. But frequent pauses for no reason are irritating and break the listeners' concentration. Pauses become even more irritating when the speaker fills them in with distracting nonwords such as *uh, like, you know,* and *OK.*

● (3) lack of vocal emphasis (gain emphasis by varying pitch, pace, and volume), and

Lack of Vocal Emphasis. A secret of good speaking is to give words their proper emphasis by varying the manner of speaking. You can do this by (1) varying the pitch of your voice, (2) varying the pace of your presentation, and (3) varying the volume of your voice. As the first two techniques have already been discussed, only the use of voice volume requires comment here.

You must talk loudly enough for your entire audience to hear you, but not too loudly. Thus, the loudness—voice volume—for a large audience should be greater than that for a small audience. Regardless of audience size, however, variety in voice volume is good for interest and emphasis. It produces contrast, which is one way of emphasizing the subject matter. Some speakers incorrectly believe that the only way to show emphasis is to get louder and louder. But you can also show emphasis by going from loud to soft. The contrast with what has gone on earlier provides the emphasis. Again, variety is the key to making the voice more effective.

● (4) unpleasant voice (improvement is often possible).

Unpleasant Voice Quality. It is a hard fact of communication that some voices are more pleasant than others. Fortunately, most voices are reasonably pleasant. But some are raspy, nasal, or unpleasant in another way. Although therapy often can improve such voices, some speakers must live with them. But concentrating on variations in pitch, speed of delivery, and volume can make even the most unpleasant voice acceptable.

● You can correct the foregoing faults through self-analysis and work.

Improvement through Self-Analysis and Imitation. You can overcome any of the foregoing voice faults through self-analysis. In this day of audio and video recorders, it is easy to hear and see yourself talk. Since you know good speaking when you hear it, you should be able to improve your vocal presentation. One of the best ways to improve your presentation skills is through watching others. Watch your

This Mark Twain story carries a vital message for windy speakers:

> Some years ago in Hartford, we all went to church one hot sweltering night to hear the annual report of Mr. Hawley, a city missionary who went around finding people who needed help and didn't want to ask for it. He told of the life in cellars, where poverty resided; he gave instances of the heroism and devotion of the poor. "When a man with millions gives," he said, "we make a great deal of noise. It's noise in the wrong place, for it's the widow's mite that counts." Well, Hawley worked me up to a great pitch. I could hardly wait for him to get through. I had $400 in my pocket. I wanted to give that and borrow more to give. You could see greenbacks in every eye. But instead of passing the plate then, he kept on talking and talking, and as he talked it grew hotter and hotter, and we grew sleepier and sleepier. My enthusiasm went down, down, down, down—$100 at a clip—until finally, when the plate did come around, I stole ten cents out of it. It all goes to show how a little thing like this can lead to crime.

instructors, your peers, television personnel, professional speakers, and anyone else who gives you an opportunity. Today you can even watch top corporate executives on webcasts and video presentations. Analyze these speakers to determine what works for them and what does not. Imitate those good techniques that you think would help you and avoid the bad ones. Take advantage of any opportunity you have to practice speaking.

Use of Visuals

The spoken word is severely limited in communicating. Sound is here briefly and then gone. A listener who misses the vocal message may not have a chance to hear it again. Because of this limitation, speeches often need strong visual support: slides with talking points, charts, tables, film, and the like. Visuals may be as vital to the success of a speech as the words themselves.

- Visuals can sometimes help overcome the limitations of spoken words.

Proper Use of Design. Effective visuals are drawn from the message. They fit the one speech and the one audience.

- Use visuals for the hard parts of the message.

In selecting visuals, you should search through your presentation for topics that appear vague or confusing. Whenever a visual of some kind will help eliminate vagueness or confusion, you should use it. You should use visuals to simplify complex information and improve cohesiveness, as well as to emphasize or add interest. Visuals are truly a part of your message, and you should look at them as such.

After deciding that a topic deserves visual help, you determine what form that help should take. That is, should the visual be an outline, a chart, a diagram, a picture, or what? You should select your visuals primarily on the basis of their ability to communicate content. Simple and obvious as this suggestion may appear, people violate it all too often. They select visuals more for appearance and dramatic effect than for communication effect.[1]

- Use the type of visual (outline, chart, diagram, picture) that communicates the information best.

Types to Consider. Because no one type of visual is best for all occasions, you should have a flexible attitude toward visuals. You should know the strengths and weaknesses of each type, and you should know how to use each type effectively.

In selecting visuals, you should keep in mind the available types. You will mainly consider the various types of graphics—the charts, line graphs, tables, diagrams, and pictures—discussed in Chapter 13. Each of these types has its strengths and weaknesses and can be displayed in various ways, generally classified as nonprojected or

- Select from the various available types of visuals.

---

[1] For a revealing review on the strengths and weaknesses of slideware, see "Learning to Love PowerPoint" by David Byrne and "Power Corrupts. PowerPoint Corrupts. Absolutely." by Edward R. Tufte, both in *Wired,* September 2003.

projected. Nonprojected techniques include such media as posters, flip charts, models, handouts, and such; projected techniques include slides, transparencies, computer projections, and such.

Audience Size, Cost, and Ease of Preparation Considerations. Your choice of visuals also should be influenced by the audience size and formality, the cost of preparing and using the media (visuals), and the ease and time of preparation. The table below illustrates how the different media fare on these dimensions, helping guide you to the best choice for your particular needs.

	Media	Image Quality	Audience Size	Cost	Ease of Preparation
Nonprojected	Poster	Very good	Small	$$	Medium
	Flip chart	Good	Small	$	Short
	Presentation board	Good	Small	$	Short
	Real object or model	Very good	Small	$–$$$$	Short to long
	Chalkboard or whiteboard	Fair	Medium	$	None
	Photos	Very good	Medium	$$	Short to medium
	Handouts	Excellent	Large	$–$$	Short to long
Projected	35mm slides	Very good	Large	$	Medium
	Overhead transparencies	Very good	Medium	$	Short
	Visual presenters	Very good	Medium	None	None
	TVs/VCRs	Excellent	Medium to large	$–$$$$	Short to long
	Computer projection	Very good	Medium to large	None	Short to long

• Make the visuals points of interest in your presentation.

Techniques in Using Visuals. Visuals usually carry key parts of the message. Thus, they are points of emphasis in your presentation. You blend them in with your words to communicate the message. How you do this is to some extent an individual matter, for techniques vary. They vary so much, in fact, that it would be hard to present a meaningful summary of them. It is more meaningful to present a list of dos and don'ts. Such a list follows:

• Here are specific suggestions for using visuals.

- Make certain that everyone in the audience can see the visuals. Too many or too-light lines on a chart, for example, can be hard to see. An illustration that is too small can be meaningless to people far from the speaker. Even fonts must be selected and sized for visibility.

- Explain the visual if there is any likelihood that it will be misunderstood.

- Organize the visuals as a part of the presentation. Fit them into the presentation plan.

- Emphasize the visuals. Point to them with physical action and words. Use laser presenter tools and slide animations to emphasize. Most presentation software and tablet PCs let you annotate slides easily.

- Talk to the audience—not to the visuals. Look at the visuals only when the audience should look at them. When you want the audience to look at you, you can regain attention by covering the visual or making the screen in PowerPoint white or black (toggle the W or B keys).

- Avoid blocking the listeners' views of the visuals. Make certain that the listeners' views are not blocked by lecterns, pillars, chairs, and such. Take care not to stand in anyone's line of vision.

A Summary List of Speaking Practices

• This review has covered the high points of speaking.

The foregoing review of business speaking has been selective, for the subject is broad. In fact, entire books have been devoted to it. But this review has covered the high points, especially those that you can easily transfer into practice. Perhaps even more practical is the following list of what to do and not to do in speaking.

- Organize the speech so that it leads the listeners' thoughts logically to the conclusion.

- Use language specifically adapted to the audience.

- Articulate clearly, pleasantly, and with proper emphasis. Avoid mumbling and the use of nonwords such as *ah, er, uh, like* and *OK*.

- Speak correctly, using accepted grammar and pronunciation.

- Maintain an attitude of alertness, displaying appropriate enthusiasm and confidence.

- Employ body language to best advantage. Use it to emphasize points and to assist in communicating concepts and ideas.

- Be relaxed and natural. Avoid stiffness or rigidity of physical action.

- Look the listeners in the eye and talk directly to them.

- Keep still. Avoid excessive movements, fidgeting, and other signs of nervousness.

- Punctuate the presentation with reference to visuals. Make them a part of the speech text.

- Even when faced with hostile questions or remarks, keep your temper. To lose your temper is to lose control of the presentation.

- Move surely and quickly to the conclusion. Do not leave a conclusion dangling, repeat unnecessarily, or appear unable to close.

• This summary checklist of good and bad speaking practices should prove helpful.

TEAM (COLLABORATIVE) PRESENTATIONS

Another type of presentation you may be asked to give is a group or team presentation. To give this type of presentation, you will need to use all you have learned about giving individual speeches. Also, you will need to use many of the topics discussed in Chapter 10 on collaborative writing groups. But you will need to adapt the ideas to an oral presentation setting. Some of the adaptations should be obvious. We will mention others to which you should give special thought in your team presentation.

• Group presentations require individual speaking skills plus planning for collaboration. Adapt the ideas on collaborative writing in Chapter 10 to team presentations.

First, you will need to take special care to plan the presentation—to determine the sequence of the presentation as well as the content of each team member's part. You also will need to select carefully supporting examples to build continuity from one part of the presentation to the next.

• Plan for the order of the presentation and each member's part.

Groups should plan for the physical aspects of the presentation, too. You should coordinate the type of delivery, use of notes, graphics, and styles and colors of attire to present a good image of competence and professionalism. And you should plan transitions so that the team will appear coordinated.

• Plan for the physical factors.

Another presentation aspect—physical staging—is important as well. Team members should know where to sit or stand, how visuals will be handled, how to change or adjust microphones, and how to enter and leave the speaking area.

• Plan for the physical staging.

Attention to the close of the presentation is especially strategic. Teams need to decide who will present the close and what will be said. If a summary is used, the member who presents it should attribute key points to appropriate team members. If there is to be a question-and-answer session, the team should plan how to conduct it. For example, will one member take the questions and direct them to a specific team member? Or will the audience be permitted to ask questions to specific members? Some type of final note of appreciation or thanks needs to be planned with all the team nodding in agreement or acknowledging the final comment in some way.

• Plan for the close.

In all of their extra planning activities, teams should not overlook the need to plan for rehearsal time. Teams should consider practicing the presentation in its entirety several times as a group before the actual presentation. During these rehearsals, individual members should critique thoroughly each other's contributions, offering specific ways to improve. After first rehearsal sessions, outsiders (nonteam members) might be asked

• Plan to rehearse the presentation.

to view the team's presentation and critique the group. Moreover, the team might consider videotaping the presentation so that all members can evaluate it. In addition to a more effective presentation, the team can enjoy the by-products of group cohesion and *esprit de corps* by rehearsing the presentation. Successful teams know the value of rehearsing and will build such activity into their presentation planning schedules.

These points may appear trivial, but careful attention to them will result in a polished, coordinated team presentation.

REPORTING ORALLY

- The oral report is a form of speech.

A special form of speech is the oral report. You are more likely to make oral reports than speeches in business, and the oral reports you make are likely to be important to you. Unfortunately, most of us have had little experience and even less instruction in oral reporting. Thus, the following review should be valuable to you.

A Definition of Oral Reports

- An oral report is defined as an oral presentation of factual information.

In its broadest sense, an oral report is any presentation of factual information and its interpretation using the spoken word. A business oral report would logically limit coverage to factual business information. By this definition, oral business reports cover much of the information and analysis exchanged daily in the conduct of business. They vary widely in formality. At one extreme, they cover the most routine and informal reporting situations. At the other, they include highly formal and proper presentations. Because the more informal oral exchanges are little more than routine conversations, the emphasis in the following pages is on the more formal ones. Clearly, these are the oral reports that require the most care and skill and are the most deserving of study.

Differences between Oral and Written Reports

- Oral reports differ from written reports in three ways:

Oral reports are much like written reports, so there is little need to repeat much of the previously presented material on reports. Instead, we will focus on the most significant differences between oral and written reports. Three in particular stand out.

Visual Advantages of the Written Word. The first significant difference between oral and written reports is that writing permits greater use of visuals to communicate than does speaking. With writing, you can use paragraphing to show readers the structure of the message and to make the thought units stand out. In addition, you can use punctuation to help show relationships, subordination, and qualification. These techniques improve the communication effect of the entire message.

On the other hand, when you make an oral presentation, you cannot use any of these techniques. However, you can use techniques peculiar to oral communication. For example, you can use inflection, pauses, volume emphasis, and changes in the rate of delivery. Depending on the situation, the techniques used in both oral and written reports are effective in assisting communication. But the point is that the techniques are different.

● (1) writing and speaking have unique advantages and disadvantages;

Reader Control of Written Presentation. A second significant difference between oral and written reports is that the readers of a written report, unlike the listeners to an oral report, control the pace of the communication. They can pause, reread, change their rate of reading, or stop as they choose. Since the readers set the pace, writing can be complex and still communicate. However, since the listeners to an oral report cannot control the pace of the presentation, they must grasp the intended meaning as the speaker presents the words. Because of this limiting factor, good oral reporting must be relatively simple.

● (2) the speaker controls the pace of an oral report, and the reader controls the pace of a written report; and

Emphasis on Correctness in Writing. A third significant difference between oral and written reports is the different degrees of correctness that they require. Because written reports are likely to be inspected carefully, you are likely to work for a high degree of correctness when you prepare them. That is, you are likely to follow carefully the recognized rules of grammar, punctuation, sentence structure, and so on. When you present oral reports, on the other hand, you may be more lax about following these rules. One reason is that usually oral reports are not recorded for others to inspect at their leisure. Another is that oral communication standards of correctness are less rigid than written communication standards. This statement does not imply that you should avoid good language in oral communication, however.

● (3) written reports place more stress on correctness.

The differences between writing and speaking—visual aspects, reader control, and correctness—can become planning parts to improve your oral report. You will need to identify the advantages of written reports and compensate for their lack in your oral report. Such a process is an essential preliminary step to the actual planning of oral reports.

Planning the Oral Report

As with written reports, planning is the logical first step in your work on oral reports. For short, informal oral reports, planning may be minimal. But for the more formal oral reports, particularly those involving audiences of more than one, proper planning is likely to be as involved as that for a comparable written report.

● Planning is the first step in preparing oral reports.

Determination of Report Objective. Logically, your first task in planning an oral report is to determine your objective. As prescribed for the written report in Chapter 10, you should state the report objective in clear, concise language. Then you should clearly state the factors involved in achieving this objective. This procedure gives you a guide to the information you must gather and to the framework around which you will build your presentation.

In determining your report objective, you must be aware of your general objective. That is, you must decide on your general purpose in making the presentation. Is it to persuade? To inform? To recommend? This decision will have a major influence on your development of material for presentation and perhaps even on the presentation itself.

● First determine the objective and what must be done to reach it.

Organization of Content. The procedure for organizing oral reports is similar to that for organizing written reports. You have the choice of using either the direct or indirect order. Even so, the same information is not necessarily presented in the same way orally and in writing. Time pressure, for example, might justify direct presentation for an oral report on a problem that, presented in writing, might be better arranged in the indirect order. Readers in a hurry can always skip to the conclusion or ending of the report. Listeners do not have this choice.

Although oral reports may use either the direct or indirect order, the indirect is the most logical order and by far the more widely used order. Because your audience is not likely to know the problem well, introductory remarks are needed to prepare it to receive your message. In addition, you may need such remarks to arouse interest, stimulate curiosity, or impress the audience with the importance of the subject. The main goals of the introductory remarks are to state the purpose, define unfamiliar terms, explain limitations, describe scope, and generally cover all the necessary introductory subjects (see discussion of the report introduction, Chapter 11).

In the body of the oral report, you should work toward the objective you have set. Here, too, the oral report closely resembles the written report. Division of subject matter into comparable parts, logical order, introductory paragraphs, concluding paragraphs, and the like are equally important to both forms.

The major difference in the organization of the written and the oral report is in the ending. Both forms may end with a conclusion, a recommendation, a summary, or a combination of the three. But the oral report is likely to have a final summary, whether or not it has a conclusion or a recommendation. In a sense, this final summary serves the purpose of an executive summary by bringing together all the really important information, analyses, conclusions, and recommendations in the report. It also assists the memory by emphasizing the points that should stand out. Oral and nonverbal emphasis techniques should help your audience remember your key points.

PRESENTING VIRTUALLY

One new venue for oral presentations is the virtual or online venue. While videoconferencing has been around for years, several factors seem to be driving the use of this technology now. Some of these factors are negative—high costs of travel in both dollars and time and widely dispersed business operations. But there are positives working as well, including both better technology and high speed networks. With better hardware and more widely accessible connections to the Internet, several companies have developed easy-to-use, web-based applications. WebEx, once the defacto standard in this area, now has competitors with such products as Citrix's GoToMeeting, Microsoft's Live Meeting, Marcomedia's Breeze, Horizon's Wimba, and more. And the affordable costs make this technology attractive to both large and small businesses for presentations to both large and small audiences.

Understanding the nature of this technology, the differences between virtual and face-to-face presentations, and some techniques to use with it will become more important as its use in business grows.

A Definition of Virtual Presentations

A virtual presentation is one usually delivered from a desktop over the Internet to an audience located anywhere in the world where there is Internet access. While it could be delivered with both audio and video components, so the audience could see and hear the presenter, about 80 percent of today's users view PowerPoint slides on the Internet and listen over a phone line. Usually no other special hardware or costly software is needed. These presentations can also be recorded, allowing audiences to view them at different times as well at different places.

Virtual presentations are being used in businesses in many of the same ways face-to-face presentations are used—to inform and to persuade. They can improve productivity by giving even remote employees up-to-date information and training, avoiding down time for travel and reducing travel costs. They can allow sales people to reach broader audiences as well as highly targeted specialized audiences worldwide.

Differences between Face-to-Face and Virtual Presentations

The major difference between face-to-face and virtual presentations is that the dynamics have changed—the speaker cannot see the audience and sometimes the audience cannot see the speaker. Some argue that being able to see the presenter is not critical, and the technology has given us some tools to help the speaker get feedback from the audience. In Figure 15–1, you can see some of the tools available to the viewer using Microsoft's LiveMeeting. Each viewer can configure the screen to his or her preference.

- Virtual presenters cannot see their audience; most audiences today do not see the presenter.

For this particular meeting the presenter loaded a still picture of himself, which many viewers appreciate. The list of attendees shows that 545 people are present and gives their sign-on names. It also shows a seating chart with most of the audience indicating in green that the speaker should proceed; however, there is a significant number of red boxes turned on, indicating that some want the presenter to slow down. Also, it includes a chat box for real-time questions and answers. Obviously, the speaker cannot present and type answers to questions at the same time, so this feature is usually used when an assistant is available. And the predominant window here is the slide being discussed. Viewers often run this window at full screen size, toggling back to the other tools as needed. Presenters can also poll the audience during a presentation and display the results immediately.

To deliver a virtual presentation effectively, a presenter needs to do some preliminary, delivery, and closing activities. First is to choose a user-friendly, simple technology. Then send out announcements of the presentation along with a note encouraging the audience to pretest their systems before the designated start time for the presentation. If needed, you might want to arrange to have a technical person on hand to troubleshoot, anticipating that some will have trouble connecting, others will fall behind, and occasionally your time will expire. With a technical person on hand, these typical problems can be resolved quickly. Also, you'll need to arrange ahead of time for an assistant if you need one. And you need to create something for early arrivers at your presentation to view in the first 5 to 10 minutes before you start. This could be an announcement, news of an upcoming presentation, or information about your products and services. You will also want to tell participants where additional information is available, including your slides, video recording of the presentation, and other business links.

- Effective virtual presenters employ some unique preliminary, delivery, and closing techniques.

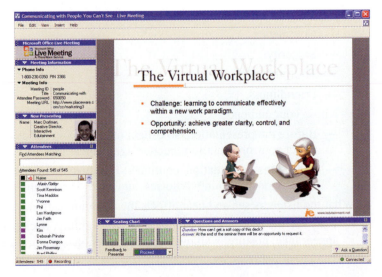

Figure 15–1

Microsoft's LiveMeeting has several tools that can enhance the interaction between the speaker and audience.

- Effective virtual presenters often use a variety of technological tools to keep their audiences attention.

- Effective virtual presenters manage the timing carefully.

The delivery of your presentation will be much like that for other presentations, except you will be doing it from your desktop using a headphone. You may want to use the highlighter or an animation effects tool in PowerPoint to help you emphasize key points that you would otherwise physically point to in a face-to-face presentation. You will want to plan breaks where you will poll or quiz the audience or handle questions that have come in through the chat tool. If you use the presenter's view in PowerPoint, you can set the timer to help you do this at regular intervals as well as gauge the timing through the questions and speed feedback.

In the closing, you will want to allow time to evaluate the success of your presentation as well as to handle questions and answers. Watching your time is critical because some systems will drop you if you exceed your requested time.

Overall, presenting virtually requires the same keys to success as other presentations—careful planning, attentive delivery, and practice.

SUMMARY BY LEARNING OBJECTIVES

1 Select and organize a subject for effective formal presentation to a specific audience.

1. Consider the following suggestions in selecting and organizing a speech.
   - Begin by selecting an appropriate topic—one in your area of specialization and of interest to your audience.
   - Organize the message (probably by introduction, body, conclusion).
   - Consider an appropriate greeting ("Ladies and Gentlemen," "Friends").
   - Design the introduction to meet these goals:
     — Arouse interest with a story, humor, or such.
     — Introduce the subject (theme).
     — Prepare the reader to receive the message.
   - Use indirect order presentation to persuade and direct order for other cases.
   - Organize like a report: divide and subdivide, usually by factors.
   - Select the most appropriate ending, usually restating the subject and summarizing.
   - Consider using a climactic close.
   - Choose the best manner of presentation.
     — Extemporaneous is usually best.
     — Memorizing is risky.
     — Reading is difficult unless you are skilled.

2 Describe how personal aspects and audience analysis contribute to formal presentations.

2. To improve your speaking, take these steps:
   - Work on these characteristics of a good speaker:
     — Confidence.
     — Sincerity.
     — Thoroughness.
     — Friendliness.
   - Know your audience.
     — Before the presentation, size them up—looking for characteristics that affect your presentation (gender, age, education).
     — During the presentation, continue to analyze them, looking at facial expressions, listening to noises, and such—and adapt to them.

3 Explain the use of voice quality and physical aspects such as posture, walking, facial expression, and gestures in effective oral communication.

3. What the listeners see and hear affects the communication.
   - They see the physical environment (stage, lighting, background), personal appearance, posture, walking, facial expressions, gestures, and such.
   - They hear your voice.

— For best effect, vary the pitch and speed.

— Give appropriate vocal emphasis.

— Cultivate a pleasant quality.

4. Use visuals whenever they help communicate.

- Select the types that do the best job.

- Blend the visuals into your speech, making certain that the audience sees and understands them.

- Organize your visuals as a part of your message.

- Emphasize the visuals by pointing to them.

- Talk to the audience, not the visuals.

- Do not block your audience's view of the visuals.

4 Plan for visuals to support speeches and oral reports.

5. Group presentations have special problems.

- They require all the skills of individual presentation.

- In addition, they require extra planning to

— Reduce overlap and provide continuity.

— Provide smooth transitions between presentations.

— Coordinate questions and answers.

5 Work effectively with a group in preparing and making a team presentation.

6. Business oral reports are spoken communications of factual business information and its interpretation.

- Written and oral reports differ in three significant ways.

— Written reports permit more use of visual helps to communication (paragraphing, punctuation, and such); oral reports allow voice inflection, pauses, and the like.

— Oral reports permit the speaker to exercise greater control over the pace of the presentation; readers of a written report control the pace.

— Written reports place more emphasis on writing correctness (grammar, punctuation, etc.).

- Plan oral reports just as you do written ones.

— First, determine your objective and state its factors.

— Next, organize the report, using either indirect or direct order.

— Divide the body based on your purpose, keeping the divisions comparable and using introductory/concluding paragraphs, logical order, and the like.

— End the report with a final summary—a sort of ending executive summary.

6 Define oral reports and differentiate between them and written reports on the basis of their advantages, disadvantages, and organization.

7. Advances in hardware and software along with increases in broadband speeds and Internet access have spawned the growth of virtual presentations in business.

- In virtual presentations the speaker cannot see the audience and often the audience cannot see the speaker. But today's software helps bridge this gap.

- Before delivering a virtual presentation, the speaker should plan for the technology being used, announcements mailed to the audience ahead of the meeting, system testing, assistance for presentation support from technical and non-technical sides, and material for early arrivers to view.

- During the delivery, the speaker should plan intereaction with polling or quizzing, take regular breaks for feedback and questions, and be attentive to the feedback from the audience on speed of delivery.

- In closing, the speaker should allow ample time for both questions and evaluation.

- Overall, the virtual presentation like the face-to-face presentation requires planning, attentive delivery, and practice.

7 Plan and deliver presentations virtually.

1 Assume that you must prepare a speech on the importance of making good grades for an audience of college students. Develop some attention-gaining ideas for the introduction of this speech. Do the same for a climactic close for the speech.

2 When is an extemporaneous presentation desirable? When should a speech be read? Discuss.

3 Explain how a speaker's personal characteristics influence the meanings of his or her spoken words.

4 An employee presented an oral report to an audience of 27 middle- and upper-level administrators. Then she presented the same information to three top executives. Note some of the probable differences between the two presentations.

5 Explain how feedback can be used in making a speech.

6 One's manner of dress, choice of hairstyle, physical characteristics, and the like are personal. They should have no influence on any form of oral communication. Discuss.

7 By description (or perhaps by example), identify good and bad postures and walking practices for speaking.

8 Explain how facial expressions can miscommunicate.

9 Give some illustrations of gestures that can be used to communicate more than one meaning. Demonstrate them.

10 "We are born with voices—some good, some bad, and some in between. We have no choice but to accept what we have been given." Comment.

11 What should be the determining factors in the use of visuals (graphics)?

12 Discuss (or demonstrate) some good and bad techniques of using visuals.

13 In presenting an oral report to a group composed of fellow workers as well as some bosses, a worker is harassed by the questions of a fellow worker who is trying to embarrass him. What advice would you give the worker? Would your advice be different if the critic were one of the bosses? What if the speaker were a boss and the critic a worker? Discuss.

14 Give examples of ways a team could provide continuity between members through the use of supporting examples. Be specific.

15 Explain the principal differences between written and oral reports.

16 Compare the typical organization plans of oral and written reports. Note the major differences between the two kinds of plans.

17 Explain the principal differences between face-to-face and virtual presentations.

Speeches (face-to-face or Virtual)

Since a speech can be made on almost any topic, it is not practical to list topics for speeches. You or your instructor can generate any number of interesting and timely topics in a short time. Whatever topic you select, you will need to determine the goals clearly, to work out the facts of the situation, and to set a time limit.

Oral Reports

Most of the written report problems presented in the problem section following Chapter 11 also can serve as oral report problems. The following problems, however, are especially suitable for oral presentation.

1 Survey the major business publications for information about the outlook for the national (or world) economy for the coming year. Then present a summary report to the directors of Allied Department Stores, Inc.

2 Select a current technological innovation for business use and report it to a company's top administrators (you select the company). You will describe the innovation and point out how it will benefit the company. If appropriate, you may recommend its purchase.

3 Report to a meeting of a wildlife-protection organization on the status of an endangered species. You will need to gather the facts through research, probably in wildlife publications.

4 A national chain of _____ (your choice) is opening an outlet in your city. You have been assigned the task of reviewing site possibilities. Gather the pertinent information and make an oral recommendation to the board of directors.

5 The Future Business Leaders Club at your old high school has asked you to report to it on the nature and quality of business study at your college. You will

cover all the factors that you think high school students need to know. Include visuals in your presentation.

6 As representative of a travel agency, present a travel package on _____ (place or places of your choice) to the members of the Adventurer Travel Club. You will describe places to be visited, and you will cover all the essential details: dates, hotels, guide service, meals, costs, manner of travel, and so on.

7 As a member of an investment club, report to the membership on whether the club should purchase shares of Time Warner (TWX), Clear Channel Communications (CCU), and Yahoo (YHOO). Your report will cover past performance, current status, and future prospects for the short and long run.

8 Look through current newspapers, magazines, the web, and so on, and get the best available information on the job outlook for this year's college graduates. You will want to look at each major field separately. You also may want to show variations by geographic area, degree, and schools. Present your findings in a well-organized and illustrated oral report.

9 Present a plan for improving some phase of operation on your campus (registration, academic honesty, housing, grade appeals, library, cafeteria, traffic, curricula, athletics, computer labs, or the like).

10 Present an objective report on some legislation of importance to business (right-to-work laws, ethics, environmental controls, taxes, or the like). Take care to present evidence and reasoning from all the major viewpoints. Support your presentation with facts, figures, and so on whenever they will help. Prepare visual supports.

11 Assume that you are being considered by a company of your choice for a job of your choice. Your prospective employer has asked you to make a _____ -minute report (your instructor will specify) on your qualifications. You may project your education to the date you will be on the job market, making assumptions that are consistent with your record to date.

12 Prepare and present a report on how individuals may reduce their federal or state income tax payments. You probably will want to emphasize the most likely sources of tax savings, such as tax sheltering and avoiding common errors.

13 Make a presentation to a hypothetical group of investors that will get you the investment money you need for a purpose of your choice. Your purpose could be to begin a new business, to construct a building, to develop land—whatever interests you. Make your presentation as real (or realistic) as you can. And support your appeal with visuals.

14 As chairperson of the site-selection committee of the National Federation of Business Executives, present a report on your committee's recommendation. The committee has selected a city and a convention hotel (you may choose each). Your report will give your recommendation and the reasons that support it. For class purposes, you may make up whatever facts you may need about the organization and its convention requirements and about the hotel. But use real facts about the city.

15 As a buyer of men's (or women's) clothing, report to the sales personnel of your store on the fashions for the coming season. You may get the necessary information from publications in the field.

16 The top administrators of your company have asked you to look into the matter of whether the company should own automobiles, lease automobiles, or pay mileage costs on employee-owned automobiles. (Automobiles are used by sales personnel.) Gather the best available information on the matter and report it to the top administrators. You may make up any company facts you need, but make them realistic.

Named one of the "25 Most Influential Global Executives" (*Time* magazine/CNN) and one of *Fortune* magazine's "50 most powerful women in business," Andrea Jung is widely recognized for connecting Avon's international operations into a global "Company for Women." By setting up and listening to an advisory council from every level of the company, Jung has revitalized the 140-country sales force and increased sales around the globe. Being able to adapt to cultural and market differences is essential to communicating with customers.

"Avon does business in more than 100 countries, and engaging in an active dialogue with women is critical in helping us meet the beauty and lifestyle aspirations of our 5 million Avon Sales Representatives and 300 million customers from diverse cultures. We are a major global corporation but our roots are in local communities, and the person-to-person relationships we build through our direct sales model are a source of competitive advantage."

Andrea Jung, Chairman and CEO,
Avon Products, Inc.

chapter sixteen

Techniques of Cross-Cultural Communication

LEARNING OBJECTIVES

Upon completing this chapter, you will be able to describe the major barriers to cross-cultural communication and how to overcome them. To reach this goal, you should be able to

1   Explain why communicating clearly across cultures is important to business.

2   Define culture and explain its effects on cross-cultural communication.

3   Describe cultural differences in body positions and movements and use this knowledge effectively in communicating.

4   Describe cultural differences in views and practices concerning time, space, odors, and such and use this knowledge effectively in communicating.

5   Explain the language equivalency problem as a cause of miscommunication.

6   Describe what one can do to overcome the language equivalency problem.

Cross-Cultural Communication

To introduce yourself to this chapter, assume the position of assistant to the president of Thatcher-Stone and Company, a small manufacturer of computer components. Your boss, gregarious old Vernon Thatcher, invited you to join him at a luncheon meeting with a group of Asian business executives in which negotiations for the sale of Thatcher-Stone products would be opened. Because Thatcher-Stone's domestic sales have been lagging, the company badly needs these customers.

The Asian guests entered the room, bowing as introductions were made. Mr. Thatcher attempted to put them at ease. "No need to do that," he said. "I'm just plain Vernon Thatcher. Just relax and make yourself at home." You noticed that the Asians appeared bewildered. They appeared even more bewildered when early in the meeting Mr. Thatcher made this statement: "We've only got the lunch hour, gents. I know you'll appreciate getting right down to business."

Throughout the meeting Mr. Thatcher was in his best conversational mood—laughing, backslapping, telling jokes. But none of this seemed to make an impression on the guests. They seemed confused to you. They smiled and were extremely polite, but they seemed to understand little of what Mr. Thatcher was saying. Although he tried again and again to move to business talk, they did not respond. The meeting ended pleasantly, but without a sale.

"They're a strange people," Mr. Thatcher commented when he got back to his office. "They have a lot to learn about doing business. It doesn't look like they're going to deal with us, does it?" Mr. Thatcher was right in his last comment. They did not.

As you review the meeting, you cannot help but feel that Mr. Thatcher spoiled the deal, for he failed miserably in communicating with the Asians. The fact is that there is much to know about communicating in cross-cultural settings. The goal of this chapter is to introduce you to this issue.

Technological advances in communication, travel, and transportation have made business increasingly global. This trend is expected to continue in the foreseeable future. Thus, the chances are good that you will have to communicate with people from other cultures.

- Business has become more global.

Both large and small businesses want you to be able to communicate clearly with those from other cultures for several reasons. A primary reason is that businesses sell their products and services both domestically and internationally. Being able to communicate with others helps you be more successful in understanding customers' needs, communicating how your company can meet these needs, and winning their business. Another reason is that in addition to being a more effective worker, you will be more efficient both within and outside your company. You will be able to work harmoniously with those from other cultures, creating a more comfortable and productive workplace. Furthermore, if cultural barriers are eliminated, you will be able to hire good people despite their differences. Also, you will avoid problems stemming solely from misinterpretations. A final reason is that your attention to communicating clearly with those from other cultures will enrich your business and personal life.

- Communicating across cultures effectively improves your productivity and efficiency and promotes harmonious work environments.

In preparing to communicate with people from other cultures, you might well begin by reviewing the instructions given in this book. Most of them fit all people. But many do not, especially those involving message writing. To determine which do not, you must study the differences among cultures, for cultural differences are at the root of the exceptions. In addition, you must look at the special problems that our language presents to those who use it as a second language. It is around these two problem areas that this review of cross-cultural communication is organized.

- Cross-cultural communication involves understanding cultural differences and overcoming language problems.

PROBLEMS OF CULTURAL DIFFERENCES

A study of the role of culture in international communication properly begins with two qualifying statements. First, culture is often improperly assumed to be the cause of miscommunication. Often it is confused with the other human elements involved. We must

- Two qualifying statements begin this study of culture: (1) It is improperly blamed for some miscommunication.

TECHNOLOGY IN BRIEF

Web Tools for Cross-Cultural Communication

The Internet is a rich source of cross-cultural information for business communicators. Not only can you find information about places where you might be doing business, but you can use some interactive websites to help you with information and tools for your communication. One of these, shown below, is a currency converter, allowing you to convert from one currency to another. In this example, U.S. dollars are converted to Indian rupees. These converters are set up to use regularly updated exchange rates, so you can quote prices in both U.S. dollars and other currency. The web page example at the bottom right is part of a site that helps you learn some of the language of your customers. This site shows a word or phrase in English and the second language, as well as gives you an audio pronunciation of it. Learning a few words in your customers' language is both helpful and courteous. The other sites you see listed here include a site where you can get world time, a resource desk that provides updated site reviews regularly, and a site with helpful cultural information and some discussion groups on doing business in various countries. More links are available on the text website.

Other good sites:

http://www.timeticker.com/
http://globaledge.msu.edu/ibrd/ibrd.asp
http://www.NationMaster.com

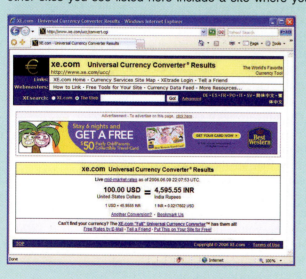

remember that communication between people of different cultures involves the same problems of human behavior that are involved when people of the same culture communicate. In either case, people can be belligerent, arrogant, prejudiced, insensitive, or biased. The miscommunication these types of behavior cause is not a product of culture.

- (2) It is easy to overgeneralize cultural practices.

Second, one must take care not to overgeneralize the practices within a culture. We say this even though some of the statements we make in the following paragraphs are overgeneralized. But we have little choice. In covering the subject, it is necessary to make generalizations such as "Latin Americans do this" or "Arabs do that" in order to emphasize a point. But the truth of the matter is that in all cultures, subcultures are present; and common practice in one segment of a culture may be unheard of by other segments. Within a culture townspeople differ from country dwellers, the rich differ from the poor, and the educated differ from the uneducated. Clearly, the subject of culture is highly complex and should not be reduced to simple generalizations.

- Culture is the shared ways groups of people view the world.

Culture has been defined in many ways. The classic definition most useful in this discussion is one derived from anthropology: *Culture* is "a way of life of a group of

A squatting position is quite natural for this woman as she conducts business.

people . . . the stereotyped patterns of learning behavior, which are handed down from one generation to the next through means of language and imitation."[1] Similarly, a modern definition is that culture is "the shared ways in which groups of people understand and interpret the world."[2]

While we can all talk on wireless phones and drink Coca-Cola at McDonald's, these activities can be interpreted very differently in different cultures. A Coke at McDonald's in America and a conversation on a wireless phone in Israel may be common occurrences, but in Moscow a trip to McDonald's is a status symbol, as is a wireless phone. In other words, people living in different countries have developed not only different ways to interpret events; they have different habits, values, and ways of relating to one another.

These differences are a major source of problems when people of different cultures try to communicate. Unfortunately, people tend to view the ways of their culture as normal and the ways of other cultures as bad, wrong, peculiar, or such. This is called *ethnocentrism,* and it can be disastrous to effective communication across cultures. One way to overcome this tendency is to become more culturally intelligent by developing a higher level of cultural sensitivity to many dimensions of culture. The way one becomes more sensitive is to learn more about the culture and of be mindful of the differences. Two of the dimensions that impact communications are the cultural differences in (1) body positions and movements and (2) views and practices concerning various factors of human relationships (time, space, intimacy, and so on).

- Two major kinds of cultural differences affect communication.

Body Positions and Movements

One might think that the positions and movements of the body are much the same for all people. But such is not the case. These positions and movements differ by culture, and the differences can affect communication. For example, in our culture most people

- Body positions and movements differ among cultures. For example, in some cultures, people sit; in other cultures, they squat.

[1] V. Barnouw, *Culture and Personality* (Chicago: Dorsey Press, 1963) 4.

[2] Fons Trompenaars and Peter Woolliams, *Business across Cultures* (London:Capstone, 2003) 53.

Carefully Present and Receive a Business Card in Japan

In Japan, it is considered bad manners to go to a business meeting without a business card, or *meishi*. There are a number of ways to present the card, but receiving it is an art, too. If you want to make a good impression on the presenter, receive it in both hands, especially when the other party is senior in age or status or a potential customer. Be careful not to fiddle with the card or put it in your rear pocket—that is considered crude. Put it in some distinctive case. Those who do business in both countries often have their business cards translated on the back, as the examples here show.

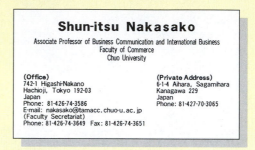

sit when they wish to remain in one place for some time, but in much of the world people squat. Because we do not squat, we tend to view squatting as primitive. This view obviously affects our communication with people who squat, for what we see when we communicate is a part of the message. But how correct is this view? Actually, squatting is a very normal body position. Our children squat quite naturally—until their elders teach them to sit. Who is to say that sitting is more advanced or better?

For another example, people from our culture who visit certain Asian countries are likely to view the fast, short steps taken by the inhabitants as peculiar or funny and to view our longer strides as normal. And when people from our culture see the inhabitants of these countries bow on meeting and leaving each other, they are likely to interpret the bowing as a sign of subservience or weakness. Similarly, people from our culture see standing up as the appropriate thing to do on certain occasions (as when someone enters the room), whereas people from some other cultures do not.

As you know, movements of certain body parts (especially the hands) are a vital form of human communication. Some of these movements have no definite meaning even within a culture. But some have clear meanings, and these meanings may differ by culture. To us an up-and-down movement of the head means yes and a side-to-side movement of the head means no. These movements may mean nothing at all or something quite different to people from cultures in which thrusting the head forward, raising the eyebrows, jerking the head to one side, or lifting the chin are used to convey similar meanings.

In addition, the two-fingered "victory" sign is as clear to us as any of our hand gestures. To an Australian, whose culture is not vastly different from ours, the sign has a most vulgar meaning. The "OK" sign is terribly rude and insulting in such diverse

- Manners of walking differ among cultures.

- Communication with body parts (hands, arms, head, etc.) varies by culture.

- Hand gestures differ by culture.

places as Russia, Germany, and Brazil.[3] In Japan, a similar sign represents money. If a businessperson completing a contract gave this sign, the Japanese might think they needed to give more money, perhaps even a bribe. Even the widely used "thumbs up" sign for "things are going well" could get you into trouble in countries from Nigeria to Australia. In our culture a side-by-side hand movement can be interpreted to mean "hello." The same movement can be interpreted to mean "go away" or "no" in India.[4] And so it is with many of our other body movements. They differ widely, even within cultures.

The meanings that movements of our eyes convey also vary by culture. In North America, we are taught not to look over the heads of our audience but to maintain eye contact in giving formal speeches. In informal talking, we are encouraged to look at others but not to stare. In Indonesia, looking directly at people, especially those in higher positions and older, is considered to be disrespectful. On the other hand, our practices of eye contact are less rigorous than those of the British and Germans. Unless one understands these cultural differences, how one uses eye movement can be interpreted as being impolite on the one hand or being shy on the other.

Touching and particularly handshaking differences are important to understand in cross-cultural communication. This is made difficult by other cultures adopting Western greetings. However, some cultures, like the Chinese, do not like much touching. They will give a handshake you might perceive as weak. Other cultures that like touching will give you greetings ranging from full embraces and kisses to nose rubbing. If you can avoid judging others from different cultures on their greeting based on your standards for others like you, you can seize the opportunity to access the cultural style of another. Here are some types of handshakes by culture.

Culture	Handshakes
Americans	Firm
Germans	Brusque, firm, repeated upon arrival and departure
French	Light, quick, not offered to superiors, repeated upon arrival and departure
British	Soft
Hispanics	Moderate grasp, repeated frequently
Latin Americans	Firm, long-lasting
Middle Easterners	Gentle, repeated frequently
Asians	Gentle; for some, shaking hands is unfamiliar and uncomfortable (an exception to this is the Korean, who generally has a firm handshake)
Arabs	Gentle, kisses on both cheeks

In our culture, smiles are viewed positively in most situations. But in some other cultures (notably African cultures), a smile is regarded as a sign of weakness in certain situations (such as bargaining). Receiving a gift or touching with the left hand is a serious breach of etiquette among Muslims, for they view the left hand as unclean. We attach no such meaning to the left hand. And so it is with other body movements—arching the eyebrows, positioning the fingers, raising the arms, and many more. All cultures use body movements in communicating, but in different ways.

Views and Practices Concerning Factors of Human Relationships

Probably causing even more miscommunication than differences in body positions and movements are the different attitudes of different cultures toward various factors

---

[3] Roger E. Axtell, *Gestures: The Dos and Taboos of Body Language around the World* (New York: John Wiley & Sons, 1998) 43.

[4] Jane Lasky, "Watch Your Body Language in Asia," *Austin American-Statesman* 17 Oct. 1999: D2.

A Classic Defense of Cultural Difference

The classic "ugly American" was traveling in a faraway land. He had been critical of much of what he experienced—the food, the hotels, the customs in general. One day he came upon a funeral. He observed that the mourners placed food on the grave—and left it there.

"What a stupid practice!" he exclaimed to his native host. "Do your people actually think that the dead person will eat the food?"

At this point, the host had taken all the insults he could handle for one day. So he replied, "Our dead will eat the food as soon as your dead smell the flowers you place on their graves."

of human relationships. For illustrative purposes, we will review seven major factors: time, space, odors, frankness, intimacy of relationships, values, and expression of emotions.

- Views about time differ widely. Some cultures stress punctuality; some do not.

Time. In our culture, people tend to be monochronic. They regard time as something that must be planned for the most efficient use. They strive to meet deadlines, to be punctual, to conduct business quickly, and to work on a schedule.

In some other cultures (especially those of the Middle East and some parts of Asia), people are polychronic, viewing time in a more relaxed way. They see planning as unwise and unnecessary. Being late to a meeting, a social function, or such is of little consequence to them. In fact, some of them hold the view that important people should be late to show that they are busy. In business negotiations, the people in these cultures move at a deliberately slow pace, engaging in casual talk before getting to the main issue. It is easy to see how such different views of time can cause people from different cultures to have serious communication problems.

- Space is viewed differently by different cultures. In some cultures, people want to be far apart; in other cultures, they want to be close.

Space. People from different cultures often vary in their attitudes toward space. Even people from the same culture may have different space preferences, as noted in Chapter 14. North Americans tend to prefer about two feet or so of distance between themselves and those with whom they speak. But in some cultures (some Arabian and South American cultures), people stand closer to each other; not following this practice is considered impolite and bad etiquette. For another example, North Americans view personal space as a right and tend to respect this right of others; thus, they stand in line and wait their turn. People from some other cultures view space as belonging to all. Thus, they jostle for space when boarding trains, standing at ticket counters, shopping in stores, and such. In encounters between people whose cultures have such different attitudes toward space, actions are likely to be misinterpreted.

- Some cultures view body odors as bad; others view them as normal.

Odors. People from different cultures may have different attitudes toward body odors. To illustrate, Americans work hard to neutralize body odors or cover them up and view those with body odors as dirty and unsanitary. On the other hand, in some Asian cultures people view body odors not as something to be hidden but as something that friends should experience. Some of the people from these cultures believe that it is an act of friendship to "breathe the breath" of the person with whom they converse and to feel their presence by smelling. Clearly, encounters between people with such widely differing attitudes could lead to serious miscommunication.

- Low-context cultures are more frank and explicit than high-context cultures.

Frankness. North Americans tend to be relatively frank or explicit in their relationships with others, quickly getting to the point and perhaps being blunt and sharp in doing so. Germans and Israelis are even more frank than Americans. Asians tend to

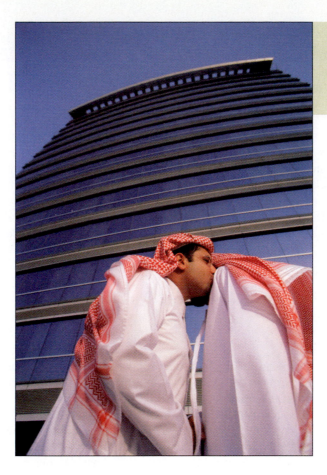

be far more reticent or implicit and sometimes go to great lengths to save face or not to offend. Americans belong to a low-context culture, a culture that explicitly shares all relevant background information in our communication. Asians, on the other hand, belong to a high-context culture, extracting limited background information and thus communicating more implicitly.[5] Thus, Asians may appear evasive, roundabout, and indecisive to North Americans; and North Americans may appear harsh, impolite, and aggressive to Asians. Phone customs may be an exception, especially among the Chinese, who tend to end telephone calls abruptly after their purpose has been accomplished. North Americans, on the other hand, tend to move on to friendly talk and clearly prepare the listener for the end of the call.

Intimacy of Relationships. In many cultures, strict social classes exist, and class status determines how intimately people are addressed and treated in communication. For this reason, a person from such a culture might quiz a person from another culture to determine that person's class status. Questions concerning occupation, income, title, origin, and such might be asked. People from cultures that stress human equality are apt to take offense at such questioning about class status. This difference in attitude toward class status also is illustrated by differences in the familiarity of address. Some Americans are quick to use first names. This practice is offensive to people from some other cultures, notably the English and the Germans, who expect such intimate address only from long-standing acquaintances.

- Intimacy among people varies in different cultures.

Similarly, how people view superior–subordinate relations can vary by culture. The dominant view in Latin America, for example, is a strong boss with weak subordinates doing as the boss directs. In sharp contrast is the somewhat democratic work

- How people view superior–subordinate relations also differs.

---

[5] Iris Varner and Linda Beamer, *Intercultural Communication in the Global Workplace,* 3rd ed. (New York: McGraw-Hill/Irwin, 2005) 27.

While the 2008 Olympics in Beijing will bring the world's best athletes together, it will also likely highlight many of the cultural differences between Asians and Americans. One of the primary differences has already made headlines—the endorsements and sponsorships of athletes. Most Americans view these deals as something the gold medalist athletes have earned—even deserve. However, the Chinese view their athletes as part of a team of coaches, trainers, doctors, and the state, all of whom are entitled to share in a part of any endorsement deals. In fact, in order to participate in the games, one Chinese gold-medalist, Guo Jingjing, had to apologize to the public for her own financial ambitions with "I belong to the nation." This collectivism value is one that shows up when Eastern businesses meet Western businesses, too.

Hannah Beech, "An Olympian Takes a Dive," *Time Asia* 7 February 2005, 24 June 2006
<www.time.com/time/asia/magazine/0,13674,501050207,00.html>.

arrangement of the Japanese in which much of the decision making is by consensus. Most in our culture view as appropriate an order between these extremes. These widely differing practices have led to major communication problems in joint business ventures involving people from these cultures.

- So does the role of women.

The role of women varies widely by culture. In North America, we continue to move toward a generally recognized goal of equality. In many Islamic cultures, the role of women is quite different. To many in our culture, the practices of the people of these other cultures suggest severe restriction of human rights. In the view of the people of these cultures, their practices are in accord with their religious convictions. They see us as being the ones out of step.

- Each culture has different values concerning such matters as attitude toward work,

Values. Also differing by culture are our values—how we evaluate the critical matters in life. Americans, for example, have been indoctrinated with the Protestant work ethic. It is the belief that if one puts hard work ahead of pleasure, success will follow. The product of this thinking is an emphasis on planning, working efficiently, and maximizing production. Of course, not all of us subscribe to this ethic, but it is a strong force in the thinking of many in our culture. The prevailing view in some other cultures is quite different. In India, for example, the major concern is for spiritual and human well-being. The view of work is relaxed, and productivity is, at best, a secondary concern.

- employee–employer relations,

Views about the relationships of employers and employees also may differ by culture. North American workers expect to change companies in their career a number of times; and they expect companies to fire them from time to time. Employees expect to move freely from job to job, and they expect employers to hire and fire as their needs change. Expectations are quite different in some other cultures. In Japan, for example, employment tends to be for a lifetime. The company is viewed much like a family, with loyalty expected from employees and employer. Such differences have caused misunderstandings in American–Japanese joint ventures.

- and authority.

How employees view authority is yet another question that cultures view differently. We North Americans generally accept authority, yet we fiercely maintain the rights of the individual. In many Third World cultures, workers accept a subservient role passively. Autocratic rule is expected—even wanted.

- Social behavior varies by culture, such as practices concerning affection, laughter, and emotion.

Expression of Emotions. From culture to culture, differences in social behavior have developed. To illustrate, some Asian cultures strongly frown upon public displays of affection—in fact, they consider them crude and offensive. Westerners, on the other hand, accept at least a moderate display of affection. To Westerners, laughter is a spontaneous display of pleasure, but in some cultures (Japanese, for one), laughter also can be a controlled behavior—to be used in certain social situations. Even such emotional displays as sorrow are influenced by culture. In some Middle Eastern cultures, sorrow is expressed with loud, seemingly uncontrolled wailing. In similar situations, Westerners typically respond with subdued and controlled emotions, which could be seen as cold and uncaring by Middle Easterners.

We all have observed the emotion and animation that people of the Mediterranean cultures display as they communicate. And we have seen the more subdued communication of others—notably northern Europeans. The first group tends to see the second as disinterested and lacking in friendliness. The second sees the first as excitable, emotional, perhaps even unstable.

- Included is the degree of animation displayed.

Many more such practices exist. Some cultures combine business and social pleasure; others do not. Some expect to engage in aggressive bargaining in business transactions; others prefer straightforward dealings. Some talk loudly and with emotion; others communicate orally in a subdued manner. Some communicate with emphasis on economy of expression; others communicate with an abundance of verbiage.

- Many more such practices exist.

The comparisons could go on and on, for there are countless differences in cultures. But it is not necessary to review them all. What is important is that we recognize their existence, that we are mindful of them, and that we understand them. We should guard against ethnocentrism, the use of one's own cultural values as standards for determining meaning in cross-cultural communication.

- We must recognize them, look for them, and understand them.

Effects on Business Communication Techniques

The foregoing examples illustrate only a few of the numerous differences that exist among cultures. Books have been written on the subject. Our objective here is only to establish the point that the differences among cultures affect communication between people of different cultures.

- Cultural differences affect communication.

The communication techniques presented in this book should be modified to fit the culture involved. Keep in mind that this book was written for our culture. Much of what we say does not apply to other cultures, especially our coverage of the basic message situations—those concerning directness and indirectness. People in Asian cultures, for example, generally favor a somewhat indirect approach for messages we would treat directly. They begin with an identification of context—that is, a description of the situation the message concerns.[6] They use what appears to us as exaggerated politeness and slowness in moving the message. In fact, some of our direct messages would be regarded as rude by people in these cultures.[7]

- Our communication techniques are not universally acceptable.

Our persuasive appeals may be rejected in India, where views of an older, more highly developed morality lead to thinking different from ours.[8] Even the British, whose culture we think of as resembling our own, have message practices that differ from ours. They especially differ in the treatment of negative situations. They prefer an approach that we would regard as blunt and calloused. They would regard our goodwill strategies as insincere and evasive.

- The Indians and even the British have practices different from ours.

And so it is with the many other cultures of the world. Our practices just do not fit into them. What to do about this problem? You have no choice but to become a student of culture. You must learn the cultures of those with whom you communicate. Don't expect them to understand your culture, although many of them do. With your recipient's culture in mind, you then modify your communication accordingly.

- You must modify your communications to fit the culture of your recipient.

---

[6] Varner and Beamer 145.

[7] Richard M. Hodgetts, Fred Luthans, and Jonathan Doh, *International Management: Culture, Strategy, and Behavior* (New York: McGraw-Hill/Irwin, 2006) 190.

[8] Varner and Beamer 152.

PROBLEMS OF LANGUAGE

The people on earth use more than 3,000 languages. Because few of us can learn more than one or two other languages well, problems of miscommunication are bound to occur in international communication.

Lack of Language Equivalency

Unfortunately, wide differences among languages make precisely equivalent translations difficult. One reason for such differences is that languages are based on the concepts, experiences, views, and such of the cultures that developed them. And different cultures have different concepts, experiences, views, and such. For example, we think of a florist as someone who sells flowers and related items in a store. In some cultures, however, flowers are sold by street vendors, mainly women and children. Obviously, our *florist* does not have a precise equivalent in the language of such cultures.

Similarly, our *supermarket* has no equivalent in some languages. The French have no word to distinguish between *house* and *home, mind* and *brain,* and *man* and *gentleman.* The Spanish have no word to distinguish between a *chairman* and a *president,* while Italians have no word for *wishful thinking.* And Russians have no words for *efficiency, challenge,* and *having fun.* However, Italians have nearly 500 words for types of pasta. And so it is with words for many other objects, actions, concepts, and such (for example, *roundup, interview, strike, tough, monopoly, domestic, feminine, responsible, aloof*).

Another explanation for the lack of language equivalency is the grammatical and syntactic differences among languages. Some languages (Urdu, for example) have no gerunds, and some have no adverbs and/or adjectives. Not all languages deal with verb mood, voice, and tense in the same way. The obvious result is that even the best translators often cannot find literal equivalents between languages.

Adding to these equivalency problems is the problem of multiple word meanings. Like English, other languages have more than one meaning for many words. Think, for example, of our numerous meanings for the simple word *run* (to move fast, to compete for office, a score in baseball, a break in a stocking, a fading of colors, and many more). Or consider the multiple meanings of such words as *fast, cat, trip, gross, ring,* and *make.* The Oxford English Dictionary uses over 15,000 words to define *what.* Unless one knows a language well, it is difficult to know which of the meanings is intended.

Within a culture, certain manners of expression may be used in a way that their dictionary translations and grammatical structures do not explain. Those within the culture understand these expressions; those outside may not. For example, we might say, "Business couldn't be better," meaning business is very good. One from another culture might understand the sentence to mean "Business is bad" (impossible to improve). Or we might say, "We could never be too nice to our customers," meaning try as we may, we couldn't be overly nice. To one from another culture, the sentence might mean "We cannot be nice to our customers."[9]

Similarly, like-meaning words can be used in different ways in different cultures. One example is the simple word *yes,* a word that has an equivalent in all languages. "The Chinese *yes,* like the Japanese *yes,* can often be understood by Americans and British as their English *yes.* But the Chinese *yes* often means 'I am listening.' Or it may be understood in English as the opposite. For example, when an American says to a Chinese counterpart, "I see you don't agree with this clause," the Chinese will usually reply, "Yes" meaning a polite agreement with the negative question: 'Yes, you are right. I do not agree with the clause.'"[10]

Overcoming such language problems is difficult. The best way, of course, is to know more than one language well, but the competence required is beyond the reach of many of us. Thus, your best course is first to be aware that translation problems exist and then to ask questions—to probe—to determine what the other person understands.

---

[9] Jensen J. Zhao, "The Chinese Approach to International Business Negotiation," *Journal of Business Communication* 37 (2000): 225.

[10] Zhao 225.

Margin notes (left column):

- Communication problems are caused by the existence of many languages.

- Differences among languages make equivalent translations difficult.

- Examples prove the point.

- Grammar and syntax differences add to the difficulty.

- So do the multiple meanings of words.

- Certain of our expressions don't mean what their dictionary and grammatical structures say they mean.

- Even words with the same meaning can differ in usage by culture.

- Overcome such language problems by knowing languages well and by questioning.

For very important oral messages, documents, or such, you might consider using a procedure called *back translating*. This procedure involves using two translators, one with first-language skills in one of the languages involved and one with first-language skills in the other language. The first translator translates the message into his or her language, and the second translator then translates the message back into the original. If the translations are good, the second translation matches the original.

- Use back translating for important communications.

Difficulties in Using English

Fortunately for us, English is the primary language of international business. This is not to say that other languages are not used in international business, for they are. When business executives from different countries have a common language, whatever it may be, they are likely to use it. For example, an executive from Iraq and an executive from Saudi Arabia would communicate with each other in Arabic, for Arabic is their common first language. For the same reason, an executive from Venezuela would use Spanish in dealing with an executive from Mexico. However, when executives have no common language, they are likely to use English. The members of the European Free Trade Association conduct all their business in English even though not one of them is a native English speaker. In the words of one international authority, "English has emerged as the *lingua franca* of world commerce in much the same way that Greek did in the ancient world of the West and Chinese did in the East."[11]

- English is the primary language of international business.

Although we can take comfort from knowing that English is the primary language of international business, we must keep in mind that it is not the primary language of many of those who use it. Since many of these users have had to learn English as a second language, they are likely to use it less fluently than we and to experience problems in understanding us. Some of their more troublesome problems are reviewed in the following pages.

- But many nonnatives have problems using English.

---

[11] Naoki Kameda, *Business Communication toward Transnationalism: The Significance of Cross-Cultural Business English and Its Role* (Tokyo: Kindaibungeisha Co., 1996) 34.

Figure 16-1

**Some Two-Word Verbs
That Confuse Nonnative
Speakers**

Verb Plus *Away*	Verb Plus *In*	Verb Plus *Out*	Verb Plus *Up*
give away	cash in	blow out	blow up
keep away	cave in	clean out	build up
lay away	close in	crowd out	call up
pass away	dig in	cut out	catch up
throw away	give in	die out	cover up
	run in	dry out	dig up
Verb Plus *Back*	take in	even out	end up
	throw in	figure out	fill up
cut back		fill out	get up
feed back		find out	hang up
keep back	**Verb Plus *Off***	give out	hold up
play back		hold out	keep up
read back	break off	lose out	look up
take back	brush off	pull out	mix up
turn back	buy off	rule out	pick up
win back	check off	tire out	save up
	clear off	wear out	shake up
	cool off	work out	shut up
Verb Plus *Down*	cut off		slow up
	finish off		wrap up
calm down	let off	**Verb Plus *Over***	
die down	mark off		**Verb Plus**
hand down	pay off	check over	**Miscellaneous**
keep down	run off	do over	**Words**
let down	send off	hold over	
lie down	slow off	pass over	bring about
mark down	shut off	put over	catch on
pin down	sound off	roll over	get across
play down	start off	run over	pass on
put down	take off	stop over	put across
run down	write off	take over	put forth
shut down		talk over	set forth
sit down		think over	
wear down		win over	

Two-Word Verbs. One of the most difficult problems for nonnative speakers of English is the use of two-word verbs. By *two-word verbs* we mean a wording consisting of (1) a verb and (2) a second element that, combined with the verb, produces a meaning that the verb alone does not have. For example, take the verb *break* and the word *up*. When combined, they have a meaning quite different from the meanings the words have alone. And look how the meaning changes when the same verb is combined with other words: *break away, break out, break in, break down.* Dictionaries are of little help to nonnatives who are seeking the meanings of these word combinations.

There are many two-word verbs—so many, in fact, that a special dictionary of them has been compiled.[12] Figure 16–1 lists some of the more common words that combine with verbs.

Of course, nonnatives studying English learn some of these word combinations, for they are part of the English language. But many of them are not covered in language textbooks or listed in dictionaries. It is apparent that we should use these word combinations sparingly when communicating with nonnative speakers of English. Whenever

---

[12] George A. Meyer, *The Two-Word Verb* (The Hague, Netherlands: Mouton, 1975).

possible, we should substitute for them words that appear in standard dictionaries. Following are some two-word verbs and suggested substitutes:

Two-Word Verbs	Suggested Substitutes
give up	surrender
speed up, hurry up	accelerate
go on, keep on	continue
put off	defer
take off	depart, remove
come down	descend
go in, come in, get in	enter
go out, come out, get out	exit, leave
blow up	explode
think up	imagine
figure out	solve
take out, take away	remove
go back, get back, be back	return

Additional problems result from the fact that some two-word verbs have noun and adjective forms. These also tend to confuse nonnatives using English. Examples of such nouns are *breakthrough, cover-up, drive-in, hookup, show-off,* and *sit-in.* Examples of such adjectives are *going away* (a going-away gift), *cover-up* (cover-up tactics), *cleanup* (cleanup work), and *turning-off* (turning-off place). Fortunately, some nouns and adjectives of this kind are commonly used and appear in standard dictionaries (words such as *hookup, feedback, breakthrough, lookout,* and *takeover*). In writing to nonnative readers, you will need to use sparingly those that do not appear in standard dictionaries.

- Some two-word verbs have noun and adjective forms. Use these sparingly.

Culturally Derived Words. Words derived from our culture also present problems. The most apparent are the slang expressions that continually come into and go out of use. Some slang expressions catch on and find a place in our dictionaries (*brunch, hobo, blurb, bogus*). But most are with us for a little while and then are gone. Examples of such short-lived slang expressions are the "twenty-three skiddoo" and "oh you kid" of the 1920s and the *ritzy, scram, natch, lousy, soused, all wet, hep, in the groove,* and *tops* of following decades. More recent slang words that are probably destined for the same fate include *nerd, wimp, earth pig, pig out, couch potato, squid, airhead,* and *cool.* Perhaps you are not aware of just how much slang we use. For an eye-opener, you have only to visit ESL: Idioms and Slang Page, <http:iteslj.org/links/ESL/ Idioms_and_Slang/>, for links to many lists.

- Culturally derived words, especially slang, cause problems.

Most slang words are not in dictionaries or on the word lists that non–English-speaking people study to learn English. The obvious conclusion is that you should not use slang in cross-cultural communication.

- So avoid slang.

Similar to and in fact overlapping slang are the words and expressions that we derive from our various activities—sports, social affairs, work, and the like. Sports especially have contributed such words, many of which are so widely used that they are part of our everyday vocabulary. From football we have *kickoff, goal-line stand,* and *over the top.* Baseball has given us *out in left field, strike out, touch base, off base, right off the bat, a steal, squeeze play, balk,* and *go to bat for.* From boxing we have *knockout, down for the count, below the belt, answer the bell,* and *on the ropes.* From other sports and from sports in general we have *jock, ace, par, stymie, from scratch, ballpark figure,* and *get the ball rolling.*

- Words derived from sports, social activities, and so on cause problems.

Similar to these words and expressions are words and expressions developed within our culture (colloquialisms). Some of these have similar meanings in other cultures, but most are difficult for nonnatives to understand. You will find some examples in Figure 16–2.

- Colloquialisms also cause problems.

Figure 16–2

Examples of Colloquialisms to Avoid with Nonnative Speakers

head for home	tuckered out	tote (carry)
have an itching palm	gumption	in a rut
grasp at straws	crying in his beer	priming the pump
flat-footed	in orbit	make heads or tails of it
on the beam	a honey	tearjerker
out to pasture	a flop	countdown
sitting duck	dope (crazy)	shortcut
in the groove	hood (gangster)	educated guess
nuts (crazy)	up the creek without a paddle	all ears
circle the wagons	a fish out of water	slower than molasses
shoot from the hip	a chicken with its head cut off	break the ice

- We use such words in everyday communication. But avoid them in cross-cultural correspondence.

If you are like most of us, many of these words and expressions are a part of your vocabulary. You use them in your everyday communicating, which is all right. They are colorful, and they can communicate clearly to those who understand them. Nonnative English speakers are not likely to understand them, however; so you will need to eliminate such words and expressions in communicating with them. You will need to use words that are clearly defined in the dictionaries that these people are likely to use in translating your message. Following are some examples:

Not This	**But This**
That's just off the top of my head.	Here's a quick idea.
He frequently shoots from the hip.	He frequently acts before he thinks.
We would be up the creek without a paddle.	We would be in a helpless situation.
They couldn't make heads or tails of the report.	They couldn't understand the report.
The sales campaign was a flop.	The sales campaign was a failure.
I'll touch base with you on this problem in August.	I'll talk with you about this problem in August.
Take an educated guess on this question.	Answer this question to the best of your knowledge.
Your sales report put us in orbit.	Your sales report pleased us very much.
We will wind down manufacturing operations in November.	We will end manufacturing operations in November.
Your prediction was right on the beam.	Your prediction was correct.
Don't let him get your goat.	Don't let him upset you.

A GENERAL SUGGESTION FOR COMMUNICATING ACROSS CULTURES

- Use simple, basic English.

In addition to the specific suggestions for improving your communication in English with nonnative English speakers, you should follow one general suggestion: Write or talk simply and clearly. Talk slowly and enunciate each word. Remember that because most nonnative speakers learned English in school, they are acquainted mainly with primary dictionary meanings and are not likely to understand slang words or shades of difference in the meanings we give words. They will understand you better if you avoid these pitfalls. In the words of two highly regarded scholars in the field, you should "educate yourself in the use of Simplified English."[13]

---

[13] Robert Sellers and Elaine Winters, *Cultural Issues in Business Communication*, 3 Nov. 2003 <http://www.bena.com/ewinters/sect1.html>.

You also will communicate better if you carefully word your questions. Be sure your questions are not double questions. Avoid "Do you want to go to dinner now or wait until after the rush hour is over?" Also, avoid the yes/no question that some cultures may have difficulty answering directly. Use more open-ended questions such as "When would you like to go to dinner?" Also, avoid negative questions such as "Aren't you going to dinner?" In some cultures a yes response confirms whether the questioner is correct; in other cultures the response is directed toward the question being asked.

Word questions carefully to elicit the response intended.

Finally, try to check and clarify your communication through continuous confirmation. Summarizing in writing also is a good idea, and today's technology enables parties to do this on the spot. It allows you to be certain you have conveyed your message and received the response accurately. Even in Britain, whose culture similar to ours, similar words can have vastly different meanings. For example, we use a billion to mean 1,000,000,000 whereas the British use it to mean 1,000,000,000,000. If a British English speaker asked to *table* another item, an American English speaker will probably interpret that as a request to put it off when the real request was to bring it to attention.[14] Continually checking for meaning and using written summaries can help ensure the accuracy of the communication process.

Continually check the accuracy of the communication.

SUMMARY BY LEARNING OBJECTIVES

1. Businesses are becoming increasingly global in their operations.
   - Being able to communicate across cultures is necessary in these operations.
   - Specifically, it helps in gaining additional business, in hiring good people, and generally in understanding and satisfying the needs of customers.

2. *Culture* may be defined as "the way of life of a group of people."
   - Cultures differ.
   - People tend to view the practices of their culture as right and those of other cultures as peculiar or wrong.
   - These views cause miscommunication.

1 Explain why communicating clearly across cultures is important to business.

2 Define culture and explain its effects on cross-cultural communication.

---

[14] Danielle Medina Walker, Thomas Walker, and Joerg Schmitz, *Doing Business Internationally: The Guide to Cross-Cultural Success,* 2nd ed. (New York: McGraw-Hill/Irwin, 2003) 211.

Describe cultural
differences in body
positions and
movements and use this
knowledge effectively in
communicating.

Describe cultural
differences in views and
practices concerning
time, space, odors,
and such and use this
knowledge effectively in
communicating.

Explain the language
equivalency problem
as a cause of
miscommunication.

Describe what one can
do to overcome the
language equivalency
problem.

3. Variations in how people of different cultures use body positions and body movements is a cause of miscommunication.
   - How people walk, gesture, smile, and such varies from culture to culture.
   - When people from different cultures attempt to communicate, each may not understand the other's body movements.
4. People in different cultures differ in their ways of relating to people.
   - Specifically, they differ in their practices and thinking concerning time, space, odors, frankness, relationships, values, and social behavior.
   - We should not use our culture's practices as standards for determining meaning.
   - Instead, we should try to understand the other culture.
5. Language equivalency problems are another major cause of miscommunication in cross-cultural communication.
   - About 3,000 languages are used on earth.
   - They differ greatly in grammar and syntax.
   - Like English, most have words with multiple meanings.
   - As a result, equivalency in translation is difficult.
6. Overcoming the language equivalency problems involves hard and tedious work.
   - The best advice is to master the language of the nonnative English speakers with whom you communicate.
   - Also, you should be aware of the problems caused by language differences.
   - Ask questions carefully to make sure you are understood.
   - For important communications, consider back translation—the technique of using two translators, the first to translate from one language to the other and the second to translate back to the original.
   - Check the accuracy of the communication with written summaries.

CRITICAL THINKING QUESTIONS

1 "Just as our culture has advanced in its technological sophistication, it has advanced in the sophistication of its body signals, gestures, and attitudes toward time, space, and such. Thus, the ways of our culture are superior to those of most other cultures." Discuss this view.

2 What are the prevailing attitudes in our culture toward the following, and how can those attitudes affect our communication with nonnatives? Discuss.

   a. Negotiation methods

   b. Truth in advertising

   c. Company–worker loyalty

   d. Women's place in society

   e. The Protestant work ethic

3 Some of our message-writing techniques are said to be unacceptable to people from such cultures as those of Japan and England.

   a. Which techniques in particular do you think would be most inappropriate in these cultures?

   b. Why?

4 Think of English words (other than text examples) that probably do not have a precise equivalent in some other culture. Tell how you would attempt to explain each of these words to a person from that culture.

5 Select a word with at least five meanings. List those meanings and tell how you would communicate each of them to a nonnative.

6 From newspapers or magazines, find and bring to class 10 sentences containing words and expressions that a nonnative English speaker would not be likely to understand. Rewrite the sentences for this reader.

7 Is conversational style appropriate in writing to nonnative readers? Discuss.

8 Interview a nonnative speaker of English about communication differences between cultures he or she has experienced. Report your findings to the class in a 10-minute presentation.

9 Research a non–English-speaking country on the Internet or in your library. Look for ways in which business communication can vary by culture. Report your work to the class in a short presentation.

10 Explain ethnocentrism in relation to the communication model in Chapter 1.

11 On a recent trip to India, Mr. Yang, a prominent Chinese executive, dined with his client Himanshu Jain. Mr. Yang commented that the food was spicy, which Mr. Jain interpreted as an opportunity to discuss Indian cuisine. After lengthy explanations, Mr. Yang commented again that the food was spicy.

What happened here? What barrier is likely getting in the way of clear communication? (Adapted from Danielle Medina Walker, Thomas Walker, and Joerg Schmitz, *Doing Business Internationally: The Guide to Cross-Cultural Success,* [New York: McGraw-Hill, 2003] 237.)

CRITICAL THINKING EXERCISES

Instructions: Rewrite the following sentences for a nonnative English speaker.

1 Last year our laboratory made a breakthrough in design that really put sales in orbit.

2 You will need to pin down Mr. Wang to put across the need to tighten up expenses.

3 Recent losses have us on the ropes now, but we expect to get out of the hole by the end of the year.

4 We will kick off the advertising campaign in February, and in April we will bring out the new products.

5 Maryellen gave us a ballpark figure on the project, but I think she is ready to back down from her estimate.

6 We will back up any of our products that are not up to par.

7 Mr. Maghrabi managed to straighten out and become our star salesperson.

8 Now that we have cut back on our telemarketing, we will have to build up our radio advertising.

9 If you want to improve sales, you should stay with your prospects until they see the light.

10 We should be able to bring about a savings of 8 or 10 grand.

chapter seventeen

Correctness of Communication

The Effects of Correctness on Communication

Play the role of Mike Rook, a purchasing agent for Hewlett-Packard, and read through today's mail. The first letter comes from Joe Spivey, sales manager, B and B Manufacturing Company. You have not met the writer, though you talked to him on the phone a few days ago. At that time, you were favorably impressed with Spivey's enthusiasm and ability, and with B and B. In fact, you assumed that after he gave you the information you needed about B and B's products and services, you would begin buying from it.

As you read Spivey's letter, however, you are startled. "Could this be the same person I talked with?" you ask yourself. There in the first paragraph is an *it don't,* a clear error of subject–verb agreement. Farther down, an *it's* is used to show possession rather than *its.* Spivey apparently uses the sprinkle system for placing commas—that is, he sprinkles them wherever his whims direct. His commas often fall in strange places. For example, he writes, "Our salespeople, say the Rabb Company engineers, will verify the durability of Ironskin protective coating," but you think he means "Our salespeople say the Rabb Company engineers will verify the durability of Ironskin protective coating." The two sentences, which differ only in their punctuation, have distinctly different meanings. Spivey's message is filled with such errors.

In general, you now have a lower opinion of Spivey and his company. Perhaps you'll have to take a long look at B and B's products and services. After all, the products and services that a company provides are closely related to the quality of its people.

The problem just described is a very real one in business. Image does influence the success of both companies and people. And correctness in writing influences image. Thus, you will want to make certain that your writing is correct, so that it helps form a favorable image both of you and of your company. The material presented in the pages that follow should help you in that effort.

The correctness of your communication will be important to you and your company. It will be important to you because people will judge you by it, and how they judge you will help determine your success in life. It will be important to your company because it will help convey the image of competence that companies like. People judge a company by how its employees act, think, talk, and write. Company executives want such judgments to be favorable.

- People judge you and your company by the correctness of your communication.

THE NATURE OF CORRECTNESS

Not all people agree that there are standards for correct communication. In fact, some people think there should be no general standards of this kind, that whatever communicates in a given case is all right. Businesspeople, however, generally accept the standards for correct usage that educated people have developed over the years. These are the standards that you have studied in your English composition classes and that appear in textbooks. Businesspeople expect you to follow them.

- Businesspeople expect you to follow the generally accepted standards of English.

These standards of correctness have one basic purpose: to assist in communicating. To some people the standards of correctness appear arbitrary or unnecessary. But such is not the case. They are designed to reduce misunderstanding—to make communication more precise. When you communicate precisely, you practice good ethics by meeting your reader's needs for understandable messages. It is only in this light that we can justify studying them.

- These standards of correctness assist in communicating.

The practical value of these standards is easily illustrated. Take, for example, the following two sentences. Their words are the same; only their punctuation differs. But what a difference the punctuation makes!

"The teacher," said the student, "is careless."

The teacher said, "The student is careless."

Can You Detect the Differences in Meaning the Punctuation Makes?

What's the latest dope?
What's the latest, dope?

The groom was asked to call the guests names as they arrived.
The groom was asked to call the guests' names as they arrived.

A clever dog knows it's master.
A clever dog knows its master.

Everyone, I know, has a problem.
Everyone I know has a problem.

Do not break your bread or roll in your soup.
Do not break your bread, or roll in your soup.

She ate a half-fried chicken.
She ate a half fried chicken.

I left him convinced he was a fool.
I left him, convinced he was a fool.

In the parade will be several hundred children, carrying flags and many important officials.
In the parade will be several hundred children, carrying flags, and many important officials.

The play ended, happily.
The play ended happily.

Thirteen people knew the secret, all told.
Thirteen people knew the secret; all told.

Or what about the following pair of sentences? Who is speaking, the Democrats or the Republicans? The commas make a difference.

> The Democrats, say the Republicans, will win.
> The Democrats say the Republicans will win.

Here are two more sentences. The difference here needs no explanation.

> He looked at her stern.
> He looked at her sternly.

- The following review covers the major standards. They are coded for your convenience.

- Take the self-analysis test to determine your present knowledge of the standards.

Because the standards of correctness are important to your communication in business, this chapter will review them. The review is not complete, for much more space would be needed for complete coverage. But the major standards are covered, those that most often present problems in your writing. For your convenience, the standards are coded with symbols (letters and numbers). You should find these symbols useful in identifying the standards. Your instructor should find them useful as grading marks to identify errors in your writing.

You probably already know many of the standards of correctness, so the following information will not all be new to you. To help you determine how much you know and do not know, you should take the self-analysis test at the end of the chapter or on the textbook website. This will enable you to study the standards selectively. Because the self-analysis test covers only the more frequently used standards, however, you would be wise to review the entire chapter.

STANDARDS FOR PUNCTUATION

The following explanations cover the most important standards for correctness in punctuation. For reasons of accuracy, the explanations use some technical words. Even so, the illustrations should make the standards clear.

Apostrophe: Apos 1

Use the apostrophe to show the possessive case of nouns and indefinite pronouns. If the word does not end in *s,* add an apostrophe and an *s*. If the word ends in *s,* add only an apostrophe.

- Use the apostrophe to show possession.

Nominative Form	Possessive Form
company	company's
employee	employee's
someone	someone's
companies	companies'
employees	employees'

Proper names and singular nouns ending in *s* sounds are exceptions. To such words you may add either an apostrophe and an *s* or just an apostrophe. Add only an apostrophe to the nominative plural.

Nominative Form	Possessive Form
Texas (singular)	Texas's, Texas'
Jones (singular)	Jones's, Jones'
Joneses (plural)	Joneses'
countess (singular)	countess's, countess'
boss (singular)	boss's

Apos 2

Use an apostrophe to mark the place in a contraction where letters are omitted. Do not use it to make personal pronouns possessive (its, hers).

- Mark omissions in contractions with the apostrophe.

> it is = it's
> has not = hasn't
> cannot = can't

Brackets: Bkts

Set off in brackets words that you wish to insert in a quotation.

- Use brackets to set off words that you insert in a quotation.

> "The use of this type of mentor [the personal coach] may still be increasing."
>
> "Direct supervision has diminished in importance during the past decade [the report was written in 2005], when 63 percent of the reporting business firms that started programs used teams."

Colon: Cln 1

Use the colon to introduce an enumeration, a formal quotation, or a statement of explanation.

- Use the colon to introduce formal statements.

> *Enumeration:* Working in this department are three classes of support: clerical support, computer support, and customer support.
>
> *Formal quotation:* President Hartung had this to say about the proposal: "Any such movement that fails to get the support of the workers from all divisions fails to get my support."
>
> *Explanation:* At this time the company was pioneering a new marketing idea: It was attempting to sell customized products directly to consumers through its website.

Cln 2

- Do not use the colon when it breaks the thought flow.

Do not use the colon when the thought of the sentence should continue without interruption. If introducing a list by a colon, the colon should be preceded by a word that explains or identifies the list.

> *Not this:* Cities in which new sales offices are in operation are: Fort Smith, Texarkana, Lake Charles, Jackson, and Biloxi.
>
> *But this:* Cities in which new sales offices are in operation are Fort Smith, Texarkana, Lake Charles, Jackson, and Biloxi.
>
> *Or this:* Cities with new sales offices are as follows: Fort Smith, Texarkana, Lake Charles, Jackson, and Biloxi.

Comma: Cma 1

- Use the comma to separate clauses connected by *and, but, or,* and *nor.*

Use the comma to separate independent (main) clauses connected by a coordinating conjunction. Some coordinating conjunctions are *and, but, or,* and *nor.* (An independent clause has a subject and a verb and stands by itself. A coordinating conjunction connects clauses, words, or phrases of equal rank.)

> Only two components of the index declined, and these two account for only 12 percent of the total weight of the index.
>
> New hybrid automobiles are moving at record volumes, but used-car sales are lagging behind the record pace set two years ago.

Make exceptions to this rule, however, in the case of compound sentences consisting of short and closely connected clauses.

> We sold and the price dropped.
>
> Sometimes we win and sometimes we lose.

Cma 2–1

- Use the comma to separate (1) items in a series and

Separate the items listed in a series by commas. In order to avoid misinterpretation of the rare instances in which some of the items listed have compound constructions, it is always good to include the comma between the last two items (before the final conjunction).

> Good copy must cover facts with accuracy, sincerity, honesty, and conviction.
>
> Direct advertising can be used to introduce salespeople, fill in between salespeople's calls, cover territory where salespeople cannot be maintained, and keep pertinent reference material in the hands of prospects.
>
> The DuPont Color Popularity Report conducted in 2005 indicated that in North America silver, white, blue, and black cars were the top five colors favored by the public.

Cma 2–2

Separate coordinate adjectives in a series by commas if they modify the same noun and if no *and* connects them. A good test to determine whether adjectives are coordinate is to insert an *and* between them. If the *and* does not change the meaning, the adjectives are coordinate.

● (2) adjectives in a series.

> Miss Pratt has been a reliable, faithful, efficient employee for 20 years.
>
> We guarantee that this is a good, clean car.
>
> Blue office furniture is Mr. Orr's recommendation for the new conference room. (*Office furniture* is practically a compound noun; *blue* modifies both words.)
>
> A big crescent wrench proved to be best for the task. (The *and* won't fit between *big* and *crescent*.)

Cma 3

Set off nonrestrictive modifiers by commas. By a *nonrestrictive modifier* we mean a modifier that could be omitted from the sentence without changing its meaning. Restrictive modifiers (those that restrict the words they modify to one particular object) are not set off by commas. A restrictive modifier cannot be left out of the sentence without changing its meaning.

● Use commas to set off nonrestrictive modifiers (those that could be left out without changing the meaning of the sentence).

> *Restrictive:* The salesperson who sells the most will get a bonus. (*Who sells the most* restricts the meaning to a particular salesperson.)
>
> *Nonrestrictive:* Diana Chan, who was the company's top salesperson for the year, was awarded a bonus. (If the clause *who was the company's top salesperson for the year* is omitted, the meaning of the sentence is not changed.)
>
> *Restrictive:* J. Ward & Company is the firm that employs most of the physically disabled in this area.
>
> *Nonrestrictive:* J. Ward & Company, the firm that employs most of the physically disabled in this area, has gained the admiration of the community.

Notice that some modifiers can be either restrictive or nonrestrictive, depending on the writer's intended meaning.

> *Restrictive:* All the cars that were damaged in the flood were sold at a discount. (Implies that some of the cars were not damaged.)
>
> *Nonrestrictive:* All the cars, which were damaged by the flood, were sold at a discount. (Implies that the entire fleet of cars was damaged.)

Cma 4–1

Use commas to set off parenthetical expressions. A parenthetic expression consists of words that interrupt the normal flow of the sentence. In a sense, they appear to be "stuck in." In many instances, they are simply words out of normal order. For example, the sentence "A full-page, black-and-white advertisement was run in the *Daily Bulletin*" contains a parenthetical expression when the word order is altered: "An advertisement, full-page and in black and white, was run in the *Daily Bulletin*."

● Use commas to set off (1) parenthetical expressions (comments "stuck in"),

> This practice, it is believed, will lead to financial ruin.
>
> Merck, as *The Wall Street Journal* reports, has sharply increased its alliance activity.

Although in such cases you may use dashes or the parentheses in place of commas, the three marks differ in the degree to which they separate the enclosed words from the rest of the sentence. The comma is the weakest of the three, and it is best used when the material set off is closely related to the surrounding words. Dashes are stronger marks than commas and are used when the material set off tends to be long or contains internal punctuation marks. Parentheses, the strongest of the three, are primarily used to enclose material that helps explain or supplement the main words of the sentence.

Cma 4–2

Use commas to set off an appositive (a noun or a noun and its modifiers inserted to explain another noun) from the rest of the sentence. In a sense, appositives are parenthetical expressions, for they interrupt the normal flow of the sentence.

> UPS, our primary shipper, is leasing a new distribution center in China.
> St. Louis, home office of our Midwest district, will be the permanent site of our annual sales meeting.
> President Cartwright, a self-educated woman, is the leading advocate of online training for employees.

But appositives that are required for the sentence meaning are not set off by commas.

> The word *liabilities* is not understood by most people.
> Our next shipment will come on the ship *Alberta*.

Cma 4–3

Set off parenthetical words include such transitional expressions as *however, in fact, of course, for example,* and *consequently* with commas.

> It is apparent, therefore, that the buyers' resistance was caused by an overvigorous sales campaign.
> After the first experiment, for example, the traffic flow increased 10 percent.
> The company, however, will be forced to adopt a more competitive pricing strategy.

Included in this group of parenthetical words may be introductory interjections (*oh, alas*) and responsive expressions (*yes, no, surely, indeed, well,* and *and so on*). But if the words are strongly exclamatory or are not closely connected with the rest of the sentence, they may be punctuated as a sentence. (*No. Yes. Indeed.*)

> Yes, the decision to increase product placement advertising has been made.
> Oh, contribute whatever you think is appropriate.

Cma 4–4

When more than one unit appears in a date or an address, set off the units by commas.

> *One unit:* December 30 is the date of our annual inventory.
> *One unit:* The company has one outlet in Ohio.
> *More than one unit:* December 30, 1906, is the date the Johnston Company first opened its doors.
> *More than one unit:* Richmond, Virginia, is the headquarters of the new sales district.

Cma 5–1

Use the comma after a subordinate clause that precedes the main clause.

> Although it is durable, this package does not have eye appeal.
> Since there was little store traffic on aisle 13, the area was converted into storage space.

Cma 5–2

Place a comma after an introductory verbal phrase. A verbal phrase is one that contains some verb derivative: a gerund, a participle, or an infinitive.

> *Gerund phrase:* After gaining the advantage, we failed to press on to victory.
> *Participle phrase:* Realizing his mistake, Ron instructed his direct reports to keep a record of all salvaged equipment.

Infinitive phrase: To increase the turnover of automobile accessories, we must first improve their display area.

Cma 6–1

Use the comma only for good reason. It is not a mark to be inserted indiscriminately at the writer's whim. As a rule, the use of commas should be justified by one of the standard practices previously noted.

Do not be tricked into putting a comma between the subject and the verb.

The thought that he could not afford to fail spurred him on. (No comma after *fail.*)

● Do not use the comma without good reason, such as between the subject and the verb.

Cma 6–2

Take exception to the preceding standards wherever the insertion of a comma will help clarity of expression.

Not this: From the beginning inventory methods of Hill Company have been haphazard.

But this: From the beginning, inventory methods of Hill Company have been haphazard.

Not this: Ever since she has been a model worker.

But this: Ever since, she has been a model worker.

● Use the comma wherever it helps clarity.

Dash: Dsh

Use the dash to set off an element for emphasis or to show interrupted thought. In particular, use it with long parenthetical expressions or parenthetical expressions containing internal punctuation (see Cma 4–1). Most word processing software will usually allow you to insert a dash with a special character code. Depending on the software, you either insert the code through a combination of keystrokes or by selecting the character from a character map. You can also make the dash by striking the hyphen twice, without spacing before or after.

Budgets for some past years—2006, for example—were prepared without consulting the department heads.

The test proved that the new process is simple, effective, accurate—and more expensive.

Only one person—the supervisor in charge—has authority to approve a policy exception.

If you want a voice in the government—vote.

● Use the dash to show interruption or emphasis.

Exclamation Mark: Ex

Use the exclamation mark at the end of a sentence or an exclamatory fragment to show strong emotion. But use it sparingly; never use it with trivial ideas.

We've done it again!

Congratulations! Your outstanding performance review qualifies you for merit pay.

● Use exclamation marks to show strong feeling.

Hyphen: Hpn 1

Use the hyphen to indicate the division of a word at the end of the line. You must divide between syllables. It is generally impractical to leave a one-letter syllable at the end of a line (*a-bove*) or to carry over a two-letter syllable to the next line (*expens-es*).

If you turn on the hyphenation feature of your word processing software, you can let it automatically take care of hyphenating words. This feature permits you to set a hyphenation range. The wider the range, the fewer words that will be hyphenated and the more ragged your margin; the narrower the range, the more words that will be hyphenated and the smoother your right margin. You also have the option of controlling

● Mark word divisions with hyphens.

the hyphenation you desire. You can accept what the program recommends, suggest a different place to hyphenate, or tell it not to hyphenate.

Hpn 2–1

- Place hyphens between the parts of compound words.

Place hyphens between the parts of some compound words. Generally, the hyphen is used whenever its absence would confuse the meaning of the words.

Compound nouns: brother-in-law, cure-all, city-state, foreign-born

Compound numbers twenty-one through ninety-nine: fifty-five, eighty-one

Compound adjectives (two or more words used before a noun as a single adjective): *long-term* contract, *50-gallon* drum, *five-day* grace period, *end-of-month* clearance

Prefixes (most have been absorbed into the word): co-organizer, ex-chairperson, anti-inflation, self-sufficient

Hpn 2–2

- Do not place hyphens between (1) proper names and

A proper name used as a compound adjective needs no hyphen or hyphens to hold it together as a visual unit for the reader. The capitals perform that function.

Correct: a Lamar High School student

Correct: a United Airlines pilot

Hpn 2–3

- (2) words that only follow each other.

Two or more modifiers in normal grammatical form and order need no hyphens. Particularly, a phrase consisting of an unmistakable adverb (one ending in *ly*) modifying an adjective or participle that in turn modifies a noun shows normal grammatical order and is readily grasped by the reader without the benefit of the hyphen. But an adverb not ending in *ly* is joined to its adjective or participle by the hyphen.

No hyphen needed: a poorly drawn chart

Use the hyphen: a well-prepared chart

Italics: Ital 1

- Use italics for (1) publication titles,

For the use of italics for book titles, see QM 4. Note that italics also are used for titles of periodicals, works of art, long musical compositions, and names of naval vessels and aircraft.

Ital 2

- (2) foreign words and abbreviations, and

Italicize rarely used foreign words—if you must use them (*wunderbar, keiretsu, oobeya*). After a foreign word is widely accepted, however, it does not need to be italicized (carpe diem, faux pas, verboten). A current dictionary is a good source for information on which foreign words are italicized.

Ital 3

- (3) a word used as its own name.

Italicize a word, letter, or figure used as its own name. Without this device, we could not write this set of rules. Note the use of italics throughout to label name words.

The little word *sell* is still in the dictionary.

The pronoun *which* should always have a noun as a clear antecedent. (Without the italics, this one becomes a fragment.)

Parentheses: Parens

- Set off parenthetical words with parentheses.

Use the parenthesis to set off words that are parenthetical or are inserted to explain or supplement the principal message (see Cma 4–1).

PART 6   Cross-Cultural Communication, Correctness, Technology, Research

Software Enhances the Usefulness of Reference Tools

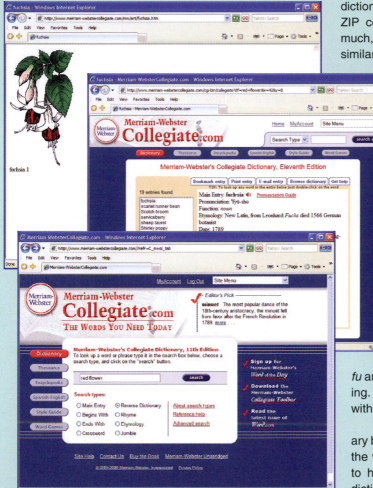

Electronic reference tools, like reference books, allow writers to look up facts when they need them. All kinds of reference materials are available electronically, from dictionaries to grammar and style guides, encyclopedias, ZIP code directories, quotation databases, maps, and much, much more. These programs vary widely in their similarities to and differences from print reference books.

Often they enhance the printed form, giving the user more ways to use them. Electronic dictionaries let you search for words the traditional way, with wildcards, as soundalikes (homophones), by words in their definition, and more. In the bottom screen, you see a search on the Merriam-Webster website for the word *fuchsia* in a reverse dictionary by searching its definition for the words *red* and *flower*. As you can see in the middle screen, the software identified 19 words with these search terms. Sometime you may recognize the word the minute you see it on the list; other times you'll need to review the definitions and perhaps check any illustrations. If you were unsure of the spelling, you could search by its beginning or ending letters. Also, you may know the word begins with *fu* and ends with *a,* but not know the middle of the spelling. You could use the asterisk (*) wildcard, searching with *fu*a* to find it.

Electronic dictionaries go beyond the printed dictionary by providing audio as well. The user here, looking up the word *fuchsia,* would simply click on the sound icon to hear the word pronounced. Additionally, electronic dictionaries often link to other definitions to help users understand the meaning when words in the definition are unclear. Such dictionaries, as well as all reference software, help writers to choose words that communicate clearly and to be correct in their writing.

David Rick's phenomenal illustrations (*Blunders in International Business,* 2006) show readers that even large corporations make incredible mistakes.

As soon as Owen Smith was elected chairperson (the vote was almost 2 to 1), he introduced his plan for reorganization.

Period: Pd 1

Use the period to indicate the end of a declarative sentence, an imperative statement, or a courteous request.

- End a declarative sentence, an imperative statement, or a courteous request with a period.

Declarative sentence: The survey will be completed and returned by October 26.

Imperative statement: Complete and return the survey by October 26.

Courteous request: Will you please complete and return the survey by October 26?

Pd 2

• Use periods in abbreviations.

Use periods after abbreviations or initials.

> Ph.D., Co., Inc., a.m., etc.

But omit the periods and use all capitals in the initials or acronyms of agencies, networks, associations, and such: IRS, NBC, OPEC, EEC.

Pd 3

• Use a series of periods to show omissions.

Use ellipses (a series of periods) to indicate the omission of words from a quoted passage. If the omitted part consists of something less than a sentence, three periods are customarily placed at the point of omission (a fourth period is added if the omission is a sentence or more). If the omitted part is a paragraph or more, however, a full line of periods is used. In all cases, the periods are separated by spaces.

> Logical explanations, however, have been given by authorities in the field. Some attribute the decline . . . to recent changes in the state's economy. . . .
> . . . .
> Added to the labor factor is the high cost of raw material, which has tended to eliminate many marginal producers. Moreover, the rising cost of electric power in recent years may have shifted the attention of many industry leaders to other forms of production.

Question Mark: Q

• End direct questions with the question mark.

Place a question mark at the end of sentences that are direct questions.

> What are the latest quotations on Disney common stock?
> Will this campaign help sell Microsoft products?

But do not use the question mark with indirect questions.

> The president was asked whether this campaign would help sell Microsoft products.
> He asked me what the latest quotations on Disney common stock were.

Quotation Marks: QM 1

• Use quotation marks to enclose a speaker's or writer's exact words.

Use quotation marks to enclose the exact words of a speaker or, if the quotation is short, the exact words of a writer.

Short written quotations are quotations of four lines or less, although authorities do not agree on this point. Some suggest three lines—others up to eight. Longer written quotations are best displayed without quotation marks and with an indented right and left margin.

> *Short written quotation:* Ben Bernanke sums up his presentation with this statement: "The central bank will remain vigilant to ensure that recent increases in inflation do not become chronic."
> *Oral quotation:* "This really should bring on a production slowdown," said Ms. Kuntz.

If a quotation is broken by explanation or reference words, each part of the quotation is enclosed in quotation marks.

> "Will you be specific," he asked, "in recommending a course of action?"

QM 2

• Use single quotation marks for a quotation within a quotation.

Enclose a quotation within a quotation with single quotation marks.

> Professor Dalbey said, "It has been a long time since I have heard a student say, 'Prof, we need more writing assignments.'"

QM 3

Always place periods and commas inside quotation marks. Place semicolons and colons outside the quotation marks. Place question marks and exclamation points inside if they apply to the quoted passage only and outside if they apply to the whole sentence.

> "If we are patient," he said, "we will reach this year's goals." (The comma and the period are within the quotation marks.)
>
> "Is there a quorum?" he asked. (The question mark belongs to the quoted passage.)
>
> Which of you said, "I know where the error lies"? (The question mark applies to the entire sentence.)
>
> I conclude only this from the union's promise to "force the hand of management": A strike will be its trump card.

● Periods and commas go inside quotation marks; semicolons and colons go outside; question marks and exclamation points go inside when they apply to the quoted part and outside when they apply to the entire sentence.

QM 4

Enclose in quotation marks the titles of parts of publications (articles in a magazine, chapters in a book). But italicize the titles of whole publications or underline if you are handwriting.

> The third chapter of the book *Elementary Statistical Procedure* is titled "Concepts of Sampling."
>
> Anne Fisher's timely article, "Fatal Mistakes When Starting a New Job," appears in the current issue of *Fortune*.

● Use quotation marks to enclose titles of parts of a publication.

Semicolon: SC 1

Use the semicolon to separate independent clauses that are not connected by a conjunction.

> The new contract provides wage increases; the original contract emphasized shorter hours.

Covered by this standard are independent clauses connected by conjunctive adverbs (transitional expressions) such as *however, nevertheless, therefore, then, moreover,* and *besides*.

> The survey findings indicated a need to revise the policy; nevertheless, the president did not approve the proposed revision.
>
> Small-town buyers favor the old model; therefore, the board concluded that both models should be marketed.

● Use the semicolon to separate independent clauses not connected by a conjunction.

SC 2

You may use the semicolon to separate independent clauses joined by *and, but, or,* or *nor* (coordinating conjunctions) if the clauses are long or if they have other punctuation in them. In such situations, you may also use the semicolon for special emphasis.

> The OCAW and the NUPNG, rivals from the beginning of the new industry, have shared almost equally in the growth of membership; but the OCAW predominates among workers in the petroleum-products crafts, including pipeline construction and operation, and the NUPNG leads in memberships of chemical workers.
>
> The market price was $6; but we paid $10.

● You may choose to separate with a semicolon independent clauses joined by a conjunction.

SC 3

Separate by semicolons the items in a list when the items have commas in them.

> The following gains were made in the February year-to-year comparison: Fort Worth, 7,300; Dallas, 4,705; Lubbock, 2,610; San Antonio, 2,350; Waco, 2,240; Port Arthur, 2,170; and Corpus Christi, 1,420.

● Use the semicolon to separate items in a list when the items contain commas.

Spell Check

Eye halve a spelling chequer
It came with my pea sea
It plainly marques four my revue
Miss steaks eye kin knot sea.

Eye strike a key and type a word
And weight four it two say
Weather eye am wrong oar write
It shows me strait a weigh.

As soon as a mist aches is maid
It nose bee fore two long
And eye can put the error rite
Its rare lea ever wrong.

Eye have run this poem threw it
I am shore your pleased two no
Its letter perfect awl the weigh
My chequer tolled me sew.

—Sauce unknown

Elected for the new term were Anna T. Zelnak, attorney from Cincinnati; Wilbur T. Hoffmeister, stockbroker and president of Hoffmeister Associates of Baltimore; and William P. Peabody, a member of the faculty of the University of Georgia.

SC 4

- Use the semicolon only between equal units.

Use the semicolon between equal (coordinate) units only. Do not use it to attach a dependent clause or phrase to an independent clause.

> *Not this:* The flood damaged much of the equipment in Building 113; making it necessary for management to close the area and suspend some employees.
>
> *But this:* The flood damaged much of the equipment in Building 113, making it necessary for management to close the area and suspend some employees.
>
> *Or this:* The flood damaged much of the equipment in Building 113; thus, it was necessary for management to close the area and suspend some employees.

STANDARDS FOR GRAMMAR

Like the review of punctuation standards, the following summary of grammatical standards is not intended as a complete handbook on the subject. Rather, it is a summary of the major trouble spots that business writers encounter. If you learn these grammatical principles, you should be able to write with the correctness expected in business.

Adjective–Adverb Confusion: AA

- Do not use adjectives for adverbs.

Do not use adjectives for adverbs or adverbs for adjectives. Adjectives modify only nouns and pronouns; and adverbs modify verbs, adjectives, or other adverbs.

Possibly the chief source of this confusion occurs in statements in which the modifier follows the verb. If the modifier refers to the subject, an adjective should be used. If it refers to the verb, an adverb is needed.

Not this: She filed the records *quick*.

But this: She filed the records *quickly*. (Refers to the verb.)

Not this: John doesn't feel *badly*.

But this: John doesn't feel *bad*. (Refers to the noun.)

Not this: The new cars look *beautifully*.

But this: The new cars look *beautiful*. (Refers to the noun.)

It should be noted that many words are both adjective and adverb (*little, well, fast, much*). And some adverbs have two forms, one the same as the adjective and the other with *ly* (*slow* and *slowly, cheap* and *cheaply, quick* and *quickly*).

Acceptable: All our drivers are instructed to drive slow.

Acceptable: All our drivers are instructed to drive slowly.

Subject–Verb Agreement: Agmt SV

Nouns and their verbs must agree in number. A plural noun must have a plural verb form; a singular noun must have a singular verb form.

- Verbs must agree in number with their subjects.

Not this: Expenditures for miscellaneous equipment *was* expected to decline. (Expenditures is plural, so its verb must be plural.)

But this: Expenditures for miscellaneous equipment *were* expected to decline.

Not this: The *president,* as well as the staff, *were* not able to attend. (*President* is the subject, and the number is not changed by the modifying phrase.)

But this: The *president,* as well as the staff, *was* not able to attend.

Not this: There's several reasons why we should act.

But this: There are several reasons why we should act.

Compound subjects (two or more nouns joined by *and*) require plural verbs.

- Compound subjects require plural verbs.

Not this: The *salespeople* and their *manager is* in favor of the proposal. (*Salespeople* and *manager* make a compound subject, but *is* is singular.)

But this: The *salespeople* and their *manager are* in favor of the proposal.

Not this: Received in the morning delivery *was* an *ink cartridge* and two *reams* of copy paper. (*Ink cartridge* and *reams* are the subjects; the verb must be plural.)

But this: Received in the morning delivery *were* an *ink cartridge* and two *reams* of copy paper.

Collective nouns may be either singular or plural, depending on the meaning intended.

- Collective nouns may be singular or plural.

The *committee have* carefully *studied* the proposal. (*Committee* is thought of as separate individuals.)

The *committee has* carefully *studied* the proposal. (The *committee* is thought of as a unit.)

As a rule, the pronouns *anybody, anyone, each, either, everyone, everybody, neither, nobody, somebody,* and *someone* take a singular verb. The word *none* may be either singular or plural, depending on whether it is used to refer to one unit or to more than one unit.

- The pronouns listed here are singular.

Either of the advertising campaigns *is* costly.

Nobody who watches the clock *is* successful.

None of the workers *understands* his assignment.

None of the workers *understand* their assignments.

Adverbial Noun Clause: AN

Do not use an adverbial clause as a noun clause. Clauses beginning with *because, when, where, if,* and similar adverbial connections are not properly used as subjects, objects, or complements of verbs.

- Do not use an adverbial clause as a noun clause.

Not this: The reason was *because* he did not submit a report.
But this: The reason was *that* he did not submit a report.

Not this: A time-series graph is *where* (or *when*) changes in an index such as wholesale prices are indicated.
But this: A time-series graph is the picturing of . . .

Awkward: Awk

- Avoid awkward writing.

Avoid awkward writing. By *awkward writing* we mean word arrangements that are unconventional, uneconomical, or simply not the best for quick understanding.

Dangling Modifiers: Dng

- Avoid dangling modifiers (those that do not clearly modify a specific word).

Avoid the use of modifiers that do not clearly modify the right word in the sentence. Such modifiers are said to dangle. They are both illogical and confusing. You can usually correct sentences containing dangling constructions by inserting the noun or pronoun that the modifier describes or by changing the dangling part to a complete clause.

Not this: Believing that credit customers should have advance notice of the sale, special letters were mailed to them.
But this: Believing that credit customers should have advance notice of the sale, we mailed special letters to them. (Improvement is made by inserting the pronoun modified.)
Or this: Because we believed that credit customers should have advance notice of the sale, special letters were mailed to them. (Improvement is made by changing the dangling element to a complete clause.)

Dangling modifiers are of four principal types: participial phrases, elliptical clauses, gerund phrases, and infinitive phrases.

Not this: Believing that District 7 was not being thoroughly covered, an additional salesperson was assigned to the area. (Dangling participial phrase.)
But this: Believing that District 7 was not being thoroughly covered, the sales manager assigned an additional salesperson to the area.

Not this: By working hard, your goal can be reached. (Dangling gerund phrase.)
But this: By working hard, you can reach your goal.

Not this: To succeed at this job, long hours and hard work must not be shunned. (Dangling infinitive phrase.)
But this: To succeed at this job, one must not shun long hours and hard work.

Not this: While waiting on a customer, the watch was stolen. (Dangling elliptical clause—a clause without a noun or verb.)
But this: While the salesperson was waiting on a customer, the watch was stolen.

- Some introductory phrases are permitted to dangle.

However, several generally accepted introductory phrases are permitted to dangle. Included in this group are *generally speaking, confidentially speaking, taking all things into consideration,* and such expressions as *in boxing, in welding,* and *in farming.*

Generally speaking, business activity is at an all-time high.
In farming, the land must be prepared long before planting time.
Taking all things into consideration, this applicant is the best for the job.

Sentence Fragment: Frag

- Avoid sentence fragments (words used as a sentence that are not a sentence).

Avoid the sentence fragment. Although the sentence fragment may sometimes be used to good effect, as in sales writing, it is best avoided by all but the most skilled writers. The sentence fragment consists of any group of words that are used as if they were a sentence but are not a sentence. Probably the most frequent cause of sentence fragments is the use of a subordinate clause as a sentence.

Not this: Believing that you will want an analysis of sales for November. We have sent you the figures.

But this: Believing that you will want an analysis of sales for November, we have sent you the figures.

Not this: He declared that such a procedure would not be practical. And that it would be too expensive in the long run.

But this: He declared that such a procedure would not be practical and that it would be too expensive in the long run.

Pronouns: Pn 1

Make certain that the word each pronoun refers to (its antecedent) is clear. Failure to conform to this standard causes confusion, particularly in sentences in which two or more nouns are possible antecedents or the antecedent is far away from the pronoun.

- A pronoun should refer clearly to a preceding word.

Not this: When the president objected to Mr. Carter, he told him to mind his own business. (Who told whom?)

But this: When the president objected to Mr. Carter, Mr. Carter told him to mind his own business.

Not this: The mixture should not be allowed to boil; so when you do it, watch the temperature gauge. (*It* doesn't have an antecedent.)

But this: The mixture should not be allowed to boil; so when conducting the experiment, watch the temperature gauge.

Not this: The Model *Q* is being introduced this year. Ads in *USA Today, The Wall Street Journal,* and big-city newspapers over the country are designed to get sales off to a good start. It is especially designed for the business person who is not willing to pay a big price.

But this: The Model *Q* is being introduced this year. Ads in *USA Today, The Wall Street Journal,* and big-city newspapers over the country are designed to get sales off to a good start. The new model is especially designed for the business person who is not willing to pay a big price.

Confusion may sometimes result from using a pronoun with an implied antecedent.

Not this: Because of the disastrous freeze in the citrus belt, it is necessary that most of them be replanted.

But this: Because of the disastrous freeze in the citrus belt, most of the citrus orchards must be replanted.

Except when the reference of *which, that,* and *this* is perfectly clear, it is wise to avoid using these pronouns to refer to the whole idea of a preceding clause. Many times you can make the sentence clear by using a clarifying noun following the pronoun.

- Usually avoid using *which, that,* and *this* to refer to broad ideas.

Not this (following a detailed presentation of the writer's suggestion for improving the company suggestion plan): This should be put into effect without delay.

But this: This suggestion plan should be put into effect right away.

Confusion may also result when using a pronoun with a group noun as the antecedent. For reference to the group as a singular entity:

Not this: The committee gave their decision on the new proposal they reviewed.

But this: The committee gave its decision on the new proposal it reviewed.

For reference to the group as individual units:

Not this: The presenter polled the audience for its interpretation on the data.

But this: The presenter polled the audience for their interpretation on the data.

Pn 2

The number of the pronoun should agree with the number of its antecedent (the word it stands for). If the antecedent is singular, its pronoun must be singular. If the antecedent is plural, its pronoun must be plural.

- The number of a pronoun should be the same as that of the word to which the pronoun refers.

Not this: Taxes and insurance are expenses in any business, and it must be considered carefully in anticipating profits.

But this: Taxes and insurance are expenses in any business, and they must be considered carefully in anticipating profits.

Not this: Everybody should plan for their retirement. (Such words as *everyone, everybody,* and *anybody* are singular.)

But this: Everybody should plan for his or her retirement.

Pn 3

- Use the correct case of pronoun.

Take care to use the correct case of the pronoun. If the pronoun serves as the subject of the verb, or if it follows a form of the infinitive *to be,* use a pronoun in the nominative case. (The nominative personal pronouns are *I, you, he, she, it, we,* and *they*).

He will record the minutes of the meeting.

I think it will be he.

If the pronoun is the object of a preposition or a verb, or if it is the subject of an infinitive, use the objective case. (The objective personal pronouns are *me, you, him, her, it, us, them.*)

Not this: This transaction is between you and *he.* (*He* is nominative and cannot be the object of the preposition *between.*)

But this: This transaction is between you and *him.*

Not this: Because the investigator praised Ms. Smith and *I,* we were promoted.

But this: Because the investigator praised Ms. Smith and *me,* we were promoted.

The case of a relative pronoun (*who, whom*) is determined by the pronoun's use in the clause it introduces. One good way of determining which case to use is to substitute the personal pronoun for the relative pronoun. If the case of the personal pronoun that fits is nominative, use *who.* If it is objective, use *whom.*

George Cutler is the salesperson *who* won the award. (*He,* nominative, could be substituted for the relative pronoun; therefore, nominative *who* should be used.)

George Cutler is the salesperson *whom* you recommended. (Objective *him* could be substituted; thus, objective *whom* is used.)

The possessive case is used for pronouns that immediately precede a gerund (a verbal noun ending in *ing*).

Our selling of the stock frightened some of the conservative members of the board.

Her accepting the money ended her legal claim to the property.

Parallelism: Prl

- Express equal thoughts in parallel (equal) grammatical form.

Parts of a sentence that express equal thoughts should be parallel (the same) in grammatical form. Parallel constructions are logically connected by the coordinating conjunctions *and, but,* and *or.* Care should be taken to see that the sentence elements connected by these conjunctions are of the same grammatical type. That is, if one of the parts is a noun, the other parts also should be nouns. If one of the parts is an infinitive phrase, the other parts also should be infinitive phrases.

Not this: The company objectives for the coming year are to match last year's sales volume, higher earnings, and improving customer relations.

But this: The company objectives for the coming year are to match last year's sales volume, to increase earnings, and to improve customer relations.

Not this: Writing copy may be more valuable experience than to make layouts.

But this: Writing copy may be more valuable experience than making layouts.

Not this: The questionnaire asks for this information: number of employees, what is our union status, and how much do we pay.

But this: The questionnaire asks for this information: number of employees, union affiliation, and pay rate.

Tense: Tns

The tense of each verb, infinitive, and participle should reflect the logical time of happening of the statement. Every statement has its place in time. To communicate that place exactly, you must select your tenses carefully.

● The tense of each verb should show the logical time of happening.

Tns 1

Use present tense for statements of fact that are true at the time of writing.

Not this: Boston was not selected as a site for the headquarters because it *was* too near the coast. (Boston is still near the coast, isn't it?)

But this: Boston was not selected as a site for the headquarters because it *is* too near the coast.

● Use present tense for current happenings.

Tns 2

Use past tense in statements covering a definite past event or action.

Not this: Mr. Burns *says* to me, "Bill, you'll never become an auditor."

But this: Mr. Burns *said* to me, "Bill, you'll never become an auditor."

● Use past tense for past happenings.

Tns 3

The time period reflected by the past participle (*having been . . .*) is earlier than that of its governing verb. The present participle (*being . . .*) reflects the same time period as that of its governing verb.

Not this: These debentures are among the oldest on record, *being* issued in early 1937.

But this: These debentures are among the oldest on record, *having been* issued in early 1937.

Not this: Ms. Sloan, *having been* the top salesperson on the force, was made sales manager. (Possible but illogical.)

But this: Ms. Sloan, *being* the top salesperson on the force, was made sales manager.

● The past participle (*having been . . .*) indicates a time earlier than that of the governing verb, and the present participle (*being . . .*) indicates the same period as that of the governing verb.

Tns 4

Verbs in subordinate clauses are governed by the verb in the main clause. When the main verb is in the past tense, you should usually also place the subordinate verb in a past tense (past, past perfect, or present perfect).

I *noticed* [past tense] the discrepancy, and then I *remembered* [same time as main verb] the incidents that had caused it.

If the time of the subordinate clause is earlier than that of the main verb in past tense, use past perfect tense for the subordinate verb.

Not this: In early July, we *noticed* [past] that he *exceeded* [logically should be previous to main verb] his quota three times.

But this: In early July, we *noticed* that he *had exceeded* his quota three times.

The present perfect tense is used for the subordinate clause when the time of this clause is subsequent to the time of the main verb.

Not this: Before the war we *contributed* [past] generously, but lately we *forget* [should be a time subsequent to the time of the main verb] our duties.

But this: Before the war we *contributed* generously, but lately we *have forgotten* our duties.

● Verbs in the principal clause govern those in subordinate clauses.

● Present perfect tense (*have . . .*) refers to the indefinite past.

Tns 5

The present perfect tense does not logically refer to a definite time in the past. Instead, it indicates time somewhere in the indefinite past.

● Use of present perfect tense indicates time somewhere in the indefinite past.

Not this: We *have audited* your records on July 31 of 2005 and 2006.
But this: We *audited* your records on July 31 of 2005 and 2006.
Or this: We *have audited* your records twice in the past.

Word Use: WU

- Use words correctly.

Misused words call attention to themselves and detract from the writing. The possibilities of error in word use are infinite; the following list contains only a few of the common errors of this kind.

Don't Use	Use
a long ways	a long way
and etc.	etc.
anywheres	anywhere
continue on	continue
different than	different from
have got to	must
in back of	behind
in hopes of	in hope of
in regards to	in regard to
inside of	within
kind of satisfied	somewhat satisfied
nowhere near	not nearly
nowheres	nowhere
over with	over
seldom ever	seldom
try and come	try to come

Wrong Word: WW

- Check the spelling and meanings of words carefully.

Wrong words refer to meaning one word and using another. Sometimes these words are confused by their spelling and sometimes by their meanings. Since the spell checker won't find these errors, you need to proofread carefully to eliminate them. Here are a few examples:

affect	effect
among	between
bow	bough
capital	capitol
cite	sight, site
collision	collusion
complement	compliment
cooperation	corporation
deferential	differential
desert	dessert
except	accept
implicit	explicit
imply	infer
plane	plain
principal	principle
stationary	stationery

STANDARDS FOR THE USE OF NUMBERS: NO

Quantities may be spelled out or expressed as numerals. Whether to use one form or the other is often a perplexing question. It is especially perplexing to business writers, for much of their work deals with quantitative subjects. Because the proper expression of quantities is vital to business writers, the following notes on the use of numbers are presented.

No 1

Although authorities do not agree on number usage, business writers would do well to follow the rule of nine. By this rule, you spell out numbers nine and below. You use figures for numbers above nine.

> The auditor found 13 discrepancies in the stock records.
>
> The auditor found nine discrepancies in the stock records.

Apply the rule to both ordinal and cardinal numbers:

> She was the seventh applicant.
>
> She was the 31st applicant.

● Spell out numbers nine and under, and use figures for higher numbers, except as follows:

No 2

Make an exception to the rule of nine when a number begins a sentence. Spell out all numbers in this position.

> Seventy-three bonds and six debentures were destroyed.
>
> Eighty-nine strikers picketed the north entrance.

● Spell out numbers that begin a sentence.

No 3

In comparisons, keep all numbers in the same form. If any number requires numeral form, use numerals for all the numbers.

> We managed to salvage 3 printers, 1 scanner, and 13 monitors.

● Keep in the same form all numbers in comparisons.

No 4

Use numerals for all percentages.

> Sales increases over last year were 9 percent on automotive parts, 14 percent on hardware, and 23 percent on appliances.

On whether to use the percent sign (%) or the word, authorities differ. One good rule to follow is to use the percentage sign in papers that are scientific or technical and the word in all others. Also, it is conventional to use the sign following numbers in graphics. The trend in business appears to be toward using the sign. Consistent use of either is correct.

● Use numerals for percentages.

No 5

Present days of the month in figure form when the month precedes the day.

> June 29, 2008.

When days of the month appear alone or precede the month, they may be either spelled out or expressed in numeral form according to the rule of nine.

> I will be there on the 13th.
>
> The union scheduled the strike vote for the eighth.
>
> Ms. Millican signed the contract on the seventh of July.
>
> Sales have declined since the 14th of August.

● Use figures for days of the month when the month precedes the day.

No 6

For dates, use either day, month, year or month, day, year sequence, the latter with year set off by commas.

Use either of the two orders for date information. One, preferred by *The Chicago Manual of Style,* is day, month, and year:

> On 29 June 2008 we introduced a new product line.

The other is the conventional sequence of month, day, and year. This order requires that the year be set off by commas:

> On June 29, 2008, we introduced a new product line.

No 7

Present amounts like other numbers, spelling units when numbers are spelled and using appropriate symbols or abbreviations when in figures.

Present money amounts as you would other numbers. If you spell out the number, also spell out the unit of currency.

> Twenty-seven dollars

If you present the number as a figure, use the $ with U.S. currency and the appropriate abbreviation or symbol with other currencies.

U.S., Canada, and Mexico	US $27.33, Can $27.33, Mex $27.33
Euro countries	€202.61
Japan	¥2,178.61
Thailand	฿7,489.91

No 8

Usually spell indefinite numbers and amounts.

Usually spell out indefinite numbers and amounts.

> Over a million people live there.
> The current population is about four hundred thousand.
> Bill Gates's net worth is in the billions.

No 9

Spell out fractions that stand alone or begin a sentence. Use numerics with whole numbers and in technical contexts.

Spell out a fraction such as *one-half* that stands alone (without a whole number) or begins a sentence. However, if this results in long and awkward wording or if the context is technical, use the numeric form.

> Two-thirds of all jobs in the United States are jobs in the information industry.
> The median price of a home rose by 6½ percent this year.

No 10

Only use both words and figures for legal reasons.

Except in legal documents, do not express amounts in both figures and words.

> *For legal purposes:* 25 (twenty-five)
> *For business use:* either the figure or the word, depending on circumstance

SPELLING: SP

Spell words correctly. Use the dictionary.

Misspelling is probably the most frequently made error in writing. And it is the least excusable. It is inexcusable because all one needs to do to virtually eliminate the error is to use a dictionary and a spell checker. Unfortunately, spell checkers cannot detect a correctly spelled, but misused, word.

See Figure 17–1 for the 80 most commonly misspelled words.

We must memorize to spell. Thus, becoming a good speller involves long, hard work. Even so, you can improve your spelling significantly with relatively little effort. Studies show that fewer than 100 words account for most spelling errors. So if you will learn to spell these most troublesome words, you will go a long way toward solving your spelling problems. Eighty of these words appear in Figure 17–1. Although

Figure 17–1

Eighty of the Most Frequently Misspelled Words

absence	desirable	irritable	pursue
accessible	despair	leisure	questionnaire
accommodate	development	license	receive
achieve	disappear	misspelling	recommend
analyze	disappoint	necessary	repetition
argument	discriminate	ninety	ridiculous
assistant	drunkenness	noticeable	seize
balloon	embarrassment	occasionally	separate
benefited	equivalent	occurrence	sergeant
category	exceed	panicky	sheriff
cede	existence	parallel	succeed
changeable	forty	paralyze	suddenness
committee	grammar	pastime	superintendent
comparative	grievous	persistent	supersede
conscience	holiday	possesses	surprise
conscious	incidentally	predictable	truly
deductible	indispensable	privilege	until
definitely	insistent	proceed	vacuum
dependent	irrelevant	professor	vicious
description	irresistible	pronunciation	weird

English spelling follows little rhyme or reason, a few helpful rules exist. You would do well to learn and use them.

Rules for Word Plurals

1. To form the plurals of most words, add *s.*

> price, prices
> quote, quotes

2. To form the plurals of words ending in *s, sh, ch,* and *x,* usually add *es* to the singular.

> boss, bosses
> relinquish, relinquishes
> glitch, glitches
> tax, taxes

● These three rules cover plurals for most words.

3. To form the plural of words ending in *y,* if a consonant precedes the *y,* drop the *y* and add *ies.* But if the *y* is preceded by a vowel, add *s.*

> company, companies
> medley, medleys
> key, keys

Other Spelling Rules

1. Words ending in *ce* or *ge* do not drop the *e* when adding *ous* or *able.*

> charge, chargeable
> change, changeable
> notice, noticeable
> service, serviceable

● These rules cover four other trouble areas of spelling.

2. Words ending in *l* do not drop the *l* when adding *ly.*

> final, finally
> principal, principally

3. Words ending in silent *e* usually drop the *e* when adding a suffix beginning with a vowel.

> have, having
> believe, believable
> dine, dining
> time, timing

4. Place *i* before *e* except after *c*.

> relieve   conceive
> believe   receive

Exception: when the word is sounded as long *a*.

> neighbor   weigh

Exceptions:

either	Fahrenheit	height
seize	surfeit	efficient
sufficient	neither	foreign
leisure	ancient	seizure
weird	financier	codeine
forfeit	seismograph	sovereign
deficient	science	counterfeit

CAPITALIZATION: CAP

● Capitalize all proper names and the beginning words of sentences.

Use capitals for the first letters of proper names. Exceptions include names designed or used by the owner to begin with lowercase such as eBay, iOmega, and nVidia. Common examples are these:

> *Streets:* 317 East Boyd Avenue
> *Geographic places:* Chicago, Indiana, Finland
> *Companies:* Qualcomm
> *Title preceding names:* President Watkins
> *Titles of books, articles, poems: Getting Things Done: The Art of Stress-Free Prodoctirity*
> *First words of sentences and complimentary closes*
> *The word* **number** *(or its abbreviation) when used with a figure to identify something:* Our supply of No. 10 envelopes is running low.

As noted earlier, other standards are useful in clear communication. But those covered in the preceding pages will help you through most of your writing problems. By using them, you can give your writing the precision that good communication requires. For further references on this topic, you will find several links to more detailed sources on the textbook website. You also will find some interactive self-tests there to help you review this material.

CRITICAL THINKING QUESTIONS

Correct any punctuation or grammar errors you can find in the following sentences. Explain your corrections.

1 Charles E. Baskin the new member of the advisory committee has been an employee for seven years.

2 The auditor asked us, "If all members of the work group had access to the petty cash fund?"

3 Our January order consisted of the following items; two dozen Post-it pads, cube size, one dozen desk blotters, 20 by 32 inches, and one dozen gel roller pens, permanent black.

4 The truth of the matter is, that the union representative had not informed the workers of the decision.

5 Sales for the first quarter were the highest in history, profits declined for the period.

6 We suggest that you use a mild soap for best results but detergents will not harm the product.

7 Employment for October totaled 12,741 an increase of 3.1 percent over September.

8 It would not be fair however to consider only this point.

9 It is the only shrink resistant antiwrinkle and inexpensive material available.

10 Todd Thatcher a supervisor in our company is accused of the crime.

11 Mr. Goodman made this statement, "Contrary to our expectations, Smith and Company will lose money this year."

12 I bought and he sold.

13 Soon we saw George Sweeney who is the auditor for the company.

14 Sold in light medium and heavy weight this paper has been widely accepted.

15 Because of a common belief that profits are too high we will have to cut our prices on most items.

16 Such has been the growth of the cities most prestigious firm, H.E. Klauss and Company.

17 In 2006 we were advised in fact we were instructed to accept this five year contract.

18 Henrys goofing off has gotten him into trouble.

19 Cyrus B. Henshaw who was our leading salesperson last month is the leading candidate for the position.

20 The sales representative who secures the most new accounts will receive a bonus.

21 The word phone which is short for telephone should be avoided in formal writing.

22 In last months issue of Fortune appeared Johnson's latest article Tiger! The Sky's the Limit for Golf.

23 Yes he replied this is exactly what we mean.

24 Why did he say John it's too late?

25 Place your order today, it is not too late.

26 We make our plans on a day to day basis.

27 There is little accuracy in the 60 day forecast.

28 The pre Christmas sale will extend over twenty six days.

29 We cannot tolerate any worker's failure to do their duty.

30 An assortment of guns, bombs, burglar tools, and ammunition were found in the seller.

31 If we can be certain that we have the facts we can make our decision soon.

32 This one is easy to make. If one reads the instructions carefully.

33 This is the gift he received from you and I.

34 A collection of short articles on the subject were printed.

35 If we can detect only a tenth of the errors it will make us realize the truth.

36 She takes criticism good.

37 There was plenty of surprises at the meeting.

38 It don't appear that we have made much progress.

39 The surface of these products are smooth.

40 Everybody is expected to do their best.

41 The brochures were delivered to John and I early Sunday morning.

42 Who did he recommend for the job.

43 We were given considerable money for the study.

44 He seen what could happen when administration breaks down.

45 One of his conclusions is that the climate of the region was not desirable for our purposes.

46 Smith and Rogers plans to buy the Moline plant.

47 The committee feels that no action should be taken.

48 Neither of the workers found their money.

49 While observing the employees, the work flow was operating at peak perfection.

50 The new building is three stories high, fifteen years old, solid brick construction, and occupies a corner lot.

51 They had promised to have completed the job by noon.

52 Jones has been employed by Kimberly Clark for twenty years.

53 Wilson and myself will handle the job.

54 Each man and woman are expected to abide by this rule.

55 The boiler has been inspected on April 1 and May 3.

56 To find problems and correcting them takes up most of my work time.

57 The case of canned goods were distributed to the homeless.

58 The motor ran uneven.

59 All are expected except John and she.

60 Everyone here has more ability than him.

A SELF-ADMINISTERED DIAGNOSTIC TEST OF CORRECTNESS

The following test is designed to give you a quick measure of your ability to handle some of the most troublesome punctuation and grammar situations. First, correct all the errors in each sentence. Then turn to Appendix A for the recommended corrections and the symbols for the punctuation and grammar standards involved. Next, study the standards that you violate.

1 An important fact about this keyboard is, that it has the patented "ergonomic design".

2 Goods received on Invoice 2741 are as follows; 3 dozen blue denim shirts, size 15–33, 4 mens gortex gloves, brown, size large, and 5 dozen assorted socks.

3 James Silver president of the new union had the priviledge of introducing the speaker.

4 We do not expect to act on this matter however until we hear from you.

5 Shipments through September 20, 2007 totaled 69,485 pounds an increase of 17 percent over the year ago total.

6 Brick is recommended as the building material but the board is giving serious consideration to a substitute.

7 Markdowns for the sale total $34,000, never before has the company done anything like this.

8 After long experimentation a wear resistant high grade and beautiful stocking has been perfected.

9 Available in white green and blue this paint is sold by dealers all over the country.

10 Julie Jahn who won the trip is our most energetic salesperson.

11 Good he replied, sales are sure to increase.

12 Hogan's article Retirement? Never!, printed in the current issue of Management Review, is really a part of his book A Report on Worker Security.

13 Formal announcement of our Labor Day sale will be made in thirty two days.

14 Each day we encounter new problems. Although they are solved easily.

15 A list of models, sizes, and prices of both competing lines are being sent to you.

16 The manager could not tolerate any employee's failing to do their best.

17 A series of tests were completed only yesterday.

18 There should be no misunderstanding between you and I.

19 He run the accounting department for five years.

20 This report is considerable long.

21 Who did you interview for the position?

22 The report concluded that the natural resources of the Southwest was ideal for the chemical industry.

23 This applicant is six feet in height, 28 years old, weighs 165 pounds, and has had eight years' experience.

24 While reading the report, a gust of wind came through the window, blowing papers all over the room.

25 The sprinkler system has been checked on July 1 and September 3.

chapter eighteen

Technology-Enabled Communication

LEARNING OBJECTIVES

Upon completing this chapter, you will be able to describe the role of technology in business communication. To reach this goal, you should be able to

1 Explain how technology helps in constructing messages.

2 Identify appropriate tools for different stages in the writing process.

3 Discuss how technology helps in the presentation of messages.

4 Discuss various ways to transmit messages and the hardware currently used.

5 Describe how technology assists in collaboration.

6 Discuss what impact future developments in technology might have on business communication.

Business Communication Is Technology . . . Is Lesikar

In today's competitive work environment, technology and business communication go hand in hand. That's why the chapter you are about to read in *Business Communication: Making Connections in a Digital World* is also featured as an enhanced chapter with more material on the Web. It will be regularly updated by the authors to ensure the inclusion of the latest developments in technology that impact the world of business communication.

So visit our website often at **www.mhhe.com/lesikar11e** to get the most up-to-date information about the technological changes that affect the way we communicate in business. We look forward to your feedback.

Using Technology in Communication Tasks

The company that hired you after your recent graduation is looking into ways the information technology (IT) department can empower its employees with technological support. Your new boss has asked you to be on the team that is to propose new ideas. The boss has told you that this team, composed of employees from a variety of divisions, will discuss hardware, software, and the Internet. One of the main focuses will be on identifying ways to help employees improve their day-to-day communication.

This chapter is designed to help you—to give you a picture of where we are now and where we may be going. It provides a structure for continuing to build your understanding of how future technology will assist you in communication tasks.

• Technology assists with both the tedious and creative writing tasks.

Technological tools can enhance the uniquely human ability to communicate. But as with any set of tools, how one uses them determines their degree of effectiveness. By using your mind both to create messages and to focus the technology appropriately, you can improve the quality of your communication.

Appropriately used, technology can assist individuals and groups with both the routine work related to writing as well as the creative, thinking aspects. William Zinsser, author of *On Writing Well,* compares one tool—the word processor—to a dishwasher. He describes it as liberating one from a chore that's not creative and that saps one's energy. As you'll learn, several technological tools assist you in this fashion. George Gilder, publisher of the *Gilder Technology Report,* believes that the new technologies affirm our intellectual power and creativity. And Bill Gates, chairman of Microsoft, predicts that technology will help leverage our abilities to find, use, and share information. He also predicts that the tablet PCs will be widely used on college campuses. As bandwidth increases infinitely and videogaming collaboration pushes genres, Gates believes that technology will change the dynamics of all kinds of work—not just IT. Paul Saffo, Director of the Institute for the Future in Memo Park, California, believes we are at the beginning of a revolutionary age. As technology helps move us from mass media to personalized media, it will change the way people live and work.

When you think of enhancing the communication process with technology, you probably first think of using word processing software on a personal computer. While that is one important tool, numerous other hardware, software, and web-based tools can help improve your communication. These tools help with the construction, presentation, and transmission of messages as well as with collaboration.

TOOLS FOR CONSTRUCTING MESSAGES

• Computer tools can be used throughout the writing process.

Computer tools for constructing written messages can be associated with the different stages of the writing process: planning, gathering and collecting information, analyzing and organizing information, and writing and rewriting. In the past, many of these tools were discrete tools. But today, as we move toward greater convergence, they often work seamlessly together. And, of course, these tools work on a variety of devices attached to networks. The more skilled you become with each of these tools, the better they serve you.

Computer Tools for Planning

• Outlining or brainstorming programs help in planning the content of a message.

Whether you are writing a short message or a long report, you can use a computer to help you plan both the document and the writing project. In planning the content of the document, *outlining* or *concept-mapping* tools are useful. You can brainstorm, listing

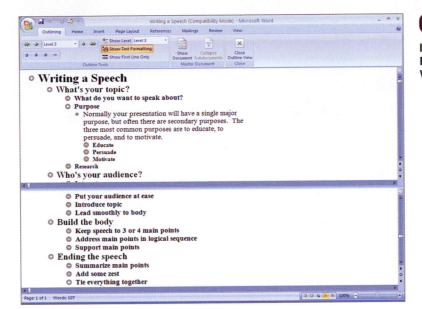

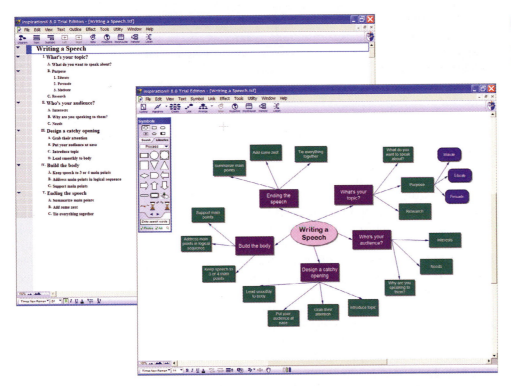

Figure 18–2

Illustration of a Concept-Mapping Tool for Planning

your ideas as they occur to you. Later you tag related ideas, asking the software to group them. Outlining tools are included in most word processors. One way to use an outliner is with a split screen, as shown in Figure 18–1. In one part of the screen you'll see one part of your outline and in the other part, another section of the document you are writing. Today's large-screen monitors make this an effective use. Another way you can use an outliner is as a separate document. In this case your outline is held in memory; you can toggle back and forth to view it or work with the outline and document side by side using a widescreen display. A discrete or specialty tool for planning is a concept-mapping/idea-generation program. As you see in Figure 18–2 above, the program Inspiration provides both a visual and an outlining mode, which allows users to toggle back and forth or work primarily in the mode that suits their particular tasks. You can also use these tools on your handheld personal digital assistant (PDA) or smartphone.

Figure 18–3

Illustration of a
Web-Based Project
Management Tool for
Planning a Long Report

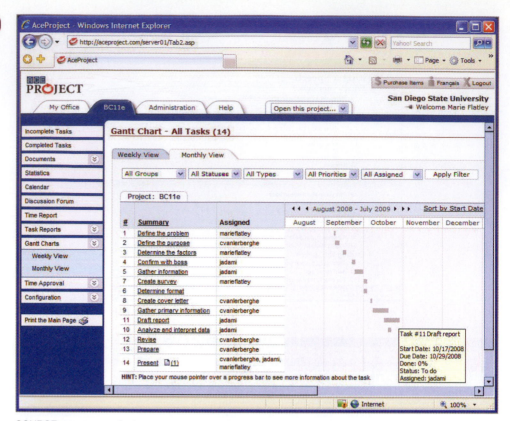

SOURCE: www.aceproject.com

- Project management
  programs assist in
  identifying tasks and
  allocating resources.

When you are working on a long writing project, several projects, or one carried over a long time, *project management programs* are excellent for planning the project. They allow you to identify all the tasks needed to complete the project, to determine how much time each task might take, and to generate a time-and-task chart (commonly called a Gantt chart). Also, they help you keep track of your progress and determine how to reallocate your resources to complete the project on time or within budget. You can see an example of a Gantt chart created using a web-based tool in Figure 18–3.

- Personal information
  management programs
  assist with time
  management.

Finding time for writing, of course, is one of the major challenges for businesspeople. By using *personal information management (PIM)* tools, you can plan time for completing writing projects. These time-management tools are essentially annotated electronic calendars. However, they are excellent planning tools for scheduling your writing tasks. They will remind you of tasks to complete and days remaining before a document needs to be finished. These tools are readily available. One such desktop tool is Microsoft Outlook. It can be synced with many handheld PDAs and smartphones as well as web-based PIM sites. But you can choose from a slew of other time-management tools as well. These offer a variety of ways to help you plan time for writing tasks, from day-to-day scheduling to longer-term planning. Figure 18–4 shows the way one tool looks. The bell icon shows that this writer set an alarm to have the computer remind him or her when it was time to write. The alarm sounds and the window opens at the designated time with a precise message of what needs to be done.

Some research identifies planning as the primary step that separates good writers from others. However, few writers have discovered the full power of electronic planning tools. Using the powerful features that both project management and PIM tools provide will give you the potential to produce high-quality work in a timely fashion.

Computer Tools for Gathering and Collecting Information

Before you can write, you have to have something to say. Sometimes you may be writing about your own ideas, but often you will supplement them with facts. Gathering facts or data is one of the most important jobs of the writer. Today you will want to combine your manual search for facts with electronic searches. The computer can help you find a variety of information quickly and accurately because today much of our published information is available electronically. In fact, some kinds of information are only available electronically. In Chapter 19, you will learn ways to find and evaluate the information you find online and in commercial databases.

● When you need information for a writing task, consider conducting an electronic search.

While technology makes constructing documents with graphics easy, writers still need to carefully review the messages they send.

- Data can be gathered from internal or external computers.

What you are looking for are facts. The facts you need may be found in either internal or external databases. Your report due today at 1:00 PM might be on the current inventory of your off-site manufacturing product line. You could simply connect to your company's computer at noon and download the most recent data before completing your report. However, if you need to project the number of completed units by the end of the month, you also may need to connect to your supplier's computer to check the inventory of the parts you will need to complete your units. In this case, you will be using your computer to find facts both internally (from within your company) and externally (from your suppliers).

Most libraries now allow both internal and external access to their online catalogs and databases. This means you can use the online catalog from within the library or from anywhere outside the library. Most college networks also allow you to connect to the library resources from campus computer labs, dormitories, and remote offices. And many colleges are installing wireless networks, allowing users within range and with wireless capabilities on laptops, PDAs, and smartphones to access their library resources.

You also can gather facts on the Internet. This expands your resources immensely beyond your local library. Not only can you reach the Library of Congress, but you also can search libraries in other countries. You can gather information from blogs and other sources not available in any library anywhere. While you do need to be especially critical of the sources of your facts, knowing how to use the Internet effectively to gather information can give you a tremendous competitive advantage. Chapter 19 gives you more details on using the Internet to gather business information.

Currently you can use technology such as Google News Alert or RSS feeds to push the information you want to you. By completing a profile at a content provider's website, you will create a filter so the kind of information pushed to you is the kind you want. You also can use software agents to monitor sources and notify you when information you specify is available. And, of course, you can rerun the results page that you have saved from a search using a well-designed search strategy. The new results page will be updated to reflect the information available at the moment. (See Technology in Brief in Chapter 19.)

- Database tools provide a convenient way to collect information.

Once you have gathered the facts, you will want to store them in some organized fashion so you can retrieve them readily when needed. *Database tools* will help you immensely here. If your company is interested in developing a new product for a newly defined market niche, you may want to collect information about the targeted market, potential suppliers of components of your new product, sites for producing the product, projected labor costs, and so on. You could do this simply by entering the facts of publication and abstracted information in your individually designed form created with database tools. The source information you have collected will be available whenever you need it. You can search and sort it on any of the categories (called fields) you set up on your data entry screen.

- Specialty tools help you collect facts, too.

Variations of the generic database are specialty tools such as EndNote, ProCite, Reference Manager, RefWorks, and others. These specialty programs allow you to enter information automatically as you transfer reference information from a wide variety of online databases. Figure 18–5 gives you an example of a web-based data manager, RefWorks. Many schools allow their students access to this tool, or you can subscribe individually.

Another tool that can help writers manage and retrieve information is OneNote. This tool enables users to collect all types of digital files from handwritten, typed, and scanned text to photos as well as audio and video records. Its powerful search function retrieves words from text, pictures, and even recordings. Furthermore, the digital notebooks can be shared and used simultaneously from any place. You can see a video demo of this tool online as well as take a self-paced, e-learning course.

In Chapter 19, which discusses business research methods, you will learn about other online information providers for business information. The major point to remember is that in business it is not necessarily what you know that really counts, but what you can find out. No one can know all there is to know about a subject, but those who are skilled at using a computer to gather information will find it a real asset.

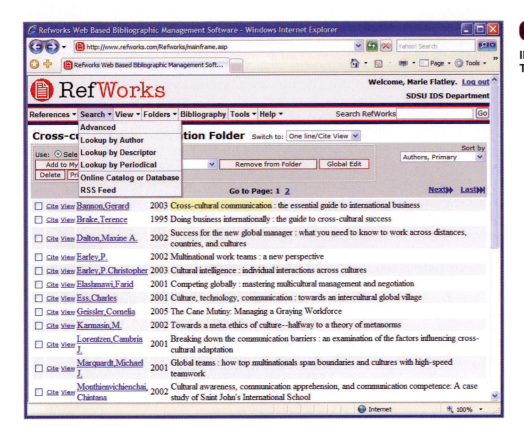

Figure 18–5

Illustration of a Specialty
Tool for Collecting Data

Computer Tools for Analyzing and Organizing

Three tools that writers find useful in analyzing data are statistics, graphics, and spreadsheet tools. Since sometimes you cannot say very much about raw numbers, combining them or viewing them in different ways gives you a clearer picture of their meaning. Today, some very sophisticated *statistical programs* have been made user-friendly, allowing those with little computer expertise to use them easily. Some programs will even query you about the nature of your data and recommend which statistical tests to use. Also, most *spreadsheet programs* will compute a broad range of statistics to help writers give meaningful interpretations to data.

Graphics programs help writers in several ways. First, graphics reveal trends and relationships in data that are often hard to cull from raw data. This helps writers understand clearly the meaning of their data. New data visualization tools, which allow users to graph and parse huge amounts of data, go further. These tools give users the power to explore what their data mean from multiple perspectives, as well as revealing where no data exist. These tools help users gain insights other tools cannot provide. Second, graphics programs help writers explain more clearly to readers what the data mean. For example, you can direct the reader to look at the red and blue lines for the last five years on a line chart, noting the trend of increasing rate of return. You can create graphics easily with all three tools. Also, most of these tools have features that allow you to annotate the graphic, directing the reader's attention to some particular aspect of the graph. You no longer have to be a graphic artist to create clear, good-looking graphics.

Outlining or *concept-mapping programs* are organizing tools for the writer as well as planning tools. Once you have captured your ideas and grouped related ideas, you can rearrange items into a meaningful order, organizing with the reader in mind. You also can collapse or expand the outline to view as few or as many levels as you want. This lets you see a macro view or big picture of your document as well as a micro or detailed view, so you can check for consistency at all levels.

- Computer programs help you analyze and interpret data with statistics and graphics.

- Graphics programs help you understand the data and create graphics.

- Outlining and concept-mapping programs help you organize your information.

Computer Tools for Writing

Word processing software is clearly the dominant writing tool of most writers. Today's word processors allow you to use other writing tools from within the word processor or that integrate seamlessly with it. Other computer writing tools that help writers include *spelling checkers, thesauruses, grammar and style checkers, reference resources, graphics, drawing packages, voice recognition tools,* and *information rights management.* The following discussion of these computer writing tools will point out how they can be used as well as caution you about any limitations.

- Word processing helps you capture, manipulate, edit, and revise your messages.

- Insert, delete, move and copy, and search and replace enable you to do what the terms suggest.

Word Processing Software. By liberating you from tiresome chores, word processing gives you time to spend on revising, editing, and other document-polishing efforts. Some of the most common features of word processing software for revising and editing include insert/delete, move and copy, and search and replace.

Insert allows the writer to add characters at any point, while *delete* lets the writer delete characters. You can change your mind and undo the most recent insert and delete changes. Some writers rarely delete text, moving the text to the end of the file or to another file for possible future use. The search and replace feature can be used in several ways. One way might be to search for the name in a file of someone who got married, retired, or was promoted and replace that name with the new name. Usually the writer decides whether to replace automatically every occurrence of the item or to check each occurrence. The search feature is usually used to find a particular word, name, or place. However, sometimes writers add asterisks or other symbols to mark copy or to add remarks or reminders—similar to the way one would use the bookmark feature. Later they search for those symbols to find the points in the document that need attention. You will find that these common features will be useful over and over.

- Basic math calculates columns and sorting arranges information in an order.

Two other useful features of word processing are basic math and simple sorting. The basic math feature lets the writer enter columns or rows of numbers, leaving the calculation job for the program. The sorting feature lets the writer enter columns or rows of words, leaving the alphabetic sorting for the program. While these are useful features of word processing programs, the writer has to be careful to enter or mark the copy exactly the way the software needs it to do the proper calculating or sorting.

- The tables feature also allows you to do simple math with data and to sort them.

The tables feature is another tool that enables you to do simple math and sort. It works similarly to a spreadsheet by allowing you to enter formulas in table cells, freeing you from the math. You also can link a table to a spreadsheet. When numbers change in the linked spreadsheet, they are automatically changed in the table with which they are linked. The tables feature allows formatting individual cells, rows, and columns. It is useful for presenting both data and textual material in rows and columns.

- The hidden text feature permits inserting information that is not printed until you choose to print it.

Another nice feature of many word processing programs is the hidden text or comment feature. If you insert the proper symbol, the comments that follow will be recorded in the file but not printed unless you tell the software to print them. Teachers can use this feature to put test answers in files but not on the test; later they can print a second copy and direct the software to print the comments. This feature can be used for reminders, detailed information, and such. For example, one might note that the vice president directed that an exception to company policy be granted under some special circumstances. Or one might leave a reminder to verify the statistics presented at a particular point in a document. In Figure 18–6, you can see both the display of a comment and the printed document without the comment.

- Hyphenation and format change enable you to control evenness of right margin.

Two additional editing features involve the physical presentation of documents. These features are hyphenation and format change. Both help you change how the physical output looks. Hyphenation, for example, is a feature that helps the right margin appear less ragged than when it is not used. A ragged margin does not usually bother most people on a full page with full-length lines; however, when one is using a short line without hyphenating, the right margin can be distracting if it appears ragged.

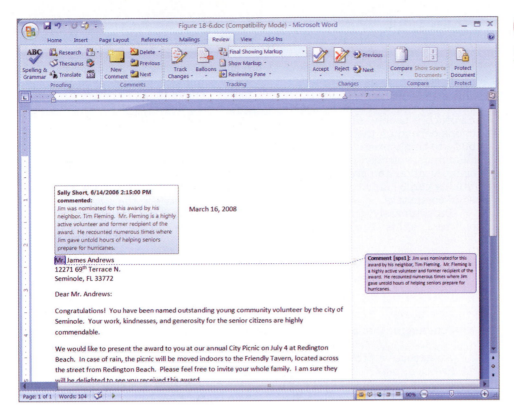

Figure 18–6

Illustration of the Comment Tool for Reviewing

The example of column text in Figure 18–7, with and without hyphenation, illustrates how hyphenation can smooth out a ragged right margin. Word's reveal formatting feature and WordPerfect's reveal codes also help you change margins, tabs, spacing, and so on. Formatting is particularly useful when you are changing letterheads, paper sizes, type styles, or binding. It allows you to experiment easily to find the most appropriate form to present the document to the reader.

Since revising and editing are extremely important to turning out well-written business documents, these are tools you will use often.

Some other word processing features that make the writing job easier are footnoting, table of contents generating, and index building. Most high-end word processors include the footnoting feature. It allows the writer to mark the place where the footnote occurs, entering the footnote at that point. The software then keeps track of the line count, placing each footnote at the bottom of the page on which it occurs, as well as numbering the footnotes consecutively. Also, the program will move a footnote if the

- Footnoting, table of contents generating, and index building are features that make writing easier.

Computers, Human Intellect, and Organizational Nervous

An executive provides vision and direction, makes decisions, diagnoses and solves problems, negotiates, convinces, and selects and coaches people. All these actions depend on the executive's ability to think creatively and communicate clearly; clear communication and creative thinking can be enhanced by the use of computers.

Unfortunately, most people don't realize this. The computer's role as a valuable thinking tool

seems to be a secret. Instead, many intelligent people, even today, believe that computers are best suited to clerical and administrative tasks. They see the computer as only a convenience or an operational necessity. I see the computer as an extension of the human brain.

An understanding of the connection between the evolution of the human mind and computers takes us back in time.

Note the ragged margin before the hyphenation feature is turned on.

Computers, Human Intellect, and Organizational Nervous

An executive provides vision and direction, makes decisions, diagnoses and solves problems, negotiates, convinces, and selects and coaches people. All these actions depend on the executive's ability to think creatively and communicate clearly; clear communication and creative thinking can be enhanced by the use of computers.

Unfortunately, most people don't realize this. The computer's role as a valuable thinking tool

seems to be a secret. Instead, many intelligent people, even today, believe that computers are best suited to clerical and administrative tasks. They see the computer as only a convenience or an operational necessity. I see the computer as an extension of the human brain.

An understanding of the connection between the evolution of the human mind and computers takes us back in time.

Note that after the hyphenation feature is used, the right margin is smoothed out.

text associated with it is moved. In Word 2007, a resource manager helps writers keep track of a wide variety of sources by completing a form that prompts for items needed to thoroughly document a source. It also helps format citations and generates bibliographies. In the illustration in Figure 18–8, you see the location of this feature on the Reference ribbon with the MLA format selected.

Another chore that word processing software assists with is table of contents generation. Using the particular tagging system your program requires, you simply tell the software to generate the table of contents. In some cases you get to select from a variety of formats, and in other cases you can define the format. Closely related to the table of contents generator is the index builder. The writer simply tags the words to be indexed, includes cross-references, and creates a list of words, and the program builds an alphabetic index with associated page numbers. This procedure is particularly helpful with long, frequently referenced documents.

- Using advanced word processing features saves time.

Word processing also has four other features that save the writer from having to reenter the same information: merge, macros, QuickWords and AutoText, and headers and footers. The merge feature permits you to combine one form document with a document containing variable data. Merge is particularly useful in early- and late-stage collection messages, where names and amounts are variable but the message content is the same. Another feature, called *macros,* allows you to enter any characters you want to call up at the command of a few keystrokes. This feature is useful for calling up form paragraphs for answering commonly occurring questions as well as for bringing

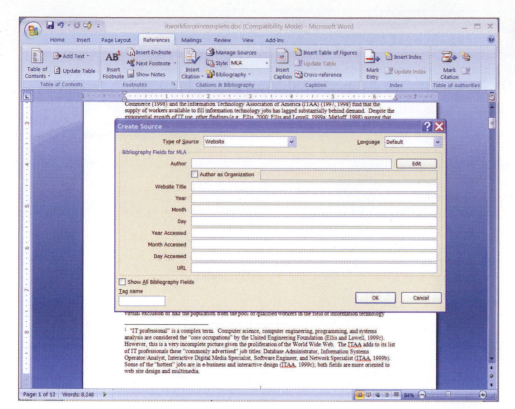

Figure 18–8

Illustration of the Citation Builder Tool for Writing

up repeatedly used memo headings or letter closings. QuickWords and AutoText features in WordPerfect and Word help users automatically complete frequently entered, long, or difficult terms and phrases. You simply begin entering the phrase and the software gives you the option of completing it for you. Headers and footers also let the program enter repeated information at the top and bottom of pages as well as count and print the page numbers.

Other special features of word processing programs help with using columns and fonts, importing graphics and spreadsheet files, and so on. Knowing how to apply fully the features of the word processing software you use will definitely make writing and revising easier for you.

- Learn to apply fully the features of your word processor.

Spelling Checkers. Along with AutoText and QuickWords, spelling checkers are tools business writers rely on daily. However, they are effective only if the writer uses them. And they are only effective at identifying words that are not in their dictionary. Therefore, spellers could miss some of your mistakes. Mistakes you will want to watch out for include wrong-word errors such as *compliment* for *complement* or *imply* for *infer*. A spell checker also will miss errors such as *desert* for *dessert* or misused words such as *good* for *well*. In addition, if any misspelled words have inadvertently been added to its dictionary, the speller will skip those words too. Therefore, careful proofreading is still in order after a document has been checked with a spelling program. Taking care to proofread carefully is a simple courtesy your reader will appreciate.

- Spelling checkers supplement proofreading but do not replace it.

Thesaurus Software. While a few serious writers may have a bound thesaurus on hand, most use a digital thesaurus with great ease and efficiency. The ease of popping up a window with suggested synonyms is hard to beat. Most word processors include a thesaurus; however, several good web-based programs are available. You may have noticed that the Merriam-Webster website includes an online thesaurus; you can access it on the site or through the Merriam-Webster toolbar if you have installed it. The thesaurus is a powerful tool, and the computer has made it faster to use and easier to access.

- The electronic thesaurus gives easy access to synonyms.

Backing up Frequently Is the Writer's Responsibility

Most writers know how difficult it is to create a document, much less recreate it, so they are willing to spend a little time to protect their investment. In the Save Options dialog box of Word (Word Options/Save in Office 2007), a writer can set up the program to fit his or her needs. Here a writer elected to have Word always create a backup file, to run these backups every 10 minutes, and to do it in the background. This writer could have also asked Word to allow fast saves, which only save the changes but take more disk space. This type of saving helps protect from systems that go down unexpectedly whether from crashes, power outages, accidents, or viruses.

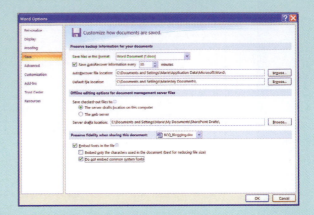

To protect your documents further, you might want to vary the backup media you use. If your computer is damaged or becomes infected with a computer virus, you still have copies of your files. This media could range from simple backups on disks or USB drives to backups at off-site locations. Individuals can do this with subscriptions on Internet hosts such as X-drive, idrive, and others, or on a smaller scale one can find free space at Yahoo Briefcase, school computers, and sometimes an Internet service provider.

Backing up is an easy, inexpensive form of insurance for a writer.

- Grammar and style checkers are only suggestion systems.

Grammar and Style Checkers. The value of grammar and style checkers is often debated. Unlike spelling programs, which are easily able to identify "wrong" words (words that are not in their dictionaries), grammar and style checkers identify "possible problems" with "suggestions" for revision. It is then your responsibility to decide whether the "possible problem" is a problem and whether the "suggestion" is the best solution. Making this decision requires that you have a good understanding of basic grammar. One recent study of accounting students' writing identified their most common writing errors. When a grammar checker was run on these common errors, fewer than half were detected. Microsoft Word found only 3 of the 13 errors and suggested 3 correct revisions; WordPerfect found 6 of the 13 errors, but only 5 of the 6 revisions were appropriate.[1] However, these programs are improving rapidly, adding expert system techniques to identify "possible problems" in context more accurately.

- They also evaluate a variety of other elements of writing quality.

In addition to checking grammar, style, word usage, and punctuation, these programs now report readability, strength, descriptive, and jargon indexes. They also perform sentence structure analysis, suggesting that you use simpler sentences, vary the sentence beginnings, use more or fewer prepositional phrases, and make various other changes. Grammar and style checkers also identify "possible problems" with specific words that might be slang, jargon, misspelled, misused, negative, or difficult for readers to understand. A complementary feature, Word Count, reports statistics for number of pages, words, characters, paragraphs, and lines. An example of the interactive use of one grammar checker is shown in Figure 18–9.

- Although often criticized, this tool is improving.

While the debate goes on, the tool is getting better. Recent versions address some of the issues concerning writers. For example, recent versions of grammar and style checkers are much more flexible than older versions. If you are writing in an informal environment where your boss finds beginning sentences with "And" and "But" acceptable, you can turn off the rule that would identify those beginnings as problems. Also,

---

[1] G. E. Whittenburg and Marie E. Flatley, "The Most Common Writing Errors Made by Accounting Students," *Proceedings of the Western Decision Sciences Institute* (Reno: Western Decision Sciences Institute, 1998).

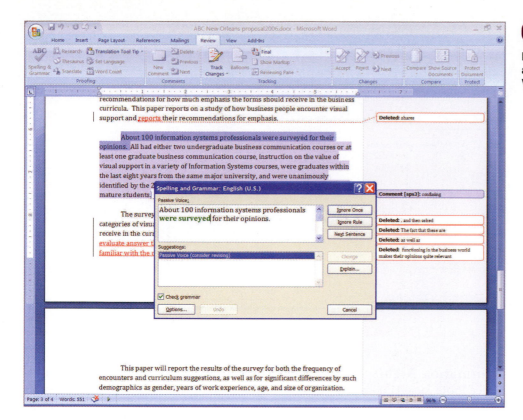

Figure 18–9

Illustration of a Spelling and Grammar Checker for Writing

you can choose the level of writing your intended audience wants. These are just a few examples of the flexibility in the newest versions of grammar and style checkers.

Grammar and style checkers are definitely important for the business writer. But, as with all tools, the more appropriately you use them the better job they do for you.

Reference Programs. Reference programs are just what their name suggests—programs that access or act like reference books such as dictionaries, style manuals, ZIP code directories, and so on. While once these reference programs were on CDs, many dictionaries, thesauruses, encyclopedias, books of quotations, ZIP code directories, world almanacs, and other references are now on the Web. They include such things as pronunciation of words in audio form and pictures, including video and animation. The Merriam-Webster website includes two good reference sources—an encyclopedia and a style guide. Chapter 19 and the textbook website identify many of these locations.

- A wide variety of reference books is available for easy access.

Graphics and Drawing Tools. Graphics and drawing tools are becoming more important for the writer every day. Not only are these programs becoming easier to use, but also you can now launch them from within your word processor. In most cases, your drawing is pasted into your document at the point you left it. The introduction of ready-made graphs and pictures (called clip art), low-cost scanners and digital cameras, and photo libraries has made it easier to supplement text with professional-looking graphics. You learned how to use graphics effectively in Chapter 13. The important point to remember here is that the computer enables you to enhance textual communication easily with a variety of graphics.

- Graphics and draw programs assist in supplementing textual materials with visuals.

Speech Recognition Tools. Recently several companies have introduced some good tools for continuous voice input. Although they are priced favorably, they have not yet gained wide acceptance in most businesses. However, as businesspeople begin to realize how easily they can compose their messages by talking to their computer systems and even editing through voice commands, their acceptance is likely to grow.

- Speech input is new technology that will free the writer from keying messages.

Figure 18–10

Illustration of Information Rights Management for Writing

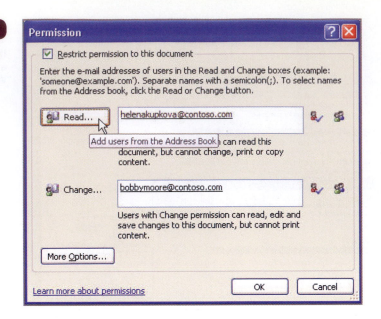

Information Rights Management (IRM). Following the lead of Microsoft's Office Professional 2003, many writing programs now give writers the ability to specify how their documents are shared, controlled, and used. Until this time writers had little control over a document once it was transmitted; one could password protect a document or perhaps encrypt it, but both were awkward and a bit complicated to use. The new set of IRM tools is easy to use and much more powerful than these old methods. As you can see in Figure 18–10, the permission dialog box allows users to easily set a variety of features.

Writers can determine how their documents are shared by specifying who can read, change, or have full control over them. Additionally, the writer can set an expiration date on these permissions. Not only do these features help businesses prevent sensitive information from getting into the wrong hands either accidentally or intentionally, but they also give writers control over documents once they leave their computers. If only certain people have permissions, forwarded and copied files will be protected from unauthorized use just as print copies can be.

IRM tools will likely cause many businesses to establish practices or policies on the kinds of permissions required for various types of information to protect their intellectual property. Perhaps this will help decrease in-box clutter as writers begin to think about who really needs the document and for how long.

As you have learned, technology is certainly an important tool for the writer in constructing messages. While word processing is the writer's primary tool in constructing a message, a wide variety of other tools will help in the planning, gathering and collecting, analyzing and organizing, and writing stages.

TOOLS FOR PRESENTING MESSAGES

After you have completed the document, you need to consider how to present it. This decision involves both software and hardware choices.

Software

- Today's software gives the writer many options for presenting messages.

Today you can publish your document in print or digital form. For print publication, you can use desktop publishing software or word processing software. Desktop publishing software is particularly good for layout of long documents that combine text, graphics, and design elements such as long reports, newsletters, manuals, and proposals. This software enables you to present professional-looking documents. Word processors are also capable of combining these elements. Most are capable of doing nearly 80 percent of the tasks that full-featured desktop publishing software can do if you take advantage of their features.

For electronic publication, you also can use these programs to generate files in hypertext markup language (html) or portable document file (pdf) format. In addition to the text, graphics, and design elements, digital documents can contain links, audio, and video elements. At the moment, authoring software is more fully featured for creating html documents (web documents). Web documents allow the writer to have some control over the presentation of the document, but today's browsers allow the reader to override the web documents and present them in a format the reader prefers. Also, browsers often display these html documents differently; therefore, it is the writer's responsibility to test the documents (at least in the default mode) on the most commonly used browsers to ensure that the look of their documents does not distract from or interfere with the message content. Some writers prefer to keep this control and create electronic documents in pdf, a format that gives the writer control over both the content and look.

Coincidentally, professionals engaged in designing documents for publication have the same major objective as writers—to communicate effectively. Professionals aim for designs that attract the reader but do not distract. Also, they understand that the most successful publications are those in which the design enhances or complements the meaning of the writer.

With publishing programs, you can break out of the traditional-looking page with its roots in the typewriter era to give the reader the best-looking, most readable document possible. However, to do this, you need to know about some basic design principles. Attention to the importance of the effect of design on communication was clearly pointed out with the butterfly ballot discussion in the Bush/Gore presidential election. These principles cover three areas: layout, typography, and art. See Appendix B for a discussion of these key areas of document design.

Hardware

Software is just one component of presenting a message; hardware is another. If the software has features that your printer or other output device cannot print or display, the features are useless. On the other hand, if your hardware has features that your software cannot produce, they, too, are useless. Both must work together to produce your message.

- Your choice of output hardware is critical to the appearance of your message.

The most common output device is still the printer. Depending on the formality of your communication, you may find yourself using ink-jet printers for one type of message and laser printers for others. In circumstances where you must have the best-looking documents, you may even use typeset output. Appearance does convey a message, and the hardware you choose to complete the presentation of your document is an important consideration.

Digital documents have different hardware considerations. The cross-platform formats—portable document format (pdf) and rich text format (rtf)—are used to prepare documents that keep their formatting. While they can be printed out, many will be read on the screen. In Word 2007, Microsoft created new fonts that were optimized for reading on the screen with Clear Type. Some of these include Calibri, Cambria, and Constantia. Other fonts are better read on paper. And because writers can use links within a document, the reading order of a digital document may vary substantially from the order for the same document in print form. Keeping the readers apprised of where they are at all times within a document is important. Also, it is important always to give a reader ways to move around the document; including buttons and keystroke alternatives is essential.

- Print and some electronic documents give the writer control of appearance.

TOOLS FOR TRANSMITTING MESSAGES

Transmitting means sending the message. The medium in which you choose to transmit a message communicates to the receiver the importance you attach to the message. Usually a written message gets more attention than an oral message, and a special delivery

- The medium in which you choose to send your message is important.

© ZITS Partnership. King Features Syndicate.

or urgent message gets more attention than an ordinary message. Even the method of special delivery chosen conveys a message. The client who electronically sends you the document you requested is perceived differently from the client who sends it on paper through Federal Express. Knowing what technologies are available to transmit the message will help you decide which is the most appropriate medium to use.

Technologies for sending a variety of oral and visual messages are widely used in business. One ubiquitous technology for oral communication is the mobile phone. Once predominantly used in cars, mobile phones can be used in any area of the country equipped for them. With a phone that fits in the palm of the hand, businesspeople can now be reached for important calls as well as conduct business from otherwise inaccessible places. Once like dumb bricks, today's devices are small and smart. Most of today's mobile phones have memories that enable users to reach others with just a few clicks or through voice input, as well as by dialing a complete number. Mobile phones can enable businesspeople to make more productive use of their time. However, the courteous user will be discreet about the time and place of use. Most people do not want to overhear your business calls; therefore, it is best to make them where using your mobile phone will not disturb others. And when in doubt, ask before you make that intrusive call.

As mentioned in Chapter 14, another widely used oral communication technology is the voice messaging system. Not only do these systems answer phones, direct calls, and take messages, but they also act as voice storage systems. For example, you can ask the system to retrieve messages for a particular date or from a particular person. You also can take a message you receive, annotate it with your voice message, and pass it along to another person's voice mailbox. You can even record a message for the system to deliver to several people's voice mailboxes at a specified time. By eliminating telephone tag and interruptions, this technology, too, improves the productivity of those using it.

One technology that combines oral and video communication effectively is videoconferencing. While it has been around for a while, advancements in optical fibers, bandwidth, and software and chip technology will push videoconferencing into even more favor. New developments are making the systems better and lowering the costs. Videoconferencing systems save travel time and expense, and they help eliminate many scheduling problems. Even small and medium-sized companies can afford desktop conferencing systems with inexpensive video cameras. Already available and widely used in Asia, phone systems are being used to send video email as well as to conduct real-time video messaging. Use of this technology is likely to be seen in the United States soon.

Technology also gives us the option of adding audio and video to our written messages. The sounds can be words dictated and attached to a document, or they can be sounds from other sources such as sound clip libraries. Sounds can be used to add interest, emphasis, and clarity to a document. Video also can be added to

- Mobile technology expands the physical environment of the message sender.

- Voice messaging systems are gaining business use.

- Videoconferencing combines oral and video media.

- Technology enables us to add audio and video to our written documents.

Using wireless technology to transmit messages allows you and your receiver to communicate anywhere and any time, but courtesy in taking and placing calls should be exercised.

email. In fact, many current video email systems simply attach video files to email messages. With digital convergence we will see a growth in the use of the compound document.

Written communication, on the other hand, can be transmitted effectively with proven technologies: facsimile, email, text messaging, instant messaging, and blogs.

Facsimile transmission (fax) uses telephone lines and Internet connections to send a copy of the document. Faxing is much like photocopying or printing, but the copy is delivered elsewhere. You need to know the telephone number of the receiving fax in order to send the message, and someone on the receiving end usually needs to check for the fax. Currently, you also can use the Internet to send or retrieve a fax. Many companies are setting up these systems on their company portals so users can send and retrieve faxes from their desktops.

Email transmissions work with a variety of sending devices. The desktop computer is probably the widest used at this point, but businesspeople may use other wireless devices, such as the Blackberry, Palm, and PocketPC.

Another form of written communication is text messaging. Text messages are typically limited to 160 characters and are sent through phones or the Internet to the receiver's phone. Text messages are similar to email and fax in that users need to check for them although the phone could alert them to incoming messages.

Written communication can also be transmitted with instant messaging (IM) tools. Although widely used by teens in the United States, IM has not been used much as a productivity tool in business. However, with IM programs available on mobile phones, its business use is sure to grow. Still, many businesses worry about security and choose not to use this tool. However, IBM recently introduced new server tools that enable companies to run IM securely. With a large user base already comfortable using the technology and more secure systems, it is likely that businesses will begin to use them internally and perhaps with suppliers and customers when appropriate.

- Facsimile, email, text messaging, instant messaging, and blogs are widely used for transmitting written messages.

- Blogs are both an efficient and effective tool for conveying and sharing ideas.

Finally, a newer medium that has gained rapid adoption for both business and personal use is the weblog or blog. It is an easy-to-use medium that incorporates words, pictures, and sounds readily and where users can post ideas and comment on others' ideas. Many of today's businesses are running them internally, enabling teams to work together efficiently by sharing their knowledge both within their team and company-wide. Blogs enable the teams to be efficient as well as creative by recording everyone's contribution, thus eliminating redundancies. And the content of blogs can be easily saved to comply with Sarbanes-Oxley requirements and searched or mined to help build new ideas.

- Although they communicate in writing, these tools are viewed as informal.

- So use them appropriately.

All these tools are being effectively used for transmitting messages. However, while they have the advantage of immediacy, they are a less formal means of transmission than sending a printed document. You need to evaluate carefully the need for formality in choosing your transmission medium.

Knowing that you have a choice of media for transmitting the message and knowing how to use each one are both important in order to choose the most appropriate medium. Because this technology is developing rapidly, you need to make it a priority to keep up-to-date on the latest developments.

TOOLS FOR COLLABORATION

- Computer tools assist groups on a wide variety of tasks.

As discussed in Chapter 10, collaborative writing or group writing tasks occur regularly in business, and they vary widely in the form and nature of the work. However, a wide range of computer tools is available to support various aspects of the process. These tools for computer-supported collaborative work group writing can generally be divided into two classifications: asynchronous and synchronous. Asynchronous tools are used for different-time/different-place collaboration; synchronous tools, on the other hand, are used for same-time/anyplace collaboration.

Asynchronous Computer Tools

- Several computer tools assist the traditional group.

Asynchronous tools include word processing, discussion forums, and electronic mail. Word processing features useful in group writing include commenting and reviewing. Commenting allows you to insert comments or questions in a document written by someone else but not change it. Reviewing allows others to edit your documents, which can appear as strikeouts (for deletions) or underlining (for insertions). Different colors can be assigned to different kinds of changes, so you can see at a glance the nature and location of the changes. The writer can view the document and decide whether to accept or reject each suggestion. As shown in Figure 18–11, the writer can see the reviewer's suggestions when viewing a document either by moving the cursor over the spot where a comment was made or by viewing comments in the margins.

- Discussion tools are useful when distance or time makes getting together difficult.

Another type of group writing tool is the discussion tool. The output from this kind of tool can take the form of blogs or of threaded discussions such as those used in Blackboard or other classroom management programs. Such tools are useful when groups have a difficult time meeting due to distance and time. To begin, the lead writer enters some text. Others access the system, review the text, and enter their own comments. All members of the group can review all the comments. In some systems, group members have anonymity, but others maintain audit trails so comments can be attributed to specific group members. While discussion entries are usually arranged as threaded discussions with comments on topics grouped together, blogs are arranged chronologically as the origin of their name—weblog—implies. Although blogs are used asynchronously, some become so popular that they can become a form of group chatting when users are connected at the same time. Blogs also often are capable of being set up as RSS feeds, pushing new postings to a feed reader or the desktop and freeing the reader from having to go to a particular source to view the newest postings.

Figure 18–11

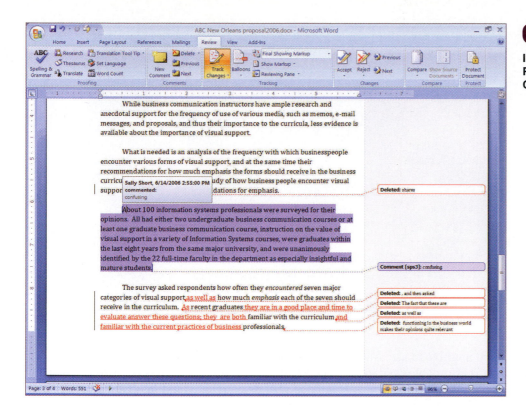

Electronic mail (email) provides a means for one writer to send a message to others. Unlike discussions, in these systems access to others' mailboxes is restricted. While you can distribute messages to a whole group, you do not have access to messages one member sends to someone else.

- Electronic mail permits communicating to intended receivers only.

All these tools are designed to work the way groups have traditionally worked. The planning, writing, and revising occur much the way they occur in traditional groups. However, the tools contribute to improvements in both speed and the quality of the final documents.

Synchronous Computer Tools

Synchronous computer tools are used by all group members at the same time. However, they can be used either at the same place or at different places. Same-place tools are generally referred to as electronic meeting systems (EMS). Different-place tools are sometimes called whiteboard or virtual collaborative tools.

- Collaborative writing is helped by group authoring tools.

With the same-place EMS tools, a facilitator conducts the meeting and operates the software that runs on a network. The facilitator may start the group with a question or statement. The group members will comment on the statement through their computers simultaneously and anonymously. For example, members may brainstorm new company policy statements and comment on them. The group under the direction of the facilitator might use other EMS tools to group related comments, rank-order them, and vote for the final policy statement. This kind of EMS collaborative tool has been shown to produce significantly higher quality output than non-computer-supported meetings.

- Collaborative tools change the group process and improve its output quality.

With the different-place collaborative tools, one member of the group initiates the process either on a network or through Internet connections. This tool often provides both a chat box and audio connection where users can talk to each other, a video connection where members can see each other, and a place where a shared document can be viewed and manipulated. The software can be set for different levels and types of control. The use of this technology became more widely accepted after 9/11 when people needed to meet but were hesitant to travel. They are also becoming more widely used as broadband speeds improve and new web-based applications become easier and

- Web-based collaborative tools are easy to use, cost effective, and convenient.

more intuitive to use. And with several companies competing in this marketplace, the cost is affordable even for the smallest of businesses. Today, businesspeople are using these virtual meeting tools locally as well as nationally and internationally for both cost and convenience reasons.

A LOOK TO THE FUTURE

- Computer tools will continue to enhance the communication process,

In addition to the technology discussed this far, you can anticipate further rapid advancements. Joseph Tucci, president and CEO of EMC Corporation, believes that innovation will continue forever and that companies will continue to use it to help improve productivity. While some of this innovation is happening in academic institutions such as MIT's Media Lab, much of it is happening at large companies such as IBM, Intel, Microsoft, Yahoo!, and Google. These companies have some of their brightest, most creative people working on technologies for both the near term and the longer term. In the near term, Bill Gates predicts the miniaturization of the PC and mobile phones becoming as rich as our current desktops. Intel is working on chip improvements for better power management, giving us the longer battery life needed for this kind of improvement. Internet TV and video will soon become a more widely used technology. And email will get better, too. Not only will offensive, malicious, and deceptive email become a thing of the past, but through the use of data mining tools businesses will be able to better understand their people and their strengths. They will be able to identify experts on a variety of subjects as well as discover new ideas. HP is already beginning to mine its email to "harvest organizational knowledge." Two of the biggest near-term changes that Bill Gates foresees relate to the explosion of web services and mash ups (integrated web services) and the growth of social networking. These tools have the potential to define new digital workstyles and lifestyles for us.

In the longer term, Microsoft research is working on ways to eliminate repetitive tasks, freeing us up for more productive work. Software that learns and understands how we work will be able to act as experts, giving us suggestions when needed. And search will be transformed in a couple of ways. We will be able to interact with programs orally and in natural language, and accessing information will become seamless. Using social networks we will be able to direct our efforts into the most useful places.

- but humans will continue to form the messages.

However, whatever form these developments take, human minds will continue to control message formulation. In fact, there is no evidence whatsoever that the need for messages communicated in writing and speaking will decrease. Even more important, there is absolutely no evidence that these messages can be handled in a way that does not require basic writing and speaking skills. Business communication is here to stay. In fact, the increasing advancement of the technology of the future is likely to require more—not less—of it.

SUMMARY BY LEARNING OBJECTIVES

1. Technology helps a writer construct messages through every step of the writing process including

   - Planning,
   - Gathering and collecting information,
   - Analyzing and organizing information, and
   - Writing and rewriting.

1 Explain how technology helps in constructing messages.

2. Each stage of the writing process has a set of tools most appropriate for the tasks in that stage. These include the following:

   - Outlining or concept-mapping, project management, and personal information management programs for planning;
   - Database programs and reference managers for gathering and collecting information; and
   - Statistical, spreadsheet, graphics, and outlining or concept-mapping tools for analyzing and organizing information, and word processing, spelling, thesaurus, grammar and style checking, reference, graphics, drawing, and voice recognition, and information rights management programs for writing.

2 Identify appropriate tools for different stages in the writing process.

3. Technology helps in the presentation of documents with both sophisticated hardware and software.

   - Software contributes with publishing features that combine text, graphics, links, audio, and video and that promote good layout and design.
   - Hardware contributes in the printing and display of documents.

3 Discuss how technology helps in the presentation of messages.

4. Communicators have a variety of choices of media for transmitting their messages.

   - Oral messages can be sent by mobile phone, voice messaging systems, and sound clips.
   - Videoconferencing technology combines oral and visual messages.
   - Written messages can be transmitted by fax, email, text messaging, instant messaging, and blogs.

4 Discuss various ways to transmit messages and the hardware currently used.

5. A range of software tools assists groups of writers in asynchronous and synchronous writing environments.

   - Asynchronous tools such as word processing, discussions, blogs, and email are used for different-time/different-place collaboration.
   - Synchronous tools allow writers to work on a document at the same time. Electronic meeting system tools are used for same-time/same-place writing, and collaboration tools are used for same-time/different-place writing.

5 Describe how technology assists in collaboration.

6. Business leaders believe technology will continue to advance. Future developments are expected to enhance present technologies, making them better and easier to use. Researchers at large companies are working on a variety of projects, including many search and social networking areas. Future developments will likely mean more need for good basic communication skills.

6 Discuss what impact future developments in technology might have on business communication.

1 Explain how technology can help the writer with both creative and tedious writing tasks.

2 Identify specific software tools that assist with constructing written messages. Explain what each does.

3 Word processing programs are the writer's primary tool. Identify five basic features and two advanced features useful to business writers.

4 Discuss the advantages and disadvantages of spelling checkers and grammar and style checkers.

5 Describe ways that graphics software helps writers.

6 Brainstorm some practices or policies that businesses might develop for using the Information Rights Management (IRM) tool effectively.

7 Explain what a writer should know about layout and design and why it is important.

8 Identify various ways that business writers can transmit oral and written messages.

9 How can technology assist in collaboration?

10 What can we expect to see in future technological developments that will affect business communication?

CRITICAL THINKING EXERCISES

1 Investigate the school and/or local libraries to determine what current (or future) computer sources will help one find information for business. Report your findings to the class.

2 Compile an annotated list of at least 10 websites with good links to business sources. Three of these links should be for local business information.

3 Locate six examples of video and audio clips you might use in a business document. Describe the examples along with a brief explanation of a good use in a business document.

4 Identify where computers, printers, scanners, wireless hot spots, and other tools are available at or around your college. Prepare a table with this information, listing times available as well as any costs. Also, be sure to include computer configurations and programs available.

5 Choose a feature from your word processor (such as index, table of contents, templates, or citation builder) that

you have not used much. Learn how to use it and create an example of its use in a business document. Write a brief description of its application.

6 Select a dozen idioms from a reference book (found online or in print) that seem common to you. Type these into your word processor and run the file through a grammar and style checker. Print a copy of the results and bring it to class for discussion.

7 List five text messaging shortcuts (B4, BTW, B2U) that you use or know of along with your meaning. Then ask three different people to tell you what each shortcut means. Write a short report of your results.

8 From a current computer magazine, find an article that relates to communication in business. Write a one-paragraph reaction to it and post it to a blog specified by your instructor.

chapter nineteen

Business Research Methods

LEARNING OBJECTIVES

Upon completing this chapter, you will be able to design and implement a plan for conducting the research needed for a business report. To reach this goal, you should be able to

1 Explain the difference between primary and secondary research.

2 Gather secondary sources using direct and indirect research methods.

3 Evaluate website reliability.

4 Describe the procedures for searching through company records.

5 Conduct an experiment for a business problem.

6 Design an observational study for a business problem.

7 Use sampling to conduct a survey.

8 Construct a questionnaire, develop a working plan, and conduct a pilot test for a survey.

9 Analyze and interpret information clearly and completely for your reader.

INTRODUCTORY SITUATION

Business Research Methods

Introduce yourself to this chapter by assuming the position of administrative assistant to Carmen Bergeron, the vice president for human resources for Pinnacle Industries. Today at a meeting of administrators, someone commented about the low morale among sales representatives since last year's merger with Price Corporation. The marketing vice president immediately came to the defense of her area, claiming that there is no proof of the statement—that in fact the opposite is true. Others joined in with their views, and in time a heated discussion developed. In an effort to ease tensions, Ms. Bergeron suggested that her office conduct a survey of employees "to learn the truth of the matter." The administrators liked the idea.

After the meeting, Ms. Bergeron called you in to tell you that you would be the one to do the research. And she wants the findings in report form in time for next month's meeting. She didn't say much more. No doubt she thinks your college training equipped you to handle the assignment.

Now you must do the research. This means you will have to work out a plan for a survey. Specifically, you will have to select a sample, construct a questionnaire, devise an interview procedure, conduct interviews, record findings—and more. All these activities require much more than a casual understanding of research. There are right ways and wrong ways of going about them. How to do them right is the subject of this chapter.

- The two basic forms of research are secondary research (getting information from published sources) and primary research (getting information firsthand).

You can collect the information you need for your report by using the two basic forms of research: secondary research and primary research. Secondary research is research utilizing material that someone else has published—periodicals, brochures, books, electronic publications, and such. This research may be the first form of research that you use in some problems (see The Preliminary Investigation in Chapter 10). Primary research is research that uncovers information firsthand. It is research that produces new findings.

To be effective as a report writer, you should be familiar with the techniques of both secondary and primary research. A brief summary of each appears in the following pages.

SECONDARY RESEARCH

- Secondary research can be a rich source of information if you know what to look for and where to look.

Secondary research materials are potentially the least costly, the most accessible, and the most complete source of information. However, to take full advantage of the available materials, you must know what you are looking for and where and how to find it.

The task can be complex and challenging. You can meet the challenge if you become familiar with the general arrangement of a library or other repositories of secondary materials and if you learn the techniques of finding those materials. Also, research must be orderly if it is to be reliable and complete.

- Keep track of the sources you gather in an orderly way.

In the past, researchers used a card system to help them keep track of the sources they identified. This card system could be combined with and adapted to a computer system quite easily. The manual system of organization required that the researcher complete two sets of cards. One set was simply a bibliography card set, containing complete information about sources. A researcher numbered these cards consecutively as the sources were identified. A second set of cards contained the notes from each source. Each of these cards was linked to its source through the number of the source in the bibliography card set.

Since the computer systems in today's libraries often allow users to print, download, email, or transfer directly the citations they find from the indexes and databases, it makes sense to identify each with a unique number rather than recopy the source to a card. Not only is the resulting list more legible than one's handwriting, but it is also complete. Some researchers cut their printouts apart and tape them to a master sheet. Others enter these items in databases they build. And still others export items directly into specialty databases, letting the software organize and number them. With the widespread use of notebook and laptop computers, many researchers are taking notes on computers rather than cards. These notes can be linked to the original source by number as in the manual system.

No matter whether you use a manual, combined, or computer system, using an orderly system is essential.

Finding Publication Collections

The first step in an orderly search for printed information is to determine where to begin. The natural place, of course, is a library. However, since different types of libraries offer different kinds of collections, it is helpful to know what types of libraries are available and to be familiar with their contents.

General libraries are the best known and the most accessible. General libraries, which include college, university, and most public libraries, are called *general* to the extent that they contain all kinds of materials. Many general libraries, however, have substantial collections in certain specialized areas.

Libraries that limit their collections to one type or just a few types of material are considered *special libraries*. Many such libraries are private and do not invite routine public use of their materials. Still, they will frequently cooperate on research projects that they consider relevant and worthwhile.

Among the special libraries are those libraries of private businesses. As a rule, such libraries are designed to serve the sponsoring company and provide excellent information in the specialized areas of its operations. Company libraries are less accessible than other specialized libraries, but a written inquiry explaining the nature and purpose of a project or an introduction from someone known to the company can help you gain access to them.

Special libraries are also maintained by various types of associations—for example, trade organizations, professional and technical groups, chambers of commerce, and labor unions. Like company libraries, association libraries may provide excellent coverage of highly specialized areas. Although such libraries develop collections principally for members or a research staff, they frequently make resources available to others engaged in reputable research.

A number of public and private research organizations also maintain specialized libraries. The research divisions of big-city chambers of commerce and the bureaus of research of major universities, for example, keep extensive collections of material containing statistical and general information on a local area. State agencies collect similar data. Again, though these materials are developed for a limited audience, they are often made available upon request.

Several guides are available in the reference department of most general libraries to help you determine what these research centers and special libraries offer and whom to contact for permission to use their collections. The *American Library Directory* is a geographic listing of libraries in the United States and Canada. It gives detailed information on libraries, including special interests and collections. It covers all public libraries as well as many corporate and association libraries. Also, the Special Libraries Association has chapters in many large cities that publish directories for their chapter areas. Particularly helpful in identifying the information available in research centers is *The Research Centers Directory.* Published by The Gale Group, it lists the research activities, publications, and services of 7,500 university-related and other nonprofit organizations. It is supplemented between editions by a related publication, *New Research Centers.*

The Gale Group also publishes a comprehensive three-volume guide to special library collections, *The Directory of Special Libraries and Information Centers.* Volume one, *Subject Directory of Special Libraries and Information Centers,* describes the contents and services of 23,300 information centers, archives, and special and research libraries, and it contains a detailed subject index. Volume two, *Geographic and Personnel Indexes,* includes the address and telephone number of the facility and

- A library is the natural place to begin secondary research.

- General libraries offer the public a wide variety of information sources.

- Special libraries have limited collections and circulation and can be owned by

- private business,

- associations, and

- research organizations.

- Consult a directory to determine what special libraries offer.

the name and title of the individual in charge. The third volume, *New Special Libraries*, is a periodic supplement to the first. One particularly good source to an organized collection of links to online libraries is at <http://sunsite.berkeley.edu/libweb/>. This site is organized geographically but also allows one to search by library type, name, and other information.

Taking the Direct Approach

You can begin your research using the direct approach, but you must be familiar with basic references.

When you have found the appropriate library for your research, you are ready for the next challenge. With the volume of material available, how will you find what you need? Many cost-conscious businesses are hiring professionals to find information for them. These professionals' charges range from $60 to $120 per hour in addition to any online charges incurred. Other companies like to keep their information gathering more confidential; some employ company librarians, and others expect their employees to gather the information. If you know little about how material is arranged in a library or online, you will waste valuable time on a probably fruitless search. However, if you are familiar with certain basic reference materials, you may be able to proceed directly to the information you seek. And if the direct approach does not work, there are several effective indirect methods of finding the material you need.

The direct approach is especially effective with quantitative or factual information.

Taking the direct approach is advisable when you seek quantitative or factual information. The reference section of your library is where you should start. There, either on your own or with the assistance of a research librarian, you can discover any number of timely and comprehensive sources of facts and figures. Although you cannot know all these sources, as a business researcher you should be familiar with certain basic ones. These sources are available in either print or electronic forms. You should be able to use both.

Encyclopedias offer both general and detailed information.

Encyclopedias. Encyclopedias are the best-known sources of direct information and are particularly valuable when you are just beginning a search. They offer background material and other general information that give you a helpful introduction to the area under study. Individual articles or sections of articles are written by experts in the field and frequently include a short bibliography.

Of the general encyclopedias, two worthy of special mention are *Encyclopedia Americana* and *Encyclopaedia Britannica*. *Britannica* online now requires a subscription at britannica.com. Others gaining wide use and acceptance are *Grolier's Multimedia Encyclopedia* and *Microsoft Encarta*. These are available either online and updated regularly, for sale in software outlets, or even bundled with multimedia computer systems. Also helpful are such specialized encyclopedias as the *Encyclopedia of Banking and Finance*, the *Encyclopedia of Business and Finance*, the *Encyclopedia of Small Business*, the *Encyclopedia of Advertising*, and the *Encyclopedia of Emerging Industries*.

Biographical directories offer information about influential people.

Biographical Directories. A direct source of biographical information about leading figures of today or of the past is a biographical directory. The best-known biographical directories are *Who's Who in America* and *Who's Who in the World*, annual publications that summarize the lives of living people who have achieved prominence. Similar publications provide coverage by geographic area: *Who's Who in the East* and *Who's Who in the South and Southwest*, for example. For biographical information about prominent Americans of the past, the *Dictionary of American Biography* is useful. You also can find biographical information under the reference section of *Lexis-Nexis Academic Universe*. In addition to links to biographical directories, links to news stories about the person also are provided.

Specialized publications will help you find information on people in particular professions. Among the most important of these are *Who's Who in Finance and Industry; Standard & Poor's Register of Corporations, Directors, and Executives; Who's Who in Insurance;* and *Who's Who in Technology*. Nearly all business and professional areas are covered by some form of directory.

Today much secondary research can be done online accessing a variety of databases, directories, and Internet sites.

Almanacs. Almanacs are handy guides to factual and statistical information. Simple, concise, and selective in their presentation of data, they should not be underestimated as references. *The World Almanac and Book of Facts,* published by Funk & Wagnalls, is an excellent general source of facts and statistics. The *Time Almanac* is another excellent source for a broad range of statistical data. One of its strongest areas is information on the world. The *New York Times Almanac* presents much of its data in tables. It has excellent coverage of business and the economy. *The Jobs Rated Almanac* by Les Krantz ranks 250 jobs on factors such as salary, dress, benefits, and more.

- Almanacs provide factual and statistical information.

Almanacs are available online as well. Infoplease.com offers broad coverage of topics, including a business section at <http://www.infoplease.com/almanacs.html>. A more specialized almanac, *The Writer's Almanac,* is a daily extension of Garrison Keillor's radio show sponsored by Minnesota Public Radio.

Trade Directories. For information about individual businesses or the products they make, buy, or sell, directories are the references to consult. Directories compile details in specific areas of interest and are variously referred to as *catalogs, listings, registers,* or *source books.* Some of the more comprehensive directories indispensable in general business research are the following: *The Million Dollar Directory* (a listing of U.S. companies compiled by Dun & Bradstreet), *Thomas Register of American Manufacturers* (free on the web at <http://www.thomasregister.com>), and *The Datapro Directory.* Some directories that will help you determine linkages between parent entities and their subsidiaries include *America's Corporate Families* and *Who Owns Whom* (both compiled by Dun & Bradstreet) as well as the *Directory of Corporate Affiliations.* Thousands of directories exist—so many, in fact, that there is a directory called *Directories in Print.*

- Trade directories publish information about individual businesses and products.

Government Publications. Governments (national, state, local, etc.) publish hundreds of thousands of titles each year. In fact, the U.S. government is the world's largest publisher. Surveys, catalogs, pamphlets, periodicals—there seems to be no limit to the information that various bureaus, departments, and agencies collect and make available to the public. The challenge of working with government publications, therefore, is finding your way through this wealth of material to the specifics you need. That task sometimes can be so complex as to require indirect research methods. However, if you are familiar with a few key sources, the direct approach will often produce good results. And at this time, many government publications are moving rapidly to the web.

In the United States, it may be helpful to consult the *Monthly Catalog of U.S. Government Publications.* Issued by the Superintendent of Documents, it includes a comprehensive listing of annual and monthly publications and an alphabetical index of the issuing agencies. It can be searched online at <http://www.gpoaccess.gov/cgp/>. The Superintendent of Documents also issues *Selected United States Government Publications,* a monthly list of general-interest publications that are sold to the public.

Routinely available are a number of specialized publications that are invaluable in business research. These include *Census of Population, Census of Housing, Annual Housing Survey, Consumer Income, Population Characteristics, Census of Governments, Census of Retail Trade, Census of Manufacturers, Census of Agriculture, Census of Construction Industries, Census of Transportation, Census of Service Industries, Census of Wholesale Trade,* and *Census of Mineral Industries.* The *Statistical Abstract of the United States* is another invaluable publication, as are the *Survey of Current Business,* the *Monthly Labor Review,* the *Occupational Outlook Quarterly,* and the *Federal Reserve Bulletin.* To say the least, government sources are extensive.

Dictionaries. Dictionaries are helpful for looking up meanings, spellings, and pronunciations of words or phrases. Electronic dictionaries add other options; they include pronunciation in audio files and let you find words when you know the meaning only. Dictionaries are available in both general and specialized versions. While it might be nice to own an unabridged dictionary, an abridged collegiate or desk dictionary will answer most of your questions. You should be aware that the name *Webster* can be legally used by any dictionary publisher. Also, dictionaries often include added features such as style manuals, signs, symbols, and weights and measures. Because dictionaries reflect usage, you want to be sure the one you use is current. Not only are new words being added, but spellings and meanings change, too. Several good dictionaries are the *American Heritage Dictionary,* the *Funk & Wagnalls Standard Dictionary,* the *Random House Webster's College Dictionary,* and *Merriam-Webster's Collegiate Dictionary.* To have the most current dictionary available at your fingertips (through toolbars), you may want to subscribe to one such as Merriam-Webster at <http://www.m-w.com/>.

Specialized dictionaries concentrate on one functional area. Some business dictionaries are the *Dictionary of Business Terms, The Blackwell Encyclopedic Dictionary of Management Information Systems, The Blackwell Encyclopedic Dictionary of Accounting, The Blackwell Encyclopedic Dictionary of Business Ethics, The Blackwell Encyclopedic Dictionary of Finance,* the *Dictionary of Taxation,* the *Dictionary of International Business Terms,* the *Concise Dictionary of Business Management,* and the *Dictionary of Marketing and Advertising.* There are also dictionaries of acronyms, initialisms, and abbreviations. Two of these are the *Acronyms, Initialisms, and Abbreviations Dictionary* and the *Abbreviations Dictionary.*

Additional Statistical Sources. Today's businesses rely heavily on statistical information. Not only is this information helpful in the day-to-day business operations, but it also is helpful in planning future products, expansions, and strategies. Some of this information can be found in the publications previously mentioned, especially the government publications. More is available online and can be seen long before it is printed. Even more is available from the various public and private sources described in Figure 19.1.

List of Resources by Research Question. Sources with web addresses provided are available to the general public.

How do I find business news and trends?

ABI Inform Complete on ProQuest

Business & Company Resource Center

Business & Industry Database (includes articles from over 900 trade publications)

Business Source Premier

Factiva (includes Dow Jones and Reuters Newswires and *The Wall Street Journal,* plus more than 8,000 other sources from around the world)

LexisNexis Academic, News and Business sections

Wilson OmniFile Full Text Mega

How do I find information about companies?

The Annual Reports Library (<http://www.zpub.com/sf/arl/>)

Business & Company Resource Center

Companies' own websites

D&B's (Dunn & Bradstreet's) *International Million Dollar Database*

D&B's *Million Dollar Database*

Factiva

Hoover's Online

LexisNexis Academic, Business section

Marketline (basic information about 10,000 global companies, including the United States)

Mergent Online (information about 11,000 U.S. and 17,000 international companies)

SEC Filings and Forms (EDGAR) (includes 10-K reports and annual reports)

Standard & Poor's Net Advantage

Thomson Research (Disclosure provides information about 12,000 U.S. companies; Worldscope covers both U.S. and international company filings)

Value Line Research Center

How do I find information about particular industries?

Business Insight

Global Market Information Database

ICON Group International (see Industry Reports, Country Reports, and Culture Statistics)

IBISWorld

MarketLine

MarketResearch.com Academic

MergentOnline, Industry Reports

Plunkett Research Online

Standard & Poor's Net Advantage, Industries section

How do I find biographical and contact information for business people?

American Business Directory (<http://library.dialog.com/bluesheets/html/bl0531.html>)

Biographical Dictionary of American Business Leaders

Biography Reference Bank

D&B's (Dunn & Bradstreet's) *Million Dollar Database*

LexisNexis Academic, Reference/Biographical Information section

Standard & Poor's Net Advantage (see Register of Executives)

Who's Who in Finance and Business (includes Biography Resource Center)

How do I find information provided by the US government?

Business.gov (government rules and regulations, research, resources)

Fedstats (<http://www.fedstats.gov/>)

STAT-USA (includes State of the Nation Library)

U.S. Bureau of Labor Statistics (< http://stats.bls.gov.proxy.libraries.uc.edu/>; comprehensive employment and economic data, including Monthly Labor Review and Occupational Outlook Handbook)

U.S. Census Bureau (<http://www.census.gov>; links to Statistical Abstract of the United States)

U.S. Government Printing Office (<http://www.gpoaccess.gov>; comprehensive site for U.S. government publications)

U.S. Small Business Administration (<http://www.sba.gov/>)

How do I find out about other countries and international trade?

Europa World Yearbooks

Global Market Information Database

SourceOECD (from the Organisation for Economic Cooperation and Development)

STAT-USA/Internet (<http://www.stat-usa.gov>)

U.S. Library of Congress, Country Studies (<http:// http://lcweb2.loc.gov>)

U.S. State Department information (<http://www.state.gov>)

The World Factbook (<http://www.cia.gov/cia/publications/factbook/>)

WDI Online (the World Bank's World Development Indicators)

Yahoo!'s country links (<http://dir.yahoo.com/Regional/Countries/>)

How do I find information about cities?

American FactFinder (<http://factfinder.census.gov/home/saff/main.html?_lang=en>)

Cities' own websites

Country and City Data Books (<http://fisher.lib.virginia.edu/collections/stats/ccdb/>)

Sourcebook America (CD-ROM)

Cities of the World (4-volume reference book)

Compiled with the assistance of Wahib Nasrallah, Business Reference Librarian, University of Cincinnati.

In order to facilitate the collection and retrieval of statistical data for industry, the U.S. government developed a classification system called the Standard Industrial Classification (SIC) code. In the 1930s, this system used a four-digit code for all manufacturing and nonmanufacturing industries.

In 1997, the U.S. government introduced a new industrial classification system—the North American Industry Classification System (NAICS)—to replace the SIC code. The new system is more flexible than the old one and accounts for changes in the global economy by allowing the United States, Mexico, and Canada to compare economic and financial statistics better. It has also been expanded to include new sectors such as the information sector; the health care and social assistance sector; and the professional, scientific, and technical services sector. The United States and Canada began using this system in 1997, and Mexico in 1998. The first NAICS-based statistics were issued in 1999 and are just beginning to be used.

Some of the basic comprehensive publications include the *Statistical Abstract of the United States* and *Standard & Poor's Statistical Service*. These sources are a starting point when you are not familiar with more specialized sources. They include historical data on American industry, commerce, labor, and agriculture; industry data by SIC (and soon NAICS) codes; and numerous indexes such as producer price indexes, housing indexes, and stock price indexes. Additionally, the *Statistical Abstract of the United States* contains an extremely useful guide to sources of statistics.

If you are not certain where to find statistics, you may find various guides useful. The *American Statistics Index* is an index to statistics published by all government agencies. It identifies the agency, describes the statistics, and provides access by category. The *Encyclopedia of Business Information Sources* provides a list of information sources along with names of basic statistical sources. The *Statistical Reference Index* publishes statistics from sources other than the government, such as trade and professional associations. These three directories will help direct you to specialized statistics when you need them.

Business Information Services. Business services are private organizations that supply a variety of information to business practitioners, especially investors. Libraries also subscribe to their publications, giving business researchers ready access to yet another source of valuable, timely data.

Mergent, Inc., one of the best-known of such organizations, publishes a weekly *Manual* in each of five business areas: industrials, over-the-counter (OTC) industrials, international banks and finance, and municipals and governments. These reports primarily summarize financial data and operating facts on all major American companies, providing information that an investor needs to evaluate the investment potential of individual securities or of fields as a whole. *Corporation Records,* published by Standard & Poor's Corporation, presents similar information in loose-leaf form. Both Mergent and Standard & Poor's provide a variety of related services, including *Moody's Investors' Advisory Service* and *Value Line Investment Survey.*

Another organization whose publications are especially helpful to business researchers is The Gale Group, Inc. Gale provides several business services, including publications featuring forecasts and market data by country, product, and company. Its online Business and Company Resource Center is particularly useful. This database provides access to hundreds of thousands of company records, allowing users to search by company name, ticker symbol, and SIC and NAICS codes. It provides links to the full text of news and magazine articles, company profiles, investment reports, and even legal actions and suits. Users can print the information as well as email it to others.

International Sources. In today's global business environment, we often need information outside our borders. Many of the sources we have discussed have counterparts with international information. *Principal International Businesses* lists basic information on major companies located around the world. *Major Companies of Europe* and *Japan Company Handbook* are two sources providing facts on companies in their respective areas. The *International Encyclopedia of the Social Sciences* covers all

- A new classification system will enable users to compare economic and financial statistics better.

- Basic publications provide broad coverage and source listings for more detailed statistics.

- Guides help you locate sources.

- Private business services collect and publish data. Many such reports are available in public and university libraries.

- Statistical information for the international business environment is available in a wide range of documents.

important areas of social science, including biographies of acclaimed persons in these areas. General and specialized dictionaries are available, too. The *International Business Dictionary and References* includes commonly used business terms in several languages. You will even be able to find trade names in the *International Brands and Their Companies,* published by The Gale Group. For bibliographies and abstracts, one good source is the *Foreign Commerce Handbook.* Even statistical information is available in sources such as the *Index to International Statistics, Statistical Yearbook,* and online at the United Nations Department of Economic and Social Affairs Statistical Division, <http://unstats.un.org/unsd/>. Additionally, the U.S. Bureau of Labor Statistics at <http://www.bls.gov/bls/other.htm> provides links to many countries' statistical portals. With the help of translation tools (see the textbook website for several tools), you can get information you want directly. In addition, libraries usually contain many references for information on international marketing, exporting, tax, and trade.

Using Indirect Methods

If you cannot move directly to the information you need, you must use indirect methods to find it. The first step in this approach is preparing a bibliography or a list of prospective sources. The next two steps are gathering the publications in your bibliography and systematically checking them for the information you need.

These two steps are elementary but nonetheless important. Your acquisition of secondary materials must be thorough. You should not depend solely on the material you find on the shelves of your library. Rather, you should use interlibrary loan services and database and Internet searches. And you should gather company or government documents. All checking of the sources must be equally thorough. For each source, review the pages cited in your bibliographic reference. Then take time to learn about the publication by reviewing its table of contents, its index, and the endnotes or footnotes related to the pages you are researching. You should be familiar with both the source and the context of all the information you plan to report; they are as significant as the information itself.

However, the first step, preparing the bibliography, is still the most demanding and challenging task in indirect research. It is, therefore, helpful to review what this task involves.

The Online Catalog. Today most libraries use electronic catalogs to list their holdings, giving one numerous ways to locate sources. As you can see from the main menu screen of one system in Figure 19–2, you can locate sources by the standard Author, Words, Title, and Subject options as well as a few other options. Additionally, this menu gives you tips on how to use the catalog. Becoming familiar with these tips is highly recommended, especially for the systems you access frequently. By using effective and efficient searching techniques, you will reap many rewards.

Two options you need to understand clearly are Words and Subject. When you select the Words option, the system will ask you to enter keywords. It will then search for only those exact words in several of each record's fields, missing all those records using slightly different wording. However, when you select Subject, the system will ask you to enter the Library of Congress subject heading. While you must know the exact heading, sometimes it will cross-reference headings such as suggesting you *See Intercultural Communication* when you enter *cross-cultural communication.* A Subject search will find all those holdings on the subject, including those with different wording such as *intercultural communication, international communication, global communication,* and *diversity.* If you ran multiple searches under the Word option using these terms, you would still miss those titles without the keywords, such as Robert Axtell's book *Dos and Taboos around the World.* With a Subject search, you might even find a management book with a chapter on intercultural communication; however, the book's emphasis might be on something else, such as crisis management, negotiation, or conflict resolution.

- When you cannot find secondary materials directly, try the indirect approach. Start by preparing a bibliography of needed sources.

- Gather all available publications. Check each systematically for the information you need.

- A library's online catalog lists its holdings.

- Electronic catalogs give many search options.

Figure 19–2

A Menu for an Online
Catalog

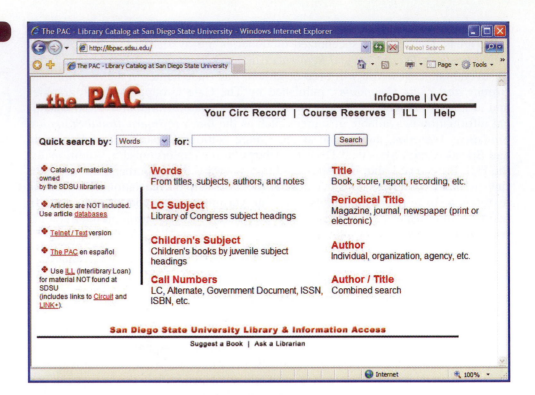

Figure 19–3

Illustration of Online
Search Results

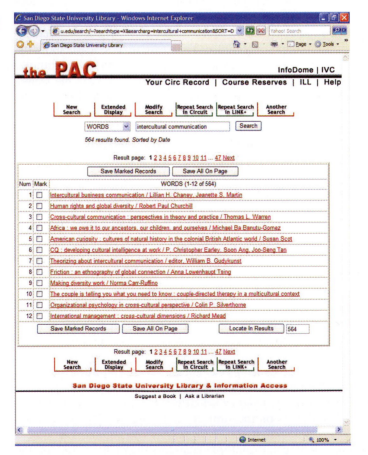

The online catalog never gets tired. If you key in the words accurately, it will always produce a complete and accurate list of sources. Let us look at a few results from a subject search on *intercultural communication*. Notice in Figure 19–3 that the system found 564 sources. Assume that these are more than you really want; so you decide to select

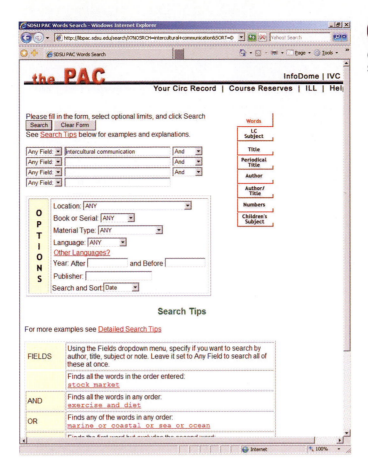

Figure 19–4

Options for Limiting Your Search

the Modify Search option, shown both at the bottom and top of the screen, to limit your search. This system then gives you options for limiting your search (see Figure 19–4). You decide to limit the search by material type and year, telling it you want it to find all sources that are books after 2004 (see Figure 19–5). As you can see in Figure 19–6, 36 entries were found. When you ask the system to display a record, it brings up the screen shown in Figure 19–7. Not only will you find the title and author, but you also will find complete bibliographic information, the call number, and the status, along with subjects associated with this book. Furthermore, the system gives you more options, including options helpful in exporting the information, such as MARC Display and Save to List.

The online catalog is a useful source of information about your library's holdings. Learning how to use it effectively will save you time and will help your searches be fast and accurate.

Online Databases. The online catalog helps you identify books and other holdings in your library. To identify articles published in newspapers, magazines, or journals, you will need to consult an index, either a general one or one that specializes in the field you are researching. Regularly updated indexes are available both online and in the reference section of most libraries.

If you are like most business researchers today, you will start your search for periodical literature in an online database. As the sophistication and capacity of computer technology have improved, much of the information that was once routinely recorded in print form and accessed through directories, encyclopedias, and indexes is now stored electronically in computer files. These files, known as *databases,* are accessed through the use of search strategies. However, one first needs to identify which databases to use.

While there are many databases produced by private and government information services, some of those most useful to business researchers are *ABI/Inform, Factiva, Lexis-Nexis Academic,* and the *Business and Industry Database. ABI/Inform* is one of

- To identify articles for your list of prospective sources, consult an index.

- Computer databases hold much of the information recorded in print and accessed through indexes.

- Knowing which online databases to use helps business researchers find the kind of information they need.

Figure 19–5

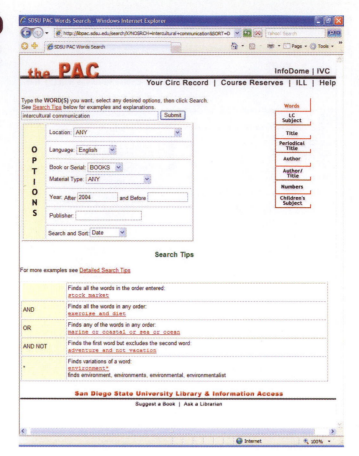

Figure 19–6

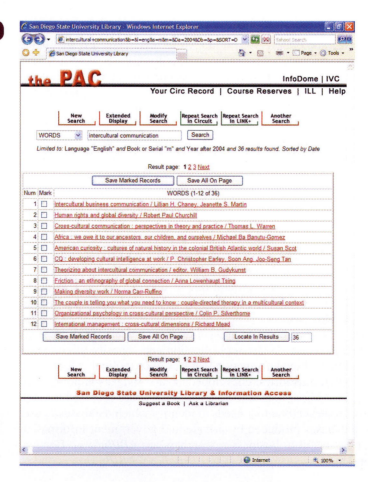

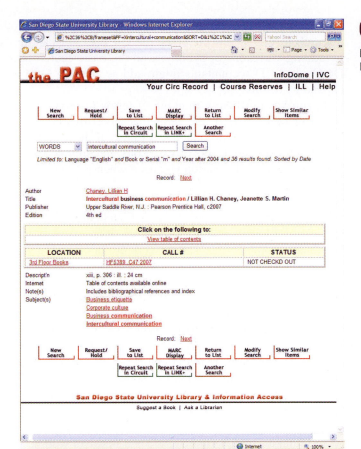

Figure 19–7

Illustration of a Retrieved Record

the most complete databases, providing access to hundreds of business research journals as well as important industry trade publications. Most of the articles are included in full text or with lengthy summaries. It allows basic, guided, and natural language searching. *Factiva,* on the other hand, provides access to current business, general, and international news, including access to various editions of *The Wall Street Journal.* It also includes current information on U.S. public companies and industries. Similarly, *Lexis-Nexis* offers access to the current business and international articles, providing them in full text. Additionally, it includes legal and reference information. Finally, the *Business and Industry Database* covers over 1,000 trade publications, emphasizing facts, figures, and key events. Over 60 percent of its contents are full text, and the remaining include key figures and facts.

Once researchers know where to begin, their search skills become critical. A good command of Boolean logic combined with the knowledge of how to implement it in the databases (or Internet search engines) used will help researchers extract the information they need quickly and accurately. Boolean logic uses three primary operators: AND, OR, and NOT. If search results yield more citations than you need, the results can be limited. Similar to the online catalog, most databases in the guided or advanced mode allow users to limit the search by article or publication type as well as by date. But the use of Boolean logic operators allows users to focus the subject matter more tightly, eliminating citations that are unrelated or tangential to the problem being discussed.

The operator AND is a narrowing term. It instructs the computer to find citations with both terms. The operator NOT is another narrowing term, instructing the computer to eliminate citations with a particular term. It should be used as a last resort because it can eliminate potentially good sources. For example, if one were searching for articles on venture capital, using the NOT term in an attempt to eliminate DotCom companies might eliminate good articles where DotCom was mentioned as an aside

● Skilled use of Boolean logic operators—AND, OR, and NOT—helps you retrieve the kind of information needed.

or even an article that compared DotCom companies to other funded companies. If a search results in few citations, the OR operator can be used to expand the search by adding variations or synonyms to the basic search term. A search for articles on DotComs AND accountants might add accounting OR comptroller OR controller to expand its results.

If you have difficulty thinking of terms to broaden your search, look at the keywords or descriptors of the items that have already been identified. Often these will give you ideas for additional terms to use. If the search still comes up short, you need to check for spelling errors or variations. Becoming skilled at using Boolean logic will help you get the information you need when you need it.

- A wide variety of business sources is available through the Internet.

The Internet. The Internet is a network of networks. It operates in a structure originally funded by the National Science Foundation. However, no one organization owns or runs this globally connected network. Its users work together to develop standards, which are still emerging. The network provides a wide variety of resources, including many useful to business. Since no one is officially in charge, finding information on the Internet can be difficult. Nevertheless, this network of loosely organized computer systems does provide some search and retrieval tools.

- Using online individual search tools will help you find files and text.

These tools can search for files as well as text on various topics. They can search both titles and the documents themselves. Since the Internet is a rapidly growing medium for publishing, the browsers and major portals incorporate links to search tools. Most of the links currently are to individual search engines such as AlltheWeb.com, Google, Hotbot, MSN Search, and Yahoo!. Some of these engines compile their indexes using human input, some use software robots, and some use a combination. Google, whose simple, clean screens you see in Figures 19–8 through 19–12, provides users with much more than the ability to search web pages. From the primary search page, users can search images, groups, directories, and news as well as link to advanced search and translation tools. In Figure 19–8, you may notice that the terms *venture capital women* are entered without the Boolean operator AND. Google automatically ANDs all terms,

Figure 19–8

Illustration of an Individual Web Search Engine— Google

SOURCE: Copyright © Google, Inc., reprinted with permission.

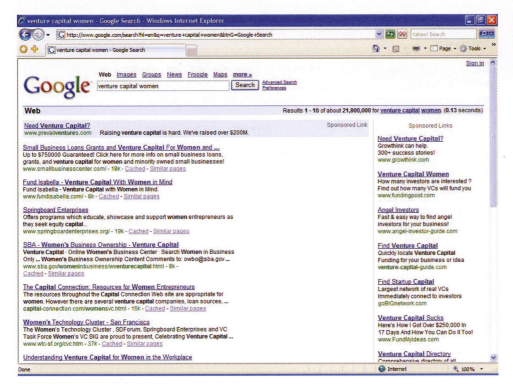

SOURCE: Copyright © Google, Inc., reprinted with permission.

Figure 19–9

An Illustration of Results from a Basic Search

SOURCE: Copyright © Google, Inc., reprinted with permission.

Figure 19–10

Illustration of the Advanced Search Feature of Google

freeing the user from having to add the operator each time a search is conducted. By hitting enter (or clicking on the Google Search button), you execute the search. Notice the result in Figure 19–9: 21,800,000 links found in .13 of a second.

To limit this search, you could use the advanced search tool shown in Figure 19–10. Notice how the first search line (**all**) uses a built-in AND operator, and the third line (**at least one**) uses a built-in OR operator. Additionally, the advanced search allows its user to limit by language, English in this case, and by type of site, .gov here. When this search was run, its results were those shown in Figure 19–11: 261,000 links found in .14 of a second. To further limit the number of links, the user could click on the phrase *Similar pages*. It would return the screen you see in Figure 19–12, showing 573 links.

These are only a few of the features of Google. By thoroughly learning the special techniques and features of the search engines you use most frequently, you will find that they can help you immensely in finding the information you need.

As search engines evolve to meet the changing needs of the Internet's content and its users, new forms of these tools are emerging as well. Metasearch tools allow searchers to enter the search terms once, running the search simultaneously with several individual search engines and compiling a combined results page. Examples of these include Dogpile, EZZwww, Ixquick, Kartoo, Mamma, Metacrawler, and Search.com. You will find links to these and other search tools on the textbook website. Figures 19–13 and 19–14 illustrate how Dogpile searches various search engines for the phrase *cross-cultural communication,* and then combines the results and presents them in an easy-to-view form.

Another type of search tool that is emerging is the specialized search engine. Examples of some of these tools are Yahoo!: People Search for finding people, Deja.com for searching newsgroups, Edgar for finding corporate information, FindLaw for gathering legal information, and Mediafinder for finding print items. There are specialty engines for finding information in finance, music, wireless, medicine, and more. These sites are sometimes referred to as the invisible web or deep web.

Another form of gathering information from the Web is through use of personal agents. These agents allow users to define the kind of information they want to gather. The information gathered can be ready and waiting when users access their personal website, such as at my.yahoo.com. Or it can be delivered by email or in the form of

- Metasearch tools help one use several individual tools more easily.

- Specialized search engines run efficient searches on clearly identified subject-related sites.

- User-defined agents help personalize information needs.

Figure 19–13

An Illustration of a Metasearch Engine— Dogpile

Figure 19–14

An Illustration of Results of a Metasearch

- Users must evaluate the results carefully for both accuracy and completeness.

"push technology," broadcast directly to the connected user's computer screen. You are using push technology if you have news/traffic/weather updates sent to you.

While these tools assist users in finding helpful web documents, it is crucial to remember that the tools are limited. You must evaluate the source of the information critically. Also, you must recognize that not all of the documents published on the Web are indexed and that no search tool covers the entire Web. Skill in using the tools plays a role, but judgment in evaluating the accuracy and completeness of the search plays an even more significant role.

Evaluating Websites

- All sources need careful evaluation; websites need special attention.

Once you have located information sources, whether print or electronic, you need to evaluate them. Most print sources include items such as author, title of publication, facts of publication, and date in a standard form; however, websites have not yet established a standard form. Additionally, the unmonitored electronic media have introduced a slew of other factors one would want to consider in evaluating the credibility of the source as well as the reliability of the content. For example, most users of search engines do not understand the extent or type of bias introduced in the order in which search engines present their results; they often rely on one exclusively to find the most relevant sites when even the best of them only index an estimated 16 percent of the Internet content.

- Research shows that many are overconfident in their ability to judge the reliability of websites.

One experimental study found that users of website information were particularly susceptible to four types of misinformation: advertising claims, government misinformation, propaganda, and even scam sites. Furthermore, the study found that users' confidence in their ability to gather reliable information was not related to their actual ability to judge the information appropriately. The results also revealed that level of education was not related to one's ability to evaluate website information accurately.[1]

- Skills can be honed by habitually asking about the purpose, qualifications, validity, and structure of websites.

One solution might be to limit one's use of information only to sites accessed through links from a trustworthy site, a site where others have evaluated the links

---

[1] Leah Graham and Panagiotis Takis Metaxas, "'Course It's True; I Saw It on the Internet!': Critical Thinking in the Internet Era," *Communications of the ACM* 46.5. (2003): 73.

Doing More Efficient Repeat Searching through Favorites

Most of the newest versions of today's browsers support tabs, enabling fast and efficient repeat searching. In the first illustration here, you can see that separate tabs were opened in Internet Explorer 7 to search cross-cultural communication in three different search engines—Alta Vista, Dogpile, and Mamma. It also shows that adding the complete group of tabs to Favorites (called bookmarking in other browsers) can be done in one click. The second illustration shows naming a folder, *Cross-Cultural Searches,* for the collection of tabs. Once they are saved there, you can repeatedly open all tabs in the folder to run all the searches simultaneously by simply clicking the folder's arrow as shown in the third illustration.

Any search that you need to do repeatedly can be set up this way once and opened whenever you need to review the most recent results.

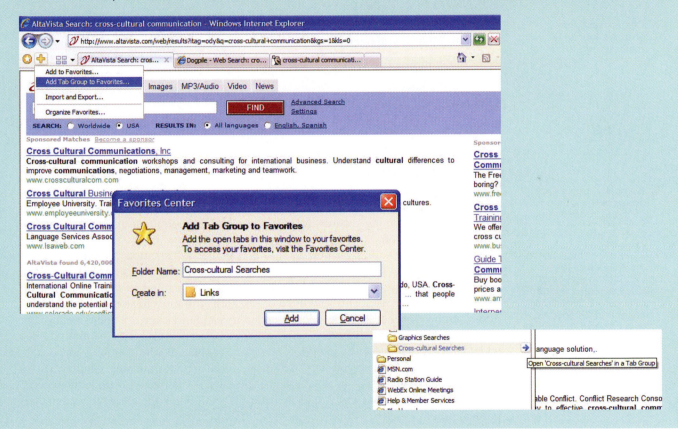

before posting them. However, these sites are clearly not comprehensive and are often late in providing links to new sources. Therefore, developing the skill and habit of evaluating websites critically is probably a better choice. This skill can be honed by getting into the habit of looking at the purpose, qualifications, validity, and structure of websites one uses.

- **Purpose.** Why was the information provided? To explain? To inform? To persuade? To sell? To share? What are the provider's biases? Who is the intended audience? What point of view does the site take? Could it possibly be ironic, a satire, or a parody?

- **Qualifications.** What are the credentials of the information provider? What is the nature of any sponsorship? Is contact information provided? Is it accurate? Is it complete—name, email address, street address, and phone? Is the information well written, clear, and organized?

- **Validity.** Where else can the information provided be found? Is the information the original source? Has the information been synthesized or abstracted accurately and in correct context? Is the information timely? When was it created? When was it posted? Has the site already been validated? Who links to it? (On Google, enter link:*url* to find links.) How long has the site existed? Is it updated regularly? Do the links work? Do they represent other views? Are they well organized? Are they annotated? Has the site received any ratings or reviews? Is cited information authentic?

- **Structure.** How is the site organized, designed, and formatted? Does its structure provide a particular emphasis? Does it appeal to its intended audience?

By critically evaluating websites you use, you will be developing a skill that will help you effectively filter the vast amount of data you encounter.

PRIMARY RESEARCH

• Primary research employs four basic methods.

When you cannot find the information you need in secondary sources, you must get it firsthand. That is, you must use primary research, which employs four basic methods:

1. A search through company records.
2. Experimentation.
3. Observation.
4. Survey.

Searching through Company Records

• Company records are an excellent source of firsthand information.

Since many of today's business problems involve various phases of company operations, a company's internal records—production data, sales records, marketing information, accounting records, and the like—are frequently an excellent source of firsthand information.

• Make sure you (1) have a clear idea of the information you need, (2) understand the terms of access and confidentiality, and (3) cooperate with company personnel.

There are no set rules on how to find and gather information through company records. Record-keeping systems vary widely from company to company. However, you are well advised to keep the following standards in mind as you conduct your investigation. First, as in any other type of research, you must have a clear idea of the information you need. Undefined, open-ended investigations are not appreciated—nor are they particularly productive. Second, you must clearly understand the ground rules under which you are allowed to review materials. Matters of confidentiality and access should be resolved before you start. And third, if you are not intimately familiar with a company's records or how to access them, you must cooperate with someone who is. The complexity and sensitivity of such materials require that they be reviewed in their proper context.

Conducting an Experiment

• Experimentation manipulates one factor and holds others constant.

The experiment is a very useful technique in business research. Originally perfected in the sciences, the experiment is an orderly form of testing. In general, it is a form of research in which you systematically manipulate one variable factor of a problem while holding all the others constant. You measure quantitatively or qualitatively any changes resulting from your manipulations. Then you apply your findings to the problem.

For example, suppose you are conducting research to determine whether a new package design will lead to more sales. You might start by selecting two test cities, taking care that they are as alike as possible on all the characteristics that might affect the problem. Then you would secure information on sales in the two cities for a specified time period before the experiment. Next, for a second specified time period, you would use the new package design in one of the cities and continue to use the old package in the other. During that period, you would keep careful sales records and check to make sure that advertising, economic conditions, competition, and other factors that might

PART 6   Cross-Cultural Communication, Correctness, Technology, Research

Figure 19–15

The Before–After
Experimental Design

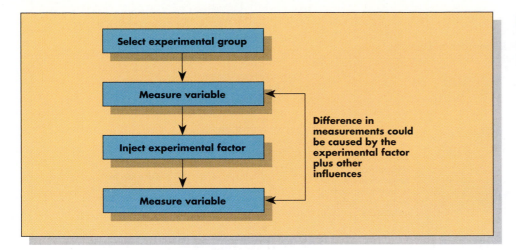

have some effect on the experiment remain unchanged. Thus, when the experimentation period is over, you can attribute any differences you found between the sales of the two cities to the change in package design.

Each experiment should be designed to fit the individual requirements of the problem. Nonetheless, a few basic designs underlie most experiments. Becoming familiar with two of the most common designs—the before–after and the controlled before–after—will give you a framework for understanding and applying this primary research technique.

- Design each experiment to fit the problem.

The Before–After Design.
The simplest experimental design is the before–after design. In this design, illustrated in Figure 19–15, you select a test group of subjects, measure the variable in which you are interested, and then introduce the experimental factor. After a specified time period, during which the experimental factor has presumably had its effect, you again measure the variable in which you are interested. If there are any differences between the first and second measurements, you may assume that the experimental factor, plus any uncontrollable factors, is the cause.

- The before–after design is the simplest. You use just one test group.

Consider the following application. Assume you are conducting research for a retail store to determine the effect of point-of-sale advertising. Your first step is to select a product for the experiment, Gillette razor blades. Second, you record sales of Gillette blades for one week, using no point-of-sale advertising. Then you introduce the experimental variable: the Gillette point-of-sale display. For the next week you again record sales of Gillette blades; and at the end of that week, you compare the results for the two weeks. Any increase in sales would presumably be explained by the introduction of the display. Thus, if 500 packages of Gillette blades were sold in the first week and 600 were sold in the second week, you would conclude that the 100 additional sales can be attributed to point-of-sale advertising.

You can probably recognize the major shortcoming of the design. It is simply not logical to assume that the experimental factor explains the entire difference in sales between the first week and the second. The sales of Gillette razor blades could have changed for a number of other reasons: changes in the weather, holiday or other seasonal influences on business activity, other advertising, and so on. At best, you have determined only that point-of-sale advertising could influence sales.

- The changes recorded in a before–after experiment may not be attributable to the experimental factor alone.

The Controlled Before–After Design.
To account for influences other than the experimental factors, you may use designs more complex than the before–after design. These designs attempt to measure the other influences by including some means of control. The simplest of these designs is the controlled before–after design.

In the controlled before–after design, you select not one group, but two: the experimental group and the control group. Before introducing the experimental factor, you measure in each group the variable to be tested. Then you introduce the experimental factor into the experimental group only.

- In the controlled before–after experiment, you use two identical test groups. You introduce the experimental factor into one group, then compare the two groups. You can attribute any difference between the two to the experimental factor.

Figure 19–16

The Controlled Before–After Experimental Design

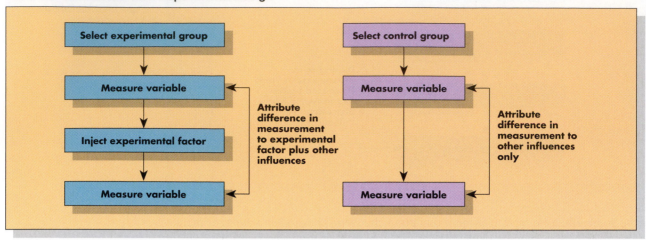

When the period allotted for the experiment is over, you again measure in each group the variable being tested. Any difference between the first and second measurements in the experimental group can be explained by two causes: the experimental factor and other influences. But the difference between the first and second measurements in the control group can be explained only by other influences, for this group was not subjected to the experimental factor. Thus, comparing the "afters" of the two groups will give you a measure of the influence of the experimental factor, as diagrammed in Figure 19–16.

In a controlled before–after experiment designed to test point-of-sale advertising, you might select Gillette razor blades and Schick razor blades and record the sales of both brands for one week. Next you introduce point-of-sale displays for Gillette only and you record sales for both Gillette and Schick for a second week. At the end of the second week, you compare the results for the two brands. Whatever difference you find in Gillette sales and Schick sales will be a fair measure of the experimental factor, independent of the changes that other influences may have brought about.

For example, without point-of-sales displays in the control group, if 400 packages of Schick blades are sold the first week and 450 packages are sold the second week, the increase of 50 packages (12.5 percent) can be attributed to influences other than the experimental factor, the point-of-sale display. If 500 packages of Gillette blades are sold the first week and 600 are sold the second week, the increase of 100 can be attributed to both the point-of-sale display and other influences. To distinguish between the two, you note that other influences accounted for the 12.5 percent increase in the sales of Schick blades. Because of the experimental control, you attribute 12.5 percent of the increase in Gillette sales to other influences as well. An increase of 12.5 percent on a base of 500 sales is 63 sales, indicating that 63 of the 100 additional Gillette sales are the result of other influences. However, the sale of 37 additional packages of Gillette blades can be attributed to point-of-sale advertising.

Using the Observation Technique

- Research by observation involves watching phenomena and recording what is seen.

Like the experiment, observation is a technique perfected in the sciences that is also useful in business research. Simply stated, observation is seeing with a purpose. It consists of watching the events involved in a problem and systematically recording what is seen. In observation, you do not manipulate the details of what you observe; you take note of situations exactly as you find them.

- This form of observation does not involve experimentation.

Note that observation as an independent research technique is different from the observation you use in recording the effects of variables introduced into a test situation. In the latter case, observation is a step in the experiment, not an end in itself. The two methods, therefore, should not be confused.

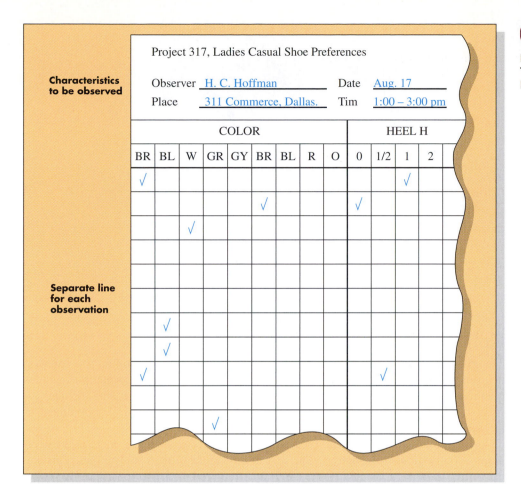

Figure 19–17

Excerpt of a Common Type of Observation Recording Form

Characteristics to be observed

Project 317, Ladies Casual Shoe Preferences

Observer H. C. Hoffman   Date Aug. 17
Place   311 Commerce, Dallas.   Tim 1:00 – 3:00 pm

Separate line for each observation

COLOR									HEEL H			
BR	BL	W	GR	GY	BR	BL	R	O	0	1/2	1	2
√											√	
					√				√			
		√										
	√											
	√											
√											√	
			√									

To see how observation works as a business technique, consider this situation. You work for a fast-food chain, such as McDonald's, that wants to check the quality and consistency of some menu items throughout the chain. By hiring observers, sometimes called mystery shoppers, you can gather information on the temperature, freshness, and speed of delivery of various menu items. This method may reveal important information that other data collection methods cannot.

Like all primary research techniques, observation must be designed to fit the requirements of the problem being considered. However, the planning stage generally requires two steps. First, you construct a recording form; second, you design a systematic procedure for observing and recording the information of interest.

- Observation requires a systematic procedure for observing and recording.

The recording form may be any tabular arrangement that permits quick and easy recording of that information. Though observation forms are hardly standardized, one commonly used arrangement (see Figure 19–17) provides a separate line for each observation. Headings at the top of the page mark the columns in which the observer will place the appropriate mark. The recording form identifies the characteristics that are to be observed and requires the recording of such potentially important details as the date, time, and place of the observation and the name of the observer.

- The recording form should enable you to record details quickly and accurately.

The observation procedure may be any system that ensures the collection of complete and representative information. But every effective observation procedure includes a clear focus, well-defined steps, and provisions for ensuring the quality of the information collected. For example, an observation procedure for determining the courtesy of employees toward customers when answering the telephone would include a detailed schedule for making calls, detailed instructions on what to ask, and provisions for dealing with different responses the observer might encounter. In short, the procedure would leave no major question unanswered.

- An effective observation procedure ensures the collection of complete and representative information.

"We sent you on a fact-finding mission and all you found were two facts?"

SOURCE: © Benita Epstein 2000. Reprinted with permission of the artist.

Collecting Information by Survey

- You can best acquire certain information by asking questions.

The premise of the survey as a method of primary research is simple: You can best acquire certain types of information by asking questions. Such information includes personal data, opinions, evaluations, and other important material. It also includes information necessary to plan for an experiment or an observation or to supplement or interpret the data that result.

- Decide which survey format and delivery will be most effective in developing the information you need.

Once you have decided to use the survey for your research, you have to make decisions about a number of matters. The first is the matter of format. The questions can range from spontaneous inquiries to carefully structured interrogations. The next is the matter of delivery. The questions can be posed in a personal interview, asked over the telephone, or presented in printed or electronic form.

- Also decide whom to interview. If the subject group is large, select a sample.

But the most important is the matter of whom to survey. Except for situations in which a small number of people are involved in the problem under study, you cannot reach all the people involved. Thus, you have to select a sample of respondents who represent the group as a whole as accurately as possible. There are several ways to select that sample, as you will see.

- Survey research is based on sampling.

Sampling as a Basis. Sampling theory forms the basis for most research by survey, though it has any number of other applications as well. Buyers of grain, for example, judge the quality of a multiton shipment by examining a few pounds. Quality-control supervisors spot-check a small percentage of products ready for distribution to determine whether production standards are being met. Auditors for large corporations sample transactions when examining the books. Sampling is generally used for economy and practicality. However, for a sample to be representative of the whole group, it must be designed properly.

- Good samples are reliable, valid, and controlled for sampling error.

Two important aspects to consider in sample design are controlling for sampling error and bias. Sampling error results when the sample is not representative of the whole group. While all samples have some degree of sampling error, you can reduce the error through techniques used to construct representative samples. These techniques fall into two groups: probability and nonprobability sampling.

Probability Sampling Techniques. Probability samples are based on chance selection procedures. Every element in the population has a known nonzero probability of selection.[2] These techniques include simple random sampling, stratified random sampling, systematic sampling, and area or cluster sampling.

---

[2] William G. Zikmund, *Business Research Methods*, 7th ed. (Mason, OH: South-Western, 2003) 279.

Survey Tools Help Writers Lay Out, Analyze, and Report Results of Questionnaires

Survey tools, both software and web-based tools, help you design professional-looking questionnaires as well as compile and analyze the data collected. Software programs help with construction and layout of questionnaires and allow you to convert the questionnaires to html format for publishing on the Web easily. Web-based programs help you create, distribute, and manage data collection for online questionnaires.

Special data entry screens assist you in selecting the types of questions and desired layout. They then arrange the questionnaire automatically while giving you the freedom to move the questions to change the ordering and arrangement if desired. The tools also let you create open-

ended questions. All of these questions can be saved in a library for reuse. Some of the tools even include libraries of surveys that can be adapted for one's particular use.

As shown, one program, SurveyMonkey.com, creates a variety of graphics, helping you see the results clearly and accurately as the questionnaires are being submitted.

Businesses can use these tools in a variety of applications, including training program evaluations, employee feedback on policies and procedures, longitudinal studies of ongoing practices such as network advertising revenues, opinion surveys of customers and potential customers, and feedback on customer satisfaction.

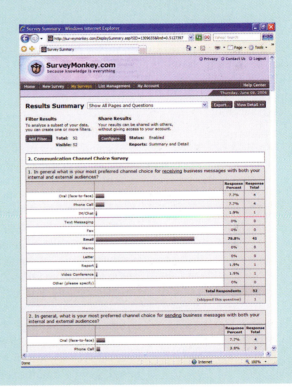

Random Sampling. Random sampling is the technique assumed in the general law of sampling. By definition, it is the sampling technique that gives every member of the group under study an equal chance of being included. To assure equal chances, you must first identify every member of the group and then, using a list or some other convenient format, record all the identifications. Next, through some chance method, you select the members of your sample.

For example, if you are studying the job attitudes of 200 employees and determine that 25 interviews will give you the information you need, you might put the names of each worker in a container, mix them thoroughly, and draw out 25. Since each of the 200 workers has an equal chance of being selected, your sample will be random and can be presumed to be representative.

• In random sampling, every item in the subject group has an equal chance of being selected.

- In stratified random sampling, the group is divided into subgroups and the sample is randomly selected from each subgroup.

Stratified Random Sampling. Stratified random sampling subdivides the group under study and makes random selections within each subgroup. The size of each subgroup is usually proportionate to that subgroup's percentage of the whole. If a subgroup is too small to yield meaningful findings, however, you may have to select a disproportionately large sample. Of course, when the study calls for statistics on the group as a whole, the actual proportion of such a subgroup must be restored.

Assume, for example, that you are attempting to determine the curriculum needs of 5,000 undergraduates at a certain college and that you have decided to survey 20 percent of the enrollment, or 1,000 students. To construct a sample for this problem, first divide the enrollment list by academic concentration: business, liberal arts, nursing, engineering, and so forth. Then draw a random sample from each of these groups, making sure that the number you select is proportionate to that group's percentage of the total undergraduate enrollment. Thus, if 30 percent of the students are majoring in business, you will randomly select 300 business majors for your sample; if 40 percent of the students are liberal arts majors, you will randomly select 400 liberal arts majors for your sample; and so on.

- In systematic sampling, the items are selected from the subject group at constant intervals.

- Select the interval randomly or scramble the order of the subject group if you want your systematic sample to be random.

Systematic Sampling. Systematic sampling, though not random in the strictest sense, is random for all practical purposes. It is the technique of taking selections at constant intervals (every nth unit) from a list of the items under study. The interval used is based, as you might expect, on the size of the list and the size of the desired sample. For example, if you want a 10 percent sample of a list of 10,000, you might select every 10th item on the list.

However, your sample would not really be random. By virtue of their designated place on the original list, items do not have an equal chance of being selected. To correct that problem, you might use an equal-chance method to determine what n to use. Thus, if you selected the number 7 randomly, you would draw the numbers 7, 17, 27, and so on to 9,997 to make up your sample. Or, if you wanted to draw every 10th item, you might first scramble the list and then select from the revised list numbers 10, 20, 30, and so on up to 10,000 and make up your sample that way.

- For an area or cluster sample, draw items from the subject group in stages. Select randomly at each stage.

Area or Cluster Sampling. In area sampling, the items for a sample are drawn in stages. This sampling technique is appropriate when the area to be studied is large and can be broken down into progressively smaller components. For example, if you want to draw an area sample for a certain city, you may use census data to divide the city into homogeneous districts. Using an equal-chance method, you then select a given number of districts to include in the next stage of your sample. Next you divide each of the selected districts into subdistricts—city blocks, for example. Continuing the process, you randomly select a given number of these blocks and subdivide each of them into households. Finally, using random sampling once more, you select the households that will constitute the sample you will use in your research.

Area or cluster sampling is not limited to geographic division, however. It is adaptable to any number of applications. For example, it is an appropriate technique to use in a survey of the employees in a given industry. An approach that you may take in this situation is to randomly select a given number of companies from a list of all the companies in the industry. Then, using organization units and selecting randomly at each level, you break down each of these companies into divisions, departments, sections, and so on until you finally identify the workers you will survey.

Nonprobability Sampling Techniques. Nonprobability samples are based on an unknown probability of any one of a population being chosen. These techniques include convenience sampling, quota sampling, and referral sampling.[3]

Convenience Sampling. A convenience sample is one whose members are convenient and economical to reach. When professors use their students as subjects for their research, they are using a convenience sample. Researchers generally use this sample to reach a large number quickly and economically. This kind of sampling is best used for exploratory research.

- Convenience samples are chosen for their convenience, their ease and economy of reaching subjects, and their appropriateness.

A form of convenience sampling is *judgment* or *expert* sampling. This technique relies on the judgment of the researcher to identify appropriate members of the sample. Illustrating this technique is the common practice of predicting the outcome of an election, based on the results in a bellwether district.

Quota Sampling. Quota sampling is another nonrandom technique. Also known as *controlled sampling,* it is used whenever the proportionate makeup of the universe under study is available. The technique requires that you refer to the composition of the universe in designing your sample, selecting items so that your sample has the same characteristics in the same proportion as that universe. Specifically, it requires that you set quotas for each characteristic that you want to consider in your research problem. Within those quotas, however, you will select individual items randomly.

- Setting quotas assures that the sample reflects the whole. Choose items randomly within each quota.

Let us say that you want to survey a college student body of 4,000 using a 10 percent sample. As Figure 19–18 illustrates, you have a number of alternatives for determining the makeup of your sample, depending on the focus of your research. Keep in mind, though, that no matter what characteristic you select, the quotas the individual segments represent must total 100 percent and the number of items in the sample must total 400. Keep in mind also that within these quotas you will use an equal-chance method to select the individual members of your sample.

Referral Sampling. Referral samples are those whose members are identified by others from a random sample. This technique is used to locate members when the population is small or hard to reach. For example, you might want to survey rolle bolle players. To get a sample large enough to make the study worthwhile, you could ask those from your town to give you the names of other players. Perhaps you are trying to survey the users of project management software. You could survey a user's group and ask those members for names of other users. You might even post your announcement on a newsgroup or listserv; users of the system would send you the names for your sample.

- Referral samples are used for small or hard-to-reach groups.

Constructing the Questionnaire. Most orderly interrogation follows a definite plan of inquiry. This plan is usually worked out in a published (print or electronic)

- Construct a questionnaire carefully so that the results it provides are both reliable and valid.

---

[3] Zikmund 279.

Figure 19–18

Example of Quota Sample

	Number in Universe	Percent of Total	Number to Be Interviewed
Total student enrollment	4,000	100	400
Sex			
Men students	2,400	60	240
Women students	1,600	40	160
Fraternity, sorority membership			
Members	1,000	25	100
Nonmembers	3,000	75	300
Marital status			
Married students	400	10	40
Single students	3,600	90	360
Class rank			
Freshmen	1,600	40	160
Sophomores	1,000	25	100
Juniors	800	20	80
Seniors	400	10	40
Graduates	200	5	20

form, called the *questionnaire.* The questionnaire is simply an orderly arrangement of the questions, with appropriate spaces provided for the answers. But simple as the finished questionnaire may appear to be, it is the subject of careful planning. You should plan carefully so that the results are *reliable;* a test of a questionnaire's reliability is its repeatability with similar results. You also want your questionnaire to be *valid,* measuring what it is supposed to measure. It is, in a sense, the outline of the analysis of the problem. In addition, it must observe certain rules. These rules sometimes vary with the problem. The more general and by far the more important ones follow.

- Avoid leading questions (questions that influence the answer).

Avoid Leading Questions. A leading question is one that in some way influences the answer. For example, the question "Is Dove your favorite bath soap?" leads the respondent to favor Dove. Some people who would say yes would name another brand if they were asked, "What is your favorite brand of bath soap?"

- Word the questions so that all the respondents understand them.

Make the Questions Easy to Understand. Questions not clearly understood by all respondents lead to error. Unfortunately, it is difficult to determine in advance just what respondents will not understand. As will be mentioned later, the best means of detecting such questions in advance is to test the questions before using them. But you can be on the alert for a few general sources of confusion.

- Vagueness of expression, difficult words, and two questions in one cause misunderstanding.

One source of confusion is vagueness of expression, which is illustrated by the ridiculous question "How do you bank?" Who other than its author knows what the question means? Another source is using words respondents do not understand, as in the question "Do you read your house organ regularly?" The words *house organ* have a specialized, not widely known meaning, and *regularly* means different things to different people. Combining two questions in one is yet another source of confusion. For example, "Why did you buy a Ford?" actually asks two questions: "What do you like about Fords?" and "What don't you like about the other automobiles?"

- Avoid questions of a personal nature.

Avoid Questions That Touch on Personal Prejudices or Pride. For reasons of pride or prejudices, people cannot be expected to answer accurately questions about certain areas of information. These areas include age, income status, morals, and personal habits. How many people, for example, would answer no to the question "Do you brush your teeth daily?" How many people would give their ages correctly? How many solid citizens would admit to fudging a bit on their tax returns? The answers are obvious.

- But if personal questions are necessary, use less direct methods.

But one may ask, "What if such information is essential to the solution of the problem?" The answer is to use less direct means of inquiry. To ascertain age, for example, investigators could ask for dates of high school graduation, marriage, or the like. From this information, they could approximate age. Or they could approximate age through observation, although this procedure is acceptable only if broad age approximations would be satisfactory. They could ask for such harmless information as occupation, residential area, and standard of living and then use that information as a basis for approximating income. Another possibility is to ask range questions such as "Are you between 18 and 24, 25 and 40, or over 40?" This technique works well with income questions, too. People are generally more willing to answer questions worded by ranges rather than specifics. Admittedly, such techniques are sometimes awkward and difficult. But they can improve on the biased results that direct questioning would obtain.

Seek Facts as Much as Possible. Although some studies require opinions, it is far safer to seek facts whenever possible. Human beings simply are not accurate reporters of their opinions. They are often limited in their ability to express themselves. Frequently, they report their opinions erroneously simply because they have never before been conscious of having them.

- Seek factual information whenever possible.

When opinions are needed, it is usually safer to record facts and then to judge the thoughts behind them. This technique, however, is only as good as the investigators' judgment. But a logical analysis of fact made by trained investigators is preferable to a spur-of-the-moment opinion.

A frequent violation of this rule results from the use of generalizations. Respondents are sometimes asked to generalize an answer from a large number of experiences over time. The question "Which magazines do you read regularly?" is a good illustration. Aside from the confusion caused by the word *regularly* and the fact that the question may tap the respondent's memory, the question forces the respondent to generalize. Would it not be better to phrase it in this way: "What magazines have you read this month?" The question could then be followed by an article-by-article check of the magazines to determine the extent of readership.

Ask Only for Information That Can Be Remembered. Since the memory of all human beings is limited, the questionnaire should ask only for information that the respondents can be expected to remember. To make sure that this is done, you need to know certain fundamentals of memory.

- Ask only for information that can be remembered.

Recency is the foremost fundamental. People remember insignificant events that occurred within the past few hours. By the next day, they will forget some. A month later they may not remember any. One might well remember, for example, what one ate for lunch on the day of the inquiry, and perhaps one might remember what one ate for lunch a day, or two days, or three days earlier. But one would be unlikely to remember what one ate for lunch a year earlier.

- Memory is determined by three fundamentals: (1) recency,

The second fundamental of memory is that significant events may be remembered over long periods. One may long remember the first day of school, the day of one's wedding, an automobile accident, a Christmas Day, and the like. In each of these examples there was an intense stimulus—a requisite for retention in memory.

- (2) intensity of stimulus, and

A third fundamental of memory is that fairly insignificant facts may be remembered over long time periods through association with something significant. Although one would not normally remember what one ate for lunch a year earlier, for example, one might remember if the date happened to be one's wedding day, Christmas Day, or one's first day at college. Obviously, the memory is stimulated not by the meal itself but by the association of the meal with something more significant.

- (3) association.

Plan the Physical Layout with Foresight. The overall design of the questionnaire should be planned to facilitate recording, analyzing, and tabulating the answers. Three major considerations are involved in such planning.

- Design the form for each recording.

First, sufficient space should be allowed for recording answers. When practical, a system for checking answers may be set up. Such a system must always provide for all possible answers, including conditional answers. For example, a direct question

- Provide sufficient space.

may provide for three possible answers: Yes _____, No _____, and Don't know _____.

Second, adequate space for identifying and describing the respondent should be provided. In some instances, such information as the age, sex, and income bracket of the respondent is vital to the analysis of the problem and should be recorded. In other instances, little or no identification is necessary.

- Arrange the questions in logical order.

Third, the best possible sequence of questions should be used. In some instances, starting with a question of high interest value may have psychological advantages. In other instances, it may be best to follow some definite order of progression. Frequently, some questions must precede others because they help explain the others. Whatever the requirements of the individual case may be, however, careful and logical analysis should be used in determining the sequence of questions.

- Provide for scaling when appropriate.

Use Scaling When Appropriate. It is sometimes desirable to measure the intensity of the respondents' feelings about something (an idea, a product, a company, and so on). In such cases, some form of scaling is generally useful.

Of the various techniques of scaling, ranking and rating deserve special mention. These are the simpler techniques and, some believe, the more practical. They are less sophisticated than some others,[4] but the more sophisticated techniques are beyond the scope of this book.

- Ranking of responses is one form.

The ranking technique consists simply of asking the respondent to rank a number of alternative answers to a question in order of preference (1, 2, 3, and so on). For example, in a survey to determine consumer preferences for toothpaste, the respondent might be asked to rank toothpastes A, B, C, D, and E in order of preference. In this example, the alternatives could be compared on the number of preferences stated for each. This method of ranking and summarizing results is reliable despite its simplicity. More complicated ranking methods (such as the use of paired comparison) and methods of recording results are also available.

- Rating is another.

The rating technique graphically sets up a scale showing the complete range of possible attitudes on a matter and assigns number values to the positions on the scale. The respondent must then indicate the position on the scale that indicates his or her attitude on that matter. Typically, the numeral positions are described by words, as the example in Figure 19–19 illustrates.

Because the rating technique deals with the subjective rather than the factual, it is sometimes desirable to use more than one question to cover the attitude being measured. Logically, the average of a person's answers to such questions gives a more reliable answer than does any single answer.

- Select the way of asking the questions (by personal contact, telephone, or mail) that gives the best sample, the lowest cost, and the best results.

Selecting the Manner of Questioning. You can get responses to the questions you need answered in three primary ways: by personal (face-to-face) contact, by telephone, or by mail (print or electronic). You should select the way that in your unique case gives the best sample, the lowest cost, and the best results. By *best sample* we mean respondents who best represent the group concerned. And *results* are the information you need. As you can see in Figure 19–20, other factors will influence your choice.

- Develop a working plan that covers all the steps and all the problems.

Developing a Working Plan. After selecting the manner of questioning, you should carefully develop a working plan for the survey. As well as you can, you should anticipate and determine how to handle every possible problem. If you are conducting a mail or Web survey, for example, you need to develop an explanatory message that moves the subjects to respond, tells them what to do, and answers all the questions they are likely to ask (see Figure 19–21). If you are conducting a personal or telephone survey, you need to cover this information in instructions to the interviewers.

---

[4] Equivalent interval techniques (developed by L. L. Thurstone), scalogram analysis (developed by Louis Guttman), and the semantic differential (developed by C. E. Osgood, G. J. Suci, and P. H. Tannenbaum) are more complex techniques.

Figure 19–19

Illustration of a Rating Question

What is your opinion of current right-to-work legislation?

Strongly oppose	Moderately oppose	Mildly oppose	Neutral	Mildly favor	Moderately favor	Strongly favor
-3	-2	-1	0	1	2	3

Figure 19–20

Comparison of Data Collection Methods

	Personal	Telephone	Online	Mail
Data collection costs	High	Medium	Low	Low
Data collection time required	Medium	Low	Medium	High
Sample size for a given budget	Small	Medium	Large	Large
Data quantity per respondent	High	Medium	Low	Low
Reaches high proportion of public	Yes	Yes	No	Yes
Reaches widely dispersed sample	No	Maybe	Yes	Yes
Reaches special locations	Yes	Maybe	No	No
Interaction with respondents	Yes	Yes	No	No
Degree of interviewer bias	High	Medium	None	None
Severity of nonresponse bias	Low	Low	High	High
Presentation of visual stimuli	Yes	No	Yes	Maybe
Field-worker training required	Yes	Yes	No	No

SOURCE: Pamela L. Alreck and Robert B. Settle, *The Survey Research Handbook,* 3rd ed. (Burr Ridge, IL: McGraw-Hill/Irwin, 2004) 33.

Figure 19–21

Illustration of a Persuasive Request Cover Message

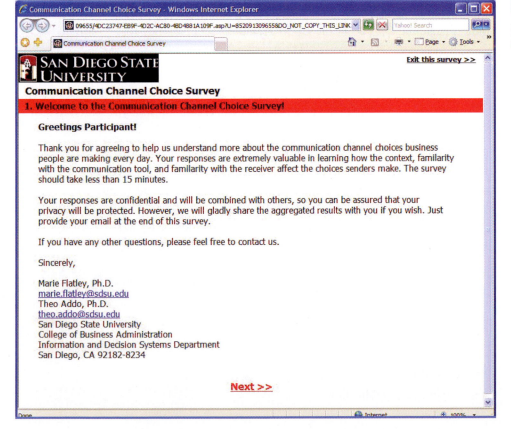

You should develop your working plan before conducting the pilot study discussed in the following section. You should test that plan in the pilot study and revise it based on the knowledge you gain from the pilot study.

- Test the questionnaire and the working plan. Make any changes needed.

Conducting a Pilot Study. Before doing the survey, it is advisable to conduct a pilot study on your questionnaire and working plan. A pilot study is a small-scale version of the actual survey. Its purpose is to test what you have planned. Based on your experience in the pilot study, you modify your questionnaire and working plan for use in the full-scale survey that follows.

Evaluating and Reporting Data

- Carefully evaluate the secondary information you find.

Gathering information is one step in processing facts for your report. You also need to evaluate it. In the case of secondary research, ask yourself questions about the writer's credibility, including methods of collecting facts and ability to draw inferences from the facts presented. Does the author draw conclusions that can be supported by the data presented? Are the sources reliable? Are the data or interpretations biased in any way? Are there any gaps or holes in the data or interpretation? You need to be a good judge of the material and feel free to discard it if it does not meet your standard for quality.

- Report statistics from primary research clearly and completely.

As for primary research, this chapter has discussed how to plan and carry out primary data collection properly. Once you have good data to work with, you must interpret them accurately and clearly for your reader (see Chapter 10 for interpreting procedure). If you are unsure of your reader's level of expertise in understanding descriptive statistics such as measures of central tendency and cross-tabulations, present the statistic and tell the reader what it means. In general, you can expect to explain the statistics from univariate, bivariate, and multivariate analyses. In many cases, graphics help tremendously because they clearly show trends and relationships. Statistical programs such as SPSS and SAS help you analyze, report, and graph your data. Finally, you have an ethical responsibility to present your data honestly and completely.

Omitting an error or limitation of the data collection is often viewed as seriously as hiding errors or variations from accepted practices. Of course, any deliberate distortion of the data, whether primary or secondary, is unethical. It is your responsibility to communicate the findings of the report accurately and clearly.

SUMMARY BY LEARNING OBJECTIVES

1 Explain the difference between primary and secondary research.

1. Primary research is firsthand research. You can conduct primary research in four major ways:
   - Looking through company records.
   - Conducting an experiment.
   - Recording observations.
   - Conducting a survey.

   Secondary research is secondhand research. You conduct secondary research in either a general library (usually public), a special library (usually private), or online.

2 Gather secondary sources using direct and indirect research methods.

2. If you need quantitative or factual information, you may be able to go directly to it, using such sources as the following:
   - Encyclopedias.
   - Biographical directories.
   - Almanacs.
   - Trade directories.
   - Government publications.
   - Dictionaries.

- Statistical sources.
- Business information services.

When you cannot go directly to the source, you use indirect methods. You may begin by searching the following sources:

- The online catalog.
- Online databases.
- The Internet.

3. Websites must be critically evaluated to ensure that the information is relevant and reliable. The skill can be honed and become habit by looking at the purpose of each site, the qualifications of the information provider, the validity of the content, and the organizational structure and design format.

3 Evaluate website reliability.

4. Company records are usually confidential. You must either ask the person responsible for the information for it or gather it yourself from company records.

4 Describe the procedures for searching through company records.

5. An experiment is an orderly form of testing. It can be designed using the before–after design or the controlled before–after design.

5 Conduct an experiment for a business problem.

- The simplest is the before–after design. It involves selecting a group of subjects, measuring the variable, introducing the experimental factor, and measuring the variable again. The difference between the two measurements is assumed to be the result of the experimental factor.

- The controlled before–after design involves selecting two groups, measuring the variable in both groups, introducing the experimental factor in one group, and then measuring the variable again in both groups. The second measurement enables you to determine the effect of the experimental factor and of other factors that might have influenced the variable between the two measurements.

6. The observation method may be defined as seeing with a purpose. It consists of watching the events involved in a problem and systematically recording what is seen. The events observed are not manipulated.

6 Design an observational study for a business problem.

7. A sample is a group representative of the whole group. The procedure for selecting the group is called sampling. A good sample is controlled for sampling error. You may use any of a variety of sample designs. Those discussed in this chapter include probability and nonprobability sampling.

7 Use sampling to conduct a survey.

- Probability sampling is based on chance selection procedures. Every element in the population has a known nonzero probability of selection. Some of the techniques are described below.

    — Simple random sampling involves chance selection, giving every member of the group under study an equal chance of being selected.

    — Stratified random sampling involves proportionate and random selection from each major subgroup of the group under study.

    — Systematic sampling involves taking selections at constant intervals (every fifth one, for example) from a complete list of the group under study.

    — Area or cluster sampling involves dividing into parts the area that contains the sample, selecting from these parts randomly, and continuing to subdivide and select until you have your desired sample size.

- Nonprobability sampling is based on an unknown probability of any one of a group being studied. Some of the techniques are described below.

    — Convenience sampling involves selecting members that are convenient, easy to reach, and appropriate as judged by the researcher.

    — Quota sampling requires that you know the proportions of certain characteristics (sex, age, education, etc.) in the group under study. You then select respondents in the same proportions.

    — Referral sampling involves building your sample from other participants' referrals.

8
Construct a
questionnaire, develop
a working plan, and
conduct a pilot test for a
survey.

8. The questions you ask should follow a definite plan, usually in the form of a questionnaire. You should construct the questionnaire carefully, ensuring that it is valid and reliable, and the questionnaire should follow these general rules.

- Avoid leading questions.
- Make the questions easy to understand (avoid vagueness, difficult words, technical words).
- Avoid questions that touch on personal prejudices or pride.
- Seek facts as much as possible.
- Ask only for what can be remembered (consider the laws of memory: recency, intensity, and association).
- Plan the layout with foresight (enough space for answers and identifying information, proper sequence of questions).
- Use scaling when appropriate.

You develop a working plan for conducting the questioning—one that covers all the possible problems and clearly explains what to do. It is usually advisable to test the questionnaire and working plan through a pilot study. This enables you to make changes in the questionnaire and improve the working plan before conducting the survey.

9
Analyze and interpret
information clearly and
completely for your
reader.

9. You need to evaluate the facts you gather from secondary research carefully before you include them in your report. Check to make sure they meet the following tests.

- Can the author draw the conclusions from the data presented?
- Are the sources reliable?
- Has the author avoided biased interpretation?
- Are there any gaps in the facts?

You must present the primary information you collect clearly and completely. It is your responsibility to explain statistics the reader may not understand.

CRITICAL THINKING QUESTIONS

1 Suggest a hypothetical research problem that would make good use of a specialized library. Justify your selection.

2 What specialized libraries are there in your community? What general libraries?

3 Under what general condition are investigators likely to be able to proceed directly to the published source of the information sought?

4 Which databases or other sources would be good sources of information for each of the following subjects?

a. Labor–management relations

b. A certain company's market share

c. Whether or not a company is being sued

d. Viewpoints on the effect of deficit financing by governments

e. The top companies, by sales, in a certain industry

f. New techniques in interviewing

g. The job outlook in a certain industry

h. Recent trends in business-related technology

i. The potential world market for a certain product

j. Government regulations for incorporating your business

k. The qualifications of a new CEO of a company

l. Promising sites for a new branch of your business

5 Use your critical skills to evaluate websites, identifying those with problems in advertising claims, government misinformation, propaganda, or scam sites.

6 What advice would you give an investigator who has been assigned a task involving analysis of internal records of several company departments?

7 Define *experimentation*. What does the technique of experimentation involve?

8 Explain the significance of keeping constant all factors other than the experimental variable of an experiment.

9 Give an example of (*a*) a problem that can best be solved through a before–after design and (*b*) a problem that can best be solved through a controlled before–after design. Explain your choices.

10 Define *observation* as a research technique.

11 Select an example of a business problem that can be solved best by observation. Explain your choice.

12 Point out violations of the rules of good questionnaire construction in the following questions. The questions do not come from the same questionnaire.

a. How many days on the average do you wear a pair of socks before changing?

b. (The first question in a survey conducted by Coca-Cola.) Have you ever drunk a Diet Coke?

c. Do you consider the ideal pay plan to be one based on straight commission or straight salary?

d. What kind of gasoline did you purchase last time?

e. How much did you pay for clothing in the past 12 months?

f. Check the word below that best describes how often you eat dessert with your noon meal.

Always

Usually

Sometimes

Never

13 Explain the difference between random sampling and convenience sampling.

14 Explain how to evaluate secondary information.

15 Discuss the writer's responsibility in explaining and reporting data.

CRITICAL THINKING EXERCISES

1 Using your imagination to supply any missing facts you may need, develop a plan for the experiment you would use in the following situations.

a. The Golden Glow Baking Company has for many years manufactured and sold cookies packaged in attractive boxes. It is considering packaging the cookies in recyclable bags and wants to conduct an experiment to determine consumer response to this change.

b. The Miller Brush Company, manufacturers of a line of household goods, has for years sold its products through conventional retail outlets. It now wants to conduct an experiment to test the possibility of selling through catalogs (or home shopping networks or the Web).

c. A national chain of drugstores wants to know whether it would profit by doubling the face value of coupons. It is willing to pay the cost of an experiment in its research for an answer.

d. The True Time Watch Company is considering the use of electronic sales displays ($49.50 each) instead of print displays ($24.50 each) in the 2,500 retail outlets that sell True Time watches. The company will conduct an experiment to determine the relative effects on sales of the two displays.

e. The Marvel Soap Company has developed a new cleaning agent that is unlike current soaps and detergents. The product is well protected by patent. The company wants to determine the optimum price for the new product through experimentation.

f. National Cereals, Inc., wants to determine the effectiveness of advertising to children. Until now, it has been aiming its appeal at parents. The company will support an experiment to learn the answer.

2 Using your imagination to supply any missing facts you may need, develop a plan for research by observation for these problems.

a. A chain of department stores wants to know what causes differences in sales by departments within stores and by stores. Some of this information it hopes to get through research by observation.

b. Your university wants to know the nature and extent of its parking problem.

c. The management of an insurance company wants to determine the efficiency and productivity of its data-entry department.

d. Owners of a shopping center want a study to determine shopping patterns of their customers. Specifically they want to know such things as what parts of town the customers come from, how they travel, how many stores they visit, and so on.

e. The director of your library wants a detailed study of library use (what facilities are used, when, by whom, and so on).

f. The management of a restaurant wants a study of its workers' efficiency in the kitchen.

3. Using your imagination to supply any missing facts you may need, develop a plan for research by survey for these problems.

a. The American Restaurant Association wants information that will give its members a picture of its customers.

The information will serve as a guide for a promotional campaign designed to increase restaurant eating. Specifically it will seek such information as who eats out, how often, where they go, how much they spend. Likewise, it will seek to determine who does not eat out and why.

b. The editor of your local daily paper wants a readership study to learn just who reads what in both print and online editions.

c. The National Beef Producers Association wants to determine the current trends in meat consumption. The association wants such information as the amount of meat people consume, whether people have changed their meat consumption habits, and so on.

d. The International Association of Publishers wants a survey of the reading habits of adults in the United States and Canada. It wants such information as who reads what, how much, when, where, and so on. It also wants to gauge reader attitude toward ebooks.

e. Your boss wants to hire an experienced computer webmaster for your company. Because you have not hired anyone in this category in five years, you were asked to survey experienced webmasters using the Web or Usenet groups to gather salary figures.

Corrections for the Self-Administered Diagnostic Test of Correctness

Following are the corrected sentences for the diagnostic test at the end of Chapter 17. The corrections are underscored, and the symbols for the standards explaining the correction follow the sentences.

1. An important fact about this keyboard is<u>,</u> that it has the patented "ergonomic design"<u>.</u>
   An important fact about this keyboard is that it has the patented "ergonomic design." *Cma 6.1, QM 3*

2. Goods received on Invoice 2741 are as follows<u>:</u> 3 dozen blue denim shirts, size 15–33<u>,</u> 4 men's gortex gloves, brown, size large and 5 dozen assorted socks.
   Goods received on Invoice 2741 are as follows: three dozen blue denim shirts, size 15–33; four men's gortex gloves, brown, size large; and five dozen assorted socks. *Cln 1, Apos 1, SC 3, No 1*

3. James Silver <u>President</u> of the new union<u>_</u>had the <u>priviledge</u> of introducing the speaker.
   James Silver, president of the new union, had the privilege of introducing the speaker. *Cma 4.2, Cap, SP*

4. We do not expect to act on this matter<u>_</u>however<u>_</u>until we hear from you.
   We do not expect to act on this matter, however, until we hear from you. *Cma 4.3*

5. Shipments through September 20, 2007<u>_</u>totaled 69,485 pounds<u>_</u>an increase of 17 percent over the year<u>_</u>ago total.
   Shipments through September 20, 2007, totaled 69,485 pounds, an increase of 17 percent over the year-ago total. *Cma 4.4, Cma 4.1, Hpn 2*

6. Brick is recommended as the building material<u>_</u>but the board is giving serious consideration to a substitute.
   Brick is recommended as the building material, but the board is giving serious consideration to a substitute. *Cma 1*

7. Markdowns for the sale total $34,000<u>,</u> never before has the company done anything like this.
   Markdowns for the sale total $34,000; never before has the company done anything like this. *SC 1*

8. After long experimentation a wear<u>_</u>resistant<u>_</u>high<u>_</u>grade<u>_</u>and beautiful stocking has been perfected.
   After long experimentation a wear-resistant, high-grade, and beautiful stocking has been perfected. *Hpn 2, Cma 2.2*

9. Available in white_green_and blue_this paint is sold by dealers all over the country.
Available in white, green, and blue, this paint is sold by dealers all over the country. *Cma 2.1, Cma 3*

10. Julie Jahn_who won the trip_is our most energetic salesperson.
Julie Jahn, who won the trip, is our most energetic salesperson. *Cma 3*

11. _Good_he replied_sales are sure to increase.
"Good," he replied. "Sales are sure to increase." *QM 1, Pd 1, Cap*

12. Hogan's article_Retirement? Never!,_printed in the current issue of Management Review, is really a part of his book A Report on Worker Security.
Hogan's article, "Retirement? Never!," printed in the current issue of *Management Review,* is really a part of his book, *A Report on Worker Security.* *Cma 4.2, QM 4, Ital 1*

13. Formal announcement of our Labor Day sale will be made in thirty-two days.
Formal announcement of our Labor Day sale will be made in 32 days. *No 1*

14. Each day we encounter new problems. Although they are solved easily.
Each day we encounter new problems, although they are solved easily. *Cma 5.1, Frag*

15. A list of models, sizes, and prices of both competing lines are being sent to you.
A list of models, sizes, and prices of both competing lines is being sent to you. *Agmt SV*

16. The manager could not tolerate any employee's failing to do their best.
The manager could not tolerate any employee's failing to do his or her best. *Pn 2*

17. A series of tests were completed only yesterday.
A series of tests was completed only yesterday. *Agmt SV*

18. There should be no misunderstanding between you and I.
There should be no misunderstanding between you and me. *Pn 3*

19. He run the accounting department for five years.
He ran the accounting department for five years. *Tns 2*

20. This report is considerable long.
This report is considerably long. *AA*

21. Who did you interview for the position?
Whom did you interview for the position? *Pn 3*

22. The report concluded that the natural resources of the Southwest was ideal for the chemical industry.
The report concluded that the natural resources of the Southwest are ideal for the chemical industry. *Agmt SV, Tns 1*

23. This applicant is six feet in height, _28 years old, weighs 165 pounds, and has had eight years' experience.
This applicant is six feet in height, is 28 years old, weighs 165 pounds, and has had eight years' experience. *Prl*

24. While _ reading the report, a gust of wind came through the window, blowing papers all over the room.
While she was reading the report, a gust of wind came through the window, blowing papers all over the room. *Dng*

25. The sprinkler system has been checked on July 1 and September 3.
The sprinkler system was checked on July 1 and September 3. *Tns 5*

Physical Presentation of Letters, Memos, and Reports

The appearance of a letter, memo, or report plays a significant role in communicating the message. Attractively presented messages reflect favorably on the writer and the writer's company. They give an impression of competence and care; and they build credibility for the writer. Their attractiveness tells the readers that the writer thinks they are important and deserving of a good-looking document. It reflects on the common courtesy of the writer. On the other hand, sloppy work reflects unfavorably on the writer, the company, and the message itself. Thus, you should want your documents to be attractively displayed.

Currently, the writer has better control over the display in print and portable document format (pdf) than in email and hypertext markup language (html). However, as applications migrate to html output and as more browsers and email programs display standardized html similarly, the writer will gain better control over these electronic displays, too. The material presented here will help you present your documents attractively and appropriately in whichever medium you choose.

Advances in word processing have finally relieved us of much of the tedious, repetitive tasks involved in presenting documents. Yesterday's hot feature in word processing programs was a feature called styles. Styles allowed writers to define and apply a set of commands or keystrokes to a single style just once and then reuse the style. Writers could format a level-one heading once and reuse its style each time they needed to format a level-one heading. Also, if a writer decided to change the level-one formatting, only the style needed to be changed, for the software automatically changed all occurrences linked to the styles. While styles let writers create formatting for use anywhere within a document, today's automated formatting with interactive assistants or templates helps writers create a variety of documents.

In addition to creating a professional image consistently, companies that use automated formatting usually are more productive. Not only will the company save time formatting documents, but the assistance also can act as a prompt to the writer. This can help ensure that all components are included. Today's full-featured word processors include automated formatting for a full range of documents and templates that can be customized to serve the precise needs of a business. They can include text, graphics, macros, styles, keyboard assignments, and custom toolbars.

Several word processors help users create customized templates from existing documents. The user simply identifies a document and the software will build the template from it, a process similar to the reverse engineering that's long been part of manufacturing.

Furthermore, automated formatting is easy to use. Some word processors use *wizards* or *experts,* and others use templates to lead one through the creation of most kinds of business documents. This is especially helpful for the first time one creates a document and for those documents that one creates infrequently. Figure B–1 illustrates the process of creating a letter using the *wizard* in Word 2003. Notice that the writer simply fills in text, clicks buttons, or checks boxes or radio buttons.

These Steps Are Followed in Creating a Basic Business Letter Using Microsoft Word 2003's Letter Wizard

Step 1 of 8

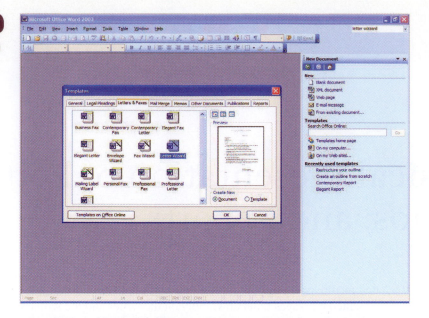

Step 2 of 8

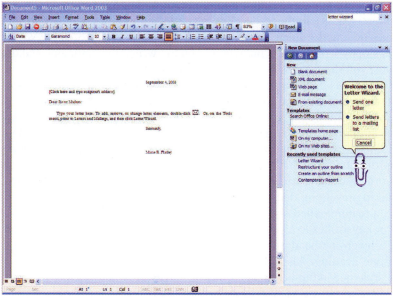

Step 3 of 8

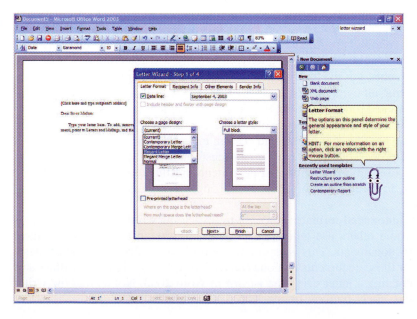

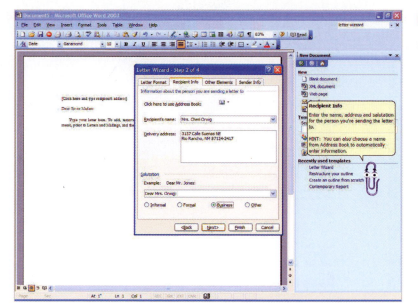

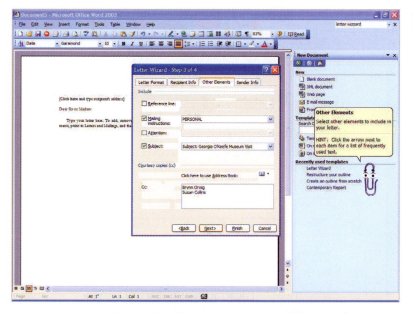

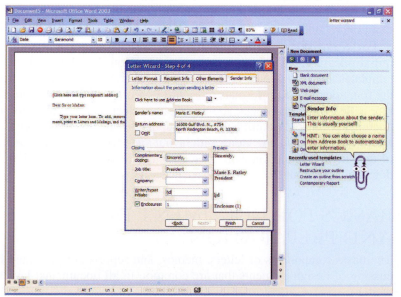

Physical Presentation of Letters, Memos, and Reports

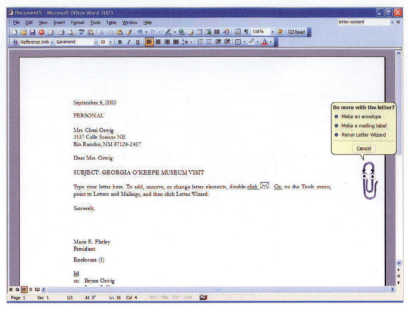

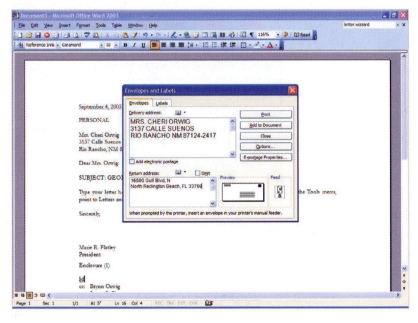

For Word 2007, Microsoft insiders report that wizards will not be included in the initial release but they may be downloadables on the Microsoft website. Document templates are available both on Microsoft's Word website and your textbook site for the four standard letter formats in Figure B–4 on page 595. In Word 2007, a new feature called Building Blocks allows users to select reusable parts to build customized documents quickly. Additionally, you will find a selection of themes that include preselected typefaces and art. Along with layout and media, these are the basic components of document design. Knowing more about these components will help you design a document that conveys your message accurately to your audience.

BASICS FOR DOCUMENT DESIGN AND PREPARATION

The basic components of letters, memos, and reports are presented here after a discussion of design elements that are common to all documents: layout, type, art, and media.

Layout Illustrations on Different Grids

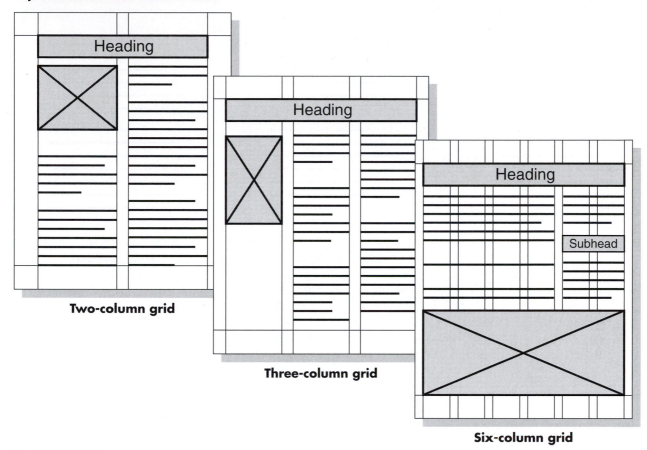

Two-column grid

Three-column grid

Six-column grid

LAYOUT

Common layout decisions involve grids, spacing, and margins. Grids are the non-printed horizontal and vertical lines that help you place elements of your document precisely on the page. The examples shown in Figure B–2 illustrate the placement of text on two-, three-, and six-column grids. You can readily see how important it is to plan for this element.

To make your document look its best, you must consider both external and internal spacing. External spacing is the white space—the space some never think about carefully. Just as volume denotes importance in writing, white space denotes importance. Surrounding text or a graphic with white spaces sets it apart, emphasizing it to the reader. Used effectively, white space also has been shown to increase the readability of your documents, giving your readers' eyes a rest. Ideally, white space should be a careful part of the design of your document.

Internal spacing refers to both vertical and horizontal spacing. The spacing between letters on a line is called _kerning_. With word processing programs, you can adjust how close the letters are to each other. These programs also allow you to adjust how close the lines are to each other vertically, called _leading_. Currently, many still refer to spacing in business documents as single or double spacing. However, this is a carryover from the typewriter era when a vertical line space was always ⅙ inch or when six lines equaled an inch. Today's software and hardware allow you to control this aspect of your document much more exactly. Deciding on the best spacing to use depends on the typeface you decide to use. In any case, you need to make a conscious decision about the spacing aspect of the layout of your documents.

Another aspect of layout is your margin settings. Ideally, you should want your document to look like a framed picture. This arrangement calls for all margins to be equal. However, some businesses use a fixed margin on all documents regardless of

Different Forms of Justification

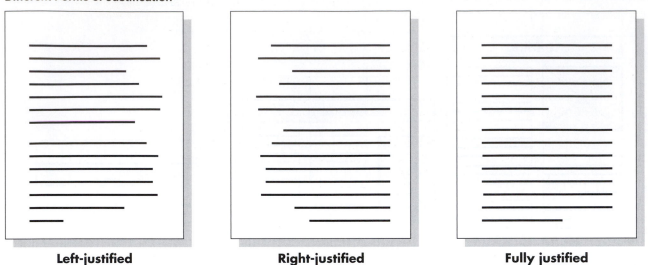

Left-justified   **Right-justified**   **Fully justified**

their length. Some do this to line up with design features on their letterhead; others believe it increases productivity. In either case, the side margins will be equal. And with today's word processors you easily make your top and bottom margins equal by telling the program to center the document vertically on the page. Although all margins will not be exactly equal, the page will still have horizontal and vertical balance. And some word processors have "make it fit" experts. With this feature, the writer tells the program the number of pages, allowing it to select such aspects as margins, font size, and spacing to fit the message to the desired space.

Today's programs also have the capability to align your type at the margins or in the center. This is called *justification*. Left justification aligns every line at the left, right justification aligns every line at the right, and full justification aligns every line at both the left and the right (see Figure B–3). Full justification takes the extra spaces between the last word and the right margin and distributes them across the line. This adds extra white spaces across the line, stopping most readers' eyes a bit. Therefore, it is usually best to set a left-justified margin and ignore the resulting ragged right margin. However, if your document's right margin is distracting, you may want to turn on the hyphenation feature. Your program will then hyphenate words at the end of lines, smoothing the raggedness of the right margin.

Type

Type is purported to influence the appearance of your document more than any other aspect. You need to make decisions on the typeface, the type style, and the type size. Typeface refers to the font or shape of the characters. Although thousands of fonts are available, they are generally classified as *serif* or *sans serif*. Serif typefaces have feet; sans serif do not. You can see this clearly in the examples that follow.

Fonts optimized for display:

Calibri is a sans serif typeface.
Cambria is a serif typeface.

Fonts optimized for print:

Times New Roman is a serif typeface.
Arial is a sans serif typeface.

Since readers use the visual cues they get from the feet to form the words in their minds, they find the text of documents easier to read if a serif typeface is used. Sans serif typefaces are particularly good for headings where clear, distinct letters are important.

Type style refers to the way the typeface can be modified. The most basic styles include normal, **bold,** *italic,* and ***bold italic.*** Depending on your software and printer, you may have other options such as outline or shadow. You usually will decide to use modifications for specific reasons. For example, you may present all actions you want the reader to take in boldface type. Or you may decide to apply different styles to different levels of headings. In any case, use of type styles should be planned.

Finally, you will need to decide on size of type. Type is measured in points. Characters one inch high are 72 points. While this is a standard measure, different typefaces in the same size often appear to be a different size. You need to consider your typeface in choosing size for your documents. Generally, body text is between 9 and 14 points, and headings are 15 points and larger.

Art

Art as used here in its broadest sense refers to drawings, graphs, photos, and other illustrations. As a writer, you primarily need to remember that art should always serve a message's purpose. Both its looks and placement must be carefully planned.

While older versions of Word let writers import a variety of art formats, Word 2007 makes it even easier for writers to insert both tables and illustrations. And its Smart-Art feature adds the ability to include lists, processes, cycles, matrices, and more by clicking looks, selecting a color, and filling in a text. But the fact that it's easy doesn't mean it should be overused either. Careful selection and placement of art are still the responsibility of the writer.

Media

The media you choose to transmit your documents also communicate. Text and instant messaging and most email today are perceived as informal media. But choosing these media communicates to the reader that you are a user of a particular technology, and its choice may be associated with the nature and quality of your business. Choosing to send your message by fax, especially an Internet-based fax, also may imply your currency with the technology. Also, sending a formatted document, an rtf file, or a pdf document as an attached file both conveys a message and gives you some control over your document's display. By choosing paper as your medium, you will have control over appearance while relinquishing control over delivery to company and mail-delivery systems.

Today, paper is still a common choice of medium.[1] In the United States, standard business paper size is 8½ by 11 inches; international business A4 (210 × 297 mm) results in paper sized slightly narrower than 8½ inches and slightly longer than 11 inches. Occasionally, half-size (5½ × 8½) or executive size (7¼ × 10½) is used for short messages. Other than these standards, you have a variety of choices to make for color, weight, texture, and such.

The most conservative color choice is white. Of course, you will find that there are numerous variations of white. In addition, there are all the colors of the palette and many tints of these colors. You want your paper to represent you, your business, and its brand but not to distract your reader from the message. The color you choose for the first page of your document should also be the color you use for the second and continuing pages. This is the color you would usually use for envelopes, too.

Some businesses even match the color of the paper with the color of their printer ink and the color of their postage meter ink. This, of course, communicates to the reader

---

[1]According to a report in the December 12, 2005, issue of the *Christian Science Monitor,* the growth rate of the sales of paper has flattened about a half percent a year to 4 percent. While the reality of the paperless office still seems far removed, digital technologies will likely slow the growth of paper sales.

that the writer or company is detail conscious. Such an image would be desirable for accountants or architects where attention to detail is perceived as a positive trait.

The weight and texture of your paper also communicate. While "cheap" paper may denote control of expenses to one reader, it may denote cost cutting to another. Usually businesses use paper with a weight of 16 to 20 pounds and a rag or cotton content of 25 to 100 percent. The higher the numbers, the higher the quality. And, of course, many readers often associate a high-quality paper with a high-quality product or service.

The choice of medium to use for your documents is important because it, too, sends a message. By being aware of these subtle messages, you will be able to choose the most appropriate medium for your situation.

With the basics taken care of, now we can move on to the specifics for the letter, memo, or report.

FORM OF BUSINESS LETTERS

The layout of a letter (its shape on the page) accounts for a major part of the impression that the appearance of the letter makes. A layout that is too wide, too narrow, too high, too low, or off-center may impress the reader unfavorably. The ideal letter layout is one that has the same shape as the space in which it is formed. It fits that space much as a picture fits a frame. That is, a rectangle drawn around the processed letter has the same shape as the space under the letterhead. The top border of the rectangle is the dateline, the left border is the line beginnings, the right border is the average line length, and the bottom border is the last line of the notations.

As to the format of the layout, any generally recognized one is acceptable. Some people prefer one format or another, and some people even think the format they prefer is the best. Automated formatting allows you to choose your own format preferences. Generally, the most popular formats are block, modified block, and simplified. These are illustrated in Figure B–4. In all formats, single-spacing in paragraphs and double-spacing between paragraphs is the general rule.

Agreement has not been reached on all the practices for setting up the parts of the letter. The following suggestions, however, follow the bulk of authoritative opinion.

Dateline. You should use the conventional date form, with month, day, and year (September 17, 2007). When you are using a word processor's date feature, be sure to select the appropriate one. If you choose to insert a date code, decide whether you want it to record when the document was created (CreateDate), last printed (PrintDate), or last saved (SaveDate). Also, recognize that abbreviated date forms such as 09-17-07 or Sept. 17, '07 are informal and leave unfavorable impressions on some people. Most word processors allow you to set up your preference and will use that preference when you use the date feature.

Return Address. In most cases, your return address is printed on the letterhead or filled in on it during automated formatting.

Inside Address. The mailing address, complete with the title of the person being addressed, makes up the inside address. Preferably, form it without abbreviations, except for commonly abbreviated words (*Dr., Mr., Mrs., Ms.*). In Word, you can use its smart tag feature to quickly and easily enter addresses stored in Outlook.

Attention Line. Some executives prefer to emphasize the company address rather than the individual offices. Thus, they address the letter to the company in the inside address and then use an attention line to direct the letter to a specific officer or department. The attention line is placed two lines below the inside address and two lines above the salutation. When used, the typical form of the attention line is

Attention: Mr. Donovan Price, Vice President

Standard Letter Formats

Full Block

Vary spacing to lengthen or shorten⬜ → *Letterhead*

April 9, 20–

Vary spacing to lengthen or shorten⬜

Ms. Mary A. Smitherman, President
Smitherman and Sons, Inc.
3107 Western Avenue
New London, CT 04320-4133

Double Space

Dear Ms. Smitherman:

Subject: Your April 14 inquiry about Mr. H.O. Abel

Double Space → *Single Space*

Sincerely,

Double Space → 3 Blank Lines⬜

Calvin C. DeWitte
Secretary-Treasurer

apc

Modified Block, Blocked Paragraphs

Letterhead → Vary spacing to lengthen or shorten⬜

September 17, 20–

Vary spacing to lengthen or shorten

Ms. Loretta R. Gunnison, President
Port City Investments, Inc.
3117 Avenue E
Seattle, WA 20103

Double Space

Dear Ms. Gunnison:

Double Space → *Single Space*

Sincerely,

THE SWANSON COMPANY

3 Blank Lines⬜ → *Double Space*

C.I. Breen, President
Helen Toohey
Manager

htl
Enc.

Modified Block, Indented Paragraphs

Letterhead → Vary spacing to lengthen or shorten⬜

September 28, 20—

Vary spacing to lengthen or shorten⬜

Sales Manager
Midwest Novelty Distributors, Inc.
4171 North 41st Street
Chicago, IL 60602

Double Space

Dear Sales Manager:

Double Space → *Single Space*

Sincerely,
3 Blank Lines⬜ → *Double Space*

Richard A. Constantine
Purchasing Agent

jep
C. Joan O. Dodge

Simplified

Vary spacing to lengthen or shorten⬜ → *Letterhead*

November 17, 20––

Vary spacing to lengthen or shorten⬜

Ms. Stephanie Palmore, President
Palmore Management Services
4110 Black Forest Road
Cincinnati, OH 48519-5539

Triple Space

ILLUSTRATION OF AMS SIMPLIFIED STYLE

Double Space

3 Blank Lines⬜

DOUGLAS SPELL
PRODUCTION MANAGER

rii

Salutation. The salutation you choose should be based on your familiarity with the reader and on the formality of the situation. As a general rule, remember that if the writer and the reader know each other well, the salutation may be by first name, *Dear Joan.* A salutation by last name, *Dear Mr. Baskin,* is appropriate in most cases.

If you do not know and cannot find out the name of the person to whom you are sending the letter, use a position title. By directing your letter to Director of Human Resources or Public Relations Manager, you are helping your letter reach the appropriate person.

Women's preferences have sharply reduced the use of *Mrs.* and *Miss.* The question many women ask is, Why distinguish between married and single women when we make no such distinction between married and single men? The logical solution is to use *Ms.* for all women, just as *Mr.* is used for all men. If you know that the woman you are writing has another preference, however, you should adhere to that preference.

Mixed or Open Punctuation. The punctuation following the salutation and the closing is either mixed or open. Mixed punctuation employs a colon after the salutation and a comma after the complimentary close. Open punctuation, on the other hand, uses no punctuation after the salutation and none after the complimentary close. These two forms are used in domestic communication. In international communication, you may see letters with closed punctuation—punctuation distinguished by commas after the lines in the return and inside addresses and a period at the end of the complimentary close.

Subject Line. So that both the sender and the receiver may quickly identify the subject of the correspondence, many offices use the subject line in their letters. The subject line tells what the letter is about. In addition, it contains any specific identifying material that may be helpful: date of previous correspondence, invoice number, order number, and the like. It is usually placed two lines below the salutation. The block may be headed in a number of ways, of which the following are representative:

> Subject: Your July 2nd inquiry about . . .
> RE: Please refer to Invoice H-320.

Second Page Heading. When the length of a letter must exceed one page, you should set up the following page or pages for quick identification. Always print such pages on plain paper (no letterhead). These two forms are the most common:

Ms. Helen E. Mann   2   May 7, 2008

Ms. Helen E. Mann
May 7, 2008
Page 2

Most standard templates automatically insert this information—name of addressee, date, and page number—on the second and following pages of your letter.

Closing. By far the most commonly used complimentary close is *Sincerely. Sincerely yours* is also used, but in recent years the *yours* has been fading away. *Truly* (with and without the *yours*) is also used, but it also has lost popularity. Such closes as *Cordially* and *Respectfully* are appropriate when their meanings fit the writer–reader relationship. A long-standing friendship, for example, would justify *Cordially;* the writer's respect for the position, prestige, or accomplishments of the reader would justify *Respectfully.* Word 2003's letter template has an insert feature that allows the writer to select the letter's closing (see Figure B–5).

Signature Block. The printed signature conventionally appears on the fourth line below the closing, beginning directly under the first letter for the block form. Most templates will insert the closing. A short name and title may appear on the same line, separated by a comma. If either the name or title is long, the title appears on the following

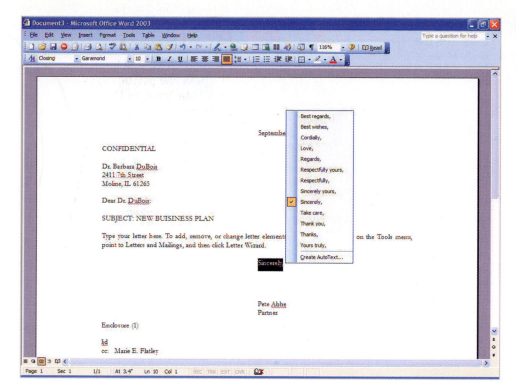

line, blocked under the name. The writer's signature appears in the space between the closing and the printed signature.

Some people prefer to have the firm name appear in the signature block—especially when the letter continues on a second page without the company letterhead. The conventional form for this arrangement places the firm name in solid capitals and blocked on the second line below the closing phrase. The typed name of the person signing the letter is on the fourth line below the firm name.

Information Notations. In the lower-left corner of the letter may appear abbreviated notations for enclosures, *Enc., Enc.—3*, and so on, and for the initials of the writer and the typist, *WEH:ga*. However, many businesses are dropping these initials since the reader does not need this information, and since most word processors allow businesses to put this information in the document summary. Also, businesses are no longer including filename notations on the letters, since readers do not need them and today's word processors can find files by searching for specific content. Indications of copies prepared for other readers also may be included: *cc: Sharon Garbett, copy to Sharon Garbett.*

Postscripts. Postscripts, commonly referred to as the PS, are placed after any notations. While rarely used in most business letters because they look like afterthoughts, they can be very effective as added punch in sales letters.

Folding. The carelessly folded letter is off to a bad start with the reader. Neat folding will complete the planned effect by (1) making the letter fit snugly in its cover, (2) making the letter easy for the reader to remove, and (3) making the letter appear neat when opened.

The two-fold pattern is the easiest. It fits the standard sheet for the long (Number 10) envelope as well as some other envelope sizes. As shown in Figure B–6, the first fold of the two-fold pattern is from the bottom up, taking a little less than a third of the sheet. The second fold goes from the top down, making exactly the same panel as the bottom segment. (This measurement will leave the recipient a quarter-inch thumbhold for easy unfolding of the letter.) Thus folded, the letter should be slipped into its envelope with the second crease toward the bottom and the center panel at the front of the envelope.

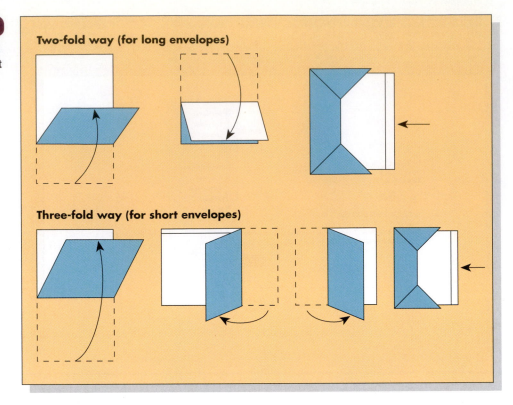

Two-fold way (for long envelopes)

Three-fold way (for short envelopes)

The three-fold pattern is necessary to fit the standard sheet into the commonly used small (Number 6¾) envelope. Its first fold is from the bottom up, with the bottom edge of the sheet riding about a quarter inch under the top edge to allow the thumbhold. (If the edges are exactly even, they are harder to separate.) The second fold is from the right side of the sheet toward the left, taking a little less than a third of the width. The third fold matches the second: from the left side toward the right, with a panel of exactly the same width. (This fold will leave a quarter-inch thumbhold at the right, for the user's convenience.) So that the letter will appear neat when unfolded, the creases should be neatly parallel with the top and sides, not at angles that produce "dog-ears" and irregular shapes. In the three-fold form, it is especially important for the side panels produced by the second and third folds to be exactly the same width; otherwise, the vertical creases are off-center and tend to throw the whole carefully planned layout off-center.

The three-fold letter is inserted into its cover with the third crease toward the bottom of the envelope and the loose edges toward the stamp end of the envelope. From habit, most recipients of business letters slit envelopes at the top and turn them facedown to extract the letter. The three-fold letter inserted as described thus gives its reader an easy thumbhold at the top of the envelope to pull it out by and a second one at the top of the sheet for easy unfolding of the whole.

Envelope Address. So that optical character recognition (OCR) equipment may be used in sorting mail, the U.S. Postal Service requests that all envelopes be typed as follows (see Figure B–7):

1. Place the address in the scannable area as shown in the white box in Figure B–7. It is best to use a sans serif font in 10 to 12 points.

2. Use a block address format.

3. Single-space.

4. Use all uppercase letters (capitals). While today's OCR equipment can read lowercase, the post office prefers uppercase.

5. Do not use punctuation, except for the hyphen in the nine-digit zip code.

6. Use the two-letter abbreviations for the U.S. states and territories and the Canadian provinces.

Form for Addressing Envelopes Recommended by the U.S. Postal Service, Publication 28

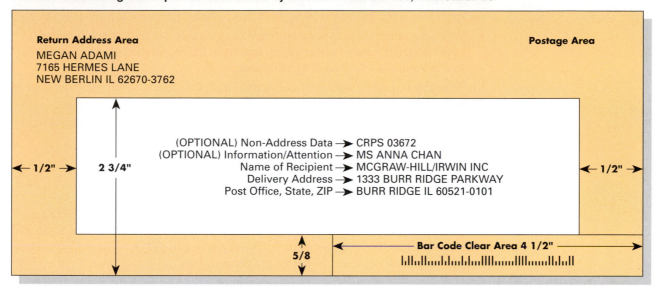

Use other address abbreviations as shown in the most recent edition of the *Post Office Directory* (see www.usps.com). When sending to a foreign country, include only the country name in uppercase on the bottom line.

States and Possessions of the United States

Alabama	AL	Kansas	KS	Northern Mariana	
Alaska	AK	Kentucky	KY	Islands	MP
American Samoa	AS	Louisiana	LA	Ohio	OH
Arizona	AZ	Maine	ME	Oklahoma	OK
Arkansas	AR	Marshall Islands	MH	Oregon	OR
California	CA	Maryland	MD	Palau	PW
Colorado	CO	Massachusetts	MA	Pennsylvania	PA
Connecticut	CT	Michigan	MI	Puerto Rico	PR
Delaware	DE	Minnesota	MN	Rhode Island	RI
District of Columbia	DC	Mississippi	MS	South Carolina	SC
Federated States of		Missouri	MO	South Dakota	SD
Micronesia	FM	Montana	MT	Tennessee	TN
Florida	FL	Nebraska	NE	Texas	TX
Georgia	GA	Nevada	NV	Utah	UT
Guam	GU	New Hampshire	NH	Vermont	VT
Hawaii	HI	New Jersey	NJ	Virginia	VA
Idaho	ID	New Mexico	NM	Virgin Islands	VI
Illinois	IL	New York	NY	Washington	WA
Indiana	IN	North Carolina	NC	West Virginia	WV
Iowa	IA	North Dakota	ND	Wyoming	WY

Canadian Provinces and Territories

Alberta	AB	Newfoundland	NF	Prince Edward Island	PE
British Columbia	BC	Northwest Territories	NT	Quebec	PQ
Manitoba	MB	Nova Scotia	NS	Saskatchewan	SK
New Brunswick	NB	Ontario	ON	Yukon Territory	YT

7. The last line of the mailing address should contain no more than 28 characters. The city should be 13 or fewer characters. Also, there should be one space between city and state; two spaces for the state or province abbreviation; two spaces between the state and zip code; and 10 characters for the zip + 4 code.

8. When the return address must be typed (it is usually printed), block it in the left corner, beginning on the second line from the top of the envelope and three spaces from the left edge of the envelope.

9. Print any on-arrival instructions (Confidential, Personal) four lines below the return address.

10. Place all notations for the post office (Special Delivery) below the stamp and at least three lines above the mailing address.

FORM OF MEMORANDUMS

Memorandums (memos) have basic components in common, but their form varies widely from organization to organization. The basic components are the heading and body. The heading has four elements: *To, From, Date,* and *Subject.* These elements are arranged in various placements, but all are present.

The body of the memo is usually single-spaced with double-spacing between paragraphs. First-level headings are frequently used in long memos. And notations for typist and enclosures are included just as they are in letters. An example of typical template format choices for memos in Word 2003 is shown in Figure B–8.

FORM OF LETTER AND MEMORANDUM REPORTS

Because letter reports are actually letters, the review of letter form presented earlier in this appendix applies to them. Memorandum reports, however, are somewhat different. The conventional memorandum form uses the introductory information: *To, From, Date, Subject.* Many large companies have stationery on which this information

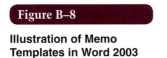

Figure B–8

Illustration of Memo Templates in Word 2003

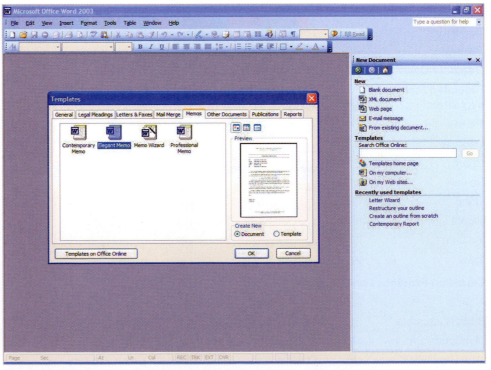

First-level Head

_____
_____
_____

Second-level Head

_____
_____
_____

Third-level Head. _____
_____
_____

  Fourth-level head. _____
_____
_____

Figure B–9

Levels of Headings. Use the placement and form of headings to indicate the structure of your report's contents. One way to do so is shown. You can modify your word processor's heading styles to suit your preferences and then easily format your different headings with these styles.

is printed or use standard macros, templates, or styles. The report text follows the introductory information.

Both letter and memorandum reports may use headings to display the topics covered. The headings are usually displayed in the margins, on separate lines, and in a different style. (see Figure B–9.) Memorandum and letter reports also may differ from ordinary letters by having illustrations (charts, tables), an appendix, and/or a bibliography.

FORM OF FORMAL REPORTS

Like letters, formal reports should be pleasing to the eye. Well-arranged reports give an impression of competence—of work professionally done. Because such an impression can affect the success of a report, you should make good use of the following review of report form.

General Information on Report Presentation

Since your formal reports are likely to be prepared with word processing programs, you will not need to know the general mechanics of manuscript preparation if you use automated formatting, as shown in the Word 2007 template in Figure B–10. However, even if you do not have to format your own reports, you should know enough about report presentation to be sure your work is done right. You cannot be certain that your report is in good form unless you know good form.

Conventional Page Layout. For the typical text page in a report, a conventional layout appears to fit the page as a picture fits a frame (see Figure B–11). This eye-pleasing layout, however, is arranged to fit the page space not covered by the binding of the report. Thus, you must allow an extra half inch or so on the left margins of the pages of a single-sided left-bound report and at the top of the pages of a top-bound report.

Special Page Layouts. Certain text pages may have individual layouts. Pages displaying major titles (first pages of chapters, tables of contents, executive summaries, and the like) conventionally have an extra half inch or so of space at the top. Figure B–12 illustrates that some special pages can be created with templates.

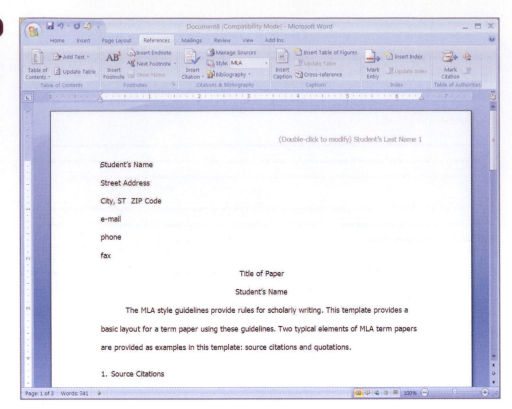

Recommended Page Layouts

Double-spaced Page

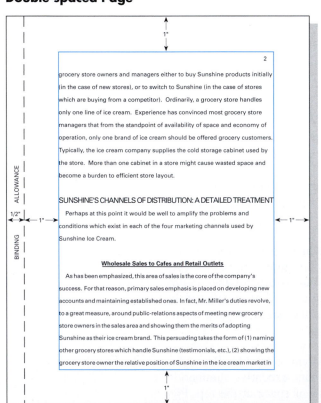

Single-spaced Page

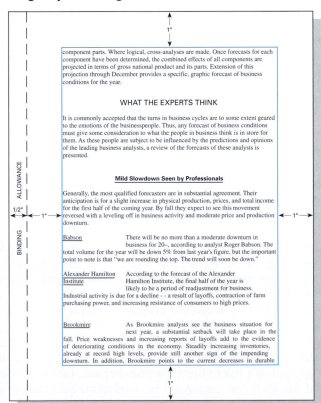

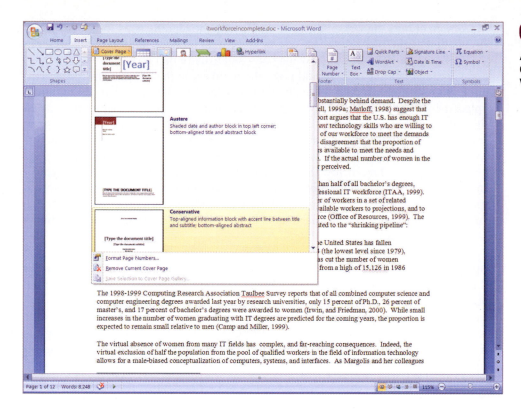

Figure B–12

An Illustration of the Cover Page Feature of Word 2007

Letters of transmittal and authorization also may have individual layouts. They are arranged in any conventional letter form. In the more formal reports, they may be carefully arranged to have the same general shape as the space in which they appear using the "make-it-fit" feature.

Choice of Spacing. It is conventional to double-space reports. This procedure stems from the old practice of double-spacing to make typed manuscripts more readable for the proofreader and printer. The practice has been carried over into work that is not to be reproduced. Advocates of double-spacing claim that it is easier to read than single-spacing, as the reader is less likely to lose line place.

In recent years, single-spacing has gained in popularity. The general practice is to single-space within paragraphs, double-space between paragraphs, and triple-space above all centered heads. Supporters of single-spacing contend that it saves space and facilitates reading, as it is like the printing that most people are accustomed to reading.

Patterns of Indentation. You should indent the paragraph beginnings of double-spaced typing. On the other hand, you should block single-spaced material because its paragraph headings are clearly marked by the blank lines between paragraphs.

No generally accepted distance of indentation exists. Some sources suggest ½ inch, and others like 1" and more. Any decision as to the best distance to use is up to you, though you would do well to follow the practice established in the office, group, or school for which you write the report. Whatever your selection, you should be consistent.

Numbering of Pages. Two systems of numbers are used in numbering the pages of the written report. Arabic numerals are conventional for the text portion, normally beginning with the first page of the introduction and continuing through the appendix. Small Roman numerals are standard for the pages preceding the text. Although these prefatory pages are all counted in the numbering sequence, the numbers generally do not appear on the pages before the table of contents. See the text website for specific instructions on how to number pages in Word.

Physical Presentation of Letters, Memos, and Reports

Placement of the numbers on the page varies with the binding used for the report. In reports bound at the top of the page, you should center all page numbers at the bottom of the page, two or three lines below the body and usually in a footer.

For left-sided binding, you should place the numbers in the upper-right corner, two or three lines above the top line, usually in the header, and right justified. Exception to this placement is customarily made for special-layout pages that have major titles and an additional amount of space displayed at the top. Such pages may include the first page of the report text; the executive summary; the table of contents; and, in very long and formal works, the first page of each major division or chapter. Numbers for these pages are centered two or three lines below the imaginary line marking the bottom of the layout.

In documents printed back-to-back, page numbers are usually placed at the top of the page even with the outside margin. Not only are today's word processing programs capable of automatically placing page numbers this way if directed, but many printers are also capable of two-sided printing.

Display of Headings. Headings are the titles of the parts of the report. Designed to lead the readers through the report, they must show at a glance the importance of the information they cover.

In showing heading importance by position, you have many choices. If your software and printer make available a variety of typefaces, you can select various progressions of font sizes and styles to fit your needs. Your goal, of course, should be to select forms that show differences in importance at first glance—much as is done in the printing of this book.

You can use any combination of form and placement that clearly shows the relative importance of the heading (Figure B–9 demonstrates one way). The one governing rule to follow in considering form and positions of headings is that no heading may have a higher-ranking form or position than any of the headings of a higher level. But you can use the same form for two successive levels of headings as long as the positions vary. And you can use the same position for two successive levels as long as the forms vary. You also can skip over any of the steps in the progression of form or position.

Mechanics and Format of the Report Parts

The foregoing notes on physical appearance apply generally to all parts of the report. But special notes are needed for the individual construction of the specific report pages. Thus you may be able to get and follow these notes, a part-by-part review of the physical construction of the formal report follows.

Title Fly. The title fly contains only the report title. Print the title in the highest-ranking form used in the report, and double-space it if you need more than one line. If your report cover has a window for the title to show through, make sure you place the title in the window.

Title Page. The title page normally contains four main areas of identification. In the typical title page, the first area of identification contains the report title. Preferably, use the highest-ranking form used in the report.

The second area of identification names the individual (or group) for whom the report has been prepared. Precede it with an identifying phrase indicating that individual's role in the report, such as "Prepared for" or "Submitted to." In addition to the recipient's name, include the identification of the recipient by title or role, company, and address, particularly if you and the recipient are from different companies.

The third area of identification names you, the writer of the report. It is also preceded by an identifying phrase—"Prepared by," "Written by," or similar wording describing your role in the report—and it also may identify title or role, company, and address. The fourth and final part of this area of information is the date of presentation or publication. Placement of the four areas of identification on the page should make for an eye-pleasing arrangement. Most word processors will help you place this page vertically.

Letters of Transmittal and Authorization. As their names imply, the letters of transmittal and authorization are actual letters. You should print them in any acceptable letter form. If the report is important, you should give the letter an ideal layout—that is one that fits the letter into a rectangle of the same shape as the space within which it is printed.

Acknowledgments. When you are indebted to the assistance of others, it is fitting that you acknowledge the indebtedness somewhere in the report. If the number is small, you may acknowledge them in the introduction of the report or in the letter of transmittal. In the rare event that you need to make numerous acknowledgments, you may construct a special section for this purpose. This section, bearing the simple title "Acknowledgments," has the same layout as any other text page on which a title is displayed.

Table of Contents. The table of contents is the report outline in its polished, finished form. It lists the major report headings with the page numbers on which those headings appear. Although not all reports require a table of contents, one should be a part of any report long enough to make such a guide helpful to the readers. Most word processors are capable of generating a table of contents—complete with page numbers. See the textbook website for a short tutorial on how to create one in Word.

The table of contents is appropriately titled "Contents" or "Table of Contents." The layout of the table of contents is the same as that used for any other report page with a title display. Below the title, set up two columns. One contains the outline headings, generally beginning with the first report part following the table of contents. You have the option of including or leaving out the outline letters and numbers.

In the table of contents, as in the body of the report, you may vary the form to distinguish different heading levels. But the form variations of the table of contents need not be the same as those used in the text of the report. The highest level of headings is usually distinguished from the other levels, and sometimes typeface differences are used to distinguish second-level headings from lower-level headings. It is acceptable to show no distinction by using plain capitals and lowercase for all levels of headings.

Table of Illustrations. The table (list) of illustrations may be either a continuation of the table of contents or a separate table. Such a table lists the graphics presented in the report in much the same way as the table of contents lists the report parts.

In constructing this table, head it with an appropriately descriptive title, such as "Table of Charts and Illustrations," or "List of Tables and Charts," or "Table of Figures." If you place the table of illustrations on a separate page, layout for this page is the same as that for any other text page with a displayed title. And if you place it as a continued part of the table of contents, you should begin it after the last contents entry.

The table consists of two columns, the first for the graphics titles and the second for the pages on which the graphics appear. The look of the table should match the format and layout of the table of contents. Line spacing form in the table of illustrations is optional, again depending on the line lengths of the entries. Preceding the title of each entry, place that entry's number; and should these numbers be Roman or otherwise require more than one digit, align the digits at the right. If your report contains two or more illustration types (tables, charts, maps, and the like) and you have given each type its own numbering sequence, you should list each type separately.

References (or Bibliography). Anytime you use another's idea, you need to give credit to the source. Sometimes business writers interweave this credit into the narrative of their text, and often they use footnotes to convey their source information. But often these sources are listed in a reference or bibliography section at the end of the report. Typically, these sections are organized alphabetically, but they also can be organized by date, subject, or type of source.

The format and content of citations vary by style used as described in Appendix E. Among the widely used formats are Chicago, MLA (Modern Language Association), and the APA (American Psychological Association) styles. The content for most items on the list of references is similar to that of the footnote. This format can be set up by the report format. Word 2007's Reference ribbon includes a reference management tool that will help you generate a bibliography in these standard formats.

Need to Improvise. The foregoing review covers most of the problems of form you will encounter in preparing reports. But there will be others. When you encounter other problems, you simply improvise an arrangement that appears right to the eye. After all, what appears right to the eye is the basis of conventional report form.

General Grading Checklist: Punctuation, Grammar, Number, Spelling, Proofreading, Technique, Strategy, and Formatting

Listed below are general grading symbols and their descriptions. These symbols give you a general idea of how to improve your writing. You will find more detailed information in your text, particularly in Chapter 17.

Punctuation

Symbol	Explanation	Description
APOS	Apostrophe	1. Use the apostrophe to show the possessive case of nouns and indefinite pronouns.
		2. Use an apostrophe to mark the place in a contraction where letters are omitted.
Bkts	Brackets	Set off in brackets words that you wish to insert in a quotation.
Cln	Colon	1. Use the colon to introduce a statement of explanation, an enumeration, or a formal quotation.
		2. Do not use the colon when the thought of the sentence should continue without interruption. If introducing a list by a colon, the colon should be preceded by a word that explains or identifies the list.
Cma	Comma	
Dsh	Dash	Use the dash to set off an element for emphasis or to show interrupted thought.
Ex	Exclamation mark	Use the exclamation mark at the end of a sentence or exclamatory fragment to show strong emotion.
Hpn	Hyphen	
Ital	Italics	
Parens	Parentheses	
Pd	Period	
Ques	Question mark	Place a question mark at the end of sentences that are direct questions.
QM	Quotation marks	Use quotation marks to enclose the exact words of a speaker or, if the quotation is short, the exact words of a writer.
SC	Semicolon	

Grammar

Symbol	Explanation	Description
AA	Adjective–adverb Confusion	Do not use adjectives for adverbs or adverbs for adjectives. Adjectives modify only nouns and pronouns; and adverbs modify verbs, adjectives, or other adverbs.
Agmt SV	Subject–verb agreement	Nouns and their verbs must agree in number.
AN	Adverbial noun clause	
Awk	Awkward	Avoid awkward writing where word arrangements are unconventional, uneconomical, or simply not the best for quick understanding.
Dng	Dangling modifier	Avoid the use of modifiers that do not logically modify a word in the sentence.
Frag	Sentence fragment	Avoid words used as a sentence that are not a sentence.
Pn	Pronoun	
Prl	Parallelism	Express equal thoughts in parallel grammatical form.
Tns	Tense	

Number

Symbol	Explanation
No	Number

Spelling

Symbol	Explanation	Description
Sp	Spelling	Spell words correctly. Use the dictionary.
Caps	Capitalization	Capitalize all proper names and the beginning words of sentences.

Proofreading

Symbol		Explanation	Description
Align	═══	Align	Line up horizontally or vertically.
Stet	*stet*	Let original stand	Don't delete.
Close	⌒	Close up	Close up space.
Del	৸	Delete	Delete.
Ins	^	Insert	Insert space, punctuation, text, or graphic.
Keep		Keep together	Keep text and/or graphic together.
LC	*lc* /	Lowercase	Use lowercase.
Caps	*cap* ═	Capitalize	Make all caps.
Mv L	[	Move left	Move left.
Mv R	]	Move right	Move right.
Cntr	] [	Center	Center.
Nl	*nl*	New line	Start new line.
Run	⌒	Run together	Run text together.
Par	#	Paragraph	Start new paragraph.
Sp O	*sp* ⊂⊃	Spell out	Spell out.
Trp	*tr* ⌒	Transpose	Transpose.

Technique

Symbol	Explanation	Description
Adp	Adaptation	Adapt to the one reader. Here your writing is above or below your reader.
Acc	Accuracy	Check for correct information.
Assign	Assignment	Needs to follow assignment.
AV	Active voice	Use active voice.
Blky	Bulky arrangement	Make your paragraphs more inviting by breaking them into shorter units of thought.
Blame	Blaming	Avoid blaming or accusing the reader.
Chop	Choppy writing	Avoid a succession of short sentences that produce an irritating effect.
COH	Coherence	Needs to be easier to follow with clear, logical development.
Copy	Copying	Avoid copying or following examples too closely. Organize around the unique facts of the case.
CTone	Conversational tone	Be natural or less formal in your word choice.
Dis	Discriminatory	Avoid using words that discriminate unnecessarily against sex, age, race, disability, or sexual orientation.
DL	Dull writing	Bring your writing back to life with vivid, concrete words.
Doc	Documentation	Cite source of information.
Emp–	Emphasis too little	Give appropriate emphasis with placement, volume, words, or mechanical means.
Emp+	Emphasis too much	Give appropriate emphasis with placement, volume, words, or mechanical means.
GW	Goodwill	Needs more goodwill.
Intp	Interpretation	Do more than just present facts. Make the data meaningful in terms of the reader's situation.
Jargon	Jargon	Avoid using jargon.
Los	Loose writing	Use words more economically. Write concisely.
Neg	Negative	Try wording more positively.
Ob	Obvious	Include only necessary information or detail.
Ord	Order of presentation	Needs clear, logical order.
Org	Organization	Needs clearer, tighter organization with setup and follow through.
Pomp	Pompous	Use more humble, sincere words.
Pre	Precise	Be more precise or concrete.
RB	Reader benefit	Needs more reader benefit.
Red	Redundant	Avoid unnecessary repetition.
Resale	Resale	Use more resale here.
RS	Rubber-stamp expression	Avoid overused phrases and time-worn words from the past.
Trans	Transition	Avoid abrupt shift of thought here.
Var	Variety	Vary the words and sentence patterns.
WU	Word use	Use words correctly. Misused words call attention to themselves and detract from the writing.
WW	Wrong word	Wrong words refer to meaning one word and using another.
YVP	You-viewpoint	Revise with the reader in mind.

Message Strategy

Symbol	Explanation	Description
O Dir	Directness needed	The opening is too slow in getting to the goal.
O Ind	Indirectness needed	The opening gets to the goal too fast.
O Qual	Quality	The opening could be improved by making it more on subject, logical, or interesting. It should also set up the rest of the message.
C Ex	Excess information	You have included more information than is needed.
C Exp	Explanation	More or better explanation is needed here.
C Id	Identification	Completely identify the situation.
C Inc	Incomplete	You have not covered all the important facts.
E AC	Action close	A drive for action is appropriate in this situation.
E AC S	Action strong	This action drive is too strong.
E AC W	Action weak	This action drive is too weak.
E IT	Individually tailored	Make your close fit the one case.
E OS	Off subject	An off-subject close is best for this case. These words recall unpleasant things in the reader's mind.

Formatting

Symbol	Explanation	Description
Lay	Layout	Use standard or specified format.
T	Type	Select a readable font for size and style.
Media	Media	Use a medium appropriate for the reader and the context

Special Grading Checklists: Messages and Reports

MESSAGES

The Opening

O Dir *Directness needed.*   This opening is too slow in getting to the goal.

O Ind *Indirectness needed.*   This opening gets to the goal too fast.

O Qual *Quality.*   This opening could be improved by making it more (1) on subject, (2) logical, or (3) interesting.

Coverage

C Ex *Excess information.*   You have included more information than is needed.

C Exp *Explanation.*   More or better explanation is needed here.

C Id *Identification.*   Completely identify the situation.

C Inc *Incomplete.*   You have not covered all the important information.

Ending

E AC *Action close.*   A drive for action is appropriate in this situation.

E AC S *Action strong.*   This action drive is too strong.

E AC W *Action weak.*   This action drive is too weak.

E IT *Individually tailored.*   Make your close fit the one case.

E OS *Off subject.*   An off-subject close is best for this case. These words recall unpleasant things in the reader's mind.

Technique

Adp *Adaptation.*   Your words should be adapted to the one reader. Here yours are (1) above or (2) below your reader.

Awk *Awkward word arrangement.*

Bky *Bulky arrangement.*   Make your paragraphs more inviting by breaking them into shorter units of thought.

Chop *Choppy writing.*   A succession of short sentences produces an irritating effect.

DL *Dull writing.*   Bring your writing back to life with vivid, concrete words.

Emp + *Emphasis, too much.*

Emp – *Emphasis, too little.* Here you have given too much or too little (as marked) emphasis by (1) placement, (2) volume, or (3) words or mechanical means.

Intp *Interpretation.* Do more than just present facts. In this situation, something more is needed. Make the data meaningful in terms of the reader's situation.

Los *Loose writing.* Use words more economically. Write concisely.

Ord *Order of presentation.* This information does not fall into a logical order. The information is mixed up and confusing.

RS *Rubber-stamp expression.* Timeworn words from the past have no place in modern business writing.

Trans *Transition.* Abrupt shift of thought here.

Effect

Conv *Conviction.* This is less convincing than it should be. More fact or a more skillful use of words is needed.

GW *Goodwill.* The message needs more goodwill. Try to make your words convey friendliness. Here you tend to be too dull and matter-of-fact.

Hur *Hurried treatment.* Your coverage of the problem appears to be hurried. Thus, it tends to leave an effect of routine or brusque treatment. Conciseness is wanted, of course, but you must not sacrifice your objectives for it.

Log *Logic.* Is this really logical? Would you do it this way in business?

Neg *Negative effect.* By word or implication, this part is more negative than it should be.

Pers + *Too persuasive.* Your words are too high-pressure for this situation.

Pers – *Not persuasive enough.* More persuasion, by either words or facts, would help your message.

Ton *Tone of the words.* Your words create a bad impression on the reader. Words work against the success of your message if they talk down, lecture, argue, accuse, and the like.

YVP *You-viewpoint.* More you-viewpoint wording and adaptation would help the overall effect of your message.

REPORTS

Title

T 1 Complete? The title should tell what the report contains. Use the five Ws and 1 H as a check for completeness (*who, what, where, when, why*—sometimes *how*).

T 2 Too long. This title is longer than it needs to be. Check it for uneconomical wording or unnecessary information.

Transmittal

LT 1 More directness is needed in the opening. The message should present the report right away.

LT 2 Content of the message needs improvement. Comments that help the readers understand or appreciate the report are appropriate.

LT 3 Do not include findings unless the report has no executive summary.

LT 4 A warm statement of your attitude toward the assignment is appropriate—often expected. You either do not make one, or the one you make is weak.

LT 5 A friendlier, more conversational style would improve the transmittal.

Executive Summary

ES 1 *(If the direct order is assigned)* Begin directly—with a statement of findings, conclusion, or recommendation.

ES 2 *(If the indirect order is assigned)* Begin with a brief review of introductory information.

ES 3 The summary of highlights should be in proportion and should include major findings, analyses, and conclusions. Your coverage here is (1) scant or (2) too detailed.

ES 4 Work for a more interesting and concise summary.

Organization—Outline/Table of Contents

O 1 This organization plan is not the best for this problem. The main sections should form a logical solution to the problem.

O 2 The order of the parts of this organizational plan is not logical. The parts should form a step-by-step route to the goal.

O 3 Do not let one major section account for the entire body of the report.

O 4 One-item subdivisions are illogical. You cannot divide an area without coming up with at least two parts.

O 5 These parts overlap. Each part should be independent of the other parts. Although some repetition and relating of parts may be desirable, outright overlap is a sign of bad organization.

O 6 More subparts are needed here. The subparts should cover all the information in the major part.

O 7 This subpart does not fit logically under this major part.

O 8 These parts are not equal in importance. Do not give them equal status in the outline.

O 9 *(If talking headings are assigned.)* These headings do not talk well.

O 10 Coordinate headings should be parallel in grammatical structure.

O 11 This (these) heading(s) is (are) too long.

O 12 Vary the wording of the headings to avoid monotonous repetition.

Introduction

I 1 This introduction does not cover exactly what the readers need to know. Although the readers' needs vary by problem, these topics are usually important: (1) origin of the problem, (2) statement of the problem, (3) methods used in researching the problem, and (4) preview of the presentation.

I 2 Coverage of this part is (1) scant or (2) too detailed.

I 3 Important information has been left out.

I 4 Findings, conclusions, and other items of information are not a part of the introduction.

Coverage

C 1 The coverage here is (1) scant or (2) too detailed.

C 2 More analysis is needed here.

C 3 Here you rely too heavily on a graphic. The text should cover the important information.

C 4 Do not lose sight of the goal of the report. Relate the information to the problem.

C 5 Clearly distinguish between fact and opinion. Label opinion as opinion.

C 6   Your analyses and conclusions need the support of more fact and authoritative opinion.

Writing

W 1   This writing should be better adapted to your readers. It appears to be (1) too heavy or (2) too light for your readers.

W 2   Avoid the overuse of passive voice.

W 3   Work for more conciseness. Try to cut down on words without sacrificing meaning.

W 4   For this report, more formal writing is appropriate. You should write consistently in impersonal (third-person) style.

W 5   A more personal style is appropriate for this report. That is, you should use more personal pronouns (*I*'s, *we*'s, *you*'s).

W 6   The change in thought is abrupt here.

    (1) Between major parts, use introductions, summaries, and conclusions to guide the readers' thinking.

    (2) Use transitional words, phrases, or sentences to relate minor parts.

W 7   Your paragraphing is questionable. Check the paragraphs for unity. Look for topic sentences.

Graphics

GA 1   You have (1) not used enough graphics or (2) used too many graphics.

GA 2   For the information presented, this graphic is (1) too large or (2) too small.

GA 3   This type of graphic is not the best for presenting the information.

GA 4   Place the graphic near the place where its contents are discussed.

GA 5   The text must tell the story, so don't just refer the reader to a figure or table and let it go at that.

GA 6   The appearance of this graphic needs improvement. This may be your best work, but it does not make a good impression on the readers.

GA 7   Refer the readers to the graphics at the times that the readers should look at them.

GA 8   Interpret the patterns in the graphic. Note central tendencies, exceptions, ranges, trends, and such.

GA 9   Refer to the graphics incidentally, in subordinate parts of sentences that comment on their content (for example, ". . . as shown in Figure 5" or "see Figure 5").

Layout and Mechanics

LM 1   The layout of this page is (1) too fat, (2) too skinny, or (3) too low, high, or off-center (as marked).

LM 2   Neat? Smudges and light type detract from the message.

LM 3   Make the margins straighter. The raggedness here offends the eye.

LM 4   The spacing here needs improvement. (1) Too much space here. (2) Not enough space here.

LM 5   Your page numbering is not the best. See the text for specific instructions.

LM 6   This page appears (1) choppy or (2) heavy.

LM 7   Your selection of type placement and style for the headings is not the best.

LM 8   This item or form is not generally acceptable.

Documentation and the Bibliography

In writing reports, you will frequently use information from other sources. Because this material is not your own, you may need to acknowledge it. Whether and how you should acknowledge it are the subject of this brief review.

WHEN TO ACKNOWLEDGE

Your decision to acknowledge or not acknowledge a source should be determined mainly on the basis of giving credit where credit is due. If you are quoting verbatim (in the original author's exact words), you must give credit. If you are paraphrasing (using someone else's ideas in your own words), you should give credit unless the material covered is general knowledge.

Today many colleges have academic honesty or academic integrity policies. Businesses, too, have similar ethics policies and codes. Following the policies not only ensures that you get full credit for your own work and develop the thinking and writing skills that will be helpful to you the rest of your life, but it also helps you build an ethical character. This character leads others to trust you, serving you well both professionally and personally.

Plagiarism, presenting another's work as your own, and falsifying data are two unethical practices plaguing schools and businesses alike. These practices range from carefully planned, intentional acts to careless, unintentional acts. However, the results are similar. Presenting another's work as your own steals from the creator—often depriving not only the author of the financial rewards honestly earned but also the whole support staff of editors, artists, designers, and production and distribution workers. Plagiarism is also stealing from classmates who write their own papers, but just as important, a cheater loses the opportunity to develop good writing and thinking skills. Additionally, plagiarism affects your reputation as well as the reputation of those in your class, your school, and those who have graduated from your school. It may also affect your family and friends. Falsifying data is equally malicious, especially when others rely on the information you present to make decisions. Worse yet, if you are successful in passing off falsified or plagiarized work as your own, it sets you up to behave unethically in the future. One writer for *The New York Times* recently wrote stories creating facts where he had none. After he did it once and fooled his boss and readers, he continued until he was caught. In addition to being fired and publicly humiliated, his actions brought into question the reporting practices and credibility of *The New York Times*.

In your writing tasks, you can eliminate such problems by following these guidelines.

Write Your Own Papers. Do not buy, beg, or borrow papers from others. Not only are instructors adept at spotting plagiarism, they now have powerful search engines and access to large databases of student papers. These databases even contain papers

Quotation Marks, Citation, Both, or Neither?

For both ethical and complete communication, you should make clear where your words and content come from. To decide whether to use quotation marks, a citation (naming the source of the material), both, or neither, follow these rules of thumb:

- When the content is general knowledge and you use your own words, you need neither quotation marks nor a citation.

  Example: Microsoft is a developer of computer technology.

  You have not borrowed any special words, so you do not need quotation marks. And since anyone would agree with this general claim, you do not need to cite a source.

- When the content is specialized knowledge but you use either your own words or the only words that can be used, you need to cite but do not need quotation marks.

  Example: Microsoft was founded in 1975 ("Microsoft at 30").

  This is not a generally known fact, so you need a citation, but your words are a common way to state this plain fact, so you do not need quotation marks.

- When you use striking or biased language from a source, whether about a well-known fact or not, you need both a citation and quotation marks.

  Example: Microsoft "was founded upon an ambitious dream" in 1975 ("Microsoft at 30").

  Here, you are using Microsoft's own evocative language, so you need quotation marks—and whenever you have a quote, you need to cite the source.

  The chart below summarizes this advice:

You . . .	Use Quotation Marks	Cite the Source	Do Neither
Used a **well-known fact** and **your own or ordinary language**			✓
Used a **special fact** from a source; used **your own language**		✓	
Used **the source's unique wording** (whether for a well-known or special fact)	✓	✓	

submitted recently. Tweaking these papers to fit your assignment does not get past these tools, which report percentages of similarity to other works. If you are going to go to all this work to copy a paper, you might as well do the work yourself and gain the benefits.

Give Credit to All Ideas That Are Not Your Own. Not only do you need to cite exact quotes, but you also need to cite paraphrased material when the ideas come from someplace else. Changing a few words does not make an idea either original or paraphrased. Also be sure to cite charts, tables, photos, and graphics. Give credit to adapted material as well. When in doubt, cite the source.

Use Discipline and Technological Tools to Manage the Data You Gather. Some unintentional problems arise when writers cannot retrieve the information they know they have collected and read, leading them to cite inaccurately or falsely. While making the information-gathering phase of research easier, the Internet has made managing the vast amount of information one finds a major task. By disciplining yourself to follow strict organizing practices, you will find retrieving the information easier when you need it. If you have ever used a money management program to manage your bank accounts, you know that it makes gathering tax information and preparing your tax return much easier. Similarly, tools such as EndNote or RefWorks (presented in Chapter 19) help tremendously, but only if one uses the tools faithfully.

Ask Your Instructor or School's Librarian When You Need Help. Both these people want to help you learn how to document appropriately. They will probably be more approachable if you have shown you have tried to find the answer to your question and if you are asking well before the final hour.

HOW TO ACKNOWLEDGE

You can acknowledge sources by citing them in the text, using one of a number of reference systems. Three of the most commonly used systems are the Chicago (*The Chicago Manual of Style*), MLA (Modern Language Association), and APA (American Psychological Association). Although they are similar, they differ somewhat in format, as you will see in the following pages. Because students tend to be most familiar with MLA format, we will review it first.[1] Then we will illustrate the Chicago and APA systems to note primary differences.

After you have selected a system, you must choose a method of acknowledgment. Two methods are commonly used in business: (1) parenthetical references within the text and (2) footnote references. A third method, endnote references, is sometimes used, although it appears to be losing favor. Only the first two are discussed here.

The Parenthetical Citation Method

The parenthetical method of citing sources is widely used in both academia and business. It is called "parenthetical" because it involves putting the author's last name or other identifying information in parentheses immediately following the cited material. This reference is keyed to an alphabetical reference list—variously labeled "Works Cited," "References," or "Bibliography," or given a custom-made title—that appears at the end of the report. Readers thus see a brief reference to your sources as they read your text, and, if and when they are interested in the full reference information, they go to the list of references and use your citation to find that information in the alphabetical list. The following examples in MLA format show how in-text citations and reference-list entries work together. (For a fuller discussion of how to prepare the reference list, see "The Reference List or Bibliography" on pages 625–626.)

A work with one author:

In-text citation: (Smith 47)

If you are citing the whole work, omit the page number. If you are citing more than one work by the same author, provide a short form of the title as well, as in "(Smith, *Bioblogs* 47)."

Reference-list citation:

Smith, Michael Holley. *Bioblogs: Résumés for the 21st Century.* New York: HarperCollins, 2006.

A work with two or three authors or editors:

In-text citation: (Solomon, Taylor, and Tyler 18)

Reference-list citation:

Solomon, Amy, Terry Taylor, and Lori Tyler. *100% Job Search Success.* Clifton Park, NY: Thomson Delmar Learning, 2006.

---

[1] Examples included here follow Joseph Gibaldi, *MLA Handbook for Writers of Research Papers,* 6th ed. (New York: MLA, 2003).

A work with more than three authors or editors:

In-text citation: (Lewis et al. 115)

Reference-list citation:

Lewis, Laurie K., et al. "Advice on Communicating during Organizational Change: The Content of Popular Press Books." *Journal of Business Communication* 43 (2006): 113–137.

A work by a corporate or government author:

In-text citation: (US Environmental Protection Agency 88)

Reference-list citation:

U.S. Environmental Protection Agency. Office of Air and Radiation. *Healthy Buildings, Healthy People: A Vision for the 21st Century.* Oct. 2001. 17 Sept. 2006 <http://www.epa.gov/iaq/hbhp/hbhp_report.pdf>.

A work with no author identified:

In-text citation: ("Why")

Reference-list citation:

"Why Internal Communications Fail When Branding Change to Employees." *PR News* 5 June 2006: 1. Access Intelligence. 21 Aug. 2006 <http://www.prandmarketing.com/search>.

If citing more than one work in one parenthetical reference:

In-text citation: (Griffiths; Tieger, Barron-Tieger, and Tiger)

Notice that the authors for the different works are put in alphabetical order, separated by a semicolon (multiple authors for the same work stay in their original order).

Reference-list citations:

Griffiths, Bob. *Do What You Love for the Rest of Your Life: A Practical Guide to Career Change and Personal Renewal.* New York: Ballantine, 2003.

Tieger, Paul D., Barbara Barron-Tieger, and Barbara Tiger. *Do What You Are: Discover the Perfect Career for You through the Secrets of Personality Type.* Boston: Little, Brown, 2001.

In practice, you may find that it feels more natural to work your sources of information into your sentences rather than naming them in parentheses. For example, rather than write "E-learning has become a multi-billion-dollar industry (Jacobs 8)," you might write "According to Jeff Jacobs, e-learning has become a multi-billion-dollar industry" (8). Or, if you were citing the whole work rather than a particular page, you would not even need the parenthetical citation. The reader could still find the corresponding entry in the reference list by using the source information in the sentence—in this case, the author's name. Use your sense of good style and readability to decide whether to work the source into the sentence or to name it in parentheses.

Remember that the goal of this, or any, citation method is to enable your readers to identify, verify, and evaluate the sources of your information. At every point in your report, your reader should be able to tell exactly where the information came from. Include citations whenever you believe that the source isn't understood. If you are providing lengthy information from one source, you usually need to cite it only once per paragraph. When you move to a new paragraph, though, you should cite it again, just to confirm for your reader that you are still basing your discussion on that source.

When placing parenthetical references in your text, put them at the end of a sentence or in some other logical break in your text, and put them before any mark of punctuation that occurs there. Here are two examples:

Palmeri observes that particular organizational contexts "will often both hinder and support the organization's writing goals" (60).

Collaborative writing is pervasive in the workplace (Couture and Rymer; Ede and Lunsford), and it can be particularly difficult when the collaborators come from different organizational cultures (Spilka).

The Footnote Method

Footnotes are a second means used to acknowledge sources. Two types of footnotes are used in business documents: citation footnotes and discussion footnotes. The emphasis here is on the citation footnote, but the uses of the discussion footnote also will be presented.

Citation Footnotes. A common way to acknowledge sources is by footnotes; that is, the references are placed at the bottom of the page and are keyed to the text material by superscripts (raised Arabic numbers). The numbering sequence of the superscripts is consecutive—by page, by chapter, or by the whole work. The footnotes are placed inside the page layout, single-spaced, and indented or blocked just as the text is typed.

If your footnotes include the complete facts about the cited sources, then you do not need to include a bibliography unless you believe that your reader would appreciate a list of references at the end as well. Thus, in addition to saving time and trouble for the writer, footnotes can be a convenience to business readers, keeping them from having to flip back and forth from the text to a bibliography as they read. You will need to learn your word-processing program's features for creating superscripts and placing the footnotes at the bottom of the page.

Although footnote form varies from one source to another, one generally accepted procedure is the MLA style presented here. With this method, the facts about the source are provided in the order shown below. The following lists give all the possible items in an entry. The items listed should be used as needed.

Book

1. *Name of the author, in normal order*. If a source has two or three authors, all are named. If a source has more than three authors, the name of the first author followed by the Latin et al. or its English equivalent "and others" may be used.

2. *Capacity of the author.* Needed only when the person named is actually not the author of the book but an editor, compiler, or the like.

3. *Chapter name.* Necessary only in the rare instances in which the chapter title helps the reader find the source.

4. *Book title.* Usually placed in italics. However, if the font used does not allow the reader to easily discriminate between italics and normal style, use underlining to help the reader see the title more clearly. But be sure to avoid underlining if the document will be posted to the Web so the reader will not confuse it with an active link.

5. *Edition.*

6. *Location of publisher.* If more than one city is listed on the title page, the one listed first should be used. If the population exceeds half a million, the name of the city is sufficient; otherwise, the city and state (or province) are best given.

7. *Publishing company.*

8. *Date.* Year of publication. If revised, year of latest revision.

9. *Page or pages.* Specific page or inclusive pages on which the cited material is found.

10. *URL for Internet sources or indication of the media (CD, DVD).*

The following are examples of book entries:

Book by single author:

[1] Michael Holley Smith, *Bioblogs: Résumés for the 21st Century* (New York: HarperCollins, 2006) 47.

Book by multiple authors:

[1] Amy Solomon, Terry Taylor, and Lori Tyler, *100% Job Search Success* (Clifton Park, NY: Thomson Delmar Learning, 2006) 60.

Edited collection (if citing the whole work):

[1] Julian Barling, E. Kevin Kelloway, and Michael R. Frone, ed., *Handbook of Work Stress* (Thousand Oaks, CA: Sage, 2005).

An article or chapter in an edited collection or reference work:

[1] Terry A. Beehr and Sharon Glazer, "Organization Role Stress," *Handbook of Work Stress,* eds. Julian Barling, E. Kevin Kelloway, and Michael R. Frone (Thousand Oaks, CA: Sage, 2005) 8.

[2] "Business Law," *Encyclopaedia Britannica Online, Academic Edition,* 2006, 17 June 2006 <http://search.eb.com.proxy.libraries.uc.edu/eb/article-9018282>.

Ebook:

[1] Jim Collins, *Level 5 Leadership: The Triumph of Humility and Fierce Resolve (HBR Enhanced Edition),* 2005: 15, *Harvard Business Review,* 19 June 2006 <http://www.amazon.com/gp/product/B00005REID/103-2194016-4411802?v= glance&n=551440#citebody>.

Government publication:

[1] US Environmental Protection Agency, Office of Air and Radiation, *Healthy Buildings, Healthy People: A Vision for the 21st Century,* Oct. 2001: 92, 17 Sept. 2006 <http://www.epa.gov/iaq/hbhp/hbhp_report.pdf>.

Magazine or Journal Article

1. *Name.* Frequently, no author is given. In such cases, the entry may be skipped, or if it is definitely known to be anonymous, the word *anonymous* may be placed in the entry.

2. *Article title.* Typed within quotation marks.

3. *Periodical title.* Set in italics.

4. *Publication identification.* Complete date for magazines. For journals, volume number (and issue number if necessary), followed by year.

5. *Page or pages* (if applicable).

6. *Database information* (if applicable).

7. *URL* (if accessed online).

Examples of magazine and journal entries are shown below:

Print magazine article:

[1] Bridget McCrea, "Creating Connections," *Black Enterprise* June 2006: 72.

Print magazine article acquired through an online database:

[1] Bridget McCrea, "Creating Connections," *Black Enterprise* June 2006: 72, *ABI/ Inform,* ProQuest, University of Cincinnati, University Libraries, 20 July 2006 <http://proquest.umi.com.proxy.libraries.uc.edu/pqdweb?did=1050459991&sid= 4&Fmt=4&clientId=5468&RQT=309&VName=PQD>.

Print magazine article acquired from the Internet:

[1] "Why Internal Communications Fail When Branding Change to Employees," *PR News* 5 June 2006: 1, Access Intelligence, 21 Aug. 2006 <http://www.prandmarketing.com/search>.

Article from an online magazine or the online edition of a magazine:

[1] Coco Masters, "Yogurt Nation: How Kid-Friendly Marketing and an Explosion of Products Are Turning an Ancient Food into America's Top Snack," *Time Online Edition,* 30 May 2006, 8 July 2006 <http://www.time.com/time/insidebiz/article/ 0,9171,1198925,00.html>.

Journal article (pages numbered consecutively throughout the year):

[1] Laurie K. Lewis et al., "Advice on Communicating during Organizational Change: The Content of Popular Press Books," *Journal of Business Communication* 43 (2006): 114. (If acquired online, add the online information as shown for magazine articles.)

Journal article (pages of each issue numbered separately):

[1] Kathryn Yates, "Internal Communication Effectiveness Enhances Bottom-line Results," *Journal of Organizational Excellence* 25.3 (2006): 71. (If acquired online, add the online information as shown for magazine articles.)

Book review:

[1] Joshua Tusin, rev. of *Writing and Presenting a Business Plan,* by Carolyn A. Boulger, *Business Communication Quarterly* 69.2 (2006): 227.

Newspaper Article

1. *Source description.* If article is signed, give author's name. Otherwise, give description of article, such as "Associated Press dispatch" or "Editorial."

2. *Main head (title) of article.* Typed within quotation marks.

3. *Newspaper title.* Set in italics. City and state (or province) names inserted in brackets if place names do not appear in newspaper title. State (or province) names not needed in case of very large cities, such as New York, Toronto, and Los Angeles.

4. *Date of publication.*

5. *Edition* (such as "natl. ed") if applicable.

6. *Section and page.*

7. *Database information* (if applicable).

8. *URL* (if accessed online).

The following are typical newspaper article entries:

Print article:

[1] M. P. McQueen, "Employers Offer Help Fighting ID Theft: As Security Breaches Proliferate, New Benefit Aims to Cut Time Workers Spend Restoring Their Name," *The Wall Street Journal* 24 May 2006, Eastern ed.: D1. (If acquired through a database, add the online information as shown for magazine articles.)

Online article:

[1] "New Service Allows Workgroups to Share Information Online," *Telecomworldwire* 9 June 2006: 1, *ABI/Inform,* ProQuest, University of Cincinnati, University Libraries, 20 June 2006 <http://proquest.umi.com.proxy.libraries.uc.edu/pqdweb?did=1052805181&sid=1&Fmt=3&clientId=5468&RQT=309&VName=PQD>.

Letter or Document

1. *Name of writer* (with title and organization where helpful).

2. *Nature of communication.*

3. *Name of recipient* (with title and organization where helpful).

4. *Date of writing.*

5. *Where filed.*

Two examples follow:

[1] Thomas McLaughlin, CEO, McLaughlin Body Company, Letter to Linda Hittle, 1 Dec. 2007.

[2] Farm Markets of Ohio, Affiliate of The Ohio Farm Bureau Federation, brochure.

Information from a Database

1. *Name of author(s) or owner in normal order.*
2. *Title,* in quotes or italics as appropriate.
3. *Source of information* (such as newswire service or journal title).
4. *Volume, issue number, and date* (if applicable).
5. *Page numbers* (if any).
6. *The word "abstract"* (if applicable).
7. *Database information.*
8. *Date of access.*
9. *URL*

Some examples of entries for information found in databases are the following. (To format an entry for a periodical article retrieved through a database, see the earlier examples for magazines, journals, and newspapers.)

Full-text record:

[1] Dana Knight, Daniel Lee, and Madhusmita Bora, "A New Way of Doing Business Is Scandal's Legacy," Knight-Ridder Tribune Business News 26 May 2006, *LexisNexis Academic,* Gale Group, University of Cincinnati, University Libraries, 20 June 2006 <http://web.lexis-nexis.com.proxy.libraries. uc.edu/universe/document?_m=022472255b7d5b07f34cfebc2cc19c66&_ docnum=7&wchp=dGLbVlb-zSkVb&_md5=50e784ae1d73b7653839430022c0c 6cb>.

Abstract-only record:

[1] Brett Sheehan, "From Cotton Mill to Business Empire," *The American Historical Review* 109.5 (2004): 1548, abstract, *Humanities Abstracts,* University of Cincinnati, OhioLink, 22 June 2006 <http://rave.ohiolink.edu.proxy.libraries. uc.edu/databases/record/huai/BHUM05104647>.

Other kinds of information:

[1] "The Procter & Gamble Company: Fact Sheet," *Hoover's Online,* Hoover's, 2006, University of Cincinnati, University Libraries, 30 June 2006 <http://premium.hoovers.com.proxy.libraries.uc.edu/subscribe/co/factsheet. xhtml?ID=rrtrrffryrjxtk>.

Other Electronic Material

1. *Name of author or owner of site in normal order.*
2. *Title of document,* in italics or quotes as appropriate.
3. *Title of complete work* (if applicable), in italics.
4. *Type of material* (if not obvious).
5. *Date of publication.* If revised, last revision.
6. *Date accessed* (if appropriate).
7. *Complete URL.* If the length exceeds the line length, break after a forward slash.

Typical entries for other kinds of electronic material follow.

Website:

[1] *Amazon.com,* 2006, 11 July 2006 <http://www.amazon.com/gp/homepage.html/ 103-2194016-4411802>.

Document from a website:

[1] eMarketer, "What Comes before Search? Behavioral Targeting: Enabling Online Marketers to Reach Consumers Earlier in the Purchase Cycle," white paper, Sept. 2004, 25 June 2006 <https://www.emarketer.com/Reports/Whitepaper. aspx?behavior_white_sep04&emailPdf=Y>.

Blog:

[1] Douglas Kersten, "How to Build a Bulletproof Startup," weblog comment, *The Small Business Blog,* 31 May 2006, 17 June 2006 <http://www.allbusiness.com/blog/TheSmallBusinessBlog/3882/005783.html>.

Online radio program:

[1] Debbie Elliot, "All Things Considered," NPR, 10 June 2006, 11 June 2006 <http://www.npr.org/templates/archives/rundown_archive_hub.php>.

Email message:

[1] John Bryan, Associate Professor, University of Cincinnati, "Internship Opportunity," email to the author, 7 May 2006.

Listserv message:

[1] Jeff Viorst, "My Favorite Communication Case," online posting, 8 Sept. 2006 bizcom@biz.cath.vt.edu.

CD-ROM:

[1] "Human-factors Engineering," *Britannica 2006 Deluxe Edition,* CD-ROM.

The Digital Object Identifier (DOI) citation method, currently being developed, looks promising for providing reliable and permanent electronic source identification.[2] The DOI can be used to identify text, audio, images, software, and such. It was originally developed by a consortium of publishers interested in protecting intellectual content while enabling Internet commerce.[3] The Patricia Seybold Group predicts "that within five years every article, track of music, or other digital asset will be tagged with a unique Digital Object Identifier."[4]

Here is how one might use the DOI in a footnote:

[1] Carol Acord and Sharon Garbett, "Learning Entrepreneurship Skills through Successful Ventures in Areas of Personal Interest," *Journal of Business Research* 65.1 (2005), doi:10.1965/jbr.2005.1022, http://www.jbr.org/links/doi/10.1965/jbr.2005.1022.

The types of entries discussed in the preceding paragraphs are those most likely to be used. Yet many unusual types of publications (conference proceedings, computer programs, audiotapes, maps, patents, podcasts, webcasts) are likely to come up. When they do, you should classify the source by the form it most closely resembles: a book or a periodical. Then you should construct the entry that describes the source completely and accurately. Frequently, you will need to improvise—to use your best judgment in determining the source description.

Subsequent References. Writers used to use the Latin abbreviations *Ibid.* (which means "in the same place") and *Op. cit.* ("in the work cited") to refer back to earlier footnotes. These have largely been replaced by abbreviated forms of the original footnote entries. Usually the author's last name followed by the relevant page number is adequate for a previously cited work:

[4] Beehr and Glaser 34.

If you happen to have cited two or more works by the same author, simply add a short form of the title after the author's name to distinguish this source from the others:

[4] Beehr and Glaser, "Organization" 34.

---

[2] For updates on the development of this important international standard, check with the International DOI Foundation at <http://www.doi.org/>.

[3] Bill Rosenblatt, "Solving the Dilemma of Copyright Protection Online," *Journal of Electronic Publishing,* University of Michigan Press, 1 Aug. 2006 <http://www.press.umich.edu/jep/03-02/doi.html>.

[4] Patricia B. Seybold, *Protecting Your Digital Assets: Technical Journal Publishers Lead the Way Using Digital Object Identifiers,* 2003: 3, Patricia Sey bold Group, 13 Feb. 2003 <http://www.doi.org/topics/Protect_Digital_Acess.pdf>.

Discussion Footnotes. In sharp contrast with traditional footnotes are discussion footnotes. Through discussion footnotes, the writer strives to explain a part of the text, to amplify the discussion of a certain topic, to make cross-references to other parts of the report, and the like. The following examples illustrate some possibilities of this footnote type.

Cross-Reference:

[1] See the principle of inflection points on page 72.

Amplification of Discussion and Cross-Reference:

[2] Lyman Bryson says the same thing: "Every communication is different for every receiver even in the same context. No one can estimate the variation of understanding that there may be among receivers of the same message conveyed in the same vehicle when the receivers are separated in either space or time" (see *Communication of Ideas* 5).

PRESENTATION OF QUOTED AND PARAPHRASED INFORMATION

You may use data obtained from secondary sources in two ways. You may paraphrase the information (cast it in your own words), or you may use it verbatim (exactly as the original author worded it). In typing paraphrased material, you need not distinguish it from the remainder of the report text. Material you use verbatim, however, must be clearly distinguished.

The procedure for marking this difference is simple. If the quoted passage is short (about 10 lines or less), place it within the text and with quotation marks before and after it. Set off longer quotations from the margins, without quotation marks, as shown in the example below. If the text is double-spaced, further distinguish the quoted passage by single-spacing it.

Of those opposing the issue, Logan Wilson makes this penetrating observation:

It is a curious paradox that academicians display a scientific attitude toward every universe of inquiry except that which comprises their own profession. . . . Lacking precise qualitative criteria, administrators are prone to fall back upon rather crude quantitative measures as a partial substitute. For example, student evaluations of teachers often lack acceptable reliability and validity statistics. And when they are administered is quite illogical. Moreover, most statements on them relate to contextual factors—office hours, fairness of tests, and such—and not to acquiring knowledge itself. Yet administrators use quantitative scores from these instruments to the minute fraction of a point to assess teaching quality. Multiple measures of teaching performance with an emphasis on student learning would bring a more rational approach to teaching as one dimension of academic responsibility. (201)

These logical, straightforward, and simple arguments of the critics of teacher evaluation appear to be irrefutable.

Frequently, you will find it best to break up or use only fragments of the quoted author's work. Because omissions may distort the meaning of a passage, you must clearly indicate them, using ellipsis points (a series of three periods typed with intervening spaces) where material is left out. If an omission begins before or after the end of a sentence, you must use four periods—one for the final punctuation plus three for the ellipsis points. A passage with such omissions is the following:

Many companies have undertaken to centralize in the hands of specially trained correspondents the handling of the outgoing email. Usually, centralization has been accomplished by the firm's employment of a correspondence supervisor. . . . The supervisor may guide the work of correspondents . . . , or the company may employ a second technique.

In long quotations it is conventional to show omission of a paragraph or more by a full line of periods, typed with intervening spaces (see example in Pd 3, Chapter 17).

THE REFERENCE LIST OR BIBLIOGRAPHY

A bibliography is an orderly list of resources on a particular subject. Usually it provides the full reference information for sources cited in parentheses in the text, as described in the section on parenthetical citation, and is labeled "References" or "List of Works Cited." But sometimes the bibliography is itself the main information product. For example, if someone asked you to compile a list of resources on e-learning, you would prepare your findings in the form of a bibliography, probably preceded by some introductory text. And if someone asked you to provide a brief description with each entry as well, you would prepare what is known as an annotated bibliography. If your bibliography is extensive, you might precede it with a fly page containing the title ("Bibliography" or a custom title such as "List of E-learning Sources"). You could also organize your entries by category, with subheadings (for example, "Books," "Periodicals," and "Internet Resources"). If your report has an appendix, the bibliography follows it.

As with footnotes, variations in bibliographic style are numerous, but in MLA style, the information for a bibliography entry follows the order described in this chapter's section on footnotes (pp. 619-624). There are significant differences, however, between footnote and bibliography format. The latter uses periods rather than commas between the major components of an entry. Bibliographies also have these distinguishing traits:

1. The author's name is listed in reverse order—surname first—for the purpose of alphabetizing. If an entry has more than one author, however, only the name of the first author is reversed.

2. The entry is generally presented in hanging-indention form. That is, the second and subsequent lines of an entry begin some uniform distance (usually about one-half inch) to the right of the beginning point of the first line. The purpose of this indented pattern is to make the alphabetized first line stand out.

3. The entry gives the inclusive pages of articles, but not for books, and does not refer to any one page or passage.

4. Second and subsequent references to publications of the same author are indicated by a line formed by three hyphens. But this line may be used only if the entire authorship is the same in the consecutive publications. For example, the line could not be used if consecutive entries have one common author but different coauthors.

The following is a bibliography made up of some examples discussed in this chapter:

Works Cited

Beehr, Terry A., and Sharon Glazer. "Organization Role Stress." *Handbook of Work Stress*. Eds. Julian Barling, E. Kevin Kelloway, and Michael R. Frone. Thousand Oaks, CA: Sage, 2005. 7–34.

Bryan, John. Associate Professor. University of Cincinnati. "Internship Opportunity." Email to the author. 7 May 2006.

Griffiths, Bob. *Do What You Love for the Rest of Your Life: A Practical Guide to Career Change and Personal Renewal*. New York: Ballantine, 2003.

McCrea, Bridget. "Creating Connections." *Black Enterprise* June 2006: 72. *ABI/Inform*. ProQuest. 20 July 2006 <http://proquest.umi.com.proxy.libraries. uc.edu/pqdweb?did=1050459991&sid=4&Fmt=4&clientId=5468&RQT=30 9&VName=PQD>.

"New Service Allows Workgroups to Share Information Online." *Telecomworldwire* 9 June 2006: 1. *ABI/Inform*. ProQuest. University of Cincinnati. University Libraries. 20 June 2006 <http://proquest.umi.com. proxy.libraries.uc.edu/pqdweb?did=1052805181&sid=1&Fmt=3&clientId= 5468&RQT=309&VName=PQD>.

"The Procter & Gamble Company: Fact Sheet." *Hoover's Online.* Hoover's. 2006. University of Cincinnati. University Libraries. 30 June 2006 <http://premium.hoovers.com.proxy.libraries.uc.edu/subscribe/co/factsheet.xhtml?ID=rrtrrffryrjxtk>.

Smith, Michael Holley. *Bioblogs: Résumés for the 21st Century.* New York: HarperCollins, 2006.

Tieger, Paul D., Barbara Barron-Tieger, and Barbara Tiger. *Do What You Are: Discover the Perfect Career for You through the Secrets of Personality Type.* Boston: Little, Brown, 2001.

Yates, Kathryn. "Internal Communication Effectiveness Enhances Bottom-line Results." *Journal of Organizational Excellence* 25.3 (2006): 71–77.

DIFFERENCES IN MLA, CHICAGO, AND APA FORMATS

As noted previously, the Chicago and APA systems differ somewhat from the MLA style presented in preceding pages. The primary differences are shown in the following illustrations.

Notice that the Chicago and APA styles emphasize the date of publication more than the MLA style does, while the MLA style, which provides complete author names, emphasizes the source of authority more.

Parenthetical Citation

MLA: (Solomon, Taylor, and Tyler 60)

Chicago: (Solomon, Taylor, and Tyler 2006, 60)

APA: (Solomon, Taylor, & Tyler, 2006, p. 60)

Footnote—Book

MLA:

[1] Amy Solomon, Terry Taylor, and Lori Tyler, *100% Job Search Success* (Clifton Park, NY: Thomson Delmar Learning, 2006) 60.

Chicago:

[1] Amy Solomon, Terry Taylor, and Lori Tyler, *100% Job Search Success* (Clifton Park, NY: Thomson Delmar Learning, 2006), 60.

APA:

(Does not use citation footnotes)

Footnote—Periodical:

MLA:

[1] Kathryn Yates, "Internal Communication Effectiveness Enhances Bottom-line Results," *Journal of Organizational Excellence* 25.3 (2006): 71.

Chicago:

[1] Kathryn Yates, "Internal Communication Effectiveness Enhances Bottom-line Results," *Journal of Organizational Excellence* 25, no. 3 (2006): 71.

APA:

(Does not use citation footnotes)

Bibliography Entry—Book

MLA:

Tieger, Paul D., Barbara Barron-Tieger, and Barbara Tiger. *Do What You Are: Discover the Perfect Career for You through the Secrets of Personality Type.* Boston: Little, Brown, 2001.

Chicago:

Tieger, Paul D., Barbara Barron-Tieger, and Barbara Tiger. 2001. *Do what you are: Discover the perfect career for you through the secrets of personality type.* Boston: Little, Brown.

APA:

Tieger, P. D., Barron-Tieger, B., & Tiger, B. (2001). *Do what you are: Discover the perfect career for you through the secrets of personality type.* Boston: Little, Brown.

Bibliography Entry—Periodical:

MLA:

Yates, Kathryn. "Internal Communication Effectiveness Enhances Bottom-line Results." *Journal of Organizational Excellence* 25.3 (2006): 71–77.

Chicago:

Yates, K. 2006. Internal communication effectiveness enhances bottom-line results. *Journal of Organizational Excellence* 25 (3): 71–77.

APA:

Yates, K. (2006). Internal communication effectiveness enhances bottom-line results. *Journal of Organizational Excellence, 25*(3), 71–77.

Whatever system you decide to use, use only one within a document and always be complete, accurate, and consistent.

PHOTO CREDITS

Page 1: Courtesy of Norm Fjeldheim

Page 6: Courtesy of John Deere

Page 9 top: © Bob Daemmrich/PhotoEdit

Page 9 bottom: © PhotoDisc/Getty Images

Page 23: Photo by Steve Grayson/WireImage.com

Page 27: Courtesy of Stephanie Crown

Page 38: © Digital Vision/Getty Images

Page 53: © Digital Vision

Page 57: © Joaquin Palting/Getty Images

Page 73: © Comstock/PictureQuest

Page 78: Courtesy of Stephanie Crown

Page 85: Courtesy of Dell Inc.

Page 94: © Image Source/WireImage.com

Page 96: © Justin Lane/epa/CORBIS

Page 113: © Jean Louid Batt/Getty Images

Page 119: Alexander Walter/Getty Images

Page 127: © Comstock/PictureQuest

Page 167: Courtesy of Stephanie Crown

Page 177: © Greg Pease/Getty Images

Page 204: © Jim Whitmer

Page 222: Courtesy of Stephanie Crown

Page 242: © Bob Daemmrich/The Image Works

Page 266: © Mike Greenlar/The Image Works

Page 276: © Digital Vision

Page 291: AP/Wide World Photos

Page 297: © Digital Vision

Page 299: © Keith Brofsky/ Getty Images

Page 318: © Stockbyte/Getty Images

Page 327: © Digital Vision/Getty Images

Page 331: © Comstock/PictureQuest

Page 346: © PhotoDisc/AGE Fotostock

Page 375: © Blend Images/Getty Images

Page 385, 433: © Royalty-Free/CORBIS

Page 439: Courtesy of Liz Claiborne Inc.

Page 444: © Digital Vision/Getty Images

Page 453: © Eric Audras/Photoalto/PictureQuest

Page 454: © John A. Rizzo/Getty Images

Page 465, 467, 474: © Digital Vision/Getty Images

Page 483: Avon Products

Page 487: © Luca Tettoni/Imagestate

Page 491: © Gulfimages/Getty Images

Page 531: © Royalty-Free/CORBIS

Page 543: © Tipp Howell/Getty Images

Page 546: AP/Wide World Photos

Page 553: © LWA-Dann Tardif/CORBIS

Page 574: © Richard Lord/PhotoEdit

Page numbers followed by n indicate notes.